Blackstone's Statutes on

IT and e-Commerce

Blackstone's Statutes Series

Edited by subject specialists

Commercial and Consumer Law
Francis Rose

Company Law
Derek French

Contract, Tort, and Restitution
Francis Rose

Criminal Justice and Sentencing
Barry Mitchell and Salim Farrar

Criminal Law
Peter Glazebrook

EU Treaties and Legislation
Nigel Foster

Employment Law
Richard Kidner

Environmental Legislation
Donald McGillivray

Evidence
Phil Huxley

Family Law
Mika Oldham

Intellectual Property
Andrew Christie and Stephen Gare

International Human Rights Documents
Sandy Ghandhi

International Law Documents
Malcolm D. Evans

IT and e-Commerce
Steve Hedley and Tanya Aplin

Media Law
Richard Caddell and Howard Johnson

Medical Law
Anne E. Morris and Michael A. Jones

Property Law
Meryl Thomas

Public Law and Human Rights
Peter Wallington and Robert G. Lee

UK and EC Competition Documents
Kirsty Middleton

Trusted in over
a million exams

www.oxfordtextbooks.co.uk/orc/statutes

Blackstone's Statutes on
IT and e-Commerce

4th edition

edited by

Steve Hedley
Professor of Law, University College, Cork

Tanya Aplin
Reader in Intellectual Property Law, King's College, London

OXFORD
UNIVERSITY PRESS

OXFORD
UNIVERSITY PRESS

Great Clarendon Street, Oxford OX2 6DP
United Kingdom

Oxford University Press is a department of the University of Oxford.
It furthers the University's objective of excellence in research, scholarship,
and education by publishing worldwide. Oxford is a registered trade mark of
Oxford University Press in the UK and in certain other countries

First published by Blackstone Press
First edition 2002
Second edition 2004
Third edition 2006
Fourth edition 2008
Reprinted 2012

British Library Cataloguing in Publication Data
Data available

Library of Congress Cataloging in Publication Data
Data available

ISBN 978-0-19-923821-7

Printed and bound by CPI Group (UK) Ltd, Croydon, CR0 4YY

Contents

Alphabetical contents

Editors' preface

The pace of legislative change in relation to the Internet has not slowed since the last edition, though it is noticeable that the changes are more to do with detail than with substance. They are none the less important for that, however, and if anything they emphasise the difficulties of those having to work from (much amended and re-ordered) primary materials. With this in mind we have produced what we hope is a comprehensive collection of official instruments relating to IT and e-commerce.

As to content, we have aimed to reproduce the main provisions relating to IT, e-commerce and data protection. More and more of the material is now Internet-specific or at least IT-specific, though there remains a substantial quantity of general statutes, minimally amended to make them applicable to the Internet. We have tried to be comprehensive as to the law of data protection. With regrets, we have decided not to venture into the area of public information and freedom of information (a move which could very easily have doubled the size of the book!).

As to jurisdiction, our main concern has been with the UK. As with the previous edition, we have included a substantial amount of EU law (in addition to the UK statutory instruments implementing the EU directives). We have retained the selection of international materials, but have omitted foreign statutes in order to focus upon EU law.

As to timing, we have reproduced the text in force at the time of writing (May 2008). Where the text is an amended one, we have indicated this by [square brackets].

A book of this kind is, almost necessarily, out of date some weeks before it is printed. For those who need to be up to the minute, we recommend our Online Resource Centre at **www.oxfordtextbooks. co.uk/orc/statutes/.**

We would like to thank Melanie Jackson, Kate Hickey and all at OUP for the competence and speed with which they have handled this edition. We are also grateful to the following organisations for granting us permission to reproduce extracts of their respective publications in this book:

WIPO—WIPO Copyright Treaty 1996 and Agreed Statements[1]

WTO—Agreement on Trade Related Aspects of Intellectual Property Rights 1994

We would be delighted to hear comments and suggestions from any users of this book.

Tanya Aplin
tanya.aplin@kcl.ac.uk

Steve Hedley
s.hedley@ucc.ie

May 2008

---

[1] Material originally provided by the World Intellectual Property Organisation (WIPO), the owner of the copyright. The Secretariat of WIPO assumes no liability or responsibility with regard to the transformation or translation of this data.

UK Statutes

Obscene Publications Act 1959

(1959, c. 66)

An Act to amend the law relating to the publication of obscene matter; to provide for the protection of literature; and to strengthen the law concerning pornography. [29th July 1959]

1 Test of obscenity

(1) For the purposes of this Act an article shall be deemed to be obscene if its effect or (where the article comprises two or more distinct items) the effect of any one of its items is, if taken as a whole, such as to tend to deprave and corrupt persons who are likely, having regard to all relevant circumstances, to read, see or hear the matter contained or embodied in it.

(2) In this Act "article" means any description of article containing or embodying matter to be read or looked at or both, any sound record, and any film or other record of a picture or pictures.

(3) For the purposes of this Act a person publishes an article who—

(a) distributes, circulates, sells, lets on hire, gives, or lends it, or who offers it for sale or for letting on hire; or

(b) in the case of an article containing or embodying matter to be looked at or a record, shows, plays or projects it [, or, where the matter is data stored electronically, transmits that data].

[(4) For the purposes of this Act a person also publishes an article to the extent that any matter recorded on it is included by him in a programme included in a programme service.

(5) Where the inclusion of any matter in a programme so included would, if that matter were recorded matter, constitute the publication of an obscene article for the purposes of this Act by virtue of subsection (4) above, this Act shall have effect in relation to the inclusion of that matter in that programme as if it were recorded matter.

(6) In this section "programme" and "programme service" have the same meaning as in the Broadcasting Act 1990.]

2 Prohibition of publication of obscene matter

(1) Subject as hereinafter provided, any person who, whether for gain or not, publishes an obscene article [or who has an obscene article for publication for gain (whether gain to himself or gain to another)] shall be liable—

(a) on summary conviction to a fine not exceeding [the prescribed sum] or to imprisonment for a term not exceeding six months;

(b) on conviction on indictment to a fine or to imprisonment for a term not exceeding three years or both.

(2) [...]

(3) A prosecution [...] for an offence against this section shall not be commenced more than two years after the commission of the offence.

[(3A) Proceedings for an offence under this section shall not be instituted except by or with the consent of the Director of Public Prosecutions in any case where the article in question is a moving picture film of a width of not less than sixteen millimetres and the relevant publication or the only other publication which followed or could reasonably have been expected to follow from the relevant publication took place or (as the case may be) was to take place in the course of [an exhibition of a film]; and in this subsection "the relevant publication" means—

    (a) in the case of any proceedings under this section for publishing an obscene article, the publication in respect of which the defendant would be charged if the proceedings were brought; and

    (b) in the case of any proceedings under this section for having an obscene article for publication for gain, the publication which, if the proceedings were brought, the defendant would be alleged to have had in contemplation.]

    (4) A person publishing an article shall not be proceeded against for an offence at common law consisting of the publication of any matter contained or embodied in the article where it is of the essence of the offence that the matter is obscene.

    [(4A) Without prejudice to subsection (4) above, a person shall not be proceeded against for an offence at common law—

    (a) in respect of [an exhibition of a film] or anything said or done in the course of [an exhibition of a film], where it is of the essence of the common law offence that the exhibition or, as the case may be, what was said or done was obscene, indecent, offensive, disgusting or injurious to morality; or

    (b) in respect of an agreement to give [an exhibition of a film] or to cause anything to be said or done in the course of such an exhibition where the common law offence consists of conspiring to corrupt public morals or to do any act contrary to public morals or decency.]

    (5) A person shall not be convicted of an offence against this section if he proves that he had not examined the article in respect of which he is charged and had no reasonable cause to suspect that it was such that his publication of it would make him liable to be convicted of an offence against this section.

    (6) In any proceedings against a person under this section the question whether an article is obscene shall be determined without regard to any publication by another person unless it could reasonably have been expected that the publication by the other person would follow from publication by the person charged.

    [(7) In this section "exhibition of a film" has the meaning given in paragraph 15 of Schedule 1 to the Licensing Act 2003.]

Obscene Publications Act 1964

(1964, c. 74)

An Act to strengthen the law for preventing the publication for gain of obscene matter and the publication of things intended for the production of obscene matter.   [31st July 1964]

1   Obscene articles intended for publication for gain

    (1) [*Amends the Obscene Publications Act 1959, above.*]

    (2) For the purpose of any proceedings for an offence against the said section 2 a person shall be deemed to have an article for publication for gain if with a view to such publication he has the article in his ownership, possession or control.

    (3) In proceedings brought against a person under the said section 2 for having an obscene article for publication for gain the following provisions shall apply in place of subsections (5) and (6) of that section, that is to say,—

    (a) he shall not be convicted of that offence if he proves that he had not examined the article and had no reasonable cause to suspect that it was such that his having it would make him liable to be convicted of an offence against that section; and

    (b) the question whether the article is obscene shall be determined by reference to such publication for gain of the article as in the circumstances it may reasonably be inferred he had in contemplation and to any further publication that could reasonably be expected to follow from it, but not to any other publication.

(4) Where articles are seized under section 3 of the Obscene Publications Act 1959 (which provides for the seizure and forfeiture of obscene articles kept for publication for gain), and a person is convicted under section 2 of that Act of having them for publication for gain, the court on his conviction shall order the forfeiture of those articles:

Provided that an order made by virtue of this subsection (including an order so made on appeal) shall not take effect until the expiration of the ordinary time within which an appeal in the matter of the proceedings in which the order was made may be instituted or, where such an appeal is duly instituted, until the appeal is finally decided or abandoned; and for this purpose—

(a) an application for a case to be stated or for leave to appeal shall be treated as the institution of an appeal; and

(b) where a decision on appeal is subject to a further appeal, the appeal shall not be deemed to be finally decided until the expiration of the ordinary time within which a further appeal may be instituted or, where a further appeal is duly instituted, until the further appeal is finally decided or abandoned.

(5) References in section 3 of the Obscene Publications Act 1959 and this section to publication for gain shall apply to any publication with a view to gain, whether the gain is to accrue by way of consideration for the publication or in any other way.

Patents Act 1977

(1977, c. 37)

An Act to establish a new law of patents applicable to future patents and applications for patents; to amend the law of patents applicable to existing patents and applications for patents; to give effect to certain international conventions on patents; and for connected purposes.   [29th July 1977]

PART I NEW DOMESTIC LAW

Patentability

1   Patentable inventions

(1) A patent may be granted only for an invention in respect of which the following conditions are satisfied, that is to say—

(a) the invention is new;

(b) it involves an inventive step;

(c) it is capable of industrial application;

(d) the grant of a patent for it is not excluded by subsections (2) and (3) [or section 4A] below;

and references in this Act to a patentable invention shall be construed accordingly.

(2) It is hereby declared that the following (among other things) are not inventions for the purposes of this Act, that is to say, anything which consists of—

(a) a discovery, scientific theory or mathematical method;

(b) a literary, dramatic, musical or artistic work or any other aesthetic creation whatsoever;

(c) a scheme, rule or method for performing a mental act, playing a game or doing business, or a program for a computer;

(d) the presentation of information;

but the foregoing provision shall prevent anything from being treated as an invention for the purposes of this Act only to the extent that a patent or application for a patent relates to that thing as such.

[(3) A patent shall not be granted for an invention the commercial exploitation of which would be contrary to public policy or morality.

(4) For the purposes of subsection (3) above exploitation shall not be regarded as contrary to public policy or morality only because it is prohibited by any law in force in the United Kingdom or any part of it.]

(5) The Secretary of State may by order vary the provisions of subsection (2) above for these purpose of maintaining them in conformity with developments in science and technology; and no such order shall be made unless a draft of the order has been laid before, and approved by resolution of, each House of Parliament.

2   Novelty

(1) An invention shall be taken to be new if it does not form part of the state of the art.

(2) The state of the art in the case of an invention shall be taken to comprise all matter (whether a product, a process, information about either, or anything else) which has at any time before the priority date of that invention been made available to the public (whether in the United Kingdom or elsewhere) by written or oral description, by use or in any other way.

(3) The state of the art in the case of an invention to which an application for a patent or a patent relates shall be taken also to comprise matter contained in an application for another patent which was published on or after the priority date of that invention, if the following conditions are satisfied, that is to say—

> (a) that matter was contained in the application for that other patent both as filed and as published; and
>
> (b) the priority date of that matter is earlier than that of the invention.

(4) For the purposes of this section the disclosure of matter constituting an invention shall be disregarded in the case of a patent or an application for a patent if occurring later than the beginning of the period of six months immediately proceeding the date of filing the application for the patent and either—

> (a) the disclosure was due to, or made in consequence of, the matter having been obtained unlawfully or in breach of confidence by any person—
>
> > (i) from the inventor or from any other person to whom the matter was made available in confidence by the inventor or who obtained it from the inventor because he or the inventor believed that he was entitled to obtain it; or
> >
> > (ii) from any other person to whom the matter was made available in confidence by any person mentioned in sub-paragraph (i) above or in this subparagraph or who obtained it from any person so mentioned because he or the person from whom he obtained it believed that he was entitled to obtain it;
>
> (b) the disclosure was made in breach of confidence by any person who obtained the matter in confidence from the inventor or from any other person to whom it was made available, or who obtained it, from the inventor; or
>
> (c) the disclosure was due to, or made in consequence of the inventor displaying the invention at an international exhibition and the applicant states, on filing the application, that the invention has been so displayed and also, within the prescribed period, files written evidence in support of the statement complying with any prescribed conditions.

(5) In this section references to the inventor include references to any proprietor of the invention for the time being.

(6) [...]

3   Inventive step

An invention shall be taken to involve an inventive step if it is not obvious to a person skilled in the art, having regard to any matter which forms part of the state of the art by virtue only of section 2(2) above (and disregarding section 2(3) above).

4   Industrial application

(1) Subject to subsection (2) below, an invention shall be taken to be capable of industrial application if it can be made or used in any kind of industry, including agriculture.

(2) [repealed]

(3) [repealed]

[4A   Methods of treatment or diagnosis

(1) A patent shall not be granted for the invention of—

    (a) a method of treatment of the human or animal body by surgery or therapy, or

    (b) a method of diagnosis practised on the human or animal body.

(2) Subsection (1) above does not apply to an invention consisting of a substance or composition for use in any such method.

(3) In the case of an invention consisting of a substance or composition for use in any such method, the fact that the substance or composition forms part of the state of the art shall not prevent the invention from being taken to be new if the use of the substance or composition in any such method does not form part of the state of the art.

(4) In the case of an invention consisting of a substance or composition for a specific use in any such method, the fact that the substance or composition forms part of the state of the art shall not prevent the invention from being taken to be new if that specific use does not form part of the state of the art.]

5   Priority date

(1) For the purposes of this Act the priority date of an invention to which an application for a patent relates and also of any matter (whether or not the same as the invention) contained in any such application is, except as provided by the following provisions of this Act, the date of filing the application.

(2) If in or in connection with an application for a patent (the application in suit) a declaration is made, whether by the applicant or any predecessor in title of his, complying with the relevant requirements of rules and specifying one or more earlier relevant applications for the purposes of this section made by the applicant or a predecessor in title of his and [the application in suit has a date of filing during the period allowed under subsection (2A)(a) or (b) below], then—

    (a) if an invention to which the application in suit relates is supported by matter disclosed in the earlier relevant application or applications, the priority date of that invention shall instead of being the date of filing the application in suit be the date of filing the relevant application in which that matter was disclosed or, if it was disclosed in more than one relevant application, the earliest of them;

    (b) the priority date of any matter contained in the application in suit which was also disclosed in the earlier relevant application or applications shall be the date of filing the relevant application in which that matter was disclosed or, if it was disclosed in more than one relevant application, the earliest of them.

[(2A) The periods are—

    (a) the period of twelve months immediately following the date of filing of the earlier specified relevant application, or if there is more than one, of the earliest of them; and

    (b) where the comptroller has given permission under subsection (2B) below for a late declaration to be made under subsection (2) above, the period commencing immediately after the end of the period allowed under paragraph (a) above and ending at the end of the prescribed period.

(2B) The applicant may make a request to the comptroller for permission to make a late declaration under subsection (2) above.

(2C) The comptroller shall grant a request made under subsection (2B) above if, and only if—

    (a) the request complies with the relevant requirements of rules; and

    (b) the comptroller is satisfied that the applicant's failure to file the application in suit within the period allowed under subsection (2A)(a) above was unintentional.]

(3) Where an invention or other matter contained in the application in suit was also disclosed in two earlier relevant applications filed by the same applicant as in the case of the application in suit or a predecessor in title of his and the second of those relevant applications was specified in or

in connection with the application in suit, the second of those relevant applications shall, so far as concerns that invention or matter, be disregarded unless—

    (a) it was filed in or in respect of the same country as the first; and

    (b) not later than the date of filing the second, the first (whether or not so specified) was unconditionally withdrawn, or was abandoned or refused, without—

        (i)   having been made available to the public (whether in the United Kingdom or elsewhere);

        (ii) leaving any rights outstanding; and

        (iii) having served to establish a priority date in relation to another application, wherever made.

(4) The foregoing provisions of this section shall apply for determining the priority date of an invention for which a patent has been granted as they apply for determining the priority date of an invention to which an application for that patent relates.

(5) In this section "relevant application" means any of the following applications which has a date of filing, namely—

    (a) an application for a patent under this Act:

    (b) an application in or for a convention country (specified under section 90 below) for protection in respect of an invention or an application which, in accordance with the law of a convention country or a treaty or international convention to which a convention country is a party, is equivalent to such an application.

[(6) References in subsection (5) above to a convention country include references to a country, other than the United Kingdom, which is a member of the World Trade Organisation.]

Right to apply for and obtain a patent and be mentioned as inventor

7 Right to apply for and obtain a patent

(1) Any person may make an application for a patent either alone or jointly with another.

(2) A patent for an invention may be granted—

    (a) primarily to the inventor or joint inventors;

    (b) in preference to the foregoing, to any person or persons who, by virtue of any enactment or rule of law, or any foreign law or treaty or international convention, or by virtue of an enforceable term of any agreement entered into with the inventor before the making of the invention, was or were at the time of the making of the invention entitled to the whole of the property in it (other than equitable interests) in the United Kingdom;

    (c) in any event, to the successor or successors in title of any person or persons mentioned in paragraph (a) or (b) above or any person so mentioned and the successor or successors in title of another person so mentioned;

and to no other person.

(3) In this Act "inventor" in relation to an invention means the actual deviser of the invention and "joint inventor" shall be construed accordingly.

(4) Except so far as the contrary is established, a person who makes an application for a patent shall be taken to be the person who is entitled under subsection (2) above to be granted a patent and two or more persons who make such an application jointly shall be taken to be the persons so entitled.

Applications

14 Making of application

(1) Every application for a patent—

    (a) shall be made in the prescribed form and shall be filed at the Patent Office in the prescribed manner; [...]

[(1A) Where an application for a patent is made, the fee prescribed for the purpose of this subsection ("the application fee") shall be paid not later than the end of the period prescribed for the purposes of section 15(10)(c) below.]

(2) Every application for a patent shall contain—

    (a) a request for the grant of a patent;

    (b) a specification containing a description of the invention, a claim or claims and any drawing referred to in the description or any claim; and

    (c) an abstract;

but the foregoing provision shall not prevent an application being initiated by documents complying with section 15(1) below.

(3) The specification of an application shall disclose the invention in a manner which is clear enough and complete enough for the invention to be performed by a person skilled in the art.

(4) [...]

(5) The claim or claims shall—

    (a) define the matter for which the applicant seeks protection;

    (b) be clear and concise;

    (c) be supported by the description; and

    (d) relate to one invention or to a group of inventions which are so linked as to form a single inventive concept.

(6) Without prejudice to the generality of subsection (5)(d) above, rules may provide for treating two or more inventions as being so linked as to form a single inventive concept for the purposes of this Act.

(7) The purpose of the abstract is to give technical information and on publication it shall not form part of the state of the art by virtue of section 2(3) above, and the comptroller may determine whether the abstract adequately fulfills its purpose and, if it does not, may reframe it so that it does.

(8) [...]

(9) An application for a patent may be withdrawn at any time before the patent is granted and any withdrawal of such an application may not be revoked.

[(10) Subsection (9) above does not affect the power of the comptroller under section 117(1) below to correct an error or mistake in a withdrawal of an application for a patent.]

[15 Date of filing application

(1) Subject to the following provisions of this Act, the date of filing an application for a patent shall be taken to be the earliest date on which documents filed at the Patent Office to initiate the application satisfy the following conditions—

    (a) the documents indicate that a patent is sought;

    (b) the documents identify the person applying for a patent or contain information sufficient to enable that person to be contacted by the Patent Office; and

    (c) the documents contain either—

        (i) something which is or appears to be a description of the invention for which a patent is sought; or

        (ii) a reference, complying with the relevant requirements of rules, to an earlier relevant application made by the applicant or a predecessor in title of his.

(2) It is immaterial for the purposes of subsection (1)(c)(i) above—

    (a) whether the thing is in, or is accompanied by a translation into, a language accepted by the Patent Office in accordance with rules;

    (b) whether the thing otherwise complies with the other provisions of this Act and with any relevant rules.

(3) Where documents filed at the Patent Office to initiate an application for a patent satisfy one or more of the conditions specified in subsection (1) above, but do not satisfy all those conditions, the comptroller shall as soon as practicable after the filing of those documents notify the applicant of what else must be filed in order for the application to have a date of filing.

(4) Where documents filed at the Patent Office to initiate an application for a patent satisfy all the conditions specified in subsection (1) above, the comptroller shall as soon as practicable after the filing of the last of those documents notify the applicant of—

(a) the date of filing the application, and

(b) the requirements that must be complied with, and the periods within which they are required by this Act or rules to be complied with, if the application is not to be treated as having been withdrawn.

(5) Subsection (6) below applies where—

(a) an application has a date of filing by virtue of subsection (1) above;

(b) within the prescribed period the applicant files at the Patent Office—

(i) a drawing, or

(ii) part of the description of the invention for which a patent is sought, and

(c) that drawing or that part of the description was missing from the application at the date of filing.

(6) Unless the applicant withdraws the drawing or the part of the description filed under subsection (5)(b) above ("the missing part") before the end of the prescribed period—

(a) the missing part shall be treated as included in the application; and

(b) the date of filing the application shall be the date on which the missing part is filed at the Patent Office.

(7) Subsection (6)(b) above does not apply if—

(a) on or before the date which is the date of filing the application by virtue of subsection (1) above a declaration is made under section 5(2) above in or in connection with the application;

(b) the applicant makes a request for subsection (6)(b) above not to apply; and

(c) the request complies with the relevant requirements of rules and is made within the prescribed period.

(8) Subsections (6) and (7) above do not affect the power of the comptroller under section 117(1) below to correct an error or mistake.

(9) Where, after an application for a patent has been filed and before the patent is granted—

(a) a new application is filed by the original applicant or his successor in title in accordance with rules in respect of any part of the matter contained in the earlier application, and

(b) the conditions mentioned in subsection (1) above are satisfied in relation to the new application (without the new application contravening section 76 below),

the new application shall be treated as having, as its date of filing, the date of filing the earlier application.

(10) Where an application has a date of filing by virtue of this section, the application shall be treated as having been withdrawn if any of the following applies—

(a) the applicant fails to file at the Patent Office, before the end of the prescribed period, one or more claims and the abstract;

(b) where a reference to an earlier relevant application has been filed as mentioned in subsection (1)(c)(ii) above—

(i) the applicant fails to file at the Patent Office, before the end of the prescribed period, a description of the invention for which the patent is sought;

(ii) the applicant fails to file at the Patent Office, before the end of the prescribed period, a copy of the application referred to, complying with the relevant requirements of rules;

(c) the applicant fails to pay the application fee before the end of the prescribed period;

(d) the applicant fails, before the end of the prescribed period, to make a request for a search under section 17 below and pay the search fee.

(11) In this section "relevant application" has the meaning given by section 5(5) above.]

[15A   Preliminary examination

(1) The comptroller shall refer an application for a patent to an examiner for a preliminary examination if—

 (a) the application has a date of filing;

 (b) the application has not been withdrawn or treated as withdrawn; and

 (c) the application fee has been paid.

(2) On a preliminary examination of an application the examiner shall—

 (a) determine whether the application complies with those requirements of this Act and the rules which are designated by the rules as formal requirements for the purposes of this Act; and

 (b) determine whether any requirements under section 13(2) or 15(10) above remain to be complied with.

(3) The examiner shall report to the comptroller his determinations under subsection (2) above.

(4) If on the preliminary examination of an application it is found that—

 (a) any drawing referred to in the application, or

 (b) part of the description of the invention for which the patent is sought,

is missing from the application, then the examiner shall include this finding in his report under subsection (3) above.

(5) Subsections (6) to (8) below apply if a report is made to the comptroller under subsection (3) above that not all the formal requirements have been complied with.

(6) The comptroller shall specify a period during which the applicant shall have the opportunity—

 (a) to make observations on the report, and

 (b) to amend the application so as to comply with those requirements (subject to section 76 below).

(7) The comptroller may refuse the application if the applicant fails to amend the application as mentioned in subsection (6)(b) above before the end of the period specified by the comptroller under that subsection.

(8) Subsection (7) above does not apply if—

 (a) the applicant makes observations as mentioned in subsection (6)(a) above before the end of the period specified by the comptroller under that subsection, and

 (b) as a result of the observations, the comptroller is satisfied that the formal requirements have been complied with.

(9) If a report is made to the comptroller under subsection (3) above—

 (a) that any requirement of section 13(2) or 15(10) above has not been complied with; or

 (b) that a drawing or part of the description of the invention has been found to be missing,

then the comptroller shall notify the applicant accordingly.]

25   Term of patent

(1) A patent granted under this Act shall be treated for the purposes of the following provisions of this Act as having been granted, and shall take effect, on the date on which notice of its grant is published in the journal and, subject to subsection (3) below, shall continue in force until the end of the period of 20 years beginning with the date of filing the application for the patent or with such other date as may be prescribed.

Property in patents and applications, and registration

30   Nature of, and transactions in, patents and applications for patents

(1) Any patent or application for a patent is personal property (without being a thing in action), and any patent or any such application and rights in or under it may be transferred, created or granted in accordance with subsections (2) to (7) below.

(2) Subject to section 36(3) below, any patent or any such application, or any right in it, may be assigned or mortgaged.

(3) Any patent or any such application or right shall vest by operation of law in the same way as any other personal property and may be vested by an assent of personal representatives.

(4) Subject to section 36(3) below, a licence may be granted under any patent or any such application for working the invention which is the subject of the patent or the application; and—

(a) to the extent that the licence so provides, a sub-licence may be granted under any such licence and any such licence or sub-licence may be assigned or mortgaged; and

(b) any such licence or sub-licence shall vest by operation of law in the same way as any other personal property and may be vested by an assent of personal representatives.

(5) Subsections (2) to (4) above shall have effect subject to the following provisions of this Act.

(6) Any of the following transactions, that is to say—

(a) any assignment or mortgage of a patent or any such application, or any right in a patent or any such application;

(b) any assent relating to any patent or any such application or right;

shall be void unless it is in writing and is signed by or on behalf of [the assignor or mortgagor] (or, in the case of an assent or other transaction by a personal representative, by or on behalf of the personal representative) [. . .]

[(6A) If a transaction mentioned in subsection (6) above is by a body corporate, references in that subsection to such a transaction being signed by or on behalf of the assignor or mortgagor shall be taken to include references to its being under the seal of the body corporate.]

(7) An assignment of a patent or any such application or a share in it, and an exclusive licence granted under any patent or any such application, may confer on the assignee or licensee the right of the assignor or licensor to bring proceedings by virtue of section 61 or 69 below for a previous infringement or to bring proceedings under section 58 below for a previous act.

36   Co-ownership of patents and applications for patents

(1) Where a patent is granted to two or more persons, each of them shall, subject to any agreement to the contrary, be entitled to an equal undivided share in the patent.

(2) Where two or more persons are proprietors of a patent, then, subject to the provisions of this section and subject to any agreement to the contrary—

(a) each of them shall be entitled, by himself or his agents, to do in respect of the invention concerned, for his own benefit and without the consent of or the need to account to the other or others, any act which would apart from this subsection and section 55 below, amount to an infringement of the patent concerned; and

(b) any such act shall not amount to an infringement of the patent concerned.

(3) Subject to the provisions of sections 8 and 12 above and section 37 below and to any agreement for the time being in force, where two or more persons are proprietors of a patent one of them shall not without the consent of the other or others [—

(a) amend the specification of the patent or apply for such an amendment to be allowed or for the patent to be revoked, or

(b)] grant a licence under the patent or assign or mortgage a share in the patent or in Scotland cause or permit security to be granted over it.

[. . .]

37   Determination of right to patent after grant

(1) [After a patent has been granted for an invention any person having or claiming a proprietary interest in or under the patent may refer to the comptroller the question—

(a) who is or are the true proprietor or proprietors of the patent,

(b) whether the patent should have been granted to the person or persons to whom it was granted, or

(c) whether any right in or under the patent should be transferred or granted to any other person or persons;

and the comptroller shall determine the question and make such order as he thinks fit to give effect to the determination.]

[...]

(5) On any such reference no order shall be made under this section transferring the patent to which the reference relates on the ground that the patent was granted to a person not so entitled, and no order shall be made under subsection (4) above on that ground, if the reference was made after the end of the period of two years beginning with the date of the grant, unless it is shown that any person registered as a proprietor of the patent knew at the time of the grant or, as the case may be, of the transfer of the patent to him that he was not entitled to the patent.

(6) An order under this section shall not be so made as to affect the mutual rights or obligations of trustees or of the personal representatives of a deceased person, or their rights or obligations as such.

[...]

Employees' inventions

39 Right to employees' inventions

(1) Notwithstanding anything in any rule of law, an invention made by an employee shall, as between him and his employer, be taken to belong to his employer for the purposes of this Act and all other purposes if—

(a) it was made in the course of the normal duties of the employee or in the course of duties falling outside his normal duties, but specifically assigned to him, and the circumstances in either case were such that an invention might reasonably be expected to result from the carrying out of his duties; or

(b) the invention was made in the course of the duties of the employee and, at the time of making the invention, because of the nature of his duties and the particular responsibilities arising from the nature of his duties he had a special obligation to further the interests of the employer's undertaking.

(2) Any other invention made by an employee shall, as between him and his employer, be taken for those purposes to belong to the employee.

[(3) Where by virtue of this section an invention belongs, as between him and his employer, to an employee, nothing done—

(a) by or on behalf of the employee or any person claiming under him for the purposes of pursuing an application for a patent, or

(b) by any person for the purpose of performing or working the invention,

shall be taken to infringe any copyright or design right to which, as between him and his employer, his employer is entitled in any model or document relating to the invention.]

40 Compensation of employees for certain inventions

[(1) Where it appears to the court or the comptroller on an application made by an employee within the prescribed period that—

(a) the employee has made an invention belonging to the employer for which a patent has been granted,

(b) having regard among other things to the size and nature of the employer's undertaking, the invention or the patent for it (or the combination of both) is of outstanding benefit to the employer, and

(c) by reason of those facts it is just that the employee should be awarded compensation to be paid by the employer,

the court or the comptroller may award him such compensation of an amount determined under section 41 below.]

(2) Where it appears to the court or the comptroller on an application made by an employee within the prescribed period that—

(a) a patent has been granted for an invention made by and belonging to the employee;

(b) his rights in the invention, or in any patent or application for a patent for the invention, have since the appointed day been assigned to the employer or an exclusive licence under the patent or application has since the appointed day been granted to the employer;

(c) the benefit derived by the employee from the contract of assignment, assignation or grant or any ancillary contract ("the relevant contract") is inadequate in relation to the benefit derived by the employer from [the invention or the patent for it (or both)]; and

(d) by reason of those facts it is just that the employee should be awarded compensation to be paid by the employer in addition to the benefit derived from the relevant contract;

the court or the comptroller may award him such compensation of an amount determined under section 41 below.

(3) Subsections (1) and (2) above shall not apply to the invention of an employee where a relevant collective agreement provides for the payment of compensation in respect of inventions of the same description as that invention to employees of the same description as that employee.

(4) Subsection (2) above shall have effect notwithstanding anything in the relevant contract or any agreement applicable to the invention (other than any such collective agreement).

(5) If it appears to the comptroller on an application under this section that the application involves matters which would more properly be determined by the court, he may decline to deal with it.

(6) In this section—

"the prescribed period", in relation to proceedings before the court, means the period prescribed by rules of court, and

"relevant collective agreement" means a collective agreement within the meaning of [the Trade Union and Labour Relations (Consolidation) Act 1992], made by or on behalf of a trade union to which the employee belongs, and by the employer or an employers' association to which the employer belongs which is in force at the time of the making of the invention.

(7) References in this section to an invention belonging to an employer or employee are references to it so belonging as between the employer and the employee.

41   Amount of compensation

[(1) An award of compensation to an employee under section 40(1) or (2) above shall be such as will secure for the employee a fair share (having regard to all the circumstances) of the benefit which the employer has derived, or may reasonably be expected to derive, from any of the following—

(a) the invention in question;

(b) the patent for the invention;

(c) the assignment, assignation or grant of—

(i)   the property or any right in the invention, or

(ii)   the property in, or any right in or under, an application for the patent,

to a person connected with the employer.]

(2) For the purposes of subsection (1) above the amount of any benefit derived or expected to be derived by an employer from the assignment, assignation or grant of—

(a) the property in, or any right in or under, a patent for the invention or an application for such a patent; or

(b) the property or any right in the invention;

to a person connected with him shall be taken to be the amount which could reasonably be expected to be so derived by the employer if that person had not been connected with him.

(3) Where the Crown or a Research Council in its capacity as employer assigns or grants the property in, or any right in or under, an invention, patent or application for a patent to a body having among its functions that of developing or exploiting inventions resulting from public research and does so for no consideration or only a nominal consideration, any benefit derived from the invention, patent or application by that body shall be treated for the purposes of the foregoing provisions of this section as so derived by the Crown or, as the case may be, Research Council.

In this subsection "Research Council" means a body which is a Research Council for the purposes of the Science and Technology Act 1965 [or the Arts and Humanities Research Council (as defined by section 1 of the Higher Education Act 2004)].

(4) In determining the fair share of the benefit to be secured for an employee in respect of [...] an invention which has always belonged to an employer, the court or the comptroller shall, among

other things, take the following matters into account, that is to say—

    (a) the nature of the employee's duties, his remuneration and the other advantages he derives or has derived from his employment or has derived in relation to the invention under this Act;

    (b) the effort and skill which the employee has devoted to making the invention;

    (c) the effort and skill which any other person has devoted to making the invention jointly with the employee concerned, and the advice and other assistance contributed by any other employee who is not a joint inventor of the invention; and

    (d) the contribution made by the employer to the making, developing and working of the invention by the provision of advice, facilities and other assistance, by the provision of opportunities and by his managerial and commercial skill and activities.

(5) In determining the fair share of the benefit to be secured for an employee in respect of [. . .] an invention which originally belonged to him, the court or the comptroller shall, among other things, take the following matters into account, that is to say—

    (a) any conditions in a licence or licences granted under this Act or otherwise in respect of the invention or the patent [for it];

    (b) the extent to which the invention was made jointly by the employee with any other person; and

    (c) the contribution made by the employer to the making, developing and working of the invention as mentioned in subsection (4)(d) above.

(6) Any order for the payment of compensation under section 40 above may be an order for the payment of a lump sum or for periodical payment, or both.

(7) Without prejudice to [section 12 of the Interpretation Act 1978] which provides that a statutory power may in general be exercised from time to time), the refusal of the court or the comptroller to make any such order on an application made by an employee under section 40 above shall not prevent a further application being made under that section by him or any successor in title of his.

(8) Where the court or the comptroller has made any such order, the court or he may on the application of either the employer or the employee vary or discharge it or suspend any provision of the order and revive any provision so suspended, and section 40(5) above shall apply to the application as it applies to an application under that section.

(9) In England and Wales any sums awarded by the comptroller under section 40 above shall, if a county court so orders, be recoverable by execution issued from the county court or otherwise as if they were payable under an order of that court.

(10) In Scotland an order made under section 40 above by the comptroller for the payment of any sums may be enforced in like manner as [an extract registered decree arbitral bearing a warrant for execution issued by the sheriff court of any sheriffdom in Scotland].

(11) In Northern Ireland an order made under section 40 above by the comptroller for the payment of any sums may be enforced as if it were a money judgment.

42   Enforceability of contracts relating to employees' inventions

(1) This section applies to any contract (whenever made) relating to inventions made by an employee, being a contract entered into by him—

    (a) with the employer (alone or with another); or

    (b) with some other person at the request of the employer or in pursuance of the employee's contract of employment.

(2) Any term in a contract to which this section applies which diminishes the employee's rights in inventions of any description made by him after the appointed day and the date of the contract, or in or under patents for those inventions or applications for such patents, shall be unenforceable against him to the extent that it diminishes his rights in an invention of that description so made, or in or under a patent for such an invention or an application for any such patent.

(3) Subsection (2) above shall not be construed as derogating from any duty of confidentiality owed to his employer by an employee by virtue of any rule of law or otherwise.

(4) This section applies to any arrangement made with a Crown employee by or on behalf of the Crown as his employer as it applies to any contract made between an employee and an employer other than the Crown, and for the purposes of this section "Crown employee" means a person employed under or for the purposes of a government department or any officer or body exercising on behalf of the Crown functions conferred by any enactment [or a person serving in the naval, military or air forces of the Crown].

43   Supplementary

(1) Sections 39 to 42 above shall not apply to an invention made before the appointed day.

(2) Sections 39 to 42 above shall not apply to an invention made by an employee unless at the time he made the invention one of the following conditions was satisfied in his case, that is to say—

(a) he was mainly employed in the United Kingdom; or

(b) he was not mainly employed anywhere or his place of employment could not be determined, but his employer had a place of business in the United Kingdom to which the employee was attached, whether or not he was also attached elsewhere.

(3) In sections 39 to 42 above and this section, except so far as the context otherwise requires, references to the making of an invention by an employee are references to his making it alone or jointly with any other person, but do not include references to his merely contributing advice or other assistance in the making of an invention by another employee.

(4) Any references [in sections 39 to 42] above to a patent and to a patent being granted are respectively references to a patent or other protection and to its being granted whether under the law of the United Kingdom or the law in force in any other country or under any treaty or international convention.

(5) For the purposes of sections 40 and 41 above the benefit derived or expected to be derived by an employer from [an invention or patent] shall, where he dies before any award is made under section 40 above in respect of [it], include any benefit derived or expected to be derived from [it] by his personal representatives or by any person in whom it was vested by their assent.

[(5A) For the purposes of sections 40 and 41 above the benefit derived or expected to be derived by an employer from an invention shall not include any benefit derived or expected to be derived from the invention after the patent for it has expired or has been surrendered or revoked.]

(6) Where an employee dies before an award is made under section 40 above in respect of a patented invention made by him, his personal representatives or their successors in title may exercise his right to make or proceed with an application for compensation under subsection (1) or (2) of that section.

(7) In sections 40 and 41 above and this section "benefit" means benefit in money or money's worth.

(8) Section 533 of the Income and Corporation Taxes Act 1970 (definition of connected persons) shall apply for determining for the purposes of section 41(2) above whether one person is connected with another as it applies for determining that question for the purposes of the Tax Acts.

Infringement

60   Meaning of infringement

(1) Subject to the provisions of this section, a person infringes a patent for an invention if, but only if, while the patent is in force, he does any of the following things in the United Kingdom in relation to the invention without the consent of the proprietor of the patent, that is to say—

(a) where the invention is a product, he makes, disposes of, offers to dispose of, uses or imports the product or keeps it whether for disposal or otherwise;

(b) where the invention is a process, he uses the process or he offers it for use in the United Kingdom when he knows, or it is obvious to a reasonable person in the circumstances, that its use there without the consent of the proprietor would be an infringement of the patent;

(c) where the invention is a process, he disposes of, offers to dispose of, uses or imports any product obtained directly by means of that process or keeps any such product whether for disposal or otherwise.

(2) Subject to the following provisions of this section, a person (other than the proprietor of the patent) also infringes a patent for an invention if, while the patent is in force and without the consent of the proprietor, he supplies or offers to supply in the United Kingdom a person other than a licensee or other person entitled to work the invention with any of the means, relating to an essential element of the invention, for putting the invention into effect when he knows, or it is obvious to a reasonable person in the circumstances, that those means are suitable for putting, and are intended to put, the invention into effect in the United Kingdom.

(3) Subsection (2) above shall not apply to the supply or offer of a staple commercial product unless the supply or the offer is made for the purpose of inducing the person supplied or, as the case may be, the person to whom the offer is made to do an act which constitutes an infringement of the patent by virtue of subsection (1) above.

(4) [...]

(5) An act which, apart from this subsection, would constitute an infringement of a patent for an invention shall not do so if—

   (a) it is done privately and for purposes which are not commercial;

   (b) it is done for experimental purposes relating to the subject-matter of the invention;

   (c) it consists of the extemporaneous preparation in a pharmacy of a medicine for an individual in accordance with a prescription given by a registered medical or dental practitioner or consists of dealing with a medicine so prepared;

   (d) it consists of the use, exclusively for the needs of a relevant ship, of a product or process in the body of such a ship or in its machinery, tackle, apparatus or other accessories, in a case where the ship has temporarily or accidentally entered the internal or territorial waters of the United Kingdom;

   (e) it consists of the use of a product or process in the body or operation of a relevant aircraft, hovercraft or vehicle which has temporarily or accidentally entered or is crossing the United Kingdom (including the air space above it and its territorial waters) or the use of accessories for such a relevant aircraft, hovercraft or vehicle;

   (f) it consists of the use of an exempted aircraft which has lawfully entered or is lawfully crossing the United Kingdom as aforesaid or of the importation into the United Kingdom, or the use or storage there, of any part of accessory for such an aircraft.

   [(g) it consists of the use by a farmer of the product of his harvest for propagation or multiplication by him on his own holding, where there has been a sale of plant propagating material to the farmer by the proprietor of the patent or with his consent for agricultural use;

   (h) it consists of the use of an animal or animal reproductive material by a farmer for an agricultural purpose following a sale to the farmer, by the proprietor of the patent or with his consent, of breeding stock or other animal reproductive material which constitutes or contains the patented invention.

   (i) it consists of—

      (i) an act done in conducting a study, test or trial which is necessary for and is conducted with a view to the application of paragraphs 1 to 5 of article 13 of Directive 2001/82/EC or paragraphs 1 to 4 of article 10 of Directive 2001/83/EC, or

      (ii) any other act which is required for the purpose of the application of those paragraphs].

   [...]

61 Proceedings for infringement of patent

(1) Subject to the following provisions of this Part of this Act, civil proceedings may be brought in the court by the proprietor of a patent in respect of any act alleged to infringe the patent and (without prejudice to any other jurisdiction of the court) in those proceedings a claim may be made—

   (a) for an injunction or interdict restraining the defendant or defender from any apprehended act of infringement;

   (b) for an order for him to deliver up or destroy any patented product in relation to which the patent is infringed or any article in which that product is inextricably comprised;

(c) for damages in respect of the infringement;

(d) for an account of the profits derived by him from the infringement;

(e) for a declaration or declarator that the patent is valid and has been infringed by him.

(2) The court shall not, in respect of the same infringement, both award the proprietor of a patent damages and order that he shall be given an account of the profits.

(3) The proprietor of a patent and any other person may by agreement with each other refer to the comptroller the question whether that other person has infringed the patent and on the reference the proprietor of the patent may make any claim mentioned in subsection (1)(c) or (e) above.

(4) Except so far as the context requires, in the following provisions of this Act—

(a) any reference to proceedings for infringement and the bringing of such proceedings includes a reference to a reference under subsection (3) above and the making of such a reference;

(b) any reference to a [claimant] or pursuer includes a reference to the proprietor of the patent; and

(c) any reference to a defendant or defender includes a reference to any other party to the reference.

(5) If it appears to the comptroller on a reference under subsection (3) above that the question referred to him would more properly be determined by the court, he may decline to deal with it and the court shall have jurisdiction to determine the question as if the reference were proceedings brought in the court.

(6) Subject to the following provisions of this Part of this Act, in determining whether or not to grant any kind of relief claimed under this section and the extent of the relief granted the court or the comptroller shall apply the principles applied by the court in relation to that kind of relief immediately before the appointed day.

[(7) If the comptroller awards any sum by way of damages on a reference under subsection (3) above, then—

(a) in England and Wales, the sum shall be recoverable, if a county court so orders, by execution issued from the county court or otherwise as if it were payable under an order of that court;

(b) in Scotland, payment of the sum may be enforced in like manner as an extract registered decree arbitral bearing a warrant for execution issued by the sheriff court of any sheriffdom in Scotland;

(c) in Northern Ireland, payment of the sum may be enforced as if it were a money judgment.]

64   Right to continue use begun before priority date

[(1) Where a patent is granted for an invention, a person who in the United Kingdom before the priority date of the invention—

(a) does in good faith an act which would constitute an infringement of the patent if it were in force, or

(b) makes in good faith effective and serious preparations to do such an act,

has the right to continue to do the act or, as the case may be, to do the act, notwithstanding the grant of the patent; but this right does not extend to granting a licence to another person to do the act.

(2) If the act was done, or the preparations were made, in the course of a business, the person entitled to the right conferred by subsection (1) may—

(a) authorise the doing of that act by any partners of his for the time being in that business, and

(b) assign that right, or transmit it on death (or in the case of a body corporate on its dissolution), to any person who acquires that part of the business in the course of which the act was done or the preparations were made.

(3) Where a product is disposed of to another in exercise of the rights conferred by subsection (1) or (2), that other and any person claiming through him may deal with the product in the same way as if it had been disposed of by the registered proprietor of the patent.]

66 Proceedings infringement by a co-owner

(1) In the application of section 60 above to a patent of which there are two or more joint proprietors the reference to the proprietor shall be construed—

(a) in relation to any act, as a reference to that proprietor or those proprietors who, by virtue of section 36 above or any agreement referred to in that section, is or are entitled to do that act without its amounting to an infringement; and

(b) in relation to any consent, as a reference to that proprietor or those proprietors who, by virtue of section 36 above or any such agreement, is or are the proper person or persons to give the requisite consent.

(2) One of two or more joint proprietors of a patent may without the concurrence of the others bring proceedings in respect of an act alleged to infringe the patent, but shall not do so unless the others are made parties to the proceedings; but any of the others made a defendant or defender shall not be liable for any costs or expenses unless he enters an appearance and takes part in the proceedings.

67 Proceedings for infringement by exclusive licensee

(1) Subject to the provisions of this section, the holder of an exclusive licence under a patent shall have the same right as the proprietor of the patent to bring proceedings in respect of any infringement of the patent committed after the date of the licence; and references to the proprietor of the patent in the provisions of this Act relating to infringement shall be construed accordingly.

(2) In awarding damages or granting any other relief in any such proceedings the court or the comptroller shall take into consideration any loss suffered or likely to be suffered by the exclusive licensee as such as a result of the infringement, or, as the case may be, the profits derived from the infringement, so far as it constitutes an infringement of the rights of the exclusive licensee as such.

(3) In any proceedings taken by an exclusive licensee by virtue of this section the proprietor of the patent shall be made a party to the proceedings, but if made a defendant or defender shall not be liable for any costs or expenses unless he enters an appearance and takes part in the proceedings.

70 Remedy for groundless threats of infringement proceedings

(1) Where a person (whether or not the proprietor of, or entitled to any right in, a patent) by circulars, advertisements or otherwise threatens another person with proceedings for any infringement of a patent, a person aggrieved by the threats (whether or not he is the person to whom the threats are made) may, subject to subsection (4) below, bring proceedings in the court against the person making the threats, claiming any relief mentioned in subsection (3) below.

[(2) In any such proceedings the claimant or pursuer shall, subject to subsection (2A) below, be entitled to the relief claimed if he proves that the threats were so made and satisfies the court that he is a person aggrieved by them.

(2A) If the defendant or defender proves that the acts in respect of which proceedings were threatened constitute or, if done, would constitute an infringement of a patent—

(a) the claimant or pursuer shall be entitled to the relief claimed only if he shows that the patent alleged to be infringed is invalid in a relevant respect;

(b) even if the claimant or pursuer does show that the patent is invalid in a relevant respect, he shall not be entitled to the relief claimed if the defendant or defender proves that at the time of making the threats he did not know, and had no reason to suspect, that the patent was invalid in that respect.]

(3) The said relief is—

(a) a declaration or declarator to the effect that the threats are unjustifiable;

(b) an injunction or interdict against the continuance of the threats; and

(c) damages in respect of any loss which the [claimant] or pursuer has sustained by the threats.

[(4) Proceedings may not be brought under this section for—

(a) a threat to bring proceedings for an infringement alleged to consist of making or importing a product for disposal or of using a process, or

(b) a threat, made to a person who has made or imported a product for disposal or used a process, to bring proceedings for an infringement alleged to consist of doing anything else in relation to that product or process.

(5) For the purposes of this section a person does not threaten another person with proceedings for infringement of a patent if he merely—

(a) provides factual information about the patent,

(b) makes enquiries of the other person for the sole purpose of discovering whether, or by whom, the patent has been infringed as mentioned in subsection (4)(a) above, or

(c) makes an assertion about the patent for the purpose of any enquiries so made.

(6) In proceedings under this section for threats made by one person (A) to another (B) in respect of an alleged infringement of a patent for an invention, it shall be a defence for A to prove that he used his best endeavours, without success, to discover—

(a) where the invention is a product, the identity of the person (if any) who made or (in the case of an imported product) imported it for disposal;

(b) where the invention is a process and the alleged infringement consists of offering it for use, the identity of a person who used the process;

(c) where the invention is a process and the alleged infringement is an act falling within section 60(1)(c) above, the identity of the person who used the process to produce the product in question;

and that he notified B accordingly, before or at the time of making the threats, identifying the endeavours used.]

Revocation of patents

72   Power to revoke patents on application

(1) Subject to the following provisions of this Act, the court or the comptroller may [. . .] by order revoke a patent for an invention [on the application of any person (including the proprietor of the patent)] on (but only on) any of the following grounds, that is to say—

(a)   the invention is not a patentable invention;

[(b) that the patent was granted to a person who was not entitled to be granted that patent;]

(c)   the specification of the patent does not disclose the invention clearly enough and completely enough for it to be performed by a person skilled in the art;

(d)   the matter disclosed in the specification of the patent extends beyond that disclosed in the application for the patent, as filed, or, if the patent was granted on a new application filed under section 8(3), 12 or 37(4) above or as mentioned in [section 15(9)] above, in the earlier application, as filed;

(e)   the protection conferred by the patent has been extended by an amendment which should not have been allowed.

(2) An application for the revocation of a patent on the ground mentioned in subsection (1)(b) above—

(a) may only be made by a person found by the court in an action for a declaration or declarator, or found by the court or the comptroller on a reference under section 37 above, to be entitled to be granted that patent or to be granted a patent for part of the matter comprised in the specification of the patent sought to be revoked; and

(b) may not be made if that action was commenced or that reference was made after the end of the period of two years beginning with the date of the grant of the patent sought to be revoked, unless it is shown that any person registered as a proprietor of the patent knew at the time of the grant or of the transfer of the patent to him that he was not entitled to the patent.

(3) [. . .]

(4) An order under this section may be an order for the unconditional revocation of the patent or, where the court or the comptroller determines that one of the grounds mentioned in subsection (1)

above has been established, but only so as to invalidate the patent to a limited extent, an order that the patent should be revoked unless within a specified time the specification is amended [. . .] to the satisfaction of the court or the comptroller, as the case may be.

[(4A) The reference in subsection (4) above to the specification being amended is to its being amended under section 75 below and also, in the case of a European patent (UK), to its being amended under any provision of the European Patent Convention under which the claims of the patent may be limited by amendment at the request of the proprietor.]

(5) A decision of the comptroller or on appeal from the comptroller shall not estop any party to civil proceedings in which infringcmcnt of a patent is in issue from alleging invalidity of the patent on any of the grounds referred to in subsection (1) above, whether or not any of the issues involved were decided in the said decision.

(6) Where the comptroller refuses to grant an application made to him by any person under this section, no application (otherwise than by way of appeal or by way of putting validity in issue in proceedings for infringement) may be made to the court by that person under this section in relation to the patent concerned, without the leave of the court.

(7) Where the comptroller has not disposed of an application made to him under this section, the applicant may not apply to the court under this section in respect of the patent concerned unless either—

    (a) the proprietor of the patent agrees that the applicant may so apply, or

    (b) the comptroller certifies in writing that it appears to him that the question whether the patent should be revoked is one which would more properly be determined by the court.

73 Comptroller's power to revoke patents on his own initiative

(1) If it appears to the comptroller that an invention for which a patent has been granted formed part of the state of the art by virtue only of section 2(3) above, he may on his own initiative by order revoke the patent, but shall not do so without giving the proprietor of the patent an opportunity of making any observations and of amending the specification of the patent so as to exclude any matter which formed part of the state of the art as aforesaid without contravening section 76 below.

    [. . .]

Putting validity in issue

74 Proceedings in which validity of patent may be put in issue

(1) Subject to the following provisions of this section, the validity of a patent may be put in issue—

    (a) by way of defence, in proceedings for infringement of the patent under section 61 above or proceedings under section 69 above for infringment of rights conferred by the publication of an application;

    (b) in proceedings under section 70 above;

    (c) in proceedings in which a declaration in relation to the patent is sought under section 71 above;

    (d) in proceedings before the court or the comptroller under section 72 above for the revocation of the patent;

    (e) in proceedings under section 58 above.

(2) The validity of a patent may not be put in issue in any other proceedings and, in particular, no proceedings may be instituted (whether under this Act or otherwise) seeking only a declaration as to the validity or invalidity of a patent.

(3) The only grounds on which the validity of a patent may be put in issue (whether in proceedings for revocation under section 72 above or otherwise) are the grounds on which the patent may be revoked under that section.

    [. . .]

PART III MISCELLANEOUS AND GENERAL

Supplemental

125 Extent of invention

(1) For the purposes of this Act an invention for a patent for which an application has been made or for which a patent has been granted shall, unless the context otherwise requires, be taken to be that specified in a claim of the specification of the application or patent, as the case may be, as interpreted by the description and any drawings contained in that specification, and the extent of the protection conferred by a patent or application for a patent shall be determined accordingly.

(2) It is hereby declared for the avoidance of doubt that where more than one invention is specified in any such claim, each invention may have a different priority date under section 5 above.

(3) The Protocol on the Interpretation of Article 69 of the European Patent Convention (which Article contains a provision corresponding to subsection (1) above) shall, as for the time being in force, apply for the purposes of subsection (1) above as it applies for the purposes of that Article.

130 Interpretation

(1) In this Act, except so far as the context otherwise requires—

"comptroller" means the Comptroller-General of Patents, Designs and Trade Marks;

"Convention on International Exhibitions" means the Convention relating to International Exhibitions signed in Paris on 22nd November 1928, as amended or supplemented by any protocol to that convention which is for the time being in force;

"court" means—

[(a) as respects England and Wales, the High Court or any patents county court having jurisdiction by virtue of an order under section 287 of the Copyright, Designs and Patents Act 1988;]

(b) as respects Scotland, the Court of Session;

(c) as respects Northern Ireland, the High Court in Northern Ireland;

"date of filing" means—

(a) in relation to an application for a patent made under this Act, the date which is the date of filing that application by virtue of section 15 above; and

(b) in relation to any other application, the date which, under the law of the country where the application was made or in accordance with the terms of a treaty or convention to which that country is a party, is to be treated as the date of filing that application or is equivalent to the date of filing an application in that country (whatever the outcome of the application);

"employee" means a person who works or (where the employment has ceased) worked under a contract of employment or in employment under or for the purposes of a government department [or a person who serves (or served) in the naval, military or air forces of the Crown];

"employer", in relation to an employee, means the person by whom the employee is or was employed;

"exclusive licence" means a licence from the proprietor of or applicant for a patent conferring on the licensee, or on him and persons authorised by him, to the exclusion of all other persons (including the proprietor or applicant), any right in respect of the invention to which the patent or application relates, and "exclusive licensee" and "non-exclusive licence" shall be construed accordingly;

"international exhibition" means an official or officially recognised international exhibition falling within the terms of the Convention on International Exhibitions or falling within the terms of any subsequent treaty or convention replacing that convention;

"inventor" has the meaning assigned to it by section 7 above;

"patent" means a patent under this Act;

"patented invention" means an invention for which a patent is granted and

"patented process" shall be construed accordingly;

"patented product" means a product which is a patented invention or, in relation to a patented process, a product obtained directly by means of the process or to which the process has been applied;

"priority date" means the date determined as such under section 5 above;

"published" means made available to the public (whether in the United Kingdom or elsewhere) and a document shall be taken to be published under any provision of this Act if it can be inspected as of right at any place in the United Kingdom by members of the public, whether on payment of a fee or not; and "republished" shall be construed accordingly; [...]

Protection of Children Act 1978

(1978, c. 37)

An Act to prevent the exploitation of children by making indecent photographs of them; and to penalise the distribution, showing and advertisement of such indecent photographs.   [20th July 1978]

1   Indecent photographs of children

(1) [Subject to sections 1A and 1B, it] is an offence for a person—

(a) to take, or permit to be taken [or to make], any indecent photograph [or pseudo-photograph] of a child [...]; or

(b) to distribute or show such indecent photographs [or pseudo-photographs]; or

(c) to have in his possession such indecent photographs [or pseudo-photographs], with a view to their being distributed or shown by himself or others; or

(d) to publish or cause to be published any advertisement likely to be understood as conveying that the advertiser distributes or shows such indecent photographs [or pseudo-photographs], or intends to do so.

(2) For purposes of this Act, a person is to be regarded as distributing an indecent photograph [or pseudo-photograph] if he parts with possession of it to, or exposes or offers it for acquisition by, another person.

(3) Proceedings for an offence under this Act shall not be instituted except by or with the consent of the Director of Public Prosecutions.

(4) Where a person is charged with an offence under subsection (1)(b) or (c), it shall be a defence for him to prove—

(a) that he had a legitimate reason for distributing or showing the photographs [or pseudo-photographs] or (as the case may be) having them in his possession; or

(b) that he had not himself seen the photographs [or pseudo-photographs] and did not know, nor had any cause to suspect, them to be indecent.

(5) References in the Children and Young Persons Act 1933 (except in sections 15 and 99) to the offences mentioned in Schedule 1 to that Act shall include an offence under subsection (1)(a) above.

1A   Marriage and other relationships

[(1) This section applies where, in proceedings for an offence under section 1(1)(a) of taking or making an indecent photograph of a child, or for an offence under section 1(1)(b) or (c) relating to an indecent photograph of a child, the defendant proves that the photograph was of the child aged 16 or over, and that at the time of the offence charged the child and he—

(a) were married, or

(b) lived together as partners in an enduring family relationship.

(2) Subsections (5) and (6) also apply where, in proceedings for an offence under section 1(1)(b) or (c) relating to an indecent photograph of a child, the defendant proves that the photograph was of the child aged 16 or over, and that at the time when he obtained it the child and he—

(a) were married, or

(b) lived together as partners in an enduring family relationship.

(3) This section applies whether the photograph showed the child alone or with the defendant, but not if it showed any other person.

(4) In the case of an offence under section 1(1)(a), if sufficient evidence is adduced to raise an issue as to whether the child consented to the photograph being taken or made, or as to whether the defendant reasonably believed that the child so consented, the defendant is not guilty of the offence unless it is proved that the child did not so consent and that the defendant did not reasonably believe that the child so consented.

(5) In the case of an offence under section 1(1)(b), the defendant is not guilty of the offence unless it is proved that the showing or distributing was to a person other than the child.

(6) In the case of an offence under section 1(1)(c), if sufficient evidence is adduced to raise an issue both—

   (a) as to whether the child consented to the photograph being in the defendant's possession, or as to whether the defendant reasonably believed that the child so consented, and

   (b) as to whether the defendant had the photograph in his possession with a view to its being distributed or shown to anyone other than the child,

the defendant is not guilty of the offence unless it is proved either that the child did not so consent and that the defendant did not reasonably believe that the child so consented, or that the defendant had the photograph in his possession with a view to its being distributed or shown to a person other than the child.]

1B   Exception for criminal proceedings, investigations etc.

[(1) In proceedings for an offence under section 1(1)(a) of making an indecent photograph or pseudo-photograph of a child, the defendant is not guilty of the offence if he proves that—

   (a) it was necessary for him to make the photograph or pseudo-photograph for the purposes of the prevention, detection or investigation of crime, or for the purposes of criminal proceedings, in any part of the world,

   (b) at the time of the offence charged he was a member of the Security Service, and it was necessary for him to make the photograph or pseudo-photograph for the exercise of any of the functions of the Service, or

   (c) at the time of the offence charged he was a member of GCHQ, and it was necessary for him to make the photograph or pseudo-photograph for the exercise of any of the functions of GCHQ.

(2) In this section "GCHQ" has the same meaning as in the Intelligence Services Act 1994.]

6   Punishments

(1) Offences under this Act shall be punishable either on conviction on indictment or on summary conviction.

(2) A person convicted on indictment of any offence under this Act shall be liable to imprisonment for a term of not more than [ten] years, or to a fine or to both.

(3) A person convicted summarily of any offence under this Act shall be liable—

   (a) to imprisonment for a term not exceeding six months; or

   (b) to a fine not exceeding the prescribed sum for the purposes of [section 32 of the Magistrates' Courts Act 1980] (punishment on summary conviction of offences triable either way: £1,000 or other sum substituted by order under that Act), or to both.

7   Interpretation

(1) The following subsections apply for the interpretation of this Act.

(2) References to an indecent photograph include an indecent film, a copy of an indecent photograph or film, and an indecent photograph comprised in a film.

(3) Photographs (including those comprised in a film) shall, if they show children and are indecent, be treated for all purposes of this Act as indecent photographs of children [and so as respects pseudo-photographs].

[(4) References to a photograph include—

   (a) the negative as well as the positive version; and

   (b) data stored on a computer disc or by other electronic means which is capable of conversion into a photograph.]

(5) "Film" includes any form of video-recording.

[(6) "Child", subject to subsection (8), means a person under the age of [18].

(7) "Pseudo-photograph" means an image, whether made by computer-graphics or otherwise howsoever, which appears to be a photograph.

(8) If the impression conveyed by a pseudo-photograph is that the person shown is a child, the pseudo-photograph shall be treated for all purposes of this Act as showing a child and so shall a pseudo-photograph where the predominant impression conveyed is that the person shown is a child notwithstanding that some of the physical characteristics shown are those of an adult.

(9) References to an indecent pseudo-photograph include—

(a) a copy of an indecent pseudo-photograph; and

(b) data stored on a computer disc or by other electronic means which is capable of conversion into a pseudo-photograph.]

Indecent Displays (Control) Act 1981

(1981, c. 42)

An Act to make fresh provision with respect to the public display of indecent matter; and for purposes connected therewith.   [27th July 1981]

1   Indecent displays

(1) If any indecent matter is publicly displayed the person making the display and any person causing or permitting the display to be made shall be guilty of an offence.

(2) Any matter which is displayed in or so as to be visible from any public place shall, for the purposes of this section, be deemed to be publicly displayed.

(3) In subsection (2) above, "public place", in relation to the display of any matter, means any place to which the public have or are permitted to have access (whether on payment or otherwise) while that matter is displayed except—

(a) a place to which the public are permitted to have access only on payment which is or includes payment for that display; or

(b) a shop or any part of a shop to which the public can only gain access by passing beyond an adequate warning notice;

but the exclusions contained in paragraphs (*a*) and (*b*) above shall only apply where persons under the age of 18 years are not permitted to enter while the display in question is continuing.

(4) Nothing in this section applies in relation to any matter—

[(a) included by any person in a television broadcasting service or other television programme service (within the meaning of Part I of the Broadcasting Act 1990);]

(b) included in the display of an art gallery or museum and visible only from within the gallery or museum; or

(c) displayed by or with the authority of, and visible only from within a building occupied by, the Crown or any local authority; or

(d) included in a performance of a play (within the meaning of the Theatres Act 1968); or

[(e) included in a film exhibition as defined in the Cinemas Act 1985—

(i) given in a place which as regards that exhibition is required to be licensed under section 1 of that Act or by virtue only of section 5, 7 or 8 of that Act is not required to be so licensed; or

(ii) which is an exhibition to which section 6 of that Act applies given by an exempted organisation as defined in subsection (6) of that section].

(5) In this section "matter" includes anything capable of being displayed, except that it does not include an actual human body or any part thereof; and in determining for the purpose of this section whether any displayed matter is indecent—

(a) there shall be disregarded any part of that matter which is not exposed to view; and

(b) account may be taken of the effect of juxtaposing one thing with another.

(6) A warning notice shall not be adequate for the purposes of this section unless it complies with the following requirements—

> (a) The warning notice must contain the following words, and no others—
>
> "WARNING
>
> Person passing beyond this notice will find material on display which they may consider indecent. No admittance to persons under 18 years of age."
>
> (b) The word "WARNING" must appear as a heading.
>
> (c) No pictures or other matter shall appear on the notice.
>
> (d) The notice must be so situated that no one could reasonably gain access to the shop or part of the shop in question without being aware of the notice and it must be easily legible by any person gaining such access.

4   Penalties

(1) In England and Wales, any person guilty of an offence under this Act shall be liable—

> (a) on summary conviction, to a fine not exceeding the statutory maximum; or
>
> (b) on conviction on indictment, to imprisonment for a term not exceeding two years or a fine or both.

(2) In Scotland, any person guilty of an offence under this Act shall be liable—

> (a) on summary conviction—
>
> > (i) in the district court, to a fine not exceeding £200;
> >
> > (ii) in the sheriff court, to a fine not exceeding the statutory maximum; or
>
> (b) on conviction on indictment, to imprisonment for a term not exceeding two years or a fine or both.

Civic Government (Scotland) Act 1982

(1982, c. 45)

An Act to make provision as regards Scotland [...] for prohibiting the taking of and dealing with indecent photographs of children; [...] and for connected purposes.   [28th October 1982]

PART IV OFFENCES, POWERS OF CONSTABLES, ETC.

Offences of annoying, offensive, obstructive or dangerous behaviour

52A   Possession of indecent photographs of children

(1) It is an offence for a person to have any indecent photograph [or pseudo-photograph] of a child in his possession.

(2) Where a person is charged with an offence under subsection (1), it shall be a defence for him to prove—

> (a) that he had a legitimate reason for having the photograph [or pseudo-photograph] in his possession; or
>
> (b) that he had not himself seen the photograph or [pseudo-photograph] and did not know, nor had any cause to suspect, it to be indecent; or
>
> (c) that the photograph [or pseudo-photograph] was sent to him without any prior request made by him or on his behalf and that he did not keep it for an unreasonable time.

[(3) A person shall be liable—

> (a) on summary conviction of an offence under this section to imprisonment for a period not exceeding 6 months or to a fine not exceeding level 5 on the standard scale or both;
>
> (b) on conviction on indictment of such an offence to imprisonment for a period not exceeding 5 years or to a fine or to both].

[...]

Criminal Justice Act 1988

(1988, c. 33)
An Act to [...] create a summary offence of possession of an indecent photograph of a child [...]
[29th July 1988]

PART XI MISCELLANEOUS

160   Summary offence of possession of indecent photograph of child

(1) [Subject to subsection 1A, it] is an offence for a person to have any indecent photograph [or pseudo-photograph] of a child [...] in his possession.

(2) Where a person is charged with an offence under subsection (1) above, it shall be a defence for him to prove—

    (a) that he had a legitimate reason for having the photograph [or pseudo-photograph] in his possession; or

    (b) that he had not himself seen the photograph [or pseudo-photograph] and did not know nor had any cause to suspect, it to be indecent; or

    (c) that the photograph [or pseudo-photograph] was sent to him without any prior request made by him or on his behalf and that he did not keep it for an unreasonable time.

[(2A) A person shall be liable on conviction on indictment of an offence under this section to imprisonment for a term not exceeding five years or a fine, or both.]

(3) A person shall be liable on summary conviction of an offence under this section to [imprisonment for a term not exceeding six months or] a fine not exceeding level 5 on the standard scale[, or both].

(4) Sections 1(3), 2(3), 3 and 7 of the Protection of Children Act 1978 shall have effect as if any reference in them to that Act included a reference to this section.

[160A   Marriage and other relationships

(1) This section applies where, in proceedings for an offence under section 160 relating to an indecent photograph of a child, the defendant proves that the photograph was of the child aged 16 or over, and that at the time of the offence charged the child and he—

    (a) were married [or civil partners of each other], or

    (b) lived together as partners in an enduring family relationship.

(2) This section also applies where, in proceedings for an offence under section 160 relating to an indecent photograph of a child, the defendant proves that the photograph was of the child aged 16 or over, and that at the time when he obtained it the child and he—

    (a) were married [or civil partners of each other], or

    (b) lived together as partners in an enduring family relationship.

(3) This section applies whether the photograph showed the child alone or with the defendant, but not if it showed any other person.

(4) If sufficient evidence is adduced to raise an issue as to whether the child consented to the photograph being in the defendant's possession, or as to whether the defendant reasonably believed that the child so consented, the defendant is not guilty of the offence unless it is proved that the child did not so consent and that the defendant did not reasonably believe that the child so consented.]

Copyright, Designs and Patents Act 1988

(1988, c. 48)
An Act to restate the law of copyright, with amendments; to make fresh provision as to the rights of performers and others in performances; [...] and for connected purposes.   [15th November 1988]

PART I COPYRIGHT

Chapter I Subsistence, Ownership and Duration of Copyright

Introductory

1 Copyright and copyright works

(1) Copyright is a property right which subsists in accordance with this Part in the following descriptions of work—

    (a) original literary, dramatic, musical or artistic works,

    (b) sound recordings, films [or broadcasts] and

    (c) the typographical arrangement of published editions.

(2) In this Part "copyright work" means a work of any of those descriptions in which copyright subsists.

(3) Copyright does not subsist in a work unless the requirements of this Part with respect to qualification for copyright protection are met (see section 153 and the provisions referred to there).

2 Rights subsisting in copyright works

(1) The owner of the copyright in a work of any description has the exclusive right to do the acts specified in Chapter II as the acts restricted by the copyright in a work of that description.

(2) In relation to certain descriptions of copyright work the following rights conferred by Chapter IV (moral rights) subsist in favour of the author, director or commissioner of the work, whether or not he is the owner of the copyright—

    (a) section 77 (right to be identified as author or director),

    (b) section 80 (right to object to derogatory treatment of work), and

    (c) section 85 (right to privacy of certain photographs and films).

Descriptions of work and related provisions

3 Literary, dramatic and musical works

(1) In this Part—

"literary work" means any work, other than a dramatic or musical work, which is written, spoken or sung, and accordingly includes—

    (a) a table or compilation [other than a database],

    (b) a computer program,

    [(c) preparatory design material for a computer program, and

    (d) a database];

"dramatic work" includes a work of dance or mime; and

"musical work" means a work consisting of music, exclusive of any words or action intended to be sung, spoken or performed with the music.

(2) Copyright does not subsist in a literary, dramatic or musical work unless and until it is recorded, in writing or otherwise; and references in this Part to the time at which such a work is made are to the time at which it is so recorded.

(3) It is immaterial for the purposes of subsection (2) whether the work is recorded by or with the permission of the author; and where it is not recorded by the author, nothing in that subsection affects the question whether copyright subsists in the record as distinct from the work recorded.

[3A Databases

(1) In this Part "database" means a collection of independent works, data or other materials which—

    (a) are arranged in a systematic or methodical way, and

    (b) are individually accessible by electronic or other means.

(2) For the purposes of this Part a literary work consisting of a database is original if, and only if, by reason of the selection or arrangement of the contents of the database the database constitutes the author's own intellectual creation.]

4 Artistic works

(1) In this Part "artistic work" means—

    (a) a graphic work, photograph, sculpture or collage, irrespective of artistic quality;

    (b) a work of architecture being a building or a model for a building, or

    (c) a work of artistic craftsmanship.

(2) In this Part—

"building" includes any fixed structure, and a part of a building or fixed structure;

"graphic work" includes—

    (a) any painting, drawing, diagram, map, chart or plan, and

    (b) any engraving, etching, lithograph, woodcut or similar work;

"photograph" means a recording of light or other radiation on any medium on which an image is produced or from which an image may by any means be produced, and which is not part of a film;

"sculpture" includes a cast or model made for purposes of sculpture.

[5A Sound recordings

(1) In this Part "sound recording" means—

    (a) a recording of sounds, from which the sounds may be reproduced, or

    (b) a recording of the whole or any part of a literary, dramatic or musical work, from which sounds reproducing the work or part may be produced,

regardless of the medium on which the recording is made or the method by which the sounds are reproduced or produced.

(2) Copyright does not subsist in a sound recording which is, or to the extent that it is, a copy taken from a previous sound recording.

5B Films

(1) In this Part "film" means a recording on any medium from which a moving image may by any means be produced.

(2) The sound track accompanying a film shall be treated as part of the film for the purposes of this Part.

(3) Without prejudice to the generality of subsection (2), where that subsection applies—

    (a) references in this Part to showing a film include playing the film sound track to accompany the film, [

    (b) references in this Part to playing a sound recording, or to communicating a sound recording to the public, do not include playing or communicating the film sound track to accompany the film,

    (c) references in this Part to copying a work, so far as they apply to a sound recording, do not include copying the film sound track to accompany the film, and

    (d) references in this Part to the issuing, rental or lending of copies of a work, so far as they apply to a sound recording, do not include the issuing, rental or lending of copies of the sound track to accompany the film].

(4) Copyright does not subsist in a film which is, or to the extent that it is, a copy taken from a previous film.

(5) Nothing in this section affects any copyright subsisting in a film sound track as a sound recording.

6 Broadcasts

[(1) In this Part a "broadcast" means an electronic transmission of visual images, sounds or other information which—

    (a) is transmitted for simultaneous reception by members of the public and is capable of being lawfully received by them, or

(b) is transmitted at a time determined solely by the person making the transmission for presentation to members of the public,

and which is not excepted by subsection (1A); and references to broadcasting shall be construed accordingly.

(1A) Excepted from the definition of "broadcast" is any internet transmission unless it is—

(a) a transmission taking place simultaneously on the internet and by other means,

(b) a concurrent transmission of a live event, or

(c) a transmission of recorded moving images or sounds forming part of a programme service offered by the person responsible for making the transmission, being a service in which programmes are transmitted at scheduled times determined by that person.]

(2) An encrypted transmission shall be regarded as capable of being lawfully received by members of the public only if decoding equipment has been made available to members of the public by or with the authority of the person making the transmission or the person providing the contents of the transmission.

(3) References in this Part to the person making a broadcast [or a transmission which is a broadcast] are—

(a) to the person transmitting the programme, if he has responsibility to any extent for its contents, and

(b) to any person providing the programme who makes with the person transmitting it the arrangements necessary for its transmission;

and references in this Part to a programme, in the context of broadcasting, are to any item included in a broadcast.

(4) For the purposes of this Part, the place from which a [wireless] broadcast is made is the place where, under the control and responsibility of the person making the broadcast, the programme-carrying signals are introduced into an uninterrupted chain of communication (including, in the case of a satellite transmission, the chain leading to the satellite and down towards the earth).

(4A) Subsections (3) and (4) have effect subject to section 6A (safeguards in case of certain satellite broadcasts).

(5) References in this Part to the reception of a broadcast include reception of a broadcast relayed by means of a telecommunications system.

[(5A) The relaying of a broadcast by reception and immediate re-transmission shall be regarded for the purposes of this Part as a separate act of broadcasting from the making of the broadcast which is so re-transmitted.]

(6) Copyright does not subsist in a broadcast which infringes, or to the extent that it infringes, the copyright in another broadcast [. . .]

[6A Safeguards in case of certain satellite broadcasts

(1) This section applies where the place from which a broadcast by way of satellite transmission is made is located in a country other than an EEA State and the law of that country fails to provide at least the following level of protection—

(a) exclusive rights in relation to [wireless] broadcasting equivalent to those conferred by section 20 [(infringement by communication to the public)] on the authors of literary, dramatic, musical and artistic works, films and broadcasts;

(b) a right in relation to live [wireless] broadcasting equivalent to that conferred on a performer by section 182(1)(b) (consent required for live broadcast of performance); and

(c) a right for authors of sound recordings and performers to share in a single equitable remuneration in respect of the [wireless] broadcasting of sound recordings.

(2) Where the place from which the programme-carrying signals are transmitted to the satellite ("the uplink station") is located in an EEA State—

(a) that place shall be treated as the place from which the broadcast is made, and

(b) the person operating the uplink station shall be treated as the person making the broadcast.

(3) Where the uplink station is not located in an EEA State but a person who is established in an EEA State has commissioned the making of the broadcast—

    (a) that person shall be treated as the person making the broadcast, and

    (b) the place in which he has his principal establishment in the European Economic Area shall be treated as the place from which the broadcast is made.]

[…]

8 Published editions

(1) In this Part "published edition", in the context of copyright in the typographical arrangement of a published edition, means a published edition of the whole or any part of one or more literary, dramatic or musical works.

(2) Copyright does not subsist in the typographical arrangement of a published edition if, or to the extent that, it reproduces the typographical arrangement of a previous edition.

Authorship and ownership of copyright

9 Authorship of work

(1) In this Part "author", in relation to a work, means the person who creates it.

(2) That person shall be taken to be—

    [(aa) in the case of a sound recording, the producer;

    (ab) in the case of a film, the producer and the principal director;]

    (b) in the case of a broadcast, the person making the broadcast (see section 6(3)) or, in the case of a broadcast which relays another broadcast by reception and immediate re-transmission, the person making that other broadcast;

    (c) […]

    (d) in the case of the typographical arrangement of a published edition, the publisher.

(3) In the case of a literary, dramatic, musical or artistic work which is computer-generated, the author shall be taken to be the person by whom the arrangements necessary for the creation of the work are undertaken.

(4) For the purposes of this Part a work is of "unknown authorship" if the identity of the author is unknown or, in the case of a work of joint authorship, if the identity of none of the authors is known.

(5) For the purposes of this Part the identity of an author shall be regarded as unknown if it is not possible for a person to ascertain his identity by reasonable inquiry; but if his identity is once known it shall not subsequently be regarded as unknown.

10 Works of joint authorship

(1) In this Part a "work of joint authorship" means a work produced by the collaboration of two or more authors in which the contribution of each author is not distinct from that of the other author or authors.

[(1A) A film shall be treated as a work of joint authorship unless the producer and the principal director are the same person.]

(2) A broadcast shall be treated as a work of joint authorship in any case where more than one person is to be taken as making the broadcast (see section 6(3)).

(3) References in this Part to the author of a work shall, except as otherwise provided, be construed in relation to a work of joint authorship as references to all the authors of the work.

11 First ownership of copyright

(1) The author of a work is the first owner of any copyright in it, subject to the following provisions.

(2) Where a literary, dramatic, musical or artistic work [or a film] is made by an employee in the course of his employment, his employer is the first owner of any copyright in the work subject to any agreement to the contrary.

(3) This section does not apply to Crown copyright or Parliamentary copyright (see sections 163 and 165) or to copyright which subsists by virtue of section 168 (copyright of certain international organisations).

Duration of copyright

[12   Duration of copyright in literary, dramatic, musical or artistic works

(1) The following provisions have effect with respect to the duration of copyright in a literary, dramatic, musical or artistic work.

(2) Copyright expires at the end of the period of 70 years from the end of the calendar year in which the author dies, subject as follows.

(3) If the work is of unknown authorship, copyright expires—

(a) at the end of the period of 70 years from the end of the calendar year in which the work was made, or

(b) if during that period the work is made available to the public, at the end of the period of 70 years from the end of the calendar year in which it is first so made available,

subject as follows.

(4) Subsection (2) applies if the identity of the author becomes known before the end of the period specified in paragraph (a) or (b) of subsection (3).

(5) For the purposes of subsection (3) making available to the public includes—

(a) in the case of a literary, dramatic or musical work—

(i)   performance in public, or

[(ii) communication to the public]

(b) in the case of an artistic work—

(i)   exhibition in public,

(ii)   a film including the work being shown in public, or

[(iii) communication to the public;]

but in determining generally for the purposes of that subsection whether a work has been made available to the public no account shall be taken of any unauthorised act.

(6) Where the country of origin of the work is not an EEA State and the author of the work is not a national of an EEA State, the duration of copyright is that to which the work is entitled in the country of origin, provided that does not exceed the period which would apply under subsection (2) to (5).

(7) If the work is computer-generated the above provisions do not apply and copyright expires at the end of the period of 50 years from the end of the calendar year in which the work was made.

(8) The provisions of this section are adapted as follows in relation to a work of joint authorship—

(a) the reference in subsection (2) to the death of the author shall be construed—

(i)   if the identity of all the authors is known, as a reference to the death of the last of them to die, and

(ii) if the identity of one or more of the authors is known and the identity of one or more others is not, as a reference to the death of the last whose identity is known;

(b) the reference in subsection (4) to the identity of the author becoming known shall be construed as a reference to the identity of any of the authors becoming known;

(c) the reference in subsection (6) to the author not being a national of an EEA State shall be construed as a reference to none of the authors being a national of an EEA State.

(9) This section does not apply to Crown copyright or Parliamentary copyright (see sections 163 to [166B]) or to copyright which subsists by virtue of section 168 (copyright of certain international organisations).]

[13A   Duration of copyright in sound recordings

(1) The following provisions have effect with respect to the duration of copyright in a sound recording.

[(2) Subject to subsections (4) and (5), copyright expires—

(a) at the end of the period of 50 years from the end of the calendar year in which the recording is made, or

(b) if during that period the recording is published, 50 years from the end of the calendar year in which it is first published, or

(c) if during that period the recording is not published but is made available to the public by being played in public or communicated to the public, 50 years from the end of the calendar year in which it is first so made available,

but in determining whether a sound recording has been published, played in public or communicated to the public, no account shall be taken of any unauthorised act.]

(3) [...]

(4) Where the author of a sound recording is not a national of an EEA State, the duration of copyright is that to which the sound recording is entitled in the country of which the author is a national, provided that does not exceed the period which would apply under [subsection (2)].

(5) If or to the extent that the application of subsection (4) would be at variance with an international obligation to which the United Kingdom became subject prior to 29th October 1993, the duration of copyright shall be as specified in [subsection (2)].]

[13B   Duration of copyright in films

(1) The following provisions have effect with respect to the duration of copyright in a film.

(2) Copyright expires at the end of the period of 70 years from the end of the calendar year in which the death occurs of the last to die of the following persons—

(a) the principal director,

(b) the author of the screenplay,

(c) the author of the dialogue, or

(d) the composer of music specially created for and used in the film;

subject as follows.

(3) If the identity of one or more of the persons referred to in subsection (2)(a) to (d) is known and the identity of one or more others is not, the reference in that subsection to the death of the last of them to die shall be construed as a reference to the death of the last whose identity is known.

(4) If the identity of the persons referred to in subsection (2)(a) to (d) is unknown, copyright expires at—

(a) the end of the period of 70 years from the end of the calendar year in which the film was made, or

(b) if during that period the film is made available to the public, at the end of the period of 70 years from the end of the calendar year in which it is first so made available.

(5) Subsections (2) and (3) apply if the identity of any of those persons becomes known before the end of the period specified in paragraph (a) or (b) of subsection (4).

(6) For the purposes of subsection (4) making available to the public includes—

(a) showing in public, or

[(b) communicating to the public,]

but in determining generally for the purposes of that subsection whether a film has been made available to the public no account shall be taken of any unauthorised act.

(7) Where the country of origin is not an EEA State and the author of the film is not a national of an EEA state, the duration of copyright is that to which the work is entitled in the country of origin, provided that does not exceed the period which would apply under subsections (2) to (6).

(8) In relation to a film of which there are joint authors, the reference in subsection (7) to the author not being a national of an EEA State shall be construed as a reference to none of the authors being a national of an EEA State.

(9) If in any case there is no person falling within paragraphs (a) to (d) of subsection (2), the above provisions do not apply and copyright expires at the end of the period of 50 years from the end of the calendar year in which the film was made.

(10) For the purposes of this section the identity of any of the persons referred to in subsection (2)(a) to (d) shall be regarded as unknown if it is not possible for a person to ascertain his identity by reasonable inquiry; but if the identity of any such person is once known it shall not subsequently be regarded as unknown.]

[14   Duration of copyright in broadcasts [. . .]

(1) The following provisions have effect with respect to the duration of copyright in a broadcast [. . .]

(2) Copyright in a broadcast [. . .] expires at the end of the period of 50 years from the end of the calendar year in which the broadcast was made [. . .] subject as follows.

(3) Where the author of the broadcast [. . .] is not a national of an EEA State, the duration of copyright in the broadcast [. . .] is that to which it is entitled in the country of which the author is a national, provided that does not exceed the period which would apply under sub-section (2).

(4) If or to the extent that the application of subsection (3) would be at variance with an international obligation to which the United Kingdom became subject prior to 29th October 1993, the duration of copyright shall be as specified in subsection (2).

(5) Copyright in a repeat broadcast [. . .] expires at the same time as the copyright in the original broadcast [. . .]; and accordingly no copyright arises in respect of a repeat broadcast [. . .] which is broadcast [. . .] after the expiry of the copyright in the original broadcast [. . .].

(6) A repeat broadcast [. . .] means one which is a repeat [. . .] of a broadcast previously made [. . .]

15   Duration of copyright in typographical arrangement of published editions

Copyright in the typographical arrangement of a published edition expires at the end of the period of 25 years from the end of the calendar year in which the edition was first published.

[15A   Meaning of country of origin

(1) For the purposes of the provisions of this Part relating to the duration of copyright the country of origin of a work shall be determined as follows.

(2) If the work is first published in a Berne Convention country and is not simultaneously published elsewhere, the country of origin is that country.

(3) If the work is first published simultaneously in two or more countries only one of which is a Berne Convention country, the country of origin is that country.

(4) If the work is first published simultaneously in two or more countries of which two or more are Berne Convention countries, then—

(a) if any of those countries is an EEA State, the country of origin is that country; and

(b) if none of those countries is an EEA State, the country of origin is the Berne Convention country which grants the shorter or shortest period of copyright protection.

(5) If the work is unpublished or is first published in a country which is not a Berne Convention country (and is not simultaneously published in a Berne Convention country), the country of origin is—

(a) if the work is a film and the maker of the film has his headquarters in, or is domiciled or resident in a Berne Convention country, that country;

(b) if the work is—

(i) a work of architecture constructed in a Berne Convention country, or

(ii) an artistic work incorporated in a building or other structure situated in a Berne Convention country,

that country;

(c) in any other case, the country of which the author of the work is a national.

(6) In this section—

(a) a "Berne Convention country" means a country which is a party to any Act of the International Convention for the Protection of Literary and Artistic Works signed at Berne on 9th September 1886; and

(b) references to simultaneous publication are to publication within 30 days of first publication.]

Chapter II Rights Of Copyright Owner

The acts restricted by copyright

16 The acts restricted by copyright in a work

(1) The owner of the copyright in a work has, in accordance with the following provisions of this Chapter, the exclusive right to do the following acts in the United Kingdom—

[a]   to copy the work (see section 17);

(b)   to issue copies of the work to the public (see section 18);

[(ba) to rent or lend the work to the public (see section 18A);]

(c)   to perform, show or play the work in public (see section 19);

[(d) to communicate the work to the public (see section 20);]

(e)   to make an adaptation of the work or do any of the above in relation to an adaptation (see section 21);

and those acts are referred to in this Part as the "acts restricted by the copyright".

(2) Copyright in a work is infringed by a person who without the licence of the copyright owner does, or authorises another to do, any of the acts restricted by the copyright.

(3) References in this Part to the doing of an act restricted by the copyright in a work are to the doing of it—

(a) in relation to the work as a whole or any substantial part of it, and

(b) either directly or indirectly;

and it is immaterial whether any intervening acts themselves infringe copyright.

(4) This Chapter has effect subject to—

(a) the provisions of Chapter III (acts permitted in relation to copyright works), and

(b) the provisions of Chapter VII (provisions with respect to copyright licensing).

17 Infringement of copyright by copying

(1) The copying of the work is an act restricted by the copyright in every description of copyright work; and references in this Part to copying and copies shall be construed as follows.

(2) Copying in relation to a literary, dramatic, musical or artistic work means reproducing the work in any material form.

This includes storing the work in any medium by electronic means.

(3) In relation to an artistic work copying includes the making of a copy in three dimensions of a two-dimensional work and the making of a copy in two dimensions of a three-dimensional work.

(4) Copying in relation to a film, [or broadcast] includes making a photograph of the whole or any substantial part of any image forming part of the film [or broadcast].

(5) Copying in relation to the typographical arrangement of a published edition means making a facsimile copy of the arrangement.

(6) Copying in relation to any description of work includes the making of copies which are transient or are incidental to some other use of the work.

18 Infringement by issue of copies to the public

(1) The issue to the public of copies of the work is an act restricted by the copyright in every description of copyright work.

[(2) References in this Part to the issue to the public of copies of a work are to—

(a) the act of putting into circulation in the EEA copies not previously put into circulation in the EEA by or with the consent of the copyright owner, or

(b) the act of putting into circulation outside the EEA copies not previously put into circulation in the EEA or elsewhere.

(3) References in this Part to the issue to the public of copies of a work do not include—

(a) any subsequent distribution, sale, hiring or loan of copies previously put into circulation (but see section 18A: infringement by rental or lending), or

(b) any subsequent importation of such copies into the United Kingdom or another EEA State,
except so far as paragraph (a) of subsection (2) applies to putting into circulation in the EEA copies
previously put into circulation outside the EEA.

(4) References in this Part to the issue of copies of a work include the issue of the original.]

[18A   Infringement by rental or lending of work to the public

(1) The rental or lending of copies of the work to the public is an act restricted by the
copyright in—

    (a) a literary, dramatic or musical work,

    (b) an artistic work, other than—

        (i)   a work of architecture in the form of a building or a model for a building, or

        (ii)   a work of applied art, or

    (c) a film or a sound recording.

(2) In this Part, subject to the following provisions of this section—

    (a) "rental" means making a copy of the work available for use, on terms that it will or may be
returned, for direct or indirect economic or commercial advantage, and

    (b) "lending" means making a copy of the work available for use, on terms that it will or may
be returned, otherwise than for direct or indirect economic or commercial advantage,
through an establishment which is accessible to the public.

(3) The expressions "rental" and "lending" do not include—

    (a) making available for the purpose of public performance, playing or showing in public, [or
communication to the public];

    (b) making available for the purpose of exhibition in public; or

    (c) making available for on-the-spot reference use.

(4) The expression "lending" does not include making available between establishments which
are accessible to the public.

(5) Where lending by an establishment accessible to the public gives rise to a payment the amount
of which does not go beyond what is necessary to cover the operating costs of the establishment, there
is no direct or indirect economic or commercial advantage for the purposes of this section.

(6) References in this Part to the rental or lending of copies of a work include the rental or lending of the original.]

19   Infringement by performance, showing or playing of work in public

(1) The performance of the work in public is an act restricted by the copyright in a literary, dramatic or musical work.

(2) In this Part "performance", in relation to a work—

    (a) includes delivery in the case of lectures, addresses, speeches and sermons, and

    (b) in general, includes any mode of visual or acoustic presentation, including presentation
by means of a sound recording, film, [or broadcast of the work.]

(3) The playing or showing of the work in public is an act restricted by the copyright in a sound
recording, film [or broadcast].

(4) Where copyright in a work is infringed by its being performed, played or shown in public by
means of apparatus for receiving visual images or sounds conveyed by electronic means, the person
by whom the visual images or sounds are sent, and in the case of a performance the performers, shall
not be regarded as responsible for the infringement.

[20   Infringement by communication to the public

(1) The communication to the public of the work is an act restricted by the copyright in—

    (a) a literary, dramatic, musical or artistic work,

    (b) a sound recording or film, or

    (c) a broadcast.

(2) References in this Part to communication to the public are to communication to the public by
electronic transmission, and in relation to a work include—

(a) the broadcasting of the work;

(b) the making available to the public of the work by electronic transmission in such a way that members of the public may access it from a place and at a time individually chosen by them.]

21 Infringement by making adaptation or act done in relation to adaptation

(1) The making of an adaptation of the work is an act restricted by the copyright in a literary, dramatic or musical work.

For this purpose an adaptation is made when it is recorded, in writing or otherwise.

(2) The doing of any of the acts specified in sections 17 to 20, or subsection (1) above, in relation to an adaptation of the work is also an act restricted by the copyright in a literary, dramatic or musical work.

For this purpose it is immaterial whether the adaptation has been recorded, in writing or otherwise, at the time the act is done.

(3) In this Part "adaptation"—

(a) in relation to a literary [work, other than a computer program or a database, or in relation to a] dramatic work, means—

(i) a translation of the work;

(ii) a version of a dramatic work in which it is converted into a non-dramatic work or, as the case may be, of a non-dramatic work in which it is converted into a dramatic work;

(iii) a version of the work in which the story or action is conveyed wholly or mainly by means of pictures in a form suitable for reproduction in a book, or in a newspaper, magazine or similar periodical;

[(ab) in relation to a computer program, means an arrangement or altered version of the program or a translation of it;

(ac) in relation to a database, means an arrangement or altered version of the database or a translation of it;]

(b) in relation to a musical work, means an arrangement or transcription of the work.

(4) In relation to a computer program a "translation" includes a version of the program in which it is converted into or out of a computer language or code or into a different computer language or code . . .

(5) No inference shall be drawn from this section as to what does or does not amount to copying a work.

Secondary infringement of copyright

22 Secondary infringement: importing infringing copy

The copyright in a work is infringed by a person who, without the licence of the copyright owner, imports into the United Kingdom, otherwise than for his private and domestic use, an article which is, and which he knows or has reason to believe is, an infringing copy of the work.

23 Secondary infringement: possessing or dealing with infringing copy

The copyright in a work is infringed by a person who, without the licence of the copyright owner—

(a) possesses in the course of a business,

(b) sells or lets for hire, or offers or exposes for sale or hire,

(c) in the course of a business exhibits in public or distributes, or

(d) distributes otherwise than in the course of a business to such an extent as to affect prejudicially the owner of the copyright,

an article which is, and which he knows or has reason to believe is, an infringing copy of the work.

24 Secondary infringement: providing means for making infringing copies

(1) Copyright in a work is infringed by a person who, without the licence of the copyright owner—

(a) makes,

(b) imports into the United Kingdom,

(c) possesses in the course of a business, or

(d) sells or lets for hire, or offers or exposes for sale or hire,

an article specifically designed or adapted for making copies of that work, knowing or having reason to believe that it is to be used to make infringing copies.

(2) Copyright in a work is infringed by a person who without the licence of the copyright owner transmits the work by means of a telecommunications system (otherwise than by [communication to the public]), knowing or having reason to believe that infringing copies of the work will be made by means of the reception of the transmission in the United Kingdom or elsewhere.

25   Secondary infringement: permitting use of premises for infringing performance

(1) Where the copyright in a literary, dramatic or musical work is infringed by a performance at a place of public entertainment, any person who gave permission for that place to be used for the performance is also liable for the infringement unless when he gave permission he believed on reasonable grounds that the performance would not infringe copyright.

(2) In this section "place of public entertainment" includes premises which are occupied mainly for other purposes but are from time to time made available for hire for the purposes of public entertainment.

26   Secondary infringement: provision of apparatus for infringing performance, etc.

(1) Where copyright in a work is infringed by a public performance of the work, or by the playing or showing of the work in public, by means of apparatus for—

(a) playing sound recordings,

(b) showing films, or

(c) receiving visual images or sounds conveyed by electronic means,

the following persons are also liable for the infringement.

(2) A person who supplied the apparatus, or any substantial part of it, is liable for the infringement if when he supplied the apparatus or part—

(a) he knew or had reason to believe that the apparatus was likely to be so used as to infringe copyright, or

(b) in the case of apparatus whose normal use involves a public performance, playing or showing, he did not believe on reasonable grounds that it would not be so used as to infringe copyright.

(3) An occupier of premises who gave permission for the apparatus to be brought onto the premises is liable for the infringement if when he gave permission he knew or had reason to believe that the apparatus was likely to be so used as to infringe copyright.

(4) A person who supplied a copy of a sound recording or film used to infringe copyright is liable for the infringement if when he supplied it he knew or had reason to believe that what he supplied, or a copy made directly or indirectly from it, was likely to be so used as to infringe copyright.

Infringing copies

27   Meaning of "infringing copy"

(1) In this Part "infringing copy", in relation to a copyright work, shall be construed in accordance with this section.

(2) An article is an infringing copy if its making constituted an infringement of the copyright in the work in question.

(3) An article is also an infringing copy if—

(a) it has been or is proposed to be imported into the United Kingdom, and

(b) its making in the United Kingdom would have constituted an infringement of the copyright in the work in question, or a breach of an exclusive licence agreement relating to that work.

(4) Where in any proceedings the question arises whether an article is an infringing copy and it is shown—

(a) that the article is a copy of the work, and

(b) that copyright subsists in the work or has subsisted at any time,

it shall be presumed until the contrary is proved that the article was made at a time when copyright subsisted in the work.

(5) Nothing in subsection (3) shall be construed as applying to an article which may lawfully be imported into the United Kingdom by virtue of any enforceable Community right within the meaning of section 2(1) of the European Communities Act 1972.

(6) In this Part "infringing copy" includes a copy falling to be treated as an infringing copy by virtue of any of the following provisions—

[section 31A(6) and (9) (making a single accessible copy for personal use),

section 31B(9) and (10) (multiple copies for visually impaired persons),

section 31C(2) (intermediate copies held by approved bodies),]

section 32(5) (copies made for purposes of instruction or examination),

section 35(3) (recordings made by educational establishments for educational purposes),

section 36(5) (reprographic copying by educational establishments for purposes of instruction),

section 37(3)(b) (copies made by librarian or archivist in reliance on false declaration),

section 56(2) (further copies, adaptations, &c. of work in electronic form retained on transfer of principal copy),

section 63(2) (copies made for purpose of advertising artistic work for sale),

section 68(4) (copies made for purpose of broadcast [. . .]), or

any provision of an order under section 141 (statutory licence for certain reprographic copying by educational establishments).

Chapter III Acts Permitted in Relation to Copyright Works

Introductory

28 Introductory provisions

(1) The provisions of this Chapter specify acts which may be done in relation to copyright works notwithstanding the subsistence of copyright; they relate only to the question of infringement of copyright and do not affect any other right or obligation restricting the doing of any of the specified acts.

(2) Where it is provided by this Chapter that an act does not infringe copyright, or may be done without infringing copyright, and no particular description of copyright work is mentioned, the act in question does not infringe the copyright in a work of any description.

(3) No inference shall be drawn from the description of any act which may by virtue of this Chapter be done without infringing copyright as to the scope of the acts restricted by the copyright in any description of work.

(4) The provisions of this Chapter are to be construed independently of each other, so that the fact that an act does not fall within one provision does not mean that it is not covered by another provision.

[28A Making of temporary copies

Copyright in a literary work, other than a computer program or a database, or in a dramatic, musical or artistic work, the typographical arrangement of a published edition, a sound recording or a film, is not infringed by the making of a temporary copy which is transient or incidental, which is an integral and essential part of a technological process and the sole purpose of which is to enable—

(a) a transmission of the work in a network between third parties by an intermediary; or

(b) a lawful use of the work;

and which has no independent economic significance.]

General

29   Research and private study

[(1) Fair dealing with a literary, dramatic, musical or artistic work for the purposes of research for a non-commercial purpose does not infringe any copyright in the work provided that it is accompanied by a sufficient acknowledgement.

(1B) No acknowledgement is required in connection with fair dealing for the purposes mentioned in subsection (1) where this would be impossible for reasons of practicality or otherwise.

(1C) Fair dealing with a literary, dramatic, musical or artistic work for the purposes of private study does not infringe any copyright in the work.]

(2) Fair dealing with the typographical arrangement of a published edition for the purposes [of research or private study] does not infringe any copyright in the arrangement.

(3) Copying by a person other than the researcher or student himself is not fair dealing if—

(a) in the case of a librarian, or a person acting on behalf of a librarian, he does anything which regulations under section 40 would not permit to be done under section 38 or 39 (articles or parts of published works: restriction on multiple copies of same material), or

(b) in any other case, the person doing the copying knows or has reason to believe that it will result in copies of substantially the same material being provided to more than one person at substantially the same time and for substantially the same purpose.

(4) It is not fair dealing—

(a) to convert a computer program expressed in a low level language into a version expressed in a higher level language, or

(b) incidentally in the course of so converting the program, to copy it,

(these acts being permitted if done in accordance with section 50B (decompilation)).

[(4A) It is not fair dealing to observe, study or test the functioning of a computer program in order to determine the ideas and principles which underlie any element of the program (these acts being permitted if done in accordance with section 50BA (observing, studying and testing)).]

(5) [...]

30   Criticism, review and news reporting

(1) Fair dealing with a work for the purpose of criticism or review, of that or another work or of a performance of a work, does not infringe any copyright in the work provided that it is accompanied by a sufficient acknowledgement [and provided that the work has been made available to the public.]

[(1A) For the purposes of subsection (1) a work has been made available to the public if it has been made available by any means, including—

(a) the issue of copies to the public;

(b) making the work available by means of an electronic retrieval system;

(c) the rental or lending of copies of the work to the public;

(d) the performance, exhibition, playing or showing of the work in public;

(e) the communication to the public of the work,

but in determining generally for the purposes of that subsection whether a work has been made available to the public no account shall be taken of any unauthorised act.]

(2) Fair dealing with a work (other than a photograph) for the purpose of reporting current events does not infringe any copyright in the work provided that (subject to subsection (3)) it is accompanied by a sufficient acknowledgement.

(3) No acknowledgement is required in connection with the reporting of current events by means of a sound recording, film [or broadcast where this would be impossible for reasons of practicality or otherwise].

31   Incidental inclusion of copyright material

(1) Copyright in a work is not infringed by its incidental inclusion in an artistic work, sound recording, film [or broadcast].

(2) Nor is the copyright infringed by the issue to the public of copies, or the playing showing [or communication to the public], of anything whose making was, by virtue of subsection (1), not an infringement of the copyright.

(3) A musical work, words spoken or sung with music, or so much of a sound recording [or broadcast] as includes a musical work or such words, shall not be regarded as incidentally included in another work if it is deliberately included.

Computer programs: lawful users

[50A   Back up copies

(1) It is not an infringement of copyright for a lawful user of a copy of a computer program to make any back up copy of it which it is necessary for him to have for the purposes of his lawful use.

(2) For the purposes of this section and sections 50B [, 50BA] and 50C a person is a lawful user of a computer program if (whether under a licence to do any acts restricted by the copyright in the program or otherwise), he has a right to use the program.

(3) Where an act is permitted under this section, it is irrelevant whether or not there exists any term or condition in an agreement which purports to prohibit or restrict the act (such terms being, by virtue of section 296A, void)].

[50B   Decompilation

(1) It is not an infringement of copyright for a lawful user of a copy of a computer program expressed in a low level language—

> (a) to convert it into a version expressed in a higher level language, or
>
> (b) incidentally in the course of so converting the program, to copy it,

(that is, to "decompile" it), provided that the conditions in subsection (2) are met.

(2) The conditions are that—

> (a) it is necessary to decompile the program to obtain the information necessary to create an independent program which can be operated with the program decompiled or with another program ("the permitted objective"); and
>
> (b) the information so obtained is not used for any purpose other than the permitted objective.

(3) In particular, the conditions in subsection (2) are not met if the lawful user—

> (a) has readily available to him the information necessary to achieve the permitted objective;
>
> (b) does not confine the decompiling to such acts as are necessary to achieve the permitted objective;
>
> (c) supplies the information obtained by the decompiling to any person to whom it is not necessary to supply it in order to achieve the permitted objective; or
>
> (d) uses the information to create a program which is substantially similar in its expression to the program decompiled or to do any act restricted by copyright.

(4) Where an act is permitted under this section, it is irrelevant whether or not there exists any term or condition in an agreement which purports to prohibit or restrict the act (such terms being, by virtue of section 296A, void).]

[50BA   Observing, studying and testing of computer programs

(1) It is not an infringement of copyright for a lawful user of a copy of a computer program to observe, study or test the functioning of the program in order to determine the ideas and principles which underlie any element of the program if he does so while performing any of the acts of loading, displaying, running, transmitting or storing the program which he is entitled to do.

(2) Where an act is permitted under this section, it is irrelevant whether or not there exists any term or condition in an agreement which purports to prohibit or restrict the act (such terms being, by virtue of section 296A, void).]

[50C Other acts permitted to lawful users

(1) It is not an infringement of copyright for a lawful user of a copy of a computer program to copy or adapt it, provided that the copying or adapting—

(a) is necessary for his lawful use; and

(b) is not prohibited under any term or condition of an agreement regulating the circumstances in which his use is lawful.

(2) It may, in particular, be necessary for the lawful use of a computer program to copy it or adapt it for the purpose of correcting errors in it.

(3) This section does not apply to any copying or adapting permitted under [section 50A, 50B or 50BA].]

Databases: permitted acts

[50D Acts permitted in relation to databases

(1) It is not an infringement of copyright in a database for a person who has a right to use the database or any part of the database, (whether under a licence to do any of the acts restricted by the copyright in the database or otherwise) to do, in the exercise of that right, anything which is necessary for the purposes of access to and use of the contents of the database or of that part of the database.

(2) Where an act which would otherwise infringe copyright in a database is permitted under this section, it is irrelevant whether or not there exists any term or condition in any agreement which purports to prohibit or restrict the act (such terms being, by virtue of section 296B, void).]

Typefaces

54 Use of typeface in ordinary course of printing

(1) It is not an infringement of copyright in an artistic work consisting of the design of a typeface—

(a) to use the typeface in the ordinary course of typing, composing text, typesetting or printing,

(b) to possess an article for the purpose of such use, or

(c) to do anything in relation to material produced by such use;

and this is so notwithstanding that an article is used which is an infringing copy of the work.

(2) However, the following provisions of this Part apply in relation to persons making, importing or dealing with articles specifically designed or adapted for producing material in a particular typeface, or possessing such articles for the purpose of dealing with them, as if the production of material as mentioned in subsection (1) did infringe copyright in the artistic work consisting of the design of the typeface—

section 24 (secondary infringement: making, importing, possessing or dealing with article for making infringing copy),

sections 99 and 100 (order for delivery up and right of seizure),

section 107(2) (offence of making or possessing such an article), and

section 108 (order for delivery up in criminal proceedings).

(3) The references in subsection (2) to "dealing with" an article are to selling, letting for hire, or offering or exposing for sale or hire, exhibiting in public, or distributing.

Works in electronic form

56 Transfers of copies of works in electronic form

(1) This section applies where a copy of a work in electronic form has been purchased on terms which, expressly or impliedly or by virtue of any rule of law, allow the purchaser to copy the work, or to adapt it or make copies of an adaptation, in connection with his use of it.

(2) If there are no express terms—

(a) prohibiting the transfer of the copy by the purchaser, imposing obligations which continue after a transfer, prohibiting the assignment of any licence or terminating any licence on a transfer, or

(b) providing for the terms on which a transferee may do the things which the purchaser was permitted to do,

anything which the purchaser was allowed to do may also be done without infringement of copyright by a transferee; but any copy, adaptation or copy of an adaptation made by the purchaser which is not also transferred shall be treated as an infringing copy for all purposes after the transfer.

(3) The same applies where the original purchased copy is no longer usable and what is transferred is a further copy used in its place.

(4) The above provisions also apply on a subsequent transfer, with the substitution for references in subsection (2) to the purchaser of references to the subsequent transferor.

Miscellaneous: films and sound recordings

67 Playing of sound recordings for purposes of club, society, etc.

(1) It is not an infringement of the copyright in a sound recording to play it as part of the activities of, or for the benefit of, a club, society or other organisation if the following conditions are met.

(2) The conditions are—

(a) that the organisation is not established or conducted for profit and its main objects are charitable or are otherwise concerned with the advancement of religion, education or social welfare, [...]

[(b) that the sound recording is played by a person who is acting primarily and directly for the benefit of the organisation and who is not acting with a view to gain,

(c) that the proceeds of any charge for admission to the place where the recording is to be heard are applied solely for the purposes of the organisation, and

(d) that the proceeds from any goods or services sold by, or on behalf of, the organisation—

(i) in the place where the sound recording is heard, and

(ii) on the occasion when the sound recording is played, are applied solely for the purposes of the organisation.]

Miscellaneous: broadcasts

70 Recording for purposes of time-shifting

(1) The making [in domestic premises] for private and domestic use of a recording of a broadcast [...] solely for the purpose of enabling it to be viewed or listened to at a more convenient time does not infringe any copyright in the broadcast [...] or in any work included in it.

[(2) Where a copy which would otherwise be an infringing copy is made in accordance with this section but is subsequently dealt with—

(a) it shall be treated as an infringing copy for the purposes of that dealing; and

(b) if that dealing infringes copyright, it shall be treated as an infringing copy for all subsequent purposes.

(3) In subsection (2), "dealt with" means sold or let for hire, offered or exposed for sale or hire or communicated to the public.]

[71 Photographs of broadcasts

(1) The making in domestic premises for private and domestic use of a photograph of the whole or any part of an image forming part of a broadcast, or a copy of such a photograph, does not infringe any copyright in the broadcast or in any film included in it.

(2) Where a copy which would otherwise be an infringing copy is made in accordance with this section but is subsequently dealt with—

(a) it shall be treated as an infringing copy for the purposes of that dealing; and

(b) if that dealing infringes copyright, it shall be treated as an infringing copy for all subsequent purposes.

(3) In subsection (2), "dealt with" means sold or let for hire, offered or exposed for sale or hire or communicated to the public.]

72   Free public showing or playing of broadcast

(1)The showing or playing in public of a broadcast to an audience who have not paid for admission to the place where the broadcast is to be seen or heard does not infringe any copyright in—

[(a) the broadcast;

(b) any sound recording (except so far as it is an excepted sound recording) included in it; or

(c) any film included in it.]

[(1A) For the purposes of this Part an "excepted sound recording" is a sound recording—

(a) whose author is not the author of the broadcast in which it is included; and

(b) which is a recording of music with or without words spoken or sung.

(1B) Where by virtue of subsection (1) the copyright in a broadcast shown or played in public is not infringed, copyright in any excepted sound recording included in it is not infringed if the playing or showing of that broadcast in public—

(a) forms part of the activities of an organisation that is not established or conducted for profit; or

(b) is necessary for the purposes of—

(i) repairing equipment for the reception of broadcasts;

(ii) demonstrating that a repair to such equipment has been carried out; or

(iii) demonstrating such equipment which is being sold or let for hire or offered or exposed for sale or hire.]

(2) The audience shall be treated as having paid for admission to a place—

(a) if they have paid for admission to a place of which that place forms part; or

(b) if goods or services are supplied at that place (or a place of which it forms part)—

(i) at prices which are substantially attributable to the facilities afforded for seeing or hearing the broadcast, or

(ii) at prices exceeding those usually charged there and which are partly attributable to those facilities.

(3) The following shall not be regarded as having paid for admission to a place—

(a) persons admitted as residents or inmates of the place;

(b) persons admitted as members of a club or society where the payment is only for membership of the club or society and the provision of facilities for seeing or hearing broadcasts is only incidental to the main purposes of the club or society.

(4) Where the making of the broadcast [...] was an infringement of the copyright in a sound recording or film, the fact that it was heard or seen in public by the reception of the broadcast [...] shall be taken into account in assessing the damages for that infringement.

Chapter IV Moral Rights

Right to be identified as author or director

77   Right to be identified as author or director

(1) The author of a copyright literary, dramatic, musical or artistic work, and the director of a copyright film, has the right to be identified as the author or director of the work in the circumstances mentioned in this section; but the right is not infringed unless it has been asserted in accordance with section 78.

(2) The author of a literary work (other than words intended to be sung or spoken with music) or a dramatic work has the right to be identified whenever—

(a) the work is published commercially, performed in public, [or communicated to the public]; or

(b) copies of a film or sound recording including the work are issued to the public;

and that right includes the right to be identified whenever any of those events occur in relation to an adaptation of the work as the author of the work from which the adaptation was made.

(3) The author of a musical work, or a literary work consisting of words intended to be sung or spoken with music, has the right to be identified whenever—

(a) the work is published commercially;

(b) copies of a sound recording of the work are issued to the public; or

(c) a film of which the sound-track includes the work is shown in public or copies of such a film are issued to the public;

and that right includes the right to be identified whenever any of those events occur in relation to an adaptation of the work as the author of the work from which the adaptation was made.

(4) The author of an artistic work has the right to be identified whenever—

(a) the work is published commercially or exhibited in public, or a visual image of it is [communicated to the public];

(b) a film including a visual image of the work is shown in public or copies of such a film are issued to the public; or

(c) in the case of a work of architecture in the form of a building or a model for a building, a sculpture or a work of artistic craftsmanship, copies of a graphic work representing it, or of a photograph of it, are issued to the public.

(5) The author of a work of architecture in the form of a building also has the right to be identified on the building as constructed or, where more than one building is constructed to the design, on the first to be constructed.

(6) The director of a film has the right to be identified whenever the film is shown in public, [or communicated to the public] or copies of the film are issued to the public.

(7) The right of the author or director under this section is—

(a) in the case of commercial publication or the issue to the public of copies of a film or sound recording, to be identified in or on each copy or, if that is not appropriate, in some other manner likely to bring his identity to the notice of a person acquiring a copy,

(b) in the case of identification on a building, to be identified by appropriate means visible to persons entering or approaching the building, and

(c) in any other case, to be identified in a manner likely to bring his identity to the attention of a person seeing or hearing the performance, exhibition, showing, [or communication to the public] in question;

and the identification must in each case be clear and reasonably prominent.

(8) If the author or director in asserting his right to be identified specifies a pseudonym, initials or some other particular form of identification, that form shall be used; otherwise any reasonable form of identification may be used.

(9) This section has effect subject to section 79 (exceptions to right).

78 Requirement that right be asserted

(1) A person does not infringe the right conferred by section 77 (right to be identified as author or director) by doing any of the acts mentioned in that section unless the right has been asserted in accordance with the following provisions so as to bind him in relation to that act.

(2) The right may be asserted generally, or in relation to any specified act or description of acts—

(a) on an assignment of copyright in the work, by including in the instrument effecting the assignment a statement that the author or director asserts in relation to that work his right to be identified, or

(b) by instrument in writing signed by the author or director.

(3) The right may also be asserted in relation to the public exhibition of an artistic work—

(a) by securing that when the author or other first owner of copyright parts with possession of the original, or of a copy made by him or under his direction or control, the author is identified on the original or copy, or on a frame, mount or other thing to which it is attached, or

(b) by including in a licence by which the author or other first owner of copyright authorises the making of copies of the work a statement signed by or on behalf of the person granting the licence that the author asserts his right to be identified in the event of the public exhibition of a copy made in pursuance of the licence.

(4) The persons bound by an assertion of the right under subsection (2) or (3) are—

    (a) in the case of an assertion under subsection (2)(a), the assignee and anyone claiming through him, whether or not he has notice of the assertion;

    (b) in the case of an assertion under subsection (2)(b), anyone to whose notice the assertion is brought;

    (c) in the case of an assertion under subsection (3)(a), anyone into whose hands that original or copy comes, whether or not the identification is still present or visible;

    (d) in the case of an assertion under subsection (3)(b), the licensee and anyone into whose hands a copy made in pursuance of the licence comes, whether or not he has notice of the assertion.

(5) In an action for infringement of the right the court shall, in considering remedies, take into account any delay in asserting the right.

79 Exceptions to right

(1) The right conferred by section 77 (right to be identified as author or director) is subject to the following exceptions.

(2) The right does not apply in relation to the following descriptions of work—

    (a) a computer program;

    (b) the design of a typeface;

    (c) any computer-generated work.

(3) The right does not apply to anything done by or with the authority of the copyright owner where copyright in the work originally [vested in the author's or director's employer by virtue of section 11(2) (works produced in the course of employment)].

(4) The right is not infringed by an act which by virtue of any of the following provisions would not infringe copyright in the work—

    (a) section 30 (fair dealing for certain purposes), so far as it relates to the reporting of current events by means of a sound recording, film [or broadcast];

    (b) section 31 (incidental inclusion of work in an artistic work, sound recording, film [or broadcast]);

    (c) section 32(3) (examination questions);

    (d) section 45 (parliamentary and judicial proceedings);

    (e) section 46(1) or (2) (Royal Commissions and statutory inquiries);

    (f) section 51 (use of design documents and models);

    (g) section 52 (effect of exploitation of design derived from artistic work);

    (h) [section 57 or 66A (acts permitted on assumptions as to expiry of copyright, &c.)]

(5) The right does not apply in relation to any work made for the purpose of reporting current events.

(6) The right does not apply in relation to the publication in—

    (a) a newspaper, magazine or similar periodical, or

    (b) an encyclopaedia, dictionary, yearbook or other collective work of reference,

of a literary, dramatic, musical or artistic work made for the purposes of such publication or made available with the consent of the author for the purposes of such publication.

(7) The right does not apply in relation to—

    (a) a work in which Crown copyright or Parliamentary copyright subsists, or

    (b) a work in which copyright originally vested in an international organisation by virtue of section 168,

unless the author or director has previously been identified as such in or on published copies of the work.

Right to object to derogatory treatment of work

80   Right to object to derogatory treatment of work

(1) The author of a copyright literary, dramatic, musical or artistic work, and the director of a copyright film, has the right in the circumstances mentioned in this section not to have his work subjected to derogatory treatment.

(2) For the purposes of this section—

    (a) "treatment" of a work means any addition to, deletion from or alteration to or adaptation of the work, other than—

      (i)   a translation of a literary or dramatic work, or

      (ii) an arrangement or transcription of a musical work involving no more than a change of key or register; and

    (b) the treatment of a work is derogatory if it amounts to distortion or mutilation of the work or is otherwise prejudicial to the honour or reputation of the author or director;

and in the following provisions of this section references to a derogatory treatment of a work shall be construed accordingly.

(3) In the case of a literary, dramatic or musical work the right is infringed by a person who—

    (a) publishes commercially, performs in public, [or communicates to the public] a derogatory treatment of the work; or

    (b) issues to the public copies of a film or sound recording of, or including, a derogatory treatment of the work.

(4) In the case of an artistic work the right is infringed by a person who—

    (a) publishes commercially or exhibits in public a derogatory treatment of the work, [or communicates to the public] a visual image of a derogatory treatment of the work,

    (b) shows in public a film including a visual image of a derogatory treatment of the work or issues to the public copies of such a film, or

    (c) in the case of—

      (i)   a work of architecture in the form of a model for a building,

      (ii) a sculpture, or

      (iii) a work of artistic craftsmanship,

issues to the public copies of a graphic work representing, or of a photograph of, a derogatory treatment of the work.

(5) Subsection (4) does not apply to a work of architecture in the form of a building; but where the author of such a work is identified on the building and it is the subject of derogatory treatment he has the right to require the identification to be removed.

(6) In the case of a film, the right is infringed by a person who—

    (a) shows in public, [or communicates to the public] derogatory treatment of the film; or

    (b) issues to the public copies of a derogatory treatment of the film . . .

(7) The right conferred by this section extends to the treatment of parts of a work resulting from a previous treatment by a person other than the author or director, if those parts are attributed to, or are likely to be regarded as the work of, the author or director.

(8) This section has effect subject to sections 81 and 82 (exceptions to and qualifications of right).

81   Exceptions to right

(1) The right conferred by section 80 (right to object to derogatory treatment of work) is subject to the following exceptions.

(2) The right does not apply to a computer program or to any computer-generated work.

(3) The right does not apply in relation to any work made for the purpose of reporting current events.

(4) The right does not apply in relation to the publication in—

    (a) a newspaper, magazine or similar periodical, or

    (b) an encyclopaedia, dictionary, yearbook or other collective work of reference,

of a literary, dramatic, musical or artistic work made for the purposes of such publication or made available with the consent of the author for the purposes of such publication.

Nor does the right apply in relation to any subsequent exploitation elsewhere of such a work without any modification of the published version.

(5) The right is not infringed by an act which by virtue of [section 57 or 66A (acts permitted on assumptions as to expiry of copyright, etc.)] would not infringe copyright.

(6) The right is not infringed by anything done for the purpose of—

    (a) avoiding the commission of an offence,

    (b) complying with a duty imposed by or under an enactment, or

    (c) in the case of the British Broadcasting Corporation, avoiding the inclusion in a programme broadcast by them of anything which offends against good taste or decency or which is likely to encourage or incite to crime or to lead to disorder or to be offensive to public feeling,

provided, where the author or director is identified at the time of the relevant act or has previously been identified in or on published copies of the work, that there is a sufficient disclaimer.

82 Qualification of right in certain cases

(1) This section applies to—

    (a) works in which copyright originally vested in the author's [or director's] employer by virtue of section 11(2) (works produced in course of employment) [. . .],

    (b) works in which Crown copyright or Parliamentary copyright subsists, and

    (c) works in which copyright originally vested in an international organisation by virtue of section 168.

(2) The right conferred by section 80 (right to object to derogatory treatment of work) does not apply to anything done in relation to such a work by or with the authority of the copyright owner unless the author or director—

    (a) is identified at the time of the relevant act, or

    (b) has previously been identified in or on published copies of the work;

and where in such a case the right does apply, it is not infringed if there is a sufficient disclaimer.

83 Infringement of right by possessing or dealing with infringing article

(1) The right conferred by section 80 (right to object to derogatory treatment of work) is also infringed by a person who—

    (a) possesses in the course of a business, or

    (b) sells or lets for hire, or offers or exposes for sale or hire, or

    (c) in the course of a business exhibits in public or distributes, or

    (d) distributes otherwise than in the course of a business so as to affect prejudicially the honour or reputation of the author or director,

an article which is, and which he knows or has reason to believe is, an infringing article.

(2) An "infringing article" means a work or a copy of a work which—

    (a) has been subjected to derogatory treatment within the meaning of section 80, and

    (b) has been or is likely to be the subject of any of the acts mentioned in that section in circumstances infringing that right.

False attribution of work

84 False attribution of work

(1) A person has the right in the circumstances mentioned in this section—

    (a) not to have a literary, dramatic, musical or artistic work falsely attributed to him as author, and

    (b) not to have a film falsely attributed to him as director;

and in this section an "attribution", in relation to such a work, means a statement (express or implied) as to who is the author or director.

(2) The right is infringed by a person who—

(a) issues to the public copies of a work of any of those descriptions in or on which there is a false attribution, or

(b) exhibits in public an artistic work, or a copy of an artistic work, in or on which there is a false attribution.

(3) The right is also infringed by a person who—

(a) in the case of a literary, dramatic or musical work, performs the work in public, [or communicates it to the public] as being the work of a person, or

(b) in the case of a film, shows it in public, [or communicates it to the public] as being directed by a person,

knowing or having reason to believe that the attribution is false.

(4) The right is also infringed by the issue to the public or public display of material containing a false attribution in connection with any of the acts mentioned in subsection (2) or (3).

(5) The right is also infringed by a person who in the course of a business—

(a) possesses or deals with a copy of a work of any of the descriptions mentioned in subsection (1) in or on which there is a false attribution, or

(b) in the case of an artistic work, possesses or deals with the work itself when there is a false attribution in or on it,

knowing or having reason to believe that there is such an attribution and that it is false.

(6) In the case of an artistic work the right is also infringed by a person who in the course of a business—

(a) deals with a work which has been altered after the author parted with possession of it as being the unaltered work of the author, or

(b) deals with a copy of such a work as being a copy of the unaltered work of the author,

knowing or having reason to believe that that is not the case.

(7) References in this section to dealing are to selling or letting for hire, offering or exposing for sale or hire, exhibiting in public, or distributing.

(8) This section applies where, contrary to the fact—

(a) a literary, dramatic or musical work is falsely represented as being an adaptation of the work of a person, or

(b) a copy of an artistic work is falsely represented as being a copy made by the author of the artistic work,

as it applies where the work is falsely attributed to a person as author.

Right to privacy of certain photographs and films

85   Right to privacy of certain photographs and films

(1) A person who for private and domestic purposes commissions the taking of a photograph or the making of a film has, where copyright subsists in the resulting work, the right not to have—

(a) copies of the work issued to the public,

(b) the work exhibited or shown in public, or

(c) the work [communicated to the public]

and, except as mentioned in subsection (2), a person who does or authorises the doing of any of those acts infringes that right.

(2) The right is not infringed by an act which by virtue of any of the following provisions would not infringe copyright in the work—

(a) section 31 (incidental inclusion of work in an artistic work, film, [or broadcast];

(b) section 45 (parliamentary and judicial proceedings);

(c) section 46 (Royal Commissions and statutory inquiries);

(d) section 50 (acts done under statutory authority);

(e) [section 57 or 66A (acts permitted on assumptions as to expiry of copyright, &c.)]

Supplementary

86 Duration of rights

(1) The rights conferred by section 77 (right to be identified as author or director), section 80 (right to object to derogatory treatment of work) and section 85 (right to privacy of certain photographs and films) continue to subsist so long as copyright subsists in the work.

(2) The right conferred by section 84 (false attribution) continues to subsist until 20 years after a person's death.

87 Consent and waiver of rights

(1) It is not an infringement of any of the rights conferred by this Chapter to do any act to which the person entitled to the right has consented.

(2) Any of those rights may be waived by instrument in writing signed by the person giving up the right.

(3) A waiver—

(a) may relate to a specific work, to works of a specified description or to works generally, and may relate to existing or future works, and

(b) may be conditional or unconditional and may be expressed to be subject to revocation;

and if made in favour of the owner or prospective owner of the copyright in the work or works to which it relates, it shall be presumed to extend to his licensees and successors in title unless a contrary intention is expressed.

(4) Nothing in this Chapter shall be construed as excluding the operation of the general law of contract or estoppel in relation to an informal waiver or other transaction in relation to any of the rights mentioned in subsection (1).

88 Application of provisions to joint works

(1) The right conferred by section 77 (right to be identified as author or director) is, in the case of a work of joint authorship, a right of each joint author to be identified as a joint author and must be asserted in accordance with section 78 by each joint author in relation to himself.

(2) The right conferred by section 80 (right to object to derogatory treatment of work) is, in the case of a work of joint authorship, a right of each joint author and his right is satisfied if he consents to the treatment in question.

(3) A waiver under section 87 of those rights by one joint author does not affect the rights of the other joint authors.

(4) The right conferred by section 84 (false attribution) is infringed, in the circumstances mentioned in that section—

(a) by any false statement as to the authorship of a work of joint authorship, and

(b) by the false attribution of joint authorship in relation to a work of sole authorship;

and such a false attribution infringes the right of every person to whom authorship of any description is, whether rightly or wrongly, attributed.

(5) The above provisions also apply (with any necessary adaptations) in relation to a film which was, or is alleged to have been, jointly directed, as they apply to a work which is, or is alleged to be, a work of joint authorship.

A film is "jointly directed" if it is made by the collaboration of two or more directors and the contribution of each director is not distinct from that of the other director or directors.

(6) The right conferred by section 85 (right to privacy of certain photographs and films) is, in the case of a work made in pursuance of a joint commission, a right of each person who commissioned the making of the work, so that—

(a) the right of each is satisfied if he consents to the act in question, and

(b) a waiver under section 87 by one of them does not affect the rights of the others.

89 Application of provisions to parts of works

(1) The rights conferred by section 77 (right to be identified as author or director) and section 85 (right to privacy of certain photographs and films) apply in relation to the whole or any substantial part of a work.

(2) The rights conferred by section 80 (right to object to derogatory treatment of work) and section 84 (false attribution) apply in relation to the whole or any part of a work.

Chapter V Dealings with Rights in Copyright Works

Copyright

90 Assignment and licences

(1) Copyright is transmissible by assignment, by testamentary disposition or by operation of law, as personal or moveable property.

(2) An assignment or other transmission of copyright may be partial, that is, limited so as to apply—

(a) to one or more, but not all, of the things the copyright owner has the exclusive right to do;

(b) to part, but not the whole, of the period for which the copyright is to subsist.

(3) An assignment of copyright is not effective unless it is in writing signed by or on behalf of the assignor.

(4) A licence granted by a copyright owner is binding on every successor in title to his interest in the copyright, except a purchaser in good faith for valuable consideration and without notice (actual or constructive) of the licence or a person deriving title from such a purchaser; and references in this Part to doing anything with, or without, the licence of the copyright owner shall be construed accordingly.

91 Prospective ownership of copyright

(1) Where by an agreement made in relation to future copyright, and signed by or on behalf of the prospective owner of the copyright, the prospective owner purports to assign the future copyright (wholly or partially) to another person, then if, on the copyright coming into existence, the assignee or another person claiming under him would be entitled as against all other persons to require the copyright to be vested in him, the copyright shall vest in the assignee or his successor in title by virtue of this subsection.

(2) In this Part—

"future copyright" means copyright which will or may come into existence in respect of a future work or class of works or on the occurrence of a future event; and

"prospective owner" shall be construed accordingly, and includes a person who is prospectively entitled to copyright by virtue of such an agreement as is mentioned in subsection (1).

(3) A licence granted by a prospective owner of copyright is binding on every successor in title to his interest (or prospective interest) in the right, except a purchaser in good faith for valuable consideration and without notice (actual or constructive) of the licence or a person deriving title from such a purchaser; and references in this Part to doing anything with, or without, the licence of the copyright owner shall be construed accordingly.

92 Exclusive licences

(1) In this Part an "exclusive licence" means a licence in writing signed by or on behalf of the copyright owner authorising the licensee to the exclusion of all other persons, including the person granting the licence, to exercise a right which would otherwise be exercisable exclusively by the copyright owner.

(2) The licensee under an exclusive licence has the same rights against a successor in title who is bound by the licence as he has against the person granting the licence.

Moral rights

94   Moral rights not assignable
The rights conferred by Chapter IV (moral rights) are not assignable.

95   Transmission of moral rights on death
(1) On the death of a person entitled to the right conferred by section 77 (right to identification of author or director), section 80 (right to object to derogatory treatment of work) or section 85 (right to privacy of certain photographs and films)—

    (a) the right passes to such person as he may be testamentary disposition specifically direct,

    (b) if there is no such direction but the copyright in the work in question forms part of his estate, the right passes to the person to whom the copyright passes, and

    (c) if or to the extent that the right does not pass under paragraph (a) or (b) it is exercisable by his personal representatives.

(2) Where copyright forming part of a person's estate passes in part to one person and in part to another, as for example where a bequest is limited so as to apply—

    (a) to one or more, but not all, of the things the copyright owner has the exclusive right to do or authorise, or

    (b) to part, but not the whole, of the period for which the copyright is to subsist,

any right which passes with the copyright by virtue of subsection (1) is correspondingly divided.

(3) Where by virtue of subsection (1)(a) or (b) a right becomes exercisable by more than one person—

    (a) it may, in the case of the right conferred by section 77 (right to identification of author or director), be asserted by any of them;

    (b) it is, in the case of the right conferred by section 80 (right to object to derogatory treatment of work) or section 85 (right to privacy of certain photographs and films), a right exercisable by each of them and is satisfied in relation to any of them if he consents to the treatment or act in question; and

    (c) any waiver of the right in accordance with section 87 by one of them does not affect the rights of the others.

(4) A consent or waiver previously given or made binds any person to whom a right passes by virtue of subsection (1).

(5) Any infringement after a person's death of the right conferred by section 84 (false attribution) is actionable by his personal representatives.

(6) Any damages recovered by personal representatives by virtue of this section in respect of an infringement after a person's death shall devolve as part of his estate as if the right of action had subsisted and been vested in him immediately before his death.

Chapter VI Remedies for Infringement

Rights and remedies of copyright owner

96   Infringement actionable by copyright owner
(1) An infringement of copyright is actionable by the copyright owner.

(2) In an action for infringement of copyright all such relief by way of damages, injunctions, accounts or otherwise is available to the plaintiff as is available in respect of the infringement of any other property right.

(3) This section has effect subject to the following provisions of this Chapter.

97   Provisions as to damages in infringement action
(1) Where in an action for infringement of copyright it is shown that at the time of the infringement the defendant did not know, and had no reason to believe, that copyright subsisted in the work to which the action relates, the plaintiff is not entitled to damages against him, but without prejudice to any other remedy.

(2) The court may in an action for infringement of copyright having regard to all the circumstances, and in particular to—

    (a) the flagrancy of the infringement, and

    (b) any benefit accruing to the defendant by reason of the infringement,

award such additional damages as the justice of the case may require.

101 Rights and remedies of exclusive licensee

(1) An exclusive licensee has, except against the copyright owner, the same rights and remedies in respect of matters occurring after the grant of the licence as if the licence had been an assignment.

(2) His rights and remedies are concurrent with those of the copyright owner; and references in the relevant provisions of this Part to the copyright owner shall be construed accordingly.

(3) In an action brought by an exclusive licensee by virtue of this section a defendant may avail himself of any defence which would have been available to him if the action had been brought by the copyright owner.

[101A Certain infringements actionable by a non-exclusive licensee

(1) A non-exclusive licensee may bring an action for infringement of copyright if—

    (a) the infringing act was directly connected to a prior licensed act of the licensee, and

    (b) the licence—

        (i) is in writing and is signed by or on behalf of the copyright owner; and

        (ii) expressly grants the non-exclusive licensee a right of action under this section.

(2) In an action brought under this section, the non-exclusive licensee shall have the same rights and remedies available to him as the copyright owner would have had if he had brought the action.

(3) The rights granted under this section are concurrent with those of the copyright owner and references in the relevant provisions of this Part to the copyright owner shall be construed accordingly.

(4) In an action brought by a non-exclusive licensee by virtue of this section a defendant may avail himself of any defence which would have been available to him if the action had been brought by the copyright owner.

(5) Subsections (1) to (4) of section 102 shall apply to a non-exclusive licensee who has a right of action by virtue of this section as it applies to an exclusive licensee.

(6) In this section a "non-exclusive licensee" means the holder of a licence authorising the licensee to exercise a right which remains exercisable by the copyright owner.]

102 Exercise of concurrent rights

(1) Where an action for infringement of copyright brought by the copyright owner or an exclusive licensee relates (wholly or partly) to an infringement in respect of which they have concurrent rights of action, the copyright owner or, as the case may be, the exclusive licensee may not, without the leave of the court, proceed with the action unless the other is either joined as a plaintiff or added as a defendant.

(2) A copyright owner or exclusive licensee who is added as a defendant in pursuance of subsection (1) is not liable for any costs in the action unless he takes part in the proceedings.

(3) The above provisions do not affect the granting of interlocutory relief on an application by a copyright owner or exclusive licensee alone.

(4) Where an action for infringement of copyright is brought which relates (wholly or partly) to an infringement in respect of which the copyright owner and an exclusive licensee have or had concurrent rights of action—

    (a) the court shall in assessing damages take into account—

        (i) the terms of the licence, and

        (ii) any pecuniary remedy already awarded or available to either of them in respect of the infringement;

    (b) no account of profits shall be directed if an award of damages has been made, or an account of profits has been directed, in favour of the other of them in respect of the infringement; and

(c) the court shall if an account of profits is directed apportion the profits between them as the court considers just, subject to any agreement between them;

and these provisions apply whether or not the copyright owner and the exclusive licensee are both parties to the action.

(5) The copyright owner shall notify any exclusive licensee having concurrent rights before applying for an order under section 99 (order for delivery up) or exercising the right conferred by section 100 (right of seizure); and the court may on the application of the licensee make such order under section 99 or, as the case may be, prohibiting or permitting the exercise by the copyright owner of the right conferred by section 100, as it thinks fit having regard to the terms of the licence.

Remedies for infringement of moral rights

103   Remedies for infringement of moral rights

(1) An infringement of a right conferred by Chapter IV (moral rights) is actionable as a breach of statutory duty owed to the person entitled to the right.

(2) In proceedings for infringement of the right conferred by section 80 (right to object to derogatory treatment of work) the court may, if it thinks it is an adequate remedy in the circumstances, grant an injunction on terms prohibiting the doing of any act unless a disclaimer is made, in such terms and in such manner as may be approved by the court, dissociating the author or director from the treatment of the work.

Offences

107   Criminal liability for making or dealing with infringing articles, &c

(1) A person commits an offence who, without the licence of the copyright owner—
  (a) makes for sale or hire, or
  (b) imports into the United Kingdom otherwise than for his private and domestic use, or
  (c) possesses in the course of a business with a view to committing any act infringing the copyright, or
  (d) in the course of a business—
    (i)   sells or lets for hire, or
    (ii)   offers or exposes for sale or hire, or
    (iii) exhibits in public, or
    (iv)   distributes, or
  (e) distributes otherwise than in the course of a business to such an extent as to affect prejudicially the owner of the copyright,

an article which is, and which he knows or has reason to believe is, an infringing copy of a copyright work.

(2) A person commits an offence who—
  (a) makes an article specifically designed or adapted for making copies of a particular copyright work, or
  (b) has such an article in his possession,

knowing or having reason to believe that it is to be used to make infringing copies for sale or hire or for use in the course of a business.

[(2A) A person who infringes copyright in a work by communicating the work to the public—
  (a) in the course of a business, or
  (b) otherwise than in the course of a business to such an extent as to affect prejudicially the owner of the copyright,

commits an offence if he knows or has reason to believe that, by doing so, he is infringing copyright in that work.]

(3) Where copyright is infringed (otherwise than by reception of a [communication to the public])—
  (a) by the public performance of a literary, dramatic or musical work, or
  (b) by the playing or showing in public of a sound recording or film,

any person who caused the work to be so performed, played or shown is guilty of an offence if he knew or had reason to believe that copyright would be infringed.

(4) A person guilty of an offence under subsection (1)(a), (b), (d)(iv) or (e) is liable—

    (a) on summary conviction to imprisonment for a term not exceeding six months or a fine not exceeding the statutory maximum, or both;

    (b) on conviction on indictment to a fine or imprisonment for a term not exceeding [ten] years, or both.

[(4A) A person guilty of an offence under subsection (2A) is liable—

    (a) on summary conviction to imprisonment for a term not exceeding three months or a fine not exceeding the statutory maximum, or both;

    (b) on conviction on indictment to a fine or imprisonment for a term not exceeding two years, or both.]

(5) A person guilty of any other offence under this section is liable on summary conviction to imprisonment for a term not exceeding six months or a fine not exceeding level 5 on the standard scale, or both.

(6) Sections 104 to 106 (presumptions as to various matters connected with copyright) do not apply to proceedings for an offence under this section, but without prejudice to their application in proceedings for an order under section 108 below.

110   Offence by body corporate: liability of officers

(1) Where an offence under section 107 committed by a body corporate is proved to have been committed with the consent or connivance of a director, manager, secretary or other similar officer of the body, or a person purporting to act in any such capacity, he as well as the body corporate is guilty of the offence and liable to be proceeded against and punished accordingly.

(2) In relation to a body corporate whose affairs are managed by its members "director" means a member of the body corporate.

CHAPTER IX QUALIFICATION FOR AND EXTENT OF COPYRIGHT PROTECTION

Qualification for copyright protection

153   Qualification for copyright protection

(1) Copyright does not subsist in a work unless the qualification requirements of this Chapter are satisfied as regards—

    (a) the author (see section 154), or

    (b) the country in which the work was first published (see section 155), or

    (c) in the case of a broadcast [...], the country from which the broadcast was made [...] (see section 156).

(2) Subsection (1) does not apply in relation to Crown copyright or Parliamentary copyright (see sections 163 to [166B]) or to copyright subsisting by virtue of section 168 (copyright of certain international organisations).

(3) If the qualification requirements of this Chapter, or section 163, 165 or 168, are once satisfied in respect of a work, copyright does not cease to subsist by reason of any subsequent event.

154   Qualification by reference to author

(1) A work qualifies for copyright protection if the author was at the material time a qualifying person, that is—

    (a) a British citizen, a [British overseas territories citizen], a British National (Overseas), a British Overseas citizen, a British subject or a British protected person within the meaning of the British Nationality Act 1981, or

    (b) an individual domiciled or resident in the United Kingdom or another country to which the relevant provisions of this Part extend, or

(c) a body incorporated under the law of a part of the United Kingdom or of another country to which the relevant provisions of this Part extend.

(2) Where, or so far as, provision is made by Order under section 159 (application of this Part to countries to which it does not extend), a work also qualifies for copyright protection if at the material time the author was a citizen or subject of, an individual domiciled or resident in, or a body incorporated under the law of, a country to which the Order relates.

(3) A work of joint authorship qualifies for copyright protection if at the material time any of the authors satisfies the requirements of subsection (1) or (2); but where a work qualifies for copyright protection only under this section, only those authors who satisfy those requirements shall be taken into account for the purposes of—

section 11(1) and (2) (first ownership of copyright; entitlement of author or author's employer),

[section 12 (duration of copyright), and section 9(4) (meaning of "unknown authorship") so far as it applies for the purposes of section 12, and]

section 57 (anonymous or pseudonymous works: acts permitted on assumptions as to expiry of copyright or death of author).

(4) The material time in relation to a literary, dramatic, musical or artistic work is—

(a) in the case of an unpublished work, when the work was made or, if the making of the work extended over a period, a substantial part of that period;

(b) in the case of a published work, when the work was first published or, if the author had died before that time, immediately before his death.

(5) The material time in relation to other descriptions of work is as follows—

(a) in the case of a sound recording or film, when it was made;

(b) in the case of a broadcast, when the broadcast was made;

(c) [...]

(d) in the case of the typographical arrangement of a published edition, when the edition was first published.

155   Qualification by reference to country of first publication

(1) A literary, dramatic, musical or artistic work, a sound recording or film, or the typographical arrangement of a published edition, qualifies for copyright protection if it is first published—

(a) in the United Kingdom, or

(b) in another country to which the relevant provisions of this Part extend.

(2) Where, or so far as, provision is made by Order under section 159 (application of this Part to countries to which it does not extend), such a work also qualifies for copyright protection if it is first published in a country to which the Order relates.

(3) For the purposes of this section, publication in one country shall not be regarded as other than the first publication by reason of simultaneous publication elsewhere; and for this purpose publication elsewhere within the previous 30 days shall be treated as simultaneous.

156   Qualification by reference to place of transmission

(1) A broadcast qualifies for copyright protection if it is made from [...], a place in—

(a) the United Kingdom, or

(b) another country to which the relevant provisions of this Part extend.

(2) Where, or so far as, provision is made by Order under section 159 (application of this Part to countries to which it does not extend), a broadcast [...] also qualifies for copyright protection if it is made from [...] a place in a country to which the Order relates.

Interpretation

175   Meaning of publication and commercial publication

(1) In this Part "publication", in relation to a work—

(a) means the issue of copies to the public, and

(b) includes, in the case of a literary, dramatic, musical or artistic work, making it available to the public by means of an electronic retrieval system;

and related expressions shall be construed accordingly.

(2) In this Part "commercial publication", in relation to a literary, dramatic, musical or artistic work means—

    (a) issuing copies of the work to the public at a time when copies made in advance of the receipt of orders are generally available to the public, or

    (b) making the work available to the public by means of an electronic retrieval system;

and related expressions shall be construed accordingly.

(3) In the case of a work of architecture in the form of a building, or an artistic work incorporated in a building, construction of the building shall be treated as equivalent to publication of the work.

(4) The following do not constitute publication for the purposes of this Part and references to commercial publication shall be construed accordingly—

    (a) in the case of a literary, dramatic or musical work—

        (i) the performance of the work, or

        (ii) the [communication to the public] (otherwise than for the purposes of an electronic retrieval system);

    (b) in the case of an artistic work—

        (i) the exhibition of the work,

        (ii) the issue to the public of copies of a graphic work representing, or of photographs of, a work of architecture in the form of a building or a model for a building, a sculpture or a work of artistic craftsmanship,

        (iii) the issue to the public of copies of a film including the work, or

        (iv) the [communication to the public] (otherwise than for the purposes of an electronic retrieval system);

    (c) in the case of a sound recording or film—

        (i) the work being played or shown in public, or

        (ii) the [communication to the public].

(5) References in this Part to publication or commercial publication do not include publication which is merely colourable and not intended to satisfy the reasonable requirements of the public.

(6) No account shall be taken for the purposes of this section of any unauthorised act.

178 Minor definitions

In this Part—

    "article", in the context of an article in a periodical, includes an item of any description;

    "business" includes a trade or profession;

    "collective work" means—

    (a) a work of joint authorship, or

    (b) a work in which there are distinct contributions by different authors or in which works or parts of works of different authors are incorporated;

    "computer-generated", in relation to a work, means that the work is generated by computer in circumstances such that there is no human author of the work;

    "country" includes any territory;

    "the Crown" includes the Crown in right of [the Scottish Administration or of] Her Majesty's Government in Northern Ireland or in any country outside the United Kingdom to which this Part extends;

    "electronic" means actuated by electric, magnetic, electro-magnetic, electro-chemical or electro-mechanical energy, and "in electronic form" means in a form usable only by electronic means;

    "employed", "employee", "employer" and "employment" refer to employment under a contract of service or of apprenticeship;

    "facsimile copy" includes a copy which is reduced or enlarged in scale;

    "international organisation" means an organisation the members of which include one or more states;

    "judicial proceedings" includes proceedings before any court, tribunal or person having authority to decide any matter affecting a person's legal rights or liabilities;

    "parliamentary proceedings" includes proceedings of the Northern Ireland Assembly [of the Scottish Parliament] or of the European Parliament;

["private study" does not include any study which is directly or indirectly for a commercial purpose;]

["producer", in relation to a sound recording or a film, means the person by whom the arrangements necessary for the making of the sound recording or film are undertaken;]

"rental right" means the right of a copyright owner to authorise or prohibit the rental of copies of the work (see section 18A);]

"reprographic copy" and "reprographic copying" refer to copying by means of a reprographic process;

"reprographic process" means a process—

(a) for making facsimile copies, or

(b) involving the use of an appliance for making multiple copies,

and includes, in relation to a work held in electronic form, any copying by electronic means, but does not include the making of a film or sound recording;

"sufficient acknowledgement" means an acknowledgement identifying the work in question by its title or other description, and identifying the author unless—

(a) in the case of a published work, it is published anonymously;

(b) in the case of an unpublished work, it is not possible for a person to ascertain the identity of the author by reasonable inquiry;

"sufficient disclaimer", in relation to an act capable of infringing the right conferred by section 80 (right to object to derogatory treatment of work), means a clear and reasonably prominent indication—

(a) given at the time of the act, and

(b) if the author or director is then identified, appearing along with the identification,

that the work has been subjected to treatment to which the author or director has not consented;

"telecommunications system" means a system for conveying visual images, sounds or other information by electronic means;

"typeface" includes an ornamental motif used in printing;

"unauthorised", as regards anything done in relation to a work, means done otherwise than—

(a) by or with the licence of the copyright owner, or

(b) if copyright does not subsist in the work, by or with the licence of the author or, in a case where section 11(2) would have applied, the author's employer or, in either case, persons lawfully claiming under him, or

(c) in pursuance of section 48 (copying, etc. of certain material by the Crown);

"wireless broadcast" means a broadcast by means of wireless telegraphy;]

"wireless telegraphy" means the sending of electro-magnetic energy over paths not provided by a material substance constructed or arranged for that purpose;

"writing" includes any form of notation or code, whether by hand or otherwise and regardless of the method by which, or medium in or on which, it is recorded, and "written" shall be construed accordingly.

PART VII MISCELLANEOUS AND GENERAL

[Circumvention of protection measures

296 Circumvention of technical devices applied to computer programs

(1) This section applies where—

(a) a technical device has been applied to a computer program; and

(b) a person (A) knowing or having reason to believe that it will be used to make infringing copies—

(i) manufactures for sale or hire, imports, distributes, sells or lets for hire, offers or exposes for sale or hire, advertises for sale or hire or has in his possession for commercial purposes any means the sole intended purpose of which is to facilitate the unauthorised removal or circumvention of the technical device; or

    (ii) publishes information intended to enable or assist persons to remove or circumvent the technical device.

(2) The following persons have the same rights against A as a copyright owner has in respect of an infringement of copyright—

    (a) a person—

        (i) issuing to the public copies of, or

        (ii) communicating to the public,

the computer program to which the technical device has been applied;

    (b) the copyright owner or his exclusive licensee, if he is not the person specified in paragraph (a);

    (c) the owner or exclusive licensee of any intellectual property right in the technical device applied to the computer program.

(3) The rights conferred by subsection (2) are concurrent, and sections 101(3) and 102(1) to (4) apply, in proceedings under this section, in relation to persons with concurrent rights as they apply, in proceedings mentioned in those provisions, in relation to a copyright owner and exclusive licensee with concurrent rights.

(4) Further, the persons in subsection (2) have the same rights under section 99 or 100 (delivery up or seizure of certain articles) in relation to any such means as is referred to in subsection (1) which a person has in his possession, custody or control with the intention that it should be used to facilitate the unauthorised removal or circumvention of any technical device which has been applied to a computer program, as a copyright owner has in relation to an infringing copy.

(5) The rights conferred by subsection (4) are concurrent, and section 102(5) shall apply, as respects anything done under section 99 or 100 by virtue of subsection (4), in relation to persons with concurrent rights as it applies, as respects anything done under section 99 or 100, in relation to a copyright owner and exclusive licensee with concurrent rights.

(6) In this section references to a technical device in relation to a computer program are to any device intended to prevent or restrict acts that are not authorised by the copyright owner of that computer program and are restricted by copyright.

(7) The following provisions apply in relation to proceedings under this section as in relation to proceedings under Part 1 (copyright)—

    (a) sections 104 to 106 of this Act (presumptions as to certain matters relating to copyright); and

    (b) section 72 of the Supreme Court Act 1981, section 15 of the Law Reform (Miscellaneous Provisions) (Scotland) Act 1985 and section 94A of the Judicature (Northern Ireland) Act 1978 (withdrawal of privilege against self-incrimination in certain proceedings relating to intellectual property);

and section 114 of this Act applies, with the necessary modifications, in relation to the disposal of anything delivered up or seized by virtue of subsection (4).

(8) Expressions used in this section which are defined for the purposes of Part 1 of this Act (copyright) have the same meaning as in that Part.

296ZA Circumvention of technological measures

(1) This section applies where—

    (a) effective technological measures have been applied to a copyright work other than a computer program; and

    (b) a person (B) does anything which circumvents those measures knowing, or with reasonable grounds to know, that he is pursuing that objective.

(2) This section does not apply where a person, for the purposes of research into cryptography, does anything which circumvents effective technological measures unless in so doing, or in issuing information derived from that research, he affects prejudicially the rights of the copyright owner.

(3) The following persons have the same rights against B as a copyright owner has in respect of an infringement of copyright—

    (a) a person—

        (i) issuing to the public copies of, or

        (ii) communicating to the public,

the work to which effective technological measures have been applied; and

    (b) the copyright owner or his exclusive licensee, if he is not the person specified in paragraph (a).

(4) The rights conferred by subsection (3) are concurrent, and sections 101(3) and 102(1) to (4) apply, in proceedings under this section, in relation to persons with concurrent rights as they apply, in proceedings mentioned in those provisions, in relation to a copyright owner and exclusive licensee with concurrent rights.

(5) The following provisions apply in relation to proceedings under this section as in relation to proceedings under Part 1 (copyright)—

    (a) sections 104 to 106 of this Act (presumptions as to certain matters relating to copyright); and

    (b) section 72 of the Supreme Court Act 1981, section 15 of the Law Reform (Miscellaneous Provisions) (Scotland) Act 1985 and section 94A of the Judicature (Northern Ireland) Act 1978 (withdrawal of privilege against self-incrimination in certain proceedings relating to intellectual property).

(6) Subsections (1) to (4) and (5)(b) and any other provision of this Act as it has effect for the purposes of those subsections apply, with any necessary adaptations, to rights in performances, publication right and database right.

(7) The provisions of regulation 22 (presumptions relevant to database right) of the Copyright and Rights in Databases Regulations 1997 (SI 1997/3032) apply in proceedings brought by virtue of this section in relation to database right.

296ZB Devices and services designed to circumvent technological measures

(1) A person commits an offence if he—

    (a) manufactures for sale or hire, or

    (b) imports otherwise than for his private and domestic use, or

    (c) in the course of a business—

        (i)   sells or lets for hire, or

        (ii)   offers or exposes for sale or hire, or

        (iii) advertises for sale or hire, or

        (iv)   possesses, or

        (v)   distributes, or

    (d) distributes otherwise than in the course of a business to such an extent as to affect prejudicially the copyright owner,

any device, product or component which is primarily designed, produced, or adapted for the purpose of enabling or facilitating the circumvention of effective technological measures.

(2) A person commits an offence if he provides, promotes, advertises or markets—

    (a) in the course of a business, or

    (b) otherwise than in the course of a business to such an extent as to affect prejudicially the copyright owner,

a service the purpose of which is to enable or facilitate the circumvention of effective technological measures.

(3) Subsections (1) and (2) do not make unlawful anything done by, or on behalf of, law enforcement agencies or any of the intelligence services—

    (a) in the interests of national security; or

    (b) for the purpose of the prevention or detection of crime, the investigation of an offence, or the conduct of a prosecution, and in this subsection "intelligence services" has the meaning given in section 81 of the Regulation of Investigatory Powers Act 2000.

(4) A person guilty of an offence under subsection (1) or (2) is liable—

(a) on summary conviction, to imprisonment for a term not exceeding three months, or to a fine not exceeding the statutory maximum, or both;

(b) on conviction on indictment to a fine or imprisonment for a term not exceeding two years, or both.

(5) It is a defence to any prosecution for an offence under this section for the defendant to prove that he did not know, and had no reasonable ground for believing, that—

(a) the device, product or component; or

(b) the service,

enabled or facilitated the circumvention of effective technological measures.

296ZC Devices and services designed to circumvent technological measures: search warrants and forfeiture

(1) The provisions of sections 297B (search warrants), 297C (forfeiture of unauthorised decoders: England and Wales or Northern Ireland) and 297D (forfeiture of unauthorised decoders: Scotland) apply to offences under section 296ZB with the following modifications.

(2) In section 297B the reference to an offence under section 297A(1) shall be construed as a reference to an offence under section 296ZB(1) or (2).

(3) In sections 297C(2)(a) and 297D(15) the references to an offence under section 297A(1) shall be construed as a reference to an offence under section 296ZB(1).

(4) In sections 297C and 297D references to unauthorised decoders shall be construed as references to devices, products or components for the purpose of circumventing effective technological measures.

296ZD Rights and remedies in respect of devices and services designed to circumvent technological measures

(1) This section applies where—

(a) effective technological measures have been applied to a copyright work other than a computer program; and

(b) a person (C) manufactures, imports, distributes, sells or lets for hire, offers or exposes for sale or hire, advertises for sale or hire, or has in his possession for commercial purposes any device, product or component or provides services which—

(i) are promoted, advertised or marketed for the purpose of the circumvention of, or

(ii) have only a limited commercially significant purpose or use other than to circumvent, or

(iii) are primarily designed, produced, adapted or performed for the purpose of enabling or facilitating the circumvention of,

those measures.

(2) The following persons have the same rights against C as a copyright owner has in respect of an infringement of copyright—

(a) a person—

(i) issuing to the public copies of, or

(ii) communicating to the public,

the work to which effective technological measures have been applied;

(b) the copyright owner or his exclusive licensee, if he is not the person specified in paragraph (a); and

(c) the owner or exclusive licensee of any intellectual property right in the effective technological measures applied to the work.

(3) The rights conferred by subsection (2) are concurrent, and sections 101(3) and 102(1) to (4) apply, in proceedings under this section, in relation to persons with concurrent rights as they apply, in proceedings mentioned in those provisions, in relation to a copyright owner and exclusive licensee with concurrent rights.

(4) Further, the persons in subsection (2) have the same rights under section 99 or 100 (delivery up or seizure of certain articles) in relation to any such device, product or component which a person has in his possession, custody or control with the intention that it should be used to circumvent effective technological measures, as a copyright owner has in relation to any infringing copy.

(5) The rights conferred by subsection (4) are concurrent, and section 102(5) shall apply, as respects anything done under section 99 or 100 by virtue of subsection (4), in relation to persons with concurrent rights as it applies, as respects anything done under section 99 or 100, in relation to a copyright owner and exclusive licensee with concurrent rights.

(6) The following provisions apply in relation to proceedings under this section as in relation to proceedings under Part 1 (copyright)—

(a) sections 104 to 106 of this Act (presumptions as to certain matters relating to copyright); and

(b) section 72 of the Supreme Court Act 1981, section 15 of the Law Reform (Miscellaneous Provisions) (Scotland) Act 1985 and section 94A of the Judicature (Northern Ireland) Act 1978 (withdrawal of privilege against self-incrimination in certain proceedings relating to intellectual property);

and section 114 of this Act applies, with the necessary modifications, in relation to the disposal of anything delivered up or seized by virtue of subsection (4).

(7) In section 97(1) (innocent infringement of copyright) as it applies to proceedings for infringement of the rights conferred by this section, the reference to the defendant not knowing or having reason to believe that copyright subsisted in the work shall be construed as a reference to his not knowing or having reason to believe that his acts enabled or facilitated an infringement of copyright.

(8) Subsections (1) to (5), (6)(b) and (7) and any other provision of this Act as it has effect for the purposes of those subsections apply, with any necessary adaptations, to rights in performances, publication right and database right.

(9) The provisions of regulation 22 (presumptions relevant to database right) of the Copyright and Rights in Databases Regulations 1997 (SI 1997/3032) apply in proceedings brought by virtue of this section in relation to database right.

296ZE   Remedy where effective technological measures prevent permitted acts

(1) In this section—

"permitted act" means an act which may be done in relation to copyright works, notwithstanding the subsistence of copyright, by virtue of a provision of this Act listed in Part 1 of Schedule 5A;

"voluntary measure or agreement" means—

(a) any measure taken voluntarily by a copyright owner, his exclusive licensee or a person issuing copies of, or communicating to the public, a work other than a computer program, or

(b) any agreement between a copyright owner, his exclusive licensee or a person issuing copies of, or communicating to the public, a work other than a computer program and another party,

the effect of which is to enable a person to carry out a permitted act.

(2) Where the application of any effective technological measure to a copyright work other than a computer program prevents a person from carrying out a permitted act in relation to that work then that person or a person being a representative of a class of persons prevented from carrying out a permitted act may issue a notice of complaint to the Secretary of State.

(3) Following receipt of a notice of complaint, the Secretary of State may give to the owner of that copyright work or an exclusive licensee such directions as appear to the Secretary of State to be requisite or expedient for the purpose of—

(a) establishing whether any voluntary measure or agreement relevant to the copyright work the subject of the complaint subsists; or

(b) (where it is established there is no subsisting voluntary measure or agreement) ensuring that the owner or exclusive licensee of that copyright work makes available to the complainant the means of carrying out the permitted act the subject of the complaint to the extent necessary to so benefit from that permitted act.

(4) The Secretary of State may also give directions—

(a) as to the form and manner in which a notice of complaint in subsection (2) may be delivered to him;

(b) as to the form and manner in which evidence of any voluntary measure or agreement may be delivered to him; and

(c) generally as to the procedure to be followed in relation to a complaint made under this section;

and shall publish directions given under this subsection in such manner as in his opinion will secure adequate publicity for them.

(5) It shall be the duty of any person to whom a direction is given under subsection (3)(a) or (b) to give effect to that direction.

(6) The obligation to comply with a direction given under subsection (3)(b) is a duty owed to the complainant or, where the complaint is made by a representative of a class of persons, to that representative and to each person in the class represented; and a breach of the duty is actionable accordingly (subject to the defences and other incidents applying to actions for breach of statutory duty).

(7) Any direction under this section may be varied or revoked by a subsequent direction under this section.

(8) Any direction given under this section shall be in writing.

(9) This section does not apply to copyright works made available to the public on agreed contractual terms in such a way that members of the public may access them from a place and at a time individually chosen by them.

(10) This section applies only where a complainant has lawful access to the protected copyright work, or where the complainant is a representative of a class of persons, where the class of persons have lawful access to the work.

(11) Subsections (1) to (10) apply with any necessary adaptations to—

(a) rights in performances, and in this context the expression "permitted act" refers to an act that may be done by virtue of a provision of this Act listed in Part 2 of Schedule 5A;

(b) database right, and in this context the expression "permitted act" refers to an act that may be done by virtue of a provision of this Act listed in Part 3 of Schedule 5A; and

(c) publication right.

296ZF   Interpretation of sections 296ZA to 296ZE

(1) In sections 296ZA to 296ZE, "technological measures" are any technology, device or component which is designed, in the normal course of its operation, to protect a copyright work other than a computer program.

(2) Such measures are "effective" if the use of the work is controlled by the copyright owner through—

(a) an access control or protection process such as encryption, scrambling or other transformation of the work, or

(b) a copy control mechanism,

which achieves the intended protection.

(3) In this section, the reference to—

(a) protection of a work is to the prevention or restriction of acts that are not authorised by the copyright owner of that work and are restricted by copyright; and

(b) use of a work does not extend to any use of the work that is outside the scope of the acts restricted by copyright.

(4) Expressions used in sections 296ZA to 296ZE which are defined for the purposes of Part 1 of this Act (copyright) have the same meaning as in that Part.]

[Rights management information

296ZG   Electronic rights management information

(1) This section applies where a person (D), knowingly and without authority, removes or alters electronic rights management information which—

(a) is associated with a copy of a copyright work, or

(b) appears in connection with the communication to the public of a copyright work, and where D knows, or has reason to believe, that by so doing he is inducing, enabling, facilitating or concealing an infringement of copyright.

(2) This section also applies where a person (E), knowingly and without authority, distributes, imports for distribution or communicates to the public copies of a copyright work from which electronic rights management information—

(a) associated with the copies, or

(b) appearing in connection with the communication to the public of the work, has been removed or altered without authority and where E knows, or has reason to believe, that by so doing he is inducing, enabling, facilitating or concealing an infringement of copyright.

(3) A person issuing to the public copies of, or communicating, the work to the public, has the same rights against D and E as a copyright owner has in respect of an infringement of copyright.

(4) The copyright owner or his exclusive licensee, if he is not the person issuing to the public copies of, or communicating, the work to the public, also has the same rights against D and E as he has in respect of an infringement of copyright.

(5) The rights conferred by subsections (3) and (4) are concurrent, and sections 101(3) and 102(1) to (4) apply, in proceedings under this section, in relation to persons with concurrent rights as they apply, in proceedings mentioned in those provisions, in relation to a copyright owner and exclusive licensee with concurrent rights.

(6) The following provisions apply in relation to proceedings under this section as in relation to proceedings under Part 1 (copyright)—

(a) sections 104 to 106 of this Act (presumptions as to certain matters relating to copyright); and

(b) section 72 of the Supreme Court Act 1981, section 15 of the Law Reform (Miscellaneous Provisions) (Scotland) Act 1985 and section 94A of the Judicature (Northern Ireland) Act 1978 (withdrawal of privilege against self-incrimination in certain proceedings relating to intellectual property).

(7) In this section—

(a) expressions which are defined for the purposes of Part 1 of this Act (copyright) have the same meaning as in that Part; and

(b) "rights management information" means any information provided by the copyright owner or the holder of any right under copyright which identifies the work, the author, the copyright owner or the holder of any intellectual property rights, or information about the terms and conditions of use of the work, and any numbers or codes that represent such information.

(8) Subsections (1) to (5) and (6)(b), and any other provision of this Act as it has effect for the purposes of those subsections, apply, with any necessary adaptations, to rights in performances, publication right and database right.

(9) The provisions of regulation 22 (presumptions relevant to database right) of the Copyright and Rights in Databases Regulations 1997 (SI 1997/3032) apply in proceedings brought by virtue of this section in relation to database right.]

[Computer programs

296A   Avoidance of certain terms

(1) Where a person has the use of a computer program under an agreement, any term or condition in the agreement shall be void in so far as it purports to prohibit or restrict—

(a) the making of any back up copy of the program which it is necessary for him to have for the purposes of the agreed use;

(b) where the conditions in section 50B(2) are met, the decompiling of the program; or

[(c) the observing, studying or testing the functioning of the program in accordance with section 50BA.]

(2) In this section, decompile, in relation to a computer program, has the same meaning as in section 50B.]

[296B   Avoidance of certain terms relating to databases

Where under an agreement a person has a right to use a database or part of a database, any term or condition in the agreement shall be void in so far as it purports to prohibit or restrict the performance of any act which would but for section 50D infringe the copyright in the database.]

Fraudulent reception of transmissions

297   Offence of fraudulently receiving programmes

(1) A person who dishonestly receives a programme included in a broadcasting [...] service provided from a place in the United Kingdom with intent to avoid payment of any charge applicable to the reception of the programme commits an offence and is liable on summary conviction to a fine not exceeding level 5 on the standard scale.

(2) Where an offence under this section committed by a body corporate is proved to have been committed with the consent or connivance of a director, manager, secretary or other similar officer of the body, or a person purporting to act in any such capacity, he as well as the body corporate is guilty of the offence and liable to be proceeded against and punished accordingly.

In relation to a body corporate whose affairs are managed by its members "director" means a member of the body corporate.

[297A   Unauthorised decoders

(1) A person commits an offence if he—

(a) makes, imports, distributes, sells or lets for hire or offers or exposes for sale or hire any unauthorised decoder;

(b) has in his possession for commercial purposes any unauthorised decoder;

(c) instals, maintains or replaces for commercial purposes any unauthorised decoder; or

(d) advertises any unauthorised decoder for sale or hire or otherwise promotes any unauthorised decoder by means of commercial communications.

(2) A person guilty of an offence under subsection (1) is liable—

[(a) on summary conviction, to imprisonment not exceeding six months, or a fine not exceeding the statutory maximum or to both;]

(b) on conviction on indictment, to imprisonment for a term not exceeding [ten] years, or to a fine, or to both.

(3) It is a defence to any prosecution for an offence under this section for the defendant to prove that he did not know, and had no reasonable ground for believing, that the decoder was an unauthorised decoder.

(4) In this section—

"apparatus" includes any device, component or electronic data (including software);

"conditional access technology" means any technical measure or arrangement whereby access to encrypted transmissions in an intelligible form is made conditional on prior individual authorisation;

"decoder" means any apparatus which is designed or adapted to enable (whether on its own or with any other apparatus) an encrypted transmission to be decoded;

"encrypted" includes subjected to scrambling or the operation of cryptographic envelopes, electronic locks, passwords or any other analogous application;

"transmission" means—

(a) any programme included in a broadcasting [...] service which is provided from a place in the United Kingdom or any other member State; or

(b) an information society service (within the meaning of Directive 98/34/EC of the European Parliament and of the Council of 22nd June 1998(a), as amended by Directive 98/48/EC of the European Parliament and of the Council of 20th July 1998(b)) which is provided from a place in the United Kingdom or any other member State; and

"unauthorised", in relation to a decoder, means that the decoder is designed or adapted to enable an encrypted transmission, or any service of which it forms part, to be accessed in an intelligible form without payment of the fee (however imposed) which the person making the transmission, or on whose behalf it is made, charges for accessing the transmission or service (whether by the circumvention of any conditional access technology related to the transmission or service or by any other means).]

[298 Rights and remedies in respect of apparatus, etc. for unauthorised reception of transmissions

(1) A person who—
    (a) makes charges for the reception of programmes included in a broadcasting [...] service provided from a place in the United Kingdom or any other member State,
    (b) sends encrypted transmissions of any other description from a place in the United Kingdom or any other member State, or
    (c) provides conditional access services from a place in the United Kingdom or any other member State,

is entitled to the following rights and remedies.

(2) He has the same rights and remedies against a person—
    (a) who—
        (i) makes, imports, distributes, sells or lets for hire, offers or exposes for sale or hire, or advertises for sale or hire,
        (ii) has in his possession for commercial purposes, or
        (iii) instals, maintains or replaces for commercial purposes, any apparatus designed or adapted to enable or assist persons to access the programmes or other transmissions or circumvent conditional access technology related to the programmes or other transmissions when they are not entitled to do so, or
    (b) who publishes or otherwise promotes by means of commercial communications any information which is calculated to enable or assist persons to access the programmes or other transmissions or circumvent conditional access technology related to the programmes or other transmissions when they are not entitled to do so,

as a copyright owner has in respect of an infringement of copyright.

(3) Further, he has the same rights under section 99 or 100 (delivery up or seizure of certain articles) in relation to any such apparatus as a copyright owner has in relation to an infringing copy.

(4) Section 72 of the Supreme Court Act 1981, section 15 of the Law Reform (Miscellaneous Provisions) (Scotland) Act 1985 and section 94A of the Judicature (Northern Ireland) Act 1978 (withdrawal of privilege against self-incrimination in certain proceedings relating to intellectual property) apply to proceedings under this section as to proceedings under Part I of this Act (copyright).

(5) In section 97(1) (innocent infringement of copyright) as it applies to proceedings for infringement of the rights conferred by this section, the reference to the defendant not knowing or having reason to believe that copyright subsisted in the work shall be construed as a reference to his not knowing or having reason to believe that his acts infringed the rights conferred by this section.

(6) Section 114 applies, with the necessary modifications, in relation to the disposal of anything delivered up or seized by virtue of subsection (3) above.

(7) In this section "apparatus", "conditional access technology" and "encrypted" have the same meanings as in section 297A, "transmission" includes transmissions as defined in that section and "conditional access services" means services comprising the provision of conditional access technology.]

299 Supplementary provisions as to fraudulent reception

(1) Her Majesty may by Order in Council—
    (a) provide that section 297 applies in relation to programmes included in services provided from a country or territory outside the United Kingdom, and

(b) provide that section 298 applies in relation to such programmes and to encrypted transmissions sent from such a country or territory.

(2) ...

(3) A statutory instrument containing an Order in Council under subsection (1) shall be subject to annulment in pursuance of a resolution of either House of Parliament.

(4) Where sections 297 [297A] and 298 apply in relation to a broadcasting service [...] they also apply to any service run for the person providing that service, or a person providing programmes for that service, which consists wholly or mainly in the sending by means of a telecommunications system of sounds or visual images, or both.

(5) In sections 297 and 298, and this section, "programme", "broadcasting" and "cable programme service", and related expressions, have the same meaning as in Part I (copyright).

Computer Misuse Act 1990

(1990, c. 18)

An Act to make provision for securing computer material against unauthorised access or modification; and for connected purposes.   [29th June 1990]

Computer misuse offences

1 Unauthorised access to computer material[1]

(1) A person is guilty of an offence if—

(a) he causes a computer to perform any function with intent to secure access to any program or data held in any computer [, or to enable any such access to be secured];

(b) the access he intends to secure [, or to enable to be secured,] is unauthorised; and

(c) he knows at the time when he causes the computer to perform the function that that is the case.

(2) The intent a person has to have to commit an offence under this section need not be directed at—

(a) any particular program or data;

(b) a program or data of any particular kind; or

(c) a program or data held in any particular computer.

(3) [A person guilty of an offence under this section shall be liable—

(a) on summary conviction in England and Wales, to imprisonment for a term not exceeding 12 months or to a fine not exceeding the statutory maximum or to both;

(b) on summary conviction in Scotland, to imprisonment for a term not exceeding six months or to a fine not exceeding the statutory maximum or to both;

(c) on conviction on indictment, to imprisonment for a term not exceeding two years or to a fine or to both.]

2 Unauthorised access with intent to commit or facilitate commission of further offences

(1) A person is guilty of an offence under this section if he commits an offence under section 1 above ("the unauthorised access offence") with intent—

(a) to commit an offence to which this section applies; or

(b) to facilitate the commission of such an offence (whether by himself or by any other person);

and the offence he intends to commit or facilitate is referred to below in this section as the further offence.

(2) This section applies to offences—

(a) for which the sentence is fixed by law; or

---

[1] Amendments to this section not yet in force in relation to England and Wales: see Police and Justice Act 2006, s. 53.

(b) for which a person of twenty-one years[1] of age or over (not previously convicted) may be sentenced to imprisonment for a term of five years (or, in England and Wales, might be so sentenced but for the restrictions imposed by section 33 of the Magistrates' Courts Act 1980).

(3) It is immaterial for the purposes of this section whether the further offence is to be committed on the same occasion as the unauthorised access offence or on any future occasion.

(4) A person may be guilty of an offence under this section even though the facts are such that the commission of the further offence is impossible.

(5) [A person guilty of an offence under this section shall be liable—

(a) on summary conviction in England and Wales, to imprisonment for a term not exceeding 12 months or to a fine not exceeding the statutory maximum or to both;

(b) on summary conviction in Scotland, to imprisonment for a term not exceeding six months or to a fine not exceeding the statutory maximum or to both;

(c) on conviction on indictment, to imprisonment for a term not exceeding five years or to a fine or to both.][2]

3 [Unauthorised acts with intent to impair, or with recklessness as to impairing, operation of computer, etc[3]

(1) A person is guilty of an offence if—

(a) he does any unauthorised act in relation to a computer;

(b) at the time when he does the act he knows that it is unauthorised; and

(c) either subsection (2) or subsection (3) below applies.

(2) This subsection applies if the person intends by doing the act—

(a) to impair the operation of any computer;

(b) to prevent or hinder access to any program or data held in any computer; [or]

(c) to impair the operation of any such program or the reliability of any such data [...].

(3) This subsection applies if the person is reckless as to whether the act will do any of the things mentioned in paragraphs (a) to [(c)] of subsection (2) above.

(4) The intention referred to in subsection (2) above, or the recklessness referred to in subsection (3) above, need not relate to—

(a) any particular computer;

(b) any particular program or data; or

(c) a program or data of any particular kind.

(5) In this section—

(a) a reference to doing an act includes a reference to causing an act to be done;

(b) "act" includes a series of acts;

(c) a reference to impairing, preventing or hindering something includes a reference to doing so temporarily.

(6) A person guilty of an offence under this section shall be liable—

(a) on summary conviction in England and Wales, to imprisonment for a term not exceeding 12 months or to a fine not exceeding the statutory maximum or to both;

(b) on summary conviction in Scotland, to imprisonment for a term not exceeding six months or to a fine not exceeding the statutory maximum or to both;

(c) on conviction on indictment, to imprisonment for a term not exceeding ten years or to a fine or to both.]

---

[1] An amendment to this age limit has been enacted but not yet brought into force: see Criminal Justice and Court Services Act 2000 c. 43 s. 80 and sch. 7, para. 98.

[2] Sub- section not yet in force in relation to England and Wales: see Police and Justice Act 2006, s. 53.

[3] This new section is not yet in force in relation to England and Wales: see Police and Justice Act 2006, s. 53. The amendments to it are not yet in force at all: see Serious Crime Act 2007, s. 94.

[3a   Making, supplying or obtaining articles for use in offence under section 1 or 3[1]

(1) A person is guilty of an offence if he makes, adapts, supplies or offers to supply any article intending it to be used to commit, or to assist in the commission of, an offence under section 1 or 3.

(2) A person is guilty of an offence if he supplies or offers to supply any article believing that it is likely to be used to commit, or to assist in the commission of, an offence under section 1 or 3.

(3) A person is guilty of an offence if he obtains any article with a view to its being supplied for use to commit, or to assist in the commission of, an offence under section 1 or 3.

(4) In this section "article" includes any program or data held in electronic form.

(5) A person guilty of an offence under this section shall be liable—

    (a) on summary conviction in England and Wales, to imprisonment for a term not exceeding 12 months or to a fine not exceeding the statutory maximum or to both;

    (b) on summary conviction in Scotland, to imprisonment for a term not exceeding six months or to a fine not exceeding the statutory maximum or to both;

    (c) on conviction on indictment, to imprisonment for a term not exceeding two years or to a fine or to both.]

Jurisdiction

4   Territorial scope of [offences under sections 1 to 3[2]]

(1) Except as provided below in this section, it is immaterial for the purposes of any offence under section 1 or 3 above—

    (a) whether any act or other event proof of which is required for conviction of the offence occurred in the home country concerned; or

    (b) whether the accused was in the home country concerned at the time of any such act or event.

(2) Subject to subsection (3) below, in the case of such an offence at least one significant link with domestic jurisdiction must exist in the circumstances of the case for the offence to be committed.

(3) There is no need for any such link to exist for the commission of an offence under section 1 above to be established in proof of an allegation to that effect in proceedings for an offence under section 2 above.

(4) Subject to section 8 below, where—

    (a) any such link does in fact exist in the case of an offence under section 1 above; and

    (b) commission of that offence is alleged in proceedings for an offence under section 2 above;

section 2 above shall apply as if anything the accused intended to do or facilitate in any place outside the home country concerned which would be an offence to which section 2 applies if it took place in the home country concerned were the offence in question.

(5) This section is without prejudice to any jurisdiction exercisable by a court in Scotland apart from this section.

(6) References in this Act to the home country concerned are references—

    (a) in the application of this Act to England and Wales, to England and Wales;

    (b) in the application of this Act to Scotland, to Scotland; and

    (c) in the application of this Act to Northern Ireland, to Northern Ireland.

5   Significant links with domestic jurisdiction[3]

(1) The following provisions of this section apply for the interpretation of section 4 above.

(2) In relation to an offence under section 1, either of the following is a significant link with domestic jurisdiction—

    (a) that the accused was in the home country concerned at the time when he did the act which caused the computer to perform the function; or

---

[1] This new section is not yet in force in relation to England and Wales: see Police and Justice Act 2006, s. 53.
[2] Amendment not yet in force in relation to England and Wales: see Police and Justice Act 2006, s. 53.
[3] Amendments not yet in force in relation to England and Wales: see Police and Justice Act 2006, s. 53.

(b) [that any computer containing any program or data to which the accused by doing that act secured or intended to secure unauthorised access, or enabled or intended to enable unauthorised access to be secured, was in the home country concerned at that time].

(3) In relation to an offence under section 3, either of the following is a significant link with domestic jurisdiction—

(a) that the accused was in the home country concerned at the time when he did the act which caused the unauthorised modification; or

(b) [that the unauthorised act was done in relation to a computer in the home country concerned].

6   Territorial scope of inchoate offences related to [offences under sections 1 to 3][1]

(1) On a charge of conspiracy to commit an [offence under section 1, 2 or 3 above] the following questions are immaterial to the accused's guilt—

(a) the question where any person became a party to the conspiracy; and

(b) the question whether any act, omission or other event occurred in the home country concerned.

(2) On a charge of attempting to commit an offence under section 3 above the following questions are immaterial to the accused's guilt—

(a) the question where the attempt was made; and

(b) the question whether it had an effect in the home country concerned.

(3) [...]

(4) This section does not extend to Scotland.

7   Territorial scope of inchoate offences related to offences under external law corresponding to [offences under sections 1 to 3[2]]

(1) [...]

(2) [...]

(3) The following subsections shall be inserted after section 1(1) of the Criminal Attempts Act 1981—

"(1A) Subject to section 8 of the Computer Misuse Act 1990 (relevance of external law), if this subsection applies to an act, what the person doing it had in view shall be treated as an offence to which this section applies.

(1B) Subsection (1A) above applies to an act if—

(a) it is done in England and Wales; and

(b) it would fall within subsection (1) above as more than merely preparatory to the commission of an offence under section 3 of the Computer Misuse Act 1990 but for the fact that the offence, if completed, would not be an offence triable in England and Wales."

(4) [...][3]

8   Relevance of external law

(1) A person is guilty of an offence triable by virtue of section 4(4) above only if what he intended to do or facilitate would involve the commission of an offence under the law in force where the whole or any part of it was intended to take place.

(2) [...]

(3) A person is guilty of an offence triable by virtue of section 1(1A) of the Criminal Attempts Act 1981 [...[4]] only if what he had in view would involve the commission of an offence under the law in force where the whole or any part of it was intended to take place.

---

[1] Amendments not yet in force: see Police and Justice Act 2006, s. 53 and Serious Crime Act 2007, s. 94.

[2] Amendment not yet in force: see Police and Justice Act 2006, s. 53.

[3] Repeal not yet in force: see Serious Crime Act 2007, s. 94.

[4] Repeal not yet in force: see Serious Crime Act 2007, s. 94.

(4) Conduct punishable under the law in force in any place is an offence under that law for the purposes of this section, however it is described in that law.

(5) Subject to subsection (7) below, a condition specified in [subsection (1) and (3)] above shall be taken to be satisfied unless not later than rules of court may provide the defence serve on the prosecution a notice—

    (a) stating that, on the facts as alleged with respect to the relevant conduct, the condition is not in their opinion satisfied;

    (b) showing their grounds for that opinion; and

    (c) requiring the prosecution to show that it is satisfied.

(6) In subsection (5) above the relevant conduct' means—

    (a) where the condition in subsection (1) above is in question, what the accused intended to do or facilitate;

    (b) [. . .]

    (c) where the condition in subsection (3) above is in question, what the accused had in view.

(7) The court, if it thinks fit, may permit the defence to require the prosecution to show that the condition is satisfied without the prior service of a notice under subsection (5) above.

(8) If by virtue of subsection (7) above a court of solemn jurisdiction in Scotland permits the defence to require the prosecution to show that the condition is satisfied, it shall be competent for the prosecution for that purpose to examine any witness or to put in evidence any production not included in the lists lodged by it.

(9) In the Crown Court the question whether the condition is satisfied shall be decided by the judge alone.

(10) In the High Court of Justiciary and in the sheriff court the question whether the condition is satisfied shall be decided by the judge or, as the case may be, the sheriff alone.

9 British citizenship immaterial[1]

(1) In any proceedings brought in England and Wales in respect of any offence to which this section applies it is immaterial to guilt whether or not the accused was a British citizen at the time of any act, omission or other event proof of which is required for conviction of the offence.

(2) This section applies to the following offences—

    (a) any [offence under section 1, 2 or 3 above];

    (b) [. . .]

    (c) any attempt to commit an offence under section 3 above [. . .].

Miscellaneous and general

10 Saving for certain law enforcement powers

Section 1(1) above has effect without prejudice to the operation—

    (a) in England and Wales of any enactment relating to powers of inspection, search or seizure; and

    (b) in Scotland of any enactment or rule of law relating to powers of examination, search or seizure

[and nothing designed to indicate a withholding of consent to access to any program or data from persons as enforcement officers shall have effect to make access unauthorised for the purposes of the said section 1(1).

In this section "enforcement officer" means a constable or other person charged with the duty of investigating offences; and withholding consent from a person "as" an enforcement officer of any description includes the operation, by the person entitled to control access, of rules whereby enforcement officers of that description are, as such, disqualified from membership of a class of persons who are authorised to have access].

---

[1] Amendments other than the repeal of s. 9(2)(b) not yet in force: Police and Justice Act 2006, s. 53 and Serious Crime Act 2007, s. 94.

11   Proceedings for offences under section 1

[...]¹

12   Conviction of an offence under section 1 in proceedings for an offence under section 2 or 3

[...]²

13   Proceedings in Scotland

(1) A sheriff shall have jurisdiction in respect of an offence under section 1 or 2 above if—

(a) the accused was in the sheriffdom at the time when he did the act which caused the computer to perform the function; or

(b) [any computer containing any program or data to which the accused by doing that act secured or intended to secure unauthorised access, or enabled or intended to enable unauthorised access to be secured, was in the sheriffdom at that time].

(2) A sheriff shall have jurisdiction in respect of an offence under section 3 above if—

(a) the accused was in the sheriffdom at the time when [he did the unauthorised act (or caused it to be done]; or

(b) [the unauthorised act was done in relation to a computer in the sheriffdom].

(3)–(7) [...]

(8) In proceedings in which a person is charged with an offence under section 2 or 3 above and is found not guilty or is acquitted of that charge, he may be found guilty of an offence under section 1 above if on the facts shown he could have been found guilty of that offence in proceedings for that offence [...].

(9) Subsection (8) above shall apply whether or not an offence under section 1 above has been libelled in the complaint or indictment.

(10) A person found guilty of an offence under section 1 above by virtue of subsection (8) above shall be liable, in respect of that offence, only to the penalties set out in section 1.

(11) This section extends to Scotland only.

14   Search warrants for offences under section 1

[...]³

16   Application to Northern Ireland

(1) The following provisions of this section have effect for applying this Act in relation to Northern Ireland with the modifications there mentioned.

[(1A) In section 1(3)(a)—

(a) the reference to England and Wales shall be read as a reference to Northern Ireland; and

(b) the reference to 12 months shall be read as a reference to six months.⁴]

(2) In section 2(2)(b)—

(a) the reference to England and Wales shall be read as a reference to Northern Ireland; and

(b) the reference to section 33 of the Magistrates' Courts Act 1980 shall be read as a reference to Article 46(4) of the Magistrates' Courts (Northern Ireland) Order 1981.

[(2A) In section 2(5)(a)—

(a) the reference to England and Wales shall be read as a reference to Northern Ireland; and

(b) the reference to 12 months shall be read as a reference to six months.⁵]

[(3A) In section 3(6)(a)—

(a) the reference to England and Wales shall be read as a reference to Northern Ireland; and

(b) the reference to 12 months shall be read as a reference to six months.

---

¹ Repeal not yet in force: see Police and Justice Act 2006, s. 53.
² Repeal not yet in force: see Police and Justice Act 2006, s. 53.
³ Repeal not yet in force: see Police and Justice Act 2006, s. 53.
⁴ New sub-section not yet in force: see Police and Justice Act 2006, s. 53.
⁵ New sub-section not yet in force: see Police and Justice Act 2006, s. 53.

(3B) In section 3A(5)(a)—

    (a) the reference to England and Wales shall be read as a reference to Northern Ireland; and

    (b) the reference to 12 months shall be read as a reference to six months.[1]]

(4) [Subsection (7) below shall apply in substitution for subsection (3) of section 7] [...[2]].

(5) [...]

(6) [...]

(7) The following paragraphs shall be inserted after Article 3(1) of that Order—

"(1A) Subject to section 8 of the Computer Misuse Act 1990 (relevance of external law), if this paragraph applies to an act, what the person doing it had in view shall be treated as an offence to which this Article applies.

(1B) Paragraph (1A) above applies to an act if—

    (a) it is done in Northern Ireland; and

    (b) it would fall within paragraph (1) as more than merely preparatory to the commission of an offence under section 3 of the Computer Misuse Act 1990 but for the fact that the offence, if completed, would not be an offence triable in Northern Ireland.".

(8) In section 8—

    (a) [...]

    (b) the reference in subsection (3) to section 1(1A) of the Criminal Attempts Act 1981 shall be read as a reference to Article 3(1A) of that Order.

(9) The references in sections 9(1) and 10 to England and Wales shall be read as references to Northern Ireland.

(10)–(12) [...[3]]

[16A Northern Ireland: search warrants for offences under section 1[4]

(1) Where a county court judge is satisfied by information on oath given by a constable that there are reasonable grounds for believing—

    (a) that an offence under section 1 above has been or is about to be committed in any premises, and

    (b) that evidence that such an offence has been or is about to be committed is in those premises,

he may issue a warrant authorising a constable to enter and search the premises, using such reasonable force as is necessary.

(2) The power conferred by subsection (1) above does not extend to authorising a search for material of the kinds mentioned in Article 11(2) of the Police and Criminal Evidence (Northern Ireland) Order 1989 (privileged, excluded and special procedure material).

(3) A warrant under this section—

    (a) may authorise persons to accompany any constable executing the warrant; and

    (b) remains in force for twenty-eight days from the date of its issue.

(4) In exercising a warrant issued under this section a constable may seize an article if he reasonably believes that it is evidence that an offence under section 1 above has been or is about to be committed.

(5) In this section "premises" includes land, buildings, movable structures, vehicles, vessels, aircraft and hovercraft.

(6) This section extends only to Northern Ireland.]

17 Interpretation

(1) The following provisions of this section apply for the interpretation of this Act.

(2) A person secures access to any program or data held in a computer if by causing a computer to perform any function he—

    (a) alters or erases the program or data;

    (b) copies or moves it to any storage medium other than that in which it is held or to a different location in the storage medium in which it is held;

---

[1] New sub-sections not yet in force: see Police and Justice Act 2006, s. 53.
[2] Repeal not yet in force: see Serious Crime Act 2007, s. 94.
[3] Repeal not yet in force: see Police and Justice Act 2006, s. 53.
[4] New section not yet in force: see Police and Justice Act 2006, s. 53.

    (c) uses it; or

    (d) has it output from the computer in which it is held (whether by having it displayed or in any other manner);

and references to access to a program or data (and to an intent to secure such access [or to enable such access to be secured[1]]) shall be read accordingly.

    (3) For the purposes of subsection (2)(c) above a person uses a program if the function he causes the computer to perform—

    (a) causes the program to be executed; or

    (b) is itself a function of the program.

    (4) For the purposes of subsection (2)(d) above—

    (a) a program is output if the instructions of which it consists are output; and

    (b) the form in which any such instructions or any other data is output (and in particular whether or not it represents a form in which, in the case of instructions, they are capable of being executed or, in the case of data, it is capable of being processed by a computer) is immaterial.

    (5) Access of any kind by any person to any program or data held in a computer is unauthorised if—

    (a) he is not himself entitled to control access of the kind in question to the program or data; and

    (b) he does not have consent to access by him of the kind of question to the program or data from any person who is so entitled.

[but this subsection is subject to section 10].

    (6) References to any program or data held in a computer include references to any program or data held in any removable storage medium which is for the time being in the computer; and a computer is to be regarded as containing any program or data held in any such medium.

    (7) [...[2]]

    (8) [An act done in relation to a computer is unauthorised if the person doing the act (or causing it to be done)—

    (a) is not himself a person who has responsibility for the computer and is entitled to determine whether the act may be done; and

    (b) does not have consent to the act from any such person.

In this subsection "act" includes a series of acts.[3]]

    (9) References to the home country concerned shall be read in accordance with section 4(6) above.

    (10) References to a program include references to part of a program.

18   Citation, commencement etc.

    (1) This Act may be cited as the Computer Misuse Act 1990.

    (2) This Act shall come into force at the end of the period of two months beginning with the day on which it is passed.

    (3) An offence is not committed under this Act unless every act or other event proof of which is required for conviction of the offence takes place after this Act comes into force.

Trade Marks Act 1994

(1994, c. 26)

An Act to make new provision for registered trade marks, implementing Council Directive No. 89/ 104/ EEC of 21st December 1988 to approximate the laws of the Member States relating to trade marks; to make

---

[1] Amendment not yet in force in relation to England and Wales: see Police and Justice Act 2006, s. 53.
[2] Repeal not yet in force in relation to England and Wales: see Police and Justice Act 2006, s. 53.
[3] Amendment not yet in force in relation to England and Wales: see Police and Justice Act 2006, s. 53.

provision in connection with Council Regulation (EC) No. 40/94 of 20th December 1993 on the Community trade mark; to give effect to the Madrid Protocol Relating to the International Registration of Marks of 27th June 1989, and to certain provisions of the Paris Convention for the Protection of Industrial Property of 20th March 1883, as revised and amended; and for connected purposes.

[21st July 1994]

PART I REGISTERED TRADE MARKS

Introductory

1 Trade marks

(1) In this Act a "trade mark" means any sign capable of being represented graphically which is capable of distinguishing goods or services of one undertaking from those of other undertakings.

A trade mark may, in particular, consist of words (including personal names), designs, letters, numerals or the shape of goods or their packaging.

(2) References in this Act to a trade mark include, unless the context otherwise requires, references to a collective mark (see section 49) or certification mark (see section 50).

2 Registered trade marks

(1) A registered trade mark is a property right obtained by the registration of the trade mark under this Act and the proprietor of a registered trade mark has the rights and remedies provided by this Act.

(2) No proceedings lie to prevent or recover damages for the infringement of an unregistered trade mark as such; but nothing in this Act affects the law relating to passing off.

Grounds for refusal of registration

3 Absolute grounds for refusal of registration

(1) The following shall not be registered—

    (a) signs which do not satisfy the requirements of section 1(1),

    (b) trade marks which are devoid of any distinctive character,

    (c) trade marks which consist exclusively of signs or indications which may serve, in trade, to designate the kind, quality, quantity, intended purpose, value, geographical origin, the time of production of goods or of rendering of services, or other characteristics of goods or services,

    (d) trade marks which consist exclusively of signs or indications which have become customary in the current language or in the *bona fide* and established practices of the trade:

Provided that, a trade mark shall not be refused registration by virtue of paragraph (b), (c) or (d) above if, before the date of application for registration, it has in fact acquired a distinctive character as a result of the use made of it.

(2) A sign shall not be registered as a trade mark if it consists exclusively of—

    (a) the shape which results from the nature of the goods themselves,

    (b) the shape of goods which is necessary to obtain a technical result, or

    (c) the shape which gives substantial value to the goods.

(3) A trade mark shall not be registered if it is—

    (a) contrary to public policy or to accepted principles of morality, or

    (b) of such a nature as to deceive the public (for instance as to the nature, quality or geographical origin of the goods or service).

(4) A trade mark shall not be registered if or to the extent that its use is prohibited in the United Kingdom by any enactment or rule of law or by any provision of Community law.

(5) A trade mark shall not be registered in the cases specified, or referred to, in section 4 (specially protected emblems).

(6) A trade mark shall not be registered if or to the extent that the application is made in bad faith.

4   Specially protected emblems

(1) A trade mark which consists of or contains—

(a) the Royal arms, or any of the principal armorial bearings of the Royal arms, or any insignia or device so nearly resembling the Royal arms or any such armorial bearing as to be likely to be mistaken for them or it,

(b) a representation of the Royal crown or any of the Royal flags,

(c) a representation of Her Majesty or any member of the Royal family, or any colourable imitation thereof, or

(d) words, letters or devices likely to lead persons to think that the applicant either has or recently has had Royal patronage or authorisation,

shall not be registered unless it appears to the registrar that consent has been given by or on behalf of Her Majesty or, as the case may be, the relevant member of the Royal family.

(2) A trade mark which consists of or contains a representation of—

(a) the national flag of the United Kingdom (commonly known as the Union Jack), or

(b) the flag of England, Wales, Scotland, Northern Ireland or the Isle of Man,

shall not be registered if it appears to the registrar that the use of the trade mark would be misleading or grossly offensive.

Provision may be made by rules identifying the flags to which paragraph (b) applies.

(3) A trade mark shall not be registered in the cases specified in—

section 57 (national emblems, etc. of Convention countries), or

section 58 (emblems, etc. of certain international organisations).

(4) Provision may be made by rules prohibiting in such cases as may be prescribed the registration of a trade mark which consists of or contains—

(a) arms to which a person is entitled by virtue of a grant of arms by the Crown, or

(b) insignia so nearly resembling such arms as to be likely to be mistaken for them,

unless it appears to the registrar that consent has been given by or on behalf of that person.

Where such a mark is registered, nothing in this Act shall be construed as authorising its use in any way contrary to the laws of arms.

[(5) A trade mark which consists of or contains a controlled representation within the meaning of the Olympic Symbol etc. (Protection) Act 1995 shall not be registered unless it appears to the registrar—

(a) that the application is made by the person for the time being appointed under section 1(2) of the Olympic Symbol etc. (Protection) Act 1995 (power of Secretary of State to appoint a person as the proprietor of the Olympics association right), or

(b) that consent has been given by or on behalf of the person mentioned in paragraph (a) above.]

5   Relative grounds for refusal of registration

(1) A trade mark shall not be registered if it is identical with an earlier trade mark and the goods or services for which the trade mark is applied for are identical with the goods or services for which the earlier trade mark is protected.

(2) A trade mark shall not be registered if because—

(a) it is identical with an earlier trade mark and is to be registered for goods or services similar to those for which the earlier trade mark is protected, or

(b) it is similar to an earlier trade mark and is to be registered for goods or services identical with or similar to those for which the earlier trade mark is protected,

there exists a likelihood of confusion on the part of the public, which includes the likelihood of association with the earlier trade mark.

(3) A trade mark which—

(a) is identical with or similar to an earlier trade mark, [. . .

(b) . . .]

shall not be registered if, or to the extent that, the earlier trade mark has a reputation in the United Kingdom (or, in the case of a Community trade mark [or international trade mark (EC)], in the

European Community) and the use of the later mark without due cause would take unfair advantage of, or be detrimental to, the distinctive character or the repute of the earlier trade mark.

(4) A trade mark shall not be registered if, or to the extent that, its use in the United Kingdom is liable to be prevented—

>   (a) by virtue of any rule of law (in particular, the law of passing off) protecting an unregistered trade mark or other sign used in the course of trade, or

>   (b) by virtue of an earlier right other than those referred to in subsections (1) to (3) or paragraph (a) above, in particular by virtue of the law of copyright, design right or registered designs.

A person thus entitled to prevent the use of a trade mark is referred to in this Act as the proprietor of an "earlier right" in relation to the trade mark.

(5) Nothing in this section prevents the registration of a trade mark where the proprietor of the earlier trade mark or other earlier right consents to the registration.

6   Meaning of "earlier trade mark"

(1) In this Act an "earlier trade mark" means—

>   (a) a registered trade mark, international trade mark (UK)[, Community trade mark or international trade mark (EC)] which has a date of application for registration earlier than that of the trade mark in question, taking account (where appropriate) of the priorities claimed in respect of the trade marks,

>   [(b) a Community trade mark or international trade mark (EC) which has a valid claim to seniority from an earlier registered trade mark or international trade mark (UK),

>   (ba) a registered trade mark or international trade mark (UK) which—

>> (i) has been converted from a Community trade mark or international trade mark (EC) which itself had a valid claim to seniority within paragraph (b) from an earlier trade mark, and

>> (ii) accordingly has the same claim to seniority, or]

>   (c) a trade mark which, at the date of application for registration of the trade mark in question or (where appropriate) of the priority claimed in respect of the application, was entitled to protection under the Paris Convention [or the WTO agreement] as a well known trade mark.

(2) References in this Act to an earlier trade mark include a trade mark in respect of which an application for registration has been made and which, if registered, would be an earlier trade mark by virtue of subsection (1)(a) or (b), subject to its being so registered.

(3) A trade mark within subsection (1)(a) or (b) whose registration expires shall continue to be taken into account in determining the registrability of a later mark for a period of one year after the expiry unless the registrar is satisfied that there was no *bona fide* use of the mark during the two years immediately preceding the expiry.

[6A   Raising of relative grounds in opposition proceedings in case of non-use

(1) This section applies where—

>   (a) an application for registration of a trade mark has been published,

>   (b) there is an earlier trade mark in relation to which the conditions set out in section 5(1), (2) or (3) obtain, and

>   (c) the registration procedure for the earlier trade mark was completed before the start of the period of five years ending with the date of publication.

(2) In opposition proceedings, the registrar shall not refuse to register the trade mark by reason of the earlier trade mark unless the use conditions are met.

(3) The use conditions are met if—

>   (a) within the period of five years ending with the date of publication of the application the earlier trade mark has been put to genuine use in the United Kingdom by the proprietor or with his consent in relation to the goods or services for which it is registered, or

>   (b) the earlier trade mark has not been so used, but there are proper reasons for non-use.

(4) For these purposes—

   (a) use of a trade mark includes use in a form differing in elements which do not alter the distinctive character of the mark in the form in which it was registered, and

   (b) use in the United Kingdom includes affixing the trade mark to goods or to the packaging
   of goods in the United Kingdom solely for export purposes.

(5) In relation to a Community trade mark, any reference in subsection (3) or (4) to the United
Kingdom shall be construed as a reference to the European Community.

(6) Where an earlier trade mark satisfies the use conditions in respect of some only of the goods
or services for which it is registered, it shall be treated for the purposes of this section as if it were
registered only in respect of those goods or services.

(7) Nothing in this section affects—

   (a) the refusal of registration on the grounds mentioned in section 3 (absolute grounds for
   refusal) or section 5(4) (relative grounds of refusal on the basis of an earlier right), or

   (b) the making of an application for a declaration of invalidity under section 47(2) (application on relative grounds where no consent to registration).]

7   Raising of relative grounds in case of honest concurrent use

(1) This section applies where on an application for the registration of a trade mark it appears to
the registrar—

   (a) that there is an earlier trade mark in relation to which the conditions set out in section
   5(1), (2) or (3) obtain, or

   (b) that there is an earlier right in relation to which the condition set out in section 5(4) is
   satisfied,

but the applicant shows to the satisfaction of the registrar that there has been honest concurrent use
of the trade mark for which registration is sought.

(2) In that case the registrar shall not refuse the application by reason of the earlier trade mark or
other earlier right unless objection on that ground is raised in opposition proceedings by the proprietor of that earlier trade mark or other earlier right.

(3) For the purposes of this section "honest concurrent use" means such use in the United
Kingdom, by the applicant or with his consent, as would formerly have amounted to honest concurrent use for the purposes of section 12(2) of the Trade Marks Act 1938.

(4) Nothing in this section affects—

   (a) the refusal of registration on the grounds mentioned in section 3 (absolute grounds for
   refusal), or

   (b) the making of an application for a declaration of invalidity under section 47(2) (application on relative grounds where no consent to registration).

(5) This section does not apply when there is an order in force under section 8 below.

Effects of registered trade mark

9   Rights conferred by registered trade mark

(1) The proprietor of a registered trade mark has exclusive rights in the trade mark which are
infringed by use of the trade mark in the United Kingdom without his consent.

The acts amounting to infringement, if done without the consent of the proprietor, are specified
in section 10.

(2) References in this Act to the infringement of a registered trade mark are to any such infringement of the rights of the proprietor.

(3) The rights of the proprietor have effect from the date of registration (which in accordance
with section 40(3) is the date of filing of the application for registration):

Provided that—

   (a) no infringement proceedings may be begun before the date on which the trade mark is in
   fact registered; and

   (b) no offence under section 92 (unauthorised use of trade mark, &c. in relation to goods) is
   committed by anything done before the date of publication of the registration.

10 Infringement of registered trade mark

(1) A person infringes a registered trade mark if he uses in the course of trade a sign which is identical with the trade mark in relation to goods or services which are identical with those for which it is registered.

(2) A person infringes a registered trade mark if he uses in the course of trade a sign where because—

    (a) the sign is identical with the trade mark and is used in relation to goods or services similar to those for which the trade mark is registered, or

    (b) the sign is similar to the trade mark and is used in relation to goods or services identical with or similar to those for which the trade mark is registered,

there exists a likelihood of confusion on the part of the public, which includes the likelihood of association with the trade mark.

(3) A person infringes a registered trade mark if he uses in the course of trade[, in relation to goods or services,] a sign which—

    (a) is identical with or similar to the trade mark

    (b) [...]

where the trade mark has a reputation in the United Kingdom and the use of the sign, being without due cause, takes unfair advantage of, or is detrimental to, the distinctive character or the repute of the trade mark.

(4) For the purposes of this section a person uses a sign if, in particular, he—

    (a) affixes it to goods or the packaging thereof;

    (b) offers or exposes goods for sale, puts them on the market or stocks them for those purposes under the sign, or offers or supplies services under the sign;

    (c) imports or exports goods under the sign; or

    (d) uses the sign on business papers or in advertising.

(5) A person who applies a registered trade mark to material intended to be used for labelling or packaging goods, as a business paper, or for advertising goods or services, shall be treated as a party to any use of the material which infringes the registered trade mark if when he applied the mark he knew or had reason to believe that the application of the mark was not duly authorised by the proprietor or a licensee.

(6) Nothing in the preceding provisions of this section shall be construed as preventing the use of a registered trade mark by any person for the purpose of identifying goods or services as those of the proprietor or a licensee.

But any such use otherwise than in accordance with honest practices in industrial or commercial matters shall be treated as infringing the registered trade mark if the use without due cause takes unfair advantage of, or is detrimental to, the distinctive character or repute of the trade mark.

11 Limits on effect of registered trade mark

(1) A registered trade mark is not infringed by the use of another registered trade mark in relation to goods or services for which the latter is registered (but see section 47(6) (effect of declaration of invalidity of registration)).

(2) A registered trade mark is not infringed by—

    (a) the use by a person of his own name or address,

    (b) the use of indications concerning the kind, quality, quantity, intended purpose, value, geographical origin, the time of production of goods or of rendering of services, or other characteristics of goods or services, or

    (c) the use of the trade mark where it is necessary to indicate the intended purpose of a product or service (in particular, as accessories or spare parts),

provided the use is in accordance with honest practices in industrial or commercial matters.

(3) A registered trade mark is not infringed by the use in the course of trade in a particular locality of an earlier right which applies only in that locality.

For this purpose an "earlier right" means an unregistered trade mark or other sign continuously used in relation to goods or services by a person or a predecessor in title of his from a date prior to

whichever is the earlier of—
> (a) the use of the first-mentioned trade mark in relation to those goods or services by the proprietor or a predecessor in title of his, or
> (b) the registration of the first-mentioned trade mark in respect of those goods or services in the name of the proprietor or a predecessor in title of his;

and an earlier right shall be regarded as applying in a locality if, or to the extent that, its use in that locality is protected by virtue of any rule of law (in particular, the law of passing off).

12   Exhaustion of rights conferred by registered trade mark

(1) A registered trade mark is not infringed by the use of the trade mark in relation to goods which have been put on the market in the European Economic Area under that trade mark by the proprietor or with his consent.

(2) Subsection (1) does not apply where there exist legitimate reasons for the proprietor to oppose further dealings in the goods (in particular, where the condition of the goods has been changed or impaired after they have been put on the market).

13   Registration subject to disclaimer or limitation

(1) An applicant for registration of a trade mark, or the proprietor of a registered trade mark, may—
> (a) disclaim any right to the exclusive use of any specified element of the trade mark, or
> (b) agree that the rights conferred by the registration shall be subject to a specified territorial or other limitation;

and where the registration of a trade mark is subject to a disclaimer or limitation, the rights conferred by section 9 (rights conferred by registered trade mark) are restricted accordingly.

(2) Provision shall be made by rules as to the publication and entry in the register of a disclaimer or limitation.

Infringement proceedings

14   Action for infringement

(1) An infringement of a registered trade mark is actionable by the proprietor of the trade mark.

(2) In an action for infringement all such relief by way of damages, injunctions, accounts or otherwise is available to him as is available in respect of the infringement of any other property right.

15   Order for erasure, etc. of offending sign

(1) Where a person is found to have infringed a registered trade mark, the court may make an order requiring him—
> (a) to cause the offending sign to be erased, removed or obliterated from any infringing goods, material or articles in his possession, custody or control, or
> (b) if it is not reasonably practicable for the offending sign to be erased, removed or obliterated, to secure the destruction of the infringing goods, material or articles in question.

(2) If an order under subsection (1) is not complied with, or it appears to the court likely that such an order would not be complied with, the court may order that the infringing goods, material or articles be delivered to such person as the court may direct for erasure, removal or obliteration of the sign, or for destruction, as the case may be.

21   Remedy for groundless threats of infringement proceedings

(1) Where a person threatens another with proceedings for infringement of a registered trade mark other than—
> (a) the application of the mark to goods or their packaging,
> (b) the importation of goods to which, or to the packaging of which, the mark has been applied, or
> (c) the supply of services under the mark,

any person aggrieved may bring proceedings for relief under this section.

(2) The relief which may be applied for is any of the following—

(a) a declaration that the threats are unjustifiable,

(b) an injunction against the continuance of the threats,

(c) damages in respect of any loss he has sustained by the threats;

and the plaintiff is entitled to such relief unless the defendant shows that the acts in respect of which proceedings were threatened constitute (or if done would constitute) an infringement of the registered trade mark concerned.

(3) If that is shown by the defendant, the plaintiff is nevertheless entitled to relief if he shows that the registration of the trade mark is invalid or liable to be revoked in a relevant respect.

(4) The mere notification that a trade mark is registered, or that an application for registration has been made, does not constitute a threat of proceedings for the purposes of this section.

Registered trade mark as object of property

22   Nature of registered trade mark

A registered trade mark is personal property (in Scotland, incorporeal moveable property).

23   Co-ownership of registered trade mark

(1) Where a registered trade mark is granted to two or more persons jointly, each of them is entitled, subject to any agreement to the contrary, to an equal undivided share in the registered trade mark.

(2) The following provisions apply where two or more persons are co-proprietors of a registered trade mark, by virtue of subsection (1) or otherwise.

(3) Subject to any agreement to the contrary, each co-proprietor is entitled, by himself or his agents, to do for his own benefit and without the consent of or the need to account to the other or others, any act which would otherwise amount to an infringement of the registered trade mark.

(4) One co-proprietor may not without the consent of the other or others—

(a) grant a licence to use the registered trade mark, or

(b) assign or charge his share in the registered trade mark (or, in Scotland, cause or permit security to be granted over it).

(5) Infringement proceedings may be brought by any co-proprietor, but he may not, without the leave of the court, proceed with the action unless the other, or each of the others, is either joined as a plaintiff or added as a defendant.

A co-proprietor who is thus added as a defendant shall not be made liable for any costs in the action unless he takes part in the proceedings.

Nothing in this subsection affects the granting of interlocutory relief on the application of a single co-proprietor.

(6) Nothing in this section affects the mutual rights and obligations of trustees or personal representatives, or their rights and obligations as such.

24   Assignment, etc. of registered trade mark

(1) A registered trade mark is transmissible by assignment, testamentary disposition or operation of law in the same way as other personal or moveable property.

It is so transmissible either in connection with the goodwill of a business or independently.

(2) An assignment or other transmission of a registered trade mark may be partial, that is, limited so as to apply—

(a) in relation to some but not all of the goods or services for which the trade mark is registered, or

(b) in relation to use of the trade mark in a particular manner or a particular locality.

(3) An assignment of a registered trade mark, or an assent relating to a registered trade mark, is not effective unless it is in writing signed by or on behalf of the assignor or, as the case may be, a personal representative.

Except in Scotland, this requirement may be satisfied in a case where the assignor or personal representative is a body corporate by the affixing of its seal.

(4) The above provisions apply to assignment by way of security as in relation to any other assignment.

(5) A registered trade mark may be the subject of a charge (in Scotland, security) in the same way as other personal or moveable property.

(6) Nothing in this Act shall be construed as affecting the assignment or other transmission of an unregistered trade mark as part of the good will of a business.

Licensing

28   Licensing of registered trade mark

(1) A licence to use a registered trade mark may be general or limited.
A limited licence may, in particular, apply—

    (a) in relation to some but not all of the goods or services for which the trade mark is registered, or

    (b) in relation to use of the trade mark in a particular manner or a particular locality.

(2) A licence is not effective unless it is in writing signed by or on behalf of the grantor.
Except in Scotland, this requirement may be satisfied in a case where the grantor is a body corporate by the affixing of its seal.

(3) Unless the licence provides otherwise, it is binding on a successor in title to the grantor's interest.
References in this Act to doing anything with, or without, the consent of the proprietor of a registered trade mark shall be construed accordingly.

(4) Where the licence so provides, a sub-licence may be granted by the licensee; and references in this Act to a licence or licensee include a sub-licence or sub-licensee.

29   Exclusive licences

(1) In this Act an "exclusive licence" means a licence (whether general or limited) authorising the licensee to the exclusion of all other persons, including the person granting the licence, to use a registered trade mark in the manner authorised by the licence.
The expression "exclusive licensee" shall be construed accordingly.

(2) An exclusive licensee has the same rights against a successor in title who is bound by the licence as he has against the person granting the licence.

30   General provisions as to rights of licensees in case of infringement

(1) This section has effect with respect to the rights of a licensee in relation to infringement of a registered trade mark.
The provisions of this section do not apply where or to the extent that, by virtue of section 31(1) below (exclusive licensee having rights and remedies of assignee), the licensee has a right to bring proceedings in his own name.

(2) A licensee is entitled, unless his licence, or any licence through which his interest is derived, provides otherwise, to call on the proprietor of the registered trade mark to take infringement proceedings in respect of any matter which affects his interests.

(3) If the proprietor—

    (a) refuses to do so, or

    (b) fails to do so within two months after being called upon,

the licensee may bring the proceedings in his own name as if he were the proprietor.

(4) Where infringement proceedings are brought by a licensee by virtue of this section, the licensee may not, without the leave of the court, proceed with the action unless the proprietor is either joined as a plaintiff or added as a defendant.
This does not affect the granting of interlocutory relief on an application by a licensee alone.

(5) A proprietor who is added as a defendant as mentioned in subsection (4) shall not be made liable for any costs in the action unless he takes part in the proceedings.

(6) In infringement proceedings brought by the proprietor of a registered trade mark any loss suffered or likely to be suffered by licensees shall be taken into account; and the court may give such directions as it thinks fit as to the extent to which the plaintiff is to hold the proceeds of any pecuniary remedy on behalf of licensees.

(7) The provisions of this section apply in relation to an exclusive licensee if or to the extent that he has, by virtue of section 31(1), the rights and remedies of an assignee as if he were the proprietor of the registered trade mark.

31 Exclusive licensee having rights and remedies of assignee

(1) An exclusive licence may provide that the licensee shall have, to such extent as may be provided by the licence, the same rights and remedies in respect of matters occurring after the grant of the licence as if the licence had been an assignment.

Where or to the extent that such provision is made, the licensee is entitled, subject to the provisions of the licence and to the following provisions of this section, to bring infringement proceedings, against any person other than the proprietor, in his own name.

(2) Any such rights and remedies of an exclusive licensee are concurrent with those of the proprietor of the registered trade mark; and references to the proprietor of a registered trade mark in the provisions of this Act relating to infringement shall be construed accordingly.

(3) In an action brought by an exclusive licensee by virtue of this section a defendant may avail himself of any defence which would have been available to him if the action had been brought by the proprietor of the registered trade mark.

(4) Where proceedings for infringement of a registered trade mark brought by the proprietor or an exclusive licensee relate wholly or partly to an infringement in respect of which they have concurrent rights of action, the proprietor or, as the case may be, the exclusive licensee may not, without the leave of the court, proceed with the action unless the other is either joined as a plaintiff or added as a defendant.

This does not affect the granting of interlocutory relief on an application by a proprietor or exclusive licensee alone.

(5) A person who is added as a defendant as mentioned in subsection (4) shall not be made liable for any costs in the action unless he takes part in the proceedings.

(6) Where an action for infringement of a registered trade mark is brought which relates wholly or partly to an infringement in respect of which the proprietor and an exclusive licensee have or had concurrent rights of action—

(a) the court shall in assessing damages take into account—
   (i) the terms of the licence, and
   (ii) any pecuniary remedy already awarded or available to either of them in respect of the infringement;

(b) no account of profits shall be directed if an award of damages has been made, or an account of profits has been directed, in favour of the other of them in respect of the infringement; and

(c) the court shall if an account of profits is directed apportion the profits between them as the court considers just, subject to any agreement between them.

The provisions of this subsection apply whether or not the proprietor and the exclusive licensee are both parties to the action; and if they are not both parties the court may give such directions as it thinks fit as to the extent to which the party to the proceedings is to hold the proceeds of any pecuniary remedy on behalf of the other.

(7) The proprietor of a registered trade mark shall notify any exclusive licensee who has a concurrent right of action before applying for an order under section 16 (order for delivery up); and the court may on the application of the licensee make such order under that section as it thinks fit having regard to the terms of the licence.

(8) The provisions of subsections (4) to (7) above have effect subject to any agreement to the contrary between the exclusive licensee and the proprietor.

Application for registered trade mark

32 Application for registration

(1) An application for registration of a trade mark shall be made to the registrar.

(2) The application shall contain—
- (a) a request for registration of a trade mark,
- (b) the name and address of the applicant,
- (c) a statement of the goods or services in relation to which it is sought to register the trade mark, and
- (d) a representation of the trade mark.

(3) The application shall state that the trade mark is being used, by the applicant or with his consent, in relation to those goods or services, or that he has a *bona fide* intention that it should be so used.

(4) The application shall be subject to the payment of the application fee and such class fees as may be appropriate.

Priority

35   Claim to priority of Convention application

(1) A person who has duly filed an application for protection of a trade mark in a Convention country (a "Convention application"), or his successor in title, has a right to priority, for the purposes of registering the same trade mark under this Act for some or all of the same goods or services, for a period of six months from the date of filing of the first such application.

(2) If the application for registration under this Act is made within that six-month period—
- (a) the relevant date for the purposes of establishing which rights take precedence shall be the date of filing of the first Convention application, and
- (b) the registrability of the trade mark shall not be affected by any use of the mark in the United Kingdom in the period between that date and the date of the application under this Act.

(3) Any filing which in a Convention country is equivalent to a regular national filing, under its domestic legislation or an international agreement, shall be treated as giving rise to the right of priority.

A "regular national filing" means a filing which is adequate to establish the date on which the application was filed in that country, whatever may be the subsequent fate of the application.

(4) A subsequent application concerning the same subject as the first Convention application, filed in the same Convention country, shall be considered the first Convention application (of which the filing date is the starting date of the period of priority), if at the time of the subsequent application—
- (a) the previous application has been withdrawn, abandoned or refused, without having been laid open to public inspection and without leaving any rights outstanding, and
- (b) it has not yet served as a basis for claiming a right of priority.

The previous application may not thereafter serve as a basis for claiming a right of priority.

(5) Provision may be made by rules as to the manner of claiming a right to priority on the basis of a Convention application.

(6) A right to priority arising as a result of a Convention application may be assigned or otherwise transmitted, either with the application or independently.

The reference in subsection (1) to the applicant's "successor in title" shall be construed accordingly.

Duration, renewal and alteration of registered trade mark

42   Duration of registration

(1) A trade mark shall be registered for a period of ten years from the date of registration.

(2) Registration may be renewed in accordance with section 43 for further periods of ten years.

43   Renewal of registration

(1) The registration of a trade mark may be renewed at the request of the proprietor, subject to payment of a renewal fee.

(2) Provision shall be made by rules for the registrar to inform the proprietor of a registered trade mark, before the expiry of the registration, of the date of expiry and the manner in which the registration may be renewed.

(3) A request for renewal must be made, and the renewal fee paid, before the expiry of the registration.

Failing this, the request may be made and the fee paid within such further period (of not less than six months) as may be prescribed, in which case an additional renewal fee must also be paid within that period.

(4) Renewal shall take effect from the expiry of the previous registration.

(5) If the registration is not renewed in accordance with the above provisions, the registrar shall remove the trade mark from the register.

Provision may be made by rules for the restoration of the registration of a trade mark which has been removed from the register, subject to such conditions (if any) as may be prescribed.

(6) The renewal or restoration of the registration of a trade mark shall be published in the prescribed manner.

44   Alteration of registered trade mark

(1) A registered trade mark shall not be altered in the register, during the period of registration or on renewal.

(2) Nevertheless, the registrar may, at the request of the proprietor, allow the alteration of a registered trade mark where the mark includes the proprietor's name or address and the alteration is limited to alteration of that name or address and does not substantially affect the identity of the mark.

(3) Provision shall be made by rules for the publication of any such alteration and the making of objections by any person claiming to be affected by it.

Surrender, revocation and invalidity

45   Surrender of registered trade mark

(1) A registered trade mark may be surrendered by the proprietor in respect of some or all of the goods or services for which it is registered.

(2) Provision may be made by rules—

(a) as to the manner and effect of a surrender, and

(b) for protecting the interests of other persons having a right in the registered trade mark.

46   Revocation of registration

(1) The registration of a trade mark may be revoked on any of the following grounds—

(a) that within the period of five years following the date of completion of the registration procedure it has not been put to genuine use in the United Kingdom, by the proprietor or with his consent, in relation to the goods or services for which it is registered, and there are no proper reasons for non-use;

(b) that such use has been suspended for an uninterrupted period of five years, and there are no proper reasons for non-use;

(c) that, in consequence of acts or inactivity of the proprietor, it has become the common name in the trade for a product or service for which it is registered;

(d) that in consequence of the use made of it by the proprietor or with his consent in relation to the goods or services for which it is registered, it is liable to mislead the public, particularly as to the nature, quality or geographical origin of those goods or services.

(2) For the purposes of subsection (1) use of a trade mark includes use in a form differing in elements which do not alter the distinctive character of the mark in the form in which it was registered, and use in the United Kingdom includes affixing the trade mark to goods or to the packaging of goods in the United Kingdom solely for export purposes.

(3) The registration of a trade mark shall not be revoked on the ground mentioned in subsection (1)(a) or (b) if such use as is referred to in that paragraph is commenced or resumed after the expiry of the five year period and before the application for revocation is made:

Provided that, any such commencement or resumption of use after the expiry of the five year period but within the period of three months before the making of the application shall be disregarded unless preparations for the commencement or resumption began before the proprietor became aware that the application might be made.

(4) An application for revocation may be made by any person, and may be made either to the registrar or to the court, except that—

(a) if proceedings concerning the trade mark in question are pending in the court, the application must be made to the court; and

(b) if in any other case the application is made to the registrar, he may at any stage of the proceedings refer the application to the court.

(5) Where grounds for revocation exist in respect of only some of the goods or services for which the trade mark is registered, revocation shall relate to those goods or services only.

(6) Where the registration of a trade mark is revoked to any extent, the rights of the proprietor shall be deemed to have ceased to that extent as from—

(a) the date of the application for revocation, or

(b) if the registrar or court is satisfied that the grounds for revocation existed at an earlier date, that date.

47 Grounds for invalidity of registration

(1) The registration of a trade mark may be declared invalid on the ground that the trade mark was registered in breach of section 3 or any of the provisions referred to in that section (absolute grounds for refusal of registration).

Where the trade mark was registered in breach of subsection (1)(b), (c) or (d) of that section, it shall not be declared invalid if, in consequence of the use which has been made of it, it has after registration acquired a distinctive character in relation to the goods or services for which it is registered.

(2) The registration of a trade mark may be declared invalid on the ground—

(a) that there is an earlier trade mark in relation to which the conditions set out in section 5(1), (2) or (3) obtain, or

(b) that there is an earlier right in relation to which the condition set out in section 5(4) is satisfied,

unless the proprietor of that earlier trade mark or other earlier right has consented to the registration.

[(2A) But the registration of a trade mark may not be declared invalid on the ground that there is an earlier trade mark unless—

(a) the registration procedure for the earlier trade mark was completed within the period of five years ending with the date of the application for the declaration,

(b) the registration procedure for the earlier trade mark was not completed before that date, or

(c) the use conditions are met.

(2B) The use conditions are met if—

(a) within the period of five years ending with the date of the application for the declaration the earlier trade mark has been put to genuine use in the United Kingdom by the proprietor or with his consent in relation to the goods or services for which it is registered, or

(b) it has not been so used, but there are proper reasons for non-use.

(2C) For these purposes—

(a) use of a trade mark includes use in a form differing in elements which do not alter the distinctive character of the mark in the form in which it was registered, and

(b) use in the United Kingdom includes affixing the trade mark to goods or to the packaging of goods in the United Kingdom solely for export purposes.

(2D) In relation to a Community trade mark, any reference in subsection (2B) or (2C) to the United Kingdom shall be construed as a reference to the European Community.

(2E) Where an earlier trade mark satisfies the use conditions in respect of some only of the goods or services for which it is registered, it shall be treated for the purposes of this section as if it were registered only in respect of those goods or services.]

(3) An application for a declaration of invalidity may be made by any person, and may be made either to the registrar or to the court, except that—

    (a) if proceedings concerning the trade mark in question are pending in the court, the application must be made to the court; and

    (b) if in any other case the application is made to the registrar, he may at any stage of the proceedings refer the application to the court.

(4) In the case of bad faith in the registration of a trade mark, the registrar himself may apply to the court for a declaration of the invalidity of the registration.

(5) Where the grounds of invalidity exist in respect of only some of the goods or services for which the trade mark is registered, the trade mark shall be declared invalid as regards those goods or services only.

(6) Where the registration of a trade mark is declared invalid to any extent, the registration shall to that extent be deemed never to have been made:

Provided that this shall not affect transactions past and closed.

48 Effect of acquiescence

(1) Where the proprietor of an earlier trade mark or other earlier right has acquiesced for a continuous period of five years in the use of a registered trade mark in the United Kingdom, being aware of that use, there shall cease to be any entitlement on the basis of that earlier trade mark or other right—

    (a) to apply for a declaration that the registration of the later trade mark is invalid, or

    (b) to oppose the use of the later trade mark in relation to the goods or services in relation to which it has been so used,

unless the registration of the later trade mark was applied for in bad faith.

(2) Where subsection (1) applies, the proprietor of the later trade mark is not entitled to oppose the use of the earlier trade mark or, as the case may be, the exploitation of the earlier right, notwithstanding that the earlier trade mark or right may no longer be invoked against his later trade mark.

PART II COMMUNITY TRADE MARKS AND INTERNATIONAL MATTERS

The Paris Convention: supplementary provisions

56 Protection of well-known trade marks: Article 6 bis

(1) References in this Act to a trade mark which is entitled to protection under the Paris Convention [or the WTO agreement] as a well known trade mark are to a mark which is well-known in the United Kingdom as being the mark of a person who—

    (a) is a national of a Convention country, or

    (b) is domiciled in, or has a real and effective industrial or commercial establishment in, a Convention country,

whether or not that person carries on business, or has any goodwill, in the United Kingdom.

References to the proprietor of such a mark shall be construed accordingly.

(2) The proprietor of a trade mark which is entitled to protection under the Paris Convention [or the WTO agreement] as a well known trade mark is entitled to restrain by injunction the use in the United Kingdom of a trade mark which, or the essential part of which, is identical or similar to his mark, in relation to identical or similar goods or services, where the use is likely to cause confusion.

This right is subject to section 48 (effect of acquiescence by proprietor of earlier trade mark).

(3) Nothing in subsection (2) affects the continuation of any *bona fide* use of a trade mark begun before the commencement of this section.

PART IV MISCELLANEOUS AND GENERAL PROVISIONS

Miscellaneous

100   Burden of proving use of trade mark

If in any civil proceedings under this Act a question arises as to the use to which a registered trade mark has been put, it is for the proprietor to show what use has been made of it.

Defamation Act 1996

(1996, c. 31)

An Act to amend the law of defamation and to amend the law of limitation with respect to actions for defamation or malicious falsehood.   [4th July 1996]

Responsibility for publication

1   Responsibility for publication

(1) In defamation proceedings a person has a defence if he shows that—

(a) he was not the author, editor or publisher of the statement complained of,

(b) he took reasonable care in relation to its publication, and

(c) he did not know, and had no reason to believe, that what he did caused or contributed to the publication of a defamatory statement.

(2) For this purpose "author", "editor" and "publisher" have the following meanings, which are further explained in subsection (3)—

"author" means the originator of the statement, but does not include a person who did not intend that his statement be published at all;

"editor" means a person having editorial or equivalent responsibility for the content of the statement or the decision to publish it; and

"publisher" means a commercial publisher, that is, a person whose business is issuing material to the public, or a section of the public, who issues material containing the statement in the course of that business.

(3) A person shall not be considered the author, editor or publisher of a statement if he is only involved—

(a) in printing, producing, distributing or selling printed material containing the statement;

(b) in processing, making copies of, distributing, exhibiting or selling a film or sound recording (as defined in Part I of the Copyright, Designs and Patents Act 1988) containing the statement;

(c) in processing, making copies of, distributing or selling any electronic medium in or on which the statement is recorded, or in operating or providing any equipment, system or service by means of which the statement is retrieved, copied, distributed or made available in electronic form;

(d) as the broadcaster of a live programme containing the statement in circumstances in which he has no effective control over the maker of the statement;

(e) as the operator of or provider of access to a communications system by means of which the statement is transmitted, or made available, by a person over whom he has no effective control.

In a case not within paragraphs (a) to (e) the court may have regard to those provisions by way of analogy in deciding whether a person is to be considered the author, editor or publisher of a statement.

(4) Employees or agents of an author, editor or publisher are in the same position as their employer or principal to the extent that they are responsible for the content of the statement or the decision to publish it.

(5) In determining for the purposes of this section whether a person took reasonable care, or had reason to believe that what he did caused or contributed to the publication of a defamatory statement, regard shall be had to—

(a) the extent of his responsibility for the content of the statement or the decision to publish it,

(b) the nature or circumstances of the publication, and

(c) the previous conduct or character of the author, editor or publisher.

(6) This section does not apply to any cause of action which arose before the section came into force.

Supplementary provisions

17 Interpretation

(1) In this Act—

"publication" and "publish", in relation to a statement, have the meaning they have for the purposes of the law of defamation generally, but "publisher" is specially defined for the purposes of section 1;

"statement" means words, pictures, visual images, gestures or any other method of signifying meaning; . . .

Data Protection Act 1998

(1998, c. 29)

An Act to make new provision for the regulation of the processing of information relating to individuals, including the obtaining, holding, use or disclosure of such information.   [16th July 1998]

PART I PRELIMINARY

1 Basic interpretative provisions

(1) In this Act, unless the context otherwise requires—

"data" means information which—

(a) is being processed by means of equipment operating automatically in response to instructions given for that purpose,

(b) is recorded with the intention that it should be processed by means of such equipment,

(c) is recorded as part of a relevant filing system or with the intention that it should form part of a relevant filing system, [. . .]

(d) does not fall within paragraph (a), (b) or (c) but forms part of an accessible record as defined by section 68; [or

(e) is recorded information held by a public authority and does not fall within any of paragraphs (a) to (d);]

"data controller" means, subject to subsection (4), a person who (either alone or jointly or in common with other persons) determines the purposes for which and the manner in which any personal data are, or are to be, processed;

"data processor", in relation to personal data, means any person (other than an employee of the data controller) who processes the data on behalf of the data controller;

"data subject" means an individual who is the subject of personal data;

"personal data" means data which relate to a living individual who can be identified—

(a) from those data, or

(b) from those data and other information which is in the procession of, or is likely to come into the possession of, the data controller,

and includes any expression of opinion about the individual and any indication of the intentions of the data controller or any other person in respect of the individual;

"processing", in relation to information or data, means obtaining, recording or holding the information or data or carrying out any operation or set of operations on the information or data, including—

    (a) organisation, adaptation or alteration of the information or data,

    (b) retrieval, consultation or use of the information or data,

    (c) disclosure of the information or data by transmission, dissemination or otherwise making available, or

    (d) alignment, combination, blocking, erasure or destruction of the information or data;

["public authority" means a public authority as defined by the Freedom of Information Act 2000 or a Scottish public authority as defined by the Freedom of Information (Scotland) Act 2002;]

"relevant filing system" means any set of information relating to individuals to the extent that, although the information is not processed by means of equipment operating automatically in response to instructions given for that purpose, the set is structured, either by reference to individuals or by reference to criteria relating to individuals, in such a way that specific information relating to a particular individual is readily accessible.

    (2) In this Act, unless the context otherwise requires—

    (a) "obtaining" or "recording", in relation to personal data, includes obtaining or recording the information to be contained in the data, and

    (b) "using" or "disclosing", in relation to personal data, includes using or disclosing the information contained in the data.

    (3) In determining for the purposes of this Act whether any information is recorded with the intention—

    (a) that it should be processed by means of equipment operating automatically in response to instructions given for that purpose, or

    (b) that it should form part of a relevant filing system,

it is immaterial that it is intended to be so processed or to form part of such a system only after being transferred to a country or territory outside the European Economic Area.

    (4) Where personal data are processed only for purposes for which they are required by or under any enactment to be processed, the person on whom the obligation to process the data is imposed by or under that enactment is for the purposes of this Act the data controller.

    [(5) In paragraph (e) of the definition of "data" in subsection (1), the reference to information "held" by a public authority shall be construed in accordance with section 3(2) of the Freedom of Information Act 2000 or section 3(2), (4) and (5) of the Freedom of Information (Scotland) Act 2002.

    (6) Where—

    (a) section 7 of the Freedom of Information Act 2000 prevents Parts I to V of that Act or

    (b) section 7(1) of the Freedom of Information (Scotland) Act 2002 prevents that Act,

from applying to certain information held by a public authority, that information is not to be treated for the purposes of paragraph (e) of the definition of "data" in subsection (1) as held by a public authority.]

2   Sensitive personal data

In this Act "sensitive personal data" means personal data consisting of information as to—

    (a) the racial or ethnic origin of the data subject,

    (b) his political opinions,

    (c) his religious beliefs or other beliefs of a similar nature,

    (d) whether he is a member of a trade union (within the meaning of the Trade Union and Labour Relations (Consolidation) Act 1992 c. 52. 1992),

    (e) his physical or mental health or condition,

    (f) his sexual life,

    (g) the commission or alleged commission by him of any offence, or

    (h) any proceedings for any offence committed or alleged to have been committed by him, the disposal of such proceedings or the sentence of any court in such proceedings.

3   The special purposes

In this Act "the special purposes" means any one or more of the following—

(a) the purposes of journalism,

(b) artistic purposes, and

(c) literary purposes.

4   The data protection principles

(1) References in this Act to the data protection principles are to the principles set out in Part I of Schedule 1.

(2) Those principles are to be interpreted in accordance with Part II of Schedule 1.

(3) Schedule 2 (which applies to all personal data) and Schedule 3 (which applies only to sensitive personal data) set out conditions applying for the purposes of the first principle; and Schedule 4 sets out cases in which the eighth principle does not apply.

(4) Subject to section 27(1), it shall be the duty of a data controller to comply with the data protection principles in relation to all personal data with respect to which he is the data controller.

5   Application of Act

(1) Except as otherwise provided by or under section 54, this Act applies to a data controller in respect of any data only if—

(a) the data controller is established in the United Kingdom and the data are processed in the context of that establishment, or

(b) the data controller is established neither in the United Kingdom nor in any other EEA State but uses equipment in the United Kingdom for processing the data otherwise than for the purposes of transit through the United Kingdom.

(2) A data controller falling within subsection (1)(b) must nominate for the purposes of this Act a representative established in the United Kingdom.

(3) For the purposes of subsections (1) and (2), each of the following is to be treated as established in the United Kingdom—

(a) an individual who is ordinarily resident in the United Kingdom,

(b) a body incorporated under the law of, or of any part of, the United Kingdom,

(c) a partnership or other unincorporated association formed under the law of any part of the United Kingdom, and

(d) any person who does not fall within paragraph (a), (b) or (c) but maintains in the United Kingdom—

(i)   an office, branch or agency through which he carries on any activity, or

(ii) a regular practice;

and the reference to establishment in any other EEA State has a corresponding meaning.

6   The Commissioner and the Tribunal

[(1) For the purposes of this Act and of the Freedom of Information Act 2000 there shall be an officer known as the Information Commissioner (in this Act referred to as "the Commissioner").]

(2) The Commissioner shall be appointed by Her Majesty by Letters Patent.

[(3) For the purposes of this Act and of the Freedom of Information Act 2000 there shall be a Tribunal known as the Information Tribunal (in this Act referred to as "the Tribunal").]

(4) The Tribunal shall consist of—

(a) a chairman appointed by the Lord Chancellor after consultation with the [Secretary of State],

(b) such number of deputy chairmen so appointed as the Lord Chancellor may determine, and

(c) such number of other members appointed by the [Secretary of State] as he may determine.

(5) The members of the Tribunal appointed under subsection (4)(a) and (b) shall be—

(a) [persons who satisfy the judicial-appointment eligibility condition on a 5-year basis],

(b) advocates or solicitors in Scotland of at least [5] years' standing, or

(c) members of the bar of Northern Ireland or [solicitors of the Court of Judicature of Northern Ireland] of at least [5] years' standing[1].

(6) The members of the Tribunal appointed under subsection (4)(c) shall be—

(a) persons to represent the interests of data subjects,

[(aa) persons to represent the interests of those who make requests for information under the Freedom of Information Act 2000,]

(b) persons to represent the interests of data controllers [and

(bb) persons to represent the interests of public authorities].

(7) Schedule 5 has effect in relation to the Commissioner and the Tribunal.

PART II RIGHTS OF DATA SUBJECTS AND OTHERS

7 Right of access to personal data[2]

(1) Subject to the following provisions of this section and to [sections 8, 9 and 9A] an individual is entitled—

(a) to be informed by any data controller whether personal data of which that individual is the data subject are being processed by or on behalf of that data controller,

(b) if that is the case, to be given by the data controller a description of—

(i) the personal data of which that individual is the data subject,

(ii) the purposes for which they are being or are to be processed, and

(iii) the recipients or classes of recipients to whom they are or may be disclosed,

(c) to have communicated to him in an intelligible form—

(i) the information constituting any personal data of which that individual is the data subject, and

(ii) any information available to the data controller as to the source of those data, and

(d) where the processing by automatic means of personal data of which that individual is the data subject for the purpose of evaluating matters relating to him such as, for example, his performance at work, his creditworthiness, his reliability or his conduct, has constituted or is likely to constitute the sole basis for any decision significantly affecting him, to be informed by the data controller of the logic involved in that decision-taking.

(2) A data controller is not obliged to supply any information under subsection (1) unless he has received—

(a) a request in writing, and

(b) except in prescribed cases, such fee (not exceeding the prescribed maximum) as he may require.

[(3) Where a data controller—

(a) reasonably requires further information in order to satisfy himself as to the identity of the person making a request under this section and to locate the information which that person seeks, and

(b) has informed him of that requirement,

the data controller is not obliged to comply with the request unless he is supplied with that further information.]

(4) Where a data controller cannot comply with the request without disclosing information relating to another individual who can be identified from that information, he is not obliged to comply with the request unless—

(a) the other individual has consented to the disclosure of the information to the person making the request, or

---

[1] Amendments to this sub-section not yet in force: see Constitutional Reform Act 2005, s. 148 and Tribunals, Courts and Enforcement Act 2007, s. 148.

[2] The effect of the section is modified in certain contexts: see SI 2000/413 (Health), 2000/414 (Education) and 2000/415 and 2000/467 (Social Work).

(b) it is reasonable in all the circumstances to comply with the request without the consent of the other individual.

(5) In subsection (4) the reference to information relating to another individual includes a reference to information identifying that individual as the source of the information sought by the request; and that subsection is not to be construed as excusing a data controller from communicating so much of the information sought by the request as can be communicated without disclosing the identity of the other individual concerned, whether by the omission of names or other identifying particulars or otherwise.

(6) In determining for the purposes of subsection (4)(b) whether it is reasonable in all the circumstances to comply with the request without the consent of the other individual concerned, regard shall be had, in particular, to—

    (a) any duty of confidentiality owed to the other individual,

    (b) any steps taken by the data controller with a view to seeking the consent of the other individual,

    (c) whether the other individual is capable of giving consent, and

    (d) any express refusal of consent by the other individual.

(7) An individual making a request under this section may, in such cases as may be prescribed, specify that his request is limited to personal data of any prescribed description.

(8) Subject to subsection (4), a data controller shall comply with a request under this section promptly and in any event before the end of the prescribed period beginning with the relevant day.

(9) If a court is satisfied on the application of any person who has made a request under the foregoing provisions of this section that the data controller in question has failed to comply with the request in contravention of those provisions, the court may order him to comply with the request.

(10) In this section—

"prescribed" means prescribed by the [Secretary of State] by regulations;

"the prescribed maximum" means such amount as may be prescribed;

"the prescribed period" means forty days or such other period as may be prescribed;

"the relevant day", in relation to a request under this section, means the day on which the data controller receives the request or, if later, the first day on which the data controller has both the required fee and the information referred to in subsection (3).

(11) Different amounts or periods may be prescribed under this section in relation to different cases.

8   Provisions supplementary to section 7

(1) The [Secretary of State] may by regulations provide that, in such cases as may be prescribed, a request for information under any provision of subsection (1) of section 7 is to be treated as extending also to information under other provisions of that subsection.

(2) The obligation imposed by section 7(1)(c)(i) must be complied with by supplying the data subject with a copy of the information in permanent form unless—

    (a) the supply of such a copy is not possible or would involve disproportionate effort, or

    (b) the data subject agrees otherwise;

and where any of the information referred to in section 7(1)(c)(i) is expressed in terms which are not intelligible without explanation the copy must be accompanied by an explanation of those terms.

(3) Where a data controller has previously complied with a request made under section 7 by an individual, the data controller is not obliged to comply with a subsequent identical or similar request under that section by that individual unless a reasonable interval has elapsed between compliance with the previous request and the making of the current request.

(4) In determining for the purposes of subsection (3) whether requests under section 7 are made at reasonable intervals, regard shall be had to the nature of the data, the purpose for which the data are processed and the frequency with which the data are altered.

(5) Section 7(1)(d) is not to be regarded as requiring the provision of information as to the logic involved in any decision-taking if, and to the extent that, the information constitutes a trade secret.

(6) The information to be supplied pursuant to a request under section 7 must be supplied by reference to the data in question at the time when the request is received, except that it may take account of any amendment or deletion made between that time and the time when the information is supplied, being an amendment or deletion that would have been made regardless of the receipt of the request.

(7) For the purposes of section 7(4) and (5) another individual can be identified from the information being disclosed if he can be identified from that information, or from that and any other information which, in the reasonable belief of the data controller, is likely to be in, or to come into, the possession of the data subject making the request.

9   Application of section 7 where data controller is credit reference agency

(1) Where the data controller is a credit reference agency, section 7 has effect subject to the provisions of this section.

(2) An individual making a request under section 7 may limit his request to personal data relevant to his financial standing, and shall be taken to have so limited his request unless the request shows a contrary intention.

(3) Where the data controller receives a request under section 7 in a case where personal data of which the individual making the request is the data subject are being processed by or on behalf of the data controller, the obligation to supply information under that section includes an obligation to give the individual making the request a statement, in such form as may be prescribed by the [Secretary of State] by regulations, of the individual's rights—

    (a) under section 159 of the Consumer Credit Act 1974, and

    (b) to the extent required by the prescribed form, under this Act.

[9A   Unstructured personal data held by public authorities

(1) In this section "unstructured personal data" means any personal data falling within paragraph (e) of the definition of "data" in section 1(1), other than information which is recorded as part of, or with the intention that it should form part of, any set of information relating to individuals to the extent that the set is structured by reference to individuals or by reference to criteria relating to individuals.

(2) A public authority is not obliged to comply with subsection (1) of section 7 in relation to any unstructured personal data unless the request under that section contains a description of the data.

(3) Even if the data are described by the data subject in his request, a public authority is not obliged to comply with subsection (1) of section 7 in relation to unstructured personal data if the authority estimates that the cost of complying with the request so far as relating to those data would exceed the appropriate limit.

(4) Subsection (3) does not exempt the public authority from its obligation to comply with paragraph (a) of section 7(1) in relation to the unstructured personal data unless the estimated cost of complying with that paragraph alone in relation to those data would exceed the appropriate limit.

(5) In subsections (3) and (4) "the appropriate limit" means such amount as may be prescribed by the [Secretary of State] by regulations, and different amounts may be prescribed in relation to different cases.

(6) Any estimate for the purposes of this section must be made in accordance with regulations under section 12(5) of the Freedom of Information Act 2000.]

10   Right to prevent processing likely to cause damage or distress

(1) Subject to subsection (2), an individual is entitled at any time by notice in writing to a data controller to require the data controller at the end of such period as is reasonable in the circumstances to cease, or not to begin, processing, or processing for a specified purpose or in a specified manner, any personal data in respect of which he is the data subject, on the ground that, for specified reasons—

    (a) the processing of those data or their processing for that purpose or in that manner is causing or is likely to cause substantial damage or substantial distress to him or to another, and

    (b) that damage or distress is or would be unwarranted.

(2) Subsection (1) does not apply—

(a) in a case where any of the conditions in paragraphs 1 to 4 of Schedule 2 is met, or

(b) in such other cases as may be prescribed by the [Secretary of State] by order.

(3) The data controller must within twenty-one days of receiving a notice under subsection (1) ("the data subject notice") give the individual who gave it a written notice—

(a) stating that he has complied or intends to comply with the data subject notice, or

(b) stating his reasons for regarding the data subject notice as to any extent unjustified and the extent (if any) to which he has complied or intends to comply with it.

(4) If a court is satisfied, on the application of any person who has given a notice under subsection (1) which appears to the court to be justified (or to be justified to any extent), that the data controller in question has failed to comply with the notice, the court may order him to take such steps for complying with the notice (or for complying with it to that extent) as the court thinks fit.

(5) The failure by a data subject to exercise the right conferred by subsection (1) or section 11(1) does not affect any other right conferred on him by this Part.

11   Right to prevent processing for purposes of direct marketing

(1) An individual is entitled at any time by notice in writing to a data controller to require the data controller at the end of such period as is reasonable in the circumstances to cease, or not to begin, processing for the purposes of direct marketing personal data in respect of which he is the data subject.

(2) If the court is satisfied, on the application of any person who has given a notice under subsection (1), that the data controller has failed to comply with the notice, the court may order him to take such steps for complying with the notice as the court thinks fit.

[(2A) This section shall not apply in relation to the processing of such data as are mentioned in paragraph (1) of regulation 8 of the Telecommunications (Data Protection and Privacy) Regulations 1999 (processing of telecommunications billing data for certain marketing purposes) for the purposes mentioned in paragraph (2) of that regulation.]

(3) In this section "direct marketing" means the communication (by whatever means) of any advertising or marketing material which is directed to particular individuals.

12   Rights in relation to automated decision-taking

(1) An individual is entitled at any time, by notice in writing to any data controller, to require the data controller to ensure that no decision taken by or on behalf of the data controller which significantly affects that individual is based solely on the processing by automatic means of personal data in respect of which that individual is the data subject for the purpose of evaluating matters relating to him such as, for example, his performance at work, his creditworthiness, his reliability or his conduct.

(2) Where, in a case where no notice under subsection (1) has effect, a decision which significantly affects an individual is based solely on such processing as is mentioned in subsection (1)—

(a) the data controller must as soon as reasonably practicable notify the individual that the decision was taken on that basis, and

(b) the individual is entitled, within twenty-one days of receiving that notification from the data controller, by notice in writing to require the data controller to reconsider the decision or to take a new decision otherwise than on that basis.

(3) The data controller must, within twenty-one days of receiving a notice under subsection (2) (b) ("the data subject notice") give the individual a written notice specifying the steps that he intends to take to comply with the data subject notice.

(4) A notice under subsection (1) does not have effect in relation to an exempt decision; and nothing in subsection (2) applies to an exempt decision.

(5) In subsection (4) "exempt decision" means any decision—

(a) in respect of which the condition in subsection (6) and the condition in subsection (7) are met, or

(b) which is made in such other circumstances as may be prescribed by the [Secretary of State] by order.

(6) The condition in this subsection is that the decision—

    (a) is taken in the course of steps taken—

        (i) for the purpose of considering whether to enter into a contract with the data subject,

        (ii) with a view to entering into such a contract, or

        (iii) in the course of performing such a contract, or

    (b) is authorised or required by or under any enactment.

(7) The condition in this subsection is that either—

    (a) the effect of the decision is to grant a request of the data subject, or

    (b) steps have been taken to safeguard the legitimate interests of the data subject (for example, by allowing him to make representations).

(8) If a court is satisfied on the application of a data subject that a person taking a decision in respect of him ("the responsible person") has failed to comply with subsection (1) or (2)(b), the court may order the responsible person to reconsider the decision, or to take a new decision which is not based solely on such processing as is mentioned in subsection (1).

(9) An order under subsection (8) shall not affect the rights of any person other than the data subject and the responsible person.

13 Compensation for failure to comply with certain requirements

(1) An individual who suffers damage by reason of any contravention by a data controller of any of the requirements of this Act is entitled to compensation from the data controller for that damage.

(2) An individual who suffers distress by reason of any contravention by a data controller of any of the requirements of this Act is entitled to compensation from the data controller for that distress if—

    (a) the individual also suffers damage by reason of the contravention, or

    (b) the contravention relates to the processing of personal data for the special purposes.

(3) In proceedings brought against a person by virtue of this section it is a defence to prove that he had taken such care as in all the circumstances was reasonably required to comply with the requirement concerned.

14 Rectification, blocking, erasure and destruction

(1) If a court is satisfied on the application of a data subject that personal data of which the applicant is the subject are inaccurate, the court may order the data controller to rectify, block, erase or destroy those data and any other personal data in respect of which he is the data controller and which contain an expression of opinion which appears to the court to be based on the inaccurate data.

(2) Subsection (1) applies whether or not the data accurately record information received or obtained by the data controller from the data subject or a third party but where the data accurately record such information, then—

    (a) if the requirements mentioned in paragraph 7 of Part II of Schedule I have been complied with, the court may, instead of making an order under subsection (1), make an order requiring the data to be supplemented by such statement of the true facts relating to the matters dealt with by the data as the court may approve, and

    (b) if all or any of those requirements have not been complied with, the court may, instead of making an order under that subsection, make such order as it thinks fit for securing compliance with those requirements with or without a further order requiring the data to be supplemented by such a statement as is mentioned in paragraph (a).

(3) Where the court—

    (a) makes an order under subsection (1), or

    (b) is satisfied on the application of a data subject that personal data of which he was the data subject and which have been rectified, blocked, erased or destroyed were inaccurate,

it may, where it considers it reasonably practicable, order the data controller to notify third parties to whom the data have been disclosed of the rectification, blocking, erasure or destruction.

(4) If a court is satisfied on the application of a data subject—

    (a) that he has suffered damage by reason of any contravention by a data controller of any of the requirements of this Act in respect of any personal data, in circumstances entitling him to compensation under section 13, and

    (b) that there is a substantial risk of further contravention in respect of those data in such circumstances,

the court may order the rectification, blocking, erasure or destruction of any of those data.

(5) Where the court makes an order under subsection (4) it may, where it considers it reasonably practicable, order the data controller to notify third parties to whom the data have been disclosed of the rectification, blocking, erasure or destruction.

(6) In determining whether it is reasonably practicable to require such notification as is mentioned in subsection (3) or (5) the court shall have regard, in particular, to the number of persons who would have to be notified.

15　Jurisdiction and procedure

(1) The jurisdiction conferred by sections 7 to 14 is exercisable by the High Court or a county court or, in Scotland, by the Court of Session or the sheriff.

(2) For the purpose of determining any question whether an applicant under subsection (9) of section 7 is entitled to the information which he seeks (including any question whether any relevant data are exempt from that section by virtue of Part IV) a court may require the information constituting any data processed by or on behalf of the data controller and any information as to the logic involved in any decision-taking as mentioned in section 7(1)(d) to be made available for its own inspection but shall not, pending the determination of that question in the applicant's favour, require the information sought by the applicant to be disclosed to him or his representatives whether by discovery (or, in Scotland, recovery) or otherwise.

PART III　NOTIFICATION BY DATA CONTROLLERS

16　Preliminary

(1) In this Part "the registrable particulars", in relation to a data controller, means—

    (a)　his name and address,

    (b)　if he has nominated a representative for the purposes of this Act, the name and address of the representative,

    (c)　a description of the personal data being or to be processed by or on behalf of the data controller and of the category or categories of data subject to which they relate,

    (d)　a description of the purpose or purposes for which the data are being or are to be processed,

    (e)　a description of any recipient or recipients to whom the data controller intends or may wish to disclose the data,

    (f)　the names, or a description of, any countries or territories outside the European Economic Area to which the data controller directly or indirectly transfers, or intends or may wish directly or indirectly to transfer, the data,

    [(ff)　where the data controller is a public authority, a statement of that fact,] and

    (g)　in any case where—

        (i) personal data are being, or are intended to be, processed in circumstances in which the prohibition in subsection (1) of section 17 is excluded by subsection (2) or (3) of that section, and

        (ii) the notification does not extend to those data,

a statement of that fact.

(2) In this Part—

"fees regulations" means regulations made by the [Secretary of State] under section 18(5) or 19(4) or (7);

"notification regulations" means regulations made by the [Secretary of State] under the other provisions of this Part;

"prescribed", except where used in relation to fees regulations, means prescribed by notification regulations.

(3) For the purposes of this Part, so far as it relates to the addresses of data controllers—

(a) the address of a registered company is that of its registered office, and

(b) the address of a person (other than a registered company) carrying on a business is that of his principal place of business in the United Kingdom.

17 Prohibition on processing without registration

(1) Subject to the following provisions of this section, personal data must not be processed unless an entry in respect of the data controller is included in the register maintained by the Commissioner under section 19 (or is treated by notification regulations made by virtue of section 19(3) as being so included).

(2) Except where the processing is assessable processing for the purposes of section 22, subsection (1) does not apply in relation to personal data consisting of information which falls neither within paragraph (a) of the definition of "data" in section 1(1) nor within paragraph (b) of that definition.

(3) If it appears to the [Secretary of State] that processing of a particular description is unlikely to prejudice the rights and freedoms of data subjects, notification regulations may provide that in such cases as may be prescribed, subsection (1) is not to apply in relation to processing of that description.

(4) Subsection (1) does not apply in relation to any processing whose sole purpose is the maintenance of a public register.

18 Notification by data controllers

(1) Any data controller who wishes to be included in the register maintained under section 19 shall give a notification to the Commissioner under this section.

(2) A notification under this section must specify in accordance with notification regulations—

(a) the registrable particulars, and

(b) a general description of measures to be taken for the purpose of complying with the seventh data protection principle.

(3) Notification regulations made by virtue of subsection (2) may provide for the determination by the Commissioner, in accordance with any requirements of the regulations, of the form in which the registrable particulars and the description mentioned in subsection (2)(b) are to be specified, including in particular the detail required for the purposes of section 16(1)(c), (d), (e) and (f) and subsection (2)(b).

(4) Notification regulations may make provision as to the giving of notification—

(a) by partnerships, or

(b) in other cases where two or more persons are the data controllers in respect of any personal data.

(5) The notification must be accompanied by such fee as may be prescribed by fees regulations.

(6) Notification regulations may provide for any fee paid under subsection (5) or section 19(4) to be refunded in prescribed circumstances.

19 Register of notifications

(1) The Commissioner shall—

(a) maintain a register of persons who have given notification under section 18, and

(b) make an entry in the register in pursuance of each notification received by him under that section from a person in respect of whom no entry as data controller was for the time being included in the register.

(2) Each entry in the register shall consist of—

(a) the registrable particulars notified under section 18 or, as the case requires, those particulars as amended in pursuance of section 20(4), and

    (b) such other information as the Commissioner may be authorised or required by notification regulations to include in the register.

(3) Notification regulations may make provision as to the time as from which any entry in respect of a data controller is to be treated for the purposes of section 17 as having been made in the register.

(4) No entry shall be retained in the register for more than the relevant time except on payment of such fee as may be prescribed by fees regulations.

(5) In subsection (4) "the relevant time" means twelve months or such other period as may be prescribed by notification regulations; and different periods may be prescribed in relation to different cases.

(6) The Commissioner—

    (a) shall provide facilities for making the information contained in the entries in the register available for inspection (in visible and legible form) by members of the public at all reasonable hours and free of charge, and

    (b) may provide such other facilities for making the information contained in those entries available to the public free of charge as he considers appropriate.

(7) The Commissioner shall, on payment of such fee, if any, as may be prescribed by fees regulations, supply any member of the public with a duly certified copy in writing of the particulars contained in any entry made in the register.

20　Duty to notify changes

(1) For the purpose specified in subsection (2), notification regulations shall include provision imposing on every person in respect of whom an entry as a data controller is for the time being included in the register maintained under section 19 a duty to notify to the Commissioner, in such circumstances and at such time or times and in such form as may be prescribed, such matters relating to the registrable particulars and measures taken as mentioned in section 18(2)(b) as may be prescribed.

(2) The purpose referred to in subsection (1) is that of ensuring, so far as practicable, that at any time—

    (a) the entries in the register maintained under section 19 contain current names and addresses and describe the current practice or intentions of the data controller with respect to the processing of personal data, and

    (b) the Commissioner is provided with a general description of measures currently being taken as mentioned in section 18(2)(b).

(3) Subsection (3) of section 18 has effect in relation to notification regulations made by virtue of subsection (1) as it has effect in relation to notification regulations made by virtue of subsection (2) of that section.

(4) On receiving any notification under notification regulations made by virtue of subsection (1), the Commissioner shall make such amendments of the relevant entry in the register maintained under section 19 as are necessary to take account of the notification.

21　Offences

(1) If section 17(1) is contravened, the data controller is guilty of an offence.

(2) Any person who fails to comply with the duty imposed by notification regulations made by virtue of section 20(1) is guilty of an offence.

(3) It shall be a defence for a person charged with an offence under subsection (2) to show that he exercised all due diligence to comply with the duty.

22　Preliminary assessment by Commissioner

(1) In this section "assessable processing" means processing which is of a description specified in an order made by the [Secretary of State] as appearing to him to be particularly likely—

    (a) to cause substantial damage or substantial distress to data subjects, or

    (b) otherwise significantly to prejudice the rights and freedoms of data subjects.

(2) On receiving notification from any data controller under section 18 or under notification regulations made by virtue of section 20 the Commissioner shall consider—

(a) whether any of the processing to which the notification relates is assessable processing, and

(b) if so, whether the assessable processing is likely to comply with the provisions of this Act.

(3) Subject to subsection (4), the Commissioner shall, within the period of twenty-eight days beginning with the day on which he receives a notification which relates to assessable processing, give a notice to the data controller stating the extent to which the Commissioner is of the opinion that the processing is likely or unlikely to comply with the provisions of this Act.

(4) Before the end of the period referred to in subsection (3) the Commissioner may, by reason of special circumstances, extend that period on one occasion only by notice to the data controller by such further period not exceeding fourteen days as the Commissioner may specify in the notice.

(5) No assessable processing in respect of which a notification has been given to the Commissioner as mentioned in subsection (2) shall be carried on unless either—

(a) the period of twenty-eight days beginning with the day on which the notification is received by the Commissioner (or, in a case falling within subsection (4), that period as extended under that subsection) has elapsed, or

(b) before the end of that period (or that period as so extended) the data controller has received a notice from the Commissioner under subsection (3) in respect of the processing.

(6) Where subsection (5) is contravened, the data controller is guilty of an offence.

(7) The [Secretary of State] may by order amend subsections (3), (4) and (5) by substituting for the number of days for the time being specified there a different number specified in the order.

23 Power to make provision for appointment of data protection supervisors

(1) The [Secretary of State] may by order—

(a) make provision under which a data controller may appoint a person to act as a data protection supervisor responsible in particular for monitoring in an independent manner the data controller's compliance with the provisions of this Act, and

(b) provide that, in relation to any data controller who has appointed a data protection supervisor in accordance with the provisions of the order and who complies with such conditions as may be specified in the order, the provisions of this Part are to have effect subject to such exemptions or other modifications as may be specified in the order.

(2) An order under this section may—

(a) impose duties on data protection supervisors in relation to the Commissioner, and

(b) confer functions on the Commissioner in relation to data protection supervisors.

24 Duty of certain data controllers to make certain information available

(1) Subject to subsection (3), where personal data are processed in a case where—

(a) by virtue of subsection (2) or (3) of section 17, subsection (1) of that section does not apply to the processing, and

(b) the data controller has not notified the relevant particulars in respect of that processing under section 18,

the data controller must, within twenty-one days of receiving a written request from any person, make the relevant particulars available to that person in writing free of charge.

(2) In this section "the relevant particulars" means the particulars referred to in paragraphs (a) to (f) of section 16(1).

(3) This section has effect subject to any exemption conferred for the purposes of this section by notification regulations.

(4) Any data controller who fails to comply with the duty imposed by subsection (1) is guilty of an offence.

(5) It shall be a defence for a person charged with an offence under subsection (4) to show that he exercised all due diligence to comply with the duty.

25 Functions of Commissioner in relation to making of notification regulations

(1) As soon as practicable after the passing of this Act, the Commissioner shall submit to the [Secretary of State] proposals as to the provisions to be included in the first notification regulations.

(2) The Commissioner shall keep under review the working of notification regulations and may from time to time submit to the [Secretary of State] proposals as to amendments to be made to the regulations.

(3) The Secretary of State may from time to time require the Commissioner to consider any matter relating to notification regulations and to submit to him proposals as to amendments to be made to the regulations in connection with that matter.

(4) Before making any notification regulations, the [Secretary of State] shall—

    (a) consider any proposals made to him by the Commissioner under subsection (2) or (3), and

    (b) consult the Commissioner.

26 Fees regulations

(1) Fees regulations prescribing fees for the purposes of any provision of this Part may provide for different fees to be payable in different cases.

(2) In making any fees regulations, the [Secretary of State] shall have regard to the desirability of securing that the fees payable to the Commissioner are sufficient to offset—

    (a) the expenses incurred by the Commissioner and the Tribunal in discharging their functions [under this Act] and any expenses of the [Secretary of State] in respect of the Commissioner or the Tribunal [so far as attributable to their functions under this Act], and

    (b) to the extent that the [Secretary of State] considers appropriate—

        (i) any deficit previously incurred (whether before or after the passing of this Act) in respect of the expenses mentioned in paragraph (a), and

        (ii) expenses incurred or to be incurred by the [Lord Chancellor] in respect of the inclusion of any officers or staff of the Commissioner in any scheme under section 1 of the Superannuation Act 1972.

PART IV EXEMPTIONS

27 Preliminary

(1) References in any of the data protection principles or any provision of Parts II and III to personal data or to the processing of personal data do not include references to data or processing which by virtue of this Part are exempt from that principle or other provision.

(2) In this Part "the subject information provisions" means—

    (a) the first data protection principle to the extent to which it requires compliance with paragraph 2 of Part II of Schedule 1, and

    (b) section 7.

(3) In this Part "the non-disclosure provisions" means the provisions specified in subsection (4) to the extent to which they are inconsistent with the disclosure in question.

(4) The provisions referred to in subsection (3) are—

    (a) the first data protection principle, except to the extent to which it requires compliance with the conditions in Schedules 2 and 3,

    (b) the second, third, fourth and fifth data protection principles, and

    (c) sections 10 and 14(1) to (3).

(5) Except as provided by this Part, the subject information provisions shall have effect notwithstanding any enactment or rule of law prohibiting or restricting the disclosure, or authorising the withholding, of information.

28   National security

(1) Personal data are exempt from any of the provisions of—

    (a) the data protection principles,

    (b) Parts II, III and V, and

    (c) [Section 54A and] 55,

if the exemption from that provision is required for the purpose of safeguarding national security.

(2) Subject to subsection (4), a certificate signed by a Minister of the Crown certifying that exemption from all or any of the provisions mentioned in subsection (1) is or at any time was required for the purpose there mentioned in respect of any personal data shall be conclusive evidence of that fact.

(3) A certificate under subsection (2) may identify the personal data to which it applies by means of a general description and may be expressed to have prospective effect.

(4) Any person directly affected by the issuing of a certificate under subsection (2) may appeal to the Tribunal against the certificate.

(5) If on an appeal under subsection (4), the Tribunal finds that, applying the principles applied by the court on an application for judicial review, the Minister did not have reasonable grounds for issuing the certificate, the Tribunal may allow the appeal and quash the certificate.

(6) Where in any proceedings under or by virtue of this Act it is claimed by a data controller that a certificate under subsection (2) which identifies the personal data to which it applies by means of a general description applies to any personal data, any other party to the proceedings may appeal to the Tribunal on the ground that the certificate does not apply to the personal data in question and, subject to any determination under subsection (7), the certificate shall be conclusively presumed so to apply.

(7) On any appeal under subsection (6), the Tribunal may determine that the certificate does not so apply.

(8) A document purporting to be a certificate under subsection (2) shall be received in evidence and deemed to be such a certificate unless the contrary is proved.

(9) A document which purports to be certified by or on behalf of a Minister of the Crown as a true copy of a certificate issued by that Minister under subsection (2) shall in any legal proceedings be evidence (or, in Scotland, sufficient evidence) of that certificate.

(10) The power conferred by subsection (2) on a Minister of the Crown shall not be exercisable except by a Minister who is a member of the Cabinet or by the Attorney General or the [Advocate General for Scotland].

(11) No power conferred by any provision of Part V may be exercised in relation to personal data which by virtue of this section are exempt from that provision.

(12) Schedule 6 shall have effect in relation to appeals under subsection (4) or (6) and the proceedings of the Tribunal in respect of any such appeal.

29   Crime and taxation

(1) Personal data processed for any of the following purposes—

    (a) the prevention or detection of crime,

    (b) the apprehension or prosecution of offenders, or

    (c) the assessment or collection of any tax or duty or of any imposition of a similar nature,

are exempt from the first data protection principle (except to the extent to which it requires compliance with the conditions in Schedules 2 and 3) and section 7 in any case to the extent to which the application of those provisions to the data would be likely to prejudice any of the matters mentioned in this subsection.

(2) Personal data which—

    (a) are processed for the purpose of discharging statutory functions, and

    (b) consist of information obtained for such a purpose from a person who had it in his possession for any of the purposes mentioned in subsection (1),

are exempt from the subject information provisions to the same extent as personal data processed for any of the purposes mentioned in that subsection.

(3) Personal data are exempt from the non-disclosure provisions in any case in which—

    (a) the disclosure is for any of the purposes mentioned in subsection (1), and

    (b) the application of those provisions in relation to the disclosure would be likely to prejudice any of the matters mentioned in that subsection.

(4) Personal data in respect of which the data controller is a relevant authority and which—

    (a) consist of a classification applied to the data subject as part of a system of risk assessment which is operated by that authority for either of the following purposes—

        (i) the assessment or collection of any tax or duty or any imposition of a similar nature, or

        (ii) the prevention or detection of crime, or apprehension or prosecution of offenders, where the offence concerned involves any unlawful claim for any payment out of, or any unlawful application of, public funds, and

    (b) are processed for either of those purposes,

are exempt from section 7 to the extent to which the exemption is required in the interests of the operation of the system.

(5) In subsection (4)—

"public funds" includes funds provided by any Community institution;

"relevant authority" means—

    (a) a government department,

    (b) a local authority, or

    (c) any other authority administering housing benefit or council tax benefit.

30   Health, education and social work

(1) The [Secretary of State] may by order exempt from the subject information provisions, or modify those provisions in relation to, personal data consisting of information as to the physical or mental health or condition of the data subject.

(2) The [Secretary of State] may by order exempt from the subject information provisions, or modify those provisions in relation to—

    (a) personal data in respect of which the data controller is the proprietor of, or a teacher at, a school, and which consist of information relating to persons who are or have been pupils at the school, or

    (b) personal data in respect of which the data controller is an education authority in Scotland, and which consist of information relating to persons who are receiving, or have received, further education provided by the authority.

(3) The [Secretary of State] may by order exempt from the subject information provisions, or modify those provisions in relation to, personal data of such other descriptions as may be specified in the order, being information—

    (a) processed by government departments or local authorities or by voluntary organisations or other bodies designated by or under the order, and

    (b) appearing to him to be processed in the course of, or for the purposes of, carrying out social work in relation to the data subject or other individuals;

but the [Secretary of State] shall not under this subsection confer any exemption or make any modification except so far as he considers that the application to the data of those provisions (or of those provisions without modification) would be likely to prejudice the carrying out of social work.

(4) An order under this section may make different provision in relation to data consisting of information of different descriptions.

(5) In this section—

"education authority" and "further education" have the same meaning as in the Education (Scotland) Act 1980 ("the 1980 Act"), and

"proprietor"—

    (a) in relation to a school in England or Wales, has the same meaning as in the Education Act 1996,

    (b) in relation to a school in Scotland, means—
        (i)   […]
        (ii) in the case of an independent school, the proprietor within the meaning of the 1980 Act, and
        (iii) in the case of a grant-aided school, the managers within the meaning of the 1980 Act, and
        (iv) in the case of a public school, the education authority within the meaning of the 1980 Act, and
    (c) in relation to a school in Northern Ireland, has the same meaning as in the Education and Libraries (Northern Ireland) Order 1986 and includes, in the case of a controlled school, the Board of Governors of the school.

31 Regulatory activity

(1) Personal data processed for the purposes of discharging functions to which this subsection applies are exempt from the subject information provisions in any case to the extent to which the application of those provisions to the data would be likely to prejudice the proper discharge of those functions.

(2) Subsection (1) applies to any relevant function which is designed—
    (a) for protecting members of the public against—
        (i)   financial loss due to dishonesty, malpractice or other seriously improper conduct by, or the unfitness or incompetence of, persons concerned in the provision of banking, insurance, investment or other financial services or in the management of bodies corporate,
        (ii) financial loss due to the conduct of discharged or undischarged bankrupts, or
        (iii) dishonesty, malpractice or other seriously improper conduct by, or the unfitness or incompetence of, persons authorised to carry on any profession or other activity,
    (b) for protecting charities [or community interest companies] against misconduct or mismanagement (whether by trustees[, directors] or other persons) in their administration,
    (c) for protecting the property of charities [or community interest companies] from loss or misapplication,
    (d) for the recovery of the property of charities [or community interest companies],
    (e) for securing the health, safety and welfare of persons at work, or
    (f) for protecting persons other than persons at work against risk to health or safety arising out of or in connection with the actions of persons at work.

(3) In subsection (2) "relevant function" means—
    (a) any function conferred on any person by or under any enactment,
    (b) any function of the Crown, a Minister of the Crown or a government department, or
    (c) any other function which is of a public nature and is exercised in the public interest.

(4) Personal data processed for the purpose of discharging any function which—
    (a) is conferred by or under any enactment on—
        (i)   the Parliamentary Commissioner for Administration,
        (ii)   the Commission for Local Administration in England [or], the Commission for Local Administration in Wales […],
        (iii) the Health Service Commissioner for England [or], the Health Service Commissioner for Wales […],
        [(iv) the Public Services Ombudsman for Wales,]
        (v)   the Assembly Ombudsman for Northern Ireland, […]
        (vi)   the Northern Ireland Commissioner for Complaints, [or]
        [(vii) the Scottish Public Services Ombudsman, and]
    (b) is designed for protecting members of the public against—
        (i)   maladministration by public bodies,
        (ii)   failures in services provided by public bodies, or
        (iii) a failure of a public body to provide a service which it was a function of the body to provide,

are exempt from the subject information provisions in any case to the extent to which the application of those provisions to the data would be likely to prejudice the proper discharge of that function.

[(4A) Personal data processed for the purpose of discharging any function which is conferred by or under Part XVI of the Financial Services and Markets Act 2000 on the body established by the Financial Services Authority for the purposes of that Part are exempt from the subject information provisions in any case to the extent to which the application of those provisions to the data would be likely to prejudice the proper discharge of the function.]

[(4B) Personal data processed for the purposes of discharging any function of the Legal Services Board are exempt from the subject information provisions in any case to the extent to which the application of those provisions to the data would be likely to prejudice the proper discharge of the function.

(4C) Personal data processed for the purposes of the function of considering a complaint under the scheme established under Part 6 of the Legal Services Act 2007 (legal complaints) are exempt from the subject information provisions in any case to the extent to which the application of those provisions to the data would be likely to prejudice the proper discharge of the function.[1]]

(5) Personal data processed for the purpose of discharging any function which—

    (a) is conferred by or under any enactment on [the Office of Fair Trading] and

    (b) is designed—

        (i)   for protecting members of the public against conduct which may adversely affect their interests by persons carrying on a business,

        (ii) for regulating agreements or conduct which have as their object or effect the prevention, restriction or distortion of competition in connection with any commercial activity, or

        (iii) for regulating conduct on the part of one or more undertakings which amounts to the abuse of a dominant position in a market,

are exempt from the subject information provisions in any case to the extent to which the application of those provisions to the data would be likely to prejudice the proper discharge of that function.

[(5A) Personal data processed by a CPC enforcer for the purpose of discharging any function conferred on such a body by or under the CPC Regulation are exempt from the subject information provisions in any case to the extent to which the application of those provisions to the data would be likely to prejudice the proper discharge of that function.

(5B) In subsection (5A)—

    (a) "CPC enforcer" has the meaning given to it in section 213(5A) of the Enterprise Act 2002 but does not include the Office of Fair Trading;

    (b) "CPC Regulation" has the meaning given to it in section 235A of that Act.]

[(6) Personal data processed for the purpose of the function of considering a complaint under [section 14 of the NHS Redress Act 2006,] section 113(1) or (2) or 114(1) or (3) of the Health and Social Care (Community Health and Standards) Act 2003, or section 24D, 26, 26ZA or 26ZB of the Children Act 1989, are exempt from the subject information provisions in any case to the extent to which the application of those provisions to the data would be likely to prejudice the proper discharge of that function.]

[(7) Personal data processed for the purpose of discharging any function which is conferred by or under Part 3 of the Local Government Act 2000 on—

    (a) the monitoring officer of a relevant authority,

    (b) an ethical standards officer, or

    (c) the Public Services Ombudsman for Wales,

are exempt from the subject information provisions in any case to the extent to which the application of those provisions to the data would be likely to prejudice the proper discharge of that function.

(8) In subsection (7)—

    (a) "relevant authority" has the meaning given by section 49(6) of the Local Government Act 2000, and

---

[1] These two new sub-sections are not yet in force: see Legal Services Act 2007, s. 211.

　　(b) any reference to the monitoring officer of a relevant authority, or to an ethical standards officer,

has the same meaning as in Part 3 of that Act.]

32　Journalism, literature and art

　　(1)　Personal data which are processed only for the special purposes are exempt from any provision to which this subsection relates if—

　　　　(a) the processing is undertaken with a view to the publication by any person of any journalistic, literary or artistic material,

　　　　(b) the data controller reasonably believes that, having regard in particular to the special importance of the public interest in freedom of expression, publication would be in the public interest, and

　　　　(c) the data controller reasonably believes that, in all the circumstances, compliance with that provision is incompatible with the special purposes.

　　(2)　Subsection (1) relates to the provisions of—

　　　　(a)　the data protection principles except the seventh data protection principle,

　　　　(b)　section 7,

　　　　(c)　section 10,

　　　　(d)　section 12,

　　　　(dd) [section 12A,] and

　　　　(e)　section 14(1) to (3).

　　(3)　In considering for the purposes of subsection (1)(b) whether the belief of a data controller that publication would be in the public interest was or is a reasonable one, regard may be had to his compliance with any code of practice which—

　　　　(a) is relevant to the publication in question, and

　　　　(b) is designated by the [Secretary of State] by order for the purposes of this subsection.

　　(4)　Where at any time ("the relevant time") in any proceedings against a data controller under section 7(9), 10(4), 12(8) [,12A(3)] or 14 or by virtue of section 13 the data controller claims, or it appears to the court, that any personal data to which the proceedings relate are being processed—

　　　　(a) only for the special purposes, and

　　　　(b) with a view to the publication by any person of any journalistic, literary or artistic material which, at the time twenty-four hours immediately before the relevant time, had not previously been published by the data controller,

the court shall stay the proceedings until either of the conditions in subsection (5) is met.

　　(5)　Those conditions are—

　　　　(a) that a determination of the Commissioner under section 45 with respect to the data in question takes effect, or

　　　　(b) in a case where the proceedings were stayed on the making of a claim, that the claim is withdrawn.

　　(6)　For the purposes of this Act "publish", in relation to journalistic, literary or artistic material, means make available to the public or any section of the public.

33　Research, history and statistics

　　(1)　In this section—

"research purposes" includes statistical or historical purposes;

"the relevant conditions", in relation to any processing of personal data, means the conditions—

　　　　(a) that the data are not processed to support measures or decisions with respect to particular individuals, and

　　　　(b) that the data are not processed in such a way that substantial damage or substantial distress is, or is likely to be, caused to any data subject.

　　(2)　For the purposes of the second data protection principle, the further processing of personal data only for research purposes in compliance with the relevant conditions is not to be regarded as incompatible with the purposes for which they were obtained.

(3) Personal data which are processed only for research purposes in compliance with the relevant conditions may, notwithstanding the fifth data protection principle, be kept indefinitely.

(4) Personal data which are processed only for research purposes are exempt from section 7 if—

(a) they are processed in compliance with the relevant conditions, and

(b) the results of the research or any resulting statistics are not made available in a form which identifies data subjects or any of them.

(5) For the purposes of subsections (2) to (4) personal data are not to be treated as processed otherwise than for research purposes merely because the data are disclosed—

(a) to any person, for research purposes only,

(b) to the data subject or a person acting on his behalf,

(c) at the request, or with the consent, of the data subject or a person acting on his behalf, or

(d) in circumstances in which the person making the disclosure has reasonable grounds for believing that the disclosure falls within paragraph (a), (b) or (c).

[33A   Manual data held by public authorities

(1) Personal data falling within paragraph (e) of the definition of "data" in section 1(1) are exempt from—

(a) the first, second, third, fifth, seventh and eighth data protection principles,

(b) the sixth data protection principle except so far as it relates to the rights conferred on data subjects by sections 7 and 14,

(c) sections 10 to 12,

(d) section 13, except so far as it relates to damage caused by a contravention of section 7 or of the fourth data protection principle and to any distress which is also suffered by reason of that contravention,

(e) Part III, and

(f) section 55.

(2) Personal data which fall within paragraph (e) of the definition of "data" in section 1(1) and relate to appointments or removals, pay, discipline, superannuation or other personnel matters, in relation to—

(a) service in any of the armed forces of the Crown,

(b) service in any office or employment under the Crown or under any public authority, or

(c) service in any office or employment, or under any contract for services, in respect of which power to take action, or to determine or approve the action taken, in such matters is vested in Her Majesty, any Minister of the Crown, the National Assembly for Wales, any Northern Ireland Minister (within the meaning of the Freedom of Information Act 2000) or any public authority,

are also exempt from the remaining data protection principles and the remaining provisions of Part II.]

34   Information available to the public by or under enactment

(1) Personal data are exempt from—

(a) the subject information provisions,

(b) the fourth data protection principle and section 14(1) to (3), and

(c) the non-disclosure provisions,

if the data consist of information which the data controller is obliged by or under any enactment [other than an enactment contained in the Freedom of Information Act 2000] to make available to the public, whether by publishing it, by making it available for inspection, or otherwise and whether gratuitously or on payment of a fee.

35   Disclosures required by law or made in connection with legal proceedings etc.

(1) Personal data are exempt from the non-disclosure provisions where the disclosure is required by or under any enactment, by any rule of law or by the order of a court.

(2) Personal data are exempt from the non-disclosure provisions where the disclosure is necessary—

    (a) for the purpose of, or in connection with, any legal proceedings (including prospective legal proceedings), or

    (b) for the purpose of obtaining legal advice,

or is otherwise necessary for the purposes of establishing, exercising or defending legal rights.

[35A   Parliamentary privilege

Personal data are exempt from—

    (a) the first data protection principle, except to the extent to which it requires compliance with the conditions in Schedules 2 and 3,

    (b) the second, third, fourth and fifth data protection principles,

    (c) section 7, and

    (d) sections 10 and 14(1) to (3),

if the exemption is required for the purpose of avoiding an infringement of the privileges of either House of Parliament.]

36   Domestic purposes

Personal data processed by an individual only for the purposes of that individual's personal, family or household affairs (including recreational purposes) are exempt from the data protection principles and the provisions of Parts II and III.

37   Miscellaneous exemptions

Schedule 7 (which confers further miscellaneous exemptions) has effect.

38   Powers to make further exemptions by order

(1) The [Secretary of State] may by order exempt from the subject information provisions personal data consisting of information the disclosure of which is prohibited or restricted by or under any enactment if and to the extent that he considers it necessary for the safeguarding of the interests of the data subject or the rights and freedoms of any other individual that the prohibition or restriction ought to prevail over those provisions.

(2) The [Secretary of State] may by order exempt from the nondisclosure provisions any disclosures of personal data made in circumstances specified in the order, if he considers the exemption is necessary for the safeguarding of the interests of the data subject or the rights and freedoms of any other individual.

39   Transitional relief

Schedule 8 (which confers transitional exemptions) has effect.

PART V ENFORCEMENT

40   Enforcement notices

(1) If the Commissioner is satisfied that a data controller has contravened or is contravening any of the data protection principles, the Commissioner may serve him with a notice (in this Act referred to as "an enforcement notice") requiring him, for complying with the principle or principles in question, to do either or both of the following—

    (a) to take within such time as may be specified in the notice, or to refrain from taking after such time as may be so specified, such steps as are so specified, or

    (b) to refrain from processing any personal data, or any personal data of a description specified in the notice, or to refrain from processing them for a purpose so specified or in a manner so specified, after such time as may be so specified.

(2) In deciding whether to serve an enforcement notice, the Commissioner shall consider whether the contravention has caused or is likely to cause any person damage or distress.

(3) An enforcement notice in respect of a contravention of the fourth data protection principle which requires the data controller to rectify, block, erase or destroy any inaccurate data may also

require the data controller to rectify, block, erase or destroy any other data held by him and containing an expression of opinion which appears to the Commissioner to be based on the inaccurate data.

(4) An enforcement notice in respect of a contravention of the fourth data protection principle, in the case of data which accurately record information received or obtained by the data controller from the data subject or a third party, may require the data controller either—

> (a) to rectify, block, erase or destroy any inaccurate data and any other data held by him and containing an expression of opinion as mentioned in subsection (3), or
>
> (b) to take such steps as are specified in the notice for securing compliance with the requirements specified in paragraph 7 of Part II of Schedule I and, if the Commissioner thinks fit, for supplementing the data with such statement of the true facts relating to the matters dealt with by the data as the Commissioner may approve.

(5) Where—

> (a) an enforcement notice requires the data controller to rectify, block, erase or destroy any personal data, or
>
> (b) the Commissioner is satisfied that personal data which have been rectified, blocked, erased or destroyed had been processed in contravention of any of the data protection principles,

an enforcement notice may, if reasonably practicable, require the data controller to notify third parties to whom the data have been disclosed of the rectification, blocking, erasure or destruction; and in determining whether it is reasonably practicable to require such notification regard shall be had, in particular, to the number of persons who would have to be notified.

(6) An enforcement notice must contain—

> (a) a statement of the data protection principle or principles which the Commissioner is satisfied have been or are being contravened and his reasons for reaching that conclusion, and
>
> (b) particulars of the rights of appeal conferred by section 48.

(7) Subject to subsection (8), an enforcement notice must not require any of the provisions of the notice to be complied with before the end of the period within which an appeal can be brought against the notice and, if such an appeal is brought, the notice need not be complied with pending the determination or withdrawal of the appeal.

(8) If by reason of special circumstances the Commissioner considers that an enforcement notice should be complied with as a matter of urgency he may include in the notice a statement to that effect and a statement of his reasons for reaching that conclusion; and in that event subsection (7) shall not apply but the notice must not require the provisions of the notice to be complied with before the end of the period of seven days beginning with the day on which the notice is served.

(9) Notification regulations (as defined by section 16(2)) may make provision as to the effect of the service of an enforcement notice on any entry in the register maintained under section 19 which relates to the person on whom the notice is served.

(10) This section has effect subject to section 46(1).

41 Cancellation of enforcement notice

(1) If the Commissioner considers that all or any of the provisions of an enforcement notice need not be complied with in order to ensure compliance with the data protection principle or principles to which it relates, he may cancel or vary the notice by written notice to the person on whom it was served.

(2) A person on whom an enforcement notice has been served may, at any time after the expiry of the period during which an appeal can be brought against that notice, apply in writing to the Commissioner for the cancellation or variation of that notice on the ground that, by reason of a change of circumstances, all or any of the provisions of that notice need not be complied with in order to ensure compliance with the data protection principle or principles to which that notice relates.

42 Request for assessment

(1) A request may be made to the Commissioner by or on behalf of any person who is, or believes himself to be, directly affected by any processing of personal data for an assessment as to whether it

is likely or unlikely that the processing has been or is being carried out in compliance with the provisions of this Act.

(2) On receiving a request under this section, the Commissioner shall make an assessment in such manner as appears to him to be appropriate, unless he has not been supplied with such information as he may reasonably require in order to—

    (a) satisfy himself as to the identity of the person making the request, and

    (b) enable him to identify the processing in question.

(3) The matters to which the Commissioner may have regard in determining in what manner it is appropriate to make an assessment include—

    (a) the extent to which the request appears to him to raise a matter of substance,

    (b) any undue delay in making the request, and

    (c) whether or not the person making the request is entitled to make an application under section 7 in respect of the personal data in question.

(4) Where the Commissioner has received a request under this section he shall notify the person who made the request—

    (a) whether he has made an assessment as a result of the request, and

    (b) to the extent that he considers appropriate, having regard in particular to any exemption from section 7 applying in relation to the personal data concerned, of any view formed or action taken as a result of the request.

43   Information notices

(1) If the Commissioner—

    (a) has received a request under section 42 in respect of any processing of personal data, or

    (b) reasonably requires any information for the purpose of determining whether the data controller has complied or is complying with the data protection principles,

he may serve the data controller with a notice (in this Act referred to as "an information notice") requiring the data controller, within such time as is specified in the notice, to furnish the Commissioner, in such form as may be so specified, with such information relating to the request or to compliance with the principles as is so specified.

(2) An information notice must contain—

    (a) in a case falling within subsection (1)(a), a statement that the Commissioner has received a request under section 42 in relation to the specified processing, or

    (b) in a case falling within subsection (1)(b), a statement that the Commissioner regards the specified information as relevant for the purpose of determining whether the data controller has complied, or is complying, with the data protection principles and his reasons for regarding it as relevant for that purpose.

(3) An information notice must also contain particulars of the rights of appeal conferred by section 48.

(4) Subject to subsection (5), the time specified in an information notice shall not expire before the end of the period within which an appeal can be brought against the notice and, if such an appeal is brought, the information need not be furnished pending the determination or withdrawal of the appeal.

(5) If by reason of special circumstances the Commissioner considers that the information is required as a matter of urgency, he may include in the notice a statement to that effect and a statement of his reasons for reaching that conclusion, and in that event subsection (4) shall not apply, but the notice shall not require the information to be furnished before the end of the period of seven days beginning with the day on which the notice is served.

(6) A person shall not be required by virtue of this section to furnish the Commissioner with any information in respect of—

    (a) any communication between a professional legal adviser and his client in connection with the giving of legal advice to the client with respect to his obligations, liabilities or rights under this Act, or

(b) any communication between a professional legal adviser and his client, or between such an adviser or his client and any other person, made in connection with or in contemplation of proceedings under or arising out of this Act (including proceedings before the Tribunal) and for the purposes of such proceedings.

(7) In subsection (6) references to the client of a professional legal adviser include references to any person representing such a client.

(8) A person shall not be required by virtue of this section to furnish the Commissioner with any information if the furnishing of that information would, by revealing evidence of the commission of any offence other than an offence under this Act, expose him to proceedings for that offence.

(9) The Commissioner may cancel an information notice by written notice to the person on whom it was served.

(10) This section has effect subject to section 46(3).

44   Special information notices

(1) If the Commissioner—
  (a) has received a request under section 42 in respect of any processing of personal data, or
  (b) has reasonable grounds for suspecting that, in a case in which proceedings have been stayed under section 32, the personal data to which the proceedings relate—
    (i) are not being processed only for the special purposes, or
    (ii) are not being processed with a view to the publication by any person of any journalistic, literary or artistic material which has not previously been published by the data controller,

he may serve the data controller with a notice (in this Act referred to as a "special information notice") requiring the data controller, within such time as is specified in the notice, to furnish the Commissioner, in such form as may be so specified, with such information as is so specified for the purpose specified in subsection (2).

(2) That purpose is the purpose of ascertaining—
  (a) whether the personal data are being processed only for the special purposes, or
  (b) whether they are being processed with a view to the publication by any person of any journalistic, literary or artistic material which has not previously been published by the data controller.

(3) A special information notice must contain—
  (a) in a case falling within paragraph (a) of subsection (1), a statement that the Commissioner has received a request under section 42 in relation to the specified processing, or
  (b) in a case falling within paragraph (b) of that subsection, a statement of the Commissioner"s grounds for suspecting that the personal data are not being processed as mentioned in that paragraph.

(4) A special information notice must also contain particulars of the rights of appeal conferred by section 48.

(5) Subject to subsection (6), the time specified in a special information notice shall not expire before the end of the period within which an appeal can be brought against the notice and, if such an appeal is brought, the information need not be furnished pending the determination or withdrawal of the appeal.

(6) If by reason of special circumstances the Commissioner considers that the information is required as a matter of urgency, he may include in the notice a statement to that effect and a statement of his reasons for reaching that conclusion; and in that event subsection (5) shall not apply, but the notice shall not require the information to be furnished before the end of the period of seven days beginning with the day on which the notice is served.

(7) A person shall not be required by virtue of this section to furnish the Commissioner with any information in respect of—
  (a) any communication between a professional legal adviser and his client in connection with the giving of legal advice to the client with respect to his obligations, liabilities or rights under this Act, or

(b) any communication between a professional legal adviser and his client, or between such an adviser or his client and any other person, made in connection with or in contemplation of proceedings under or arising out of this Act (including proceedings before the Tribunal) and for the purposes of such proceedings.

(8) In subsection (7) references to the client of a professional legal adviser include references to any person representing such a client.

(9) A person shall not be required by virtue of this section to furnish the Commissioner with any information if the furnishing of that information would, by revealing evidence of the commission of any offence other than an offence under this Act, expose him to proceedings for that offence.

(10) The Commissioner may cancel a special information notice by written notice to the person on whom it was served.

45   Determination by Commissioner as to the special purposes

(1) Where at any time it appears to the Commissioner (whether as a result of the service of a special information notice or otherwise) that any personal data—

(a) are not being processed only for the special purposes, or

(b) are not being processed with a view to the publication by any person of any journalistic, literary or artistic material which has not previously been published by the data controller,

he may make a determination in writing to that effect.

(2) Notice of the determination shall be given to the data controller; and the notice must contain particulars of the right of appeal conferred by section 48.

(3) A determination under subsection (1) shall not take effect until the end of the period within which an appeal can be brought and, where an appeal is brought, shall not take effect pending the determination or withdrawal of the appeal.

46   Restriction on enforcement in case of processing for the special purposes

(1) The Commissioner may not at any time serve an enforcement notice on a data controller with respect to the processing of personal data for the special purposes unless—

(a) a determination under section 45(1) with respect to those data has taken effect, and

(b) the court has granted leave for the notice to be served.

(2) The court shall not grant leave for the purposes of subsection (1)(b) unless it is satisfied—

(a) that the Commissioner has reason to suspect a contravention of the data protection principles which is of substantial public importance, and

(b) except where the case is one of urgency, that the data controller has been given notice, in accordance with rules of court, of the application for leave.

(3) The Commissioner may not serve an information notice on a data controller with respect to the processing of personal data for the special purposes unless a determination under section 45(1) with respect to those data has taken effect.

47   Failure to comply with notice

(1) A person who fails to comply with an enforcement notice, an information notice or a special information notice is guilty of an offence.

(2) A person who, in purported compliance with an information notice or a special information notice—

(a) makes a statement which he knows to be false in a material respect, or

(b) recklessly makes a statement which is false in a material respect, is guilty of an offence.

(3) It is a defence for a person charged with an offence under subsection (1) to prove that he exercised all due diligence to comply with the notice in question.

48   Rights of appeal

(1) A person on whom an enforcement notice, an information notice or a special information notice has been served may appeal to the Tribunal against the notice.

(2) A person on whom an enforcement notice has been served may appeal to the Tribunal against the refusal of an application under section 41(2) for cancellation or variation of the notice.

(3) Where an enforcement notice, an information notice or a special information notice contains a statement by the Commissioner in accordance with section 40(8), 43(5) or 44(6) then, whether or not the person appeals against the notice, he may appeal against—

(a) the Commissioner's decision to include the statement in the notice, or

(b) the effect of the inclusion of the statement as respects any part of the notice.

(4) A data controller in respect of whom a determination has been made under section 45 may appeal to the Tribunal against the determination.

(5) Schedule 6 has effect in relation to appeals under this section and the proceedings of the Tribunal in respect of any such appeal.

49   Determination of appeals

(1) If on an appeal under section 48(1) the Tribunal considers—

(a) that the notice against which the appeal is brought is not in accordance with the law, or

(b) to the extent that the notice involved an exercise of discretion by the Commissioner, that he ought to have exercised his discretion differently,

the Tribunal shall allow the appeal or substitute such other notice or decision as could have been served or made by the Commissioner; and in any other case the Tribunal shall dismiss the appeal.

(2) On such an appeal, the Tribunal may review any determination of fact on which the notice in question was based.

(3) If on an appeal under section 48(2) the Tribunal considers that the enforcement notice ought to be cancelled or varied by reason of a change in circumstances, the Tribunal shall cancel or vary the notice.

(4) On an appeal under subsection (3) of section 48 the Tribunal may direct—

(a) that the notice in question shall have effect as if it did not contain any such statement as is mentioned in that subsection, or

(b) that the inclusion of the statement shall not have effect in relation to any part of the notice,

and may make such modifications in the notice as may be required for giving effect to the direction.

(5) On an appeal under section 48(4), the Tribunal may cancel the determination of the Commissioner.

(6) Any party to an appeal to the Tribunal under section 48 may appeal from the decision of the Tribunal on a point of law to the appropriate court; and that court shall be—

(a) the High Court of Justice in England if the address of the person who was the appellant before the Tribunal is in England or Wales,

(b) the Court of Session if that address is in Scotland, and

(c) the High Court of Justice in Northern Ireland if that address is in Northern Ireland.

(7) For the purposes of subsection (6)—

(a) the address of a registered company is that of its registered office, and

(b) the address of a person (other than a registered company) carrying on a business is that of his principal place of business in the United Kingdom.

50   Powers of entry and inspection

Schedule 9 (powers of entry and inspection) has effect.

PART VI MISCELLANEOUS AND GENERAL

Functions of Commissioner

51   General duties of Commissioner

(1) It shall be the duty of the Commissioner to promote the following of good practice by data controllers and, in particular, so to perform his functions under this Act as to promote the observance of the requirements of this Act by data controllers.

(2) The Commissioner shall arrange for the dissemination in such form and manner as he considers appropriate of such information as it may appear to him expedient to give to the public about

the operation of this Act, about good practice, and about other matters within the scope of his functions under this Act, and may give advice to any person as to any of those matters.

(3) Where—

(a) the [Secretary of State] so directs by order, or

(b) the Commissioner considers it appropriate to do so,

the Commissioner shall, after such consultation with trade associations, data subjects or persons representing data subjects as appears to him to be appropriate, prepare and disseminate to such persons as he considers appropriate codes of practice for guidance as to good practice.

(4) The Commissioner shall also—

(a) where he considers it appropriate to do so, encourage trade associations to prepare, and to disseminate to their members, such codes of practice, and

(b) where any trade association submits a code of practice to him for his consideration, consider the code and, after such consultation with data subjects or persons representing data subjects as appears to him to be appropriate, notify the trade association whether in his opinion the code promotes the following of good practice.

(5) An order under subsection (3) shall describe the personal data or processing to which the code of practice is to relate, and may also describe the persons or classes of persons to whom it is to relate.

(6) The Commissioner shall arrange for the dissemination in such form and manner as he considers appropriate of—

(a) any Community finding as defined by paragraph 15(2) of Part II of Schedule 1,

(b) any decision of the European Commission, under the procedure provided for in Article 31(2) of the Data Protection Directive, which is made for the purposes of Article 26(3) or (4) of the Directive, and

(c) such other information as it may appear to him to be expedient to give to data controllers in relation to any personal data about the protection of the rights and freedoms of data subjects in relation to the processing of personal data in countries and territories outside the European Economic Area.

(7) The Commissioner may, with the consent of the data controller, assess any processing of personal data for the following of good practice and shall inform the data controller of the results of the assessment.

(8) The Commissioner may charge such sums as he may with the consent of the [Secretary of State] determine for any services provided by the Commissioner by virtue of this Part.

(9) In this section—

"good practice" means such practice in the processing of personal data as appears to the Commissioner to be desirable having regard to the interests of data subjects and others, and includes (but is not limited to) compliance with the requirements of this Act;

"trade association" includes any body representing data controllers.

52   Reports and codes of practice to be laid before Parliament

(1) The Commissioner shall lay annually before each House of Parliament a general report on the exercise of his functions under this Act.

(2) The Commissioner may from time to time lay before each House of Parliament such other reports with respect to those functions as he thinks fit.

(3) The Commissioner shall lay before each House of Parliament any code of practice prepared under section 51(3) for complying with a direction of the [Secretary of State], unless the code is included in any report laid under subsection (1) or (2).

53   Assistance by Commissioner in cases involving processing for the special purposes

(1) An individual who is an actual or prospective party to any proceedings under section 7(9), 10(4), 12(8)[, 12A(3)] or 14 or by virtue of section 13 which relate to personal data processed for the special purposes may apply to the Commissioner for assistance in relation to those proceedings.

(2) The Commissioner shall, as soon as reasonably practicable after receiving an application under subsection (1), consider it and decide whether and to what extent to grant it, but he shall not grant the application unless, in his opinion, the case involves a matter of substantial public importance.

(3) If the Commissioner decides to provide assistance, he shall, as soon as reasonably practicable after making the decision, notify the applicant, stating the extent of the assistance to be provided.

(4) If the Commissioner decides not to provide assistance, he shall, as soon as reasonably practicable after making the decision, notify the applicant of his decision and, if he thinks fit, the reasons for it.

(5) In this section—
    (a) references to "proceedings" include references to prospective proceedings, and
    (b) "applicant", in relation to assistance under this section, means an individual who applies for assistance.

(6) Schedule 10 has effect for supplementing this section.

54   International co-operation

(1) The Commissioner—
    (a) shall continue to be the designated authority in the United Kingdom for the purposes of Article 13 of the Convention, and
    (b) shall be the supervisory authority in the United Kingdom for the purposes of the Data Protection Directive.

(2) The [Secretary of State] may by order make provision as to the functions to be discharged by the Commissioner as the designated authority in the United Kingdom for the purposes of Article 13 of the Convention.

(3) The [Secretary of State] may by order make provision as to co-operation by the Commissioner with the European Commission and with supervisory authorities in other EEA States in connection with the performance of their respective duties and, in particular, as to—
    (a) the exchange of information with supervisory authorities in other EEA States or with the European Commission, and
    (b) the exercise within the United Kingdom at the request of a supervisory authority in another EEA State, in cases excluded by section 5 from the application of the other provisions of this Act, of functions of the Commissioner specified in the order.

(4) The Commissioner shall also carry out any data protection functions which the [Secretary of State] may by order direct him to carry out for the purpose of enabling Her Majesty's Government in the United Kingdom to give effect to any international obligations of the United Kingdom.

(5) The Commissioner shall, if so directed by the [Secretary of State], provide any authority exercising data protection functions under the law of a colony specified in the direction with such assistance in connection with the discharge of those functions as the [Secretary of State] may direct or approve, on such terms (including terms as to payment) as the [Secretary of State] may direct or approve.

(6) Where the European Commission makes a decision for the purposes of Article 26(3) or (4) of the Data Protection Directive under the procedure provided for in Article 31(2) of the Directive, the Commissioner shall comply with that decision in exercising his functions under paragraph 9 of Schedule 4 or, as the case may be, paragraph 8 of that Schedule.

(7) The Commissioner shall inform the European Commission and the supervisory authorities in other EEA States—
    (a) of any approvals granted for the purposes of paragraph 8 of Schedule 4, and
    (b) of any authorisations granted for the purposes of paragraph 9 of that Schedule.

(8) In this section—
"the Convention" means the Convention for the Protection of Individuals with regard to Automatic Processing of Personal Data which was opened for signature on 28th January 1981;
"data protection functions" means functions relating to the protection of individuals with respect to the processing of personal information.

[54A   Inspection of overseas information systems

(1) The Commissioner may inspect any personal data recorded in—

    (a) the Schengen information system,

    (b) the Europol information system,

    (c) the Customs information system.

(2) The power conferred by subsection (1) is exercisable only for the purpose of assessing whether or not any processing of the data has been or is being carried out in compliance with this Act.

(3) The power includes power to inspect, operate and test equipment which is used for the processing of personal data.

(4) Before exercising the power, the Commissioner must give notice in writing of his intention to do so to the data controller.

(5) But subsection (4) does not apply if the Commissioner considers that the case is one of urgency.

(6) Any person who—

    (a) intentionally obstructs a person exercising the power conferred by subsection (1), or

    (b) fails without reasonable excuse to give any person exercising the power any assistance he may reasonably require,

is guilty of an offence.

(7) In this section—

"the Customs information system" means the information system established under Chapter II of the Convention on the Use of Information Technology for Customs Purposes,

"the Europol information system" means the information system established under Title II of the Convention on the Establishment of a European Police Office,

"the Schengen information system" means the information system established under Title IV of the Convention implementing the Schengen Agreement of 14th June 1985, or any system established in its place in pursuance of any Community obligation.]

Unlawful obtaining etc. of personal data

55   Unlawful obtaining etc. of personal data

(1) A person must not knowingly or recklessly, without the consent of the data controller—

    (a) obtain or disclose personal data or the information contained in personal data, or

    (b) procure the disclosure to another person of the information contained in personal data.

(2) Subsection (1) does not apply to a person who shows—

    (a) that the obtaining, disclosing or procuring—

        (i)   was necessary for the purpose of preventing or detecting crime, or

        (ii) was required or authorised by or under any enactment, by any rule of law or by the order of a court,

    (b) that he acted in the reasonable belief that he had in law the right to obtain or disclose the data or information or, as the case may be, to procure the disclosure of the information to the other person,

    (c) that he acted in the reasonable belief that he would have had the consent of the data controller if the data controller had known of the obtaining, disclosing or procuring and the circumstances of it, or

    (d) that in the particular circumstances the obtaining, disclosing or procuring was justified as being in the public interest.

(3) A person who contravenes subsection (1) is guilty of an offence.

(4) A person who sells personal data is guilty of an offence if he has obtained the data in contravention of subsection (1).

(5) A person who offers to sell personal data is guilty of an offence if—

    (a) he has obtained the data in contravention of subsection (1), or

    (b) he subsequently obtains the data in contravention of that subsection.

(6) For the purposes of subsection (5), an advertisement indicating that personal data are or may be for sale is an offer to sell the data.

(7) Section 1(2) does not apply for the purposes of this section; and for the purposes of subsections (4) to (6), "personal data" includes information extracted from personal data.

(8) References in this section to personal data do not include references to personal data which by virtue of section 28 [or 33A] are exempt from this section.

Records obtained under data subject's right of access

56 Prohibition of requirement as to production of certain records[1]

(1) A person must not, in connection with—

(a) the recruitment of another person as an employee,

(b) the continued employment of another person, or

(c) any contract for the provision of services to him by another person,

require that other person or a third party to supply him with a relevant record or to produce a relevant record to him.

(2) A person concerned with the provision (for payment or not) of goods, facilities or services to the public or a section of the public must not, as a condition of providing or offering to provide any goods, facilities or services to another person, require that other person or a third party to supply him with a relevant record or to produce a relevant record to him.

(3) Subsections (1) and (2) do not apply to a person who shows—

(a) that the imposition of the requirement was required or authorised by or under any enactment, by any rule of law or by the order of a court, or

(b) that in the particular circumstances the imposition of the requirement was justified as being in the public interest.

(4) Having regard to the provisions of Part V of the Police Act 1997 (certificates of criminal records etc.), the imposition of the requirement referred to in subsection (1) or (2) is not to be regarded as being justified as being in the public interest on the ground that it would assist in the prevention or detection of crime.

(5) A person who contravenes subsection (1) or (2) is guilty of an offence.

(6) In this section "a relevant record" means any record which—

(a) has been or is to be obtained by a data subject from any data controller specified in the first column of the Table below in the exercise of the right conferred by section 7, and

(b) contains information relating to any matter specified in relation to that data controller in the second column,

and includes a copy of such a record or a part of such a record.

Table

Data controller	Subject-matter
1. Any of the following persons— (a) a chief officer of police of a police force in England and Wales. (b) a chief constable of a police force in Scotland. (c) [Chief Constable of the Police Service of Northern Ireland]. (d) [the Director General of the Serious Organised Crime Agency] . . .	(a) Convictions. (b) Cautions.
2. The Secretary of State.	(a) Convictions. (b) Cautions.

Cont.

---

[1] The section was in effect from 16 July 1998, but only in so far as it conferred power to make subordinate legislation (see s. 75).

Data controller	Subject-matter
	(c) His functions under [section 92 of the Powers of the Criminal Courts (Sentencing) Act 2000], section 205(2) or 208 of the Criminal Procedure (Scotland) Act 1995 or section 73 of the Children and Young Persons Act (Northern Ireland) 1968 in relation to any person sentenced to detention. (d) His functions under the Prison Act 1952, the Prisons (Scotland) Act 1989 or the Prison Act (Northern Ireland) 1953 in relation to any person imprisoned or detained. (e) His functions under the Social Security Contributions and Benefits Act 1992, the Social Security Administration Act 1992 or the Jobseekers Act 1995. (f) His functions under Part V of the Police Act 1997.
3. The Department of Health and Social Services for Northern Ireland.	Its functions under the Social Security Contributions and Benefits (Northern Ireland) Act 1992, the Social Security Administration (Northern Ireland) Act 1992 or the Jobseekers (Northern Ireland) Order 1995.

[(6A) A record is not a relevant record to the extent that it relates, or is to relate, only to personal data falling within paragraph (e) of the definition of "data" in section 1(1).]

(7) In the Table in subsection (6)—

"caution" means a caution given to any person in England and Wales or Northern Ireland in respect of an offence which, at the time when the caution is given, is admitted;

"conviction" has the same meaning as in the Rehabilitation of Offenders Act 1974 or the Rehabilitation of Offenders (Northern Ireland) Order 1978.

(8) The [Secretary of State] may by order amend—

    (a) the Table in subsection (6), and

    (b) subsection (7).

(9) For the purposes of this section a record which states that a data controller is not processing any personal data relating to a particular matter shall be taken to be a record containing information relating to that matter.

(10) In this section "employee" means an individual who—

    (a) works under a contract of employment, as defined by section 230(2) of the Employment Rights Act 1996, or

    (b) holds any office,

whether or not he is entitled to remuneration; and "employment" shall be construed accordingly.

57   Avoidance of certain contractual terms relating to health records

(1) Any term or condition of a contract is void in so far as it purports to require an individual—

    (a) to supply any other person with a record to which this section applies, or with a copy of such a record or a part of such a record, or

    (b) to produce to any other person such a record, copy or part.

(2) This section applies to any record which—

    (a) has been or is to be obtained by a data subject in the exercise of the right conferred by section 7, and

    (b) consists of the information contained in any health record as defined by section 68(2).

Information provided to Commissioner or Tribunal

58   Disclosure of information

No enactment or rule of law prohibiting or restricting the disclosure of information shall preclude a person from furnishing the Commissioner or the Tribunal with any information necessary for the discharge of their functions under this Act [or the Freedom of Information Act 2000].

59   Confidentiality of information

(1) No person who is or has been the Commissioner, a member of the Commissioner's staff or an agent of the Commissioner shall disclose any information which—

(a) has been obtained by, or furnished to, the Commissioner under or for the purposes of [the information Acts],

(b) relates to an identified or identifiable individual or business, and

(c) is not at the time of the disclosure, and has not previously been, available to the public from other sources,

unless the disclosure is made with lawful authority.

(2) For the purposes of subsection (1) a disclosure of information is made with lawful authority only if, and to the extent that—

(a) the disclosure is made with the consent of the individual or of the person for the time being carrying on the business,

(b) the information was provided for the purpose of its being made available to the public (in whatever manner) under any provision of [the information Acts],

(c) the disclosure is made for the purposes of, and is necessary for, the discharge of—

(i)   any functions under [the information Acts], or

(ii) any Community obligation,

(d) the disclosure is made for the purposes of any proceedings, whether criminal or civil and whether arising under, or by virtue of, [the information Acts], or otherwise, or

(e) having regard to the rights and freedoms or legitimate interests of any person, the disclosure is necessary in the public interest.

(3) Any person who knowingly or recklessly discloses information in contravention of subsection (1) is guilty of an offence.

[(4) In this section "the information Acts" means this Act and the Freedom of Information Act 2000.]

General provisions relating to offences

60   Prosecutions and penalties

(1) No proceedings for an offence under this Act shall be instituted—

(a) in England or Wales, except by the Commissioner or by or with the consent of the Director of Public Prosecutions;

(b) in Northern Ireland, except by the Commissioner or by or with the consent of the Director of Public Prosecutions for Northern Ireland.

(2) A person guilty of an offence under any provision of this Act other than [section 54A and] paragraph 12 of Schedule 9 is liable—

(a) on summary conviction, to a fine not exceeding the statutory maximum, or

(b) on conviction on indictment, to a fine.

(3) A person guilty of an offence under [section 54A and] paragraph 12 of Schedule 9 is liable on summary conviction to a fine not exceeding level 5 on the standard scale.

(4) Subject to subsection (5), the court by or before which a person is convicted of—

(a) an offence under section 21(1), 22(6), 55 or 56,

(b) an offence under section 21(2) relating to processing which is assessable processing for the purposes of section 22, or

(c) an offence under section 47(1) relating to an enforcement notice,

may order any document or other material used in connection with the processing of personal data and appearing to the court to be connected with the commission of the offence to be forfeited, destroyed or erased.

(5) The court shall not make an order under subsection (4) in relation to any material where a person (other than the offender) claiming to be the owner of or otherwise interested in the material applies to be heard by the court, unless an opportunity is given to him to show cause why the order should not be made.

61   Liability of directors etc.

(1) Where an offence under this Act has been committed by a body corporate and is proved to have been committed with the consent or connivance of or to be attributable to any neglect on the part of any director, manager, secretary or similar officer of the body corporate or any person who was purporting to act in any such capacity, he as well as the body corporate shall be guilty of that offence and be liable to be proceeded against and punished accordingly.

(2) Where the affairs of a body corporate are managed by its members subsection (1) shall apply in relation to the acts and defaults of a member in connection with his functions of management as if he were a director of the body corporate.

(3) Where an offence under this Act has been committed by a Scottish partnership and the contravention in question is proved to have occurred with the consent or connivance of, or to be attributable to any neglect on the part of, a partner, he as well as the partnership shall be guilty of that offence and shall be liable to be proceeded against and punished accordingly.

Amendments of Consumer Credit Act 1974

62   Amendments of Consumer Credit Act 1974

(1) In section 158 of the Consumer Credit Act 1974 (duty of agency to disclose filed information)—
  (a) in subsection (1)—
      (i)   in paragraph (a) for "individual" there is substituted "partnership or other unincorporated body of persons not consisting entirely of bodies corporate", and
      (ii) for "him" there is substituted "it",
  (b) in subsection (2), for "his" there is substituted "the consumer"'s', and
  (c) in subsection (3), for "him" there is substituted "the consumer".

(2) In section 159 of that Act (correction of wrong information) for subsection (1) there is substituted—
  "(1) Any individual (the 'objector') given—
      (a) information under section 7 of the Data Protection Act 1998 by a credit reference agency, or
      (b) information under section 158,
who considers that an entry in his file is incorrect, and that if it is not corrected he is likely to be prejudiced, may give notice to the agency requiring it either to remove the entry from the file or amend it."

(3) In subsections (2) to (6) of that section—
  (a) for "consumer", wherever occurring, there is substituted "objector", and
  (b) for "Director", wherever occurring, there is substituted "the relevant authority".

(4) After subsection (6) of that section there is inserted—
  "(7) The Data Protection Commissioner may vary or revoke any order made by him under this section.

(8) In this section 'the relevant authority' means—
  (a) where the objector is a partnership or other unincorporated body of persons, the Director, and
  (b) in any other case, the Data Protection Commissioner."

(5) In section 160 of that Act (alternative procedure for business consumers)—
  (a) in subsection (4)—
      (i)   for "him" there is substituted "to the consumer", and
      (ii) in paragraphs (a) and (b) for "he" there is substituted "the consumer" and for "his" there is substituted "the consumer"'s', and
  (b) after subsection (6) there is inserted—
  "(7) In this section 'consumer' has the same meaning as in section 158."

General

63   Application to Crown

(1) This Act binds the Crown.

(2) For the purposes of this Act each government department shall be treated as a person separate from any other government department.

(3) Where the purposes for which and the manner in which any personal data are, or are to be, processed are determined by any person acting on behalf of the Royal Household, the Duchy of Lancaster or the Duchy of Cornwall, the data controller in respect of those data for the purposes of this Act shall be—

    (a) in relation to the Royal Household, the Keeper of the Privy Purse,

    (b) in relation to the Duchy of Lancaster, such person as the Chancellor of the Duchy appoints, and

    (c) in relation to the Duchy of Cornwall, such person as the Duke of Cornwall, or the possessor for the time being of the Duchy of Cornwall, appoints.

(4) Different persons may be appointed under subsection (3)(b) or (c) for different purposes.

(5) Neither a government department nor a person who is a data controller by virtue of subsection (3) shall be liable to prosecution under this Act, but [sections 54A and] 55 and paragraph 12 of Schedule 9 shall apply to a person in the service of the Crown as they apply to any other person.

[63A   Application to Parliament

(1) Subject to the following provisions of this section and to section 35A, this Act applies to the processing of personal data by or on behalf of either House of Parliament as it applies to the processing of personal data by other persons

(2) Where the purposes for which and the manner in which any personal data are, or are to be, processed are determined by or on behalf of the House of Commons, the data controller in respect of those data for the purposes of this Act shall be the Corporate Officer of that House.

(3) Where the purposes for which and the manner in which any personal data are, or are to be, processed are determined by or on behalf of the House of Lords, the data controller in respect of those data for the purposes of this Act shall be the Corporate Officer of that House.

(4) Nothing in subsection (2) or (3) is to be taken to render the Corporate Officer of the House of Commons or the Corporate Officer of the House of Lords liable to prosecution under this Act, but section 55 and paragraph 12 of Schedule 9 shall apply to a person acting on behalf of either House as they apply to any other person.]

64   Transmission of notices etc. by electronic or other means

(1) This section applies to—

    (a) a notice or request under any provision of Part II,

    (b) a notice under subsection (1) of section 24 or particulars made available under that subsection, or

    (c) an application under section 41(2),

but does not apply to anything which is required to be served in accordance with rules of court.

(2) The requirement that any notice, request, particulars or application to which this section applies should be in writing is satisfied where the text of the notice, request, particulars or application—

    (a) is transmitted by electronic means,

    (b) is received in legible form, and

    (c) is capable of being used for subsequent reference.

(3) The [Secretary of State] may by regulations provide that any requirement that any notice, request, particulars or application to which this section applies should be in writing is not to apply in such circumstances as may be prescribed by the regulations.

65   Service of notices by Commissioner

(1) Any notice authorised or required by this Act to be served on or given to any person by the Commissioner may—

    (a) if that person is an individual, be served on him—

        (i) by delivering it to him, or

        (ii) by sending it to him by post addressed to him at his usual or last-known place of residence or business, or

        (iii) by leaving it for him at that place;

(b) if that person is a body corporate or unincorporate, be served on that body—

    (i) by sending it by post to the proper officer of the body at its principal office, or

    (ii) by addressing it to the proper officer of the body and leaving it at that office;

(c) if that person is a partnership in Scotland, be served on that partnership—

    (i) by sending it by post to the principal office of the partnership, or

    (ii) by addressing it to that partnership and leaving it at that office.

(2) In subsection (1)(b) "principal office", in relation to a registered company, means its registered office and "proper officer", in relation to any body, means the secretary or other executive officer charged with the conduct of its general affairs.

(3) This section is without prejudice to any other lawful method of serving or giving a notice.

66 Exercise of rights in Scotland by children

(1) Where a question falls to be determined in Scotland as to the legal capacity of a person under the age of sixteen years to exercise any right conferred by any provision of this Act, that person shall be taken to have that capacity where he has a general understanding of what it means to exercise that right.

(2) Without prejudice to the generality of subsection (1), a person of twelve years of age or more shall be presumed to be of sufficient age and maturity to have such understanding as is mentioned in that subsection.

67 Orders, regulations and rules

(1) Any power conferred by this Act on the [Secretary of State] to make an order, regulations or rules shall be exercisable by statutory instrument.

(2) Any order, regulations or rules made by the [Secretary of State] under this Act may—

(a) make different provision for different cases, and

(b) make such supplemental, incidental, consequential or transitional provision or savings as the [Secretary of State] considers appropriate;

and nothing in section 7(11), 19(5), 26(1) or 30(4) limits the generality of paragraph (a).

(3) Before making—

(a) an order under any provision of this Act other than section 75(3),

(b) any regulations under this Act other than notification regulations (as defined by section 16(2)),

the [Secretary of State] shall consult the Commissioner.

(4) A statutory instrument containing (whether alone or with other provisions) an order under—

section 10(2)(b),

section 12(5)(b),

section 22(1),

section 30,

section 32(3),

section 38,

section 56(8),

paragraph 10 of Schedule 3, or

paragraph 4 of Schedule 7,

shall not be made unless a draft of the instrument has been laid before and approved by a resolution of each House of Parliament.

(5) A statutory instrument which contains (whether alone or with other provisions)—

(a) an order under—

section 22(7),

section 23,

section 51(3),

section 54(2), (3) or (4),

paragraph 3, 4 or 14 of Part II of Schedule 1,

paragraph 6 of Schedule 2,

paragraph 2, 7 or 9 of Schedule 3,

paragraph 4 of Schedule 4,

paragraph 6 of Schedule 7,

  (b) regulations under section 7 which—

     (i)   prescribe cases for the purposes of subsection (2)(b),

    (ii) are made by virtue of subsection (7), or

   (iii) relate to the definition of "the prescribed period",

  (c) regulations under section 8(1)[, 9(3) or 9A(5)],

  (d) regulations under section 64,

  (e) notification regulations (as defined by section 16(2)), or

  (f) rules under paragraph 7 of Schedule 6,

and which is not subject to the requirement in subsection (4) that a draft of the instrument be laid before and approved by a resolution of each House of Parliament, shall be subject to annulment in pursuance of a resolution of either House of Parliament.

  (6) A statutory instrument which contains only—

  (a) regulations prescribing fees for the purposes of any provision of this Act, or

  (b) regulations under section 7 prescribing fees for the purposes of any other enactment,

shall be laid before Parliament after being made.

68   Meaning of "accessible record"

  (1) In this Act "accessible record" means—

  (a) a health record as defined by subsection (2),

  (b) an educational record as defined by Schedule 11, or

  (c) an accessible public record as defined by Schedule 12.

  (2) In subsection (1)(a) "health record" means any record which—

  (a) consists of information relating to the physical or mental health or condition of an individual, and

  (b) has been made by or on behalf of a health professional in connection with the care of that individual.

69   Meaning of "health professional"

  (1) In this Act "health professional" means any of the following—

  (a)   a registered medical practitioner,

  (b)   a registered dentist as defined by section 53(1) of the Dentists Act 1984,

  [(c) a registered dispensing optician or a registered optometrist within the meaning of the Opticians Act 1989,]

  (d) [a registered pharmacist or registered pharmacy technician within the meaning of the Pharmacists and Pharmacy Technicians Order 2007] or a registered person as defined by Article 2(2) of the Pharmacy (Northern Ireland) Order 1976,

  [(e) a registered nurse or midwife,]

  (f)   a registered osteopath as defined by section 41 of the Osteopaths Act 1993,

  (g)   a registered chiropractor as defined by section 43 of the Chiropractors Act 1994,

  (h)   any person who is registered as a member of a profession to which [the Health Professions Order 2001] for the time being extends,

  (i)   a clinical psychologist [or child psychotherapist],

  (j)   […]

  (k)   a scientist employed by such a body as head of a department.

  (2) In subsection (1)(a) "registered medical practitioner" includes any person who is provisionally registered under section 15 or 21 of the Medical Act 1983 and is engaged in such employment as is mentioned in subsection (3) of that section.

  (3) In subsection (1) "health service body" means—

  (a) [a Strategic Health Authority established under section 13 of the National Health Service Act 2006],

(b)   a Special Health Authority established under section 11 of that Act,

[(bb)   a Primary Care Trust established under section 18 of the National Health Service Act 2006,]

[(bbb)   a Local Health Board established under section 11 of the National Health Service (Wales) Act 2006,]

(c)   a Health Board within the meaning of the National Health Service (Scotland) Act 1978,

(d)   a Special Health Board within the meaning of that Act,

(e)   the managers of a State Hospital provided under section 102 of that Act,

(f)   a National Health Service trust first established under section 5 of the National Health Service and Community Care Act 1990[, section 25 of the National Health Service Act 2006, section 18 of the National Health Service (Wales) Act 2006] or section 12A of the National Health Service (Scotland) Act 1978,

[(fa)   an NHS foundation trust;]

(g)   a Health and Social Services Board established under Article 16 of the Health and Personal Social Services (Northern Ireland) Order 1972,

(h)   a special health and social services agency established under the Health and Personal Social Services (Special Agencies) (Northern Ireland) Order 1990, or

(i)   a Health and Social Services trust established under Article 10 of the Health and Personal Social Services (Northern Ireland) Order 1991.

70 Supplementary definitions

(1) In this Act, unless the context otherwise requires—

"business" includes any trade or profession;

"the Commissioner" means [the Information Commissioner];

"credit reference agency" has the same meaning as in the Consumer Credit Act 1974;

"the Data Protection Directive" means Directive 95/46/EC on the protection of individuals with regard to the processing of personal data and on the free movement of such data;

"EEA State" means a State which is a contracting party to the Agreement on the European Economic Area signed at Oporto on 2nd May 1992 as adjusted by the Protocol signed at Brussels on 17th March 1993;

"enactment" includes an enactment passed after this Act [and any enactment comprised in, or in any instrument made under, an Act of the Scottish Parliament];

"government department" includes a Northern Ireland department and any body or authority exercising statutory functions on behalf of the Crown;

"Minister of the Crown" has the same meaning as in the Ministers of the Crown Act 1975;

"public register" means any register which pursuant to a requirement imposed—

(a) by or under any enactment, or

(b) in pursuance of any international agreement,

is open to public inspection or open to inspection by any person having a legitimate interest;

"pupil"—

(a) in relation to a school in England and Wales, means a registered pupil within the meaning of the Education Act 1996,

(b) in relation to a school in Scotland, means a pupil within the meaning of the Education (Scotland) Act 1980, and

(c) in relation to a school in Northern Ireland, means a registered pupil within the meaning of the Education and Libraries (Northern Ireland) Order 1986;

"recipient", in relation to any personal data, means any person to whom the data are disclosed, including any person (such as an employee or agent of the data controller, a data processor or an employee or agent of a data processor) to whom they are disclosed in the course of processing the data for the data controller, but does not include any person to whom disclosure is or may be made as a result of, or with a view to, a particular inquiry by or on behalf of that person made in the exercise of any power conferred by law;

"registered company" means a company registered under the enactments relating to companies for the time being in force in the United Kingdom;

"school"—

    (a) in relation to England and Wales, has the same meaning as in the Education Act 1996,

    (b) in relation to Scotland, has the same meaning as in the Education (Scotland) Act 1980, and

    (c) in relation to Northern Ireland, has the same meaning as in the Education and Libraries (Northern Ireland) Order 1986;

"teacher" includes—

    (a) in Great Britain, head teacher, and

    (b) in Northern Ireland, the principal of a school;

"third party", in relation to personal data, means any person other than—

    (a) the data subject,

    (b) the data controller, or

    (c) any data processor or other person authorised to process data for the data controller or processor;

"the Tribunal" means [the Information Tribunal].

(2) For the purposes of this Act data are inaccurate if they are incorrect or misleading as to any matter of fact.

71 Index of defined expressions

The following Table shows provisions defining or otherwise explaining expressions used in this Act (other than provisions defining or explaining an expression only used in the same section or Schedule)—

accessible record	section 68
address (in Part III)	section 16(3)
Business	section 70(1)
the Commissioner	section 70(1)
credit reference agency	section 70(1)
Data	section 1(1)
data controller	sections 1(1) and (4) and 63(3)
data processor	section 1(1)
the Data Protection Directive	section 70(1)
data protection principles	section 4 and Schedule 1
data subject	section 1(1)
disclosing (of personal data)	section 1(2)(b)
EEA State	section 70(1)
Enactment	section 70(1)
enforcement notice	section 40(1)
fees regulations (in Part III)	section 16(2)
government department	section 70(1)
health professional	section 69
inaccurate (in relation to data)	section 70(2)
information notice	section 43(1)
Minister of the Crown	section 70(1)
the non-disclosure provisions (in Part IV)	section 27(3)
notification regulations (in Part III)	section 16(2)

obtaining (of personal data)	section 1(2)(a)
personal data	section 1(1)
prescribed (in Part III)	section 16(2)
processing (of information or data)	section 1(1) and paragraph 5 of Schedule 8
[public authority]	section 1(1)
public register	section 70(1)
publish (in relation to journalistic, literary or artistic material)	section 32(6)
pupil (in relation to a school)	section 70(1)
recipient (in relation to personal data)	section 70(1)
recording (of personal data)	section 1(2)(a)
registered company	section 70(1)
registrable particulars (in Part III)	section 16(1)
relevant filing system	section 1(1)
School	section 70(1)
sensitive personal data	section 2
Special information notice	section 44(1)
the special purposes	section 3
the subject information provisions (in Part IV)	section 27(2)
Teacher	section 70(1)
third party (in relation to processing of personal data)	section 70(1)
the Tribunal	section 70(1)
using (of personal data)	section 1(2)(b).

72 Modifications of Act

During the period beginning with the commencement of this section and ending with 23rd October 2007, the provisions of this Act shall have effect subject to the modifications set out in Schedule 13.

73 Transitional provisions and savings

Schedule 14 (which contains transitional provisions and savings) has effect.

74 Minor and consequential amendments and repeals and revocations

(1) Schedule 15 (which contains minor and consequential amendments) has effect.

(2) The enactments and instruments specified in Schedule 16 are repealed or revoked to the extent specified.

75 Short title, commencement and extent

(1) This Act may be cited as the Data Protection Act 1998.

(2) The following provisions of this Act—

(a) sections 1 to 3,

(b) section 25(1) and (4),

(c) section 26,

(d) sections 67 to 71,

(e) this section,

(f) paragraph 17 of Schedule 5,

(g) Schedule 11,

(h) Schedule 12, and

(i) so much of any other provision of this Act as confers any power to make subordinate legislation,

shall come into force on the day on which this Act is passed.

(3) The remaining provisions of this Act shall come into force on such day as the [Secretary of State] may by order appoint; and different days may be appointed for different purposes.

(4) The day appointed under subsection (3) for the coming into force of section 56 must not be earlier than the first day on which sections 112, 113 and 115 of the Police Act 1997 (which provide for the issue by the Secretary of State of criminal conviction certificates, criminal record certificates and enhanced criminal record certificates) are all in force.

[(4A) Subsection (4) does not apply to section 56 so far as that section relates to a record containing information relating to—

      (a) the Secretary of State's functions under the Safeguarding Vulnerable Groups Act 2006 or the Safeguarding Vulnerable Groups (Northern Ireland) Order 2007, or

      (b) the Independent Barring Board's functions under that Act or that Order.[1]]

(5) Subject to subsection (6), this Act extends to Northern Ireland.

(6) Any amendment, repeal or revocation made by Schedule 15 or 16 has the same extent as that of the enactment or instrument to which it relates.

SCHEDULES

SCHEDULE 1   THE DATA PROTECTION PRINCIPLES

PART I THE PRINCIPLES

1. Personal data shall be processed fairly and lawfully and, in particular, shall not be processed unless—

      (a) at least one of the conditions in Schedule 2 is met, and

      (b) in the case of sensitive personal data, at least one of the conditions in Schedule 3 is also met.

2. Personal data shall be obtained only for one or more specified and lawful purposes, and shall not be further processed in any manner incompatible with that purpose or those purposes.

3. Personal data shall be adequate, relevant and not excessive in relation to the purpose or purposes for which they are processed.

4. Personal data shall be accurate and, where necessary, kept up to date.

5. Personal data processed for any purpose or purposes shall not be kept for longer than is necessary for that purpose or those purposes.

6. Personal data shall be processed in accordance with the rights of data subjects under this Act.

7. Appropriate technical and organisational measures shall be taken against unauthorised or unlawful processing of personal data and against accidental loss or destruction of, or damage to, personal data.

8. Personal data shall not be transferred to a country or territory outside the European Economic Area unless that country or territory ensures an adequate level of protection for the rights and freedoms of data subjects in relation to the processing of personal data.

PART II INTERPRETATION OF THE PRINCIPLES IN PART I

The first principle

1.—(1) In determining for the purposes of the first principle whether personal data are processed fairly, regard is to be had to the method by which they are obtained, including in particular

---

[1] This new sub-section is not yet in force: see the Safeguarding Vulnerable Groups Act 2006, s. 65.

whether any person from whom they are obtained is deceived or misled as to the purpose or purposes for which they are to be processed.

(2) Subject to paragraph 2, for the purposes of the first principle data are to be treated as obtained fairly if they consist of information obtained from a person who—

    (a) is authorised by or under any enactment to supply it, or

    (b) is required to supply it by or under any enactment or by any convention or other instrument imposing an international obligation on the United Kingdom.

2.—(1) Subject to paragraph 3, for the purposes of the first principle personal data are not to be treated as processed fairly unless—

    (a) in the case of data obtained from the data subject, the data controller ensures so far as practicable that the data subject has, is provided with, or has made readily available to him, the information specified in subparagraph (3), and

    (b) in any other case, the data controller ensures so far as practicable that, before the relevant time or as soon as practicable after that time, the data subject has, is provided with, or has made readily available to him, the information specified in sub-paragraph (3).

(2) In sub-paragraph (1)(b) "the relevant time" means—

    (a) the time when the data controller first processes the data, or

    (b) in a case where at that time disclosure to a third party within a reasonable period is envisaged—

        (i) if the data are in fact disclosed to such a person within that period, the time when the data are first disclosed,

        (ii) if within that period the data controller becomes, or ought to become, aware that the data are unlikely to be disclosed to such a person within that period, the time when the data controller does become, or ought to become, so aware, or

        (iii) in any other case, the end of that period.

(3) The information referred to in sub-paragraph (1) is as follows, namely—

    (a) the identity of the data controller,

    (b) if he has nominated a representative for the purposes of this Act, the identity of that representative,

    (c) the purpose or purposes for which the data are intended to be processed, and

    (d) any further information which is necessary, having regard to the specific circumstances in which the data are or are to be processed, to enable processing in respect of the data subject to be fair.

3.—(1) Paragraph 2(1)(b) does not apply where either of the primary conditions in sub-paragraph (2), together with such further conditions as may be prescribed by the [Secretary of State] by order, are met.

(2) The primary conditions referred to in sub-paragraph (1) are—

    (a) that the provision of that information would involve a disproportionate effort, or

    (b) that the recording of the information to be contained in the data by, or the disclosure of the data by, the data controller is necessary for compliance with any legal obligation to which the data controller is subject, other than an obligation imposed by contract.

4.—(1) Personal data which contain a general identifier falling within a description prescribed by the [Secretary of State] by order are not to be treated as processed fairly and lawfully unless they are processed in compliance with any conditions so prescribed in relation to general identifiers of that description.

(2) In sub-paragraph (1) "a general identifier" means any identifier (such as, for example, a number or code used for identification purposes) which—

    (a) relates to an individual, and

    (b) forms part of a set of similar identifiers which is of general application.

The second principle

5. The purpose or purposes for which personal data are obtained may in particular be specified—

(a) in a notice given for the purposes of paragraph 2 by the data controller to the data subject, or

(b) in a notification given to the Commissioner under Part III of this Act.

6. In determining whether any disclosure of personal data is compatible with the purpose or purposes for which the data were obtained, regard is to be had to the purpose or purposes for which the personal data are intended to be processed by any person to whom they are disclosed.

The fourth principle

7. The fourth principle is not to be regarded as being contravened by reason of any inaccuracy in personal data which accurately record information obtained by the data controller from the data subject or a third party in a case where—

(a) having regard to the purpose or purposes for which the data were obtained and further processed, the data controller has taken reasonable steps to ensure the accuracy of the data, and

(b) if the data subject has notified the data controller of the data subject's view that the data are inaccurate, the data indicate that fact.

The sixth principle

8. A person is to be regarded as contravening the sixth principle if, but only if—

(a) he contravenes section 7 by failing to supply information in accordance with that section,

(b) he contravenes section 10 by failing to comply with a notice given under subsection (1) of that section to the extent that the notice is justified or by failing to give a notice under subsection (3) of that section,

(c) he contravenes section 11 by failing to comply with a notice given under subsection (1) of that section . . .

(d) he contravenes section 12 by failing to comply with a notice given under subsection (1) or (2)(b) of that section or by failing to give a notification under subsection (2)(a) of that section or a notice under subsection (3) of that section

[or

(e) he contravenes section 12A by failing to comply with a notice given under subsection (1) of that section to the extent that the notice is justified].

The seventh principle

9. Having regard to the state of technological development and the cost of implementing any measures, the measures must ensure a level of security appropriate to—

(a) the harm that might result from such unauthorised or unlawful processing or accidental loss, destruction or damage as are mentioned in the seventh principle, and

(b) the nature of the data to be protected.

10. The data controller must take reasonable steps to ensure the reliability of any employees of his who have access to the personal data.

11. Where processing of personal data is carried out by a data processor on behalf of a data controller, the data controller must in order to comply with the seventh principle—

(a) choose a data processor providing sufficient guarantees in respect of the technical and organisational security measures governing the processing to be carried out, and

(b) take reasonable steps to ensure compliance with those measures.

12. Where processing of personal data is carried out by a data processor on behalf of a data controller, the data controller is not to be regarded as complying with the seventh principle unless—

(a) the processing is carried out under a contract—

(i) which is made or evidenced in writing, and

(ii) under which the data processor is to act only on instructions from the data controller, and

(b) the contract requires the data processor to comply with obligations equivalent to those imposed on a data controller by the seventh principle.

The eighth principle

13. An adequate level of protection is one which is adequate in all the circumstances of the case, having regard in particular to—

  (a) the nature of the personal data,

  (b) the country or territory of origin of the information contained in the data,

  (c) the country or territory of final destination of that information,

  (d) the purposes for which and period during which the data are intended to be processed,

  (e) the law in force in the country or territory in question,

  (f) the international obligations of that country or territory,

  (g) any relevant codes of conduct or other rules which are enforceable in that country or territory (whether generally or by arrangement in particular cases), and

  (h) any security measures taken in respect of the data in that country or territory.

14. The eighth principle does not apply to a transfer falling within any paragraph of Schedule 4, except in such circumstances and to such extent as the [Secretary of State] may by order provide.

15.—(1) Where—

  (a) in any proceedings under this Act any question arises as to whether the requirement of the eighth principle as to an adequate level of protection is met in relation to the transfer of any personal data to a country or territory outside the European Economic Area, and

  (b) a Community finding has been made in relation to transfers of the kind in question,

that question is to be determined in accordance with that finding.

(2) In sub-paragraph (1) "Community finding" means a finding of the European Commission, under the procedure provided for in Article 31(2) of the Data Protection Directive, that a country or territory outside the European Economic Area does, or does not, ensure an adequate level of protection within the meaning of Article 25(2) of the Directive.

SCHEDULE 2 CONDITIONS RELEVANT FOR PURPOSES OF THE FIRST PRINCIPLE: PROCESSING OF ANY PERSONAL DATA

1. The data subject has given his consent to the processing.

2. The processing is necessary—

  (a) for the performance of a contract to which the data subject is a party, or

  (b) for the taking of steps at the request of the data subject with a view to entering into a contract.

3. The processing is necessary for compliance with any legal obligation to which the data controller is subject, other than an obligation imposed by contract.

4. The processing is necessary in order to protect the vital interests of the data subject.

5. The processing is necessary—

  (a)   for the administration of justice,

  [(aa) for the exercise of any functions of either House of Parliament,]

  (b)   for the exercise of any functions conferred on any person by or under any enactment,

  (c)   for the exercise of any functions of the Crown, a Minister of the Crown or a government department, or

  (d)   for the exercise of any functions of a public nature exercised in the public interest by any person.

6.—(1) The processing is necessary for the purposes of legitimate interests pursued by the data controller or by the third party or parties to whom the data are disclosed, except where the processing is unwarranted in any particular case by reason of prejudice to the rights and freedoms or legitimate interests of the data subject.

(2) The [Secretary of State] may by order specify particular circumstances in which this condition is, or is not, to be taken to be satisfied.

SCHEDULE 3 CONDITIONS RELEVANT FOR PURPOSES OF THE FIRST PRINCIPLE: PROCESSING OF SENSITIVE PERSONAL DATA

1. The data subject has given his explicit consent to the processing of the personal data.

2.—(1) The processing is necessary for the purposes of exercising or performing any right or obligation which is conferred or imposed by law on the data controller in connection with employment.

(2) The [Secretary of State] may by order—

    (a) exclude the application of sub-paragraph (1) in such cases as may be specified, or

    (b) provide that, in such cases as may be specified, the condition in sub-paragraph (1) is not to be regarded as satisfied unless such further conditions as may be specified in the order are also satisfied.

3. The processing is necessary—

    (a) in order to protect the vital interests of the data subject or another person, in a case where—

        (i) consent cannot be given by or on behalf of the data subject, or

        (ii) the data controller cannot reasonably be expected to obtain the consent of the data subject, or

    (b) in order to protect the vital interests of another person, in a case where consent by or on behalf of the data subject has been unreasonably withheld.

4. The processing—

    (a) is carried out in the course of its legitimate activities by any body or association which—

        (i) is not established or conducted for profit, and

        (ii) exists for political, philosophical, religious or trade-union purposes,

    (b) is carried out with appropriate safeguards for the rights and freedoms of data subjects,

    (c) relates only to individuals who either are members of the body or association or have regular contact with it in connection with its purposes, and

    (d) does not involve disclosure of the personal data to a third party without the consent of the data subject.

5. The information contained in the personal data has been made public as a result of steps deliberately taken by the data subject.

6. The processing—

    (a) is necessary for the purpose of, or in connection with, any legal proceedings (including prospective legal proceedings),

    (b) is necessary for the purpose of obtaining legal advice, or

    (c) is otherwise necessary for the purposes of establishing, exercising or defending legal rights.

7.—(1) The processing is necessary—

    (a)   for the administration of justice,

    [(aa) for the exercise of any functions of either House of Parliament,]

    (b)   for the exercise of any functions conferred on any person by or under an enactment, or

    (c)   for the exercise of any functions of the Crown, a Minister of the Crown or a government department.

(2) The [Secretary of State] may by order—

    (a) exclude the application of sub-paragraph (1) in such cases as may be specified, or

    (b) provide that, in such cases as may be specified, the condition in sub paragraph (1) is not to be regarded as satisfied unless such further conditions as may be specified in the order are also satisfied.

[7A.—(1) The processing—

    (a) is either—

        (i) the disclosure of sensitive personal data by a person as a member of an anti-fraud organisation or otherwise in accordance with any arrangements made by such an organisation; or

(ii) any other processing by that person or another person of sensitive personal data so disclosed; and

(b) is necessary for the purposes of preventing fraud or a particular kind of fraud.

(2) In this paragraph "an anti-fraud organisation" means any unincorporated association, body corporate or other person which enables or facilitates any sharing of information to prevent fraud or a particular kind of fraud or which has any of these functions as its purpose or one of its purposes.[1]]

8.—(1) The processing is necessary for medical purposes and is undertaken by—

(a) a health professional, or

(b) a person who in the circumstances owes a duty of confidentiality which is equivalent to that which would arise if that person were a health professional.

(2) In this paragraph "medical purposes" includes the purposes of preventative medicine, medical diagnosis, medical research, the provision of care and treatment and the management of healthcare services.

9.—(1) The processing—

(a) is of sensitive personal data consisting of information as to racial or ethnic origin,

(b) is necessary for the purpose of identifying or keeping under review the existence or absence of equality of opportunity or treatment between persons of different racial or ethnic origins, with a view to enabling such equality to be promoted or maintained, and

(c) is carried out with appropriate safeguards for the rights and freedoms of data subjects.

(2) The [Secretary of State] may by order specify circumstances in which processing falling within sub-paragraph (1)(a) and (b) is, or is not, to be taken for the purposes of sub-paragraph (1)(c) to be carried out with appropriate safeguards for the rights and freedoms of data subjects.

10. The personal data are processed in circumstances specified in an order made by the [Secretary of State] for the purposes of this paragraph.

SCHEDULE 4 CASES WHERE THE EIGHTH PRINCIPLE DOES NOT APPLY

1. The data subject has given his consent to the transfer.

2. The transfer is necessary—

(a) for the performance of a contract between the data subject and the data controller, or

(b) for the taking of steps at the request of the data subject with a view to his entering into a contract with the data controller.

3. The transfer is necessary—

(a) for the conclusion of a contract between the data controller and a person other than the data subject which—

(i)   is entered into at the request of the data subject, or

(ii)   is in the interests of the data subject, or

(b) for the performance of such a contract.

4.—(1) The transfer is necessary for reasons of substantial public interest.

(2) The [Secretary of State] may by order specify—

(a) circumstances in which a transfer is to be taken for the purposes of sub paragraph (1) to be necessary for reasons of substantial public interest, and

(b) circumstances in which a transfer which is not required by or under an enactment is not to be taken for the purpose of sub-paragraph (1) to be necessary for reasons of substantial public interest.

5. The transfer—

(a) is necessary for the purpose of, or in connection with, any legal proceedings (including prospective legal proceedings),

---

[1] This new paragraph is not yet in force: see the Serious Crime Act 2007, s. 94(1).

(b) is necessary for the purpose of obtaining legal advice, or

(c) is otherwise necessary for the purposes of establishing, exercising or defending legal rights.

6. The transfer is necessary in order to protect the vital interests of the data subject.

7. The transfer is of part of the personal data on a public register and any conditions subject to which the register is open to inspection are complied with by any person to whom the data are or may be disclosed after the transfer.

8. The transfer is made on terms which are of a kind approved by the Commissioner as ensuring adequate safeguards for the rights and freedoms of data subjects.

9. The transfer has been authorised by the Commissioner as being made in such a manner as to ensure adequate safeguards for the rights and freedoms of data subjects.

SCHEDULE 5 THE DATA PROTECTION COMMISSIONER AND THE DATA PROTECTION TRIBUNAL

PART I THE COMMISSIONER

Status and capacity

1.—(1) The corporation sole by the name of the Data Protection Registrar established by the Data Protection Act 1984 shall continue in existence by the name of [the Information Commissioner].

(2) The Commissioner and his officers and staff are not to be regarded as servants or agents of the Crown.

Tenure of office

2.—(1) Subject to the provisions of this paragraph, the Commissioner shall hold office for such term not exceeding five years as may be determined at the time of his appointment.

(2) The Commissioner may be relieved of his office by Her Majesty at his own request.

(3) The Commissioner may be removed from office by Her Majesty in pursuance of an Address from both Houses of Parliament.

(4) The Commissioner shall in any case vacate his office—

(a) on completing the year of service in which he attains the age of sixty-five years, or

(b) if earlier, on completing his fifteenth year of service.

(5) Subject to sub-paragraph (4), a person who ceases to be Commissioner on the expiration of his term of office shall be eligible for re-appointment, but a person may not be re-appointed for a third or subsequent term as Commissioner unless, by reason of special circumstances, the person's re-appointment for such a term is desirable in the public interest.

Salary etc.

3.—(1) There shall be paid—

(a) to the Commissioner such salary, and

(b) to or in respect of the Commissioner such pension,

as may be specified by a resolution of the House of Commons.

(2) A resolution for the purposes of this paragraph may—

(a) specify the salary or pension,

(b) provide that the salary or pension is to be the same as, or calculated on the same basis as, that payable to, or to or in respect of, a person employed in a specified office under, or in a specified capacity in the service of, the Crown, or

(c) specify the salary or pension and provide for it to be increased by reference to such variables as may be specified in the resolution.

(3) A resolution for the purposes of this paragraph may take effect from the date on which it is passed or from any earlier or later date specified in the resolution.

(4) A resolution for the purposes of this paragraph may make different provision in relation to the pension payable to or in respect of different holders of the office of Commissioner.

(5) Any salary or pension payable under this paragraph shall be charged on and issued out of the Consolidated Fund.

(6) In this paragraph "pension" includes an allowance or gratuity and any reference to the payment of a pension includes a reference to the making of payments towards the provision of a pension.

Officers and staff

4.—(1) The Commissioner—

(a) shall appoint a deputy commissioner [or two deputy commissioners], and

(b) may appoint such number of other officers and staff as he may determine.

[(1A) The Commissioner shall, when appointing any second deputy commissioner, specify which of the Commissioner's functions are to be performed, in the circumstances referred to in paragraph 5(1), by each of the deputy commissioners.]

(2) The remuneration and other conditions of service of the persons appointed under this paragraph shall be determined by the Commissioner.

(3) The Commissioner may pay such pensions, allowances or gratuities to or in respect of the persons appointed under this paragraph, or make such payments towards the provisions of such pensions, allowances or gratuities, as he may determine.

(4) The references in sub-paragraph (3) to pensions, allowances or gratuities to or in respect of the persons appointed under this paragraph include references to pensions, allowances or gratuities by way of compensation to or in respect of any of those persons who suffer loss of office or employment.

(5) Any determination under sub-paragraph (1)(b), (2) or (3) shall require the approval of the [Secretary of State].

(6) The Employers' Liability (Compulsory Insurance) Act 1969 shall not require insurance to be effected by the Commissioner.

5.—(1) The deputy commissioner [or deputy commissioners] shall perform the functions conferred by this Act [or the Freedom of Information Act 2000] on the Commissioner during any vacancy in that office or at any time when the Commissioner is for any reason unable to act.

(2) Without prejudice to sub-paragraph (1), any functions of the Commissioner under this Act [or the Freedom of Information Act 2000] may, to the extent authorised by him, be performed by any of his officers or staff.

Authentication of seal of the Commissioner

6. The application of the seal of the Commissioner shall be authenticated by his signature or by the signature of some other person authorised for the purpose.

Presumption of authenticity of documents issued by the Commissioner

7. Any document purporting to be an instrument issued by the Commissioner and to be duly executed under the Commissioner's seal or to be signed by or on behalf of the Commissioner shall be received in evidence and shall be deemed to be such an instrument unless the contrary is shown.

Money

8. The [Secretary of State] may make payments to the Commissioner out of money provided by Parliament.

9.—(1) All fees and other sums received by the Commissioner in the exercise of his functions under this Act [, under section 159 of the Consumer Credit Act 1974 or under the Freedom of Information Act 2000] shall be paid by him to the [Secretary of State].

(2) Sub-paragraph (1) shall not apply where the [Secretary of State], with the consent of the Treasury, otherwise directs.

(3) Any sums received by the [Secretary of State] under sub-paragraph (1) shall be paid into the Consolidated Fund.

Accounts

10.—(1) It shall be the duty of the Commissioner—

(a) to keep proper accounts and other records in relation to the accounts,

(b) to prepare in respect of each financial year a statement of account in such form as the [Secretary of State] may direct, and

(c) to send copies of that statement to the Comptroller and Auditor General on or before 31st August next following the end of the year to which the statement relates or on or before such earlier date after the end of that year as the Treasury may direct.

(2) The Comptroller and Auditor General shall examine and certify any statement sent to him under this paragraph and lay copies of it together with his report thereon before each House of Parliament.

(3) In this paragraph "financial year" means a period of twelve months beginning with 1st April.

Application of Part I in Scotland

11. Paragraphs 1(1), 6 and 7 do not extend to Scotland.

PART II THE TRIBUNAL

Tenure of office

12.—(1) Subject to the following provisions of this paragraph, a member of the Tribunal shall hold and vacate his office in accordance with the terms of his appointment and shall, on ceasing to hold office, be eligible for re-appointment.

(2) Any member of the Tribunal may at any time resign his office by notice in writing to the Lord Chancellor [(in the case of the chairman or a deputy chairman) or to the Secretary of State (in the case of any other member)].

(3) A person who is the chairman or deputy chairman of the Tribunal shall vacate his office on the day on which he attains the age of seventy years; but this sub-paragraph is subject to section 26(4) to (6) of the Judicial Pensions and Retirement Act 1993 (power to authorise continuance in office up to the age of seventy-five years).

Salary etc.

13. The [Secretary of State] shall pay to the members of the Tribunal out of money provided by Parliament such remuneration and allowances as he may determine.

Officers and staff

14. The [Secretary of State] may provide the Tribunal with such officers and staff as he thinks necessary for the proper discharge of its functions.

Expenses

15. Such expenses of the Tribunal as the [Secretary of State] may determine shall be defrayed by the [Secretary of State] out of money provided by Parliament.

. . .

SCHEDULE 6 APPEAL PROCEEDINGS

Hearing of appeals

1. For the purpose of hearing and determining appeals or any matter preliminary or incidental to an appeal the Tribunal shall sit at such times and in such places as the chairman or a deputy chairman may direct and may sit in two or more divisions.

Constitution of Tribunal in national security cases

2.—(1) The Lord Chancellor shall from time to time designate, from among the chairman and deputy chairman appointed by him under section 6(4)(a) and (b), those persons who are to be capable of hearing appeals under section 28(4) or (6) [or under section 60(1) or (4) of the Freedom of Information Act 2000].

(2) A designation under sub-paragraph (1) may at any time be revoked by the Lord Chancellor.

[(3) The Lord Chancellor may make, or revoke, a designation under this paragraph only with the concurrence of all of the following—

    (a) the Lord Chief Justice;

    (b) the Lord President of the Court of Session;

    (c) the Lord Chief Justice of Northern Ireland.

(4) The Lord Chief Justice of England and Wales may nominate a judicial office holder (as defined in section 109(4) of the Constitutional Reform Act 2005) to exercise his functions under sub-paragraph (3) so far as they relate to a designation under this paragraph.

(5) The Lord President of the Court of Session may nominate a judge of the Court of Session who is a member of the First or Second Division of the Inner House of that Court to exercise his functions under sub-paragraph (3) so far as they relate to a designation under this paragraph.

(6) The Lord Chief Justice of Northern Ireland may nominate any of the following to exercise his functions under sub-paragraph (3) so far as they relate to a designation under this paragraph—

    (a) the holder of one of the offices listed in Schedule 1 to the Justice (Northern Ireland) Act 2002;

    (b) a Lord Justice of Appeal (as defined in section 88 of that Act).[1]]

[3.—(1) The Tribunal shall be duly constituted—

    (a) for an appeal under section 28(4) or (6) in any case where the application of paragraph 6(1) is excluded by rules under paragraph 7, or

    (b) for an appeal under section 60(1) or (4) of the Freedom of Information Act 2000,

if it consists of three of the persons designated under paragraph 2(1), of whom one shall be designated by the Lord Chancellor to preside.

(2) The Lord Chancellor may designate a person to preside under this paragraph only with the concurrence of all of the following—

    (a) the Lord Chief Justice of England and Wales;

    (b) the Lord President of the Court of Session;

    (c) the Lord Chief Justice of Northern Ireland.

(3) The Lord Chief Justice of England and Wales may nominate a judicial office holder (as defined in section 109(4) of the Constitutional Reform Act 2005) to exercise his functions under this paragraph.

(4) The Lord President of the Court of Session may nominate a judge of the Court of Session who is a member of the First or Second Division of the Inner House of that Court to exercise his functions under this paragraph.

(5) The Lord Chief Justice of Northern Ireland may nominate any of the following to exercise his functions under this paragraph—

    (a) the holder of one of the offices listed in Schedule 1 to the Justice (Northern Ireland) Act 2002;

    (b) a Lord Justice of Appeal (as defined in section 88 of that Act).[1]]

Constitution of Tribunal in other cases

4.—(1) Subject to any rules made under paragraph 7, the Tribunal shall be duly constituted for an appeal under section 48(1), (2) or (4) if it consists of—

    (a) the chairman or a deputy chairman (who shall preside), and

---

[1] These amendments and those in para. 4 take effect when so appointed under Constitutional Reform Act 2005, s. 148(1).

(b) an equal number of the members appointed respectively in accordance with paragraphs (a) and (b) of section 6(6).

[(1A) Subject to any rules made under paragraph 7, the Tribunal shall be duly constituted for an appeal under section 57(1) or (2) of the Freedom of Information Act 2000 if it consists of—

(a) the chairman or a deputy chairman (who shall preside), and

(b) an equal number of the members appointed respectively in accordance with paragraphs (aa) and (bb) of section 6(6).]

(2) The members who are to constitute the Tribunal in accordance with sub-paragraph (1) [or (1A)] shall be nominated by the chairman or, if he is for any reason unable to act, by a deputy chairman.*

Determination of questions by full Tribunal

5. The determination of any question before the Tribunal when constituted in accordance with paragraph 3 or 4 shall be according to the opinion of the majority of the members hearing the appeal.

Ex parte proceedings

6.—(1) Subject to any rules made under paragraph 7, the jurisdiction of the Tribunal in respect of an appeal under section 28(4) or (6) shall be exercised ex parte by one or more persons designated under paragraph 2(1).

(2) Subject to any rules made under paragraph 7, the jurisdiction of the Tribunal in respect of an appeal under section 48(3) shall be exercised ex parte by the chairman or a deputy chairman sitting alone.

Rules of procedure

7. (1) The [Secretary of State] may make rules for [regulating—

(a) the exercise of the rights of appeal conferred—

    (i) by sections 28(4) and (6) and 48, and

    (ii) by sections 57(1) and (2) and section 60(1) and (4) of the Freedom of Information Act 2000, and

(b) the practice and procedure of the Tribunal].

(2) Rules under this paragraph may in particular make provision—

(a) with respect to the period within which an appeal can be brought and the burden of proof on an appeal,

[(aa) for the joinder of any other person as a party to any proceedings on an appeal under the Freedom of Information Act 2000,

(ab) for the hearing of an appeal under this Act with an appeal under the Freedom of Information Act 2000,]

(b) for the summoning (or, in Scotland, citation) of witnesses and the administration of oaths,

(c) for securing the production of documents and material used for the processing of personal data,

(d) for the inspection, examination, operation and testing of any equipment or material used in connection with the processing of personal data,

(e) for the hearing of an appeal wholly or partly in camera,

(f) for hearing an appeal in the absence of the appellant or for determining an appeal without a hearing,

(g) for enabling an appeal under section 48(1) against an information notice to be determined by the chairman or a deputy chairman,

(h) for enabling any matter preliminary or incidental to an appeal to be dealt with by the chairman or a deputy chairman,

(i) for the awarding of costs or, in Scotland, expenses,

(j) for the publication of reports of the Tribunal's decisions, and

(k) for conferring on the Tribunal such ancillary powers as the Secretary of State thinks necessary for the proper discharge of its functions.

(3) In making rules under this paragraph which relate to appeals under section 28(4) or (6) the Secretary of State shall have regard, in particular, to the need to secure that information is not disclosed contrary to the public interest.

Obstruction etc.

8.—(1) If any person is guilty of any act or omission in relation to proceedings before the Tribunal which, if those proceedings were proceedings before a court having power to commit for contempt, would constitute contempt of court, the Tribunal may certify the offence to the High Court or, in Scotland, the Court of Session.

(2) Where an offence is so certified, the court may inquire into the matter and, after hearing any witness who may be produced against or on behalf of the person charged with the offence, and after hearing any statement that may be offered in defence, deal with him in any manner in which it could deal with him if he had committed the like offence in relation to the court.

SCHEDULE 7 MISCELLANEOUS EXEMPTIONS

Confidential references given by the data controller

1. Personal data are exempt from section 7 if they consist of a reference given or to be given in confidence by the data controller for the purposes of—

(a) the education, training or employment, or prospective education, training or employment, of the data subject,

(b) the appointment, or prospective appointment, of the data subject to any office, or

(c) the provision, or prospective provision, by the data subject of any service.

Armed forces

2. Personal data are exempt from the subject information provisions in any case to the extent to which the application of those provisions would be likely to prejudice the combat effectiveness of any of the armed forces of the Crown.

Judicial appointments and honours

3. Personal data processed for the purposes of—

(a) assessing any person's suitability for judicial office or the office of Queen's Counsel, or

(b) the conferring by the Crown of any honour [or dignity],

are exempt from the subject information provisions.

4. [(1)] The [Secretary of State] may by order exempt from the subject information provisions personal data processed for the purposes of assessing any person's suitability for—

(a) employment by or under the Crown, or

(b) any office to which appointments are made by Her Majesty, by a Minister of the Crown or by a [Northern Ireland authority].

[(2) In this paragraph "Northern Ireland authority" means the First Minister, the deputy First Minister, a Northern Ireland Minister or a Northern Ireland department.]

Management forecasts etc.

5. Personal data processed for the purposes of management forecasting or management planning to assist the data controller in the conduct of any business or other activity are exempt from the subject information provisions in any case to the extent to which the application of those provisions would be likely to prejudice the conduct of that business or other activity.

Corporate finance

6.—(1) Where personal data are processed for the purposes of, or in connection with, a corporate finance service provided by a relevant person—

    (a) the data are exempt from the subject information provisions in any case to the extent to which either—

        (i) the application of those provisions to the data could affect the price of any instrument which is already in existence or is to be or may be created, or

        (ii) the data controller reasonably believes that the application of those provisions to the data could affect the price of any such instrument, and

    (b) to the extent that the data are not exempt from the subject information provisions by virtue of paragraph (a), they are exempt from those provisions if the exemption is required for the purpose of safeguarding an important economic or financial interest of the United Kingdom.

(2) For the purposes of sub-paragraph (1)(b) the [Secretary of State] may by order specify—

    (a) matters to be taken into account in determining whether exemption from the subject information provisions is required for the purpose of safeguarding an important economic or financial interest of the United Kingdom, or

    (b) circumstances in which exemption from those provisions is, or is not, to be taken to be required for that purpose.

(3) In this paragraph—

"corporate finance service" means a service consisting in—

    (a) underwriting in respect of issues of, or the placing of issues of, any instrument,

    (b) advice to undertakings on capital structure, industrial strategy and related matters and advice and service relating to mergers and the purchase of undertakings, or

    (c) services relating to such underwriting as is mentioned in paragraph (a);

"instrument" means any instrument listed in [section C of Annex I to Directive 2004/39/EC of the European Parliament and of the Council of 21 April 2004 on markets in financial instruments];

"price" includes value;

"relevant person" means—

    [(a) any person who, by reason of any permission he has under Part IV of the Financial Services and Markets Act 2000, is able to carry on a corporate finance service without contravening the general prohibition, within the meaning of section 19 of that Act;

    (b) an EEA firm of the kind mentioned in paragraph 5(a) or (b) of Schedule 3 to that Act which has qualified for authorisation under paragraph 12 of that Schedule, and may lawfully carry on a corporate finance service;

    (c) any person who is exempt from the general prohibition in respect of any corporate finance service—

        (i) as a result of an exemption order made under section 38(1) of that Act, or

        (ii) by reason of section 39(1) of that Act (appointed representatives);

    (cc) any person, not falling within paragraph (a), (b) or (c) who may lawfully carry on a corporate finance service without contravening the general prohibition;]

    (d) any person who, in the course of his employment, provides to his employer a service falling within paragraph (b) or (c) of the definition of "corporate finance service", or

    (e) any partner who provides to other partners in the partnership a service falling within either of those paragraphs.

Negotiations

7. Personal data which consist of records of the intentions of the data controller in relation to any negotiations with the data subject are exempt from the subject information provisions in any case to the extent to which the application of those provisions would be likely to prejudice those negotiations.

Examination marks

8.—(1) Section 7 shall have effect subject to the provisions of sub-paragraphs (2) to (4) in the case of personal data consisting of marks or other information processed by a data controller—

(a) for the purpose of determining the results of an academic, professional or other examination or of enabling the results of any such examination to be determined, or

(b) in consequence of the determination of any such results.

(2) Where the relevant day falls before the day on which the results of the examination are announced, the period mentioned in section 7(8) shall be extended until—

(a) the end of five months beginning with the relevant day, or

(b) the end of forty days beginning with the date of the announcement,

whichever is the earlier.

(3) Where by virtue of sub-paragraph (2) a period longer than the prescribed period elapses after the relevant day before the request is complied with, the information to be supplied pursuant to the request shall be supplied both by reference to the data in question at the time when the request is received and (if different) by reference to the data as from time to time held in the period beginning when the request is received and ending when it is complied with.

(4) For the purposes of this paragraph the results of an examination shall be treated as announced when they are first published or (if not published) when they are first made available or communicated to the candidate in question.

(5) In this paragraph—

"examination" includes any process for determining the knowledge, intelligence, skill or ability of a candidate by reference to his performance in any test, work or other activity;

"the prescribed period" means forty days or such other period as is for the time being prescribed under section 7 in relation to the personal data in question;

"relevant day" has the same meaning as in section 7.

Examination scripts etc.

9.—(1) Personal data consisting of information recorded by candidates during an academic, professional or other examination are exempt from section 7.

(2) In this paragraph "examination" has the same meaning as in paragraph 8.

Legal professional privilege

10. Personal data are exempt from the subject information provisions if the data consist of information in respect of which a claim to legal professional privilege [or, in Scotland, to confidentiality of communications], could be maintained in legal proceedings.

Self-incrimination

11.—(1) A person need not comply with any request or order under section 7 to the extent that compliance would, by revealing evidence of the commission of any offence other than an offence under this Act, expose him to proceedings for that offence.

(2) Information disclosed by any person in compliance with any request or order under section 7 shall not be admissible against him in proceedings for an offence under this Act.

SCHEDULE 8 TRANSITIONAL RELIEF

PART I INTERPRETATION OF SCHEDULE

1.—(1) For the purposes of this Schedule, personal data are "eligible data" at any time if, and to the extent that, they are at that time subject to processing which was already under way immediately before 24th October 1998.

(2) In this Schedule—

"eligible automated data" means eligible data which fall within paragraph (a) or (b) of the definition of "data" in section 1(1);

"eligible manual data" means eligible data which are not eligible automated data;

"the first transitional period" means the period beginning with the commencement of this Schedule and ending with 23rd October 2001;

"the second transitional period" means the period beginning with 24th October 2001 and ending with 23rd October 2007.

PART II EXEMPTIONS AVAILABLE BEFORE 24TH OCTOBER 2001

Manual data

2.—(1) Eligible manual data, other than data forming part of an accessible record, are exempt from the data protection principles and Parts II and III of this Act during the first transitional period.

(2) This paragraph does not apply to eligible manual data to which paragraph 4 applies.

3.—(1) This paragraph applies to—

    (a) eligible manual data forming part of an accessible record, and

    (b) personal data which fall within paragraph (d) of the definition of "data" in section 1(1) but which, because they are not subject to processing which was already under way immediately before 24th October 1998, are not eligible data for the purposes of this Schedule.

(2) During the first transitional period, data to which this paragraph applies are exempt from—

    (a) the data protection principles, except the sixth principle so far as relating to sections 7 and 12A,

    (b) Part II of this Act, except—

        (i) section 7 (as it has effect subject to section 8) and section 12A, and

        (ii) section 15 so far as relating to those sections, and

    (c) Part III of this Act.

4.—(1) This paragraph applies to eligible manual data which consist of information relevant to the financial standing of the data subject and in respect of which the data controller is a credit reference agency.

(2) During the first transitional period, data to which this paragraph applies are exempt from—

    (a) the data protection principles, except the sixth principle so far as relating to section 7 and 12A,

    (b) Part II of this Act, except—

        (i) section 7 (as it has effect subject to section 8 and 9) and section 12A, and

        (ii) section 15 so far as relating to those sections, and

    (c) Part III of this Act.

Processing otherwise than by reference to the data subject

5. During the first transitional period, for the purposes of this Act (apart from paragraph 1), eligible automated data are not to be regarded as being "processed" unless the processing is by reference to the data subject.

Payrolls and accounts

6.—(1) Subject to sub-paragraph (2), eligible automated data processed by a data controller for one or more of the following purposes—

    (a) calculating amounts payable by way of remuneration or pensions in respect of service in any employment or office or making payments of, or of sums deducted from, such remuneration or pensions, or

(b) keeping accounts relating to any business or other activity carried on by the data controller or keeping records of purchases, sales or other transactions for the purpose of ensuring that the requisite payments are made by or to him in respect of those transactions or for the purpose of making financial or management forecasts to assist him in the conduct of any such business or activity,

are exempt from the data protection principles and Parts II and III of this Act during the first transitional period.

(2) It shall be a condition of the exemption of any eligible automated data under this paragraph that the data are not processed for any other purpose, but the exemption is not lost by any processing of the eligible data for any other purpose if the data controller shows that he had taken such care to prevent it as in all the circumstances was reasonably required.

(3) Data processed only for one or more of the purposes mentioned in sub-paragraph (1)(a) may be disclosed—

    (a) to any person, other than the data controller, by whom the remuneration or pensions in question are payable,

    (b) for the purpose of obtaining actuarial advice,

    (c) for the purpose of giving information as to the persons in any employment or office for use in medical research into the health of, or injuries suffered by, persons engaged in particular occupations or working in particular places or areas,

    (d) if the data subject (or a person acting on his behalf) has requested or consented to the disclosure of the data either generally or in the circumstances in which the disclosure in question is made, or

    (e) if the person making the disclosure has reasonable grounds for believing that the disclosure falls within paragraph (d).

(4) Data processed for any of the purposes mentioned in sub-paragraph (1) may be disclosed—

    (a) for the purpose of audit or where the disclosure is for the purpose only of giving information about the data controller's financial affairs, or

    (b) in any case in which disclosure would be permitted by any other provision of this Part of this Act if sub-paragraph (2) were included among the non-disclosure provisions.

(5) In this paragraph "remuneration" includes remuneration in kind and "pensions" includes gratuities or similar benefits.

Unincorporated members' clubs and mailing lists

7. Eligible automated data processed by an unincorporated members' club and relating only to the members of the club are exempt from the data protection principles and Parts II and III of this Act during the first transitional period.

8. Eligible automated data processed by a data controller only for the purposes of distributing, or recording the distribution of, articles or information to the data subjects and consisting only of their names, addresses or other particulars necessary for effecting the distribution, are exempt from the data protection principles and Parts II and III of this Act during the first transitional period.

9. Neither paragraph 7 nor paragraph 8 applies to personal data relating to any data subject unless he has been asked by the club or data controller whether he objects to the data relating to him being processed as mentioned in that paragraph and has not objected.

10. It shall be a condition of the exemption of any data under paragraph 7 that the data are not disclosed except as permitted by paragraph 11 and of the exemption under paragraph 8 that the data are not processed for any purpose other than that mentioned in that paragraph or as permitted by paragraph 11, but—

    (a) the exemption under paragraph 7 shall not be lost by any disclosure in breach of that condition, and

    (b) the exemption under paragraph 8 shall not be lost by any processing in breach of that condition,

if the data controller shows that he had taken such care to prevent it as in all the circumstances was reasonably required.

11. Data to which paragraph 10 applies may be disclosed—

    (a) if the data subject (or a person acting on his behalf) has requested or consented to the disclosure of the data either generally or in the circumstances in which the disclosure in question is made,

    (b) if the person making the disclosure has reasonable grounds for believing that the disclosure falls within paragraph (a), or

    (c) in any case in which disclosure would be permitted by any other provision of this Part of this Act if paragraph 10 were included among the non-disclosure provisions.

Back-up data

12. Eligible automated data which are processed only for the purpose of replacing other data in the event of the latter being lost, destroyed or impaired are exempt from section 7 during the first transitional period.

Exemption of all eligible automated data from certain requirements

13.—(1) During the first transitional period, eligible automated data are exempt from the following provisions—

    (a) the first data protection principle to the extent to which it requires compliance with—

        (i) paragraph 2 of Part II of Schedule 1,

        (ii) the conditions in Schedule 2, and

        (iii) the conditions in Schedule 3,

    (b) the seventh data protection principle to the extent to which it requires compliance with paragraph 12 of Part II of Schedule 1;

    (c) the eighth data protection principle,

    (d) in section 7(1), paragraphs (b), (c)(ii) and (d),

    (e) sections 10 and 11,

    (f) section 12, and

    (g) section 13, except so far as relating to—

        (i) any contravention of the fourth data protection principle,

        (ii) any disclosure without the consent of the data controller,

        (iii) loss or destruction of data without the consent of the data controller, or

        (iv) processing for the special purposes.

  (2) The specific exemptions conferred by sub-paragraph (1)(a), (c) and (e) do not limit the data controller's general duty under the first data protection principle to ensure that processing is fair.

PART III EXEMPTIONS AVAILABLE AFTER 23RD OCTOBER 2001 BUT BEFORE 24TH OCTOBER 2007

14.—(1) This paragraph applies to—

    (a) eligible manual data which were held immediately before 24th October 1998, and

    (b) personal data which fall within paragraph (d) of the definition of "data" in section 1(1) but do not fall within paragraph (a) of this sub-paragraph,

but does not apply to eligible manual data to which the exemption in paragraph 16 applies.

  (2) During the second transitional period, data to which this paragraph applies are exempt from the following provisions—

    (a) the first data protection principle except to the extent to which it requires compliance with paragraph 2 of Part II of Schedule 1,

    (b) the second, third, fourth and fifth data protection principles, and

    (c) section 14(1) to (3).

[14A.—(1) This paragraph applies to personal data which fall within paragraph (e) of the definition of "data" in section 1(1) and do not fall within paragraph 14(1)(a), but does not apply to eligible manual data to which the exemption in paragraph 16 applies.

(2) During the second transitional period, data to which this paragraph applies are exempt from—

(a) the fourth data protection principle, and

(b) section 14(1) to (3).]

PART IV EXEMPTIONS AFTER 23RD OCTOBER 2001 FOR HISTORICAL RESEARCH

15. In this Part of this Schedule "the relevant conditions" has the same meaning as in section 33.

16.—(1) Eligible manual data which are processed only for the purpose of historical research in compliance with the relevant conditions are exempt from the provisions specified in sub-paragraph (2) after 23rd October 2001.

(2) The provisions referred to in sub-paragraph (1) are—

(a) the first data protection principle except in so far as it requires compliance with paragraph 2 of Part II of Schedule 1,

(b) the second, third, fourth and fifth data protection principles, and

(c) section 14(1) to (3).

17.—(1) After 23rd October 2001 eligible automated data which are processed only for the purpose of historical research in compliance with the relevant conditions are exempt from the first data protection principle to the extent to which it requires compliance with the conditions in Schedules 2 and 3.

(2) Eligible automated data which are processed—

(a) only for the purpose of historical research,

(b) in compliance with the relevant conditions, and

(c) otherwise than by reference to the data subject,

are also exempt from the provisions referred to in sub-paragraph (3) after 23rd October 2001.

(3) The provisions referred to in sub-paragraph (2) are—

(a) the first data protection principle except in so far as it requires compliance with paragraph 2 of Part II of Schedule 1,

(b) the second, third, fourth and fifth data protection principles, and

(c) section 14(1) to (3).

18. For the purposes of this Part of this Schedule personal data are not to be treated as processed otherwise than for the purpose of historical research merely because the data are disclosed—

(a) to any person, for the purpose of historical research only,

(b) to the data subject or a person acting on his behalf,

(c) at the request, or with the consent, of the data subject or a person acting on his behalf, or

(d) in circumstances in which the person making the disclosure has reasonable grounds for believing that the disclosure falls within paragraph (a), (b) or (c).

PART V EXEMPTION FROM SECTION 22

19. Processing which was already under way immediately before 24th October 1998 is not assessable processing for the purposes of section 22.

SCHEDULE 9 POWERS OF ENTRY AND INSPECTION

Issue of warrants

1.—(1) If a circuit judge [or a District Judge (Magistrates' Courts)[1]] is satisfied by information on oath supplied by the Commissioner that there are reasonable grounds for suspecting—

(a) that a data controller has contravened or is contravening any of the data protection principles, or

(b) that an offence under this Act has been or is being committed,

---

[1] Amendment not yet in force: see Courts Act 2003, s. 110(1).

and that evidence of the contravention or of the commission of the offence is to be found on any premises specified in the information, he may, subject to sub-paragraph (2) and paragraph 2, grant a warrant to the Commissioner.

(2) A judge shall not issue a warrant under this Schedule in respect of any personal data processed for the special purposes unless a determination by the Commissioner under section 45 with respect to those data has taken effect.

(3) A warrant issued under sub-paragraph (1) shall authorise the Commissioner or any of his officers or staff at any time within seven days of the date of the warrant to enter the premises, to search them, to inspect, examine, operate and test any equipment found there which is used or intended to be used for the processing of personal data and to inspect and seize any documents or other material found there which may be such evidence as is mentioned in that sub-paragraph.

2.—(1) A judge shall not issue a warrant under this Schedule unless he is satisfied—

(a) that the Commissioner has given seven days notice in writing to the occupier of the premises in question demanding access to the premises, and

(b) that either—

(i) access was demanded at a reasonable hour and was unreasonably refused,

or

(ii) although entry to the premises was granted, the occupier unreasonably refused to comply with a request by the Commissioner or any of the Commissioner's officers or staff to permit the Commissioner or the officer or member of staff to do any of the things referred to in paragraph 1(3), and

(c) that the occupier, has, after the refusal, been notified by the Commissioner of the application for the warrant and has had an opportunity of being heard by the judge on the question whether or not it should be issued.

(2) Sub-paragraph (1) shall not apply if the judge is satisfied that the case is one of urgency or that compliance with those provisions would defeat the object of the entry.

3. A judge who issues a warrant under this Schedule shall also issue two copies of it and certify them clearly as copies.

Execution of warrants

4. A person executing a warrant issued under this Schedule may use such reasonable force as may be necessary.

5. A warrant issued under this Schedule shall be executed at a reasonable hour unless it appears to the person executing it that there are grounds for suspecting that the evidence in question would not be found if it were so executed.

6. If the person who occupies the premises in respect of which a warrant is issued under this Schedule is present when the warrant is executed, he shall be shown the warrant and supplied with a copy of it; and if that person is not present a copy of the warrant shall be left in a prominent place on the premises.

7.—(1) A person seizing anything in pursuance of a warrant under this Schedule shall give a receipt for it if asked to do so.

(2) Anything so seized may be retained for so long as is necessary in all the circumstances but the person in occupation of the premises in question shall be given a copy of anything that is seized if he so requests and the person executing the warrant considers that it can be done without undue delay.

Matters exempt from inspection and seizure

8. The powers of inspection and seizure conferred by a warrant issued under this Schedule shall not be exercisable in respect of personal data which by virtue of section 28 are exempt from any of the provisions of this Act.

9.—(1) Subject to the provisions of this paragraph, the powers of inspection and seizure conferred by a warrant issued under this Schedule shall not be exercisable in respect of—

(a) any communication between a professional legal adviser and his client in connection with the giving of legal advice to the client with respect to his obligations, liabilities or rights under this Act, or

(b) any communication between a professional legal adviser and his client, or between such an adviser or his client and any other person, made in connection with or in contemplation of proceedings under or arising out of this Act (including proceedings before the Tribunal) and for the purposes of such proceedings.

(2) Sub-paragraph (1) applies also to—

(a) any copy or other record of any such communication as is there mentioned, and

(b) any document or article enclosed with or referred to in any such communication if made in connection with the giving of any advice or, as the case may be, in connection with or in contemplation of and for the purposes of such proceedings as are there mentioned.

(3) This paragraph does not apply to anything in the possession of any person other than the professional legal adviser or his client or to anything held with the intention of furthering a criminal purpose.

(4) In this paragraph references to the client of a professional legal adviser include references to any person representing such a client.

10. If the person in occupation of any premises in respect of which a warrant is issued under this Schedule objects to the inspection or seizure under the warrant of any material on the grounds that it consists partly of matters in respect of which those powers are not exercisable, he shall, if the person executing the warrant so requests, furnish that person with a copy of so much of the material as is not exempt from those powers.

Return of warrants

11. A warrant issued under this Schedule shall be returned to the court from which it was issued—

(a) after being executed, or

(b) if not executed within the time authorised for its execution;

and the person by whom any such warrant is executed shall make an endorsement on it stating what powers have been exercised by him under the warrant.

Offences

12. Any person who—

(a) intentionally obstructs a person in the execution of a warrant issued under this Schedule, or

(b) fails without reasonable excuse to give any person executing such a warrant such assistance as he may reasonably require for the execution of the warrant,

is guilty of an offence.

Vessels, vehicles etc.

13. In this Schedule "premises" includes any vessel, vehicle, aircraft or hovercraft, and references to the occupier of any premises include references to the person in charge of any vessel, vehicle, aircraft or hovercraft.

Scotland and Northern Ireland

14. In the application of this Schedule to Scotland—

(a) for any reference to a circuit judge there is substituted a reference to the sheriff,

(b) for any reference to information on oath there is substituted a reference to evidence on oath, and

(c) for the reference to the court from which the warrant was issued there is substituted a reference to the sheriff clerk.

15. In the application of this Schedule to Northern Ireland—

(a) for any reference to a circuit judge there is substituted a reference to a county court judge, and

(b) for any reference to information on oath there is substituted a reference to a complaint on oath.

SCHEDULE 10 FURTHER PROVISIONS RELATING TO ASSISTANCE UNDER SECTION 53

1. In this Schedule "applicant" and "proceedings" have the same meaning as in section 53.

2. The assistance provided under section 53 may include the making of arrangements for, or for the Commissioner to bear the costs of—

    (a) the giving of advice or assistance by a solicitor or counsel, and

    (b) the representation of the applicant, or the provision to him of such assistance as is usually given by a solicitor or counsel—

        (i) in steps preliminary or incidental to the proceedings, or

        (ii) in arriving at or giving effect to a compromise to avoid or bring an end to the proceedings.

3. Where assistance is provided with respect to the conduct of proceedings—

    (a) it shall include an agreement by the Commissioner to indemnify the applicant (subject only to any exceptions specified in the notification) in respect of any liability to pay costs or expenses arising by virtue of any judgment or order of the court in the proceedings,

    (b) it may include an agreement by the Commissioner to indemnify the applicant in respect of any liability to pay costs or expenses arising by virtue of any compromise or settlement arrived at in order to avoid the proceedings or bring the proceedings to an end, and

    (c) it may include an agreement by the Commissioner to indemnify the applicant in respect of any liability to pay damages pursuant to an undertaking given on the grant of interlocutory relief (in Scotland, an interim order) to the applicant.

4. Where the Commissioner provides assistance in relation to any proceedings, he shall do so on such terms, or make such other arrangements, as will secure that a person against whom the proceedings have been or are commenced is informed that assistance has been or is being provided by the Commissioner in relation to them.

5. In England and Wales or Northern Ireland, the recovery of expenses incurred by the Commissioner in providing an applicant with assistance (as taxed or assessed in such manner as may be prescribed by rules of court) shall constitute a first charge for the benefit of the Commissioner—

    (a) on any costs which, by virtue of any judgment or order of the court, are payable to the applicant by any other person in respect of the matter in connection with which the assistance is provided, and

    (b) on any sum payable to the applicant under a compromise or settlement arrived at in connection with that matter to avoid or bring to an end any proceedings.

6. In Scotland, the recovery of such expenses (as taxed or assessed in such manner as may be prescribed by rules of court) shall be paid to the Commissioner, in priority to other debts—

    (a) out of any expenses which, by virtue of any judgment or order of the court, are payable to the applicant by any other person in respect of the matter in connection with which the assistance is provided, and

    (b) out of any sum payable to the applicant under a compromise or settlement arrived at in connection with that matter to avoid or bring to an end any proceedings.

SCHEDULE 11 EDUCATIONAL RECORDS

Meaning of "educational record"

1. For the purposes of section 68 "educational record" means any record to which paragraph 2, 5 or 7 applies.

England and Wales

2. This paragraph applies to any record of information which—

    (a) is processed by or on behalf of the governing body of, or a teacher at, any school in England and Wales specified in paragraph 3,

(b) relates to any person who is or has been a pupil at the school, and

(c) originated from or was supplied by or on behalf of any of the persons specified in paragraph 4,

other than information which is processed by a teacher solely for the teacher's own use.

3. The schools referred to in paragraph 2(a) are—

(a) a school maintained by a local education authority, and

(b) a special school, as defined by section 6(2) of the Education Act 1996, which is not so maintained.

4. The persons referred to in paragraph 2(c) are—

(a) an employee of the local education authority which maintains the school,

(b) in the case of—

(i) a voluntary aided, foundation or foundation special school (within the meaning of the School Standards and Framework Act 1998), or

(ii) a special school which is not maintained by a local education authority,

a teacher or other employee at the school (including an educational psychologist engaged by the Governing body under a contract for services),

(c) the pupil to whom the record relates, and

(d) a parent, as defined by section 576(1) of the Education Act 1996, of that pupil.

Scotland

5. This paragraph applies to any record of information which is processed—

(a) by an education authority in Scotland, and

(b) for the purpose of the relevant function of the authority,

other than information which is processed by a teacher solely for the teacher's own use.

6. For the purposes of paragraph 5—

(a) "education authority" means an education authority within the meaning of the Education (Scotland) Act 1980 ("the 1980 Act") [...]

(b) "the relevant function" means, in relation to each of those authorities, their function under section 1 of the 1980 Act and section 7(1) of the 1989 Act, and

(c) information processed by an education authority is processed for the purpose of the relevant function of the authority if the processing relates to the discharge of that function in respect of a person—

(i) who is or has been a pupil in a school provided by the authority, or

(ii) who receives, or has received, further education (within the meaning of the 1980 Act) so provided.

Northern Ireland

7.—(1) This paragraph applies to any record of information which—

(a) is processed by or on behalf of the Board of Governors of, or a teacher at, any grant-aided school in Northern Ireland,

(b) relates to any person who is or has been a pupil at the school, and

(c) originated from or was supplied by or on behalf of any of the persons specified in paragraph 8,

other than information which is processed by a teacher solely for the teacher's own use.

(2) In sub-paragraph (1) "grant-aided school" has the same meaning as in the Education and Libraries (Northern Ireland) Order 1986.

8. The persons referred to in paragraph 7(1) are—

(a) a teacher at the school,

(b) an employee of an education and library board, other than such a teacher,

(c) the pupil to whom the record relates, and

(d) a parent (as defined by Article 2(2) of the Education and Libraries (Northern Ireland) Order 1986) of that pupil.

England and Wales: transitory provisions

9.—(1) Until the appointed day within the meaning of section 20 of the School Standards and Framework Act 1998, this Schedule shall have effect subject to the following modifications.

(2) Paragraph 3 shall have effect as if for paragraph (b) and the "and" immediately preceding it there were substituted—

"(aa) a grant-maintained school, as defined by section 183(1) of the Education Act 1996,

(ab) a grant-maintained special school, as defined by section 337(4) of that Act, and

(b) a special school, as defined by section 6(2) of that Act, which is neither a maintained special school, as defined by section 337(3) of that Act, nor a grant-maintained special school."

(3) Paragraph 4(b)(i) shall have effect as if for the words from "foundation", in the first place where it occurs, to "1998)" there were substituted "or grant-maintained school".

SCHEDULE 12[1] ACCESSIBLE PUBLIC RECORDS

Meaning of "accessible public record"

1. For the purposes of section 68 "accessible public record" means any record which is kept by an authority specified—

(a) as respects England and Wales, in the Table in paragraph 2,

(b) as respects Scotland, in the Table in paragraph 4, or

(c) as respects Northern Ireland, in the Table in paragraph 6,

and is a record of information of a description specified in that Table in relation to that authority.

Housing and social services records: England and Wales

2. The following is the Table referred to in paragraph 1(a).

Table of authorities and information

The authorities	The accessible information
Housing Act local authority.	Information held for the purpose of any of the authority's tenancies.
Local social services authority.	Information held for any purpose of the authority's social services functions.

3.—(1)The following provisions apply for the interpretation of the Table in paragraph 2.

(2) Any authority which, by virtue of section 4(e) of the Housing Act 1985, is a local authority for the purpose of any provision of that Act is a "Housing Act local authority" for the purposes of this Schedule, and so is any housing action trust established under Part III of the Housing Act 1988.

(3) Information contained in records kept by a Housing Act local authority is "held for the purpose of any of the authority's tenancies" if it is held for any purpose of the relationship of landlord and tenant of a dwelling which subsists, has subsisted or may subsist between the authority and any individual who is, has been or, as the case may be, has applied to be, a tenant of the authority.

(4) Any authority which, by virtue of section 1 or 12 of the Local Authority Social Services Act 1970, is or is treated as a local authority for the purposes of that Act is a "local social services authority" for the purposes of this Schedule; and information contained in records kept by such an authority is "held for any purpose of the authority's social services functions" if it is held for the purpose of any past, current or proposed exercise of such a function in any case.

[1] Deletions from paras 4–5 have yet to be brought into effect: see the Housing (Scotland) Act 2001 a.s.p. 10, ss. 112–113 and sch. 10.

(5) Any expression used in paragraph 2 or this paragraph and in Part II of the Housing Act 1985 or the Local Authority Social Services Act 1970 has the same meaning as in that Act.

Housing and social services records: Scotland

4. The following is the Table referred to in paragraph 1(b).

Table of authorities and information

The authorities	The accessible information
Local authority. Scottish Homes. Social work authority.	Information held for the purpose of any of the body's tenancies.
	Information held for any purpose of the authority's functions under the Social Work (Scotland) Act 1968 and the enactments referred to in section 5(1B) of that Act.

5.—(1)The following provisions apply for the interpretation of the Table in paragraph 4.

(2) "Local authority" means—

(a) a council constituted under section 2 of the Local Government etc. (Scotland) Act 1994,

(b) a joint board or joint committee of two or more of those councils, or

(c) any trust under the control of such a council.

(3) Information contained in records kept by a local authority or Scottish Homes is held for the purpose of any of their tenancies if it is held for any purpose of the relationship of landlord and tenant of a dwelling-house which subsists, has subsisted or may subsist between the authority or, as the case may be, Scottish Homes and any individual who is, has been or, as the case may be, has applied to be a tenant of theirs.

(4) "Social work authority" means a local authority for the purposes of the Social Work (Scotland) Act 1968; and information contained in records kept by such an authority is held for any purpose of their functions if it is held for the purpose of any past, current or proposed exercise of such a function in any case.

Housing and social services records: Northern Ireland

6. The following is the Table referred to in paragraph 1(c).

Table of authorities and information

The authorities	The accessible information
The Northern Ireland Housing Executive.	Information held for the purpose of any of the Executive's tenancies.
A Health and Social Services Board.	Information held for the purpose of any past, current or proposed exercise by the Board of any function exercisable, by virtue of directions under Article 17(1) of the Health and Personal Social Services (Northern Ireland) Order 1972, by the Board on behalf of the Department of Health and Social Services with respect to the administration of personal social services under— (a) the Children and Young Persons Act (Northern Ireland) 1968; (b) the Health and Personal Social Services (Northern Ireland) Order 1972; (c) Article 47 of the Matrimonial Causes (Northern Ireland) Order 1978; (d) Article 11 of the Domestic Proceedings (Northern Ireland) Order 1980;

Cont.

The authorities	The accessible information
	(e) the Adoption (Northern Ireland) Order 1987; or (f) (the Children (Northern Ireland) Order 1995.
An HSS trust.	Information held for the purpose of any past, current or proposed exercise by the trust of any function exercisable, by virtue of an authorisation under Article 3(1) of the Health and Personal Social Services (Northern Ireland) Order 1994, by the trust on behalf of a Health and Social Services Board with respect to the administration of personal social services under any statutory provision mentioned in the last preceding entry.

7.—(1) This paragraph applies for the interpretation of the Table in paragraph 6.

(2) Information contained in records kept by the Northern Ireland Housing Executive is "held for the purpose of any of the Executive's tenancies" if it is held for any purpose of the relationship of landlord and tenant of a dwelling which subsists, has subsisted or may subsist between the Executive and any individual who is, has been or, as the case may be, has applied to be, a tenant of the Executive.

Electronic Communications Act 2000

(2000, c. 7)

An Act to make provision to facilitate the use of electronic communications and electronic data storage; to make provision about the modification of licences granted under section 7 of the Telecommunications Act 1984; and for connected purposes.   [25th May 2000]

[. . .]

PART II FACILITATION OF ELECTRONIC COMMERCE, DATA STORAGE, ETC.

7   Electronic signatures and related certificates

(1) In any legal proceedings—

(a) an electronic signature incorporated into or logically associated with a particular electronic communication or particular electronic data, and

(b) the certification by any person of such a signature,

shall each be admissible in evidence in relation to any question as to the authenticity of the communication or data or as to the integrity of the communication or data.

(2) For the purposes of this section an electronic signature is so much of anything in electronic form as—

(a) is incorporated into or otherwise logically associated with any electronic communication or electronic data; and

(b) purports to be so incorporated or associated for the purpose of being used in establishing the authenticity of the communication or data, the integrity of the communication or data, or both.

(3) For the purposes of this section an electronic signature incorporated into or associated with a particular electronic communication or particular electronic data is certified by any person if that person (whether before or after the making of the communication) has made a statement confirming that—

(a) the signature,

(b) a means of producing, communicating or verifying the signature, or

(c) a procedure applied to the signature,

is (either alone or in combination with other factors) a valid means of establishing the authenticity of the communication or data, the integrity of the communication or data, or both.

8   Power to modify legislation

(1) Subject to subsection (3), the appropriate Minister may by order made by statutory instrument modify the provisions of—

   (a) any enactment or subordinate legislation, or
   (b) any scheme, licence, authorisation or approval issued, granted or given by or under any enactment or subordinate legislation,

in such manner as he may think fit for the purpose of authorising or facilitating the use of electronic communications or electronic storage (instead of other forms of communication or storage) for any purpose mentioned in subsection (2).

(2) Those purposes are—

   (a) the doing of anything which under any such provisions is required to be or may be done or evidenced in writing or otherwise using a document, notice or instrument;
   (b) the doing of anything which under any such provisions is required to be or may be done by post or other specified means of delivery;
   (c) the doing of anything which under any such provisions is required to be or may be authorised by a person's signature or seal, or is required to be delivered as a deed or witnessed;
   (d) the making of any statement or declaration which under any such provisions is required to be made under oath or to be contained in a statutory declaration;
   (e) the keeping, maintenance or preservation, for the purposes or in pursuance of any such provisions, of any account, record, notice, instrument or other document;
   (f) the provision, production or publication under any such provisions of any information or other matter;
   (g) the making of any payment that is required to be or may be made under any such provisions.

(3) The appropriate Minister shall not make an order under this section authorising the use of electronic communications or electronic storage for any purpose, unless he considers that the authorisation is such that the extent (if any) to which records of things done for that purpose will be available will be no less satisfactory in cases where use is made of electronic communications or electronic storage than in other cases.

(4) Without prejudice to the generality of subsection (1), the power to make an order under this section shall include power to make an order containing any of the following provisions—

   (a) provision as to the electronic form to be taken by any electronic communications or electronic storage the use of which is authorised by an order under this section;
   (b) provision imposing conditions subject to which the use of electronic communications or electronic storage is so authorised;
   (c) provision, in relation to cases in which any such conditions are not satisfied, for treating anything for the purposes of which the use of such communications or storage is so authorised as not having been done;
   (d) provision, in connection with anything so authorised, for a person to be able to refuse to accept receipt of something in electronic form except in such circumstances as may be specified in or determined under the order;
   (e) provision, in connection with any use of electronic communications so authorised, for intermediaries to be used, or to be capable of being used, for the transmission of any data or for establishing the authenticity or integrity of any data;
   (f) provision, in connection with any use of electronic storage so authorised, for persons satisfying such conditions as may be specified in or determined under the regulations to carry out functions in relation to the storage;
   (g) provision, in relation to cases in which the use of electronic communications or electronic storage is so authorised, for the determination of any of the matters mentioned in subsection (5), or as to the manner in which they may be proved in legal proceedings;

(h) provision, in relation to cases in which fees or charges are or may be imposed in connection with anything for the purposes of which the use of electronic communications or electronic storage is so authorised, for different fees or charges to apply where use is made of such communications or storage;

(i) provision, in relation to any criminal or other liabilities that may arise (in respect of the making of false or misleading statements or otherwise) in connection with anything for the purposes of which the use of electronic communications or electronic storage is so authorised, for corresponding liabilities to arise in corresponding circumstances where use is made of such communications or storage;

(j) provision requiring persons to prepare and keep records in connection with any use of electronic communications or electronic storage which is so authorised;

(k) provision requiring the production of the contents of any records kept in accordance with an order under this section;

(l) provision for a requirement imposed by virtue of paragraph (j) or (k) to be enforceable at the suit or instance of such person as may be specified in or determined in accordance with the order;

(m) any such provision, in relation to electronic communications or electronic storage the use of which is authorised otherwise than by an order under this section, as corresponds to any provision falling within any of the preceding paragraphs that may be made where it is such an order that authorises the use of the communications or storage.

(5) The matters referred to in subsection (4)(g) are—

(a) whether a thing has been done using an electronic communication or electronic storage;

(b) the time at which, or date on which, a thing done using any such communication or storage was done;

(c) the place where a thing done using such communication or storage was done;

(d) the person by whom such a thing was done; and

(e) the contents, authenticity or integrity of any electronic data.

(6) An order under this section—

(a) shall not (subject to paragraph (b)) require the use of electronic communications or electronic storage for any purpose; but

(b) may make provision that a period of notice specified in the order must expire before effect is given to a variation or withdrawal of an election or other decision which—

(i) has been made for the purposes of such an order; and

(ii) is an election or decision to make use of electronic communications or electronic storage.

(7) The matters in relation to which provision may be made by an order under this section do not include any matter under the care and management of the Commissioners of Inland Revenue or any matter under the care and management of the Commissioners of Customs and Excise.

(8) In this section references to doing anything under the provisions of any enactment include references to doing it under the provisions of any subordinate legislation the power to make which is conferred by that enactment.

9   Section 8 orders

(1) In this Part "the appropriate Minister" means (subject to subsections (2) and (7) and section 10(1))—

(a) in relation to any matter with which a department of the Secretary of State is concerned, the Secretary of State;

(b) in relation to any matter with which the Treasury is concerned, the Treasury; and

(c) in relation to any matter with which any Government department other than a department of the Secretary of State or the Treasury is concerned, the Minister in charge of the other department.

(2) Where in the case of any matter—

(a) that matter falls within more than one paragraph of subsection (1),

(b) there is more than one such department as is mentioned in paragraph (c) of that subsection that is concerned with that matter, or

(c) both paragraphs (a) and (b) of this subsection apply,

references, in relation to that matter, to the appropriate Minister are references to any one or more of the appropriate Ministers acting (in the case of more than one) jointly.

(3) Subject to subsection (4) and section 10(6), a statutory instrument containing an order under section 8 shall be subject to annulment in pursuance of a resolution of either House of Parliament.

(4) Subsection (3) does not apply in the case of an order a draft of which has been laid before Parliament and approved by a resolution of each House.

(5) An order under section 8 may—

(a) provide for any conditions or requirements imposed by such an order to be framed by reference to the directions of such persons as may be specified in or determined in accordance with the order;

(b) provide that any such condition or requirement is to be satisfied only where a person so specified or determined is satisfied as to specified matters.

(6) The provision made by such an order may include—

(a) different provision for different cases;

(b) such exceptions and exclusions as the person making the order may think fit; and

(c) any such incidental, supplemental, consequential and transitional provision as he may think fit;

and the provision that may be made by virtue of paragraph (c) includes provision modifying any enactment or subordinate legislation or any scheme, licence, authorisation or approval issued, granted or given by or under any enactment or subordinate legislation.

(7) In the case of any matter which is not one of the reserved matters within the meaning of the Scotland Act 1998 or in respect of which functions are, by virtue of section 63 of that Act, exercisable by the Scottish Ministers instead of by or concurrently with a Minister of the Crown, this section and section 8 shall apply to Scotland subject to the following modifications—

(a) subsections (1) and (2) of this section are omitted;

(b) any reference to the appropriate Minister is to be read as a reference to the Secretary of State;

(c) any power of the Secretary of State, by virtue of paragraph (b), to make an order under section 8 may also be exercised by the Scottish Ministers with the consent of the Secretary of State; and

(d) where the Scottish Ministers make an order under section 8—

(i) any reference to the Secretary of State (other than a reference in this subsection) shall be construed as a reference to the Scottish Ministers; and

(ii) any reference to Parliament or to a House of Parliament shall be construed as a reference to the Scottish Parliament.

10   Modification in relation to Welsh matters

(1) For the purposes of the exercise of the powers conferred by section 8 in relation to any matter the functions in respect of which are exercisable by the National Assembly for Wales, the appropriate Minister is the Secretary of State.

(2) Subject to the following provisions of this section, the powers conferred by section 8, so far as they fall within subsection (3), shall be exercisable by the National Assembly for Wales, as well as by the appropriate Minister.

(3) The powers conferred by section 8 fall within this subsection to the extent that they are exercisable in relation to—

(a) the provisions of any subordinate legislation made by the National Assembly for Wales;

(b) so much of any other subordinate legislation as makes provision the power to make which is exercisable by that Assembly;

(c) any power under any enactment to make provision the power to make which is so exercisable;

(d) the giving, sending or production of any notice, account, record or other document or of any information to or by a body mentioned in subsection (4); or

(e) the publication of anything by a body mentioned in subsection (4).

(4) Those bodies are—

(a) the National Assembly for Wales;

(b) any body specified in Schedule 4 to the Government of Wales Act 1998 (Welsh public bodies subject to reform by that Assembly);

(c) any other such body as may be specified for the purposes of this section by an order made by the Secretary of State with the consent of that Assembly.

(5) The National Assembly for Wales shall not make an order under section 8 except with the consent of the Secretary of State.

(6) Section 9(3) shall not apply to any order made under section 8 by the National Assembly for Wales.

(7) Nothing in this section shall confer any power on the National Assembly for Wales to modify any provision of the Government of Wales Act 1998.

(8) The power of the Secretary of State to make an order under subsection (4)(c)—

(a) shall include power to make any such incidental, supplemental, consequential and transitional provision as he may think fit; and

(b) shall be exercisable by statutory instrument subject to annulment in pursuance of a resolution of either House of Parliament.

PART III MISCELLANEOUS AND SUPPLEMENTAL

Telecommunications licences

11 [. . .]

12 [. . .]

Supplemental

13 Ministerial expenditure etc.

There shall be paid out of money provided by Parliament—

(a) any expenditure incurred by the Secretary of State for or in connection with the carrying out of his function under this Act; and

(b) any increase attributable to this Act in the sums which are payable out of money so provided under any other Act.

14 Prohibition on key escrow requirements

(1) Subject to subsection (2), nothing in this Act shall confer any power on any Minister of the Crown, on the Scottish Ministers, on the National Assembly for Wales or on any person appointed under section 3—

(a) by conditions of an approval under Part I, or

(b) by any regulations or order under this Act,

to impose a requirement on any person to deposit a key for electronic data with another person.

(2) Subsection (1) shall not prohibit the imposition by an order under section 8 of—

(a) a requirement to deposit a key for electronic data with the intended recipient of electronic communications comprising the data; or

(b) a requirement for arrangements to be made, in cases where a key for data is not deposited with another person, which otherwise secure that the loss of a key, or its becoming unusable, does not have the effect that the information contained in a record kept in pursuance of any provision made by or under any enactment or subordinate legislation becomes inaccessible or incapable of being put into an intelligible form.

(3) In this section "key', in relation to electronic data, means any code, password, algorithm, key or other data the use of which (with or without other keys)—

(a) allows access to the electronic data, or

(b) facilitates the putting of the electronic data into an intelligible form;

and references in this section to depositing a key for electronic data with a person include references to doing anything that has the effect of making the key available to that person.

15   General interpretation

(1) In this Act, except in so far as the context otherwise requires—

"document" includes a map, plan, design, drawing, picture or other image;

"communication" includes a communication comprising sounds or images or both and a communication effecting a payment;

"electronic communication" means a communication transmitted (whether from one person to another, from one device to another or from a person to a device or vice versa)—

(a) by means of [an electronic communications network]; or

(b) by other means but while in an electronic form;

"enactment" includes—

(a) an enactment passed after the passing of this Act,

(b) an enactment comprised in an Act of the Scottish Parliament, and

(c) an enactment contained in Northern Ireland legislation,

but does not include an enactment contained in Part I or II of this Act;

"modification" includes any alteration, addition or omission, and cognate expressions shall be construed accordingly;

"record" includes an electronic record; and

"subordinate legislation" means—

(a) any subordinate legislation (within the meaning of the Interpretation Act 1978);

(b) any instrument made under an Act of the Scottish Parliament; or

(c) any statutory rules (within the meaning of the Statutory Rules (Northern Ireland) Order 1979).

(2) In this Act—

(a) references to the authenticity of any communication or data are references to any one or more of the following—

(i)   whether the communication or data comes from a particular person or other source;

(ii)   whether it is accurately timed and dated;

(iii)   whether it is intended to have legal effect;

and

(b) references to the integrity of any communication or data are references to whether there has been any tampering with or other modification of the communication or data.

(3) References in this Act to something's being put into an intelligible form include references to its being restored to the condition in which it was before any encryption or similar process was applied to it.

16   Short title, commencement, extent

(1) This Act may be cited as the Electronic Communications Act 2000.

(2) Part I of this Act and sections 7, 11 and 12 shall come into force on such day as the Secretary of State may by order made by statutory instrument appoint; and different days may be appointed under this subsection for different purposes.

(3) An order shall not be made for bringing any of Part I of this Act into force for any purpose unless a draft of the order has been laid before Parliament and approved by a resolution of each House.

(4) If no order for bringing Part I of this Act into force has been made under subsection (2) by the end of the period of five years beginning with the day on which this Act is passed, that Part shall, by virtue of this subsection, be repealed at the end of that period.

(5) This Act extends to Northern Ireland.

Regulation of Investigatory Powers Act 2000

(2000, c. 23)

An Act to make provision for and about the interception of communications, the acquisition and disclosure of data relating to communications, the carrying out of surveillance, the use of covert human intelligence sources and the acquisition of the means by which electronic data protected by encryption or passwords may be decrypted or accessed; to provide for Commissioners and a tribunal with functions and jurisdiction in relation to those matters, to entries on and interferences with property or with wireless telegraphy and to the carrying out of their functions by the Security Service, the Secret Intelligence Service and the Government Communications Headquarters; and for connected purposes.

[28th July 2000]

PART I COMMUNICATIONS

Chapter I Interception

Unlawful and authorised interception

1   Unlawful interception

(1) It shall be an offence for a person intentionally and without lawful authority to intercept, at any place in the United Kingdom, any communication in the course of its transmission by means of—

    (a) a public postal service; or

    (b) a public telecommunication system.

(2) It shall be an offence for a person—

    (a) intentionally and without lawful authority, and

    (b) otherwise than in circumstances in which his conduct is excluded by subsection (6) from criminal liability under this subsection,

to intercept, at any place in the United Kingdom, any communication in the course of its transmission by means of a private telecommunication system.

(3) Any interception of a communication which is carried out at any place in the United Kingdom by, or with the express or implied consent of, a person having the right to control the operation or the use of a private telecommunication system shall be actionable at the suit or instance of the sender or recipient, or intended recipient, of the communication if it is without lawful authority and is either—

    (a) an interception of that communication in the course of its transmission by means of that private system; or

    (b) an interception of that communication in the course of its transmission, by means of a public telecommunication system, to or from apparatus comprised in that private telecommunication system.

(4) Where the United Kingdom is a party to an international agreement which—

    (a) relates to the provision of mutual assistance in connection with, or in the form of, the interception of communications,

    (b) requires the issue of a warrant, order or equivalent instrument in cases in which assistance is given, and

    (c) is designated for the purposes of this subsection by an order made by the Secretary of State,

it shall be the duty of the Secretary of State to secure that no request for assistance in accordance with the agreement is made on behalf of a person in the United Kingdom to the competent authorities of a country or territory outside the United Kingdom except with lawful authority.

(5) Conduct has lawful authority for the purposes of this section if, and only if—

    (a) it is authorised by or under section 3 or 4;

    (b) it takes place in accordance with a warrant under section 5 ("an interception warrant"); or

(c) it is in exercise, in relation to any stored communication, of any statutory power that is exercised (apart from this section) for the purpose of obtaining information or of taking possession of any document or other property;

and conduct (whether or not prohibited by this section) which has lawful authority for the purposes of this section by virtue of paragraph (a) or (b) shall also be taken to be lawful for all other purposes.

(6) The circumstances in which a person makes an interception of a communication in the course of its transmission by means of a private telecommunication system are such that his conduct is excluded from criminal liability under subsection (2) if—

(a) he is a person with a right to control the operation or the use of the system; or

(b) he has the express or implied consent of such a person to make the interception.

(7) A person who is guilty of an offence under subsection (1) or (2) shall be liable—

(a) on conviction on indictment, to imprisonment for a term not exceeding two years or to a fine, or to both;

(b) on summary conviction, to a fine not exceeding the statutory maximum.

(8) No proceedings for any offence which is an offence by virtue of this section shall be instituted—

(a) in England and Wales, except by or with the consent of the Director of Public Prosecutions;

(b) in Northern Ireland, except by or with the consent of the Director of Public Prosecutions for Northern Ireland.

2   Meaning and location of "interception" etc.

(1) In this Act—

"postal service" means any service which—

(a) consists in the following, or in any one or more of them, namely, the collection, sorting, conveyance, distribution and delivery (whether in the United Kingdom or elsewhere) of postal items; and

(b) is offered or provided as a service the main purpose of which, or one of the main purposes of which, is to make available, or to facilitate, a means of transmission from place to place of postal items containing communications;

"private telecommunication system" means any telecommunication system which, without itself being a public telecommunication system, is a system in relation to which the following conditions are satisfied—

(a) it is attached, directly or indirectly and whether or not for the purposes of the communication in question, to a public telecommunication system; and

(b) there is apparatus comprised in the system which is both located in the United Kingdom and used (with or without other apparatus) for making the attachment to the public telecommunication system;

"public postal service" means any postal service which is offered or provided to, or to a substantial section of, the public in any one or more parts of the United Kingdom;

"public telecommunications service" means any telecommunications service which is offered or provided to, or to a substantial section of, the public in any one or more parts of the United Kingdom;

"public telecommunication system" means any such parts of a telecommunication system by means of which any public telecommunications service is provided as are located in the United Kingdom;

"telecommunications service" means any service that consists in the provision of access to, and of facilities for making use of, any telecommunication system (whether or not one provided by the person providing the service); and

"telecommunication system" means any system (including the apparatus comprised in it) which exists (whether wholly or partly in the United Kingdom or elsewhere) for the purpose of facilitating the transmission of communications by any means involving the use of electrical or electro-magnetic energy.

(2) For the purposes of this Act, but subject to the following provisions of this section, a person intercepts a communication in the course of its transmission by means of a telecommunication system if, and only if, he—

    (a) so modifies or interferes with the system, or its operation,

    (b) so monitors transmissions made by means of the system, or

    (c) so monitors transmissions made by wireless telegraphy to or from apparatus comprised in the system,

as to make some or all of the contents of the communication available, while being transmitted, to a person other than the sender or intended recipient of the communication.

(3) References in this Act to the interception of a communication do not include references to the interception of any communication broadcast for general reception.

(4) For the purposes of this Act the interception of a communication takes place in the United Kingdom if, and only if, the modification, interference or monitoring or, in the case of a postal item, the interception is effected by conduct within the United Kingdom and the communication is either—

    (a) intercepted in the course of its transmission by means of a public postal service or public telecommunication system; or

    (b) intercepted in the course of its transmission by means of a private telecommunication system in a case in which the sender or intended recipient of the communication is in the United Kingdom.

(5) References in this Act to the interception of a communication in the course of its transmission by means of a postal service or telecommunication system do not include references to—

    (a) any conduct that takes place in relation only to so much of the communication as consists in any traffic data comprised in or attached to a communication (whether by the sender or otherwise) for the purposes of any postal service or telecommunication system by means of which it is being or may be transmitted; or

    (b) any such conduct, in connection with conduct falling within paragraph (a), as gives a person who is neither the sender nor the intended recipient only so much access to a communication as is necessary for the purpose of identifying traffic data so comprised or attached.

(6) For the purposes of this section references to the modification of a telecommunication system include references to the attachment of any apparatus to, or other modification of or interference with—

    (a) any part of the system; or

    (b) any wireless telegraphy apparatus used for making transmissions to or from apparatus comprised in the system.

(7) For the purposes of this section the times while a communication is being transmitted by means of a telecommunication system shall be taken to include any time when the system by means of which the communication is being, or has been, transmitted is used for storing it in a manner that enables the intended recipient to collect it or otherwise to have access to it.

(8) For the purposes of this section the cases in which any contents of a communication are to be taken to be made available to a person while being transmitted shall include any case in which any of the contents of the communication, while being transmitted, are diverted or recorded so as to be available to a person subsequently.

(9) In this section "traffic data", in relation to any communication, means—

    (a) any data identifying, or purporting to identify, any person, apparatus or location to or from which the communication is or may be transmitted,

    (b) any data identifying or selecting, or purporting to identify or select, apparatus through which, or by means of which, the communication is or may be transmitted,

    (c) any data comprising signals for the actuation of apparatus used for the purposes of a telecommunication system for effecting (in whole or in part) the transmission of any communication, and

    (d) any data identifying the data or other data as data comprised in or attached to a particular communication, but that expression includes data identifying a computer file or computer program access to which is obtained, or which is run, by means of the communication to the extent only that the file or program is identified by reference to the apparatus in which it is stored.

(10) In this section—

(a) references, in relation to traffic data comprising signals for the actuation of apparatus, to a telecommunication system by means of which a communication is being or may be transmitted include references to any telecommunication system in which that apparatus is comprised; and

(b) references to traffic data being attached to a communication include references to the data and the communication being logically associated with each other;

and in this section "data", in relation to a postal item, means anything written on the outside of the item.

(11) In this section "postal item" means any letter, postcard or other such thing in writing as may be used by the sender for imparting information to the recipient, or any packet or parcel.

3   Lawful interception without an interception warrant

(1) Conduct by any person consisting in the interception of a communication is authorised by this section if the communication is one which, or which that person has reasonable grounds for believing, is both—

(a) a communication sent by a person who has consented to the interception; and

(b) a communication the intended recipient of which has so consented.

(2) Conduct by any person consisting in the interception of a communication is authorised by this section if—

(a) the communication is one sent by, or intended for, a person who has consented to the interception; and

(b) surveillance by means of that interception has been authorised under Part II.

(3) Conduct consisting in the interception of a communication is authorised by this section if—

(a) it is conduct by or on behalf of a person who provides a postal service or a telecommunications service; and

(b) it takes place for purposes connected with the provision or operation of that service or with the enforcement, in relation to that service, of any enactment relating to the use of postal services or telecommunications services.

(4) Conduct by any person consisting in the interception of a communication in the course of its transmission by means of wireless telegraphy is authorised by this section if it takes place—

(a) with the authority of a designated person under [section 48 of the Wireless Telegraphy Act 2006 (interception and disclosure of wireless telegraphy messages)]; and

(b) for purposes connected with anything falling within subsection (5).

(5) Each of the following falls within this subsection—

[(a) the grant of wireless telegraphy licences under the Wireless Telegraphy Act 2006;]

(b) the prevention or detection of anything which constitutes interference with wireless telegraphy; and

(c) the enforcement of [—

(i) any provision of Part 2 (other than Chapter 2 and sections 27 to 31) or Part 3 of that Act, or

(ii) any enactment not falling within sub-paragraph (i),]

that relates to such interference.

4   Power to provide for lawful interception

(1) Conduct by any person ("the interceptor") consisting in the interception of a communication in the course of its transmission by means of a telecommunication system is authorised by this section if—

(a) the interception is carried out for the purpose of obtaining information about the communications of a person who, or who the interceptor has reasonable grounds for believing, is in a country or territory outside the United Kingdom;

 (b) the interception relates to the use of a telecommunications service provided to persons in that country or territory which is either—
  (i) a public telecommunications service; or
  (ii) a telecommunications service that would be a public telecommunications service if the persons to whom it is offered or provided were members of the public in a part of the United Kingdom;
 (c) the person who provides that service (whether the interceptor or another person) is required by the law of that country or territory to carry out, secure or facilitate the interception in question;
 (d) the situation is one in relation to which such further conditions as may be prescribed by regulations made by the Secretary of State are required to be satisfied before conduct may be treated as authorised by virtue of this subsection; and
 (e) the conditions so prescribed are satisfied in relation to that situation.

 (2)　Subject to subsection (3), the Secretary of State may by regulations authorise any such conduct described in the regulations as appears to him to constitute a legitimate practice reasonably required for the purpose, in connection with the carrying on of any business, of monitoring or keeping a record of—
 (a) communications by means of which transactions are entered into in the course of that business; or
 (b) other communications relating to that business or taking place in the course of its being carried on.

 (3)　Nothing in any regulations under subsection (2) shall authorise the interception of any communication except in the course of its transmission using apparatus or services provided by or to the person carrying on the business for use wholly or partly in connection with that business.

 (4)　Conduct taking place in a prison is authorised by this section if it is conduct in exercise of any power conferred by or under any rules made under section 47 of the Prison Act 1952, section 39 of the Prisons (Scotland) Act 1989 or section 13 of the Prison Act (Northern Ireland) 1953 (prison rules).

 (5)　Conduct taking place in any hospital premises where high security psychiatric services are provided is authorised by this section if it is conduct in pursuance of, and in accordance with, any direction given under section 17 of the National Health Service Act 1977 (directions as to the carrying out of their functions by health bodies) to the body providing those services at those premises.

 (6)　Conduct taking place in a state hospital is authorised by this section if it is conduct in pursuance of, and in accordance with, any direction given to the State Hospitals Board for Scotland under section 2(5) of the National Health Service (Scotland) Act 1978 (regulations and directions as to the exercise of their functions by health boards) as applied by Article 5(1) of and the Schedule to The State Hospitals Board for Scotland Order 1995 (which applies certain provisions of that Act of 1978 to the State Hospitals Board).

 (7)　In this section references to a business include references to any activities of a government department, of any public authority or of any person or office holder on whom functions are conferred by or under any enactment.

 (8)　In this section—
"government department" includes any part of the Scottish Administration, a Northern Ireland department and [the Welsh Assembly Government];
"high security psychiatric services" has the same meaning as in [section 4 of the National Health Service Act 2006];
"hospital premises" has the same meaning as in section 4(3) of that Act; and
"state hospital" has the same meaning as in the National Health Service (Scotland) Act 1978.

 (9)　In this section "prison" means—
 (a) any prison, young offender institution, young offenders centre or remand centre which is under the general superintendence of, or is provided by, the Secretary of State under the Prison Act 1952 or the Prison Act (Northern Ireland) 1953, or
 (b) any prison, young offenders institution or remand centre which is under the general superintendence of the Scottish Ministers under the Prisons (Scotland) Act 1989,

and includes any contracted out prison, within the meaning of Part IV of the Criminal Justice Act 1991 or section 106(4) of the Criminal Justice and Public Order Act 1994, and any legalised police cells within the meaning of section 14 of the Prisons (Scotland) Act 1989.

5 Interception with a warrant

(1) Subject to the following provisions of this Chapter, the Secretary of State may issue a warrant authorising or requiring the person to whom it is addressed, by any such conduct as may be described in the warrant, to secure any one or more of the following—

(a) the interception in the course of their transmission by means of a postal service or tele-communication system of the communications described in the warrant;

(b) the making, in accordance with an international mutual assistance agreement, of a request for the provision of such assistance in connection with, or in the form of, an interception of communications as may be so described;

(c) the provision, in accordance with an international mutual assistance agreement, to the competent authorities of a country or territory outside the United Kingdom of any such assistance in connection with, or in the form of, an interception of communications as may be so described;

(d) the disclosure, in such manner as may be so described, of intercepted material obtained by any interception authorised or required by the warrant, and of related communications data.

(2) The Secretary of State shall not issue an interception warrant unless he believes—

(a) that the warrant is necessary on grounds falling within subsection (3); and

(b) that the conduct authorised by the warrant is proportionate to what is sought to be achieved by that conduct.

(3) Subject to the following provisions of this section, a warrant is necessary on grounds falling within this subsection if it is necessary—

(a) in the interests of national security;

(b) for the purpose of preventing or detecting serious crime;

(c) for the purpose of safeguarding the economic well-being of the United Kingdom; or

(d) for the purpose, in circumstances appearing to the Secretary of State to be equivalent to those in which he would issue a warrant by virtue of paragraph (b), of giving effect to the provisions of any international mutual assistance agreement.

(4) The matters to be taken into account in considering whether the requirements of subsection (2) are satisfied in the case of any warrant shall include whether the information which it is thought necessary to obtain under the warrant could reasonably be obtained by other means.

(5) A warrant shall not be considered necessary on the ground falling within subsection (3)(c) unless the information which it is thought necessary to obtain is information relating to the acts or intentions of persons outside the British Islands.

(6) The conduct authorised by an interception warrant shall be taken to include—

(a) all such conduct (including the interception of communications not identified by the warrant) as it is necessary to undertake in order to do what is expressly authorised or required by the warrant;

(b) conduct for obtaining related communications data; and

(c) conduct by any person which is conduct in pursuance of a requirement imposed by or on behalf of the person to whom the warrant is addressed to be provided with assistance with giving effect to the warrant.

Interception warrants

6 Application for issue of an interception warrant

(1) An interception warrant shall not be issued except on an application made by or on behalf of a person specified in subsection (2).

(2) Those persons are—
- (a)   the Director-General of the Security Service;
- (b)   the Chief of the Secret Intelligence Service;
- (c)   the Director of GCHQ;
- (d)   the Director General of the [Serious Organised Crime Agency];
- [(da) the Director General of the Scottish Crime and Drug Enforcement Agency;]
- (e)   the Commissioner of Police of the Metropolis;
- (f)   the [Chief Constable of the Police Service of Northern Ireland];
- (g)   the chief constable of any police force maintained under or by virtue of section 1 of the Police (Scotland) Act 1967;
- (h)   the Commissioners of Customs and Excise;
- (i)   the Chief of Defence Intelligence;
- (j)   a person who, for the purposes of any international mutual assistance agreement, is the competent authority of a country or territory outside the United Kingdom.

(3) An application for the issue of an interception warrant shall not be made on behalf of a person specified in [paragraph (a), (b), (c), (e), (f), (g), (h), (i) or (j) of] subsection (2) except by a person holding office under the Crown.

7   Issue of warrants

(1) An interception warrant shall not be issued except—
- (a) under the hand of the Secretary of State [or, in the case of a warrant issued by the Scottish Ministers (by virtue of provision made under section 63 of the Scotland Act 1998), a member of the Scottish Executive]; or
- (b) in a case falling within subsection (2)[(a) or (b)], under the hand of a senior official[; or
- (c) in a case falling within subsection (2)(aa), under the hand of a member of the staff of the Scottish Administration who is a member of the Senior Civil Service and who is designated by the Scottish Ministers as a person under whose hand a warrant may be issued in such a case].

(2) Those cases are—
- (a)   an urgent case in which the Secretary of State has himself expressly authorised the issue of the warrant in that case; and
- [(aa) an urgent case in which the Scottish Ministers have themselves (by virtue of provision made under section 63 of the Scotland Act 1998) expressly authorised the use of the warrant in that case and a statement of that fact is endorsed on the warrant; and]
- (b)   a case in which the warrant is for the purposes of a request for assistance made under an international mutual assistance agreement by the competent authorities of a country or territory outside the United Kingdom and either—
  - (i) it appears that the interception subject is outside the United Kingdom; or
  - (ii) the interception to which the warrant relates is to take place in relation only to premises outside the United Kingdom.

(3) An interception warrant—
- (a) must be addressed to the person falling within section 6(2) by whom, or on whose behalf, the application for the warrant was made; and
- (b) in the case of a warrant issued under the hand of a senior official, must contain, according to whatever is applicable—
  - (i) one of the statements set out in subsection (4); and
  - (ii) if it contains the statement set out in subsection (4)(b), one of the statements set out in subsection (5).

(4) The statements referred to in subsection (3)(b)(i) are—
- (a) a statement that the case is an urgent case in which the Secretary of State has himself expressly authorised the issue of the warrant;

    (b) a statement that the warrant is issued for the purposes of a request for assistance made under an international mutual assistance agreement by the competent authorities of a country or territory outside the United Kingdom.

(5) The statements referred to in subsection (3)(b)(ii) are—

    (a) a statement that the interception subject appears to be outside the United Kingdom;

    (b) a statement that the interception to which the warrant relates is to take place in relation only to premises outside the United Kingdom.

8　Contents of warrants

(1) An interception warrant must name or describe either—

    (a) one person as the interception subject; or

    (b) a single set of premises as the premises in relation to which the interception to which the warrant relates is to take place.

(2) The provisions of an interception warrant describing communications the interception of which is authorised or required by the warrant must comprise one or more schedules setting out the addresses, numbers, apparatus or other factors, or combination of factors, that are to be used for identifying the communications that may be or are to be intercepted.

(3) Any factor or combination of factors set out in accordance with subsection (2) must be one that identifies communications which are likely to be or to include—

    (a) communications from, or intended for, the person named or described in the warrant in accordance with subsection (1); or

    (b) communications originating on, or intended for transmission to, the premises so named or described.

(4) Subsections (1) and (2) shall not apply to an interception warrant if—

    (a) the description of communications to which the warrant relates confines the conduct authorised or required by the warrant to conduct falling within subsection (5); and

    (b) at the time of the issue of the warrant, a certificate applicable to the warrant has been issued by the Secretary of State certifying—

       (i) the descriptions of intercepted material the examination of which he considers necessary; and

       (ii) that he considers the examination of material of those descriptions necessary as mentioned in section 5(3)(a), (b) or (c).

(5) Conduct falls within this subsection if it consists in—

    (a) the interception of external communications in the course of their transmission by means of a telecommunication system; and

    (b) any conduct authorised in relation to any such interception by section 5(6).

(6) A certificate for the purposes of subsection (4) shall not be issued except under the hand of the Secretary of State.

9　Duration, cancellation and renewal of warrants

(1) An interception warrant—

    (a) shall cease to have effect at the end of the relevant period; but

    (b) may be renewed, at any time before the end of that period, by an instrument under the hand of the Secretary of State [or, in the case of a warrant issued by the Scottish Ministers (by virtue of provision made under section 63 of the Scotland Act 1998), a member of the Scottish Executive] or, in a case falling within section 7(2)(b), under the hand of a senior official.

(2) An interception warrant shall not be renewed under subsection (1) unless the Secretary of State believes that the warrant continues to be necessary on grounds falling within section 5(3).

(3) The Secretary of State shall cancel an interception warrant if he is satisfied that the warrant is no longer necessary on grounds falling within section 5(3).

(4) The Secretary of State shall cancel an interception warrant if, at any time before the end of the relevant period, he is satisfied in a case in which—

     (a) the warrant is one which was issued containing the statement set out in section 7(5)(a) or has been renewed by an instrument containing the statement set out in subsection (5)(b)(i) of this section, and

     (b) the latest renewal (if any) of the warrant is not a renewal by an instrument under the hand of the Secretary of State,

that the person named or described in the warrant as the interception subject is in the United Kingdom.

(5) An instrument under the hand of a senior official that renews an interception warrant must contain—

     (a) a statement that the renewal is for the purposes of a request for assistance made under an international mutual assistance agreement by the competent authorities of a country or territory outside the United Kingdom; and

     (b) whichever of the following statements is applicable—

         (i) a statement that the interception subject appears to be outside the United Kingdom;

         (ii) a statement that the interception to which the warrant relates is to take place in relation only to premises outside the United Kingdom.

(6) In this section "the relevant period"—

     (a) in relation to an unrenewed warrant issued in a case falling within section 7(2)(a) under the hand of a senior official, means the period ending with the fifth working day following the day of the warrant's issue;

     [(ab) in relation to an unrenewed warrant which is endorsed under the hand of the Secretary of State with a statement that the issue of the warrant is believed to be necessary on grounds falling within section 5(3)(a) or (c), means the period of six months beginning with the day of the warrant's issue;]

     (b) in relation to a renewed warrant the latest renewal of which was by an instrument endorsed under the hand of the Secretary of State with a statement that the renewal is believed to be necessary on grounds falling within section 5(3)(a) or (c), means the period of six months beginning with the day of the warrant's renewal; and

     (c) in all other cases, means the period of three months beginning with the day of the warrant's issue or, in the case of a warrant that has been renewed, of its latest renewal.

10   Modification of warrants and certificates

(1) The Secretary of State may at any time—

     (a) modify the provisions of an interception warrant; or

     (b) modify a section 8(4) certificate so as to include in the certified material any material the examination of which he considers to be necessary as mentioned in section 5(3)(a), (b) or (c).

(2) If at any time the Secretary of State considers that any factor set out in a schedule to an interception warrant is no longer relevant for identifying communications which, in the case of that warrant, are likely to be or to include communications falling within section 8(3)(a) or (b), it shall be his duty to modify the warrant by the deletion of that factor.

(3) If at any time the Secretary of State considers that the material certified by a section 8(4) certificate includes any material the examination of which is no longer necessary as mentioned in any of paragraphs (a) to (c) of section 5(3), he shall modify the certificate so as to exclude that material from the certified material.

(4) Subject to subsections (5) to (8), a warrant or certificate shall not be modified under this section except by an instrument under the hand of the Secretary of State or of a senior official.

[(4A) Subject to subsections (5A), (6) and (8), a warrant issued by the Scottish Ministers (by virtue of provision made under section 63 of the Scotland Act 1998) shall not be modified under this section except by an instrument under the hand of a member of the Scottish Executive or a member of the staff of the Scottish Administration who is a member of the Senior Civil Service and is designated by the Scottish Ministers as a person under whose hand an instrument may be issued in such a case (in this section referred to as "a designated official").]

(5) Unscheduled parts of an interception warrant shall not be modified under the hand of a senior official except in an urgent case in which—

    (a) the Secretary of State has himself expressly authorised the modification; and

    (b) a statement of that fact is endorsed on the modifying instrument.

[(5A) Unscheduled parts of an interception warrant issued by the Scottish Ministers shall not be modified under the hand of a designated official except in an urgent case in which—

    (a) they have themselves (by virtue of provision made under section 63 of the Scotland Act 1998) expressly authorised the modification; and

    (b) a statement of that fact is endorsed on the modifying instrument.]

[(6) Subsection (4) authorises the modification of the scheduled parts of an interception warrant under the hand of a senior official who is either—

    (a) the person to whom the warrant is addressed, or

    (b) a person holding a position subordinate to that person,

only if the applicable condition specified in subsection (6A) is satisfied and a statement that the condition is satisfied is endorsed on the modifying instrument.

(6A) The applicable condition is—

    (a) in the case of an unrenewed warrant, that the warrant is endorsed with a statement that the issue of the warrant is believed to be necessary in the interests of national security; and

    (b) in the case of a renewed warrant, that the instrument by which it was last renewed is endorsed with a statement that the renewal is believed to be necessary in the interests of national security.]

(7) A section 8(4) certificate shall not be modified under the hand of a senior official except in an urgent case in which—

    (a) the official in question holds a position in respect of which he is expressly authorised by provisions contained in the certificate to modify the certificate on the Secretary of State's behalf; or

    (b) the Secretary of State has himself expressly authorised the modification and a statement of that fact is endorsed on the modifying instrument.

(8) Where modifications in accordance with this subsection are expressly authorised by provision contained in the warrant, the scheduled parts of an interception warrant may, in an urgent case, be modified by an instrument under the hand of—

    (a) the person to whom the warrant is addressed; or

    (b) a person holding any such position subordinate to that person as may be identified in the provisions of the warrant.

(9) Where—

    (a) a warrant or certificate is modified by an instrument under the hand of a person other than the Secretary of State [or, as the case may be, the Scottish Ministers (by virtue of provision made under section 63 of the Scotland Act 1998)], and

    (b) a statement for the purposes of subsection (5)(b)[, (5A)(b)][, (6)] or (7)(b) is endorsed on the instrument, or the modification is made under subsection (8),

that modification shall cease to have effect at the end of the fifth working day following the day of the instrument's issue.

(10) For the purposes of this section—

    (a) the scheduled parts of an interception warrant are any provisions of the warrant that are contained in a schedule of identifying factors comprised in the warrant for the purposes of section 8(2); and

    (b) the modifications that are modifications of the scheduled parts of an interception warrant include the insertion of an additional such schedule in the warrant;

and references in this section to unscheduled parts of an interception warrant, and to their modification, shall be construed accordingly.

11 Implementation of warrants

(1) Effect may be given to an interception warrant either—

(a) by the person to whom it is addressed; or

(b) by that person acting through, or together with, such other persons as he may require (whether under subsection (2) or otherwise) to provide him with assistance with giving effect to the warrant.

(2) For the purpose of requiring any person to provide assistance in relation to an interception warrant the person to whom it is addressed may—

(a) serve a copy of the warrant on such persons as he considers may be able to provide such assistance; or

(b) make arrangements under which a copy of it is to be or may be so served.

(3) The copy of an interception warrant that is served on any person under subsection (2) may, to the extent authorised—

(a) by the person to whom the warrant is addressed, or

(b) by the arrangements made by him for the purposes of that subsection,

omit any one or more of the schedules to the warrant.

(4) Where a copy of an interception warrant has been served by or on behalf of the person to whom it is addressed on—

(a) a person who provides a postal service,

(b) a person who provides a public telecommunications service, or

(c) a person not falling within paragraph (b) who has control of the whole or any part of a telecommunication system located wholly or partly in the United Kingdom,

it shall (subject to subsection (5)) be the duty of that person to take all such steps for giving effect to the warrant as are notified to him by or on behalf of the person to whom the warrant is addressed.

(5) A person who is under a duty by virtue of subsection (4) to take steps for giving effect to a warrant shall not be required to take any steps which it is not reasonably practicable for him to take.

(6) For the purposes of subsection (5) the steps which it is reasonably practicable for a person to take in a case in which obligations have been imposed on him by or under section 12 shall include every step which it would have been reasonably practicable for him to take had he complied with all the obligations so imposed on him.

(7) A person who knowingly fails to comply with his duty under subsection (4) shall be guilty of an offence and liable—

(a) on conviction on indictment, to imprisonment for a term not exceeding two years or to a fine, or to both;

(b) on summary conviction, to imprisonment for a term not exceeding six months or to a fine not exceeding the statutory maximum, or to both.

(8) A person's duty under subsection (4) to take steps for giving effect to a warrant shall be enforceable by civil proceedings by the Secretary of State for an injunction, or for specific performance of a statutory duty under section 45 of the Court of Session Act 1988, or for any other appropriate relief.

(9) For the purposes of this Act the provision of assistance with giving effect to an interception warrant includes any disclosure to the person to whom the warrant is addressed, or to persons acting on his behalf, of intercepted material obtained by any interception authorised or required by the warrant, and of any related communications data.

Interception capability and costs

12 Maintenance of interception capability

(1) The Secretary of State may by order provide for the imposition by him on persons who—

(a) are providing public postal services or public telecommunications services, or

(b) are proposing to do so,

of such obligations as it appears to him reasonable to impose for the purpose of securing that it is and remains practicable for requirements to provide assistance in relation to interception warrants to be imposed and complied with.

(2) The Secretary of State's power to impose the obligations provided for by an order under this section shall be exercisable by the giving, in accordance with the order, of a notice requiring the person who is to be subject to the obligations to take all such steps as may be specified or described in the notice.

(3) Subject to subsection (11), the only steps that may be specified or described in a notice given to a person under subsection (2) are steps appearing to the Secretary of State to be necessary for securing that that person has the practical capability of providing any assistance which he may be required to provide in relation to relevant interception warrants.

(4) A person shall not be liable to have an obligation imposed on him in accordance with an order under this section by reason only that he provides, or is proposing to provide, to members of the public a telecommunications service the provision of which is or, as the case may be, will be no more than—

    (a) the means by which he provides a service which is not a telecommunications service; or

    (b) necessarily incidental to the provision by him of a service which is not a telecommunications service.

(5) Where a notice is given to any person under subsection (2) and otherwise than by virtue of subsection (6)(c), that person may, before the end of such period as may be specified in an order under this section, refer the notice to the Technical Advisory Board.

(6) Where a notice given to any person under subsection (2) is referred to the Technical Advisory Board under subsection (5)—

    (a) there shall be no requirement for that person to comply, except in pursuance of a notice under paragraph (c)(ii), with any obligations imposed by the notice;

    (b) the Board shall consider the technical requirements and the financial consequences, for the person making the reference, of the notice referred to them and shall report their conclusions on those matters to that person and to the Secretary of State; and

    (c) the Secretary of State, after considering any report of the Board relating to the notice, may either—

        (i) withdraw the notice; or

        (ii) give a further notice under subsection (2) confirming its effect, with or without modifications.

(7) It shall be the duty of a person to whom a notice is given under subsection (2) to comply with the notice; and that duty shall be enforceable by civil proceedings by the Secretary of State for an injunction, or for specific performance of a statutory duty under section 45 of the Court of Session Act 1988, or for any other appropriate relief.

(8) A notice for the purposes of subsection (2) must specify such period as appears to the Secretary of State to be reasonable as the period within which the steps specified or described in the notice are to be taken.

(9) Before making an order under this section the Secretary of State shall consult with—

    (a) such persons appearing to him to be likely to be subject to the obligations for which it provides,

    (b) the Technical Advisory Board,

    (c) such persons representing persons falling within paragraph (a), and

    (d) such persons with statutory functions in relation to persons falling within that paragraph,

as he considers appropriate.

(10) The Secretary of State shall not make an order under this section unless a draft of the order has been laid before Parliament and approved by a resolution of each House.

(11) For the purposes of this section the question whether a person has the practical capability of providing assistance in relation to relevant interception warrants shall include the question whether

all such arrangements have been made as the Secretary of State considers necessary—

    (a) with respect to the disclosure of intercepted material;

    (b) for the purpose of ensuring that security and confidentiality are maintained in relation to, and to matters connected with, the provision of any such assistance; and

    (c) for the purpose of facilitating the carrying out of any functions in relation to this Chapter of the Interception of Communications Commissioner;

but before determining for the purposes of the making of any order, or the imposition of any obligation, under this section what arrangements he considers necessary for the purpose mentioned in paragraph (c) the Secretary of State shall consult that Commissioner.

    (12) In this section "relevant interception warrant"—

    (a) in relation to a person providing a public postal service, means an interception warrant relating to the interception of communications in the course of their transmission by means of that service; and

    (b) in relation to a person providing a public telecommunications service, means an interception warrant relating to the interception of communications in the course of their transmission by means of a telecommunication system used for the purposes of that service.

13 Technical Advisory Board

    (1) There shall be a Technical Advisory Board consisting of such number of persons appointed by the Secretary of State as he may by order provide.

    (2) The order providing for the membership of the Technical Advisory Board must also make provision which is calculated to ensure—

    (a) that the membership of the Technical Advisory Board includes persons likely effectively to represent the interests of the persons on whom obligations may be imposed under section 12;

    (b) that the membership of the Board includes persons likely effectively to represent the interests of the persons by or on whose behalf applications for interception warrants may be made;

    (c) that such other persons (if any) as the Secretary of State thinks fit may be appointed to be members of the Board; and

    (d) that the Board is so constituted as to produce a balance between the representation of the interests mentioned in paragraph (a) and the representation of those mentioned in paragraph (b).

    (3) The Secretary of State shall not make an order under this section unless a draft of the order has been laid before Parliament and approved by a resolution of each House.

14 Grants for interception costs

    (1) It shall be the duty of the Secretary of State to ensure that such arrangements are in force as are necessary for securing that a person who provides—

    (a) a postal service, or

    (b) a telecommunications service,

receives such contribution as is, in the circumstances of that person's case, a fair contribution towards the costs incurred, or likely to be incurred, by that person in consequence of the matters mentioned in subsection (2).

    (2) Those matters are—

    (a) in relation to a person providing a postal service, the issue of interception warrants relating to communications transmitted by means of that postal service;

    (b) in relation to a person providing a telecommunications service, the issue of interception warrants relating to communications transmitted by means of a telecommunication system used for the purposes of that service;

    (c) in relation to each description of person, the imposition on that person of obligations provided for by an order under section 12.

    (3) For the purpose of complying with his duty under this section, the Secretary of State may make arrangements for payments to be made out of money provided by Parliament.

Restrictions on use of intercepted material etc.

15   General safeguards

(1) Subject to subsection (6), it shall be the duty of the Secretary of State to ensure, in relation to all interception warrants, that such arrangements are in force as he considers necessary for securing—

   (a) that the requirements of subsections (2) and (3) are satisfied in relation to the intercepted material and any related communications data; and

   (b) in the case of warrants in relation to which there are section 8(4) certificates, that the requirements of section 16 are also satisfied.

(2) The requirements of this subsection are satisfied in relation to the intercepted material and any related communications data if each of the following—

   (a) the number of persons to whom any of the material or data is disclosed or otherwise made available,

   (b) the extent to which any of the material or data is disclosed or otherwise made available,

   (c) the extent to which any of the material or data is copied, and

   (d) the number of copies that are made,

is limited to the minimum that is necessary for the authorised purposes.

(3) The requirements of this subsection are satisfied in relation to the intercepted material and any related communications data if each copy made of any of the material or data (if not destroyed earlier) is destroyed as soon as there are no longer any grounds for retaining it as necessary for any of the authorised purposes.

(4) For the purposes of this section something is necessary for the authorised purposes if, and only if—

   (a) it continues to be, or is likely to become, necessary as mentioned in section 5(3);

   (b) it is necessary for facilitating the carrying out of any of the functions under this Chapter of the Secretary of State;

   (c) it is necessary for facilitating the carrying out of any functions in relation to this Part of the Interception of Communications Commissioner or of the Tribunal;

   (d) it is necessary to ensure that a person conducting a criminal prosecution has the information he needs to determine what is required of him by his duty to secure the fairness of the prosecution; or

   (e) it is necessary for the performance of any duty imposed on any person by the Public Records Act 1958 or the Public Records Act (Northern Ireland) 1923.

(5) The arrangements for the time being in force under this section for securing that the requirements of subsection (2) are satisfied in relation to the intercepted material or any related communications data must include such arrangements as the Secretary of State considers necessary for securing that every copy of the material or data that is made is stored, for so long as it is retained, in a secure manner.

(6) Arrangements in relation to interception warrants which are made for the purposes of subsection (1)—

   (a) shall not be required to secure that the requirements of subsections (2) and (3) are satisfied in so far as they relate to any of the intercepted material or related communications data, or any copy of any such material or data, possession of which has been surrendered to any authorities of a country or territory outside the United Kingdom; but

   (b) shall be required to secure, in the case of every such warrant, that possession of the intercepted material and data and of copies of the material or data is surrendered to authorities of a country or territory outside the United Kingdom only if the requirements of subsection (7) are satisfied.

(7) The requirements of this subsection are satisfied in the case of a warrant if it appears to the Secretary of State—

(a) that requirements corresponding to those of subsections (2) and (3) will apply, to such extent (if any) as the Secretary of State thinks fit, in relation to any of the intercepted material or related communications data possession of which, or of any copy of which, is surrendered to the authorities in question; and

(b) that restrictions are in force which would prevent, to such extent (if any) as the Secretary of State thinks fit, the doing of anything in, for the purposes of or in connection with any proceedings outside the United Kingdom which would result in such a disclosure as, by virtue of section 17, could not be made in the United Kingdom.

(8) In this section "copy", in relation to intercepted material or related communications data, means any of the following (whether or not in documentary form)—

(a) any copy, extract or summary of the material or data which identifies itself as the product of an interception, and

(b) any record referring to an interception which is a record of the identities of the persons to or by whom the intercepted material was sent, or to whom the communications data relates,

and "copied" shall be construed accordingly.

16   Extra safeguards in the case of certificated warrants

(1) For the purposes of section 15 the requirements of this section, in the case of a warrant in relation to which there is a section 8(4) certificate, are that the intercepted material is read, looked at or listened to by the persons to whom it becomes available by virtue of the warrant to the extent only that it—

(a) has been certified as material the examination of which is necessary as mentioned in section 5(3)(a), (b) or (c); and

(b) falls within subsection (2).

(2) Subject to subsections (3) and (4), intercepted material falls within this subsection so far only as it is selected to be read, looked at or listened to otherwise than according to a factor which—

(a) is referable to an individual who is known to be for the time being in the British Islands; and

(b) has as its purpose, or one of its purposes, the identification of material contained in communications sent by him, or intended for him.

(3) Intercepted material falls within subsection (2), notwithstanding that it is selected by reference to any such factor as is mentioned in paragraph (a) and (b) of that subsection, if—

(a) it is certified by the Secretary of State for the purposes of section 8(4) that the examination of material selected according to factors referable to the individual in question is necessary as mentioned in subsection 5(3)(a), (b) or (c); and

(b) the material relates only to communications sent during [a period specified in the certificate that is no longer than the permitted maximum].

[(3A) In subsection (3)(b) "the permitted maximum" means—

(a) in the case of material the examination of which is certified for the purposes of section 8(4) as necessary in the interests of national security, six months; and

(b) in any other case, three months.]

(4) Intercepted material also falls within subsection (2), notwithstanding that it is selected by reference to any such factor as is mentioned in paragraph (a) and (b) of that subsection, if—

(a) the person to whom the warrant is addressed believes, on reasonable grounds, that the circumstances are such that the material would fall within that subsection; or

(b) the conditions set out in subsection (5) below are satisfied in relation to the selection of the material.

(5) Those conditions are satisfied in relation to the selection of intercepted material if—

(a) it has appeared to the person to whom the warrant is addressed that there has been such a relevant change of circumstances as, but for subsection (4)(b), would prevent the intercepted material from falling within subsection (2);

(b) since it first so appeared, a written authorisation to read, look at or listen to the material has been given by a senior official; and

(c) the selection is made before the end of [the permitted period].

[(5A) In subsection (5)(c) "the permitted period" means—

(a) in the case of material the examination of which is certified for the purposes of section 8(4) as necessary in the interests of national security, the period ending with the end of the fifth working day after it first appeared as mentioned in subsection (5)(a) to the person to whom the warrant is addressed; and

(b) in any other case, the period ending with the end of the first working day after it first so appeared to that person.]

(6) References in this section to its appearing that there has been a relevant change of circumstances are references to its appearing either—

(a) that the individual in question has entered the British Islands; or

(b) that a belief by the person to whom the warrant is addressed in the individual's presence outside the British Islands was in fact mistaken.

17   Exclusion of matters from legal proceedings

(1) Subject to section 18, no evidence shall be adduced, question asked, assertion or disclosure made or other thing done in, for the purposes of or in connection with any legal proceedings [or Inquiries Act proceedings] which (in any manner)—

(a) discloses, in circumstances from which its origin in anything falling within subsection (2) may be inferred, any of the contents of an intercepted communication or any related communications data; or

(b) tends (apart from any such disclosure) to suggest that anything falling within subsection (2) has or may have occurred or be going to occur.

(2) The following fall within this subsection—

(a) conduct by a person falling within subsection (3) that was or would be an offence under section 1(1) or (2) of this Act or under section 1 of the Interception of Communications Act 1985;

(b) a breach by the Secretary of State of his duty under section 1(4) of this Act;

(c) the issue of an interception warrant or of a warrant under the Interception of Communications Act 1985;

(d) the making of an application by any person for an interception warrant, or for a warrant under that Act;

(e) the imposition of any requirement on any person to provide assistance with giving effect to an interception warrant.

(3) The persons referred to in subsection (2)(a) are—

(a)   any person to whom a warrant under this Chapter may be addressed;

(b)   any person holding office under the Crown;

[(c)   any member of the staff of the Serious Organised Crime Agency;] ...

[(ca) any member of the Scottish Crime and Drug Enforcement Agency;]

(e)   any person employed by or for the purposes of a police force;

(f)   any person providing a postal service or employed for the purposes of any business of providing such a service; and

(g)   any person providing a public telecommunications service or employed for the purposes of any business of providing such a service.

(4) [In this section—

"Inquiries Act proceedings" means proceedings of an inquiry under the Inquiries Act 2005;

"intercepted communications" means] any communication intercepted in the course of its transmission by means of a postal service or telecommunication system.]

18   Exceptions to section 17

(1) Section 17(1) shall not apply in relation to—

(a) any proceedings for a relevant offence;

(b)   any civil proceedings under section 11(8);

(c)   any proceedings before the Tribunal;

(d)   any proceedings on an appeal or review for which provision is made by an order under section 67(8);

[(da) any control order proceedings (within the meaning of the Prevention of Terrorism Act 2005) or any proceedings arising out of such proceedings;]

(e)   any proceedings before the Special Immigration Appeals Commission or any proceedings arising out of proceedings before that Commission; or

(f)   any proceedings before the Proscribed Organisations Appeal Commission or any proceedings arising out of proceedings before that Commission.

(2) Subsection (1) shall not, by virtue of [paragraphs (da) to (f)], authorise the disclosure of anything—

[(za) in the case of any proceedings falling within paragraph (da) to—

(i)   a person who, within the meaning of the Schedule to the Prevention of Terrorism Act 2005, is or was a relevant party to the control order proceedings; or

(ii)   any person who for the purposes of any proceedings so falling (but otherwise than by virtue of an appointment under paragraph 7 of that Schedule) represents a person falling within sub-paragraph (i);]

(a)   in the case of any proceedings falling within paragraph (e), to—

(i)   the appellant to the Special Immigration Appeals Commission; or

(ii)   any person who for the purposes of any proceedings so falling (but otherwise than by virtue of an appointment under section 6 of the Special Immigration Appeals Commission Act 1997) represents that appellant;

or

(b)   in the case of proceedings falling within paragraph (f), to—

(i)   the applicant to the Proscribed Organisations Appeal Commission;

(ii)   the organisation concerned (if different);

(iii) any person designated under paragraph 6 of Schedule 3 to the Terrorism Act 2000 to conduct proceedings so falling on behalf of that organisation; or

(iv)   any person who for the purposes of any proceedings so falling (but otherwise than by virtue of an appointment under paragraph 7 of that Schedule) represents that applicant or that organisation.

(3) Section 17(1) shall not prohibit anything done in, for the purposes of, or in connection with, so much of any legal proceedings as relates to the fairness or unfairness of a dismissal on the grounds of any conduct constituting an offence under section 1(1) or (2), 11(7) or 19 of this Act, or section 1 of the Interception of Communications Act 1985.

(4) Section 17(1)(a) shall not prohibit the disclosure of any of the contents of a communication if the interception of that communication was lawful by virtue of section 1(5)(c), 3 or 4.

(5) Where any disclosure is proposed to be or has been made on the grounds that it is authorised by subsection (4), section 17(1) shall not prohibit the doing of anything in, or for the purposes of, so much of any [...] proceedings as relates to the question whether that disclosure is or was so authorised.

(6) Section 17(1)(b) shall not prohibit the doing of anything that discloses any conduct of a person for which he has been convicted of an offence under section 1(1) or (2), 11(7) or 19 of this Act, or section 1 of the Interception of Communications Act 1985.

(7) Nothing in section 17(1) shall prohibit any such disclosure of any information that continues to be available for disclosure as is confined to—

(a)   a disclosure to a person conducting a criminal prosecution for the purpose only of enabling that person to determine what is required of him by his duty to secure the fairness of the prosecution; [...]

(b)   a disclosure to a relevant judge in a case in which that judge has ordered the disclosure to be made to him alone[; or

(c)   a disclosure to the panel of an inquiry held under the Inquiries Act 2005 in the course of which the panel has ordered the disclosure to be made to the panel alone].

(8) A relevant judge shall not order a disclosure under subsection (7)(b) except where he is satisfied that the exceptional circumstances of the case make the disclosure essential in the interests of justice.

[(8A) The panel of an inquiry shall not order a disclosure under subsection (7)(c) except where it is satisfied that the exceptional circumstances of the case make the disclosure essential to enable the inquiry to fulfil its terms of reference.]

(9) Subject to subsection (10), where in any criminal proceedings—

    (a) a relevant judge does order a disclosure under subsection (7)(b), and

    (b) in consequence of that disclosure he is of the opinion that there are exceptional circumstances requiring him to do so,

he may direct the person conducting the prosecution to make for the purposes of the proceedings any such admission of fact as that judge thinks essential in the interests of justice.

(10) Nothing in any direction under subsection (9) shall authorise or require anything to be done in contravention of section 17(1).

(11) In this section "a relevant judge" means—

    (a) any judge of the High Court or of the Crown Court or any Circuit judge;

    (b) any judge of the High Court of Justiciary or any sheriff;

    (c) [in relation to proceedings before the Court Martial, the judge advocate for those proceedings[1]]; or

    (d) any person holding any such judicial office as entitles him to exercise the jurisdiction of a judge falling within paragraph (a) or (b).

(12) In this section "relevant offence" means—

    (a) an offence under any provision of this Act;

    (b) an offence under section 1 of the Interception of Communications Act 1985;

    (c) [section 47 or 48 of the Wireless Telegraphy Act 2006];

    (d) an offence under [section 83 or 84 of the Postal Services Act 2000];

    (e) [...]

    (f) an offence under section 4 of the Official Secrets Act 1989 relating to any such information, document or article as is mentioned in subsection (3)(a) of that section;

    (g) an offence under section 1 or 2 of the Official Secrets Act 1911 relating to any sketch, plan, model, article, note, document or information which incorporates or relates to the contents of any intercepted communication or any related communications data or tends to suggest as mentioned in section 17(1)(b) of this Act;

    (h) perjury committed in the course of any proceedings mentioned in subsection (1) or (3) of this section;

    (i) attempting or conspiring to commit, or aiding, abetting, counselling or procuring the commission of, an offence falling within any of the preceding paragraphs; and

    (j) contempt of court committed in the course of, or in relation to, any proceedings mentioned in subsection (1) or (3) of this section.

(13) In subsection (12) "intercepted communication" has the same meaning as in section 17.

19 Offence for unauthorised disclosures

(1) Where an interception warrant has been issued or renewed, it shall be the duty of every person falling within subsection (2) to keep secret all the matters mentioned in subsection (3).

(2) The persons falling within this subsection are—

    (a)   the persons specified in subsection 6(2);

    (b)   every person holding office under the Crown;

    [(c) every member of the staff of the Serious Organised Crime Agency; ...]

    [(ca) every member of the Scottish Crime and Drug Enforcement Agency;]

    (e)   every person employed by or for the purposes of a police force;

---

[1] Amendment not yet in force: see the Armed Forces Act 2006, s. 383(2).

    (f) persons providing postal services or employed for the purposes of any business of providing such a service;

    (g) persons providing public telecommunications services or employed for the purposes of any business of providing such a service;

    (h) persons having control of the whole or any part of a telecommunication system located wholly or partly in the United Kingdom.

  (3) Those matters are—

    (a) the existence and contents of the warrant and of any section 8(4) certificate in relation to the warrant;

    (b) the details of the issue of the warrant and of any renewal or modification of the warrant or of any such certificate;

    (c) the existence and contents of any requirement to provide assistance with giving effect to the warrant;

    (d) the steps taken in pursuance of the warrant or of any such requirement; and

    (e) everything in the intercepted material, together with any related communications data.

  (4) A person who makes a disclosure to another of anything that he is required to keep secret under this section shall be guilty of an offence and liable—

    (a) on conviction on indictment, to imprisonment for a term not exceeding five years or to a fine, or to both;

    (b) on summary conviction, to imprisonment for a term not exceeding six months or to a fine not exceeding the statutory maximum, or to both.

  (5) In proceedings against any person for an offence under this section in respect of any disclosure, it shall be a defence for that person to show that he could not reasonably have been expected, after first becoming aware of the matter disclosed, to take steps to prevent the disclosure.

  (6) In proceedings against any person for an offence under this section in respect of any disclosure, it shall be a defence for that person to show that—

    (a) the disclosure was made by or to a professional legal adviser in connection with the giving, by the adviser to any client of his, of advice about the effect of provisions of this Chapter; and

    (b) the person to whom or, as the case may be, by whom it was made was the client or a representative of the client.

  (7) In proceedings against any person for an offence under this section in respect of any disclosure, it shall be a defence for that person to show that the disclosure was made by a legal adviser—

    (a) in contemplation of, or in connection with, any legal proceedings; and

    (b) for the purposes of those proceedings.

  (8) Neither subsection (6) nor subsection (7) applies in the case of a disclosure made with a view to furthering any criminal purpose.

  (9) In proceedings against any person for an offence under this section in respect of any disclosure, it shall be a defence for that person to show that the disclosure was confined to a disclosure made to the Interception of Communications Commissioner or authorised—

    (a) by that Commissioner;

    (b) by the warrant or the person to whom the warrant is or was addressed;

    (c) by the terms of the requirement to provide assistance; or

    (d) by section 11(9).

Interpretation of Chapter I

20 Interpretation of Chapter I

In this Chapter—

    "certified", in relation to a section 8(4) certificate, means of a description certified by the certificate as a description of material the examination of which the Secretary of State considers necessary;

    "external communication" means a communication sent or received outside the British Islands;

"intercepted material", in relation to an interception warrant, means the contents of any communications intercepted by an interception to which the warrant relates;

"the interception subject", in relation to an interception warrant, means the person about whose communications information is sought by the interception to which the warrant relates;

"international mutual assistance agreement" means an international agreement designated for the purposes of section 1(4);

"related communications data", in relation to a communication intercepted in the course of its transmission by means of a postal service or telecommunication system, means so much of any communications data (within the meaning of Chapter II of this Part) as—

(a) is obtained by, or in connection with, the interception; and
(b) relates to the communication or to the sender or recipient, or intended recipient, of the communication;

"section 8(4) certificate" means any certificate issued for the purposes of section 8(4).

Chapter II Acquisition and Disclosure of Communications Data

21 Lawful acquisition and disclosure of communications data

(1) This Chapter applies to—

(a) any conduct in relation to a postal service or telecommunication system for obtaining communications data, other than conduct consisting in the interception of communications in the course of their transmission by means of such a service or system; and
(b) the disclosure to any person of communications data.

(2) Conduct to which this Chapter applies shall be lawful for all purposes if—

(a) it is conduct in which any person is authorised or required to engage by an authorisation or notice granted or given under this Chapter; and
(b) the conduct is in accordance with, or in pursuance of, the authorisation or requirement.

(3) A person shall not be subject to any civil liability in respect of any conduct of his which—

(a) is incidental to any conduct that is lawful by virtue of subsection (2); and
(b) is not itself conduct an authorisation or warrant for which is capable of being granted under a relevant enactment and might reasonably have been expected to have been sought in the case in question.

(4) In this Chapter "communications data" means any of the following—

(a) any traffic data comprised in or attached to a communication (whether by the sender or otherwise) for the purposes of any postal service or telecommunication system by means of which it is being or may be transmitted;
(b) any information which includes none of the contents of a communication (apart from any information falling within paragraph (a)) and is about the use made by any person—
   (i) of any postal service or telecommunications service; or
   (ii) in connection with the provision to or use by any person of any telecommunications service, of any part of a telecommunication system;
(c) any information not falling within paragraph (a) or (b) that is held or obtained, in relation to persons to whom he provides the service, by a person providing a postal service or telecommunications service.

(5) In this section "relevant enactment" means—

(a) an enactment contained in this Act;
(b) section 5 of the Intelligence Services Act 1994 (warrants for the intelligence services); or
(c) an enactment contained in Part III of the Police Act 1997 (powers of the police and of [officers of Revenue and Customs]).

(6) In this section "traffic data", in relation to any communication, means—

(a) any data identifying, or purporting to identify, any person, apparatus or location to or from which the communication is or may be transmitted,

    (b) any data identifying or selecting, or purporting to identify or select, apparatus through which, or by means of which, the communication is or may be transmitted,

    (c) any data comprising signals for the actuation of apparatus used for the purposes of a telecommunication system for effecting (in whole or in part) the transmission of any communication, and

    (d) any data identifying the data or other data as data comprised in or attached to a particular communication,

but that expression includes data identifying a computer file or computer program access to which is obtained, or which is run, by means of the communication to the extent only that the file or program is identified by reference to the apparatus in which it is stored.

    (7) In this section—

    (a) references, in relation to traffic data comprising signals for the actuation of apparatus, to a telecommunication system by means of which a communication is being or may be transmitted include references to any telecommunication system in which that apparatus is comprised; and

    (b) references to traffic data being attached to a communication include references to the data and the communication being logically associated with each other;

and in this section "data", in relation to a postal item, means anything written on the outside of the item.

22   Obtaining and disclosing communications data

    (1) This section applies where a person designated for the purposes of this Chapter believes that it is necessary on grounds falling within subsection (2) to obtain any communications data.

    (2) It is necessary on grounds falling within this subsection to obtain communications data if it is necessary—

    (a) in the interests of national security;

    (b) for the purpose of preventing or detecting crime or of preventing disorder;

    (c) in the interests of the economic well-being of the United Kingdom;

    (d) in the interests of public safety;

    (e) for the purpose of protecting public health;

    (f) for the purpose of assessing or collecting any tax, duty, levy or other imposition, contribution or charge payable to a government department;

    (g) for the purpose, in an emergency, of preventing death or injury or any damage to a person's physical or mental health, or of mitigating any injury or damage to a person's physical or mental health; or

    (h) for any purpose (not falling within paragraphs (a) to (g)) which is specified for the purposes of this subsection by an order made by the Secretary of State.

    (3) Subject to subsection (5), the designated person may grant an authorisation for persons holding offices, ranks or positions with the same relevant public authority as the designated person to engage in any conduct to which this Chapter applies.

    (4) Subject to subsection (5), where it appears to the designated person that a postal or telecommunications operator is or may be in possession of, or be capable of obtaining, any communications data, the designated person may, by notice to the postal or telecommunications operator, require the operator—

    (a) if the operator is not already in possession of the data, to obtain the data; and

    (b) in any case, to disclose all of the data in his possession or subsequently obtained by him.

    (5) The designated person shall not grant an authorisation under subsection (3), or give a notice under subsection (4), unless he believes that obtaining the data in question by the conduct authorised or required by the authorisation or notice is proportionate to what is sought to be achieved by so obtaining the data.

    (6) It shall be the duty of the postal or telecommunications operator to comply with the requirements of any notice given to him under subsection (4).

(7) A person who is under a duty by virtue of subsection (6) shall not be required to do anything in pursuance of that duty which it is not reasonably practicable for him to do.

(8) The duty imposed by subsection (6) shall be enforceable by civil proceedings by the Secretary of State for an injunction, or for specific performance of a statutory duty under section 45 of the Court of Session Act 1988, or for any other appropriate relief.

(9) The Secretary of State shall not make an order under subsection (2)(h) unless a draft of the order has been laid before Parliament and approved by a resolution of each House.

23   Form and duration of authorisations and notices

(1) An authorisation under section 22(3)—

(a) must be granted in writing or (if not in writing) in a manner that produces a record of its having been granted;

(b) must describe the conduct to which this Chapter applies that is authorised and the communications data in relation to which it is authorised;

(c) must specify the matters falling within section 22(2) by reference to which it is granted; and

(d) must specify the office, rank or position held by the person granting the authorisation.

(2) A notice under section 22(4) requiring communications data to be disclosed or to be obtained and disclosed—

(a) must be given in writing or (if not in writing) must be given in a manner that produces a record of its having been given;

(b) must describe the communications data to be obtained or disclosed under the notice;

(c) must specify the matters falling within section 22(2) by reference to which the notice is given;

(d) must specify the office, rank or position held by the person giving it; and

(e) must specify the manner in which any disclosure required by the notice is to be made.

(3) A notice under section 22(4) shall not require the disclosure of data to any person other than—

(a) the person giving the notice; or

(b) such other person as may be specified in or otherwise identified by, or in accordance with, the provisions of the notice;

but the provisions of the notice shall not specify or otherwise identify a person for the purposes of paragraph (b) unless he holds an office, rank or position with the same relevant public authority as the person giving the notice.

(4) An authorisation under section 22(3) or notice under section 22(4)—

(a) shall not authorise or require any data to be obtained after the end of the period of one month beginning with the date on which the authorisation is granted or the notice given; and

(b) in the case of a notice, shall not authorise or require any disclosure after the end of that period of any data not in the possession of, or obtained by, the postal or telecommunications operator at a time during that period.

(5) An authorisation under section 22(3) or notice under section 22(4) may be renewed at any time before the end of the period of one month applying (in accordance with subsection (4) or subsection (7)) to that authorisation or notice.

(6) A renewal of an authorisation under section 22(3) or of a notice under section 22(4) shall be by the grant or giving, in accordance with this section, of a further authorisation or notice.

(7) Subsection (4) shall have effect in relation to a renewed authorisation or renewal notice as if the period of one month mentioned in that subsection did not begin until the end of the period of one month applicable to the authorisation or notice that is current at the time of the renewal.

(8) Where a person who has given a notice under subsection (4) of section 22 is satisfied—

(a) that it is no longer necessary on grounds falling within subsection (2) of that section for the requirements of the notice to be complied with, or

(b) that the conduct required by the notice is no longer proportionate to what is sought to be achieved by obtaining communications data to which the notice relates,

he shall cancel the notice.

(9) The Secretary of State may by regulations provide for the person by whom any duty imposed by subsection (8) is to be performed in a case in which it would otherwise fall on a person who is no longer available to perform it; and regulations under this subsection may provide for the person on whom the duty is to fall to be a person appointed in accordance with the regulations.

24   Arrangements for payments

(1) It shall be the duty of the Secretary of State to ensure that such arrangements are in force as he thinks appropriate for requiring or authorising, in such cases as he thinks fit, the making to postal and telecommunications operators of appropriate contributions towards the costs incurred by them in complying with notices under section 22(4).

(2) For the purpose of complying with his duty under this section, the Secretary of State may make arrangements for payments to be made out of money provided by Parliament.

25   Interpretation of Chapter II

(1) In this Chapter—

"communications data" has the meaning given by section 21(4);

"designated" shall be construed in accordance with subsection (2);

"postal or telecommunications operator" means a person who provides a postal service or telecommunications service;

"relevant public authority" means (subject to subsection (4)) any of the following—

    (a)   a police force;

    [(b)   the Serious Organised Crime Agency; ...]

    [(ba) the Scottish Crime and Drug Enforcement Agency;]

    [(d)   Her Majesty's Revenue and Customs;]

    (f)   any of the intelligence services;

    (g)   any such public authority not falling within paragraphs (a) to (f) as may be specified for the purposes of this subsection by an order made by the Secretary of State.

(2) Subject to subsection (3), the persons designated for the purposes of this Chapter are the individuals holding such offices, ranks or positions with relevant public authorities as are prescribed for the purposes of this subsection by an order made by the Secretary of State.

(3) The Secretary of State may by order impose restrictions—

    (a) on the authorisations and notices under this Chapter that may be granted or given by any individual holding an office, rank or position with a specified public authority; and

    (b) on the circumstances in which, or the purposes for which, such authorisations may be granted or notices given by any such individual.

[(3A) References in this Chapter to an individual holding an office or position with the Serious Organised Crime Agency include references to any member of the staff of that Agency.]

[(4) The Secretary of State may by order—

    (a) remove any person from the list of persons who are for the time being relevant public authorities for the purposes of this Chapter; and

    (b) make such consequential amendments, repeals or revocations in this or any other enactment as appear to him to be necessary or expedient.

(5) The Secretary of State shall not make an order under this section—

    (a) that adds any person to the list of persons who are for the time being relevant public authorities for the purposes of this Chapter, or

    (b) that by virtue of subsection (4)(b) amends or repeals any provision of an Act,

unless a draft of the order has been laid before Parliament and approved by a resolution of each House.]

PART II SURVEILLANCE AND COVERT HUMAN INTELLIGENCE SOURCES

Introductory

26 Conduct to which Part II applies

(1) This Part applies to the following conduct—

    (a) directed surveillance;

    (b) intrusive surveillance; and

    (c) the conduct and use of covert human intelligence sources.

(2) Subject to subsection (6), surveillance is directed for the purposes of this Part if it is covert but not intrusive and is undertaken—

    (a) for the purposes of a specific investigation or a specific operation;

    (b) in such a manner as is likely to result in the obtaining of private information about a person (whether or not one specifically identified for the purposes of the investigation or operation); and

    (c) otherwise than by way of an immediate response to events or circumstances the nature of which is such that it would not be reasonably practicable for an authorisation under this Part to be sought for the carrying out of the surveillance.

(3) Subject to subsections (4) to (6), surveillance is intrusive for the purposes of this Part if, and only if, it is covert surveillance that—

    (a) is carried out in relation to anything taking place on any residential premises or in any private vehicle; and

    (b) involves the presence of an individual on the premises or in the vehicle or is carried out by means of a surveillance device.

(4) For the purposes of this Part surveillance is not intrusive to the extent that—

    (a) it is carried out by means only of a surveillance device designed or adapted principally for the purpose of providing information about the location of a vehicle; or

    (b) it is surveillance consisting in any such interception of a communication as falls within section 48(4).

(5) For the purposes of this Part surveillance which—

    (a) is carried out by means of a surveillance device in relation to anything taking place on any residential premises or in any private vehicle, but

    (b) is carried out without that device being present on the premises or in the vehicle,

is not intrusive unless the device is such that it consistently provides information of the same quality and detail as might be expected to be obtained from a device actually present on the premises or in the vehicle.

(6) For the purposes of this Part surveillance which—

    (a) is carried out by means of apparatus designed or adapted for the purpose of detecting the installation or use in any residential or other premises of a television receiver (within the meaning of [Part 4 of the Communications Act 2003]), and

    (b) is carried out from outside those premises exclusively for that purpose,

is neither directed nor intrusive.

(7) In this Part—

    (a) references to the conduct of a covert human intelligence source are references to any conduct of such a source which falls within any of paragraphs (a) to (c) of subsection (8), or is incidental to anything falling within any of those paragraphs; and

    (b) references to the use of a covert human intelligence source are references to inducing, asking or assisting a person to engage in the conduct of such a source, or to obtain information by means of the conduct of such a source.

(8) For the purposes of this Part a person is a covert human intelligence source if—

    (a) he establishes or maintains a personal or other relationship with a person for the covert purpose of facilitating the doing of anything falling within paragraph (b) or (c);

(b) he covertly uses such a relationship to obtain information or to provide access to any information to another person; or

(c) he covertly discloses information obtained by the use of such a relationship, or as a consequence of the existence of such a relationship.

(9) For the purposes of this section—

(a) surveillance is covert if, and only if, it is carried out in a manner that is calculated to ensure that persons who are subject to the surveillance are unaware that it is or may be taking place;

(b) a purpose is covert, in relation to the establishment or maintenance of a personal or other relationship, if and only if the relationship is conducted in a manner that is calculated to ensure that one of the parties to the relationship is unaware of the purpose; and

(c) a relationship is used covertly, and information obtained as mentioned in subsection (8)(c) is disclosed covertly, if and only if it is used or, as the case may be, disclosed in a manner that is calculated to ensure that one of the parties to the relationship is unaware of the use or disclosure in question.

(10) In this section "private information", in relation to a person, includes any information relating to his private or family life.

(11) References in this section, in relation to a vehicle, to the presence of a surveillance device in the vehicle include references to its being located on or under the vehicle and also include references to its being attached to it.

Authorisation of surveillance and human intelligence sources

27 Lawful surveillance etc.

(1) Conduct to which this Part applies shall be lawful for all purposes if—

(a) an authorisation under this Part confers an entitlement to engage in that conduct on the person whose conduct it is; and

(b) his conduct is in accordance with the authorisation.

(2) A person shall not be subject to any civil liability in respect of any conduct of his which—

(a) is incidental to any conduct that is lawful by virtue of subsection (1); and

(b) is not itself conduct an authorisation or warrant for which is capable of being granted under a relevant enactment and might reasonably have been expected to have been sought in the case in question.

(3) The conduct that may be authorised under this Part includes conduct outside the United Kingdom.

(4) In this section "relevant enactment" means—

(a) an enactment contained in this Act;

(b) section 5 of the Intelligence Services Act 1994 (warrants for the intelligence services); or

(c) an enactment contained in Part III of the Police Act 1997 (powers of the police and of [officers of Revenue and Customs]).

28 Authorisation of directed surveillance

(1) Subject to the following provisions of this Part, the persons designated for the purposes of this section shall each have power to grant authorisations for the carrying out of directed surveillance.

(2) A person shall not grant an authorisation for the carrying out of directed surveillance unless he believes—

(a) that the authorisation is necessary on grounds falling within subsection (3); and

(b) that the authorised surveillance is proportionate to what is sought to be achieved by carrying it out.

(3) An authorisation is necessary on grounds falling within this subsection if it is necessary—

(a) in the interests of national security;

(b) for the purpose of preventing or detecting crime or of preventing disorder;

(c) in the interests of the economic well-being of the United Kingdom;

(d) in the interests of public safety;

(e) for the purpose of protecting public health;

(f) for the purpose of assessing or collecting any tax, duty, levy or other imposition, contribution or charge payable to a government department; or

(g) for any purpose (not falling within paragraphs (a) to (f)) which is specified for the purposes of this subsection by an order made by the Secretary of State.

(4) The conduct that is authorised by an authorisation for the carrying out of directed surveillance is any conduct that—

(a) consists in the carrying out of directed surveillance of any such description as is specified in the authorisation; and

(b) is carried out in the circumstances described in the authorisation and for the purposes of the investigation or operation specified or described in the authorisation.

(5) The Secretary of State shall not make an order under subsection (3)(g) unless a draft of the order has been laid before Parliament and approved by a resolution of each House.

29   Authorisation of covert human intelligence sources

(1) Subject to the following provisions of this Part, the persons designated for the purposes of this section shall each have power to grant authorisations for the conduct or the use of a covert human intelligence source.

(2) A person shall not grant an authorisation for the conduct or the use of a covert human intelligence source unless he believes—

(a) that the authorisation is necessary on grounds falling within subsection (3);

(b) that the authorised conduct or use is proportionate to what is sought to be achieved by that conduct or use; and

(c) that arrangements exist for the source's case that satisfy the requirements of subsection (5) and such other requirements as may be imposed by order made by the Secretary of State.

(3) An authorisation is necessary on grounds falling within this subsection if it is necessary—

(a) in the interests of national security;

(b) for the purpose of preventing or detecting crime or of preventing disorder;

(c) in the interests of the economic well-being of the United Kingdom;

(d) in the interests of public safety;

(e) for the purpose of protecting public health;

(f) for the purpose of assessing or collecting any tax, duty, levy or other imposition, contribution or charge payable to a government department; or

(g) for any purpose (not falling within paragraphs (a) to (f)) which is specified for the purposes of this subsection by an order made by the Secretary of State.

(4) The conduct that is authorised by an authorisation for the conduct or the use of a covert human intelligence source is any conduct that—

(a) is comprised in any such activities involving conduct of a covert human intelligence source, or the use of a covert human intelligence source, as are specified or described in the authorisation;

(b) consists in conduct by or in relation to the person who is so specified or described as the person to whose actions as a covert human intelligence source the authorisation relates; and

(c) is carried out for the purposes of, or in connection with, the investigation or operation so specified or described.

(5) For the purposes of this Part there are arrangements for the source's case that satisfy the requirements of this subsection if such arrangements are in force as are necessary for ensuring—

(a) that there will at all times be a person holding an office, rank or position with the relevant investigating authority who will have day-to-day responsibility for dealing with the source on behalf of that authority, and for the source's security and welfare;

(b) that there will at all times be another person holding an office, rank or position with the relevant investigating authority who will have general oversight of the use made of the source;

(c) that there will at all times be a person holding an office, rank or position with the relevant investigating authority who will have responsibility for maintaining a record of the use made of the source;

(d) that the records relating to the source that are maintained by the relevant investigating authority will always contain particulars of all such matters (if any) as may be specified for the purposes of this paragraph in regulations made by the Secretary of State; and

(e) that records maintained by the relevant investigating authority that disclose the identity of the source will not be available to persons except to the extent that there is a need for access to them to be made available to those persons.

(6) The Secretary of State shall not make an order under subsection (3)(g) unless a draft of the order has been laid before Parliament and approved by a resolution of each House.

(7) The Secretary of State may by order—

(a) prohibit the authorisation under this section of any such conduct or uses of covert human intelligence sources as may be described in the order; and

(b) impose requirements, in addition to those provided for by subsection (2), that must be satisfied before an authorisation is granted under this section for any such conduct or uses of covert human intelligence sources as may be so described.

(8) In this section "relevant investigating authority", in relation to an authorisation for the conduct or the use of an individual as a covert human intelligence source, means (subject to subsection (9)) the public authority for whose benefit the activities of that individual as such a source are to take place.

(9) In the case of any authorisation for the conduct or the use of a covert human intelligence source whose activities are to be for the benefit of more than one public authority, the references in subsection (5) to the relevant investigating authority are references to one of them (whether or not the same one in the case of each reference).

30   Persons entitled to grant authorisations under ss. 28 and 29

(1) Subject to subsection (3), the persons designated for the purposes of sections 28 and 29 are the individuals holding such offices, ranks or positions with relevant public authorities as are prescribed for the purposes of this subsection by an order under this section.

(2) For the purposes of the grant of an authorisation that combines—

(a) an authorisation under sections 28 or 29, and

(b) an authorisation by the Secretary of State for the carrying out of intrusive surveillance,

the Secretary of State himself shall be a person designated for the purposes of that section.

(3) An order under this section may impose restrictions—

(a) on the authorisations under sections 28 and 29 that may be granted by any individual holding an office, rank or position with a specified public authority; and

(b) on the circumstances in which, or the purposes for which, such authorisations may be granted by any such individual.

(4) A public authority is a relevant public authority for the purposes of this section—

(a) in relation to section 28 if it is specified in Part I or II of Schedule 1; and

(b) in relation to section 29 if it is specified in Part I of that Schedule.

(5) An order under this section may amend Schedule 1 by—

(a) adding a public authority to Part I or II of that Schedule;

(b) removing a public authority from that Schedule;

(c) moving a public authority from one Part of that Schedule to the other;

(d) making any change consequential on any change in the name of a public authority specified in that Schedule.

(6) Without prejudice to section 31, the power to make an order under this section shall be exercisable by the Secretary of State.

(7) The Secretary of State shall not make an order under subsection (5) containing any provision for—

(a) adding any public authority to Part I or II of that Schedule, or

(b) moving any public authority from Part II to Part I of that Schedule, unless a draft of the order has been laid before Parliament and approved by a resolution of each House.

31 Orders under s. 30 for Northern Ireland

(1) Subject to subsections (2) and (3), the power to make an order under section 30 for the purposes of the grant of authorisations for conduct in Northern Ireland shall be exercisable by the Office of the First Minister and deputy First Minister in Northern Ireland (concurrently with being exercisable by the Secretary of State).

(2) The power of the Office of the First Minister and deputy First Minister to make an order under section 30 by virtue of subsection (1) or (3) of that section shall not be exercisable in relation to any public authority other than—

(a) the Food Standards Agency;

(b) …

(c) an authority added to Schedule 1 by an order made by that Office;

(d) an authority added to that Schedule by an order made by the Secretary of State which it would (apart from that order) have been within the powers of that Office to add to that Schedule for the purposes mentioned in subsection (1) of this section.

(3) The power of the Office of the First Minister and deputy First Minister to make an order under section 30—

(a) shall not include power to make any provision dealing with an excepted matter;

(b) shall not include power, except with the consent of the Secretary of State, to make any provision dealing with a reserved matter.

(4) The power of the Office of the First Minister and deputy First Minister to make an order under section 30 shall be exercisable by statutory rule for the purposes of the Statutory Rules (Northern Ireland) Order 1979.

(5) A statutory rule containing an order under section 30 which makes provision by virtue of subsection (5) of that section for—

(a) adding any public authority to Part I or II of Schedule 1, or

(b) moving any public authority from Part II to Part I of that Schedule,

shall be subject to affirmative resolution (within the meaning of section 41(4) of the Interpretation Act (Northern Ireland) 1954).

(6) A statutory rule containing an order under section 30 (other than one to which subsection (5) of this section applies) shall be subject to negative resolution (within the meaning of section 41(6) of the Interpretation Act (Northern Ireland) 1954).

(7) An order under section 30 made by the Office of the First Minister and deputy First Minister may—

(a) make different provision for different cases;

(b) contain such incidental, supplemental, consequential and transitional provision as that Office thinks fit.

(8) The reference in subsection (2) to an addition to Schedule 1 being within the powers of the Office of the First Minister and deputy First Minister includes a reference to its being within the powers exercisable by that Office with the consent for the purposes of subsection (3)(b) of the Secretary of State.

(9) In this section "excepted matter" and "reserved matter" have the same meanings as in the Northern Ireland Act 1998; and, in relation to those matters, section 98(2) of that Act (meaning of "deals with") applies for the purposes of this section as it applies for the purposes of that Act.

32 Authorisation of intrusive surveillance

(1) Subject to the following provisions of this Part, the Secretary of State and each of the senior authorising officers shall have power to grant authorisations for the carrying out of intrusive surveillance.

(2) Neither the Secretary of State nor any senior authorising officer shall grant an authorisation for the carrying out of intrusive surveillance unless he believes—

(a) that the authorisation is necessary on grounds falling within subsection (3); and

(b) that the authorised surveillance is proportionate to what is sought to be achieved by carrying it out.

(3) Subject to the following provisions of this section, an authorisation is necessary on grounds falling within this subsection if it is necessary—

(a) in the interests of national security;

(b) for the purpose of preventing or detecting serious crime; or

(c) in the interests of the economic well-being of the United Kingdom.

[(3A) In the case of an authorisation granted by the chairman of the OFT, the authorisation is necessary on grounds falling within subsection (3) only if it is necessary for the purpose of preventing or detecting an offence under section 188 of the Enterprise Act 2002 (cartel offence).]

(4) The matters to be taken into account in considering whether the requirements of subsection (2) are satisfied in the case of any authorisation shall include whether the information which it is thought necessary to obtain by the authorised conduct could reasonably be obtained by other means.

(5) The conduct that is authorised by an authorisation for the carrying out of intrusive surveillance is any conduct that—

(a) consists in the carrying out of intrusive surveillance of any such description as is specified in the authorisation;

(b) is carried out in relation to the residential premises specified or described in the authorisation or in relation to the private vehicle so specified or described; and

(c) is carried out for the purposes of, or in connection with, the investigation or operation so specified or described.

(6) For the purposes of this section the senior authorising officers are—

(a) the chief constable of every police force maintained under section 2 of the Police Act 1996 (police forces in England and Wales outside London);

(b) the Commissioner of Police of the Metropolis and every Assistant Commissioner of Police of the Metropolis;

(c) the Commissioner of Police for the City of London;

(d) the chief constable of every police force maintained under or by virtue of section 1 of the Police (Scotland) Act 1967 (police forces for areas in Scotland);

(e) the [Chief Constable of the Police Service of Northern Ireland] and the Deputy Chief Constable of the [Police Service of Northern Ireland];

(f) the Chief Constable of the Ministry of Defence Police;

(g) the Provost Marshal of the [Royal Navy Police];

(h) the Provost Marshal of the Royal Military Police;

(i) the Provost Marshal of the Royal Air Force Police;

(j) the Chief Constable of the British Transport Police;

[(k) the Director General of the Serious Organised Crime Agency and any member of the staff of that Agency who is designated for the purposes of this paragraph by that Director General; . . .]

(m) [an officer of Revenue and Customs who is a senior official and who is designated for the purposes of this paragraph by the Commissioners for Her Majesty's Revenue and Customs; and

(n) the Chairman of the OFT.]

Police and customs authorisations

33   Rules for grant of authorisations

(1) A person who is a designated person for the purposes of section 28 or 29 by reference to his office, rank or position with a police force [. . .] shall not grant an authorisation under that section except on an application made by a member of the same force [. . .].

[(1A) A person who is a designated person for the purposes of section 28 or 29 by reference to his office or position with the Serious Organised Crime Agency shall not grant an authorisation under that section except on an application made by a member of the staff of the Agency.]

[(1B) A person who is a designated person for the purposes of section 28 or 29 by reference to his office, rank or position with the Scottish Crime and Drug Enforcement Agency shall not grant an authorisation under that section except on an application made by a police member of the Agency.]

[(2) A person who is a designated person for the purposes of section 28 or 29 by reference to office, rank or position in Her Majesty's Revenue and Customs shall not grant an authorisation under that section except on an application made by an officer of Revenue and Customs.]

(3) A person who is a senior authorising officer by reference to a police force [. . .] shall not grant an authorisation for the carrying out of intrusive surveillance except—

    (a) on an application made by a member of the same force [. . .]; and

    (b) in the case of an authorisation for the carrying out of intrusive surveillance in relation to any residential premises, where those premises are in the area of operation of that force [. . .].

[(3A) The Director General of the Serious Organised Crime Agency or a person designated for the purposes of section 32(6)(k) by that Director General shall not grant an authorisation for the carrying out of intrusive surveillance except on an application made by a member of the staff of the Agency.]

[(4) A person who is a senior authorising officer by virtue of a designation by the Commissioners for Her Majesty's Revenue and Customs shall not grant an authorisation for the carrying out of intrusive surveillance except on an application made by an officer of Revenue and Customs.]

[(4A) The chairman of the OFT shall not grant an authorisation for the carrying out of intrusive surveillance except on an application made by an officer of the OFT.]

(5) A single authorisation may combine both—

    (a) an authorisation granted under this Part by, or on the application of, an individual who is a member of a police force, [a member of the staff of the Serious Organised Crime Agency or a member of the Scottish Crime and Drug Enforcement Agency], or who is [an officer of Revenue and Customs or the Chairman or an officer of the OFT]; and

    (b) an authorisation given by, or on the application of, that individual under Part III of the Police Act 1997;

but the provisions of this Act or that Act that are applicable in the case of each of the authorisations shall apply separately in relation to the part of the combined authorisation to which they are applicable.

(6) For the purposes of this section—

    (a) the area of operation of a police force maintained under section 2 of the Police Act 1996, of the metropolitan police force, of the City of London police force or of a police force maintained under or by virtue of section 1 of the Police (Scotland) Act 1967 is the area for which that force is maintained;

    (b) the area of operation of the [Police Service of Northern Ireland] is Northern Ireland;

    (c) residential premises are in the area of operation of the Ministry of Defence Police if they are premises where the members of that police force, under section 2 of the Ministry of Defence Police Act 1987, have the powers and privileges of a constable;

    (d) residential premises are in the area of operation of the [Royal Navy Police], the Royal Military Police or the Royal Air Force Police if they are premises owned or occupied by, or used for residential purposes by, a [person subject to service law or a civilian subject to service discipline[1]];

    (e) the area of operation of the British Transport Police [. . .] is the United Kingdom;

    (f) [. . .]

and references in this section to the United Kingdom or to any part or area of the United Kingdom include any adjacent waters within the seaward limits of the territorial waters of the United Kingdom.

(7) [In subsection (6) "subject to service law" and "civilian subject to service discipline" have the same meanings as in the Armed Forces Act 2006.*]

---

[1] These amendments not yet in force: see the Armed Forces Act 2006, s. 383(2).

34   Grant of authorisations in the senior officer's absence

(1) This section applies in the case of an application for an authorisation for the carrying out of intrusive surveillance where—

(a) the application is one made by a member of a police force, [a member of the staff of the Serious Organised Crime Agency] or by [an officer of the OFT or an officer of Revenue and Customs]; and

(b) the case is urgent.

(2) If—

(a) it is not reasonably practicable, having regard to the urgency of the case, for the application to be considered by any person who is a senior authorising officer by reference to the force [or Agency] in question or, as the case may be [as chairman of the OFT or], by virtue of a designation by [the Commissioners for Her Majesty's Revenue and Customs], and

(b) it also not reasonably practicable, having regard to the urgency of the case, for the application to be considered by a person (if there is one) who is entitled, as a designated deputy of a senior authorising officer, to exercise the functions in relation to that application of such an officer,

the application may be made to and considered by any person who is entitled under subsection (4) to act for any senior authorising officer who would have been entitled to consider the application.

(3) A person who considers an application under subsection (1) shall have the same power to grant an authorisation as the person for whom he is entitled to act.

(4) For the purposes of this section—

(a) a person is entitled to act for the chief constable of a police force maintained under section 2 of the Police Act 1996 if he holds the rank of assistant chief constable in that force;

(b) a person is entitled to act for the Commissioner of Police of the Metropolis, or for an Assistant Commissioner of Police of the Metropolis, if he holds the rank of commander in the metropolitan police force;

(c) a person is entitled to act for the Commissioner of Police for the City of London if he holds the rank of commander in the City of London police force;

(d) a person is entitled to act for the chief constable of a police force maintained under or by virtue of section 1 of the Police (Scotland) Act 1967 if he holds the rank of assistant chief constable in that force;

(e) a person is entitled to act for the [Chief Constable of the Police Service of Northern Ireland], or for the Deputy Chief Constable of the [Police Service of Northern Ireland], if he holds the rank of assistant chief constable in the [Police Service of Northern Ireland];

(f) a person is entitled to act for the Chief Constable of the Ministry of Defence Police if he holds the rank of deputy or assistant chief constable in that force;

(g) a person is entitled to act for the Provost Marshal of the [Royal Navy Police] if he holds the position of assistant Provost Marshal in [that force];

(h) a person is entitled to act for the Provost Marshal of the Royal Military Police or the Provost Marshal of the Royal Air Force Police if he holds the position of deputy Provost Marshal in the police force in question;

(i) a person is entitled to act for the Chief Constable of the British Transport Police if he holds the rank of deputy or assistant chief constable in that force;

[(j) a person is entitled to act for the Director General of the Serious Organised Crime Agency if he is a person designated for the purposes of this paragraph by that Director General as a person entitled so to act in an urgent case; ...]

(l) a person is entitled to act for a person who is a senior authorising officer by virtue of a designation by [the Commissioners for Her Majesty's Revenue and Customs], if he is [a senior official] designated for the purposes of this paragraph by those Commissioners as a person entitled so to act in an urgent case;

[(m) a person is entitled to act for the chairman of the OFT if he is an officer of the OFT designated by it for the purposes of this paragraph as a person entitled so to act in an urgent case.]

(5) [...]

(6) In this section "designated deputy"—

[(a) in relation to the chief constable for a police force in England and Wales, means—

(i) the person who is the appropriate deputy chief constable for the purposes of section 12A(1) of the Police Act 1996, or

(ii) a person holding the rank of assistant chief constable who is designated to act under section 12A(2) of that Act;

(aa) in relation to the chief constable for a police force in Scotland, means—

(i) a person holding the rank of deputy chief constable and, where there is more than one person in the police force who holds that rank, who is designated as the officer having the powers and duties conferred on a deputy chief constable by section 5A(1) of the Police (Scotland) Act 1967, or

(ii) a person holding the rank of assistant chief constable who is designated to act under section 5A(2) of that Act;]

(b) in relation to the Commissioner of Police for the City of London, means a person authorised to act under section 25 of the City of London Police Act 1839;

(c) [...]

35 Notification of authorisations for intrusive surveillance

(1) Where a person grants or cancels a [police, SOCA, Revenue and Customs or OFT] authorisation for the carrying out of intrusive surveillance, he shall give notice that he has done so to an ordinary Surveillance Commissioner.

(2) A notice given for the purposes of subsection (1)—

(a) must be given in writing as soon as reasonably practicable after the grant or, as the case may be, cancellation of the authorisation to which it relates;

(b) must be given in accordance with any such arrangements made for the purposes of this paragraph by the Chief Surveillance Commissioner as are for the time being in force; and

(c) must specify such matters as the Secretary of State may by order prescribe.

(3) A notice under this section of the grant of an authorisation shall, as the case may be, either—

(a) state that the approval of a Surveillance Commissioner is required by section 36 before the grant of the authorisation will take effect; or

(b) state that the case is one of urgency and set out the grounds on which the case is believed to be one of urgency.

(4) Where a notice for the purposes of subsection (1) of the grant of an authorisation has been received by an ordinary Surveillance Commissioner, he shall, as soon as practicable—

(a) scrutinise the authorisation; and

(b) in a case where notice has been given in accordance with subsection (3)(a), decide whether or not to approve the authorisation.

(5) Subject to subsection (6), the Secretary of State shall not make an order under subsection (2)(c) unless a draft of the order has been laid before Parliament and approved by a resolution of each House.

(6) Subsection (5) does not apply in the case of the order made on the first occasion on which the Secretary of State exercises his power to make an order under subsection (2)(c).

(7) The order made on that occasion shall cease to have effect at the end of the period of forty days beginning with the day on which it was made unless, before the end of that period, it has been approved by a resolution of each House of Parliament.

(8) For the purposes of subsection (7)—

(a) the order's ceasing to have effect shall be without prejudice to anything previously done or to the making of a new order; and

(b) in reckoning the period of forty days no account shall be taken of any period during which Parliament is dissolved or prorogued or during which both Houses are adjourned for more than four days.

(9) Any notice that is required by any provision of this section to be given in writing may be given, instead, by being transmitted by electronic means.

(10) In this section references to a [police, SOCA, customs] [or OFT] authorisation are references to an authorisation granted by—

(a)   a person who is a senior authorising officer by reference to a police force [or the Serious Organised Crime Agency];

(b)   a person who is a senior authorising officer by virtue of a designation by [the Commissioners for Her Majesty's Revenue and Customs]; or

[(ba) the Chairman of the OFT; or]

(c)   a person who for the purposes of section 34 is entitled to act for a person falling within paragraph (a) or for a person falling within paragraph (b) [or for a person falling within paragraph (ba).]

36   Approval required for authorisations to take effect

(1) This section applies where an authorisation for the carrying out of intrusive surveillance has been granted on the application of—

(a)   a member of a police force;

[(b) a member of the staff of the Serious Organised Crime Agency; ...

(d)   an officer of Revenue and Customs; or

(e)   an officer of the OFT].

(2) Subject to subsection (3), the authorisation shall not take effect until such time (if any) as—

(a)   the grant of the authorisation has been approved by an ordinary Surveillance Commissioner; and

(b)   written notice of the Commissioner's decision to approve the grant of the authorisation has been given, in accordance with subsection (4), to the person who granted the authorisation.

(3) Where the person who grants the authorisation—

(a)   believes that the case is one of urgency, and

(b)   gives notice in accordance with section 35(3)(b),

subsection (2) shall not apply to the authorisation, and the authorisation shall have effect from the time of its grant.

(4) Where subsection (2) applies to the authorisation—

(a)   a Surveillance Commissioner shall give his approval under this section to the authorisation if, and only if, he is satisfied that there are reasonable grounds for believing that the requirements of section 32(2)(a) and (b) are satisfied in the case of the authorisation; and

(b)   a Surveillance Commissioner who makes a decision as to whether or not the authorisation should be approved shall, as soon as reasonably practicable after making that decision, give written notice of his decision to the person who granted the authorisation.

(5) If an ordinary Surveillance Commissioner decides not to approve an authorisation to which subsection (2) applies, he shall make a report of his findings to the most senior relevant person.

(6) In this section "the most senior relevant person" means—

(a)   where the authorisation was granted by the senior authorising officer with any police force who is not someone's deputy, that senior authorising officer;

(b)   where the authorisation was granted by the Director General of the [Serious Organised Crime Agency,] that Director General;

(c)   where the authorisation was granted by a senior authorising officer with a police force who is someone's deputy, the senior authorising officer whose deputy granted the authorisation;

[(d) where the authorisation was granted by a person designated for the purposes of section 32(6)(k), or by a person entitled to act for the Director General of the Serious Organised Crime Agency by virtue of section 34(4)(j), that Director General; ...]

(e)   [...]

(f) where the authorisation was granted by a person entitled to act for a senior authorising officer under section 34(4)(a) to (i), the senior authorising officer in the force in question who is not someone's deputy; [...]

(g) [where the authorisation was granted by an officer of Revenue and Customs, the officer of Revenue and Customs for the time being designated for the purposes of this paragraph by a written notice given to the Chief Surveillance Commissioner by the Commissioners for Her Majesty's Revenue and Customs]; and

(h) [where the authorisation was granted by the Chairman of the OFT or a person entitled to act for him by virtue of section 34(4)(m), that chairman.]

(7) The references in subsection (6) to a person's deputy are references to the following—

(a) in relation to—

(i)   a chief constable of a police force maintained under section 2 of the Police Act 1996,

(ii) the Commissioner of Police for the City of London, or

(iii) a chief constable of a police force maintained under or by virtue of section 1 of the Police (Scotland) Act 1967, to his designated deputy;

(b) in relation to the Commissioner of Police of the Metropolis, to an Assistant Commissioner of Police of the Metropolis; and

(c) in relation to the [Chief Constable of the Police Service of Northern Ireland], to the Deputy Chief Constable of the [Police Service of Northern Ireland];

and in this subsection and that subsection "designated deputy" has the same meaning as in section 34.

(8) Any notice that is required by any provision of this section to be given in writing may be given, instead, by being transmitted by electronic means.

37   Quashing of police and customs authorisations etc.

(1) This section applies where an authorisation for the carrying out of intrusive surveillance has been granted on the application of—

(a) a member of a police force;

[(b) a member of the staff of the Serious Organised Crime Agency;...

(d) an officer of Revenue and Customs; or

(e) an officer of the OFT].

(2) Where an ordinary Surveillance Commissioner is at any time satisfied that, at the time when the authorisation was granted or at any time when it was renewed, there were no reasonable grounds for believing that the requirements of section 32(2)(a) and (b) were satisfied, he may quash the authorisation with effect, as he thinks fit, from the time of the grant of the authorisation or from the time of any renewal of the authorisation.

(3) If an ordinary Surveillance Commissioner is satisfied at any time while the authorisation is in force that there are no longer any reasonable grounds for believing that the requirements of section 32(2)(a) and (b) are satisfied in relation to the authorisation, he may cancel the authorisation with effect from such time as appears to him to be the time from which those requirements ceased to be so satisfied.

(4) Where, in the case of any authorisation of which notice has been given in accordance with section 35(3)(b), an ordinary Surveillance Commissioner is at any time satisfied that, at the time of the grant or renewal of the authorisation to which that notice related, there were no reasonable grounds for believing that the case was one of urgency, he may quash the authorisation with effect, as he thinks fit, from the time of the grant of the authorisation or from the time of any renewal of the authorisation.

(5) Subject to subsection (7), where an ordinary Surveillance Commissioner quashes an authorisation under this section, he may order the destruction of any records relating wholly or partly to information obtained by the authorised conduct after the time from which his decision takes effect.

(6) Subject to subsection (7), where—

(a) an authorisation has ceased to have effect (otherwise than by virtue of subsection (2) or (4)), and

(b) an ordinary Surveillance Commissioner is satisfied that there was a time while the author-isation was in force when there were no reasonable grounds for believing that the require-ments of section 32(2)(a) and (b) continued to be satisfied in relation to the authorisation,

he may order the destruction of any records relating, wholly or partly, to information obtained at such a time by the authorised conduct.

(7) No order shall be made under this section for the destruction of any records required for pending criminal or civil proceedings.

(8) Where an ordinary Surveillance Commissioner exercises a power conferred by this section, he shall, as soon as reasonably practicable, make a report of his exercise of that power, and of his reasons for doing so—

(a) to the most senior relevant person (within the meaning of section 36); and

(b) to the Chief Surveillance Commissioner.

(9) Where an order for the destruction of records is made under this section, the order shall not become operative until such time (if any) as—

(a) the period for appealing against the decision to make the order has expired; and

(b) any appeal brought within that period has been dismissed by the Chief Surveillance Commissioner.

(10) No notice shall be required to be given under section 35(1) in the case of a cancellation under subsection (3) of this section.

38 Appeals against decisions by Surveillance Commissioners

(1) Any senior authorising officer may appeal to the Chief Surveillance Commissioner against any of the following—

(a) any refusal of an ordinary Surveillance Commissioner to approve an authorisation for the carrying out of intrusive surveillance;

(b) any decision of such a Commissioner to quash or cancel such an authorisation;

(c) any decision of such a Commissioner to make an order under section 37 for the destruc-tion of records.

(2) In the case of an authorisation granted by the designated deputy of a senior authorising office or by a person who for the purposes of section 34 is entitled to act for a senior authorising officer, that designated deputy or person shall also be entitled to appeal under this section.

(3) An appeal under this section must be brought within the period of seven days beginning with the day on which the refusal or decision appealed against is reported to the appellant.

(4) Subject to subsection (5), the Chief Surveillance Commissioner, on an appeal under this sec-tion, shall allow the appeal if—

(a) he is satisfied that there were reasonable grounds for believing that the requirements of section 32(2)(a) and (b) were satisfied in relation to the authorisation at the time in question; and

(b) he is not satisfied that the authorisation is one of which notice was given in accordance with section 35(3)(b) without there being any reasonable grounds for believing that the case was one of urgency.

(5) If, on an appeal falling within subsection (1)(b), the Chief Surveillance Commissioner—

(a) is satisfied that grounds exist which justify the quashing or cancellation under section 37 of the authorisation in question, but

(b) considers that the authorisation should have been quashed or cancelled from a differ-ent time from that from which it was quashed or cancelled by the ordinary Surveillance Commissioner against whose decision the appeal is brought,

he may modify that Commissioner's decision to quash or cancel the authorisation, and any related decision for the destruction of records, so as to give effect to the decision under section 37 that he considers should have been made.

(6) Where, on an appeal under this section against a decision to quash or cancel an authorisa-tion, the Chief Surveillance Commissioner allows the appeal he shall also quash any related order for the destruction of records relating to information obtained by the authorised conduct.

(7) In this section "designated deputy" has the same meaning as in section 34.

39   Appeals to the Chief Surveillance Commissioner: supplementary

(1) Where the Chief Surveillance Commissioner has determined an appeal under section 38, he shall give notice of his determination to both—

(a) the person by whom the appeal was brought; and

(b) the ordinary Surveillance Commissioner whose decision was appealed against.

(2) Where the determination of the Chief Surveillance Commissioner on an appeal under section 38 is a determination to dismiss the appeal, the Chief Surveillance Commissioner shall make a report of his findings—

(a) to the persons mentioned in subsection (1); and

(b) to the Prime Minister.

(3) Subsections (3) and (4) of section 107 of the Police Act 1997 (reports to be laid before Parliament and exclusion of matters from the report) apply in relation to any report to the Prime Minister under subsection (2) of this section as they apply in relation to any report under subsection (2) of that section.

(4) Subject to subsection (2) of this section, the Chief Surveillance Commissioner shall not give any reasons for any determination of his on an appeal under section 38.

40   Information to be provided to Surveillance Commissioners

It shall be the duty of—

(a)   every member of a police force,

[(b) every member of the staff of the Serious Organised Crime Agency,...

(d)   every officer of Revenue and Customs, and

(e)   every officer of the OFT,]

to comply with any request of a Surveillance Commissioner for documents or information required by that Commissioner for the purpose of enabling him to carry out the functions of such a Commissioner under sections 35 to 39.

Other authorisations

41   Secretary of State authorisations

(1) The Secretary of State shall not grant an authorisation for the carrying out of intrusive surveillance except on an application made by—

(a) a member of any of the intelligence services;

(b) an official of the Ministry of Defence;

(c) a member of Her Majesty's forces;

(d) an individual holding an office, rank or position with any such public authority as may be designated for the purposes of this section as an authority whose activities may require the carrying out of intrusive surveillance.

(2) Section 32 shall have effect in relation to the grant of an authorisation by the Secretary of State on the application of an official of the Ministry of Defence, or of a member of Her Majesty's forces, as if the only matters mentioned in subsection (3) of that section were—

(a) the interests of national security; and

(b) the purpose of preventing or detecting serious crime.

(3) The designation of any public authority for the purposes of this section shall be by order made by the Secretary of State.

(4) The Secretary of State may by order provide, in relation to any public authority, that an application for an authorisation for the carrying out of intrusive surveillance may be made by an individual holding an office, rank or position with that authority only where his office, rank or position is one prescribed by the order.

(5) The Secretary of State may by order impose restrictions—

(a) on the authorisations for the carrying out of intrusive surveillance that may be granted on the application of an individual holding an office, rank or position with any public authority designated for the purposes of this section; and

    (b) on the circumstances in which, or the purposes for which, such authorisations may be granted on such an application.

    (6) The Secretary of State shall not make a designation under subsection (3) unless a draft of the order containing the designation has been laid before Parliament and approved by a resolution of each House.

    (7) References in this section to a member of Her Majesty's forces do not include references to any member of Her Majesty's forces who is a member of a police force by virtue of his service with the [Royal Navy Police], the Royal Military Police or the Royal Air Force Police.

42   Intelligence services authorisations

    (1) The grant by the Secretary of State [or, the Scottish Ministers (by virtue of provision under section 63 of the Scotland Act 1998)] on the application of a member of one of the intelligence services of any authorisation under this Part must be made by the issue of a warrant.

    (2) A single warrant issued by the Secretary of State [or, the Scottish Ministers (by virtue of provision under section 63 of the Scotland Act 1998)] may combine both—

        (a) an authorisation under this Part; and

        (b) an intelligence services warrant;

but the provisions of this Act or the Intelligence Services Act 1994 that are applicable in the case of the authorisation under this Part or the intelligence services warrant shall apply separately in relation to the part of the combined warrant to which they are applicable.

    (3) Intrusive surveillance in relation to any premises or vehicle in the British Islands shall be capable of being authorised by a warrant issued under this Part on the application of a member of the Secret Intelligence Service or GCHQ only if the authorisation contained in the warrant is one satisfying the requirements of section 32(2)(a) otherwise than in connection with any functions of that intelligence service in support of the prevention or detection of serious crime.

    (4) Subject to subsection (5), the functions of the Security Service shall include acting on behalf of the Secret Intelligence Service or GCHQ in relation to—

        (a) the application for and grant of any authorisation under this Part in connection with any matter within the functions of the Secret Intelligence Service or GCHQ; and

        (b) the carrying out, in connection with any such matter, of any conduct authorised by such an authorisation.

    (5) Nothing in subsection (4) shall authorise the doing of anything by one intelligence service on behalf of another unless—

        (a) it is something which either the other service or a member of the other service has power to do; and

        (b) it is done otherwise than in connection with functions of the other service in support of the prevention or detection of serious crime.

    (6) In this section "intelligence services warrant" means a warrant under section 5 of the Intelligence Services Act 1994.

Grant, renewal and duration of authorisations

43   General rules about grant, renewal and duration[1]

    (1) An authorisation under this Part—

        (a) may be granted or renewed orally in any urgent case in which the entitlement to act of the person granting or renewing it is not confined to urgent cases; and

        (b) in any other case, must be in writing.

    (2) A single authorisation may combine two or more different authorisations under this Part; but the provisions of this Act that are applicable in the case of each of the authorisations shall apply separately in relation to the part of the combined authorisation to which they are applicable.

---

[1] This section is modified in its application to the detection of television receivers: see SI 2001/1057.

(3) Subject to subsections (4) and (8), an authorisation under this Part shall cease to have effect at the end of the following period—

    (a) in the case of an authorisation which—

        (i) has not been renewed and was granted either orally or by a person whose entitlement to act is confined to urgent cases, or

        (ii) was last renewed either orally or by such a person,

    the period of seventy-two hours beginning with the time when the grant of the authorisation or, as the case may be, its latest renewal takes effect;

    (b) in a case not falling within paragraph (a) in which the authorisation is for the conduct or the use of a covert human intelligence source, the period of twelve months beginning with the day on which the grant of the authorisation or, as the case may be, its latest renewal takes effect; and

    (c) in any case not falling within paragraph (a) or (b), the period of three months beginning with the day on which the grant of the authorisation or, as the case may be, its latest renewal takes effect.

(4) Subject to subsection (6), an authorisation under this Part may be renewed, at any time before the time at which it ceases to have effect, by any person who would be entitled to grant a new authorisation in the same terms.

(5) Sections 28 to 41 shall have effect in relation to the renewal of an authorisation under this Part as if references to the grant of an authorisation included references to its renewal.

(6) A person shall not renew an authorisation for the conduct or the use of a covert human intelligence source, unless he—

    (a) is satisfied that a review has been carried out of the matters mentioned in sub-section (7); and

    (b) has, for the purpose of deciding whether he should renew the authorisation, considered the results of that review.

(7) The matters mentioned in subsection (6) are—

    (a) the use made of the source in the period since the grant or, as the case may be, latest renewal of the authorisation; and

    (b) the tasks given to the source during that period and the information obtained from the conduct or the use of the source.

(8) The Secretary of State may by order provide in relation to authorisations of such descriptions as may be specified in the order that subsection (3) is to have effect as if the period at the end of which an authorisation of a description so specified is to cease to have effect were such period shorter than that provided for by that subsection as may be fixed by or determined in accordance with that order.

(9) References in this section to the time at which, or the day on which, the grant or renewal of an authorisation takes effect are references—

    (a) in the case of the grant of an authorisation to which paragraph (c) does not apply, to the time at which or, as the case may be, day on which the authorisation is granted;

    (b) in the case of the renewal of an authorisation to which paragraph (c) does not apply, to the time at which or, as the case may be, day on which the authorisation would have ceased to have effect but for the renewal; and

    (c) in the case of any grant or renewal that takes effect under subsection (2) of section 36 at a time or on a day later than that given by paragraph (a) or (b), to the time at which or, as the case may be, day on which the grant or renewal takes effect in accordance with that subsection.

(10) In relation to any authorisation granted by a member of any of the intelligence services, and in relation to any authorisation contained in a warrant issued by the Secretary of State on the application of a member of any of the intelligence services, this section has effect subject to the provisions of section 44.

44   Special rules for intelligence services authorisations

(1) Subject to subsection (2), a warrant containing an authorisation for the carrying out of intrusive surveillance—

  (a) shall not be issued on the application of a member of any of the intelligence services, and

  (b) if so issued shall not be renewed,

except under the hand of the Secretary of State [or, in the case of a warrant issued by the Scottish Ministers (by virtue of provision made under section 63 of the Scotland Act 1998), a member of the Scottish Executive].

(2) In an urgent case in which—

  (a) an application for a warrant containing an authorisation for the carrying out of intrusive surveillance has been made by a member of any of the intelligence services, and

  (b) the Secretary of State has himself [or the Scottish Ministers (by virtue of provision made under section 63 of the Scotland Act 1998) have themselves] expressly authorised the issue of the warrant in that case,

the warrant may be issued (but not renewed) under the hand of a senior official [or, as the case may be, a member of the staff of the Scottish Administration who is a member of the Senior Civil Service and is designated by the Scottish Ministers as a person under whose hand a warrant may be issued in such a case (in this section referred to as "a designated official")].

(3) Subject to subsection (6), a warrant containing an authorisation for the carrying out of intrusive surveillance which—

  (a) was issued, on the application of a member of any of the intelligence services, under the hand of a senior official [or, as the case may be, a designated official], and

  (b) has not been renewed under the hand of the Secretary of State [or, in the case of a warrant issued by the Scottish Ministers (by virtue of provision made under section 63 of the Scotland Act 1998), a member of the Scottish Executive],

shall cease to have effect at the end of the second working day following the day of the issue of the warrant, instead of at the time provided for by section 43(3).

(4) Subject to subsections (3) and (6), where any warrant for the carrying out of intrusive surveillance which is issued or was last renewed on the application of a member of any of the intelligence services, the warrant (unless renewed or, as the case may be, renewed again) shall cease to have effect at the following time, instead of at the time provided for by section 43(3), namely—

  (a) in the case of a warrant that has not been renewed, at the end of the period of six months beginning with the day on which it was issued; and

  (b) in any other case, at the end of the period of six months beginning with the day on which it would have ceased to have effect if not renewed again.

(5) Subject to subsection (6), where—

  (a) an authorisation for the carrying out of directed surveillance is granted by a member of any of the intelligence services, and

  (b) the authorisation is renewed by an instrument endorsed under the hand of the person renewing the authorisation with a statement that the renewal is believed to be necessary on grounds falling within section 32(3)(a) or (c),

the authorisation (unless renewed again) shall cease to have effect at the end of the period of six months beginning with the day on which it would have ceased to have effect but for the renewal, instead of at the time provided for by section 43(3).

(6) The Secretary of State may by order provide in relation to authorisations of such descriptions as may be specified in the order that subsection (3), (4) or (5) is to have effect as if the period at the end of which an authorisation of a description so specified is to cease to have effect were such period shorter than that provided for by that subsection as may be fixed by or determined in accordance with that order.

(7) Notwithstanding anything in section 43(2), in a case in which there is a combined warrant containing both—

  (a) an authorisation for the carrying out of intrusive surveillance, and

  (b) an authorisation for the carrying out of directed surveillance, the reference in subsection (4) of this section to a warrant for the carrying out of intrusive surveillance is a reference to the warrant so far as it confers both authorisations.

45   Cancellation of authorisations[1]

(1) The person who granted or, as the case may be, last renewed an authorisation under this Part shall cancel it if—

    (a) he is satisfied that the authorisation is one in relation to which the requirements of section 28(2)(a) and (b), 29(2)(a) and (b) or, as the case may be, 32(2)(a) and (b) are no longer satisfied; or

    (b) in the case of an authorisation under section 29, he is satisfied that arrangements for the source's case that satisfy the requirements mentioned in subsection (2)(c) of that section no longer exist.

(2) Where an authorisation under this Part was granted or, as the case may be, last renewed—

    (a) by a person entitled to act for any other person, or

    (b) by the deputy of any other person,

that other person shall cancel the authorisation if he is satisfied as to either of the matters mentioned in subsection (1).

(3) Where an authorisation under this Part was granted or, as the case may be, last renewed by a person whose deputy had power to grant it, that deputy shall cancel the authorisation if he is satisfied as to either of the matters mentioned in subsection (1).

(4) The Secretary of State may by regulations provide for the person by whom any duty imposed by this section is to be performed in a case in which it would otherwise fall on a person who is no longer available to perform it.

(5) Regulations under subsection (4) may provide for the person on whom the duty is to fall to be a person appointed in accordance with the regulations.

(6) The references in this section to a person's deputy are references to the following—

    (a) in relation to—

        (i) a chief constable of a police force maintained under section 2 of the Police Act 1996,

        (ii) the Commissioner of Police for the City of London, or

        (iii) a chief constable of a police force maintained under or by virtue of section 1 of the Police (Scotland) Act 1967,

    to his designated deputy;

    (b) in relation to the Commissioner of Police of the Metropolis, to an Assistant Commissioner of Police of the Metropolis; […]

    (c) in relation to the [Chief Constable of the Police Service of Northern Ireland], to the Deputy Chief Constable of the [Police Service of Northern Ireland];[and

    (ca) in relation to the Director General of the Scottish Crime and Drug Enforcement Agency, to the Deputy Director General of that Agency;]

    (d) […]

    (e) […]

(7) In this section "designated deputy" has the same meaning as in section 34.

Scotland

46   Restrictions on authorisations extending to Scotland

(1) No person shall grant or renew an authorisation under this Part for the carrying out of any conduct if it appears to him—

    (a) that the authorisation is not one for which this Part is the relevant statutory provision for all parts of the United Kingdom; and

    (b) that all the conduct authorised by the grant or, as the case may be, renewal of the authorisation is likely to take place in Scotland.

---

[1] On the application of this section to the detection of television receivers: see SI 2001/1057.

(2) In relation to any authorisation, this Part is the relevant statutory provision for all parts of the United Kingdom in so far as it—

    (a) is granted or renewed on the grounds that it is necessary in the interests of national security or in the interests of the economic well-being of the United Kingdom;

    (b) is granted or renewed by or on the application of a person holding any office, rank or position with any of the public authorities specified in subsection (3);

    (c) authorises conduct of a person holding an office, rank or position with any of the public authorities so specified;

    (d) authorises conduct of an individual acting as a covert human intelligence source for the benefit of any of the public authorities so specified; or

    (e) authorises conduct that is surveillance by virtue of section 48(4).

(3) The public authorities mentioned in subsection (2) are—

    (a)   each of the intelligence services;

    (b)   Her Majesty's forces;

    (c)   the Ministry of Defence;

    (d)   the Ministry of Defence Police;

    [(dza) the Civil Nuclear Constabulary;]

    [(da)   the OFT;]

    [(db)   the Serious Organised Crime Agency;]

    (e)   [the Commissioners for Her Majesty's Revenue and Customs]; and

    (f)   the British Transport Police.

(4) For the purposes of so much of this Part as has effect in relation to any other public authority by virtue of—

    (a) the fact that it is a public authority for the time being specified in Schedule 1, or

    (b) an order under subsection (1)(d) of section 41 designating that authority for the purposes of that section,

the authorities specified in subsection (3) of this section shall be treated as including that authority to the extent that the Secretary of State by order directs that the authority is a relevant public authority or, as the case may be, is a designated authority for all parts of the United Kingdom.

Supplemental provision for Part II

47   Power to extend or modify authorisation provisions

(1) The Secretary of State may by order do one or both of the following—

    (a) apply this Part, with such modifications as he thinks fit, to any such surveillance that is neither directed nor intrusive as may be described in the order;

    (b) provide for any description of directed surveillance to be treated for the purposes of this Part as intrusive surveillance.

(2) No order shall be made under this section unless a draft of it has been laid before Parliament and approved by a resolution of each House.

48   Interpretation of Part II

(1) In this Part—

"covert human intelligence source" shall be construed in accordance with section 26(8);

"directed" and "intrusive", in relation to surveillance, shall be construed in accordance with section 26(2) to (6);

["OFT" means the Office of Fair Trading]

"private vehicle" means (subject to subsection (7)(a)) any vehicle which is used primarily for the private purposes of the person who owns it or of a person otherwise having the right to use it;

"residential premises" means (subject to subsection (7)(b)) so much of any premises as is for the time being occupied or used by any person, however temporarily, for residential purposes or otherwise as living accommodation (including hotel or prison accommodation that is so occupied or used);

"senior authorising officer" means a person who by virtue of subsection (6) of section 32 is a senior authorising officer for the purposes of that section;

"surveillance" shall be construed in accordance with subsections (2) to (4);

"surveillance device" means any apparatus designed or adapted for use in surveillance.

(2) Subject to subsection (3), in this Part "surveillance" includes—

    (a) monitoring, observing or listening to persons, their movements, their conversations or their other activities or communications;

    (b) recording anything monitored, observed or listened to in the course of surveillance; and

    (c) surveillance by or with the assistance of a surveillance device.

(3) References in this Part to surveillance do not include references to—

    (a) any conduct of a covert human intelligence source for obtaining or recording (whether or not using a surveillance device) any information which is disclosed in the presence of the source;

    (b) the use of a covert human intelligence source for so obtaining or recording information; or

    (c) any such entry on or interference with property or with wireless telegraphy as would be unlawful unless authorised under—

        (i) section 5 of the Intelligence Services Act 1994 (warrants for the intelligence services); or

        (ii) Part III of the Police Act 1997 (powers of the police and of [officers of Revenue and Customs]).

(4) References in this Part to surveillance include references to the interception of a communication in the course of its transmission by means of a postal service or telecommunication system if, and only if—

    (a) the communication is one sent by or intended for a person who has consented to the interception of communications sent by or to him; and

    (b) there is no interception warrant authorising the interception.

(5) References in this Part to an individual holding an office or position with a public authority include references to any member, official or employee of that authority.

(6) For the purposes of this Part the activities of a covert human intelligence source which are to be taken as activities for the benefit of a particular public authority include any conduct of his as such a source which is in response to inducements or requests made by or on behalf of that authority.

(7) In subsection (1)—

    (a) the reference to a person having the right to use a vehicle does not, in relation to a motor vehicle, include a reference to a person whose right to use the vehicle derives only from his having paid, or undertaken to pay, for the use of the vehicle and its driver for a particular journey; and

    (b) the reference to premises occupied or used by any person for residential purposes or otherwise as living accommodation does not include a reference to so much of any premises as constitutes any common area to which he has or is allowed access in connection with his use or occupation of any accommodation.

(8) In this section—

"premises" includes any vehicle or moveable structure and any other place whatever, whether or not occupied as land;

"vehicle" includes any vessel, aircraft or hovercraft.

PART III   INVESTIGATION OF ELECTRONIC DATA PROTECTED BY ENCRYPTION ETC.

Power to require disclosure

49   Notices requiring disclosure

(1) This section applies where any protected information—

(a) has come into the possession of any person by means of the exercise of a statutory power to seize, detain, inspect, search or otherwise to interfere with documents or other property, or is likely to do so;

(b) has come into the possession of any person by means of the exercise of any statutory power to intercept communications, or is likely to do so;

(c) has come into the possession of any person by means of the exercise of any power conferred by an authorisation under section 22(3) or under Part II, or as a result of the giving of a notice under section 22(4), or is likely to do so;

(d) has come into the possession of any person as a result of having been provided or disclosed in pursuance of any statutory duty (whether or not one arising as a result of a request for information), or is likely to do so; or

(e) has, by any other lawful means not involving the exercise of statutory powers, come into the possession of any of the intelligence services, the police[, SOCA, SCDEA] or [Her Majesty's Revenue and Customs], or is likely so to come into the possession of any of those services, the police[, SOCA, SCDEA] or [Her Majesty's Revenue and Customs].

(2) If any person with the appropriate permission under Schedule 2 believes, on reasonable grounds—

(a) that a key to the protected information is in the possession of any person,

(b) that the imposition of a disclosure requirement in respect of the protected information is—

(i) necessary on grounds falling within subsection (3), or

(ii) necessary for the purpose of securing the effective exercise or proper performance by any public authority of any statutory power or statutory duty,

(c) that the imposition of such a requirement is proportionate to what is sought to be achieved by its imposition, and

(d) that it is not reasonably practicable for the person with the appropriate permission to obtain possession of the protected information in an intelligible form without the giving of a notice under this section,

the person with that permission may, by notice to the person whom he believes to have possession of the key, impose a disclosure requirement in respect of the protected information.

(3) A disclosure requirement in respect of any protected information is necessary on grounds falling within this subsection if it is necessary—

(a) in the interests of national security;

(b) for the purpose of preventing or detecting crime; or

(c) in the interests of the economic well-being of the United Kingdom.

(4) A notice under this section imposing a disclosure requirement in respect of any protected information—

(a) must be given in writing or (if not in writing) must be given in a manner that produces a record of its having been given;

(b) must describe the protected information to which the notice relates;

(c) must specify the matters falling within subsection (2)(b)(i) or (ii) by reference to which the notice is given;

(d) must specify the office, rank or position held by the person giving it;

(e) must specify the office, rank or position of the person who for the purposes of Schedule 2 granted permission for the giving of the notice or (if the person giving the notice was entitled to give it without another person's permission) must set out the circumstances in which that entitlement arose;

(f) must specify the time by which the notice is to be complied with; and

(g) must set out the disclosure that is required by the notice and the form and manner in which it is to be made;

and the time specified for the purposes of paragraph (f) must allow a period for compliance which is reasonable in all the circumstances.

(5) Where it appears to a person with the appropriate permission—

    (a) that more than one person is in possession of the key to any protected information,

    (b) that any of those persons is in possession of that key in his capacity as an officer or employee of any body corporate, and

    (c) that another of those persons is the body corporate itself or another officer or employee of the body corporate,

a notice under this section shall not be given, by reference to his possession of the key, to any officer or employee of the body corporate unless he is a senior officer of the body corporate or it appears to the person giving the notice that there is no senior officer of the body corporate and (in the case of an employee) no more senior employee of the body corporate to whom it is reasonably practicable to give the notice.

(6) Where it appears to a person with the appropriate permission—

    (a) that more than one person is in possession of the key to any protected information,

    (b) that any of those persons is in possession of that key in his capacity as an employee of a firm, and

    (c) that another of those persons is the firm itself or a partner of the firm,

a notice under this section shall not be given, by reference to his possession of the key, to any employee of the firm unless it appears to the person giving the notice that there is neither a partner of the firm nor a more senior employee of the firm to whom it is reasonably practicable to give the notice.

(7) Subsections (5) and (6) shall not apply to the extent that there are special circumstances of the case that mean that the purposes for which the notice is given would be defeated, in whole or in part, if the notice were given to the person to whom it would otherwise be required to be given by those subsections.

(8) A notice under this section shall not require the making of any disclosure to any person other than—

    (a) the person giving the notice; or

    (b) such other person as may be specified in or otherwise identified by, or in accordance with, the provisions of the notice.

(9) A notice under this section shall not require the disclosure of any key which—

    (a) is intended to be used for the purpose only of generating electronic signatures; and

    (b) has not in fact been used for any other purpose.

(10) In this section "senior officer", in relation to a body corporate, means a director, manager, secretary or other similar officer of the body corporate; and for this purpose "director", in relation to a body corporate whose affairs are managed by its members, means a member of the body corporate.

(11) Schedule 2 (definition of the appropriate permission) shall have effect.

50   Effect of notice imposing disclosure requirement

(1) Subject to the following provisions of this section, the effect of a section 49 notice imposing a disclosure requirement in respect of any protected information on a person who is in possession at a relevant time of both the protected information and a means of obtaining access to the information and of disclosing it in an intelligible form is that he—

    (a) shall be entitled to use any key in his possession to obtain access to the information or to put it into an intelligible form; and

    (b) shall be required, in accordance with the notice imposing the requirement, to make a disclosure of the information in an intelligible form.

(2) A person subject to a requirement under subsection (1)(b) to make a disclosure of any information in an intelligible form shall be taken to have complied with that requirement if—

    (a) he makes, instead, a disclosure of any key to the protected information that is in his possession; and

    (b) that disclosure is made, in accordance with the notice imposing the requirement, to the person to whom, and by the time by which, he was required to provide the information in that form.

(3) Where, in a case in which a disclosure requirement in respect of any protected information is imposed on any person by a section 49 notice—

    (a) that person is not in possession of the information,

    (b) that person is incapable, without the use of a key that is not in his possession, of obtaining access to the information and of disclosing it in an intelligible form, or

    (c) the notice states, in pursuance of a direction under section 51, that it can be complied with only by the disclosure of a key to the information.

the effect of imposing that disclosure requirement on that person is that he shall be required, in accordance with the notice imposing the requirement, to make a disclosure of any key to the protected information that is in his possession at a relevant time.

(4) Subsections (5) to (7) apply where a person ("the person given notice")—

    (a) is entitled or obliged to disclose a key to protected information for the purpose of complying with any disclosure requirement imposed by a section 49 notice; and

    (b) is in possession of more than one key to that information.

(5) It shall not be necessary, for the purpose of complying with the requirement, for the person given notice to make a disclosure of any keys in addition to those the disclosure of which is, alone, sufficient to enable the person to whom they are disclosed to obtain access to the information and to put it into an intelligible form.

(6) Where—

    (a) subsection (5) allows the person given notice to comply with a requirement without disclosing all of the keys in his possession, and

    (b) there are different keys, or combinations of keys, in the possession of that person the disclosure of which would, under that subsection, constitute compliance,

the person given notice may select which of the keys, or combination of keys, to disclose for the purpose of complying with that requirement in accordance with that subsection.

(7) Subject to subsections (5) and (6), the person given notice shall not be taken to have complied with the disclosure requirement by the disclosure of a key unless he has disclosed every key to the protected information that is in his possession at a relevant time.

(8) Where, in a case in which a disclosure requirement in respect of any protected information is imposed on any person by a section 49 notice—

    (a) that person has been in possession of the key to that information but is no longer in possession of it,

    (b) if he had continued to have the key in his possession, he would have been required by virtue of the giving of the notice to disclose it, and

    (c) he is in possession, at a relevant time, of information to which subsection (9) applies,

the effect of imposing that disclosure requirement on that person is that he shall be required, in accordance with the notice imposing the requirement, to disclose all such information to which subsection (9) applies as is in his possession and as he may be required, in accordance with that notice, to disclose by the person to whom he would have been required to disclose the key.

(9) This subsection applies to any information that would facilitate the obtaining or discovery of the key or the putting of the protected information into an intelligible form.

(10) In this section "relevant time", in relation to a disclosure requirement imposed by a section 49 notice, means the time of the giving of the notice or any subsequent time before the time by which the requirement falls to be complied with.

51 Cases in which key required

(1) A section 49 notice imposing a disclosure requirement in respect of any protected information shall not contain a statement for the purposes of section 50(3)(c) unless—

    (a) the person who for the purposes of Schedule 2 granted the permission for the giving of the notice in relation to that information, or

    (b) any person whose permission for the giving of a such a notice in relation to that information would constitute the appropriate permission under that Schedule, has given a direction that the requirement can be complied with only by the disclosure of the key itself.

(2) A direction for the purposes of subsection (1) by [the police, SOCA, SCDEA, Her Majesty's Revenue and Customs] or a member of Her Majesty's forces shall not be given—

(a)   in the case of a direction by the police or by a member of Her Majesty's forces who is a member of a police force, except by or with the permission of a chief officer of police;

[(aa) in the case of a direction by SOCA, except by or with the permission of the Director General of the Serious Organised Crime Agency;]

[(ab) in the case of a direction by SCDEA, except by or with the permission of the Director General of the Scottish Crime and Drug Enforcement Agency;]

(b)   in the case of a direction by [Her Majesty's Revenue and Customs], except by or with the permission of [the Commissioners for Her Majesty's Revenue and Customs]; or

(c)   in the case of a direction by a member of Her Majesty's forces who is not a member of a police force, except by or with the permission of a person of or above the rank of brigadier or its equivalent.

(3) A permission given for the purposes of subsection (2) by a chief officer of police, [the Director General of the Serious Organised Crime Agency, the Director General of the Scottish Crime and Drug Enforcement Agency, the Commissioners for Her Majesty's Revenue and Customs] or a person of or above any such rank as is mentioned in paragraph (c) of that subsection must be given expressly in relation to the direction in question.

(4) A person shall not give a direction for the purposes of subsection (1) unless he believes—

(a) that there are special circumstances of the case which mean that the purposes for which it was believed necessary to impose the requirement in question would be defeated, in whole or in part, if the direction were not given; and

(b) that the giving of the direction is proportionate to what is sought to be achieved by prohibiting any compliance with the requirement in question otherwise than by the disclosure of the key itself.

(5) The matters to be taken into account in considering whether the requirement of subsection (4)(b) is satisfied in the case of any direction shall include—

(a) the extent and nature of any protected information, in addition to the protected information in respect of which the disclosure requirement is imposed, to which the key is also a key; and

(b) any adverse effect that the giving of the direction might have on a business carried on by the person on whom the disclosure requirement is imposed.

(6) Where a direction for the purposes of subsection (1) is given by a chief officer of police, [by the Director General of the Serious Organised Crime Agency, the Director General of the Scottish Crime and Drug Enforcement Agency, by the Commissioners for Her Majesty's Revenue and Customs] or by a member of Her Majesty's forces, the person giving the direction shall give a notification that he has done so—

(a) in a case where the direction is given—

(i)   by a member of Her Majesty's forces who is not a member of a police force, and

(ii) otherwise than in connection with activities of members of Her Majesty's forces in Northern Ireland,

to the Intelligences Services Commissioner; and

(b) in any other case, to the Chief Surveillance Commissioner.

(7) A notification under subsection (6)—

(a) must be given not more than seven days after the day of the giving of the direction to which it relates; and

(b) may be given either in writing or by being transmitted to the Commissioner in question by electronic means.

Contributions to costs

52 Arrangements for payments for disclosure

(1) It shall be the duty of the Secretary of State to ensure that such arrangements are in force as he thinks appropriate for requiring or authorising, in such cases as he thinks fit, the making to persons to whom section 49 notices are given of appropriate contributions towards the costs incurred by them in complying with such notices.

(2) For the purpose of complying with his duty under this section, the Secretary of State may make arrangements for payments to be made out of money provided by Parliament.

Offences

53 Failure to comply with a notice

(1) A person to whom a section 49 notice has been given is guilty of an offence if he knowingly fails, in accordance with the notice, to make the disclosure required by virtue of the giving of the notice.

(2) In proceedings against any person for an offence under this section, if it is shown that that person was in possession of a key to any protected information at any time before the time of the giving of the section 49 notice, that person shall be taken for the purposes of those proceedings to have continued to be in possession of that key at all subsequent times, unless it is shown that the key was not in his possession after the giving of the notice and before the time by which he was required to disclose it.

(3) For the purposes of this section a person shall be taken to have shown that he was not in possession of a key to protected information at a particular time if—

   (a) sufficient evidence of that fact is adduced to raise an issue with respect to it; and
   (b) the contrary is not proved beyond a reasonable doubt.

(4) In proceedings against any person for an offence under this section it shall be a defence for that person to show—

   (a) that it was not reasonably practicable for him to make the disclosure required by virtue of the giving of the section 49 notice before the time by which he was required, in accordance with that notice, to make it; but
   (b) that he did make that disclosure as soon after that time as it was reasonably practicable for him to do so.

(5) A person guilty of an offence under this section shall be liable—

   (a) on conviction on indictment, to imprisonment for a term not exceeding [the appropriate maximum term] or to a fine, or to both;
   (b) on summary conviction, to imprisonment for a term not exceeding six months or to a fine not exceeding the statutory maximum, or to both.

[(5A) In subsection (5) "the appropriate maximum term" means—

   (a) in a national security case, five years; and
   (b) in any other case, two years.

(5B) In subsection (5A) "a national security case" means a case in which the grounds specified in the notice to which the offence relates as the grounds for imposing a disclosure requirement were or included a belief that the imposition of the requirement was necessary in the interests of national security.]

54 Tipping-off

(1) This section applies where a section 49 notice contains a provision requiring—

   (a) the person to whom the notice is given, and
   (b) every other person who becomes aware of it or of its contents,

to keep secret the giving of the notice, its contents and the things done in pursuance of it.

(2) A requirement to keep anything secret shall not be included in a section 49 notice except where—

    (a) it is included with the consent of the person who for the purposes of Schedule 2 granted the permission for the giving of the notice; or

    (b) the person who gives the notice is himself a person whose permission for the giving of such a notice in relation to the information in question would have constituted appropriate permission under that Schedule.

(3) A section 49 notice shall not contain a requirement to keep anything secret except where the protected information to which it relates—

    (a) has come into the possession of the police, [SOCA, SCDEA, Her Majesty's Revenue and Customs] or any of the intelligence services, or

    (b) is likely to come into the possession of the police, [SOCA, SCDEA, Her Majesty's Revenue and Customs] or any of the intelligence services,

by means which it is reasonable, in order to maintain the effectiveness of any investigation or operation or of investigatory techniques generally, or in the interests of the safety or well-being of any person, to keep secret from a particular person.

(4) A person who makes a disclosure to any other person of anything that he is required by a section 49 notice to keep secret shall be guilty of an offence and liable—

    (a) on conviction on indictment, to imprisonment for a term not exceeding five years or to a fine, or to both;

    (b) on summary conviction, to imprisonment for a term not exceeding six months or to a fine not exceeding the statutory maximum, or to both.

(5) In proceedings against any person for an offence under this section in respect of any disclosure, it shall be a defence for that person to show that—

    (a) the disclosure was effected entirely by the operation of software designed to indicate when a key to protected information has ceased to be secure; and

    (b) that person could not reasonably have been expected to take steps, after being given the notice or (as the case may be) becoming aware of it or of its contents, to prevent the disclosure.

(6) In proceedings against any person for an offence under this section in respect of any disclosure, it shall be a defence for that person to show that—

    (a) the disclosure was made by or to a professional legal adviser in connection with the giving, by the adviser to any client of his, of advice about the effect of provisions of this Part; and

    (b) the person to whom or, as the case may be, by whom it was made was the client or a representative of the client.

(7) In proceedings against any person for an offence under this section in respect of any disclosure, it shall be a defence for that person to show that the disclosure was made by a legal adviser—

    (a) in contemplation of, or in connection with, any legal proceedings; and

    (b) for the purposes of those proceedings.

(8) Neither subsection (6) nor subsection (7) applies in the case of a disclosure made with a view to furthering any criminal purpose.

(9) In proceedings against any person for an offence under this section in respect of any disclosure, it shall be a defence for that person to show that the disclosure was confined to a disclosure made to a relevant Commissioner or authorised—

    (a) by such a Commissioner;

    (b) by the terms of the notice;

    (c) by or on behalf of the person who gave the notice; or

    (d) by or on behalf of a person who—

        (i) is in lawful possession of the protected information to which the notice relates; and

        (ii) came into possession of that information as mentioned in section 49(1).

(10) In proceedings for an offence under this section against a person other than the person to whom the notice was given, it shall be a defence for the person against whom the proceedings are

brought to show that he neither knew nor had reasonable grounds for suspecting that the notice contained a requirement to keep secret what was disclosed.

(11) In this section "relevant Commissioner" means the Interception of Communications Commissioner, the Intelligence Services Commissioner or any Surveillance Commissioner or Assistant Surveillance Commissioner.

Safeguards

55   General duties of specified authorities

(1)   This section applies to—

- (a)   the Secretary of State and every other Minister of the Crown in charge of a government department;
- (b)   every chief officer of police;
- [(ba)   the Director General of the Serious Organised Crime Agency;]
- [(bb)   the Director General of the Scottish Crime and Drug Enforcement Agency;]
- (c)   [the Commissioners for Her Majesty's Revenue and Customs]; and
- (d)   every person whose officers or employees include persons with duties that involve the giving of section 49 notices.

(2)   It shall be the duty of each of the persons to whom this section applies to ensure that such arrangements are in force, in relation to persons under his control who by virtue of this Part obtain possession of keys to protected information, as he considers necessary for securing—

- (a)   that a key disclosed in pursuance of a section 49 notice is used for obtaining access to, or putting into an intelligible form, only protected information in relation to which power to give such a notice was exercised or could have been exercised if the key had not already been disclosed;
- (b)   that the uses to which a key so disclosed is put are reasonable having regard both to the uses to which the person using the key is entitled to put any protected information to which it relates and to the other circumstances of the case;
- (c)   that, having regard to those matters, the use and any retention of the key are proportionate to what is sought to be achieved by its use or retention;
- (d)   that the requirements of subsection (3) are satisfied in relation to any key disclosed in pursuance of a section 49 notice;
- (e)   that, for the purpose of ensuring that those requirements are satisfied, any key so disclosed is stored, for so long as it is retained, in a secure manner;
- (f)   that all records of a key so disclosed (if not destroyed earlier) are destroyed as soon as the key is no longer needed for the purpose of enabling protected information to be put into an intelligible form.

(3)   The requirements of this subsection are satisfied in relation to any key disclosed in pursuance of a section 49 notice if—

- (a)   the number of persons to whom the key is disclosed or otherwise made available, and
- (b)   the number of copies made of the key,

are each limited to the minimum that is necessary for the purpose of enabling protected information to be put into an intelligible form.

[(3A)   Paragraph 11 of Schedule 1 to the Serious Organised Crime and Police Act 2005 does not apply in relation to the duties of the Director General of the Serious Organised Crime Agency under this section.]

[(3B)   Paragraph 6(2) of schedule 2 to the Police, Public Order and Criminal Justice (Scotland) Act 2006 (asp 10) does not apply in relation to the duties of the Director General of the Scottish Crime and Drug Enforcement Agency under this section.]

(4)   Subject to subsection (5), where any relevant person incurs any loss or damage in consequence of—

- (a)   any breach by a person to whom this section applies of the duty imposed on him by subsection (2), or

(b) any contravention by any person whatever of arrangements made in pursuance of that subsection in relation to persons under the control of a person to whom this section applies,

the breach or contravention shall be actionable against the person to whom this section applies at the
suit or instance of the relevant person.

(5) A person is a relevant person for the purposes of subsection (4) if he is—

(a) a person who has made a disclosure in pursuance of a section 49 notice; or

(b) a person whose protected information or key has been disclosed in pursuance of such a
notice;

and loss or damage shall be taken into account for the purposes of that subsection to the extent only
that it relates to the disclosure of particular protected information or a particular key which, in the
case of a person falling with paragraph (b), must be his information or key.

(6) For the purposes of subsection (5)—

(a) information belongs to a person if he has any right that would be infringed by an unauthorised disclosure of the information; and

(b) a key belongs to a person if it is a key to information that belongs to him or he has any right
that would be infringed by an unauthorised disclosure of the key.

(7) In any proceedings brought by virtue of subsection (4), it shall be the duty of the court to have
regard to any opinion with respect to the matters to which the proceedings relate that is or has been
given by a relevant Commissioner.

(8) In this section "relevant Commissioner" means the Interception of Communications
Commissioner, the Intelligence Services Commissioner, the Investigatory Powers Commissioner for
Northern Ireland or any Surveillance Commissioner or Assistant Surveillance Commissioner.

Interpretation of Part III

56   **Interpretation of Part III**

(1) In this Part—

"chief officer of police" means any of the following—

(a) the chief constable of a police force maintained under or by virtue of section 2 of the Police
Act 1996 or section 1 of the Police (Scotland) Act 1967;

(b) the Commissioner of Police of the Metropolis;

(c) the Commissioner of Police of the City of London;

(d) the [Chief Constable of the Police Service of Northern Ireland];

(e) the Chief Constable of the Ministry of Defence Police;

(f) the Provost Marshal of the [Royal Navy Police];

(g) the Provost Marshal of the Royal Military Police;

(h) the Provost Marshal of the Royal Air Force Police;

(i) the Chief Constable of Transport Police; [...]

[...]

"electronic signature" means anything in electronic form which—

(a) is incorporated into, or otherwise logically associated with, any electronic communication or other electronic data;

(b) is generated by the signatory or other source of the communication or data; and

(c) is used for the purpose of facilitating, by means of a link between the signatory or other
source and the communication or data, the establishment of the authenticity of the communication or data, the establishment of its integrity, or both;

"key", in relation to any electronic data, means any key, code, password, algorithm or other data
the use of which (with or without other keys)—

(a) allows access to the electronic data, or

(b) facilitates the putting of the data into an intelligible form;

"the police" means—

(a) any constable [(except a constable who is a member of the staff of the Serious Organised
Crime Agency or a constable who is a member of the Scottish Crime and Drug Enforcement
Agency)];

(b) the Commissioner of Police of the Metropolis or any Assistant Commissioner of Police of the Metropolis; or

(c) the Commissioner of Police for the City of London;

"protected information" means any electronic data which, without the key to the data—

(a) cannot, or cannot readily, be accessed, or

(b) cannot, or cannot readily, be put into an intelligible form;

["SCDEA" means the Scottish Crime and Drug Enforcement Agency;]

"section 49 notice" means a notice under section 49;

["SOCA" means the Serious Organised Crime Agency or any member of the staff of the Serious Organised Crime Agency;]

"warrant" includes any authorisation, notice or other instrument (however described) conferring a power of the same description as may, in other cases, be conferred by a warrant.

(2) References in this Part to a person's having information (including a key to protected information) in his possession include references—

(a) to its being in the possession of a person who is under his control so far as that information is concerned;

(b) to his having an immediate right of access to it, or an immediate right to have it transmitted or otherwise supplied to him; and

(c) to its being, or being contained in, anything which he or a person under his control is entitled, in exercise of any statutory power and without otherwise taking possession of it, to detain, inspect or search.

(3) References in this Part to something's being intelligible or being put into an intelligible form include references to its being in the condition in which it was before an encryption or similar process was applied to it or, as the case may be, to its being restored to that condition.

(4) In this section—

(a) references to the authenticity of any communication or data are references to any one or more of the following—

(i) whether the communication or data comes from a particular person or other source;

(ii) whether it is accurately timed and dated;

(iii) whether it is intended to have legal effect;

and

(b) references to the integrity of any communication or data are references to whether there has been any tampering with or other modification of the communication or data.

SCHEDULE 1 RELEVANT PUBLIC AUTHORITIES

PART I RELEVANT AUTHORITIES FOR THE PURPOSES OF SS. 28 AND 29

Police forces etc.

1.   Any police force.

[1A. The Civil Nuclear Constabulary.

2.   The Serious Organised Crime Agency . . .]

[2A. The Scottish Crime and Drug Enforcement Agency.]

4.   The Serious Fraud Office.

[4A. The force comprising the special constables appointed under section 79 of the Harbours, Docks and Piers Clauses Act 1847 on the nomination of the Dover Harbour Board.

4B.   The force comprising the constables appointed under article 3 of the Mersey Docks and Harbour (Police) Order 1975 on the nomination of the Mersey Docks and Harbour Company.]

The intelligence services

5.   Any of the intelligence services.

The armed forces

6. Any of Her Majesty's forces.

[Revenue and Customs]

7. [Her Majesty's Revenue and Customs . . .]

Government departments

9.   [. . .]
[9ZA.   The Department for Business, Enterprise and Regulatory Reform.]
[9A.   The Department for Communities and Local Government]
10.   The Ministry of Defence.
[10ZA. The Office of the Deputy Prime Minister.
10A.   The Department for Environment, Food and Rural Affairs.]
11.   [. . .]
12.   The Department of Health.
13.   The Home Office.
[13ZA. The Ministry of Justice.]
[13A.   The Northern Ireland Office.]
14.   [. . .]
15.   [. . .]
[15A.   The Department for Transport.
15B.   The Department for Work and Pensions.]

[The Welsh Assembly Government]

16. [The Welsh Assembly Government.]

Local authorities

[17. Any county council or district council in England, a London borough council, the Common Council of the City of London in its capacity as a local authority, the Council of the Isles of Scilly, and any county council or county borough council in Wales.]

[17A. Any fire authority within the meaning of the Fire Services Act 1947 (read with paragraph 2 of Schedule 11 to the Local Government Act 1985.]

Other bodies

[17B.   The Charity Commission].
18.   The Environment Agency.
19.   The Financial Services Authority.
20.   The Food Standards Agency.
[20A.   The Gambling Commission.
20B.   The Office of Fair Trading.
20C.   The Office of the Police Ombudsman for Northern Ireland.
20D.   The Postal Services Commission.]
[20E.   The Gangmasters Licensing Authority.
20F.   The Commission for Healthcare Audit and Inspection.]
21.   [. . .]
22.   [. . .]
23.   [A universal service provider (within the meaning of the Postal Services Act 2000) acting in connection with the provision of a universal postal service (within the meaning of that Act)].
[23A.   The Office of Communications.]

[Northern Ireland authorities

23A. The Department of Agriculture and Rural Development.
23B. The Department of Enterprise, Trade and Investment.

23C. The Department of the Environment.

23D. Any district council (within the meaning of section 44 of the Interpretation Act (Northern Ireland) 1954.]

PART II RELEVANT AUTHORITIES FOR THE PURPOSES ONLY OF S. 28

The Health and Safety Executive

24.   The Health and Safety Executive.

NHS bodies in England and Wales

25. [...]

26. A Special Health Authority established under [section 28 of the National Health Service Act 2006 or section 22 of the National Health Service (Wales) Act 2006].

27. [...]

[27A. ...]

[HM Chief Inspector of Education, Children's Services and Skills]

[27B. Her Majesty's Chief Inspector of Education, Children's Services and Skills.]

The Information Commissioner

27C. The Information Commissioner.

27D. [...]

The Royal Pharmaceutical Society of Great Britain]

28. The Royal Pharmaceutical Society of Great Britain.

[Northern Ireland Authorities

29. The Department of Health, Social Services and Public Safety.

30. The Department for Regional Development.

31. The Department for Social Development.

32. The Department of Culture, Arts and Leisure.

33. The Foyle, Carlingford and Irish Lights Commission.

34. The Fisheries Conservancy Board for Northern Ireland.

35. A Health and Social Services trust established under Article 10 of the Health and Personal Services (Northern Ireland) Order 1991.

36. A Health and Social Services Board established under Article 16 of the Health and Personal Services (Northern Ireland) Order 1972.

37. The Health and Safety Executive for Northern Ireland.

38. The Northern Ireland Central Services Agency for the Health and Social Services.

39. The Fire Authority for Northern Ireland.

40. The Northern Ireland Housing Executive.]

SCHEDULE 2 PERSONS HAVING THE APPROPRIATE PERMISSION

Requirement that appropriate permission is granted by a judge

1.—(1) Subject to the following provisions of this Schedule, a person has the appropriate permission in relation to any protected information if, and only if, written permission for the giving of section 49 notices in relation to that information has been granted—

(a) in England and Wales, by a Circuit judge [or a District Judge (Magistrates' Courts)[1]];

[1] Amended section not yet in force: see Courts Act 2003, s. 110(1).

(b) in Scotland, by a sheriff; or

(c) in Northern Ireland, by a country court judge.

(2) Nothing in paragraphs 2 to 5 of this Schedule providing for the manner in which a person may be granted the appropriate permission in relation to any protected information without a grant under this paragraph shall be construed as requiring any further permission to be obtained in a case in which permission has been granted under this paragraph.

Data obtained under warrant etc.

2.—(1) This paragraph applies in the case of protected information falling within section 49(1) (a), (b) or (c) where the statutory power in question is one exercised, or to be exercised, in accordance with—

(a) a warrant issued by the Secretary of State or a person holding judicial office; or

(b) an authorisation under Part III of the Police Act 1997 (authorisation of otherwise unlawful action in respect of property).

(2) Subject to sub-paragraphs (3) to (5) and paragraph 6(1), a person has the appropriate permission in relation to that protected information (without any grant of permission under paragraph 1) if—

(a) the warrant or, as the case may be, the authorisation contained the relevant authority's permission for the giving of section 49 notices in relation to protected information to be obtained under the warrant or authorisation; or

(b) since the issue of the warrant or authorisation, written permission has been granted by the relevant authority for the giving of such notices in relation to protected information obtained under the warrant or authorisation.

(3) Only persons holding office under the Crown, the police[, SOCA, SCDEA and Her Majesty's Revenue and Customs] shall be capable of having the appropriate permission in relation to protected information obtained, or to be obtained, under a warrant issued by the Secretary of State.

(4) Only a person who—

(a) was entitled to exercise the power conferred by the warrant, or

(b) is of the description of persons on whom the power conferred by the warrant was, or could have been, conferred,

shall be capable of having the appropriate permission in relation to protected information obtained, or to be obtained, under a warrant issued by a person holding judicial office.

(5) Only the police[, SOCA, SCDEA and Her Majesty's Revenue and Customs] shall be capable of having the appropriate permission in relation to protected information obtained, or to be obtained, under an authorisation under Part III of the Police Act 1997.

(6) In this paragraph "the relevant authority"—

(a) in relation to a warrant issued by the Secretary of State, means the Secretary of State;

(b) in relation to a warrant issued by a person holding judicial office, means any person holding any judicial office that would have entitled him to issue the warrant; and

(c) in relation to protected information obtained under an authorisation under Part III of the Police Act 1997, means (subject to sub-paragraph (7)) an authorising officer within the meaning of section 93 of that Act.

(7) Section 94 of the Police Act 1997 (power of other persons to grant authorisations in urgent cases) shall apply in relation to—

(a) an application for permission for the giving of section 49 notices in relation to protected information obtained, or to be obtained, under an authorisation under Part III of that Act, and

(b) the powers of any authorising officer (within the meaning of section 93 of that Act) to grant such a permission,

as it applies in relation to an application for an authorisation under section 93 of that Act and the powers of such an officer under that section.

(8) References in this paragraph to a person holding judicial office are references to—

  (a) any judge of the Crown Court or of the High Court of Justiciary;

  (b) any sheriff;

  (c) any justice of the peace;

  (d) any resident magistrate in Northern Ireland; or

  (e) any person holding any such judicial office as entitles him to exercise the jurisdiction of a judge of the Crown Court or of a justice of the peace.

(9) Protected information that comes into a person's possession by means of the exercise of any statutory power which—

  (a) is exercisable without a warrant, but

  (b) is so exercisable in the course of, or in connection with, the exercise of another statutory power for which a warrant is required,

shall not be taken, by reason only of the warrant required for the exercise of the power mentioned in paragraph (b), to be information in the case of which this paragraph applies.

Data obtained by the intelligence services under statute but without a warrant

3.—(1) This paragraph applies in the case of protected information falling within section 49(1)(a), (b) or (c) which—

  (a) has come into the possession of any of the intelligence services or is likely to do so; and

  (b) is not information in the case of which paragraph 2 applies.

(2) Subject to paragraph 6(1), a person has the appropriate permission in relation to that protected information (without any grant of permission under paragraph 1) if written permission for the giving of section 49 notices in relation to that information has been granted by the Secretary of State.

(3) Sub-paragraph (2) applies where the protected information is in the possession, or (as the case may be) is likely to come into the possession, of both—

  (a) one or more of the intelligence services, and

  (b) a public authority which is not one of the intelligence services,

as if a grant of permission under paragraph 1 were unnecessary only where the application to the Secretary of State for permission under that sub-paragraph is made by or on behalf of a member of one of the intelligence services.

Data obtained under statute by other persons but without a warrant

4.—(1) This paragraph applies—

  (a) in the case of protected information falling within section 49(1)(a), (b) or (c) which is not information in the case of which paragraph 2 or 3 applies; and

  (b) in the case of protected information falling within section 49(1)(d) which is not information also falling within section 49(1)(a), (b) or (c) in the case of which paragraph 3 applies.

(2) Subject to paragraph 6, where—

  (a) the statutory power was exercised, or is likely to be exercised, by the police, [SOCA, SCDEA, Her Majesty's Revenue and Customs] or a member of Her Majesty's forces, or

  (b) the information was provided or disclosed, or is likely to be provided or disclosed, to the police, [SOCA, SCDEA, Her Majesty's Revenue and Customs] or a member of Her Majesty's forces, or

  (c) the information is in the possession of, or is likely to come into the possession of, the police, [SOCA, SCDEA, Her Majesty's Revenue and Customs] or a member of Her Majesty's forces,

the police, [SOCA, SCDEA, Her Majesty's Revenue and Customs] or, as the case may be, members of Her Majesty's forces have the appropriate permission in relation to the protected information, without any grant of permission under paragraph 1.

(3) In any other case a person shall not have the appropriate permission by virtue of a grant of permission under paragraph 1 unless he is a person falling within sub-paragraph (4).

(4) A person falls within this sub-paragraph if, as the case may be—

    (a) he is the person who exercised the statutory power or is of the description of persons who would have been entitled to exercise it;

    (b) he is the person to whom the protected information was provided or disclosed, or is of a description of the person the provision or disclosure of the information to whom would have discharged the statutory duty; or

    (c) he is a person who is likely to be a person falling within paragraph (a) or (b) when the power is exercised or the protected information provided or disclosed.

Data obtained without the exercise of statutory powers

5.—(1) This paragraph applies in the case of protected information falling within section 49(1 (e).

(2) Subject to paragraph 6, a person has the appropriate permission in relation to that protected information (without any grant of permission under paragraph 1) if—

    (a) the information is in the possession of any of the intelligence services, or is likely to come into the possession of any of those services; and

    (b) written permission for the giving of section 49 notices in relation to that information has been granted by the Secretary of State.

(3) Sub-paragraph (2) applies where the protected information is in the possession, or (as the case may be) is likely to come into the possession, of both—

    (a) one or more of the intelligence services, and

    (b) the police[, SOCA, SCDEA or Her Majesty's Revenue and Customs],

as if a grant of permission under paragraph 1 were unnecessary only where the application to the Secretary of State for permission under that sub-paragraph is made by or on behalf of a member of one of the intelligence services.

General requirements relating to the appropriate permission

6.—(1) A person does not have the appropriate permission in relation to any protected information unless he is either—

    (a) a person who has the protected information in his possession or is likely to obtain possession of it; or

    (b) a person who is authorised (apart from this Act) to act on behalf of such a person.

(2) Subject to sub-paragraph (3), a constable does not by virtue of paragraph 1, 4 or 5 have the appropriate permission in relation to any protected information unless—

    (a) he is of or above the rank of superintendent; or

    (b) permission to give a section 49 notice in relation to that information has been granted by a person holding the rank of superintendent, or any higher rank.

(3) In the case of protected information that has come into the police's possession by means of the exercise of powers conferred by—

    (a) section 44 of the Terrorism Act 2000 (power to stop and search), or

    (b) section 13A or 13B of the Prevention of Terrorism (Temporary Provisions) Act 1989 (which had effect for similar purposes before the coming into force of section 44 of the Terrorism Act 2000),

the permission required by sub-paragraph (2) shall not be granted by any person below the rank mentioned in section 44(4) of that Act of 2000 or, as the case may be, section 13A(1) of that Act of 1989.

[(3A) A member of the staff of the Serious Organised Crime Agency does not by virtue of paragraph 1, 4 or 5 have the appropriate permission in relation to any protected information unless permission to give a section 49 notice in relation to that information has been granted—

    (a) by the Director General; or

    (b) by a member of the staff of the Agency of or above such level as the Director General may designate for the purposes of this sub-paragraph.]

[(3B) A member of the Scottish Crime and Drug Enforcement Agency does not by virtue of paragraph 1, 4 or 5 have the appropriate permission in relation to any protected information unless—

    (a) he is of or above the rank of superintendent; or

(b) permission to give a section 49 notice in relation to that information has been granted by the Director General of that Agency;]

(4) [An officer of Revenue and Customs] does not by virtue of paragraph 1, 4 or 5 have the appropriate permission in relation to any protected information unless permission to give a section 49 notice in relation to that information has been granted—

(a) by [the Commissioners for Her Majesty's Revenue and Customs]; or

(b) by an officer of [Revenue and Customs] of or above such level as [the Commissioners] may designate for the purposes of this sub-paragraph.

(5) A member of Her Majesty's forces does not by virtue of paragraph 1, 4 or 5 have the appropriate permission in relation to any protected information unless—

(a) he is of or above the rank of lieutenant colonel or its equivalent; or

(b) permission to give a section 49 notice in relation to that information has been granted by a person holding the rank of lieutenant colonel or its equivalent, or by a person holding a rank higher than lieutenant colonel or its equivalent.

[(6) In sub-paragraph (2) "constable" does not include a constable who is a member of the staff of the Serious Organised Crime Agency or a constable who is a member of the Scottish Crime and Drug Enforcement Agency.]

Duration of permission

7.—(1) A permission granted by any person under any provision of this Schedule shall not entitle any person to give a section 49 notice at any time after the permission has ceased to have effect.

(2) Such a permission, once granted, shall continue to have effect (notwithstanding the cancellation, expiry or other discharge of any warrant or authorisation in which it is contained or to which it relates) until such time (if any) as it—

(a) expires in accordance with any limitation on its duration that was contained in its terms; or

(b) is withdrawn by the person who granted it or by a person holding any office or other position that would have entitled him to grant it.

Formalities for permissions granted by the Secretary of State

8.—A permission for the purposes of any provision of this Schedule shall not be granted by the Secretary of State except—

(a) under his hand; or

(b) in an urgent case in which the Secretary of State has expressly authorised the grant of the permission, under the hand of a senior official.

Anti-terrorism, Crime and Security Act 2001

(2001, c. 24)

An Act to amend the Terrorism Act 2000; to make further provision about terrorism and security; to provide for the freezing of assets; to make provision about immigration and asylum; to amend or extend the criminal law and powers for preventing crime and enforcing that law; to make provision about the control of pathogens and toxins; to provide for the retention of communications data; to provide for implementation of Title VI of the Treaty on European Union; and for connected purposes.   [14th December 2001]

PART 11 RETENTION OF COMMUNICATIONS DATA

102 Codes and agreements about the retention of communications data

(1) The Secretary of State shall issue, and may from time to time revise, a code of practice relating to the retention by communications providers of communications data obtained by or held by them.

(2) The Secretary of State may enter into such agreements as he considers appropriate with any communications provider about the practice to be followed by that provider in relation to the retention of communications data obtained by or held by that provider.

(3) A code of practice or agreement under this section may contain any such provision as appears to the Secretary of State to be necessary—

(a) for the purpose of safeguarding national security; or

(b) for the purposes of prevention or detection of crime or the prosecution of offenders which may relate directly or indirectly to national security.

(4) A failure by any person to comply with a code of practice or agreement under this section which is for the time being in force shall not of itself render him liable to any criminal or civil proceedings.

(5) A code of practice or agreement under this section which is for the time being in force shall be admissible in evidence in any legal proceedings in which the question arises whether or not the retention of any communications data is justified on the grounds that a failure to retain the data would be likely to prejudice national security, the prevention or detection of crime or the prosecution of offenders.

103   Procedure for codes of practice

(1) Before issuing the code of practice under section 102 the Secretary of State shall—

(a) prepare and publish a draft of the code; and

(b) consider any representations made to him about the draft;

and the Secretary of State may incorporate in the code finally issued any modifications made by him to the draft after its publication.

(2) Before publishing a draft of the code the Secretary of State shall consult with—

(a) the Information Commissioner; and

(b) the communications providers to whom the code will apply.

(3) The Secretary of State may discharge his duty under subsection (2) to consult with any communications providers by consulting with a person who appears to him to represent those providers.

(4) The Secretary of State shall lay before Parliament the draft code of practice under section 102 that is prepared and published by him under this section.

(5) The code of practice issued by the Secretary of State under section 102 shall not be brought into force except in accordance with an order made by the Secretary of State by statutory instrument.

(6) An order under subsection (5) may contain such transitional provisions and savings as appear to the Secretary of State to be necessary or expedient in connection with the coming into force of the code to which the order relates.

(7) The Secretary of State shall not make an order under this section unless a draft of the order has been laid before Parliament and approved by resolution of each House.

(8) The Secretary of State may from time to time—

(a) revise the whole or any part of the code issued under section 102; and

(b) issue the revised code.

(9) The preceding provisions of this section shall apply (with appropriate modifications) in relation to the issue of any revised code under section 102 as they apply in relation to the first issuing of the code.

(10) Subsection (9) shall not, in the case of a draft of a revised code, require the Secretary of State to consult under subsection (2) with any communications providers who would not be affected by the proposed revisions.

104   Directions about retention of communications data

[…]

105   Lapsing of powers in section 104

[…]

106   Arrangements for payments

(1) It shall be the duty of the Secretary of State to ensure that such arrangements are in force as he thinks appropriate for authorising or requiring, in such cases as he thinks fit, the making to communications providers of appropriate contributions towards the costs incurred by them—

(a) in complying with the provisions of any code of practice, agreement or direction under this Part, or

(b) as a consequence of the retention of any communications data in accordance with any such provisions.

(2) For the purpose of complying with his duty under this section, the Secretary of State may make arrangements for the payments to be made out of money provided by Parliament.

107   Interpretation of Part 11

(1) In this Part—

"communications data" has the same meaning as in Chapter 2 of Part 1 of the Regulation of Investigatory Powers Act 2000 (c. 23);

"communications provider" means a person who provides a postal service or a telecommunications service;

"legal proceedings", "postal service" and "telecommunications service" each has the same meaning as in that Act;

and any reference in this Part to the prevention or detection of crime shall be construed as if contained in Chapter 2 of Part 1 of that Act.

(2) References in this Part, in relation to any code of practice, agreement or direction, to the retention by a communications provider of any communications data include references to the retention of any data obtained by that provider before the time when the code was issued, the agreement made or the direction given, and to data already held by that provider at that time.

Land Registration Act 2002

(2002, c.9)

An Act to make provision about land registration; and for connected purposes.   [26 February 2002]

PART 8   ELECTRONIC CONVEYANCING[1]

91   Electronic dispositions: formalities

(1) This section applies to a document in electronic form where—

(a) the document purports to effect a disposition which falls within subsection (2), and

(b) the conditions in subsection (3) are met.

(2) A disposition falls within this subsection if it is–

(a) a disposition of a registered estate or charge,

(b) a disposition of an interest which is the subject of a notice in the register, or

(c) a disposition which triggers the requirement of registration,

which is of a kind specified by rules.

(3) The conditions referred to above are that—

(a) the document makes provision for the time and date when it takes effect,

(b) the document has the electronic signature of each person by whom it purports to be authenticated,

(c) each electronic signature is certified, and

(d) such other conditions as rules may provide are met.

---

[1] This Part and schedule do not apply to Scotland.

(4) A document to which this section applies is to be regarded as—

(a) in writing, and

(b) signed by each individual, and sealed by each corporation, whose electronic signature it has.

(5) A document to which this section applies is to be regarded for the purposes of any enactment as a deed.

(6) If a document to which this section applies is authenticated by a person as agent, it is to be regarded for the purposes of any enactment as authenticated by him under the written authority of his principal.

(7) If notice of an assignment made by means of a document to which this section applies is given in electronic form in accordance with rules, it is to be regarded for the purposes of any enactment as given in writing.

(8) The right conferred by section 75 of the Law of Property Act 1925 (c. 20) (purchaser's right to have the execution of a conveyance attested) does not apply to a document to which this section applies.

[(9) In relation to the execution of a document by a company in accordance with section 44(2) of the Companies Act 2006 (signature on behalf of the company)—

(a) subsection (4) above has effect in relation to paragraph (a) of that provision (signature by two authorised signatories) but not paragraph (b) (signature by director in presence of witness);

(b) the other provisions of section 44 apply accordingly (the references to a document purporting to be signed in accordance with subsection (2) of that section being read as references to its purporting to be authenticated in accordance with this section);

(c) where subsection (4) above has effect in relation to a person signing on behalf of more than one company, the requirement of subsection (6) of that section is treated as met if the document specifies the different capacities in which the person signs.]

[(9A) If subsection (3) of section 29C of the Industrial and Provident Societies Act 1965 (execution of documents) applies to a document because of subsection (4) above, subsection (5) of that section (presumption of due execution) shall have effect in relation to the document with the substitution of "authenticated" for "signed".]

(10) In this section, references to an electronic signature and to the certification of such a signature are to be read in accordance with section 7(2) and (3) of the Electronic Communications Act 2000 (c. 7).

92 Land registry network

(1) The registrar may provide, or arrange for the provision of, an electronic communications network for use for such purposes as he thinks fit relating to registration or the carrying on of transactions which—

(a) involve registration, and

(b) are capable of being effected electronically.

(2) Schedule 5 (which makes provision in connection with a network provided under subsection (1) and transactions carried on by means of such a network) has effect.

93 Power to require simultaneous registration

(1) This section applies to a disposition of—

(a) a registered estate or charge, or

(b) an interest which is the subject of a notice in the register,

where the disposition is of a description specified by rules.

(2) A disposition to which this section applies, or a contract to make such a disposition, only has effect if it is made by means of a document in electronic form and if, when the document purports to take effect—

(a) it is electronically communicated to the registrar, and

(b) the relevant registration requirements are met.

(3) For the purposes of subsection (2)(b), the relevant registration requirements are—

    (a) in the case of a registrable disposition, the requirements under Schedule 2, and

    (b) in the case of any other disposition, or a contract, such requirements as rules may provide.

(4) Section 27(1) does not apply to a disposition to which this section applies.

(5) Before making rules under this section the Lord Chancellor must consult such persons as he considers appropriate.

(6) In this section, "disposition", in relation to a registered charge, includes postponement.

94 Electronic settlement

The registrar may take such steps as he thinks fit for the purpose of securing the provision of a system of electronic settlement in relation to transactions involving registration.

95 Supplementary

Rules may—

    (a) make provision about the communication of documents in electronic form to the registrar;

    (b) make provision about the electronic storage of documents communicated to the registrar in electronic form.

SCHEDULE 5 LAND REGISTRY NETWORK

1   Access to network

(1) A person who is not a member of the land registry may only have access to a land registry network under authority conferred by means of an agreement with the registrar.

(2) An agreement for the purposes of sub-paragraph (1) ("network access agreement") may authorise access for—

    (a) the communication, posting or retrieval of information,

    (b) the making of changes to the register of title or cautions register,

    (c) the issue of official search certificates,

    (d) the issue of official copies, or

    (e) such other conveyancing purposes as the registrar thinks fit.

(3) Rules may regulate the use of network access agreements to confer authority to carry out functions of the registrar.

(4) The registrar must, on application, enter into a network access agreement with the applicant if the applicant meets such criteria as rules may provide.

2   Terms of access

(1) The terms on which access to a land registry network is authorised shall be such as the registrar thinks fit, subject to sub-paragraphs (3) and (4), and may, in particular, include charges for access.

(2) The power under sub-paragraph (1) may be used, not only for the purpose of regulating the use of the network, but also for—

    (a) securing that the person granted access uses the network to carry on such qualifying transactions as may be specified in, or under, the agreement,

    (b) such other purpose relating to the carrying on of qualifying transactions as rules may provide, or

    (c) enabling network transactions to be monitored.

(3) It shall be a condition of a network access agreement which enables the person granted access to use the network to carry on qualifying transactions that he must comply with any rules for the time being in force under paragraph 5.

(4) Rules may regulate the terms on which access to a land registry network is authorised.

3   Termination of access

(1) The person granted access by a network access agreement may terminate the agreement at any time by notice to the registrar.

(2) Rules may make provision about the termination of a network access agreement by the registrar and may, in particular, make provision about—

    (a) the grounds of termination,

    (b) the procedure to be followed in relation to termination, and

    (c) the suspension of termination pending appeal.

(3) Without prejudice to the generality of sub-paragraph (2)(a), rules under that provision may authorise the registrar to terminate a network access agreement if the person granted access—

    (a) fails to comply with the terms of the agreement,

    (b) ceases to be a person with whom the registrar would be required to enter into a network access agreement conferring the authority which the agreement confers, or

    (c) does not meet such conditions as the rules may provide.

4   Appeals

(1) A person who is aggrieved by a decision of the registrar with respect to entry into, or termination of, a network access agreement may appeal against the decision to the adjudicator.

(2) On determining an appeal under this paragraph, the adjudicator may give such directions as he considers appropriate to give effect to his determination.

(3) Rules may make provision about appeals under this paragraph.

5   Network transaction rules

(1) Rules may make provision about how to go about network transactions.

(2) Rules under sub-paragraph (1) may, in particular, make provision about dealings with the land registry, including provision about—

    (a) the procedure to be followed, and

    (b) the supply of information (including information about unregistered interests).

6   Overriding nature of network access obligations

To the extent that an obligation not owed under a network access agreement conflicts with an obligation owed under such an agreement by the person granted access, the obligation not owed under the agreement is discharged.

7   Do-it-yourself conveyancing

(1) If there is a land registry network, the registrar has a duty to provide such assistance as he thinks appropriate for the purpose of enabling persons engaged in qualifying transactions who wish to do their own conveyancing to do so by means of the network.

(2) The duty under sub-paragraph (1) does not extend to the provision of legal advice.

8   Presumption of authority

Where—

    (a) a person who is authorised under a network access agreement to do so uses the network for the making of a disposition or contract, and

    (b) the document which purports to effect the disposition or to be the contract—

        (i)   purports to be authenticated by him as agent, and

        (ii)   contains a statement to the effect that he is acting under the authority of his principal,

he shall be deemed, in favour of any other party, to be so acting.

9   Management of network transactions

(1) The registrar may use monitoring information for the purpose of managing network transactions and may, in particular, disclose such information to persons authorised to use the network, and authorise the further disclosure of information so disclosed, if he considers it is necessary or desirable to do so.

(2) The registrar may delegate his functions under sub-paragraph (1), subject to such conditions as he thinks fit.

(3) In sub-paragraph (1), "monitoring information" means information provided in pursuance of provision in a network access agreement included under paragraph 2(2)(c).

10   Supplementary

The registrar may provide, or arrange for the provision of, education and training in relation to the use of a land registry network.

11. (1) Power to make rules under paragraph 1, 2 or 3 is exercisable by the Lord Chancellor.

(2) Before making such rules, the Lord Chancellor must consult such persons as he considers appropriate.

(3) In making rules under paragraph 1 or 3(2)(a), the Lord Chancellor must have regard, in particular, to the need to secure—

(a) the confidentiality of private information kept on the network,

(b) competence in relation to the use of the network (in particular for the purpose of making changes), and

(c) the adequate insurance of potential liabilities in connection with use of the network.

12. In this Schedule—

"land registry network" means a network provided under section 92(1);

"network access agreement" has the meaning given by paragraph 1(2);

"network transaction" means a transaction carried on by means of a land registry network;

"qualifying transaction" means a transaction which—

(a) involves registration, and

(b) is capable of being effected electronically.

Communications Act 2003

(2003, c. 21)

An Act to confer functions on the Office of Communications; to make provision about the regulation of the provision of electronic communications networks and services and of the use of the electro-magnetic spectrum; to make provision about the regulation of broadcasting and of the provision of television and radio services; to make provision about mergers involving newspaper and other media enterprises and, in that connection, to amend the Enterprise Act 2002; and for connected purposes.   [17th July 2003]

Offences relating to networks and services

125   Dishonestly obtaining electronic communications services

(1) A person who—

(a) dishonestly obtains an electronic communications service, and

(b) does so with intent to avoid payment of a charge applicable to the provision of that service,

is guilty of an offence.

(2) It is not an offence under this section to obtain a service mentioned in section 297(1) of the Copyright, Designs and Patents Act 1988 (c. 48) (dishonestly obtaining a broadcasting [...] service provided from a place in the UK).

(3) A person guilty of an offence under this section shall be liable—

(a) on summary conviction, to imprisonment for a term not exceeding six months or to a fine not exceeding the statutory maximum, or to both;

(b) on conviction on indictment, to imprisonment for a term not exceeding five years or to a fine, or to both.

126   Possession or supply of apparatus etc. for contravening s. 125

(1) A person is guilty of an offence if, with an intention falling within subsection (3), he has in his possession or under his control anything that may be used—

(a) for obtaining an electronic communications service; or

(b) in connection with obtaining such a service.

(2) A person is guilty of an offence if—

(a) he supplies or offers to supply anything which may be used as mentioned in subsection (1); and

(b) he knows or believes that the intentions in relation to that thing of the person to whom it is supplied or offered fall within subsection (3).

(3) A person's intentions fall within this subsection if he intends—

(a) to use the thing to obtain an electronic communications service dishonestly;

(b) to use the thing for a purpose connected with the dishonest obtaining of such a service;

(c) dishonestly to allow the thing to be used to obtain such a service; or

(d) to allow the thing to be used for a purpose connected with the dishonest obtaining of such a service.

(4) An intention does not fall within subsection (3) if it relates exclusively to the obtaining of a service mentioned in section 297(1) of the Copyright, Designs and Patents Act 1988 (c. 48).

(5) A person guilty of an offence under this section shall be liable—

(a) on summary conviction, to imprisonment for a term not exceeding six months or to a fine not exceeding the statutory maximum, or to both; and

(b) on conviction on indictment, to imprisonment for a term not exceeding five years or to a fine, or to both.

(6) In this section, references, in the case of a thing used for recording data, to the use of that thing include references to the use of data recorded by it.

127   Improper use of public electronic communications network

(1) A person is guilty of an offence if he—

(a) sends by means of a public electronic communications network a message or other matter that is grossly offensive or of an indecent, obscene or menacing character; or

(b) causes any such message or matter to be so sent.

(2) A person is guilty of an offence if, for the purpose of causing annoyance, inconvenience or needless anxiety to another, he—

(a) sends by means of a public electronic communications network, a message that he knows to be false,

(b) causes such a message to be sent; or

(c) persistently makes use of a public electronic communications network.

(3) A person guilty of an offence under this section shall be liable, on summary conviction, to imprisonment for a term not exceeding six months or to a fine not exceeding level 5 on the standard scale, or to both.

(4) Subsections (1) and (2) do not apply to anything done in the course of providing a programme service (within the meaning of the Broadcasting Act 1990 (c. 42)).

Sexual Offences Act 2003

(2003, c. 42)

An Act to make new provision about sexual offences, their prevention and the protection of children from harm from other sexual acts, and for connected purposes.

[20th November 2003]

15   Meeting a child following sexual grooming etc.[1]

(1) A person aged 18 or over (A) commits an offence if—

(a) having met or communicated with another person (B) on at least two earlier occasions, he—

(i)   intentionally meets B, or

(ii) travels with the intention of meeting B in any part of the world,

---

[1] This section does not apply to Scotland.

(b) at the time, he intends to do anything to or in respect of B, during or after the meeting and in any part of the world, which if done will involve the commission by A of a relevant offence,

(c) B is under 16, and

(d) A does not reasonably believe that B is 16 or over.

(2) In subsection (1)—

(a) the reference to A having met or communicated with B is a reference to A having met B in any part of the world or having communicated with B by any means from, to or in any part of the world;

(b) "relevant offence" means—

(i) an offence under this Part,

(ii) an offence within any of paragraphs 61 to 92 of Schedule 3, or

(iii) anything done outside England and Wales and Northern Ireland which is not an offence within sub-paragraph (i) or (ii) but would be an offence within sub-paragraph (i) if done in England and Wales.

(3) In this section as it applies to Northern Ireland—

(a) subsection (1) has effect with the substitution of "17" for "16" in both places;

(b) subsection (2)(b)(iii) has effect with the substitution of "sub-paragraph (ii) if done in Northern Ireland" for "sub-paragraph (i) if done in England and Wales".

(4) A person guilty of an offence under this section is liable—

(a) on summary conviction, to imprisonment for a term not exceeding 6 months or a fine not exceeding the statutory maximum or both;

(b) on conviction on indictment, to imprisonment for a term not exceeding 10 years.

Gambling Act 2005

(2005, c. 19)

An Act to make provision about gambling. [7th April 2005]

PART I INTERPRETATION OF KEY CONCEPTS

Principal concepts

1 The licensing objectives

In this Act a reference to the licensing objectives is a reference to the objectives of—

(a) preventing gambling from being a source of crime or disorder, being associated with crime or disorder or being used to support crime,

(b) ensuring that gambling is conducted in a fair and open way, and

(c) protecting children and other vulnerable persons from being harmed or exploited by gambling.

2 Licensing authorities

(1) For the purposes of this Act the following are licensing authorities—

(a) in relation to England—

(i) a district council,

(ii) a county council for a county in which there are no district councils,

(iii) a London borough council,

(iv) the Common Council of the City of London, and

(v) the Council of the Isles of Scilly,

(b) in relation to Wales—

(i) a county council, and

(ii) a county borough council, and

    (c) in relation to Scotland, a licensing board constituted under section 1 of the Licensing (Scotland) Act 1976 (c. 66).

(2) For the purposes of Schedule 13, the Sub-Treasurer of the Inner Temple and the Under-Treasurer of the Middle Temple are licensing authorities.

3   Gambling

In this Act "gambling" means—

    (a) gaming (within the meaning of section 6),

    (b) betting (within the meaning of section 9), and

    (c) participating in a lottery (within the meaning of section 14 and subject to section 15).

4   Remote gambling

(1) In this Act "remote gambling" means gambling in which persons participate by the use of remote communication.

(2) In this Act "remote communication" means communication using—

    (a) the internet,

    (b) telephone,

    (c) television,

    (d) radio, or

    (e) any other kind of electronic or other technology for facilitating communication.

(3) The Secretary of State may by regulations provide that a specified system or method of communication is or is not to be treated as a form of remote communication for the purposes of this Act (and subsection (2) is subject to any regulations under this subsection).

5   Facilities for gambling

(1) For the purposes of this Act a person provides facilities for gambling if he—

    (a) invites others to gamble in accordance with arrangements made by him,

    (b) provides, operates or administers arrangements for gambling by others, or

    (c) participates in the operation or administration of gambling by others.

(2) But a person does not provide facilities for gambling for the purposes of this Act by virtue only of—

    (a) providing an article other than a gaming machine to a person who intends to use it, or may use it, in the course of any of the activities mentioned in subsection (1)(a) to (c),

    (b) providing, otherwise than in the course of providing, operating or administering arrangements for gambling or participating in the operation or administration of gambling, an article to a person who intends to use it, or may use it, for gambling, or

    (c) making facilities for remote communication available for use by—

        (i) persons carrying on any of those activities, or

        (ii) persons gambling in response to or in accordance with any of those activities.

(3) A person provides facilities for gambling (despite subsection (2)(c)) if—

    (a) he makes facilities for remote communication available for use,

    (b) the facilities are adapted or presented in such a way as to facilitate, or to draw attention to the possibility of, their use for gambling, and

    (c) the nature, adaptation or presentation of the facilities is such that—

        (i) they cannot reasonably be expected to be used for purposes other than gambling, or

        (ii) they are intended to be used wholly or mainly for gambling.

(4) The Secretary of State may by order, for the purposes of subsection (3)(c)—

    (a) provide that facilities of a specified nature, or adapted or presented in a specified way, cannot reasonably be expected to be used for purposes other than gambling;

    (b) provide that facilities of a specified nature, or adapted or presented in a specified way, can reasonably be expected to be used for purposes other than gambling;

    (c) specify criteria by which it is to be determined whether facilities can reasonably be expected to be used for purposes other than gambling;

(d) provide that facilities of a specified nature, or adapted or presented in a specified way, shall be taken as being intended to be used wholly or mainly for gambling;

(e) provide that facilities of a specified nature, or adapted or presented in a specified way, shall be taken as not being intended to be used wholly or mainly for gambling;

(f) specify criteria by which it is to be determined whether facilities are intended to be used wholly or mainly for gambling.

Terrorism Act 2006

(2006, c. 11)

An Act to make provision for and about offences relating to conduct carried out, or capable of being carried out, for purposes connected with terrorism; to amend enactments relating to terrorism; to amend the Intelligence Services Act 1994 and the Regulation of Investigatory Powers Act 2000; and for connected purposes.   [30 March 2006]

PART 1 OFFENCES

Encouragement etc of terrorism

1 Encouragement of terrorism

(1) This section applies to a statement that is likely to be understood by some or all of the members of the public to whom it is published as a direct or indirect encouragement or other inducement to them to the commission, preparation or instigation of acts of terrorism or Convention offences.

(2) A person commits an offence if—

(a) he publishes a statement to which this section applies or causes another to publish such a statement, and

(b) at the time he publishes it or causes it to be published, he—

(i) intends members of the public to be directly or indirectly encouraged or otherwise induced by the statement to commit, prepare or instigate acts of terrorism or Convention offences; or

(ii) is reckless as to whether members of the public will be directly or indirectly encouraged or otherwise induced by the statement to commit, prepare or instigate such acts or offences.

(3) For the purposes of this section, the statements that are likely to be understood by members of the public as indirectly encouraging the commission or preparation of acts of terrorism or Convention offences include every statement which—

(a) glorifies the commission or preparation (whether in the past, in the future or generally) of such acts or offences; and

(b) is a statement from which those members of the public could reasonably be expected to infer that what is being glorified is being glorified as conduct that should be emulated by them in existing circumstances.

(4) For the purposes of this section the questions how a statement is likely to be understood and what members of the public could reasonably be expected to infer from it must be determined having regard both—

(a) to the contents of the statement as a whole; and

(b) to the circumstances and manner of its publication.

(5) It is irrelevant for the purposes of subsections (1) to (3)—

(a) whether anything mentioned in those subsections relates to the commission, preparation or instigation of one or more particular acts of terrorism or Convention offences, of acts of terrorism or Convention offences of a particular description or of acts of terrorism or Convention offences generally; and,

(b) whether any person is in fact encouraged or induced by the statement to commit, prepare or instigate any such act or offence.

(6) In proceedings for an offence under this section against a person in whose case it is not proved that he intended the statement directly or indirectly to encourage or otherwise induce the commission, preparation or instigation of acts of terrorism or Convention offences, it is a defence for him to show—

(a) that the statement neither expressed his views nor had his endorsement (whether by virtue of section 3 or otherwise); and

(b) that it was clear, in all the circumstances of the statement's publication, that it did not express his views and (apart from the possibility of his having been given and failed to comply with a notice under subsection (3) of that section) did not have his endorsement.

(7) A person guilty of an offence under this section shall be liable—

(a) on conviction on indictment, to imprisonment for a term not exceeding 7 years or to a fine, or to both;

(b) on summary conviction in England and Wales, to imprisonment for a term not exceeding 12 months or to a fine not exceeding the statutory maximum, or to both;

(c) on summary conviction in Scotland or Northern Ireland, to imprisonment for a term not exceeding 6 months or to a fine not exceeding the statutory maximum, or to both.

(8) In relation to an offence committed before the commencement of section 154(1) of the Criminal Justice Act 2003 (c 44), the reference in subsection (7)(b) to 12 months is to be read as a reference to 6 months.

2   Dissemination of terrorist publications

(1) A person commits an offence if he engages in conduct falling within subsection (2) and, at the time he does so—

(a) he intends an effect of his conduct to be a direct or indirect encouragement or other inducement to the commission, preparation or instigation of acts of terrorism;

(b) he intends an effect of his conduct to be the provision of assistance in the commission or preparation of such acts; or

(c) he is reckless as to whether his conduct has an effect mentioned in paragraph (a) or (b).

(2) For the purposes of this section a person engages in conduct falling within this subsection if he—

(a) distributes or circulates a terrorist publication;

(b) gives, sells or lends such a publication;

(c) offers such a publication for sale or loan;

(d) provides a service to others that enables them to obtain, read, listen to or look at such a publication, or to acquire it by means of a gift, sale or loan;

(e) transmits the contents of such a publication electronically; or

(f) has such a publication in his possession with a view to its becoming the subject of conduct falling within any of paragraphs (a) to (e).

(3) For the purposes of this section a publication is a terrorist publication, in relation to conduct falling within subsection (2), if matter contained in it is likely—

(a) to be understood, by some or all of the persons to whom it is or may become available as a consequence of that conduct, as a direct or indirect encouragement or other inducement to them to the commission, preparation or instigation of acts of terrorism; or

(b) to be useful in the commission or preparation of such acts and to be understood, by some or all of those persons, as contained in the publication, or made available to them, wholly or mainly for the purpose of being so useful to them.

(4) For the purposes of this section matter that is likely to be understood by a person as indirectly encouraging the commission or preparation of acts of terrorism includes any matter which—

(a) glorifies the commission or preparation (whether in the past, in the future or generally) of such acts; and

(b) is matter from which that person could reasonably be expected to infer that what is being glorified is being glorified as conduct that should be emulated by him in existing circumstances.

(5) For the purposes of this section the question whether a publication is a terrorist publication in relation to particular conduct must be determined—

(a) as at the time of that conduct; and

(b) having regard both to the contents of the publication as a whole and to the circumstances in which that conduct occurs.

(6) In subsection (1) references to the effect of a person's conduct in relation to a terrorist publication include references to an effect of the publication on one or more persons to whom it is or may become available as a consequence of that conduct.

(7) It is irrelevant for the purposes of this section whether anything mentioned in subsections (1) to (4) is in relation to the commission, preparation or instigation of one or more particular acts of terrorism, of acts of terrorism of a particular description or of acts of terrorism generally.

(8) For the purposes of this section it is also irrelevant, in relation to matter contained in any article whether any person—

(a) is in fact encouraged or induced by that matter to commit, prepare or instigate acts of terrorism; or

(b) in fact makes use of it in the commission or preparation of such acts.

(9) In proceedings for an offence under this section against a person in respect of conduct to which subsection (10) applies, it is a defence for him to show—

(a) that the matter by reference to which the publication in question was a terrorist publication neither expressed his views nor had his endorsement (whether by virtue of section 3 or otherwise); and

(b) that it was clear, in all the circumstances of the conduct, that that matter did not express his views and (apart from the possibility of his having been given and failed to comply with a notice under subsection (3) of that section) did not have his endorsement.

(10) This subsection applies to the conduct of a person to the extent that—

(a) the publication to which his conduct related contained matter by reference to which it was a terrorist publication by virtue of subsection (3)(a); and

(b) that person is not proved to have engaged in that conduct with the intention specified in subsection (1)(a).

(11) A person guilty of an offence under this section shall be liable—

(a) on conviction on indictment, to imprisonment for a term not exceeding 7 years or to a fine, or to both;

(b) on summary conviction in England and Wales, to imprisonment for a term not exceeding 12 months or to a fine not exceeding the statutory maximum, or to both;

(c) on summary conviction in Scotland or Northern Ireland, to imprisonment for a term not exceeding 6 months or to a fine not exceeding the statutory maximum, or to both.

(12) In relation to an offence committed before the commencement of section 154(1) of the Criminal Justice Act 2003 (c 44), the reference in subsection (11)(b) to 12 months is to be read as a reference to 6 months.

(13) In this section—

"lend" includes let on hire, and "loan" is to be construed accordingly;

"publication" means an article or record of any description that contains any of the following, or any combination of them—

(a) matter to be read;

(b) matter to be listened to;

(c) matter to be looked at or watched.

3   Application of ss 1 and 2 to internet activity etc

(1) This section applies for the purposes of sections 1 and 2 in relation to cases where—

(a) a statement is published or caused to be published in the course of, or in connection with, the provision or use of a service provided electronically; or

(b) conduct falling within section 2(2) was in the course of, or in connection with, the provision or use of such a service.

(2) The cases in which the statement, or the article or record to which the conduct relates, is to be regarded as having the endorsement of a person ("the relevant person") at any time include a case in which—

(a) a constable has given him a notice under subsection (3);

(b) that time falls more than 2 working days after the day on which the notice was given; and

(c) the relevant person has failed, without reasonable excuse, to comply with the notice.

(3) A notice under this subsection is a notice which—

(a) declares that, in the opinion of the constable giving it, the statement or the article or record is unlawfully terrorism-related;

(b) requires the relevant person to secure that the statement or the article or record, so far as it is so related, is not available to the public or is modified so as no longer to be so related;

(c) warns the relevant person that a failure to comply with the notice within 2 working days will result in the statement, or the article or record, being regarded as having his endorsement; and

(d) explains how, under subsection (4), he may become liable by virtue of the notice if the statement, or the article or record, becomes available to the public after he has complied with the notice.

(4) Where—

(a) a notice under subsection (3) has been given to the relevant person in respect of a statement, or an article or record, and he has complied with it, but

(b) he subsequently publishes or causes to be published a statement which is, or is for all practical purposes, the same or to the same effect as the statement to which the notice related, or to matter contained in the article or record to which it related, (a "repeat statement");

the requirements of subsection (2)(a) to (c) shall be regarded as satisfied in the case of the repeat statement in relation to the times of its subsequent publication by the relevant person.

(5) In proceedings against a person for an offence under section 1 or 2 the requirements of subsection (2)(a) to (c) are not, in his case, to be regarded as satisfied in relation to any time by virtue of subsection (4) if he shows that he—

(a) has, before that time, taken every step he reasonably could to prevent a repeat statement from becoming available to the public and to ascertain whether it does; and

(b) was, at that time, a person to whom subsection (6) applied.

(6) This subsection applies to a person at any time when he—

(a) is not aware of the publication of the repeat statement; or

(b) having become aware of its publication, has taken every step that he reasonably could to secure that it either ceased to be available to the public or was modified as mentioned in subsection (3)(b).

(7) For the purposes of this section a statement or an article or record is unlawfully terrorism-related if it constitutes, or if matter contained in the article or record constitutes—

(a) something that is likely to be understood, by any one or more of the persons to whom it has or may become available, as a direct or indirect encouragement or other inducement to the commission, preparation or instigation of acts of terrorism or Convention offences; or

(b) information which—

(i) is likely to be useful to any one or more of those persons in the commission or preparation of such acts; and

(ii) is in a form or context in which it is likely to be understood by any one or more of those persons as being wholly or mainly for the purpose of being so useful.

(8) The reference in subsection (7) to something that is likely to be understood as an indirect encouragement to the commission or preparation of acts of terrorism or Convention offences includes anything which is likely to be understood as—

    (a) the glorification of the commission or preparation (whether in the past, in the future or generally) of such acts or such offences; and

    (b) a suggestion that what is being glorified is being glorified as conduct that should be emulated in existing circumstances.

(9) In this section "working day" means any day other than—

    (a) a Saturday or a Sunday;

    (b) Christmas Day or Good Friday; or

    (c) a day which is a bank holiday under the Banking and Financial Dealings Act 1971 (c 80) in any part of the United Kingdom.

Part II

Statutory instruments

The Copyright and Rights in Databases Regulations 1997

(SI 1997/3032)

PART I INTRODUCTORY PROVISIONS

1 Citation, commencement and extent

(1) These Regulations may be cited as the Copyright and Rights in Databases Regulations 1997.

(2) These Regulations come into force on 1st January 1998.

(3) These Regulations extend to the whole of the United Kingdom.

2 Implementation of Directive

(1) These Regulations make provision for the purpose of implementing—

(a) Council Directive No 96/9/EC of 11 March 1996 on the legal protection of databases, [...]

(b) certain obligations of the United Kingdom created by or arising under the EEA Agreement so far as relating to the implementation of that Directive [, and

(c) an Agreement in the form of an exchange of letters between the United Kingdom of Great Britain and Northern Ireland on behalf of the Isle of Man and the European Community extending to the Isle of Man the legal protection of databases as provided for in Chapter III of that Directive].

(2) In this Regulation "the EEA Agreement" means the Agreement on the European Economic Area signed at Oporto on 2nd May 1992, as adjusted by the Protocol signed at Brussels on 17th March 1993.

3 Interpretation

In this Regulations "the 1988 Act" means the Copyright, Designs and Patents Act 1988.

4 Scheme of the Regulations

(1) The 1988 Act is amended in accordance with the provisions of Part II of these Regulations, subject to the savings and transitional provisions in Part IV of these Regulations.

(2) Part III of these Regulations has effect subject to those savings and transitional provisions.

PART III DATABASE RIGHT

12 Interpretation

(1) In this Part—

"database" has the meaning given by section 3A(1) of the 1988 Act (as inserted by Regulation 6);

"extraction", in relation to any contents of a database, means the permanent or temporary transfer of those contents to another medium by any means or in any form;

"insubstantial", in relation to part of the contents of a database, shall be construed subject to Regulation 16(2);

"investment" includes any investment, whether of financial, human or technical resources;

"jointly", in relation to the making of a database, shall be construed in accordance with Regulation 14(6);

"lawful user", in relation to a database, means any person who (whether under a licence to do any of the acts restricted by any database right in the database or otherwise) has a right to use the database;

"maker", in relation to a database, shall be construed in accordance with Regulation 14;

"re-utilisation", in relation to any contents of a database, means making those contents available to the public by any means;

"substantial", in relation to any investment, extraction or re-utilisation, means substantial in terms of quantity or quality or a combination of both.

(2) The making of a copy of a database available for use, on terms that it will or may be returned, otherwise than for direct or indirect economic or commercial advantage, through an establishment which is accessible to the public shall not be taken for the purposes of this Part to constitute extraction or re-utilisation of the contents of the database.

(3) Where the making of a copy of a database available through an establishment which is accessible to the public gives rise to a payment the amount of which does not go beyond what is necessary to cover the costs of the establishment, there is no direct or indirect economic or commercial advantage for the purposes of paragraph (2).

(4) Paragraph (2) does not apply to the making of a copy of a database available for on-the-spot reference use.

(5) Where a copy of a database has been sold within the EEA [or the Isle of Man] by, or with the consent of, the owner of the database right in the database, the further sale within the EEA [or the Isle of Man] of that copy shall not be taken for the purposes of this Part to constitute extraction or re-utilisation of the contents of the database.

13   Database right

(1) A property right ("database right") subsists, in accordance with this Part, in a database if there has been a substantial investment in obtaining, verifying or presenting the contents of the database.

(2) For the purposes of paragraph (1) it is immaterial whether or not the database or any of its contents is a copyright work, within the meaning of Part I of the 1988 Act.

(3) This Regulation has effect subject to Regulation 18.

14   The maker of a database

(1) Subject to paragraphs (2) to (4), the person who takes the initiative in obtaining, verifying or presenting the contents of a database and assumes the risk of investing in that obtaining, verification or presentation shall be regarded as the maker of, and as having made, the database.

(2) Where a database is made by an employee in the course of his employment, his employer shall be regarded as the maker of the database, subject to any agreement to the contrary.

(3) Subject to paragraph (4), where a database is made by Her Majesty or by an officer or servant of the Crown in the course of his duties, Her Majesty shall be regarded as the maker of the database.

(4) Where a database is made by or under the direction or control of the House of Commons or the House of Lords—

(a) the House by whom, or under whose direction or control, the database is made shall be regarded as the maker of the database, and

(b) if the database is made by or under the direction or control of both Houses, the two Houses shall be regarded as the joint makers of the database.

[(4A) Where a database is made by or under the direction or control of the Scottish Parliament, the Scottish Parliamentary Corporate Body shall be regarded as the maker of the database.]

(5) For the purposes of this Part a database is made jointly if two or more persons acting together in collaboration take the initiative in obtaining, verifying or presenting the contents of the database and assume the risk of investing in that obtaining, verification or presentation.

(6) References in this Part to the maker of a database shall, except as otherwise provided, be construed, in relation to a database which is made jointly, as references to all the makers of the database.

15   First ownership of database right

The maker of a database is the first owner of database right in it.

16   Acts infringing database right

(1) Subject to the provisions of this Part, a person infringes database right in a database if, without the consent of the owner of the right, he extracts or re-utilises all or a substantial part of the contents of the database.

(2) For the purposes of this Part, the repeated and systematic extraction or re-utilisation of insubstantial parts of the contents of a database may amount to the extraction or reutilisation of a substantial part of those contents.

17   Term of protection

(1) Database right in a database expires at the end of the period of fifteen years from the end of the calendar year in which the making of a database was completed.

(2) Where a database is made available to the public before the end of the period referred to in paragraph (1), database right in the database shall expire fifteen years from the end of the calendar year in which the database was first made available to the public.

(3) Any substantial change to the contents of a database, including a substantial change resulting from the accumulation of successive additions, deletions or alterations, which would result in the database being considered to be a substantial new investment shall qualify the database resulting from that investment for its own term of protection.

(4) This Regulation has effect subject to Regulation 30.

18   Qualification for database right

(1) Database right does not subsist in a database unless, at the material time, its maker, or if it was made jointly, one or more of its makers, was—

    (a) an individual who was a national of an EEA state or habitually resident within the EEA,

    (b) a body which was incorporated under the law of an EEA state and which, at that time, satisfied one of the conditions in paragraph (2) [...],

    (c) a partnership or other unincorporated body which was formed under the law of an EEA state and which, at that time, satisfied the condition in paragraph (2)(a)[,

    (d) an individual who was habitually resident within the Isle of Man,

    (e) a body which was incorporated under the law of the Isle of Man and which, at that time, satisfied one of the conditions in paragraph (2A), or

    (f) a partnership or other unincorporated body which was formed under the law of the Isle of Man and which, at that time, satisfied the condition in paragraph (2A)(a)].

(2) The conditions mentioned in paragraphs (1)(b) and (c) are—

    (a) that the body has its central administration or principal place of business within the EEA, or

    (b) that the body has its registered office within the EEA and the body's operations are linked on an ongoing basis with the economy of an EEA state.

[(2A) The conditions mentioned in paragraphs (1)(e) and (f) are—

    (a) that the body has its central administration or principal place of business within the Isle of Man, or

    (b) that the body has its registered office within the Isle of Man and the body's operations are linked on an ongoing basis with the economy of the Isle of Man.]

(3) Paragraph (1) does not apply in any case falling within Regulation 14(4).

(4) In this Regulation—

    (a) "EEA" and "EEA state" have the meaning given by section 172A of the 1988 Act;

    (b) "the material time" means the time when the database was made, or if the making extended over a period, a substantial part of that period.

19 Avoidance of certain terms affecting lawful users

(1) A lawful user of a database which has been made available to the public in any manner shall be entitled to extract or re-utilise insubstantial parts of the contents of the database for any purpose.

(2) Where under an agreement a person has a right to use a database, or part of a database, which has been made available to the public in any manner, any term or condition in the agreement shall be void in so far as it purports to prevent that person from extracting or re-utilising insubstantial parts of the contents of the database, or of that part of the database, for any purpose.

20 Exceptions to database right

(1) Database right in a database which has been made available to the public in any manner is not infringed by fair dealing with a substantial part of its contents if—

  (a) that part is extracted from the database by a person who is apart from this paragraph a lawful user of the database,

  (b) it is extracted for the purpose of illustration for teaching or research and not for any commercial purpose, and

  (c) the source is indicated.

(2) The provisions of Schedule 1 specify other acts which may be done in relation to a database notwithstanding the existence of database right.

[20A Exceptions to database right: deposit libraries

(1) Database right in a database is not infringed by the copying of a work from the internet by a deposit library or person acting on its behalf if—

  (a) the work is of a description prescribed by regulations under section 10(5) of the 2003 Act,

  (b) its publication on the internet, or a person publishing it there, is connected with the United Kingdom in a manner so prescribed, and

  (c) the copying is done in accordance with any conditions so prescribed.

(2) Database right in a database is not infringed by the doing of anything in relation to relevant material permitted to be done under regulations under section 7 of the 2003 Act.

(3) Regulations under section 44A(3) of the 1988 Act exclude the application of paragraph (2) in relation to prescribed activities in relation to relevant material as (and to the extent that) they exclude the application of section 44A(2) of that Act in relation to those activities.

(4) In this Regulation—

  (a) "the 2003 Act" means the Legal Deposit Libraries Act 2003;

  (b) "deposit library" and "relevant material" have the same meaning as in section 7 of the 2003 Act.]

21 Acts permitted on assumption as to expiry of database right

(1) Database right in a database is not infringed by the extraction or re-utilisation of a substantial part of the contents of the database at a time when, or in pursuance of arrangements made at a time when—

  (a) it is not possible by reasonable inquiry to ascertain the identity of the maker, and

  (b) it is reasonable to assume that database right has expired.

(2) In the case of a database alleged to have been made jointly, paragraph (1) applies in relation to each person alleged to be one of the makers.

22 Presumptions relevant to database right

(1) The following presumptions apply in proceedings brought by virtue of this Part of these Regulations with respect to a database.

(2) Where a name purporting to be that of the maker appeared on copies of the database as published, or on the database when it was made, the person whose name appeared shall be presumed, until the contrary is proved—

  (a) to be the maker of the database, and

  (b) to have made it in circumstances not falling within Regulation 14(2) to (4).

(3) Where copies of the database as published bear a label or a mark stating—

(a) that a named person was the maker of the database, or

(b) that the database was first published in a specified year,

the label or mark shall be admissible as evidence of the facts stated and shall be presumed to be correct until the contrary is proved.

(4) In the case of a database alleged to have been made jointly, paragraphs (2) and (3), so far as is applicable, apply in relation to each person alleged to be one of the makers.

[23   Application of copyright provisions to database right

The following provisions of the 1988 Act apply in relation to database right and databases in which that right subsists as they apply in relation to copyright and copyright works—

sections 90 to 93 (dealing with rights in copyright works)

sections 96 to 102 (rights and remedies of copyright owner and exclusive licensee)

sections 113 and 114 (supplementary provisions in relation to delivery up)

section 115 (jurisdiction of county court and sheriff court).]

PART IV SAVINGS AND TRANSITIONAL PROVISIONS

[26   Introductory

Expressions used in this Part which are defined for the purposes of Part I of the 1988 Act have the same meaning as in that Part.]

27   General rule

Subject to Regulations 28 and 29, these Regulations apply to databases made before or after [1st January 1998].

[28   General savings

(1) Nothing in these Regulations affects any agreement made before 1st January 1998.

(2) Nothing in these Regulations affects any agreement made after 31st December 1997 and before 1st November 2003 in so far as the effect would only arise as a result of the amendment of these Regulations by the Copyright and Rights in Databases (Amendment) Regulations 2003.

(3) No act done in respect of any database, in which database right subsists by virtue of the maker of the database (or one or more of its makers) falling within one of the provisions contained in Regulations 14(4) and 18(1)(a), (b) and (c),—

(a) before 1st January 1998, or

(b) after 31st December 1997, in pursuance of an agreement made before 1st January 1998, shall be regarded as an infringement of database right in the database.

(4) No act done in respect of any database, in which database right subsists by virtue of its maker (or one or more of its makers) falling within one of the provisions contained in Regulation 18(1)(d), (e) and (f),—

(a) before 1st November 2003, or

(b) after 31st October 2003, in pursuance of an agreement made before 1st November 2003, shall be regarded as an infringement of database right in the database.]

29   Saving for copyright in certain existing databases

(1) Where a database—

(a) was created on or before 27th March 1996, and

(b) is a copyright work immediately before [1st January 1998],

copyright shall continue to subsist in the database for the remainder of its copyright term.

(2) In this Regulation "copyright term" means the period of the duration of copyright under section 12 of the 1988 Act (duration of copyright in literary, dramatic, musical or artistic works).

[30   Database right: term applicable to certain existing databases

Where—

    (a) the making of any database is completed on or after 1st January 1983, and before 1st January 1998, and

    (b) either—

        (i) the database is a database in which database right subsists by virtue of the maker of the database (or one or more of its makers) falling within one of the provisions contained in Regulations 14(4) and 18(1)(a), (b) and (c) and database right begins to subsist in the database on 1st January 1998, or

        (ii) the database is a database in which database right subsists by virtue of its maker (or one or more of its makers) falling within one of the provisions contained in Regulation 18(1)(d), (e) and (f) and database right begins to subsist in the database on 1st November 2003,

then database right shall subsist in the database for a period of fifteen years beginning with 1st January 1998.]

SCHEDULE 1   EXCEPTIONS TO DATABASE RIGHT FOR PUBLIC ADMINISTRATION

Parliamentary and judicial proceedings

1. Database right in a database is not infringed by anything done for the purposes of parliamentary or judicial proceedings or for the purposes of reporting such proceedings.

Royal Commissions and statutory inquiries

2.—(1) Database right in a database is not infringed by anything done for—

    (a) the purposes of the proceedings of a Royal Commission or statutory inquiry, or

    (b) the purpose of reporting any such proceedings held in public.

(2) Database right in a database is not infringed by the issue to the public of copies of the report of a Royal Commission or statutory inquiry containing the contents of the database.

(3) In this paragraph "Royal Commission" and "statutory inquiry" have the same meaning as in section 46 of the 1988 Act.

Material open to public inspection or on official register

3.—(1) Where the contents of a database are open to public inspection pursuant to a statutory requirement, or are on a statutory register, database right in the database is not infringed by the extraction of all or a substantial part of the contents containing factual information of any description, by or with the authority of the appropriate person, for a purpose which does not involve re-utilisation of all or a substantial part of the contents.

(2) Where the contents of a database are open to public inspection pursuant to a statutory requirement, database right in the database is not infringed by the extraction or re-utilisation of all or a substantial part of the contents, by or with the authority of the appropriate person, for the purpose of enabling the contents to be inspected at a more convenient time or place or otherwise facilitating the exercise of any right for the purpose of which the requirement is imposed.

(3) Where the contents of a database which is open to public inspection pursuant to a statutory requirement, or which is on a statutory register, contain information about matters of general scientific, technical, commercial or economic interest, database right in the database is not infringed by the extraction or re-utilisation of all or a substantial part of the contents, by or with the authority of the appropriate person, for the purpose of disseminating that information.

(4) In this paragraph—

"appropriate person" means the person required to make the contents of the database open to public inspection or, as the case may be, the person maintaining the register;

"statutory register" means a register maintained in pursuance of a statutory requirement; and "statutory requirement" means a requirement imposed by provision made by or under an enactment.

Material communicated to the Crown in the course of public business

4.—(1) This paragraph applies where the contents of a database have in the course of public business been communicated to the Crown for any purpose, by or with the licence of the owner of the database right and a document or other material thing recording or embodying the contents of the database is owned by or in the custody or control of the Crown.

(2) The Crown may, for the purpose for which the contents of the database were communicated to it, or any related purpose which could reasonably have been anticipated by the owner of the database right in the database, extract or re-utilise all or a substantial part of the contents without infringing database right in the database.

(3) The Crown may not re-utilise the contents of a database by virtue of this paragraph if the contents have previously been published otherwise than by virtue of this paragraph.

(4) In sub-paragraph (1) "public business" includes any activity carried on by the Crown.

(5) This paragraph has effect subject to any agreement to the contrary between the Crown and the owner of the database right in the database.

Public records

5. The contents of a database which are comprised in public records within the meaning of the Public Records Act 1958, the Public Records (Scotland) Act 1937 or the Public Records Act (Northern Ireland) 1923 which are open to public inspection in pursuance of that Act, may be re-utilised by or with the authority of any officer appointed under that Act, without infringement of database right in the database.

Acts done under statutory authority

6.—(1) Where the doing of a particular act is specifically authorised by an Act of Parliament, whenever passed, then, unless the Act provides otherwise, the doing of that act does not infringe database right in a database.

(2) Sub-paragraph (1) applies in relation to an enactment contained in Northern Ireland legislation as it applies in relation to an Act of Parliament.

(3) Nothing in this paragraph shall be construed as excluding any defence of statutory authority otherwise available under or by virtue of any enactment.

The Data Protection (Corporate Finance Exemption) Order 2000

(SI 2000/184)

1 Citation and commencement

(1) This Order may be cited as the Data Protection (Corporate Finance Exemption) Order 2000 and shall come into force on 1st March 2000.

(2) In this Order, "the Act" means the Data Protection Act 1998.

2 Matters to be taken into account

(1) The matter set out in paragraph (2) below is hereby specified for the purposes of paragraph 6(1)(b) of Schedule 7 to the Act (matters to be taken into account in determining whether exemption from the subject information provisions is required for the purpose of safeguarding an important economic or financial interest of the United Kingdom).

(2) The matter referred to in paragraph (1) above is the inevitable prejudicial effect on—

    (a) the orderly functioning of financial markets, or
    (b) the efficient allocation of capital within the economy,

which will result from the application (whether on an occasional or regular basis) of the subject information provisions to data to which paragraph (3) below applies.

(3) This paragraph applies to any personal data to which the application of the subject information provisions could, in the reasonable belief of the relevant person within the meaning of paragraph 6 of Schedule 7 to the Act, affect—

    (a) any decision of any person whether or not to—
        (i)   deal in,
        (ii) subscribe for, or
        (iii) issue,
        any instrument which is already in existence or is to be, or may be, created; or

    (b) any decision of any person to act or not to act in a way that is likely to have an effect on any business activity including, in particular, an effect on—
        (i)   the industrial strategy of any person (whether the strategy is, or is to be, pursued independently or in association with others),
        (ii) the capital structure of an undertaking, or
        (iii) the legal or beneficial ownership of a business or asset.

The Data Protection (Conditions under Paragraph 3 of Part II of Schedule 1) Order 2000

(SI 2000/185)

1   Citation and commencement

This Order may be cited as the Data Protection (Conditions under Paragraph 3 of Part II of Schedule 1) Order 2000 and shall come into force on 1st March 2000.

2   Interpretation

In this Order, "Part II" means Part II of Schedule 1 to the Data Protection Act 1998.

3   General provisions

(1) In cases where the primary condition referred to in paragraph 3 (2)(a) of Part II is met, the provisions of articles 4 and 5 apply.

(2) In cases where the primary condition referred to in paragraph 3(2)(b) of that Part is met by virtue of the fact that the recording of the information to be contained in the data by, or the disclosure of the data by, the data controller is not a function conferred on him by or under any enactment or an obligation imposed on him by order of a court, but is necessary for compliance with any legal obligation to which the data controller is subject, other than an obligation imposed by contract, the provisions of article 4 apply.

4   Notices in writing

(1) One of the further conditions prescribed in paragraph (2) must be met if paragraph 2(1)(b) of Part II is to be disapplied in respect of any particular data subject.

(2) The conditions referred to in paragraph (1) are that—

    (a) no notice in writing has been received at any time by the data controller from an individual, requiring that data controller to provide the information set out in paragraph 2(3) of that Part before the relevant time (as defined in paragraph 2(2) of that Part) or as soon as practicable after that time; or

    (b) where such notice in writing has been received but the data controller does not have sufficient information about the individual in order readily to determine whether he is processing personal data about that individual, the data controller shall send to the individual a written notice stating that he cannot provide the information set out in paragraph 2(3) of that Part because of his inability to make that determination, and explaining the reasons for that inability.

(3) The requirement in paragraph (2) that notice should be in writing is satisfied where the text of the notice—

(a) is transmitted by electronic means,

(b) is received in legible form, and

(c) is capable of being used for subsequent reference.

5   Further condition in cases of disproportionate effort

(1) The further condition prescribed in paragraph (2) must be met for paragraph 2(1)(b) of Part II to be disapplied in respect of any data.

(2) The condition referred to in paragraph (1) is that the data controller shall record the reasons for his view that the primary condition referred to in article 3(1) is met in respect of the data.

The Data Protection (Processing of Sensitive Personal Data) Order 2000

(SI 2000/417)

1—(1) This Order may be cited as the Data Protection (Processing of Sensitive Personal Data) Order 2000 and shall come into force on 1st March 2000.

(2) In this Order, "the Act" means the Data Protection Act 1998.

2 For the purposes of paragraph 10 of Schedule 3 to the Act, the circumstances specified in any of the paragraphs in the Schedule to this Order are circumstances in which sensitive personal data may be processed.

SCHEDULE CIRCUMSTANCES IN WHICH SENSITIVE PERSONAL DATA MAY BE PROCESSED

1.—(1) The processing—

(a) is in the substantial public interest;

(b) is necessary for the purposes of the prevention or detection of any unlawful act; and

(c) must necessarily be carried out without the explicit consent of the data subject being sought so as not to prejudice those purposes.

(2) In this paragraph, "act" includes a failure to act.

2.—(1) The processing—

(a) is in the substantial public interest;

(b) is necessary for the discharge of any function which is designed for protecting members of the public against—

(i)   dishonesty, malpractice, or other seriously improper conduct by, or the unfitness or incompetence of, any person, or

(ii)   mismanagement in the administration of, or failures in services provided by, any body or association; and

(c) must necessarily be carried out without the explicit consent of the data subject being sought so as not to prejudice the discharge of that function.

3.—(1) The disclosure of personal data—

(a) is in the substantial public interest;

(b) is in connection with—

(i)   the commission by any person of any unlawful act (whether alleged or established),

(ii)   dishonesty, malpractice, or other seriously improper conduct by, or the unfitness or incompetence of, any person (whether alleged or established), or

(iii) mismanagement in the administration of, or failures in services provided by, any body or association (whether alleged or established);

(c) is for the special purposes as defined in section 3 of the Act; and

(d) is made with a view to the publication of those data by any person and the data controller reasonably believes that such publication would be in the public interest.

(2) In this paragraph, "act" includes a failure to act.

4. The processing—

(a) is in the substantial public interest;

(b) is necessary for the discharge of any function which is designed for the provision of confidential counselling, advice, support or any other service; and

(c) is carried out without the explicit consent of the data subject because the processing—

   (i) is necessary in a case where consent cannot be given by the data subject,

   (ii) is necessary in a case where the data controller cannot reasonably be expected to obtain the explicit consent of the data subject, or

   (iii) must necessarily be carried out without the explicit consent of the data subject being sought so as not to prejudice the provision of that counselling, advice, support or other service.

5.—(1) The processing—

(a) is necessary for the purpose of—

   (i) carrying on insurance business, or

   (ii) making determinations in connection with eligibility for, and benefits payable under, an occupational pension scheme as defined in section 1 of the Pension Schemes Act 1993;

(b) is of sensitive personal data consisting of information falling within section 2(e) of the Act relating to a data subject who is the parent, grandparent, great grandparent or sibling of—

   (i) in the case of paragraph (a)(i), the insured person, or

   (ii) in the case of paragraph (a)(ii), the member of the scheme;

(c) is necessary in a case where the data controller cannot reasonably be expected to obtain the explicit consent of that data subject and the data controller is not aware of the data subject withholding his consent; and

(d) does not support measures or decisions with respect to that data subject.

(2) In this paragraph—

(a) "insurance business" means [business which consists of effecting or carrying out contracts of insurance of the following kind—

   (i) life and annuity,

   (ii) linked long term,

   (iii) permanent health,

   (iv) accident, or

   (v) sickness, and]

(b) "insured" and "member" includes an individual who is seeking to become an insured person or member of the scheme respectively.

[(2A) The definition of "insurance business" in sub-paragraph (2) above must be read with—

(a) section 22 of the Financial Services and Markets Act 2000;

(b) any relevant order under that section; and

(c) Schedule 2 to that Act.]

6. The processing—

(a) is of sensitive personal data in relation to any particular data subject that are subject to processing which was already under way immediately before the coming into force of this Order;

(b) is necessary for the purpose of—

   [(i) effecting or carrying out contracts of long-term insurance of the kind mentioned in sub-paragraph (2)(a)(i), (ii) or (iii) of paragraph 5 above.]

      (ii) establishing or administering an occupational pension scheme as defined in section 1 of the Pension Schemes Act 1993; and

  (c) either—

      (i) is necessary in a case where the data controller cannot reasonably be expected to obtain the explicit consent of the data subject and that data subject has not informed the data controller that he does not so consent, or

      (ii) must necessarily be carried out even without the explicit consent of the data subject so as not to prejudice those purposes.

7.—(1) Subject to the provisions of sub-paragraph (2), the processing—

  (a) is of sensitive personal data consisting of information falling within section 2(c) or of the Act;

  (b) is necessary for the purpose of identifying or keeping under review the existence or absence of equality of opportunity or treatment between persons—

      (i) holding different beliefs as described in section 2(c) of the Act, or

      (ii) of different states of physical or mental health or different physical or mental conditions as described in section 2(e) of the Act,

    with a view to enabling such equality to be promoted or maintained;

  (c) does not support measures or decisions with respect to any particular data subject otherwise than with the explicit consent of that data subject; and

  (d) does not cause, nor is likely to cause, substantial damage or substantial distress to the data subject or any other person.

(2) Where any individual has given notice in writing to any data controller who is processing personal data under the provisions of sub-paragraph (1) requiring that data controller to cease processing personal data in respect of which that individual is the data subject at the end of such period as is reasonable in the circumstances, that data controller must have ceased processing those personal data at the end of that period.

8.—(1) Subject to the provisions of sub-paragraph (2), the processing—

  (a) is of sensitive personal data consisting of information falling within section 2(b) of the Act;

  (b) is carried out by any person or organisation included in the register maintained pursuant to section 1 of the Registration of Political Parties Act 1998 in the course of his or its legitimate political activities; and

  (c) does not cause, nor is likely to cause, substantial damage or substantial distress to the data subject or any other person.

(2) Where any individual has given notice in writing to any data controller who is processing personal data under the provisions of sub-paragraph (1) requiring that data controller to cease processing personal data in respect of which that individual is the data subject at the end of such period as is reasonable in the circumstances, that data controller must have ceased processing those personal data at the end of that period.

9. The processing—

  (a) is in the substantial public interest;

  (b) is necessary for research purposes (which expression shall have the same meaning as in section 33 of the Act);

  (c) does not support measures or decisions with respect to any particular data subject otherwise than with the explicit consent of that data subject; and

  (d) does not cause, nor is likely to cause, substantial damage or substantial distress to the data subject or any other person.

10. The processing is necessary for the exercise of any functions conferred on a constable by any rule of law.

The Data Protection (Miscellaneous Subject Access Exemptions) Order 2000

(SI 2000/419)

1 This Order may be cited as the Data Protection (Miscellaneous Subject Access Exemptions) Order 2000 and shall come into force on 1st March 2000.

2 Personal data consisting of information the disclosure of which is prohibited or restricted by the enactments and instruments listed in the Schedule to this Order are exempt from section 7 of the Data Protection Act 1998.

SCHEDULE EXEMPTIONS FROM SECTION 7

Part I Enactments and Instruments Extending to the United Kingdom

Human fertilisation and embryology: information about the provision of treatment services, the keeping or use of gametes or embryos and whether identifiable individuals were born in consequence of treatment services.

Sections 31 and 33 of the Human Fertilisation and Embryology Act 1990.

Part II Enactments and Instruments Extending to England and Wales

Adoption records and reports

(a) [Sections 57 to 62, *77* and 79 of, and Schedule 2 to, the Adoption and Children Act 2002.

Regulation 14 of the Adoption Agencies Regulations 1983.
Regulation 41 of the Adoption Agencies Regulations 2005.
Regulation 42 of the Adoption Agencies (Wales) Regulations 2005.
Rules 5, 6, 9, 17, 18, 21, 22 and 53 of the Adoption Rules 1984.
Rules 5, 6, 9, 17, 18, 21, 22 and 32 of the Magistrates' Courts (Adoption) Rules 1984.
Rules 24, 29, 30, 65, 72, 73, *77*, 78 and 83 of the Family Procedure (Adoption) Rules 2005.]

Statement of child's special educational needs

(b) Regulation 19 of the Education (Special Educational Needs) Regulations 1994.

Parental order records and reports

(c) Sections 50 and 51 of the Adoption Act 1976 as modified by paragraphs 4(a) and (b) of Schedule 1 to the Parental Orders (Human Fertilisation and Embryology) Regulations 1994 in relation to parental orders made under section 30 of the Human Fertilisation and Embryology Act 1990.

Rules 4A.5 and 4A.9 of the Family Proceedings Rules 1991.
Rules 21E and 21I of the Family Proceedings Courts (Children Act 1989) Rules 1991.

Part III Enactments and Instruments Extending to Scotland

Adoption records and reports

(a) Section 45 of the Adoption (Scotland) Act 1978.

Regulation 23 of the Adoption Agencies (Scotland) Regulations 1996. [. . .]

Rule 67.3 of the Act of Sederunt (Rules of the Court of Session 1994) 1994.

Rules 2.12, 2.14, 2.30 and 2.33 of the Act of Sederunt (Child Care and Maintenance Rules) 1997.

Regulation 8 of the Adoption Allowance (Scotland) Regulations 1996.

Information provided by principal reporter for children's hearing

(b) Rules 5 and 21 of the Children's Hearings (Scotland) Rules 1996.

Record of child or young person's special educational needs

(c) Section 60(4) of the Education (Scotland) Act 1980.

Proviso (bb) to regulation 7(2) of the Education (Record of Needs) (Scotland) Regulations 1982.

Parental order records and reports

(d) Section 45 of the Adoption (Scotland) Act 1978 as modified by paragraph 10 of Schedule 1 to the Parental Orders (Human Fertilisation and Embryology) (Scotland) Regulations 1994 in relation to parental orders made under section 30 of the Human Fertilisation and Embryology Act 1990.

Rules 2.47 and 2.59 of the Act of Sederunt (Child Care and Maintenance Rules) 1997.

Rules 81.3 and 81.18 of the Act of Sederunt (Rules of the Court of Session 1994) 1994.

Part IV Enactments and Instruments Extending to Northern Ireland[1]

Adoption records and reports

(a) Articles 50 and 54 of the Adoption (Northern Ireland) Act 1987.

Rule 53 of Order 84 of the Rules of the Supreme Court (Northern Ireland) 1980.

Rule 22 of the County Court (Adoption) Rules (Northern Ireland) 1980.

Rule 32 of Order 50 of the County Court Rules (Northern Ireland) 1981.

Statement of child's special educational needs

(b) Regulation 17 of the Education (Special Educational Needs) Regulations (Northern Ireland) 1997.

Parental order records and reports

(c) Articles 50 and 54 of the Adoption (Northern Ireland) Order 1987 as modified by paragraph 5(a) and (e) of Schedule 2 to the Parental Orders (Human Fertilisation and Embryology) Regulations 1994 in respect of parental orders made under section 30 of the Human Fertilisation and Embryology Act 1990.

Rules 4, 5 and 16 of Order 84A of the Rules of the Supreme Court (Northern Ireland) 1980.

Rules 3, 4 and 15 of Order 50A of the County Court Rules (Northern Ireland) 1981.

The Consumer Protection (Distance Selling) Regulations 2000

(SI 2000/2334)

1 Title, commencement and extent

(1) These Regulations may be cited as the Consumer Protection (Distance Selling) Regulations 2000 and shall come into force on 31st October 2000.

(2) These Regulations extend to Northern Ireland.

---

[1] Various amendments to this Part are not in force at the time of writing: see Constitutional Reform Act 2005, s. 59(5), sch. 11, Pt. 1, para. 3(4).

2   Revocation

The Mail Order Transactions (Information) Order 1976 is hereby revoked.

3   Interpretation

(1) In these Regulations—

["the 2000 Act" means the Financial Services and Markets Act 2000;

"appointed representative" has the same meaning as in section 39(2) of the 2000 Act;

"authorised person" has the same meaning as in section 31(2) of the 2000 Act;]

"breach" means contravention by a supplier of a prohibition in, or failure to comply with a requirement of, these Regulations;

"business" includes a trade or profession;

"consumer" means any natural person who, in contracts to which these Regulations apply, is acting for purposes which are outside his business;

"court" in relation to England and Wales and Northern Ireland means a county court or the High Court, and in relation to Scotland means the Sheriff Court or the Court of Session;

"credit" includes a cash loan and any other form of financial accommodation, and for this purpose "cash" includes money in any form;

"[OFT]" means [the Office of Fair Trading];

"distance contract" means any contract concerning goods or services concluded between a supplier and a consumer under an organised distance sales or service provision scheme run by the supplier who, for the purpose of the contract, makes exclusive use of one or more means of distance communication up to and including the moment at which the contract is concluded;

"EEA Agreement" means the Agreement on the European Economic Area signed at Oporto on 2 May 1992 as adjusted by the Protocol signed at Brussels on 17 March 1993;

"enactment" includes an enactment comprised in, or in an instrument made under, an Act of the Scottish Parliament;

"enforcement authority" means the [OFT], every weights and measures authority in Great Britain, and the Department of Enterprise, Trade and Investment in Northern Ireland;

"excepted contract" means a contract such as is mentioned in regulation 5(1);

["financial service" means any service of a banking, credit, insurance, personal pension, investment or payment nature;]

"means of distance communication" means any means which, without the simultaneous physical presence of the supplier and the consumer, may be used for the conclusion of a contract between those parties; and an indicative list of such means is contained in Schedule 1;

"Member State" means a State which is a contracting party to the EEA Agreement;

"operator of a means of communication" means any public or private person whose business involves making one or more means of distance communication available to suppliers;

"period for performance" has the meaning given by regulation 19(2);

"personal credit agreement" has the meaning given by regulation 14(8);

["regulated activity" has the same meaning as in section 22 of the 2000 Act;]

"related credit agreement" has the meaning given by regulation 15(5);

"supplier" means any person who, in contracts to which these Regulations apply, is acting in his commercial or professional capacity; and

"working days" means all days other than Saturdays, Sundays and public holidays.

(2) In the application of these Regulations to Scotland, for references to an "injunction" or an "interim injunction" there shall be substituted references to an "interdict" or an "interim interdict" respectively.

4   Contracts to which these Regulations apply

These Regulations apply, subject to regulation 6, to distance contracts other than excepted contracts.

5   Excepted contracts

(1) The following are excepted contracts, namely any contract—

    (a) for the sale or other disposition of an interest in land except for a rental agreement;

(b) for the construction of a building where the contract also provides for a sale or other disposition of an interest in land on which the building is constructed, except for a rental agreement;

(c) relating to financial services [...]

(d) concluded by means of an automated vending machine or automated commercial premises;

(e) concluded with a telecommunications operator through the use of a public pay-phone;

(f) concluded at an auction.

(2) References in paragraph (1) to a rental agreement—

(a) if the land is situated in England and Wales, are references to any agreement which does not have to be made in writing (whether or not in fact made in writing) because of section 2(5)(a) of the Law of Property (Miscellaneous Provisions) Act 1989;

(b) if the land is situated in Scotland, are references to any agreement for the creation, transfer, variation or extinction of an interest in land, which does not have to be made in writing (whether or not in fact made in writing) as provided for in section 1(2) and (7) of the Requirements of Writing (Scotland) Act 1995; and

(c) if the land is situated in Northern Ireland, are references to any agreement which is not one to which section II of the Statute of Frauds, (Ireland) 1695 applies.

(3) Paragraph (2) shall not be taken to mean that a rental agreement in respect of land situated outside the United Kingdom is not capable of being a distance contract to which these Regulations apply.

6   Contracts to which only part of these Regulations apply

(1) Regulations 7 to 20 shall not apply to a contract which is a "timeshare agreement" within the meaning of the Timeshare Act 1992 and to which that Act applies.

(2) Regulations 7 to 19(1) shall not apply to—

(a) contracts for the supply of food, beverages or other goods intended for everyday consumption supplied to the consumer's residence or to his workplace by regular roundsmen; or

(b) contracts for the provision of accommodation, transport, catering or leisure services, where the supplier undertakes, when the contract is concluded, to provide these services on a specific date or within a specific period.

(3) Regulations 19(2) to (8) and 20 do not apply to a contract for a "package" within the meaning of the Package Travel, Package Holidays and Package Tours Regulations 1992 which is sold or offered for sale in the territory of the Member States.

[(4) Regulations 7 to 14, 17 to 20 and 25 do not apply to any contract which is made, and regulation 24 does not apply to any unsolicited services which are supplied, by an authorised person where the making or performance of that contract or the supply of those services, as the case may be, constitutes or is part of a regulated activity carried on by him.

(5) Regulations 7 to 9, 17 to 20 and 25 do not apply to any contract which is made, and regulation 24 does not apply to any unsolicited services which are supplied, by an appointed representative where the making or performance of that contract or the supply of those services, as the case may be, constitutes or is part of a regulated activity carried on by him.]

7   Information required prior to the conclusion of the contract

(1) Subject to paragraph (4), in good time prior to the conclusion of the contract the supplier shall—

(a) provide to the consumer the following information—

(i)   the identity of the supplier and, where the contract requires payment in advance, the supplier's address;

(ii) a description of the main characteristics of the goods or services;

(iii) the price of the goods or services including all taxes;

(iv) delivery costs where appropriate;

(v)   the arrangements for payment, delivery or performance;

(vi) the existence of a right of cancellation except in the cases referred to in regulation 13;

(vii) the cost of using the means of distance communication where it is calculated other than at the basic rate;

(viii) the period for which the offer or the price remains valid; and

(ix) where appropriate, the minimum duration of the contract, in the case of contracts for the supply of goods or services to be performed permanently or recurrently;

(b) inform the consumer if he proposes, in the event of the goods or services ordered by the consumer being unavailable, to provide substitute goods or services (as the case may be) of equivalent quality and price; and

(c) inform the consumer that the cost of returning any such substitute goods to the supplier in the event of cancellation by the consumer would be met by the supplier.

(2) The supplier shall ensure that the information required by paragraph (1) is provided in a clear and comprehensible manner appropriate to the means of distance communication used, with due regard in particular to the principles of good faith in commercial transactions and the principles governing the protection of those who are unable to give their consent such as minors.

(3) Subject to paragraph (4), the supplier shall ensure that his commercial purpose is made clear when providing the information required by paragraph (1).

(4) In the case of a telephone communication, the identity of the supplier and the commercial purpose of the call shall be made clear at the beginning of the conversation with the consumer.

8 Written and additional information

(1) Subject to regulation 9, the supplier shall provide to the consumer in writing, or in another durable medium which is available and accessible to the consumer, the information referred to in paragraph (2), either—

(a) prior to the conclusion of the contract, or

(b) thereafter, in good time and in any event—

(i) during the performance of the contract, in the case of services; and

(ii) at the latest at the time of delivery where goods not for delivery to third parties are concerned.

(2) The information required to be provided by paragraph (1) is—

(a) the information set out in paragraphs (i) to (vi) of Regulation 7(1)(a);

(b) information about the conditions and procedures for exercising the right to cancel under regulation 10, including—

(i) where a term of the contract requires (or the supplier intends that it will require) that the consumer shall return the goods to the supplier in the event of cancellation, notification of that requirement; [. . .]

(ii) information as to whether the consumer or the supplier would be responsible under these Regulations for the cost of returning any goods to the supplier, or the cost of his recovering them, if the consumer cancels the contract under regulation 10;

[(iii) in the case of a contract for the supply of services, information as to how the right to cancel may be affected by the consumer agreeing to performance of the services beginning before the end of the seven working day period referred to in regulation 12;]

(c) the geographical address of the place of business of the supplier to which the consumer may address any complaints;

(d) information about any after-sales services and guarantees; and

(e) the conditions for exercising any contractual right to cancel the contract, where the contract is of an unspecified duration or a duration exceeding one year.

(3) [. . .]

9 Services performed through the use of a means of distance communication

(1) Regulation 8 shall not apply to a contract for the supply of services which are performed through the use of a means of distance communication, where those services are supplied on only one occasion and are invoiced by the operator of the means of distance communication.

(2) But the supplier shall take all necessary steps to ensure that a consumer who is a party to a contract to which paragraph (1) applies is able to obtain the supplier's geographical address and the place of business to which the consumer may address any complaints.

10   Right to cancel

(1) Subject to regulation 13, if within the cancellation period set out in regulations 11 and 12, the consumer gives a notice of cancellation to the supplier, or any other person previously notified by the supplier to the consumer as a person to whom notice of cancellation may be given, the notice of cancellation shall operate to cancel the contract.

(2) Except as otherwise provided by these Regulations, the effect of a notice of cancellation is that the contract shall be treated as if it had not been made.

(3) For the purposes of these Regulations, a notice of cancellation is a notice in writing or in another durable medium available and accessible to the supplier (or to the other person to whom it is given) which, however expressed, indicates the intention of the consumer to cancel the contract.

(4) A notice of cancellation given under this regulation by a consumer to a supplier or other person is to be treated as having been properly given if the consumer—

    (a) leaves it at the address last known to the consumer and addressed to the supplier or other person by name (in which case it is to be taken to have been given on the day on which it was left);

    (b) sends it by post to the address last known to the consumer and addressed to the supplier or other person by name (in which case, it is to be taken to have been given on the day on which it was posted);

    (c) sends it by facsimile to the business facsimile number last known to the consumer (in which case it is to be taken to have been given on the day on which it is sent); or

    (d) sends it by electronic mail, to the business electronic mail address last known to the consumer (in which case it is to be taken to have been given on the day on which it is sent).

(5) Where a consumer gives a notice in accordance with paragraph (4)(a) or (b) to a supplier who is a body corporate or a partnership, the notice is to be treated as having been properly given if—

    (a) in the case of a body corporate, it is left at the address of, or sent to, the secretary or clerk of that body; or

    (b) in the case of a partnership, it is left with or sent to a partner or a person having control or management of the partnership business.

11   Cancellation period in the case of contracts for the supply of goods

(1) For the purpose of regulation 10, the cancellation period in the case of contracts for the supply of goods begins with the day on which the contract is concluded and ends as provided in paragraphs (2) to (5).

(2) Where the supplier complies with regulation 8, the cancellation period ends on the expiry of the period of seven working days beginning with the day after the day on which the consumer receives the goods.

(3) Where a supplier who has not complied with regulation 8 provides to the consumer the information referred to in regulation 8(2), and does so in writing or in another durable medium available and accessible to the consumer, within the period of three months beginning with the day after the day on which the consumer receives the goods, the cancellation period ends on the expiry of the period of seven working days beginning with the day after the day on which the consumer receives the information.

(4) Where neither paragraph (2) nor (3) applies, the cancellation period ends on the expiry of the period of three months and seven working days beginning with the day after the day on which the consumer receives the goods.

(5) In the case of contracts for goods for delivery to third parties, paragraphs (2) to (4) shall apply as if the consumer had received the goods on the day on which they were received by the third party.

12   Cancellation period in the case of contracts for the supply of services

(1) For the purposes of regulation 10, the cancellation period in the case of contracts for the supply of services begins with the day on which the contract is concluded and ends as provided in paragraphs (2) to (4).

(2) Where the supplier complies with regulation 8 on or before the day on which the contract is concluded, the cancellation period ends on the expiry of the period of seven working days beginning with the day after the day on which the contract is concluded.

(3) [Subject to paragraph (3A)] where a supplier who has not complied with regulation 8 on or before the day on which the contract is concluded provides to the consumer the information referred to in regulation 8(2) [. . .], and does so in writing or in another durable medium available and accessible to the consumer, within the period of three months beginning with the day after the day on which the contract is concluded, the cancellation period ends on the expiry of the period of seven working days beginning with the day after the day on which the consumer receives the information.

[(3A) Where the performance of the contract has begun with the consumer's agreement before the expiry of the period of seven working days beginning with the day after the day on which the contract was concluded and the supplier has not complied with regulation 8 on or before the day on which performance began, but provides to the consumer the information referred to in regulation 8(2) in good time during the performance of the contract, the cancellation period ends—

    (a) on the expiry of the period of seven working days beginning with the day after the day on which the consumer receives the information; or

    (b) if the performance of the contract is completed before the expiry of the period referred to in sub-paragraph (a), on the day when the performance of the contract is completed.]

(4) Where [none of paragraphs (2) to (3A) applies], the cancellation period ends on the expiry of the period of three months and seven working days beginning with the day after the day on which the contract is concluded.

13   Exceptions to the right to cancel

(1) Unless the parties have agreed otherwise, the consumer will not have the right to cancel the contract by giving notice of cancellation pursuant to regulation 10 in respect of contracts—

    [(a) for the supply of services if the performance of the contract has begun with the consumer's agreement—

        (i) before the end of the cancellation period applicable under regulation 12(2); and

        (ii) after the supplier has provided the information referred to in regulation 8(2);]

    (b) for the supply of goods or services the price of which is dependent on fluctuations in the financial market which cannot be controlled by the supplier;

    (c) for the supply of goods made to the consumer's specifications or clearly personalised or which by reason of their nature cannot be returned or are liable to deteriorate or expire rapidly;

    (d) for the supply of audio or video recordings or computer software if they are unsealed by the consumer;

    (e) for the supply of newspapers, periodicals or magazines; or

    (f) for gaming, betting or lottery services.

14   Recovery of sums paid by or on behalf of the consumer on cancellation, and return of security

(1) On the cancellation of a contract under regulation 10, the supplier shall reimburse any sum paid by or on behalf of the consumer under or in relation to the contract to the person by whom it was made free of any charge, less any charge made in accordance with paragraph (5).

(2) The reference in paragraph (1) to any sum paid on behalf of the consumer includes any sum paid by a creditor who is not the same person as the supplier under a personal credit agreement with the consumer.

(3) The supplier shall make the reimbursement referred to in paragraph (1) as soon as possible and in any case within a period not exceeding 30 days beginning with the day on which the notice of cancellation was given.

(4) Where any security has been provided in relation to the contract, the security (so far as it is so provided) shall, on cancellation under regulation 10, be treated as never having had effect and any property lodged with the supplier solely for the purposes of the security as so provided shall be returned by him forthwith.

(5) Subject to paragraphs (6) and (7), the supplier may make a charge, not exceeding the direct costs of recovering any goods supplied under the contract, where a term of the contract provides that the consumer must return any goods supplied if he cancels the contract under regulation 10 but the consumer does not comply with this provision or returns the goods at the expense of the supplier.

(6) Paragraph (5) shall not apply where—

    (a) the consumer cancels in circumstances where he has the right to reject the goods under a term of the contract, including a term implied by virtue of any enactment, or

    (b) the term requiring the consumer to return any goods supplied if he cancels the contract is an "unfair term" within the meaning of the Unfair Terms in Consumer Contracts Regulations 1999.

(7) Paragraph (5) shall not apply to the cost of recovering any goods which were supplied as substitutes for the goods ordered by the consumer.

(8) For the purposes of these Regulations, a personal credit agreement is an agreement between the consumer and any other person ("the creditor") by which the creditor provides the consumer with credit of any amount.

15   Automatic cancellation of a related credit agreement

(1) Where a notice of cancellation is given under regulation 10 which has the effect of cancelling the contract, the giving of the notice shall also have the effect of cancelling any related credit agreement.

(2) Where a related credit agreement is cancelled by virtue of paragraph (1), the supplier shall, if he is not the same person as the creditor under that agreement, forthwith on receipt of the notice of cancellation inform the creditor that the notice has been given.

(3) Where a related credit agreement is cancelled by virtue of paragraph (1)—

    (a) any sum paid by or on behalf of the consumer under, or in relation to, the credit agreement which the supplier is not obliged to reimburse under regulation 14(1) shall be reimbursed, except for any sum which, if it had not already been paid, would have to be paid under subparagraph (b);

    (b) the agreement shall continue in force so far as it relates to repayment of the credit and payment of interest, subject to regulation 16; and

    (c) subject to subparagraph (b), the agreement shall cease to be enforceable.

(4) Where any security has been provided under a related credit agreement, the security, so far as it is so provided, shall be treated as never having had effect and any property lodged with the creditor solely for the purposes of the security as so provided shall be returned by him forthwith.

(5) For the purposes of this regulation and regulation 16, a "related credit agreement" means an agreement under which fixed sum credit which fully or partly covers the price under a contract cancelled under regulation 10 is granted—

    (a) by the supplier, or

    (b) by another person, under an arrangement between that person and the supplier.

(6) For the purposes of this regulation and regulation 16—

    (a) "creditor" is a person who grants credit under a related credit agreement;

    (b) "fixed sum credit" has the same meaning as in section 10 of the Consumer Credit Act 1974;

    (c) "repayment" in relation to credit means repayment of money received by the consumer, and cognate expressions shall be construed accordingly; and

    (d) "interest" means interest on money so received.

16   Repayment of credit and interest after cancellation of a related credit agreement

(1) This regulation applies following the cancellation of a related credit agreement by virtue of regulation 15(1).

(2) If the consumer repays the whole or a portion of the credit—

    (a) before the expiry of one month following the cancellation of the credit agreement, or

    (b) in the case of a credit repayable by instalments, before the date on which the first instalment is due,

no interest shall be payable on the amount repaid.

(3) If the whole of a credit repayable by instalments is not repaid on or before the date referred to in paragraph (2)(b), the consumer shall not be liable to repay any of the credit except on receipt of a request in writing, signed by the creditor, stating the amounts of the remaining instalments (recalculated by the creditor as nearly as may be in accordance with the agreement and without extending the repayment period), but excluding any sum other than principal and interest.

(4) Where any security has been provided under a related credit agreement the duty imposed on the consumer to repay credit and to pay interest shall not be enforceable before the creditor has discharged any duty imposed on him by regulation 15(4) to return any property lodged with him as security on cancellation.

17   Restoration of goods by consumer after cancellation

(1) This regulation applies where a contract is cancelled under regulation 10 after the consumer has acquired possession of any goods under the contract other than any goods mentioned in regulation 13(1)(b) to (e).

(2) The consumer shall be treated as having been under a duty throughout the period prior to cancellation—

    (a) to retain possession of the goods, and

    (b) to take reasonable care of them.

(3) On cancellation, the consumer shall be under a duty to restore the goods to the supplier in accordance with this regulation, and in the meanwhile to retain possession of the goods and take reasonable care of them.

(4) The consumer shall not be under any duty to deliver the goods except at his own premises and in pursuance of a request in writing, or in another durable medium available and accessible to the consumer, from the supplier and given to the consumer either before, or at the time when, the goods are collected from those premises.

(5) If the consumer—

    (a) delivers the goods (whether at his own premises or elsewhere) to any person to whom, under regulation 10(1), a notice of cancellation could have been given; or

    (b) sends the goods at his own expense to such a person,

he shall be discharged from any duty to retain possession of the goods or restore them to the supplier.

(6) Where the consumer delivers the goods in accordance with paragraph (5)(a), his obligation to take care of the goods shall cease; and if he sends the goods in accordance with paragraph (5)(b), he shall be under a duty to take reasonable care to see that they are received by the supplier and not damaged in transit, but in other respects his duty to take care of the goods shall cease when he sends them.

(7) Where, at any time during the period of 21 days beginning with the day notice of cancellation was given, the consumer receives such a request as is mentioned in paragraph (4), and unreasonably refuses or unreasonably fails to comply with it, his duty to retain possession and take reasonable care of the goods shall continue until he delivers or sends the goods as mentioned in paragraph (5), but if within that period he does not receive such a request his duty to take reasonable care of the goods shall cease at the end of that period.

(8) Where—

    (a) a term of the contract provides that if the consumer cancels the contract, he must return the goods to the supplier, and

    (b) the consumer is not otherwise entitled to reject the goods under the terms of the contract or by virtue of any enactment,

paragraph (7) shall apply as if for the period of 21 days there were substituted the period of 6 months.

(9) Where any security has been provided in relation to the cancelled contract, the duty to restore goods imposed on the consumer by this regulation shall not be enforceable before the supplier has discharged any duty imposed on him by regulation 14(4) to return any property lodged with him as security on cancellation.

(10) Breach of a duty imposed by this regulation on a consumer is actionable as a breach of statutory duty.

18 Goods given in part-exchange

(1) This regulation applies on the cancellation of a contract under regulation 10 where the supplier agreed to take goods in part-exchange (the "part-exchange goods") and those goods have been delivered to him.

(2) Unless, before the end of the period of 10 days beginning with the date of cancellation, the part-exchange goods are returned to the consumer in a condition substantially as good as when they were delivered to the supplier, the consumer shall be entitled to recover from the supplier a sum equal to the part-exchange allowance.

(3) In this regulation the part-exchange allowance means the sum agreed as such in the cancelled contract, or if no such sum was agreed, such sum as it would have been reasonable to allow in respect of the part-exchange goods if no notice of cancellation had been served.

(4) Where the consumer recovers from the supplier a sum equal to the part-exchange allowance, the title of the consumer to the part-exchange goods shall vest in the supplier (if it has not already done so) on recovery of that sum.

19 Performance

(1) Unless the parties agree otherwise, the supplier shall perform the contract within a maximum of 30 days beginning with the day after the day the consumer sent his order to the supplier.

(2) Subject to paragraphs (7) and (8), where the supplier is unable to perform the contract because the goods or services ordered are not available, within the period for performance referred to in paragraph (1) or such other period as the parties agree ("the period for performance"), he shall—

    (a) inform the consumer; and

    (b) reimburse any sum paid by or on behalf of the consumer under or in relation to the contract to the person by whom it was made.

(3) The reference in paragraph (2)(b) to any sum paid on behalf of the consumer includes any sum paid by a creditor who is not the same person as the supplier under a personal credit agreement with the consumer.

(4) The supplier shall make the reimbursement referred to in paragraph (2)(b) as soon as possible and in any event within a period of 30 days beginning with the day after the day on which the period for performance expired.

(5) A contract which has not been performed within the period for performance shall be treated as if it had not been made, save for any rights or remedies which the consumer has under it as a result of the non-performance.

(6) Where any security has been provided in relation to the contract, the security (so far as it is so provided) shall, where the supplier is unable to perform the contract within the period for performance, be treated as never having had any effect and any property lodged with the supplier solely for the purposes of the security as so provided shall be returned by him forthwith.

(7) Where the supplier is unable to supply the goods or services ordered by the consumer, the supplier may perform the contract for the purposes of these Regulations by providing substitute goods or services (as the case may be) of equivalent quality and price provided that—

    (a) this possibility was provided for in the contract;

    (b) prior to the conclusion of the contract the supplier gave the consumer the information required by regulation 7(1)(b) and (c) in the manner required by regulation 7(2).

(8) In the case of outdoor leisure events which by their nature cannot be rescheduled, paragraph 2(b) shall not apply where the consumer and the supplier so agree.

20   Effect of non-performance on related credit agreement

Where a supplier is unable to perform the contract within the period for performance—

    (a) regulations 15 and 16 shall apply to any related credit agreement as if the consumer had given a valid notice of cancellation under regulation 10 on the expiry of the period for performance; and

    (b) the reference in regulation 15(3)(a) to regulation 14(1) shall be read, for the purposes of this regulation, as a reference to regulation 19(2).

21   Payment by card

(1) Subject to paragraph (4), the consumer shall be entitled to cancel a payment where fraudulent use has been made of his payment card in connection with a contract to which this regulation applies by another person not acting, or to be treated as acting, as his agent.

(2) Subject to paragraph (4), the consumer shall be entitled to be recredited, or to have all sums returned by the card issuer, in the event of fraudulent use of his payment card in connection with a contract to which this regulation applies by another person not acting, or to be treated as acting, as the consumer's agent.

(3) Where paragraphs (1) and (2) apply, in any proceedings if the consumer alleges that any use made of the payment card was not authorised by him it is for the card issuer to prove that the use was so authorised.

(4) Paragraphs (1) and (2) shall not apply to an agreement to which section 83(1) of the Consumer Credit Act 1974 applies.

(5) Section 84 of the Consumer Credit Act 1974 (misuse of credit-tokens) is amended by the insertion after subsection (3) of—

"(3A) Subsections (1) and (2) shall not apply to any use, in connection with a distance contract (other than an excepted contract), of a card which is a credit-token.

(3B) In subsection (3A), 'distance contract' and 'excepted contract' have the meanings given in the Consumer Protection (Distance Selling) Regulations 2000."

(6) For the purposes of this regulation—

"card issuer" means the owner of the card; and

"payment card" includes credit cards, charge cards, debit cards and store cards.

22   Amendments to the Unsolicited Goods and Services Act 1971

(1) The Unsolicited Goods and Services Act 1971(a) is amended as follows.

(2) Omit section 1 (rights of recipient of unsolicited goods).

(3) In subsection (1) of section 2 (demands and threats regarding payment), after "them" insert "for the purposes of his trade or business".

(4) The amendments made by this regulation apply only in relation to goods sent after the date on which it comes into force.

23   Amendments to the Unsolicited Goods and Services
(Northern Ireland) Order 1976

(1) The Unsolicited Goods and Services (Northern Ireland) Order 1976 is amended as follows.

(2) Omit Article 3 (rights of recipient of unsolicited goods).

(3) In paragraph (1) of Article 4 (demands and threats regarding payment), after "them" insert "for the purposes of his trade or business".

(4) The amendments made by this regulation apply only in relation to goods sent after the date on which it comes into force.

24   Inertia selling

(1) Paragraphs (2) and (3) apply if—

(a) unsolicited goods are sent to a person ("the recipient") with a view to his acquiring them;

(b) the recipient has no reasonable cause to believe that they were sent with a view to their being acquired for the purposes of a business; and

(c) the recipient has neither agreed to acquire nor agreed to return them.

(2) The recipient may, as between himself and the sender, use, deal with or dispose of the goods as if they were an unconditional gift to him.

(3) The rights of the sender to the goods are extinguished.

(4) A person who, not having reasonable cause to believe there is a right to payment, in the course of any business makes a demand for payment, or asserts a present or prospective right to payment, for what he knows are—

(a) unsolicited goods sent to another person with a view to his acquiring them for purposes other than those of his business, or

(b) unsolicited services supplied to another person for purposes other than those of his business,

is guilty of an offence and liable, on summary conviction, to a fine not exceeding level 4 on the standard scale.

(5) A person who, not having reasonable cause to believe there is a right to payment, in the course of any business and with a view to obtaining payment for what he knows are unsolicited goods sent or services supplied as mentioned in paragraph (4)—

(a) threatens to bring any legal proceedings, or

(b) places or causes to be placed the name of any person on a list of defaulters or debtors or threatens to do so, or

(c) invokes or causes to be invoked any other collection procedure or threatens to do so,

is guilty of an offence and liable, on summary conviction, to a fine not exceeding level 5 on the standard scale.

(6) In this regulation—

"acquire" includes hire;

"send" includes deliver;

"sender", in relation to any goods, includes—

(a) any person on whose behalf or with whose consent the goods are sent;

(b) any other person claiming through or under the sender or any person mentioned in paragraph (a); and

(c) any person who delivers the goods; and

"unsolicited" means, in relation to goods sent or services supplied to any person, that they are sent or supplied without any prior request made by or on behalf of the recipient.

(7) For the purposes of this regulation, an invoice or similar document which—

(a) states the amount of a payment, and

(b) fails to comply with [the conditions set out in Part 2 of the Schedule to the Regulatory Reform (Unsolicited Goods and Services Act 1971) (Directory Entries and Demands for Payment) Order 2005] or, as the case may be, [the requirements of regulations made under] Article 6 of the Unsolicited Goods and Services (Northern Ireland) Order 1976 applicable to it,

is to be regarded as asserting a right to the payment.

(8) Section 3A of the Unsolicited Goods and Services Act 1971 applies for the purposes of this regulation in its application to England, Wales and Scotland as it applies for the purposes of that Act.

(9) Article 6 of the Unsolicited Goods and Services (Northern Ireland) Order 1976 applies for the purposes of this regulation in its application to Northern Ireland as it applies for the purposes of that Order.

(10) This regulation applies only to goods sent and services supplied after the date on which it comes into force.

25   No contracting-out

(1) A term contained in any contract to which these Regulations apply is void if, and to the extent that, it is inconsistent with a provision for the protection of the consumer contained in these Regulations.

(2) Where a provision of these Regulations specifies a duty or liability of the consumer in certain circumstances, a term contained in a contract to which these Regulations apply, other than a term to which paragraph (3) applies, is inconsistent with that provision if it purports to impose, directly or indirectly, an additional duty or liability on him in those circumstances.

(3) This paragraph applies to a term which requires the consumer to return any goods supplied to him under the contract if he cancels it under regulation 10.

(4) A term to which paragraph (3) applies shall, in the event of cancellation by the consumer under regulation 10, have effect only for the purposes of regulation 14(5) and 17(8).

(5) These Regulations shall apply notwithstanding any contract term which applies or purports to apply the law of a non-Member State if the contract has a close connection with the territory of a Member State.

26   Consideration of complaints

(1) It shall be the duty of an enforcement authority to consider any complaint made to it about a breach unless—

    (a) the complaint appears to the authority to be frivolous or vexatious; or

    (b) another enforcement authority has notified the [OFT] that it agrees to consider the complaint.

(2) If an enforcement authority notifies the [OFT] that it agrees to consider a complaint made to another enforcement authority, the first mentioned authority shall be under a duty to consider the complaint.

(3) An enforcement authority which is under a duty to consider a complaint shall give reasons for its decision to apply or not to apply, as the case may be, for an injunction under regulation 27.

(4) In deciding whether or not to apply for an injunction in respect of a breach an enforcement authority may, if it considers it appropriate to do so, have regard to any undertaking given to it or another enforcement authority by or on behalf of any person as to compliance with these Regulations.

27   Injunctions to secure compliance with these Regulations

(1) The [OFT] or, subject to paragraph (2), any other enforcement authority may apply for an injunction (including an interim injunction) against any person who appears to the [OFT] or that authority to be responsible for a breach.

(2) An enforcement authority other than the [OFT] may apply for an injunction only where—

    (a) it has notified the [OFT] of its intention to apply at least fourteen days before the date on which the application is to be made, beginning with the date on which the notification was given; or

    (b) the [OFT] consents to the application being made within a shorter period.

(3) The court on an application under this regulation may grant an injunction on such terms as it thinks fit to secure compliance with these Regulations.

28   Notification of undertakings and orders to the [OFT]

An enforcement authority other than the [OFT] shall notify the [OFT]—

    (a) of any undertaking given to it by or on behalf of any person who appears to it to be responsible for a breach;

    (b) of the outcome of any application made by it under regulation 27 and of the terms of any undertaking given to or order made by the court;

    (c) of the outcome of any application made by it to enforce a previous order of the court.

29 Publication, information and advice

(1) The [OFT] shall arrange for the publication in such form and manner as [it] considers appropriate of—

(a) details of any undertaking or order notified to [it] under regulation 28;

(b) details of any undertaking given to [it] by or on behalf of any person as to compliance with these Regulations;

(c) details of any application made by [it] under regulation 27, and of the terms of any undertaking given to, or order made by, the court;

(d) details of any application made by the [OFT] to enforce a previous order of the court.

(2) The [OFT] may arrange for the dissemination in such form and manner as [it] considers appropriate of such information and advice concerning the operation of these Regulations as it may appear to [it] to be expedient to give to the public and to all persons likely to be affected by these Regulations.

SCHEDULE 1 INDICATIVE LIST OF MEANS OF DISTANCE COMMUNICATION

1. Unaddressed printed matter.
2. Addressed printed matter.
3. Letter.
4. Press advertising with order form.
5. Catalogue.
6. Telephone with human intervention.
7. Telephone without human intervention (automatic calling machine, audiotext).
8. Radio.
9. Videophone (telephone with screen).
10. Videotext (microcomputer and television screen) with keyboard or touch screen.
11. Electronic mail.
12. Facsimile machine (fax).
13. Television (teleshopping).

The Telecommunications (Lawful Business Practice) (Interception of Communications) Regulations 2000

(SI 2000/2699)

1 Citation and commencement

These Regulations may be cited as the Telecommunications (Lawful Business Practice) (Interception of Communications) Regulations 2000 and shall come into force on 24th October 2000.

2 Interpretation

In these Regulations—

(a) references to a business include references to activities of a government department, of any public authority or of any person or office holder on whom functions are conferred by or under any enactment;

(b) a reference to a communication as relevant to a business is a reference to—

(i) a communication—

(aa) by means of which a transaction is entered into in the course of that business, or

(bb) which otherwise relates to that business, or

(ii) a communication which otherwise takes place in the course of the carrying on of that business;

    (c) "regulatory or self-regulatory practices or procedures" means practices or procedures—
        (i) compliance with which is required or recommended by, under or by virtue of—
            (aa) any provision of the law of a member state or other state within the European Economic Area, or
            (bb) any standard or code of practice published by or on behalf of a body established in a member state or other state within the European Economic Area which includes amongst its objectives the publication of standards or codes of practice for the conduct of business, or
        (ii) which are otherwise applied for the purpose of ensuring compliance with anything so required or recommended;
    (d) "system controller" means, in relation to a particular telecommunication system, a person with a right to control its operation or use.

3 Lawful interception of a communication

    (1) For the purpose of section 1(5)(a) of the Act, conduct is authorised, subject to paragraphs (2) and (3) below, if it consists of interception of a communication, in the course of its transmission by means of a telecommunication system, which is effected by or with the express or implied consent of the system controller for the purpose of—
    (a) monitoring or keeping a record of communications—
        (i) in order to—
            (aa) establish the existence of facts, or
            (bb) ascertain compliance with regulatory or self-regulatory practices or procedures which are
                — applicable to the system controller in the carrying on of his business or
                — applicable to another person in the carrying on of his business where that person is supervised by the system controller in respect of those practices or procedures, or
            (cc) ascertain or demonstrate the standards which are achieved or ought to be achieved by persons using the system in the course of their duties, or
        (ii) in the interests of national security, or
        (iii) for the purpose of preventing or detecting crime, or
        (iv) for the purpose of investigating or detecting the unauthorised use of that or any other telecommunication system, or
        (v) where that is undertaken—
            (aa) in order to secure, or
            (bb) as an inherent part of,
            the effective operation of the system (including any monitoring or keeping of a record which would be authorised by section 3(3) of the Act if the conditions in paragraphs (a) and (b) thereof were satisfied); or
    (b) monitoring communications for the purpose of determining whether they are communications relevant to the system controller's business which fall within regulation 2(b)(i) above; or
    (c) monitoring communications made to a confidential voice-telephony counselling or support service which is free of charge (other than the cost, if any, of making a telephone call) and operated in such a way that users may remain anonymous if they so choose.
    (2) Conduct is authorised by paragraph (1) of this regulation only if—
    (a) the interception in question is effected solely for the purpose of monitoring or (where appropriate) keeping a record of communications relevant to the system controller's business;
    (b) the telecommunication system in question is provided for use wholly or partly in connection with that business;
    (c) the system controller has made all reasonable efforts to inform every person who may use the telecommunication system in question that communications transmitted by means thereof may be intercepted; and

    (d) in a case falling within—
       (i)   paragraph (1)(a)(ii) above, the person by or on whose behalf the interception is effected is a person specified in section 6(2)(a) to (i) of the Act;
      (ii)   paragraph (1)(b) above, the communication is one which is intended to be received (whether or not it has been actually received) by a person using the telecommunication system in question.

    (3) Conduct falling within paragraph (1)(a)(i) above is authorised only to the extent that [Article 5 of Directive 2002/58/EC of the European Parliament and of the Council of 12 July 2002] concerning the processing of personal data and the protection of privacy in the telecommunications sector so permits.

The Regulation of Investigatory Powers (Interception of Communications: Code of Practice) Order 2002

(SI 2002/1693)

1   Citation and commencement

The Order may be cited as the Regulation of Investigatory Powers (Interception of Communications: Code of Practice) Order 2002 and shall come into force on 1st July 2002.

2   Interception of Communications Code of Practice

The draft code of practice entitled "Interception of Communications", laid before each House of Parliament on 8th May 2002, relating to the interception of communications under Chapter I of Part I of the 2000 Act, shall come into force on 1st July 2002.

The Regulation of Investigatory Powers (Maintenance of Interception Capability) Order 2002

(SI 2002/1931)

1   Citation, commencement and interpretation

    (1) This Order may be cited as the Regulation of Investigatory Powers (Maintenance of Interception Capability) Order 2002 and shall come into force on 1st August 2002.

    (2) In this Order "service provider" means a person providing a public postal service or a public telecommunications service, or proposing to do so.

2   Interception capability

    (1) The Schedule to this Order sets out those obligations which appear to the Secretary of State reasonable to impose on service providers for the purpose of securing that it is and remains practicable for requirements to provide assistance in relation to interception warrants to be imposed and complied with.

    (2) Subject to paragraph (3) the obligations in—
      (a) Part I of the Schedule only apply to service providers who provide, or propose to provide, a public postal service; and
      (b) Part II of the Schedule only apply to service providers who provide, or propose to provide, a public telecommunications service.

    (3) The obligations in Part II of the Schedule shall not apply to service providers who—
      (a) do not intend to provide a public telecommunications service to more than 10,000 persons in any one or more parts of the United Kingdom and do not do so; or
      (b) only provide, or propose to provide, a public telecommunications service in relation to the provision of banking, insurance, investment or other financial services.

3   Interception capability notices

(1) The Secretary of State may give a service provider a notice requiring him to take all such steps falling within paragraph (2) as may be specified or described in the notice.

(2) Those steps are ones appearing to the Secretary of State to be necessary for securing that the service provider has the practical capability of meeting the obligations set out in the Schedule to this Order.

4   Referral of notices to the Technical Advisory Board

The period within which any person to whom a notice has been given under article 3 may refer the notice to the Technical Advisory Board is specified as being before the end of 28 days from the date of the notice.

SCHEDULE   OBLIGATIONS ON SERVICE PROVIDERS

Part I   Interception Capability for Public Postal Services

1. To ensure the interception and temporary retention of postal items destined for addresses in the United Kingdom for provision to the person on whose application the interception warrant was issued.

2. To provide for the interception and retention of postal items sent by identified persons where the carrier keeps records of who sent which item in the course of their normal business.

3. To maintain a system of opening, copying and resealing of any postal item carried for less than £1.

4. To comply with the obligations set out in paragraphs 1 to 3 above in such a manner that the chance of the interception subject or other unauthorised persons becoming aware of any interception is minimised.

Part II   Interception Capability for Public Telecommunication Services

5. To provide a mechanism for implementing interceptions within one working day of the service provider being informed that the interception has been appropriately authorised.

6. To ensure the interception, in their entirety, of all communications and related communications data authorised by the interception warrant and to ensure their simultaneous (i.e. in near real time) transmission to a hand-over point within the service provider's network as agreed with the person on whose application the interception warrant was issued.

7. To ensure that the intercepted communication and the related communications data will be transmitted so that they can be unambiguously correlated.

8. To ensure that the hand-over interface complies with any requirements communicated by the Secretary of State to the service provider, which, where practicable and appropriate, will be in line with agreed industry standards (such as those of the European Telecommunications Standards Institute).

9. To ensure filtering to provide only the traffic data associated with the warranted telecommunications identifier, where reasonable.

10. To ensure that the person on whose application the interception warrant was issued is able to remove any electronic protection applied by the service provider to the intercepted communication and the related communications data.

11. To enable the simultaneous interception of the communications of up to 1 in 10,000 of the persons to whom the service provider provides the public telecommunications service, provided that those persons number more than 10,000.

12. To ensure that the reliability of the interception capability is at least equal to the reliability of the public telecommunications service carrying the communication which is being intercepted.

13. To ensure that the intercept capability may be audited so that it is possible to confirm that the intercepted communications and related communications data are from, or intended for the interception subject, or originate from or are intended for transmission to, the premises named in the interception warrant.

14. To comply with the obligations set out in paragraphs 5 to 13 above in such a manner that the chance of the interception subject or other unauthorised persons becoming aware of any interception is minimised.

The Electronic Commerce (EC Directive) Regulations 2002

(SI 2002/2013)

1 Citation and commencement

(1) These Regulations may be cited as the Electronic Commerce (EC Directive) Regulations 2002 and except for regulation 16 shall come into force on 21st August 2002.

(2) Regulation 16 shall come into force on 23rd October 2002.

2 Interpretation

(1) In these Regulations and in the Schedule—

"commercial communication" means a communication, in any form, designed to promote, directly or indirectly, the goods, services or image of any person pursuing a commercial, industrial or craft activity or exercising a regulated profession, other than a communication—

    (a) consisting only of information allowing direct access to the activity of that person including a geographic address, a domain name or an electronic mail address; or

    (b) relating to the goods, services or image of that person provided that the communication has been prepared independently of the person making it (and for this purpose, a communication prepared without financial consideration is to be taken to have been prepared independently unless the contrary is shown);

"the Commission" means the Commission of the European Communities;

"consumer" means any natural person who is acting for purposes other than those of his trade, business or profession;

"coordinated field" means requirements applicable to information society service providers or information society services, regardless of whether they are of a general nature or specifically designed for them, and covers requirements with which the service provider has to comply in respect of—

    (a) the taking up of the activity of an information society service, such as requirements concerning qualifications, authorisation or notification, and

    (b) the pursuit of the activity of an information society service, such as requirements concerning the behaviour of the service provider, requirements regarding the quality or content of the service including those applicable to advertising and contracts, or requirements concerning the liability of the service provider,

but does not cover requirements such as those applicable to goods as such, to the delivery of goods or to services not provided by electronic means;

"the Directive" means Directive 2000/31/EC of the European Parliament and of the Council of 8 June 2000 on certain legal aspects of information society services, in particular electronic commerce, in the Internal Market (Directive on electronic commerce);

"EEA Agreement" means the Agreement on the European Economic Area signed at Oporto on 2 May 1992 as adjusted by the Protocol signed at Brussels on 17 March 1993;

"enactment" includes an enactment comprised in Northern Ireland legislation and comprised in, or an instrument made under, an Act of the Scottish Parliament;

"enforcement action" means any form of enforcement action including, in particular—

(a) in relation to any legal requirement imposed by or under any enactment, any action taken with a view to or in connection with imposing any sanction (whether criminal or otherwise) for failure to observe or comply with it; and

(b) in relation to a permission or authorisation, anything done with a view to removing or restricting that permission or authorisation;

"enforcement authority" does not include courts but, subject to that, means any person who is authorised, whether by or under an enactment or otherwise, to take enforcement action;

"established service provider" means a service provider who is a national of a member State or a company or firm as mentioned in Article 48 of the Treaty and who effectively pursues an economic activity by virtue of which he is a service provider using a fixed establishment in a member State for an indefinite period, but the presence and use of the technical means and technologies required to provide the information society service do not, in themselves, constitute an establishment of the provider; in cases where it cannot be determined from which of a number of places of establishment a given service is provided, that service is to be regarded as provided from the place of establishment where the provider has the centre of his activities relating to that service; references to a service provider being established or to the establishment of a service provider shall be construed accordingly;

"information society services" (which is summarised in recital 17 of the Directive as covering "any service normally provided for remuneration, at a distance, by means of electronic equipment for the processing (including digital compression) and storage of data, and at the individual request of a recipient of a service") has the meaning set out in Article 2(a) of the Directive, (which refers to Article 1(2) of Directive 98/34/EC of the European Parliament and of the Council of 22 June 1998 laying down a procedure for the provision of information in the field of technical standards and regulations, as amended by Directive 98/48/EC of 20 July 1998);

"member State" includes a State which is a contracting party to the EEA Agreement;

"recipient of the service" means any person who, for professional ends or otherwise, uses an information society service, in particular for the purposes of seeking information or making it accessible;

"regulated profession" means any profession within the meaning of either Article 1(d) of Council Directive 89/48/EEC of 21 December 1988 on a general system for the recognition of higher-education diplomas awarded on completion of professional education and training of at least three years' duration or of Article 1(f) of Council Directive 92/51/EEC of 18 June 1992 on a second general system for the recognition of professional education and training to supplement Directive 89/48/EEC;

"service provider" means any person providing an information society service;

"the Treaty" means the treaty establishing the European Community.

(2) In regulation 4 and 5, "requirement" means any legal requirement under the law of the United Kingdom, or any part of it, imposed by or under any enactment or otherwise.

(3) Terms used in the Directive other than those in paragraph (1) above shall have the same meaning as in the Directive.

3   Exclusions

(1) Nothing in these Regulations shall apply in respect of—

(a) the field of taxation;

(b) questions relating to information society services covered by the Data Protection Directive and the Telecommunications Data Protection Directive and Directive 2002/58/EC of the European Parliament and of the Council of 12th July 2002 concerning the processing of personal data and the protection of privacy in the electronic communications sector (Directive on privacy and electronic communications);

(c) questions relating to agreements or practices governed by cartel law; and

(d) the following activities of information society services—

(i)   the activities of a public notary or equivalent professions to the extent that they involve a direct and specific connection with the exercise of public authority,

(ii)   the representation of a client and defence of his interests before the courts, and

(iii) betting, gaming or lotteries which involve wagering a stake with monetary value.

[(2) These Regulations shall not apply in relation to any Act passed on or after the date these Regulations are made or in relation to the exercise of a power to legislate after that date.]

(3) In this regulation—

"cartel law" means so much of the law relating to agreements between undertakings, decisions by associations of undertakings or concerted practices as relates to agreements to divide the market or fix prices;

"Data Protection Directive" means Directive 95/46/EC of the European Parliament and of the Council of 24 October 1995 on the protection of individuals with regard to the processing of personal data and on the free movement of such data; and

"Telecommunications Data Protection Directive" means Directive 97/66/EC of the European Parliament and of the Council of 15 December 1997 concerning the processing of personal data and the protection of privacy in the telecommunications sector.

4   Internal market

(1) Subject to paragraph (4) below, any requirement which falls within the coordinated field shall apply to the provision of an information society service by a service provider established in the United Kingdom irrespective of whether that information society service is provided in the United Kingdom or another member State.

(2) Subject to paragraph (4) below, an enforcement authority with responsibility in relation to any requirement in paragraph (1) shall ensure that the provision of an information society service by a service provider established in the United Kingdom complies with that requirement irrespective of whether that service is provided in the United Kingdom or another member State and any power, remedy or procedure for taking enforcement action shall be available to secure compliance.

(3) Subject to paragraphs (4), (5) and (6) below, any requirement shall not be applied to the provision of an information society service by a service provider established in a member State other than the United Kingdom for reasons which fall within the coordinated field where its application would restrict the freedom to provide information society services to a person in the United Kingdom from that member State.

(4) Paragraphs (1), (2) and (3) shall not apply to those fields in the annex to the Directive set out in the Schedule.

(5) The reference to any requirements the application of which would restrict the freedom to provide information society services from another member State in paragraph (3) above does not include any requirement maintaining the level of protection for public health and consumer interests established by Community acts.

(6) To the extent that anything in these Regulations creates any new criminal offence, it shall not be punishable with imprisonment for more than two years or punishable on summary conviction with imprisonment for more than three months or with a fine of more than level 5 on the standard scale (if not calculated on a daily basis) or with a fine of more than £100 a day.

5   Derogations from Regulation 4

(1) Notwithstanding regulation 4(3), an enforcement authority may take measures, including applying any requirement which would otherwise not apply by virtue of regulation 4(3) in respect of a given information society service, where those measures are necessary for reasons of—

(a) public policy, in particular the prevention, investigation, detection and prosecution of criminal offences, including the protection of minors and the fight against any incitement to hatred on grounds of race, sex, religion or nationality, and violations of human dignity concerning individual persons;

(b) the protection of public health;

(c) public security, including the safeguarding of national security and defence, or

(d) the protection of consumers, including investors,

and proportionate to those objectives.

(2) Notwithstanding regulation 4(3), in any case where an enforcement authority with responsibility in relation to the requirement in question is not party to the proceedings, a court may, on the application of any person or of its own motion, apply any requirement which would otherwise not apply by virtue of regulation 4(3) in respect of a given information society service, if the application of that enactment or requirement is necessary for and proportionate to any of the objectives set out in paragraph (1) above.

(3) Paragraphs (1) and (2) shall only apply where the information society service prejudices or presents a serious and grave risk of prejudice to an objective in paragraph (1)(a) to (d).

(4) Subject to paragraphs (5) and (6), an enforcement authority shall not take the measures in paragraph (1) above, unless it—

- (a) asks the member State in which the service provider is established to take measures and the member State does not take such measures or they are inadequate; and
- (b) notifies the Commission and the member State in which the service provider is established of its intention to take such measures.

(5) Paragraph (4) shall not apply to court proceedings, including preliminary proceedings and acts carried out in the course of a criminal investigation.

(6) If it appears to the enforcement authority that the matter is one of urgency, it may take the measures under paragraph (1) without first asking the member State in which the service provider is established to take measures and notifying the Commission and the member State in derogation from paragraph (4).

(7) In a case where a measure is taken pursuant to paragraph (6) above, the enforcement authority shall notify the measures taken to the Commission and to the member State concerned in the shortest possible time thereafter and indicate the reasons for urgency.

(8) In paragraph (2), "court" means any court or tribunal.

6   General information to be provided by a person providing an information society service

(1) A person providing an information society service shall make available to the recipient of the service and any relevant enforcement authority, in a form and manner which is easily, directly and permanently accessible, the following information—

- (a) the name of the service provider;
- (b) the geographic address at which the service provider is established;
- (c) the details of the service provider, including his electronic mail address, which make it possible to contact him rapidly and communicate with him in a direct and effective manner;
- (d) where the service provider is registered in a trade or similar register available to the public, details of the register in which the service provider is entered and his registration number, or equivalent means of identification in that register;
- (e) where the provision of the service is subject to an authorisation scheme, the particulars of the relevant supervisory authority;
- (f) where the service provider exercises a regulated profession—
  - (i)   the details of any professional body or similar institution with which the service provider is registered;
  - (ii) his professional title and the member State where that title has been granted;
  - (iii) a reference to the professional rules applicable to the service provider in the member State of establishment and the means to access them; and
- (g) where the service provider undertakes an activity that is subject to value added tax, the identification number referred to in Article 22(1) of the sixth Council Directive 77/388/EEC of 17 May 1977 on the harmonisation of the laws of the member States relating to turnover taxes—Common system of value added tax: uniform basis of assessment.

(2) Where a person providing an information society service refers to prices, these shall be indicated clearly and unambiguously and, in particular, shall indicate whether they are inclusive of tax and delivery costs.

7 Commercial communications

A service provider shall ensure that any commercial communication provided by him and which constitutes or forms part of an information society service shall—

    (a) be clearly identifiable as a commercial communication;

    (b) clearly identify the person on whose behalf the commercial communication is made;

    (c) clearly identify as such any promotional offer (including any discount, premium or gift) and ensure that any conditions which must be met to qualify for it are easily accessible, and presented clearly and unambiguously; and

    (d) clearly identify as such any promotional competition or game and ensure that any conditions for participation are easily accessible and presented clearly and unambiguously.

8 Unsolicited commercial communications

A service provider shall ensure that any unsolicited commercial communication sent by him by electronic mail is clearly and unambiguously identifiable as such as soon as it is received.

9 Information to be provided where contracts are concluded by electronic means

(1) Unless parties who are not consumers have agreed otherwise, where a contract is to be concluded by electronic means a service provider shall, prior to an order being placed by the recipient of a service, provide to that recipient in a clear, comprehensible and unambiguous manner the information set out in (a) to (d) below—

    (a) the different technical steps to follow to conclude the contract;

    (b) whether or not the concluded contract will be filed by the service provider and whether it will be accessible;

    (c) the technical means for identifying and correcting input errors prior to the placing of the order; and

    (d) the languages offered for the conclusion of the contract.

(2) Unless parties who are not consumers have agreed otherwise, a service provider shall indicate which relevant codes of conduct he subscribes to and give information on how those codes can be consulted electronically.

(3) Where the service provider provides terms and conditions applicable to the contract to the recipient, the service provider shall make them available to him in a way that allows him to store and reproduce them.

(4) The requirements of paragraphs (1) and (2) above shall not apply to contracts concluded exclusively by exchange of electronic mail or by equivalent individual communications.

10 Other information requirements

Regulations 6, 7, 8 and 9(1) have effect in addition to any other information requirements in legislation giving effect to Community law.

11 Placing of the order

(1) Unless parties who are not consumers have agreed otherwise, where the recipient of the service places his order through technological means, a service provider shall—

    (a) acknowledge receipt of the order to the recipient of the service without undue delay and by electronic means; and

    (b) make available to the recipient of the service appropriate, effective and accessible technical means allowing him to identify and correct input errors prior to the placing of the order.

(2) For the purposes of paragraph (1)(a) above—

    (a) the order and the acknowledgement of receipt will be deemed to be received when the parties to whom they are addressed are able to access them; and

    (b) the acknowledgement of receipt may take the form of the provision of the service paid for where that service is an information society service.

(3) The requirements of paragraph (1) above shall not apply to contracts concluded exclusively by exchange of electronic mail or by equivalent individual communications.

12 Meaning of the term "order"

Except in relation to regulation 9(1)(c) and regulation 11(1)(b) where "order" shall be the contractual offer, "order" may be but need not be the contractual offer for the purposes of regulations 9 and 11.

13 Liability of the service provider

The duties imposed by regulations 6, 7, 8, 9(1) and 11(1)(a) shall be enforceable, at the suit of any recipient of a service, by an action against the service provider for damages for breach of statutory duty.

14 Compliance with Regulation 9(3)

Where on request a service provider has failed to comply with the requirement in regulation 9(3), the recipient may seek an order from any court having jurisdiction in relation to the contract requiring that service provider to comply with that requirement.

15 Right to rescind contract

Where a person—
(a) has entered into a contract to which these Regulations apply, and
(b) the service provider has not made available means of allowing him to identify and correct input errors in compliance with regulation 11(1)(b),

he shall be entitled to rescind the contract unless any court having jurisdiction in relation to the contract in question orders otherwise on the application of the service provider.

16 Amendments to the Stop Now Orders (E.C. Directive) Regulations 2001

(1) The Stop Now Orders (E.C. Directive) Regulations 2001 are amended as follows.
(2) In regulation 2(3), at the end there shall be added—
   "(k) regulations 6, 7, 8, 9, and 11 of the Electronic Commerce (E.C. Directive) Regulations 2002.".
(3) In Schedule 1, at the end there shall be added—
   "11. Directive 2000/31/EC of the European Parliament and of the Council of 8th June 2000 on certain legal aspects of information society services, in particular electronic commerce, in the Internal Market (Directive on Electronic Commerce).".

17 Mere conduit

(1) Where an information society service is provided which consists of the transmission in a communication network of information provided by a recipient of the service or the provision of access to a communication network, the service provider (if he otherwise would) shall not be liable for damages or for any other pecuniary remedy or for any criminal sanction as a result of that transmission where the service provider—
   (a) did not initiate the transmission;
   (b) did not select the receiver of the transmission; and
   (c) did not select or modify the information contained in the transmission.
(2) The acts of transmission and of provision of access referred to in paragraph (1) include the automatic, intermediate and transient storage of the information transmitted where:
   (a) this takes place for the sole purpose of carrying out the transmission in the communication network, and
   (b) the information is not stored for any period longer than is reasonably necessary for the transmission.

18 Caching

Where an information society service is provided which consists of the transmission in a communication network of information provided by a recipient of the service, the service provider (if he otherwise would) shall not be liable for damages or for any other pecuniary remedy or for any criminal sanction as a result of that transmission where—

(a) the information is the subject of automatic, intermediate and temporary storage where that storage is for the sole purpose of making more efficient onward transmission of the information to other recipients of the service upon their request, and

(b) the service provider—

(i) does not modify the information;

(ii) complies with conditions on access to the information;

(iii) complies with any rules regarding the updating of the information, specified in a manner widely recognised and used by industry;

(iv) does not interfere with the lawful use of technology, widely recognised and used by industry, to obtain data on the use of the information; and

(v) acts expeditiously to remove or to disable access to the information he has stored upon obtaining actual knowledge of the fact that the information at the initial source of the transmission has been removed from the network, or access to it has been disabled, or that a court or an administrative authority has ordered such removal or disablement.

19   Hosting

Where an information society service is provided which consists of the storage of information provided by a recipient of the service, the service provider (if he otherwise would) shall not be liable for damages or for any other pecuniary remedy or for any criminal sanction as a result of that storage where—

(a) the service provider—

(i) does not have actual knowledge of unlawful activity or information and, where a claim for damages is made, is not aware of facts or circumstances from which it would have been apparent to the service provider that the activity or information was unlawful; or

(ii) upon obtaining such knowledge or awareness, acts expeditiously to remove or to disable access to the information, and

(b) the recipient of the service was not acting under the authority or the control of the service provider.

20   Protection of rights

(1) Nothing in regulations 17, 18 and 19 shall—

(a) prevent a person agreeing different contractual terms; or

(b) affect the rights of any party to apply to a court for relief to prevent or stop infringement of any rights.

(2) Any power of an administrative authority to prevent or stop infringement of any rights shall continue to apply notwithstanding regulations 17, 18 and 19.

21   Defence in Criminal Proceedings: burden of proof

(1) This regulation applies where a service provider charged with an offence in criminal proceedings arising out of any transmission, provision of access or storage falling within regulation 17, 18 or 19 relies on a defence under any of regulations 17, 18 and 19.

(2) Where evidence is adduced which is sufficient to raise an issue with respect to that defence, the court or jury shall assume that the defence is satisfied unless the prosecution proves beyond reasonable doubt that it is not.

22   Notice for the purposes of actual knowledge

In determining whether a service provider has actual knowledge for the purposes of regulations 18(b)(v) and 19(a)(i), a court shall take into account all matters which appear to it in the particular circumstances to be relevant and, among other things, shall have regard to—

(a) whether a service provider has received a notice through a means of contact made available in accordance with regulation 6(1)(c), and

(b) the extent to which any notice includes—
    (i)   the full name and address of the sender of the notice;
    (ii) details of the location of the information in question; and
    (iii) details of the unlawful nature of the activity or information in question.

SCHEDULE

1. Copyright, neighbouring rights, rights referred to in Directive 87/54/EEC and Directive 96/9/EC and industrial property rights.
2. The freedom of the parties to a contract to choose the applicable law.
3. Contractual obligations concerning consumer contracts.
4. Formal validity of contracts creating or transferring rights in real estate where such contracts are subject to mandatory formal requirements of the law of the member State where the real estate is situated.
5. The permissibility of unsolicited commercial communications by electronic mail.

The Electronic Signatures Regulations 2002

(SI 2002/318)

1 Citation and commencement

These Regulations may be cited as the Electronic Signatures Regulations 2002 and shall come into force on 8th March 2002.

2 Interpretation

In these Regulations—
"advanced electronic signature" means an electronic signature—
    (a) which is uniquely linked to the signatory,
    (b) which is capable of identifying the signatory,
    (c) which is created using means that the signatory can maintain under his sole control, and
    (d) which is linked to the data to which it relates in such a manner that any subsequent change of the data is detectable;
"certificate" means an electronic attestation which links signature-verification data to a person and confirms the identity of that person;
"certification-service-provider" means a person who issues certificates or provides other services related to electronic signatures;
"Directive" means Directive 1999/93/EC of the European Parliament and of the Council on a Community framework for electronic signatures;
"electronic signature" means data in electronic form which are attached to or logically associated with other electronic data and which serve as a method of authentication;
"qualified certificate" means a certificate which meets the requirements in Schedule 1 and is provided by a certification-service-provider who fulfils the requirements in Schedule 2;
"signatory" means a person who holds a signature-creation device and acts either on his own behalf or on behalf of the person he represents;
"signature-creation data" means unique data (including, but not limited to, codes or private cryptographic keys) which are used by the signatory to create an electronic signature;
"signature-creation device" means configured software or hardware used to implement the signature-creation data;
"signature-verification data" means data (including, but not limited to, codes or public cryptographic keys) which are used for the purpose of verifying an electronic signature;
"signature-verification device" means configured software or hardware used to implement the signature-verification data;

"voluntary accreditation" means any permission, setting out rights and obligations specific to the provision of certification services, to be granted upon request by the certification-service-provider concerned by the person charged with the elaboration of, and supervision of compliance with, such rights and obligations, where the certification-service-provider is not entitled to exercise the rights stemming from the permission until he has received the decision of that person.

3   Supervision of certification-service-providers

(1) It shall be the duty of the Secretary of State to keep under review the carrying on of activities of certification-service-providers who are established in the United Kingdom and who issue qualified certificates to the public and the persons by whom they are carried on with a view to her becoming aware of the identity of those persons and the circumstances relating to the carrying on of those activities.

(2) It shall also be the duty of the Secretary of State to establish and maintain a register of certification-service-providers who are established in the United Kingdom and who issue qualified certificates to the public.

(3) The Secretary of State shall record in the register the names and addresses of those certification-service-providers of whom she is aware who are established in the United Kingdom and who issue qualified certificates to the public.

(4) The Secretary of State shall publish the register in such manner as she considers appropriate.

(5) The Secretary of State shall have regard to evidence becoming available to her with respect to any course of conduct of a certification-service-provider who is established in the United Kingdom and who issues qualified certificates to the public and which appears to her to be conduct detrimental to the interests of those persons who use or rely on those certificates with a view to making any of this evidence as she considers expedient available to the public in such manner as she considers appropriate.

4   Liability of certification-service-providers

(1) Where—
    (a) a certification-service-provider either—
        (i)   issues a certificate as a qualified certificate to the public, or
        (ii) guarantees a qualified certificate to the public,
    (b) a person reasonably relies on that certificate for any of the following matters—
        (i)   the accuracy of any of the information contained in the qualified certificate at the time of issue,
        (ii) the inclusion in the qualified certificate of all the details referred to in Schedule 1,
        (iii) the holding by the signatory identified in the qualified certificate at the time of its issue of the signature-creation data corresponding to the signature-verification data given or identified in the certificate, or
        (iv) the ability of the signature-creation data and the signature-verification data to be used in a complementary manner in cases where the certification-service-provider generates them both,
    (c) that person suffers loss as a result of such reliance, and
    (d) the certification-service-provider would be liable in damages in respect of any extent of the loss—
        (i)   had a duty of care existed between him and the person referred to in sub-paragraph (b) above, and
        (ii) had the certification-service-provider been negligent,
        then that certification-service-provider shall be so liable to the same extent notwithstanding that there is no proof that the certification-service-provider was negligent unless the certification-service-provider proves that he was not negligent.

(2) For the purposes of the certification-service-provider's liability under paragraph (1) above there shall be a duty of care between that certification-service-provider and the person referred to in paragraph (1)(b) above.

(3) Where—

    (a) a certification-service-provider issues a certificate as a qualified certificate to the public,

    (b) a person reasonably relies on that certificate,

    (c) that person suffers loss as a result of any failure by the certification-service-provider to register revocation of the certificate, and

    (d) the certification-service-provider would be liable in damages in respect of any extent of the loss—

        (i) had a duty of care existed between him and the person referred to in sub-paragraph (b) above, and

        (ii) had the certification-service-provider been negligent, then that certification-service-provider shall be so liable to the same extent notwithstanding that there is no proof that the certification-service-provider was negligent unless the certification-service-provider proves that he was not negligent.

(4) For the purposes of the certification-service-provider's liability under paragraph (3) above there shall be a duty of care between that certification-service-provider and the person referred to in paragraph (3)(b) above.

5 Data protection

(1) A certification-service-provider who issues a certificate to the public and to whom this paragraph applies in accordance with paragraph (6) below—

    (a) shall not obtain personal data for the purpose of issuing or maintaining that certificate otherwise than directly from the data subject or after the explicit consent of the data subject, and

    (b) shall not process the personal data referred to in sub-paragraph (a) above—

        (i) to a greater extent than is necessary for the purpose of issuing or maintaining that certificate, or

        (ii) to a greater extent than is necessary for any other purpose to which the data subject has explicitly consented,

unless the processing is necessary for compliance with any legal obligation, to which the certification-service-provider is subject, other than an obligation imposed by contract.

(2) The obligation to comply with paragraph (1) above shall be a duty owed to any data subject who may be affected by a contravention of paragraph (1).

(3) Where a duty is owed by virtue of paragraph (2) above to any data subject, any breach of that duty which causes that data subject to sustain loss or damage shall be actionable by him.

(4) Compliance with paragraph (1) above shall also be enforceable by civil proceedings brought by the Crown for an injunction or for an interdict or for any other appropriate relief or remedy.

(5) Paragraph (4) above shall not prejudice any right that a data subject may have by virtue of paragraph (3) above to bring civil proceedings for the contravention or apprehended contravention of paragraph (1) above.

(6) Paragraph (1) above applies to a certification-service-provider in respect of personal data only if the certification-service-provider is established in the United Kingdom and the personal data are processed in the context of that establishment.

(7) For the purposes of paragraph (6) above, each of the following is to be treated as established in the United Kingdom—

    (a) an individual who is ordinarily resident in the United Kingdom,

    (b) a body incorporated under the law of, or in any part of, the United Kingdom,

    (c) a partnership or other unincorporated association formed under the law of any part of the United Kingdom, and

    (d) any person who does not fall within sub-paragraph (a), (b) or (c) above but maintains in the United Kingdom—

        (i) an office, branch or agency through which he carries on any activity, or

        (ii) a regular practice.

(8) In this regulation—

"data subject" and "personal data" and "processing" shall have the same meanings as in section 1(1) of the Data Protection Act 1998, and

"obtain" shall bear the same interpretation as "obtaining" in section 1(2) of the Data Protection Act 1998.

SCHEDULE 1 REQUIREMENTS FOR QUALIFIED CERTIFICATES

Qualified certificates must contain:

(a) an indication that the certificate is issued as a qualified certificate;

(b) the identification of the certification-service-provider and the State in which it is established;

(c) the name of the signatory or a pseudonym, which shall be identified as such;

(d) provision for a specific attribute of the signatory to be included if relevant, depending on the purpose for which the certificate is intended;

(e) signature-verification data which correspond to signature-creation data under the control of the signatory;

(f) an indication of the beginning and end of the period of validity of the certificate;

(g) the identity code of the certificate;

(h) the advanced electronic signature of the certification-service-provider issuing it;

(i) limitations on the scope of use of the certificate, if applicable; and

(j) limits on the value of transactions for which the certificate can be used, if applicable.

SCHEDULE 2 REQUIREMENTS FOR CERTIFICATION-SERVICE-PROVIDERS ISSUING QUALIFIED CERTIFICATES

Certification-service-providers must:

(a) demonstrate the reliability necessary for providing certification services;

(b) ensure the operation of a prompt and secure directory and a secure and immediate revocation service;

(c) ensure that the date and time when a certificate is issued or revoked can be determined precisely;

(d) verify, by appropriate means in accordance with national law, the identity and, if applicable, any specific attributes of the person to which a qualified certificate is issued;

(e) employ personnel who possess the expert knowledge, experience, and qualifications necessary for the services provided, in particular competence at managerial level, expertise in electronic signature technology and familiarity with proper security procedures; they must also apply administrative and management procedures which are adequate and correspond to recognised standards;

(f) use trustworthy systems and products which are protected against modification and ensure the technical and cryptographic security of the process supported by them;

(g) take measures against forgery of certificates, and, in cases where the certification-service-provider generates signature-creation data, guarantee confidentiality during the process of generating such data;

(h) maintain sufficient financial resources to operate in conformity with the requirements laid down in the Directive, in particular to bear the risk of liability for damages, for example, by obtaining appropriate insurance;

(i) record all relevant information concerning a qualified certificate for an appropriate period of time, in particular for the purpose of providing evidence of certification for the purposes of legal proceedings. Such recording may be done electronically;

(j) not store or copy signature-creation data of the person to whom the certification-service-provider provided key management services;

(k) before entering into a contractual relationship with a person seeking a certificate to support his electronic signature inform that person by a durable means of communication of the precise terms and conditions regarding the use of the certificate, including any limitations on its use, the existence of a voluntary accreditation scheme and procedures for complaints and dispute settlement. Such information, which may be transmitted electronically, must be in writing and in readily understandable language. Relevant parts of this information must also be made available on request to third parties relying on the certificate;

(l) use trustworthy systems to store certificates in a verifiable form so that:
— only authorised persons can make entries and changes,
— information can be checked for authenticity,
— certificates are publicly available for retrieval in only those cases for which the certificate-holder's consent has been obtained, and
— any technical changes compromising these security requirements are apparent to the operator.

The Data Protection (Processing of Sensitive Personal Data) (Elected Representatives) Order 2002

(SI 2002/2905)

1. This Order may be cited as the Data Protection (Processing of Sensitive Personal Data) (Elected Representatives) Order 2002 and shall come into force on the twenty-eighth day after the day on which it is made.

2. For the purposes of paragraph 10 of Schedule 3 to the Data Protection Act 1998, the circumstances specified in any of paragraphs 3, 4, 5 or 6 in the Schedule to this Order are circumstances in which sensitive personal data may be processed.

SCHEDULE CIRCUMSTANCES IN WHICH SENSITIVE PERSONAL DATA MAY BE PROCESSED

Interpretation

1. In this Schedule, "elected representative" means—

(a) a Member of the House of Commons, a Member of the National Assembly for Wales, a Member of the Scottish Parliament or a Member of the Northern Ireland Assembly;

(b) a Member of the European Parliament elected in the United Kingdom;

(c) an elected member of a local authority within the meaning of section 270(1) of the Local Government Act 1972, namely—
(i) in England, a county council, a district council, a London borough council or a parish council,
(ii) in Wales, a county council, a county borough council or a community council;

(d) an elected mayor of a local authority within the meaning of Part II of the Local Government Act 2000;

(e) the Mayor of London or an elected member of the London Assembly;

    (f) an elected member of—
       (i)   the Common Council of the City of London, or
       (ii) the Council of the Isles of Scilly;
    (g) an elected member of a council constituted under section 2 of the Local Government etc (Scotland) Act 1994; or
    (h) an elected member of a district council within the meaning of the Local Government Act (Northern Ireland) 1972.
2. For the purposes of paragraph 1 above—
    (a) a person who is—
       (i)   a Member of the House of Commons immediately before Parliament is dissolved,
       (ii) a Member of the Scottish Parliament immediately before that Parliament is dissolved, or
       (iii) a Member of the Northern Ireland Assembly immediately before that Assembly is dissolved,

shall be treated as if he were such a member until the end of the fourth day after the day on which the subsequent general election in relation to that Parliament or Assembly is held;

    (b) a person who is a Member of the National Assembly for Wales and whose term of office comes to an end, in accordance with section 2(5)(b) of the Government of Wales Act 1998, at the end of the day preceding an ordinary election (within the meaning of section 2(4) of that Act), shall be treated as if he were such a member until the end of the fourth day after the day on which that ordinary election is held; and
    (c) a person who is an elected member of the Common Council of the City of London and whose term of office comes to an end at the end of the day preceding the annual Wardmotes shall be treated as if he were such a member until the end of the fourth day after the day on which those Wardmotes are held.

Processing by elected representatives

3. The processing—
    (a) is carried out by an elected representative or a person acting with his authority;
    (b) is in connection with the discharge of his functions as such a representative;
    (c) is carried out pursuant to a request made by the data subject to the elected representative to take action on behalf of the data subject or any other individual; and
    (d) is necessary for the purposes of, or in connection with, the action reasonably taken by the elected representative pursuant to that request.
4. The processing—
    (a) is carried out by an elected representative or a person acting with his authority;
    (b) is in connection with the discharge of his functions as such a representative;
    (c) is carried out pursuant to a request made by an individual other than the data subject to the elected representative to take action on behalf of the data subject or any other individual;
    (d) is necessary for the purposes of, or in connection with, the action reasonably taken by the elected representative pursuant to that request; and
    (e) is carried out without the explicit consent of the data subject because the processing—
       (i)   is necessary in a case where explicit consent cannot be given by the data subject,
       (ii) is necessary in a case where the elected representative cannot reasonably be expected to obtain the explicit consent of the data subject,
       (iii) must necessarily be carried out without the explicit consent of the data subject being sought so as not to prejudice the action taken by the elected representative, or
       (iv) is necessary in the interests of another individual in a case where the explicit consent of the data subject has been unreasonably withheld.

Processing limited to disclosures to elected representatives

5. The disclosure—
    (a) is made to an elected representative or a person acting with his authority;

(b) is made in response to a communication to the data controller from the elected representative, or a person acting with his authority, acting pursuant to a request made by the data subject;

(c) is of sensitive personal data which are relevant to the subject matter of that communication; and

(d) is necessary for the purpose of responding to that communication.

6. The disclosure—

(a) is made to an elected representative or a person acting with his authority;

(b) is made in response to a communication to the data controller from the elected representative, or a person acting with his authority, acting pursuant to a request made by an individual other than the data subject;

(c) is of sensitive personal data which are relevant to the subject matter of that communication;

(d) is necessary for the purpose of responding to that communication; and

(e) is carried out without the explicit consent of the data subject because the disclosure—

(i) is necessary in a case where explicit consent cannot be given by the data subject,

(ii) is necessary in a case where the data controller cannot reasonably be expected to obtain the explicit consent of the data subject,

(iii) must necessarily be carried out without the explicit consent of the data subject being sought so as not to prejudice the action taken by the elected representative, or

(iv) is necessary in the interests of another individual in a case where the explicit consent of the data subject has been unreasonably withheld.

The Electronic Commerce (EC Directive) (Extension) Regulations 2003

(SI 2003/115)

1 Citation and commencement

(1) These Regulations may be cited as the Electronic Commerce (EC Directive) (Extension) Regulations 2003.

(2) These Regulations shall come into force on 14th February 2003.

2 Application of the E-Commerce Regulations

The Electronic Commerce (EC Directive) Regulations 2002 shall apply to the enactments listed in the Schedule notwithstanding Regulation 3(2) of those Regulations.

Regulation 2   **SCHEDULE**

1. The Copyright (Visually Impaired Persons) Act 2002.

2. The Tobacco Advertising and Promotion Act 2002.

The Privacy and Electronic Communications (EC Directive) Regulations 2003

(SI 2003/2426)

1 Citation and commencement

These Regulations may be cited as the Privacy and Electronic Communications (EC Directive) Regulations 2003 and shall come into force on 11th December 2003.

2 Interpretation

(1) In these Regulations—

"bill" includes an invoice, account, statement or other document of similar character and "billing" shall be construed accordingly;

"call" means a connection established by means of a telephone service available to the public allowing two-way communication in real time;

"communication" means any information exchanged or conveyed between a finite number of parties by means of a public electronic communications service, but does not include information conveyed as part of a programme service, except to the extent that such information can be related to the identifiable subscriber or user receiving the information;

"communications provider" has the meaning given by section 405 of the Communications Act 2003;

"corporate subscriber" means a subscriber who is—

(a) a company within the meaning of section 735(1) of the Companies Act 1985;

(b) a company incorporated in pursuance of a royal charter or letters patent;

(c) a partnership in Scotland;

(d) a corporation sole; or

(e) any other body corporate or entity which is a legal person distinct from its members;

"the Directive" means Directive 2002/58/EC of the European Parliament and of the Council of 12 July 2002 concerning the processing of personal data and the protection of privacy in the electronic communications sector (Directive on privacy and electronic communications);

"electronic communications network" has the meaning given by section 32 of the Communications Act 2003;

"electronic communications service" has the meaning given by section 32 of the Communications Act 2003;

"electronic mail" means any text, voice, sound or image message sent over a public electronic communications network which can be stored in the network or in the recipient's terminal equipment until it is collected by the recipient and includes messages sent using a short message service;

"enactment" includes an enactment comprised in, or in an instrument made under, an Act of the Scottish Parliament;

"individual" means a living individual and includes an unincorporated body of such individuals;

"the Information Commissioner" and "the Commissioner" both mean the Commissioner appointed under section 6 of the Data Protection Act 1998;

"information society service" has the meaning given in regulation 2(1) of the Electronic Commerce (EC Directive) Regulations 2002;

"location data" means any data processed in an electronic communications network indicating the geographical position of the terminal equipment of a user of a public electronic communications service, including data relating to—

(f) the latitude, longitude or altitude of the terminal equipment;

(g) the direction of travel of the user; or

(h) the time the location information was recorded;

"OFCOM" means the Office of Communications as established by section 1 of the Office of Communications Act 2002;

"programme service" has the meaning given in section 201 of the Broadcasting Act 1990; "public communications provider" means a provider of a public electronic communications network or a public electronic communications service;

"public electronic communications network" has the meaning given in section 151 of the Communications Act 2003;

"public electronic communications service" has the meaning given in section 151 of the Communications Act 2003;

"subscriber" means a person who is a party to a contract with a provider of public electronic communications services for the supply of such services;

"traffic data" means any data processed for the purpose of the conveyance of a communication on an electronic communications network or for the billing in respect of that communication and includes data relating to the routing, duration or time of a communication;

"user" means any individual using a public electronic communications service; and

"value added service" means any service which requires the processing of traffic data or location data beyond that which is necessary for the transmission of a communication or the billing in respect of that communication.

(2) Expressions used in these Regulations that are not defined in paragraph (1) and are defined in the Data Protection Act 1998 shall have the same meaning as in that Act.

(3) Expressions used in these Regulations that are not defined in paragraph (1) or the Data Protection Act 1998 and are defined in the Directive shall have the same meaning as in the Directive.

(4) Any reference in these Regulations to a line shall, without prejudice to paragraph (3), be construed as including a reference to anything that performs the function of a line, and "connected", in relation to a line, is to be construed accordingly.

3 Revocation of the Telecommunications (Data Protection and Privacy) Regulations 1999

The Telecommunications (Data Protection and Privacy) Regulations 1999 and the Telecomm unica-tions (Data Protection and Privacy) (Amendment) Regulations 2000 are hereby revoked.

4 Relationship between these Regulations and the Data Protection Act 1998

Nothing in these Regulations shall relieve a person of his obligations under the Data Protection Act 1998 in relation to the processing of personal data.

5 Security of public electronic communications services

(1) Subject to paragraph (2), a provider of a public electronic communications service ("the service provider") shall take appropriate technical and organisational measures to safeguard the security of that service.

(2) If necessary, the measures required by paragraph (1) may be taken by the service provider in conjunction with the provider of the electronic communications network by means of which the service is provided, and that network provider shall comply with any reasonable requests made by the service provider for these purposes.

(3) Where, notwithstanding the taking of measures as required by paragraph (1), there remains a significant risk to the security of the public electronic communications service, the service provider shall inform the subscribers concerned of—

    (a) the nature of that risk;

    (b) any appropriate measures that the subscriber may take to safeguard against that risk; and

    (c) the likely costs to the subscriber involved in the taking of such measures.

(4) For the purposes of paragraph (1), a measure shall only be taken to be appropriate if, having regard to—

    (a) the state of technological developments, and

    (b) the cost of implementing it,

it is proportionate to the risks against which it would safeguard.

(5) Information provided for the purposes of paragraph (3) shall be provided to the subscriber free of any charge other than the cost to the subscriber of receiving or collecting the information.

6 Confidentiality of communications

(1) Subject to paragraph (4), a person shall not use an electronic communications network to store information, or to gain access to information stored, in the terminal equipment of a subscriber or user unless the requirements of paragraph (2) are met.

(2) The requirements are that the subscriber or user of that terminal equipment—

(a) is provided with clear and comprehensive information about the purposes of the storage of, or access to, that information; and

(b) is given the opportunity to refuse the storage of or access to that information.

(3) Where an electronic communications network is used by the same person to store or access information in the terminal equipment of a subscriber or user on more than one occasion, it is sufficient for the purposes of this regulation that the requirements of paragraph (2) are met in respect of the initial use.

(4) Paragraph (1) shall not apply to the technical storage of, or access to, information—

(a) for the sole purpose of carrying out or facilitating the transmission of a communication over an electronic communications network; or

(b) where such storage or access is strictly necessary for the provision of an information society service requested by the subscriber or user.

7   Restrictions on the processing of certain traffic data

(1) Subject to paragraphs (2) and (3), traffic data relating to subscribers or users which are processed and stored by a public communications provider shall, when no longer required for the purpose of the transmission of a communication, be—

(a) erased;

(b) in the case of an individual, modified so that they cease to constitute personal data of that subscriber or user; or

(c) in the case of a corporate subscriber, modified so that they cease to be data that would be personal data if that subscriber was an individual.

(2) Traffic data held by a public communications provider for purposes connected with the payment of charges by a subscriber or in respect of interconnection payments may be processed and stored by that provider until the time specified in paragraph (5).

(3) Traffic data relating to a subscriber or user may be processed and stored by a provider of a public electronic communications service if—

(a) such processing and storage are for the purpose of marketing electronic communications services, or for the provision of value added services to that subscriber or user; and

(b) the subscriber or user to whom the traffic data relate has given his consent to such processing or storage; and

(c) such processing and storage are undertaken only for the duration necessary for the purposes specified in subparagraph (a).

(4) Where a user or subscriber has given his consent in accordance with paragraph (3), he shall be able to withdraw it at any time.

(5) The time referred to in paragraph (2) is the end of the period during which legal proceedings may be brought in respect of payments due or alleged to be due or, where such proceedings are brought within that period, the time when those proceedings are finally determined.

(6) Legal proceedings shall not be taken to be finally determined—

(a) until the conclusion of the ordinary period during which an appeal may be brought by either party (excluding any possibility of an extension of that period, whether by order of a court or otherwise), if no appeal is brought within that period; or

(b) if an appeal is brought, until the conclusion of that appeal.

(7) References in paragraph (6) to an appeal include references to an application for permission to appeal.

8   Further provisions relating to the processing of traffic data under regulation 7

(1) Processing of traffic data in accordance with regulation 7(2) or (3) shall not be undertaken by a public communications provider unless the subscriber or user to whom the data relate has been provided with information regarding the types of traffic data which are to be processed and the duration of such processing and, in the case of processing in accordance with regulation 7(3), he has been provided with that information before his consent has been obtained.

(2) Processing of traffic data in accordance with regulation 7 shall be restricted to what is required for the purposes of one or more of the activities listed in paragraph (3) and shall be carried out only by the public communications provider or by a person acting under his authority.

(3) The activities referred to in paragraph (2) are activities relating to—

(a) the management of billing or traffic;

(b) customer enquiries;

(c) the prevention or detection of fraud;

(d) the marketing of electronic communications services; or

(e) the provision of a value added service.

(4) Nothing in these Regulations shall prevent the furnishing of traffic data to a person who is a competent authority for the purposes of any provision relating to the settling of disputes (by way of legal proceedings or otherwise) which is contained in, or made by virtue of, any enactment.

9   Itemised billing and privacy

(1) At the request of a subscriber, a provider of a public electronic communications service shall provide that subscriber with bills that are not itemised.

(2) OFCOM shall have a duty, when exercising their functions under Chapter 1 of Part 2 of the Communications Act 2003, to have regard to the need to reconcile the rights of subscribers receiving itemised bills with the rights to privacy of calling users and called subscribers, including the need for sufficient alternative privacy-enhancing methods of communications or payments to be available to such users and subscribers.

10   Prevention of calling line identification—outgoing calls

(1) This regulation applies, subject to regulations 15 and 16, to outgoing calls where a facility enabling the presentation of calling line identification is available.

(2) The provider of a public electronic communications service shall provide users originating a call by means of that service with a simple means to prevent presentation of the identity of the calling line on the connected line as respects that call.

(3) The provider of a public electronic communications service shall provide subscribers to the service, as respects their line and all calls originating from that line, with a simple means of preventing presentation of the identity of that subscriber's line on any connected line.

(4) The measures to be provided under paragraphs (2) and (3) shall be provided free of charge.

11   Prevention of calling or connected line identification—incoming calls

(1) This regulation applies to incoming calls.

(2) Where a facility enabling the presentation of calling line identification is available, the provider of a public electronic communications service shall provide the called subscriber with a simple means to prevent, free of charge for reasonable use of the facility, presentation of the identity of the calling line on the connected line.

(3) Where a facility enabling the presentation of calling line identification prior to the call being established is available, the provider of a public electronic communications service shall provide the called subscriber with a simple means of rejecting incoming calls where the presentation of the calling line identification has been prevented by the calling user or subscriber.

(4) Where a facility enabling the presentation of connected line identification is available, the provider of a public electronic communications service shall provide the called subscriber with a simple means to prevent, without charge, presentation of the identity of the connected line on any calling line.

(5) In this regulation "called subscriber" means the subscriber receiving a call by means of the service in question whose line is the called line (whether or not it is also the connected line).

12   Publication of information for the purposes of regulations 10 and 11

Where a provider of a public electronic communications service provides facilities for calling or connected line identification, he shall provide information to the public regarding the availability of such facilities, including information regarding the options to be made available for the purposes of regulations 10 and 11.

13 Co-operation of communications providers for the purposes of regulations 10 and 11

For the purposes of regulations 10 and 11, a communications provider shall comply with any reasonable requests made by the provider of the public electronic communications service by means of which facilities for calling or connected line identification are provided.

14 Restrictions on the processing of location data

(1) This regulation shall not apply to the processing of traffic data.

(2) Location data relating to a user or subscriber of a public electronic communications network or a public electronic communications service may only be processed—

    (a) where that user or subscriber cannot be identified from such data; or

    (b) where necessary for the provision of a value added service, with the consent of that user or subscriber.

(3) Prior to obtaining the consent of the user or subscriber under paragraph (2)(b), the public communications provider in question must provide the following information to the user or subscriber to whom the data relate—

    (a) the types of location data that will be processed;

    (b) the purposes and duration of the processing of those data; and

    (c) whether the data will be transmitted to a third party for the purpose of providing the value added service.

(4) A user or subscriber who has given his consent to the processing of data under paragraph (2)(b) shall—

    (a) be able to withdraw such consent at any time, and

    (b) in respect of each connection to the public electronic communications network in question or each transmission of a communication, be given the opportunity to withdraw such consent, using a simple means and free of charge.

(5) Processing of location data in accordance with this regulation shall—

    (a) only be carried out by—

        (i) the public communications provider in question;

        (ii) the third party providing the value added service in question; or

        (iii) a person acting under the authority of a person falling within (i) or (ii); and

    (b) where the processing is carried out for the purposes of the provision of a value added service, be restricted to what is necessary for those purposes.

15 Tracing of malicious or nuisance calls

(1) A communications provider may override anything done to prevent the presentation of the identity of a calling line where—

    (a) a subscriber has requested the tracing of malicious or nuisance calls received on his line; and

    (b) the provider is satisfied that such action is necessary and expedient for the purposes of tracing such calls.

(2) Any term of a contract for the provision of public electronic communications services which relates to such prevention shall have effect subject to the provisions of paragraph (1).

(3) Nothing in these Regulations shall prevent a communications provider, for the purposes of any action relating to the tracing of malicious or nuisance calls, from storing and making available to a person with a legitimate interest data containing the identity of a calling subscriber which were obtained while paragraph (1) applied.

16 Emergency calls

(1) For the purposes of this regulation, "emergency calls" means calls to either the national emergency call number 999 or the single European emergency call number 112. (2) In order to facilitate responses to emergency calls—

    (a) all such calls shall be excluded from the requirements of regulation 10;

(b) no person shall be entitled to prevent the presentation on the connected line of the identity of the calling line; and

(c) the restriction on the processing of location data under regulation 14(2) shall be disregarded.

17   Termination of automatic call forwarding

(1) Where—

(a) calls originally directed to another line are being automatically forwarded to a subscriber's line as a result of action taken by a third party, and

(b) the subscriber requests his provider of electronic communications services ("the subscriber's provider") to stop the forwarding of those calls,

the subscriber's provider shall ensure, free of charge, that the forwarding is stopped without any avoidable delay.

(2) For the purposes of paragraph (1), every other communications provider shall comply with any reasonable requests made by the subscriber's provider to assist in the prevention of that forwarding.

18   Directories of subscribers

(1) This regulation applies in relation to a directory of subscribers, whether in printed or electronic form, which is made available to members of the public or a section of the public, including by means of a directory enquiry service.

(2) The personal data of an individual subscriber shall not be included in a directory unless that subscriber has, free of charge, been—

(a) informed by the collector of the personal data of the purposes of the directory in which his personal data are to be included, and

(b) given the opportunity to determine whether such of his personal data as are considered relevant by the producer of the directory should be included in the directory.

(3) Where personal data of an individual subscriber are to be included in a directory with facilities which enable users of that directory to obtain access to that data solely on the basis of a telephone number—

(a) the information to be provided under paragraph (2)(a) shall include information about those facilities; and

(b) for the purposes of paragraph (2)(b), the express consent of the subscriber to the inclusion of his data in a directory with such facilities must be obtained.

(4) Data relating to a corporate subscriber shall not be included in a directory where that subscriber has advised the producer of the directory that it does not want its data to be included in that directory.

(5) Where the data of an individual subscriber have been included in a directory, that subscriber shall, without charge, be able to verify, correct or withdraw those data at any time.

(6) Where a request has been made under paragraph (5) for data to be withdrawn from or corrected in a directory, that request shall be treated as having no application in relation to an edition of a directory that was produced before the producer of the directory received the request.

(7) For the purposes of paragraph (6), an edition of a directory which is revised after it was first produced shall be treated as a new edition.

(8) In this regulation, "telephone number" has the same meaning as in section 56(5) of the Communications Act 2003 but does not include any number which is used as an internet domain name, an internet address or an address or identifier incorporating either an internet domain name or an internet address, including an electronic mail address.

19   Use of automated calling systems

(1) A person shall neither transmit, nor instigate the transmission of, communications comprising recorded matter for direct marketing purposes by means of an automated calling
system except in the circumstances referred to in paragraph (2).

(2) Those circumstances are where the called line is that of a subscriber who has previously notified the caller that for the time being he consents to such communications being sent by, or at the instigation of, the caller on that line.

(3) A subscriber shall not permit his line to be used in contravention of paragraph (1).

(4) For the purposes of this regulation, an automated calling system is a system which is capable of—

(a) automatically initiating a sequence of calls to more than one destination in accordance with instructions stored in that system; and

(b) transmitting sounds which are not live speech for reception by persons at some or all of the destinations so called.

20   Use of facsimile machines for direct marketing purposes

(1) A person shall neither transmit, nor instigate the transmission of, unsolicited communications for direct marketing purposes by means of a facsimile machine where the called line is that of—

(a) an individual subscriber, except in the circumstances referred to in paragraph (2);

(b) a corporate subscriber who has previously notified the caller that such communications should not be sent on that line; or

(c) a subscriber and the number allocated to that line is listed in the register kept under regulation 25.

(2) The circumstances referred to in paragraph (1)(a) are that the individual subscriber has previously notified the caller that he consents for the time being to such communications being sent by, or at the instigation of, the caller.

(3) A subscriber shall not permit his line to be used in contravention of paragraph (1).

(4) A person shall not be held to have contravened paragraph (1)(c) where the number allocated to the called line has been listed on the register for less than 28 days preceding that on which the communication is made.

(5) Where a subscriber who has caused a number allocated to a line of his to be listed in the register kept under regulation 25 has notified a caller that he does not, for the time being, object to such communications being sent on that line by that caller, such communications may be sent by that caller on that line, notwithstanding that the number allocated to that line is listed in the said register.

(6) Where a subscriber has given a caller notification pursuant to paragraph (5) in relation to a line of his—

(a) the subscriber shall be free to withdraw that notification at any time, and

(b) where such notification is withdrawn, the caller shall not send such communications on that line.

(7) The provisions of this regulation are without prejudice to the provisions of regulation 19.

21   Unsolicited calls for direct marketing purposes

(1) A person shall neither use, nor instigate the use of, a public electronic communications service for the purposes of making unsolicited calls for direct marketing purposes where—

(a) the called line is that of a subscriber who has previously notified the caller that such calls should not for the time being be made on that line; or

(b) the number allocated to a subscriber in respect of the called line is one listed in the register kept under regulation 26.

(2) A subscriber shall not permit his line to be used in contravention of paragraph (1).

(3) A person shall not be held to have contravened paragraph (1)(b) where the number allocated to the called line has been listed on the register for less than 28 days preceding that on which the call is made.

(4) Where a subscriber who has caused a number allocated to a line of his to be listed in the register kept under regulation 26 has notified a caller that he does not, for the time being, object to such calls being made on that line by that caller, such calls may be made by that caller on that line, notwithstanding that the number allocated to that line is listed in the said register.

(5) Where a subscriber has given a caller notification pursuant to paragraph (4) in relation to a line of his—

    (a) the subscriber shall be free to withdraw that notification at any time, and

    (b) where such notification is withdrawn, the caller shall not make such calls on that line.

22　Use of electronic mail for direct marketing purposes

(1) This regulation applies to the transmission of unsolicited communications by means of electronic mail to individual subscribers.

(2) Except in the circumstances referred to in paragraph (3), a person shall neither transmit, nor instigate the transmission of, unsolicited communications for the purposes of direct marketing by means of electronic mail unless the recipient of the electronic mail has previously notified the sender that he consents for the time being to such communications being sent by, or at the instigation of, the sender.

(3) A person may send or instigate the sending of electronic mail for the purposes of direct marketing where—

    (a) that person has obtained the contact details of the recipient of that electronic mail in the course of the sale or negotiations for the sale of a product or service to that recipient;

    (b) the direct marketing is in respect of that person's similar products and services only; and

    (c) the recipient has been given a simple means of refusing (free of charge except for the costs of the transmission of the refusal) the use of his contact details for the purposes of such direct marketing, at the time that the details were initially collected, and, where he did not initially refuse the use of the details, at the time of each subsequent communication.

(4) A subscriber shall not permit his line to be used in contravention of paragraph (2).

23　Use of electronic mail for direct marketing purposes where the identity or address of the sender is concealed

A person shall neither transmit, nor instigate the transmission of, a communication for the purposes of direct marketing by means of electronic mail—

    (a) where the identity of the person on whose behalf the communication has been sent has been disguised or concealed; or

    (b) where a valid address to which the recipient of the communication may send a request that such communications cease has not been provided.

24　Information to be provided for the purposes of regulations 19, 20 and 21

(1) Where a public electronic communications service is used for the transmission of a communication for direct marketing purposes the person using, or instigating the use of, the service shall ensure that the following information is provided with that communication—

    (a) in relation to a communication to which regulations 19 (automated calling systems) and 20 (facsimile machines) apply, the particulars mentioned in paragraph (2)(a) and (b);

    (b) in relation to a communication to which regulation 21 (telephone calls) applies, the particulars mentioned in paragraph (2)(a) and, if the recipient of the call so requests, those mentioned in paragraph (2)(b).

(2) The particulars referred to in paragraph (1) are—

    (a) the name of the person;

    (b) either the address of the person or a telephone number on which he can be reached free of charge.

25　Register to be kept for the purposes of regulation 20

(1) For the purposes of regulation 20 OFCOM shall maintain and keep up-to-date, in printed or electronic form, a register of the numbers allocated to subscribers, in respect of particular lines, who have notified them (notwithstanding, in the case of individual subscribers, that they enjoy the benefit of regulation 20(1)(a) and (2)) that they do not for the time being wish to receive unsolicited communications for direct marketing purposes by means of facsimile machine on the lines in question.

(2) OFCOM shall remove a number from the register maintained under paragraph (1) where they have reason to believe that it has ceased to be allocated to the subscriber by whom they were notified pursuant to paragraph (1).

(3) On the request of—

(a) a person wishing to send, or instigate the sending of, such communications as are mentioned in paragraph (1), or

(b) a subscriber wishing to permit the use of his line for the sending of such communications,

for information derived from the register kept under paragraph (1), OFCOM shall, unless it is not reasonably practicable so to do, on the payment to them of such fee as is, subject to paragraph (4), required by them, make the information requested available to that person or that subscriber.

(4) For the purposes of paragraph (3) OFCOM may require different fees—

(a) for making available information derived from the register in different forms or manners, or

(b) for making available information derived from the whole or from different parts of the register,

but the fees required by them shall be ones in relation to which the Secretary of State has notified OFCOM that he is satisfied that they are designed to secure, as nearly as may be and taking one year with another, that the aggregate fees received, or reasonably expected to be received, equal the costs incurred, or reasonably expected to be incurred, by OFCOM in discharging their duties under paragraphs (1), (2) and (3).

(5) The functions of OFCOM under paragraphs (1), (2) and (3), other than the function of determining the fees to be required for the purposes of paragraph (3), may be discharged on their behalf by some other person in pursuance of arrangements made by OFCOM with that other person.

26 Register to be kept for the purposes of regulation 21

(1) For the purposes of regulation 21 OFCOM shall maintain and keep up-to-date, in printed or electronic form, a register of the numbers allocated to [...] subscribers, in respect of particular lines, who have notified them that they do not for the time being wish to receive unsolicited calls for direct marketing purposes on the lines in question.

[(1A) Notifications to OFCOM made for the purposes of paragraph (1) by corporate subscribers shall be in writing.]

(2) OFCOM shall remove a number from the register maintained under paragraph (1) where they have reason to believe that it has ceased to be allocated to the subscriber by whom they were notified pursuant to paragraph (1).

[(2A) Where a number allocated to a corporate subscriber is listed in the register maintained under paragraph (1), OFCOM shall, within the period of 28 days following each anniversary of the date of that number being first listed in the register, send to the subscriber a written reminder that the number is listed in the register.]

(3) On the request of—

(a) a person wishing to make, or instigate the making of, such calls as are mentioned in paragraph (1), or

(b) a subscriber wishing to permit the use of his line for the making of such calls,

for information derived from the register kept under paragraph (1), OFCOM shall, unless it is not reasonably practicable so to do, on the payment to them of such fee as is, subject to paragraph (4), required by them, make the information requested available to that person or that subscriber.

(4) For the purposes of paragraph (3) OFCOM may require different fees—

(a) for making available information derived from the register in different forms or manners, or

(b) for making available information derived from the whole or from different parts of the register,

but the fees required by them shall be ones in relation to which the Secretary of State has notified OFCOM that he is satisfied that they are designed to secure, as nearly as may be and taking one year with another, that the aggregate fees received, or reasonably expected to be received, equal the costs incurred, or reasonably expected to be incurred, by OFCOM in discharging their duties under paragraphs (1), (2) and (3).

(5) The functions of OFCOM under paragraphs (1), (2), [(2A)] and (3), other than the function of determining the fees to be required for the purposes of paragraph (3), may be discharged on their behalf by some other person in pursuance of arrangements made by OFCOM with that other person.

27   Modification of contracts

To the extent that any term in a contract between a subscriber to and the provider of a public electronic communications service or such a provider and the provider of an electronic communications network would be inconsistent with a requirement of these Regulations, that term shall be void.

28   National security

(1) Nothing in these Regulations shall require a communications provider to do, or refrain from doing, anything (including the processing of data) if exemption from the requirement in question is required for the purpose of safeguarding national security.

(2) Subject to paragraph (4), a certificate signed by a Minister of the Crown certifying that exemption from any requirement of these Regulations is or at any time was required for the purpose of safeguarding national security shall be conclusive evidence of that fact.

(3) A certificate under paragraph (2) may identify the circumstances in which it applies by means of a general description and may be expressed to have prospective effect.

(4) Any person directly affected by the issuing of a certificate under paragraph (2) may appeal to the Tribunal against the issuing of the certificate.

(5) If, on an appeal under paragraph (4), the Tribunal finds that, applying the principles applied by a court on an application for judicial review, the Minister did not have reasonable grounds for issuing the certificate, the Tribunal may allow the appeal and quash the certificate.

(6) Where, in any proceedings under or by virtue of these Regulations, it is claimed by a communications provider that a certificate under paragraph (2) which identifies the circumstances in which it applies by means of a general description applies in the circumstances in question, any other party to the proceedings may appeal to the Tribunal on the ground that the certificate does not apply in those circumstances and, subject to any determination under paragraph (7), the certificate shall be conclusively presumed so to apply.

(7) On any appeal under paragraph (6), the Tribunal may determine that the certificate does not so apply.

(8) In this regulation—

    (a) "the Tribunal" means the Information Tribunal referred to in section 6 of the Data Protection Act 1998;

    (b) Subsections (8), (9), (10) and (12) of section 28 of and Schedule 6 to that Act apply for the purposes of this regulation as they apply for the purposes of section 28;

    (c) section 58 of that Act shall apply for the purposes of this regulation as if the reference in that section to the functions of the Tribunal under that Act included a reference to the functions of the Tribunal under paragraphs (4) to (7) of this regulation; and

    (d) subsections (1), (2) and (5)(f) of section 67 of that Act shall apply in respect of the making of rules relating to the functions of the Tribunal under this regulation.

29   Legal requirements, law enforcement etc

(1) Nothing in these Regulations shall require a communications provider to do, or refrain from doing, anything (including the processing of data)—

    (a) if compliance with the requirement in question—

        (i) would be inconsistent with any requirement imposed by or under an enactment or by a court order; or

        (ii) would be likely to prejudice the prevention or detection of crime or the apprehension or prosecution of offenders; or

(b) if exemption from the requirement in question—
  (i)   is required for the purposes of, or in connection with, any legal proceedings (including prospective legal proceedings);
  (ii) is necessary for the purposes of obtaining legal advice; or
  (iii) is otherwise necessary for the purposes of establishing, exercising or defending legal rights.

30 Proceedings for compensation for failure to comply with requirements of the regulations

(1) A person who suffers damage by reason of any contravention of any of the requirements of these Regulations by any other person shall be entitled to bring proceedings for compensation from that other person for that damage.

(2) In proceedings brought against a person by virtue of this regulation it shall be a defence to prove that he had taken such care as in all the circumstances was reasonably required to comply with the relevant requirement.

(3) The provisions of this regulation are without prejudice to those of regulation 31.

31 Enforcement—extension of Part V of the Data Protection Act 1998

(1) The provisions of Part V of the Data Protection Act 1998 and of Schedules 6 and 9 to that Act are extended for the purposes of these Regulations and, for those purposes, shall have effect subject to the modifications set out in Schedule 1.

(2) In regulations 32 and 33, "enforcement functions" means the functions of the Information Commissioner under the provisions referred to in paragraph (1) as extended by that paragraph.

(3) The provisions of this regulation are without prejudice to those of regulation 30.

32 Request that the Commissioner exercise his enforcement functions

Where it is alleged that there has been a contravention of any of the requirements of these Regulations either OFCOM or a person aggrieved by the alleged contravention may request the Commissioner to exercise his enforcement functions in respect of that contravention, but those functions shall be exercisable by the Commissioner whether or not he has been so requested.

33 Technical advice to the Commissioner

OFCOM shall comply with any reasonable request made by the Commissioner, in connection with his enforcement functions, for advice on technical and similar matters relating to electronic communications.

34 *(Amends the telecommunications (Lawful Business Practice) (Interception of Communications) regulations 2000; this amendment has been incorporated into the text of the regulation, above)*

35 Amendment to the electronic communications (universal service) order 2003

(1) In paragraphs 2(2) and 3(2) of the Schedule to the Electronic Communications (Universal Service) Order 2003, for the words "Telecommunications (Data Protection and Privacy) Regulations 1999" there shall be substituted "Privacy and Electronic Communications (EC Directive) Regulations 2003".

(2) Paragraph (1) shall have effect notwithstanding the provisions of section 65 of the Communications Act 2003 (which provides for the modification of the Universal Service Order made under that section).

36 Transitional provisions

The provisions in Schedule 2 shall have effect.

SCHEDULE 1 MODIFICATIONS FOR THE PURPOSES OF THESE REGULATIONS TO PART V OF THE DATA PROTECTION ACT 1998 AND SCHEDULES 6 AND 9 TO THAT ACT AS EXTENDED BY REGULATION 31

1. In section 40—
    (a) in subsection (1), for the words "data controller" there shall be substituted the word "person", for the words "data protection principles" there shall be substituted the words "requirements of the Privacy and Electronic Communications (EC Directive) Regulations 2003 (in this Part referred to as 'the relevant requirements')" and for the words "principle or principles" there shall be substituted the words "requirement or requirements";
    (b) in subsection (2), the words "or distress" shall be omitted;
    (c) subsections (3), (4), (5), (9) and (10) shall be omitted; and
    (d) in subsection (6)(a), for the words "data protection principle or principles" there shall be substituted the words "relevant requirement or requirements".

2. In section 41(1) and (2), for the words "data protection principle or principles", in both places where they occur, there shall be substituted the words "relevant requirement or requirements".

3. Section 42 shall be omitted.

4. In section 43—
    (a) for subsections (1) and (2) there shall be substituted the following provisions—

"(1) If the Commissioner reasonably requires any information for the purpose of determining whether a person has complied or is complying with the relevant requirements, he may serve that person with a notice (in this Act referred to as 'an information notice') requiring him, within such time as is specified in the notice, to furnish the Commissioner, in such form as may be so specified, with such information relating to compliance with the relevant requirements as is so specified.

(2) An information notice must contain a statement that the Commissioner regards the specified information as relevant for the purpose of determining whether the person has complied or is complying with the relevant requirements and his reason for regarding it as relevant for that purpose."

    (b) in subsection (6)(a), after the word "under" there shall be inserted the words "the Privacy and Electronic Communications (EC Directive) Regulations 2003 or";
    (c) in subsection (6)(b), after the words "arising out of" there shall be inserted the words "the said Regulations or"; and
    (d) subsection (10) shall be omitted.

5. Sections 44, 45 and 46 shall be omitted.

6. In section 47—
    (a) in subsection (1), for the words "an information notice or special information notice" there shall be substituted the words "or an information notice"; and
    (b) in subsection (2) the words "or a special information notice" shall be omitted.

7. In section 48—
    (a) in subsections (1) and (3), for the words "an information notice or a special information notice", in both places where they occur, there shall be substituted the words "or an information notice";
    (b) in subsection (3) for the words "43(5) or 44(6)" there shall be substituted the words "or 43(5)"; and
    (c) subsection (4) shall be omitted.

8. In section 49 subsection (5) shall be omitted.

9. In paragraph 4(1) of Schedule (6), for the words "(2) or (4)" there shall be substituted the words "or (2)".

10. In paragraph 1 of Schedule 9—

    (a) for subparagraph (1)(a) there shall be substituted the following provision—

        "(a) that a person has contravened or is contravening any of the requirements of the Privacy and Electronic Communications (EC Directive) Regulations 2003 (in this Schedule referred to as 'the 2003 Regulations') or"; and

    (b) subparagraph (2) shall be omitted.

11. In paragraph 9 of Schedule 9—

    (a) in subparagraph (1)(a) after the words "rights under" there shall be inserted the words "the 2003 Regulations or"; and

    (b) in subparagraph (1)(b) after the words "arising out of" there shall be inserted the words "the 2003 Regulations or".

SCHEDULE 2 TRANSITIONAL PROVISIONS

Interpretation

1. In this Schedule "the 1999 Regulations" means the Telecommunications (Data Protection and Privacy) Regulations 1999 and "caller" has the same meaning as in regulation 21 of the 1999 Regulations.

Directories

2. (1) Regulation 18 of these Regulations shall not apply in relation to editions of directories first published before 11th December 2003.

(2) Where the personal data of a subscriber have been included in a directory in accordance with Part IV of the 1999 Regulations, the personal data of that subscriber may remain included in that directory provided that the subscriber—

    (a) has been provided with information in accordance with regulation 18 of these Regulations; and

    (b) has not requested that his data be withdrawn from that directory.

(3) Where a request has been made under subparagraph (2) for data to be withdrawn from a directory, that request shall be treated as having no application in relation to an edition of a directory that was produced before the producer of the directory received the request.

(4) For the purposes of subparagraph (3), an edition of a directory, which is revised after it was first produced, shall be treated as a new edition.

Notifications

3. (1) A notification of consent given to a caller by a subscriber for the purposes of regulation 22(2) of the 1999 Regulations is to have effect on and after 11th December 2003 as a notification given by that subscriber for the purposes of regulation 19(2) of these Regulations.

(2) A notification given to a caller by a corporate subscriber for the purposes of regulation 23(2)(a) of the 1999 Regulations is to have effect on and after 11th December 2003 as a notification given by that subscriber for the purposes of regulation 20(1)(b) of these Regulations.

(3) A notification of consent given to a caller by an individual subscriber for the purposes of regulation 24(2) of the 1999 Regulations is to have effect on and after 11th December 2003 as a notification given by that subscriber for the purposes of regulation 20(2) of these Regulations.

(4) A notification given to a caller by an individual subscriber for the purposes of regulation 25 (2)(a) of the 1999 Regulations is to have effect on and after the 11th December 2003 as a notification given by that subscriber for the purposes of regulation 21(1) of these Regulations.

Registers kept under regulations 25 and 26

4. (1) A notification given by a subscriber pursuant to regulation 23(4)(a) of the 1999 Regulations to the Director General of Telecommunications (or to such other person as is discharging

his functions under regulation 23(4) of the 1999 Regulations on his behalf by virtue of an arrangement made under regulation 23(6) of those Regulations) is to have effect on or after 11th December 2003 as a notification given pursuant to regulation 25(1) of these Regulations.

(2) A notification given by a subscriber who is an individual pursuant to regulation 25(4)(a) of the 1999 Regulations to the Director General of Telecommunications (or to such other person as is discharging his functions under regulation 25(4) of the 1999 Regulations on his behalf by virtue of an arrangement made under regulation 25(6) of those Regulations) is to have effect on or after 11th December 2003 as a notification given pursuant to regulation 26(1) of these Regulations.

References in these regulations to OFCOM

5. In relation to times before an order made under section 411 of the Communications Act 2003 brings any of the provisions of Part 2 of Chapter 1 of that Act into force for the purpose of conferring on OFCOM the functions contained in those provisions, references to OFCOM in these Regulations are to be treated as references to the Director General of Telecommunications.

The Electronic Commerce (EC Directive) (Extension) (No. 2) Regulations 2003

(SI 2003/2500)

1   Citation and commencement

(1) These Regulations may be cited as the Electronic Commerce (EC Directive) (Extension) (No. 2) Regulations 2003.

(2) These Regulations shall come into force on 31st October 2003 immediately after the Copyright (Visually Impaired Persons) Act 2002 (Commencement) Order 2003 has come into force.

2   Application of the E-Commerce Regulations

The Electronic Commerce (EC Directive) Regulations 2002[4] ("the E-Commerce Regulations") shall apply to—

(a) the enactments listed in Part 1 of the Schedule, as amended by the Copyright and Related Rights Regulations 2003; and

(b) the enactments listed in Part 2 of the Schedule, notwithstanding regulation 3(2) of the E-Commerce Regulations.

Regulation 2   **SCHEDULE**

Part 1   Enactments Amended by the Copyright and Related Rights Regulations 2003

Acts

Copyright, Designs and Patents Act 1988 (c. 48)
Olympic Symbol etc (Protection) Act 1995 (c. 32)
Copyright (Visually Impaired Persons) Act 2002 (c. 33)

Instruments

Copyright (Recording of Folksongs for Archives) (Designated Bodies) Order 1989 (SI 1989/1012)
Copyright (Application of Provisions relating to Educational Establishments to Teachers) (No. 2) Order 1989 (SI 1989/1067) Copyright Tribunal Rules 1989 (SI 1989/1129)
Copyright (Librarians and Archivists) (Copying of Copyright Material) Regulations 1989 (SI 1989/1212)
Copyright (Certification of Licensing Scheme for Educational Recording of Broadcasts and Cable Programmes) (Educational Recording Agency Limited) Order 1990 (SI 1990/879)

Copyright (Recording for Archives of Designated Class of Broadcasts and Cable Programmes) (Designated Bodies) Order 1993 (SI 1993/74)
Copyright and Related Rights Regulations 1996 (SI 1996/2967)
Copyright (Certification of Licensing Scheme for Educational Recording of Broadcasts) (Open University) Order 2003 (SI 2003/187)

Part 2 Other Enactments

Performances (Reciprocal Protection) (Convention Countries and Isle of Man) Order 2003 (SI 2003/773)
Copyright (Application to Other Countries) (Amendment) Order 2003 (SI 2003/774)

The Regulation of Investigatory Powers (Communications Data) Order 2003

(SI 2003/3172)

1 Citation, commencement and interpretation

(1) This Order may be cited as the Regulation of Investigatory Powers (Communications Data) Order 2003 and shall come into force one month after the day on which it is made.

(2) In this Order—

"the 2000 Act" means the Regulation of Investigatory Powers Act 2000;

"authorisation" means an authorisation under section 22(3) of the 2000 Act; and

"notice" means a notice under section 22(4) of the 2000 Act.

2 Prescribed offices, ranks and positions

The offices, ranks and positions listed in columns 2 and 3 of Schedule 1 (being offices, ranks and positions with the relevant public authorities in column 1 of that Schedule) are hereby prescribed for the purposes of section 25(2) of the 2000 Act, subject to the restrictions in articles 6, 7 and 10.

3 Additional public authorities

The public authorities set out in column 1 of Parts I, III and IV of Schedule 2 are hereby specified as relevant public authorities for the purposes of section 25(1) of the 2000 Act.

4 Prescribed offices, ranks and positions in the additional public authorities

The offices, ranks and positions listed in columns 2 and 3 of Parts I, **II**, III and IV of Schedule 2 (being offices, ranks and positions with the relevant public authorities in column 1 of that Schedule) are hereby prescribed for the purposes of section 25(2) of the 2000 Act, subject to the restrictions in articles 6, 7, 8 and 9.

5 More senior offices, ranks and positions

(1) Where an office, rank or position with a relevant public authority listed in column 2 of Schedule 1 or column 2 of Schedule 2 is prescribed by virtue of article 2 or 4, all more senior offices, ranks or positions with that authority are also prescribed for the purposes of section 25(2) of the 2000 Act, subject to article 11.

(2) Where an office, rank or position with a relevant public authority is described in column 2 of Schedule 1 or column 2 of Schedule 2 by reference to an agency, unit, branch, division or other part of that authority, the reference in paragraph (1) to all more senior offices, ranks or positions with that

authority is a reference to all more senior offices, ranks or positions with that agency, unit, branch, division or part.

6   Restrictions on the granting of authorisations or the giving of notices

The restriction in this article is that an individual holding an office, rank or position which is listed in column 2 or 3 of Schedule 1 or column 2 or 3 of Schedule 2 may not grant an authorisation or give a notice unless he believes it is necessary on the grounds set out in one or more of the paragraphs of section 22(2) of the 2000 Act listed in the corresponding entry in column 4 of those Schedules.

7.   (1) The restriction in this paragraph is that an individual holding an office, rank or position which is listed in column 2 of Schedule 1 or column 2 of Schedule 2 may only grant an authorisation or give a notice that he believes is necessary on grounds other than those set out in paragraphs (a), (b), (c) and (g) of section 22(2) of the 2000 Act where that authorisation or notice satisfies the condition in paragraph (3).

(2) The restriction in this paragraph is that an individual holding an office, rank or position which is listed in column 3 of Schedule 1 or column 3 of Schedule 2 may only grant an authorisation or give a notice which satisfies the condition set out in paragraph (3).

(3) The condition referred to in paragraphs (1) and (2) is that the only communications data authorised to be obtained by the authorisation, or required to be obtained or disclosed by the notice, is communications data falling within section 21(4)(c) of the 2000 Act.

8.   (1) The restriction in this article is that an individual holding an office, rank or position which is listed in column 2 of Part II or Part III of Schedule 2 may only grant an authorisation or give a notice which satisfies the condition set out in paragraph (2).

(2) The condition referred to in paragraph (1) is that the only communications data authorised to be obtained by the authorisation, or required to be obtained or disclosed by the notice, is communications data falling within section 21(4)(b) or (c) of the 2000 Act.

9.   (1) The restriction in this article is that an individual holding an office, rank or position which is listed in column 2 of Part IV of Schedule 2 may only grant an authorisation or give a notice which satisfies the condition set out in paragraph (2).

(2) The condition referred to in paragraph (1) is that the only communications data authorised to be obtained by the authorisation, or required to be obtained or disclosed by the notice, is communications data relating to a postal service.

10.   (1) The restriction in this article is that an individual holding an office, rank or position with the Commissioners of Inland Revenue (being a relevant public authority listed in Schedule 1) may only grant an authorisation or give a notice which satisfies the condition set out in paragraph (2).

(2) The condition referred to in paragraph (1) is that the only communications data falling with section 21(4)(a) of the 2000 Act authorised to be obtained by the authorisation, or required to be obtained or disclosed by the notice is communications data relating to a postal service.

11.   The restrictions on the granting of authorisations and the giving of notices that apply to an individual holding an office, rank or position with a relevant public authority listed in column 2 of Schedule 1 or column 2 of Schedule 2 shall also apply to all individuals holding all more senior offices, ranks or positions with that authority that are prescribed by article 5.

SCHEDULE 1 INDIVIDUALS IN PUBLIC AUTHORITIES WITHIN SECTION 25(1) OF THE 2000 ACT

(1) Relevant public authorities	(2) Prescribed offices etc. (All authorisations/ notices)	(3) Additional prescribed offices etc. (Authorisations/ notices relating solely to communications data falling within section 21(4)(c))	(4) Purposes within section 22(2) for which an authorisation may be granted or a notice given
Police Forces			
A police force maintained under section 2 of the Police Act 1996 (police forces in England and Wales outside London)	Superintendent	Inspector	(a)(b)(c)(d)(e)(g)
A police force maintained under or by virtue of section 1 of the Police (Scotland) Act 1967	Superintendent	Inspector	(a)(b)(c)(d)(e)(g)
The metropolitan police force	Superintendent	Inspector	(a)(b)(c)(d)(e)(g)
The City of London police force	Superintendent	Inspector	(a)(b)(c)(d)(e)(g)
The Police Service of Northern Ireland	Superintendent	Inspector	(a)(b)(c)(d)(e)(g)
The Ministry of Defence Police	Superintendent	Inspector	(a)(b)(c)(g)
The Royal Navy RegulatingBranch	Provost Marshal	—	(a)(b)(c)(g)
The Royal Military Police	Lieutenant Colonel	Major	(a)(b)(c)(g)
The Royal Air Force Police	Wing Commander	Squadron Leader	(a)(b)(c)(g)
The British Transport Police	Superintendent	Inspector	(a)(b)(c)(d)(e)(g)
The Commissioners of Customs and Excise	Band 9	Band 7 or 8	(b)(f)
The Commissioners of Inland Revenue	Band C1	Brand C2	(b)(f)
The Intelligence Services			
Government Communications Headquarters	GC8	—	(a)(b)(c)
The Security Service	General Duties 3 or any other Officer at Level 3	General Duties 4	(a)(b)(c)
The Secret Intelligence Service	Grade 6 or equivalent	—	(a)(b)(c)
[Other Bodies			
The Serious Organised Crime Agency	Senior Manager (Grade 2)	Principal Officer (Grade 3)	(b)]

SCHEDULE 2 INDIVIDUALS IN ADDITIONAL PUBLIC AUTHORITIES SPECIFIED BY THIS ORDER

Part I

(Individuals in additional public authorities that may acquire all types of communications data within section 21(4) of the 2000 Act)

(1) Additional public authorities specified for the purposes of section 25(1) of the 2000 Act	(2) Prescribed offices etc. (All authorisations/ notices)	(3) Additional prescribed offices etc. (Authorisations/ notices relating solely to communications data falling within section 21(4)(c))	(4) Purposes within section 22(2) for which an authorisation may be granted or a notice given
The Financial Services Authority	Head of Department in EnforcementDivision	—	(b)
[The Scottish Drug Enforcement Agency, meaning the organisation known by that name and established under section 36(1)(a)(ii) of the Police (Scotland) Act 1967	Superintendent, Grade PO7 or any individual on secondment to the Scottish Drug Enforcement Agency who holds the rank of Superintendent or Grade PO7 with the police force from which that person is seconded	Inspector or any individual on secondment to the Scottish Drug Enforcement Agency who holds the rank of Inspector with the police force from which that person is seconded	(b)(d)(g)
The Civil Nuclear Constabulary	Inspector	Superintendent	(a)(b)]
The Office of the Police Ombudsman for Northern Ireland	Senior Investigating Officer	—	(b)
[The Independent Police Complaints Commission	Commissioner, Regional Director, Director of Investigations or Deputy Director of Investigations	—	(b)
The Office of Communications	Senior Enforcement Policy Manager	—	(b)
The force comprising the special constables appointed under section 79 of the Harbours, Docks and Piers Clauses Act 1847 on the nomination of the Dover Harbour Board	Superintendent	Inspector	(a)(b)(d)(e)
The force comprising the constables appointed under article 3 of the Mersey Docks and Harbour (Police) Order 1975 on the nomination of the Mersey Docks and Harbour Company	Superintendent	Inspector	(a)(b)(d)(e)]

Cont.

(1) Additional public authorities specified for the purposes of section 25(1) of the 2000 Act	(2) Prescribed offices etc. (All authorisations/ notices)	(3) Additional prescribed offices etc. (Authorisations/ notices relating solely to communications data falling within section 21(4)(c))	(4) Purposes within section 22(2) for which an authorisation may be granted or a notice given
Emergency Services			
A National Health Service trust established under section 5 of the National Health Service and Community Care Act 1990 whose functions, as specified in its Establishment Order, include the provision of emergency ambulance services	Duty Officer responsible for the Control Function	—	(g)
The Welsh Ambulance Services NHS Trust	Regional Control Manager	—	(g)
The Scottish Ambulance Service Board	Emergency Medical Dispatch Centre Officer in Charge	—	(g)
The Northern Ireland Ambulance Service Health and Social Services Trust	Control Supervisor in Ambulance Control Room	—	(g)
The Department for Transport	Area Operations Manager in the Maritime and Coastguard Agency	—	(g)
Any fire authority within the meaning of the Fire Services Act 1947 (read with paragraph 2 of Schedule 11 to the Local Government Act 1985) [or any fire and rescue authority under the Fire and Rescue Services Act 2004]	Fire Control Officer	—	(g)
A council constituted under section 2 of the Local Government etc. (Scotland) Act 1994			
[A joint fire and rescue board constituted by an amalgamation scheme under section 2 of the Fire (Scotland) Act 2005 (asp 5) or a joint fire and rescue board within the meaning of section 5 of that Act]	Fire Control Officer	—	(g)
The Fire Authority for Northern Ireland	Fire Control Officer	—	(g)

Part II

(Individuals in the public authorities specified in Part I that may only acquire communications data falling within sections 21(4)(b) and (c) of the 2000 Act)

(1) Additional public authorities specified for the purposes of section 25(1) of the 2000 Act	(2) Prescribed offices etc. (All authorisations/ notices relating to communications data falling within sections 21(4)(b) and (c))	(3) Additional prescribed offices etc. (Authorisations/ notices relating solely to communications data falling within section 21(4)(c))	(4) Purposes within section 22(2) for which an authorisation may be granted or a notice given
The Department of Trade and Industry	Deputy Inspector of Companies in Companies Investigation Branch	—	(b)
	Deputy Chief Investigation Officer in the Investigation Officers Section of Legal Services Directorate D	—	(b)
Emergency Services			
A National Health Service Trust established under section 5 of the National Health Service and Community Care Act 1990 whose functions, as specified in its Establishment Order, include the provision of emergency ambulance services	Director of Operations or Director of Control and Communications	—	(b)
The Welsh Ambulance Services NHS Trust	Director of Operations	—	(b)
The Scottish Ambulance Service Board	Director of Operations	—	(b)
The Northern Ireland Ambulance Service Health and Social Services Trust	Director of Operations	—	(b)
The Department for Transport	Principal Enforcement Officer in the Maritime and Coastguard Agency	—	(b)(d)
Any fire authority within the meaning of the Fire Services Act 1947 (read with paragraph 2 of Schedule 11 to the Local Government Act 1985) [or any fire and rescue authority under the Fire and Rescue Services Act 2004]	Principal Fire Control Officer or Divisional Officer 2	—	(b)(d)

Cont.

(1) Additional public authorities specified for the purposes of section 25(1) of the 2000 Act	(2) Prescribed offices etc (All authorisations/ notices relating to communications data falling within sections 21(4)(b) and (c))	(3) Additional prescribed offices etc. (Authorisations/ notices relating solely to communications data falling within section 21(4)(c)	(4) Purposes within section 22(2) for which an authorisation may be granted or a notice given
A council constituted under section 2 of the Local Government etc. (Scotland) Act 1994	Assistant Chief Officer, Assistant Head of Service, Service Manager or equivalent	—	(b)
[A joint fire and rescue board constituted by an amalgamation scheme under section 2 of the Fire (Scotland) Act 2005 (asp 5) or a joint fire and rescue board within the meaning of section 5 of that Act]	Principal Fire Control Officer or Divisional Officer 2	—	(b)(d)
The Fire Authority for Northern Ireland	Principal Fire Control Officer or Divisional Officer 2	—	(b)(d)

Part III

(Individuals in further additional public authorities that may only acquire communications data falling within sections 21(4) (b) and (c) of the 2000 Act)

(1) Additional public authorities specified for the purposes of section 25(1) of the 2000 Act	(2) Prescribed offices etc. (All authorisations/ notices relating to communications data falling within sections 21(4)(b) and (c))	(3) Additional prescribed offices etc. (Authorisations/ notices relating solely to communications data falling within section 21(4)(c)	(4) Purposes within section 22(2) for which an authorisation may be granted or a notice given
Government Departments			
The Department for Environment, Food and Rural Affairs	Senior Investigation Officer in DEFRA Investigation Branch	—	(b)
	Senior Investigation Officer in the Centre for Environment, Fisheries and Aquaculture Science	—	(b)
	Senior Counter Fraud Officer in the Counter Fraud and Compliance Unit of the Rural Payments Agency	—	(b)

Cont.

(1) Additional public authorities specified for the purposes of section 25(1) of the 2000 Act	(2) Prescribed offices etc. (All authorisations/ notices relating to communications data falling within sections 21(4)(b) and (c))	(3) Additional prescribed offices etc. (Authorisations/ notices relating solely to communications data falling within section 21(4)(c))	(4) Purposes within section 22(2) for which an authorisation may be granted or a notice given
The Food Standards Agency	Deputy Director of Legal Services or any Director	—	(b)(d)(e)
The Department of Health	Integrated Payband 3 (Standard 2) in the Medicines and Healthcare Products Regulatory Agency	—	(b)(d)(e)
The Home Office	Immigration Inspector in the Immigration Service	—	(b)
The Department of Enterprise, Trade and Investment for Northern Ireland	Deputy Chief Inspector in Trading Standards Service	—	(b)
Local Authorities			
Any county council or district council in England, a London borough council, the Common Council of the City of London in its capacity as a local authority, the Council of the Isles of Scilly, and any county council or county borough council in Wales	Assistant Chief Officer, Assistant Head of Service, ServiceManager or equivalent	—	(b)
A district council within the meaning of the Local Government Act (Northern Ireland) 1972	Assistant Chief Officer	—	(b)
NHS Bodies			
[NHS Business Services Authority]	[Senior Manager(not below the grade of Agenda for Change pay band 8b) in the Counter Fraud and Security Management Services division of the NHS Business Services Authority]	—	(b)
The Common Services Agency for the Scottish Health Service	Head of NHS Scotland CounterFraud Services	—	(b)
The Northern Ireland Health and Social Services Central Services Agency	Head of the Counter Fraud Unit	—	(b)

Cont.

(1) Additional public authorities specified for the purposes of section 25(1) of the 2000 Act	(2) Prescribed offices etc. (All authorisations/ notices relating to communications data falling within sections 21(4)(b) and (c))	(3) Additional prescribed offices etc. (Authorisations/ notices relating solely to communications data falling within section 21(4)(c))	(4) Purposes within section 22(2) for which an authorisation may be granted or a notice given
Other Bodies			
The Charity Commission	Senior Investigations Manager	—	(b)
The Environment Agency	Area Management Team Member	—	(b)(d)(e)
The Gaming Board for Great Britain	Chief Inspector	—	(b)
The Health and Safety Executive	Band 2 Inspector	—	(b)(d)(e)(g)
The Information Commissioner	Head of Investigations	—	(b)
The Office of Fair Trading	Director of Cartel Investigations	—	(b)
The Serious Fraud Office	Assistant Director	—	(b)
The Scottish Environment Protection Agency	Director of Operations, any other Director	—	(b)(d)(e)
A Universal Service Provider within the meaning of the Postal Services Act 2000	Senior Investigation Manager in Royal Mail Group plc	—	(b)

Part IV

(Individuals in additional public authorities that may only acquire communications data within section 21(4) of the 2000 Act relating to a postal service)

(1) Additional public authorities specified for the purposes of section 25(1) of the 2000 Act	(2) Prescribed offices etc. (All authorisations/ notices relating to communications data relating to postal services	(3) Additional prescribed offices etc. (Authorisations/ notices relating solely to communications data falling within section 21(4)(c))	(4) Purposes within section 22(2) for which an authorisation may be granted or a notice given
Postal Services Commission	Legal Adviser	—	(b)

The Retention of Communications Data (Code of Practice) Order 2003

(SI 2003/3175)

1 Citation and commencement

The Order may be cited as the Retention of Communications Data (Code of Practice) Order 2003 and shall come into force on the day after the day on which it is made.

2 Retention of communications data code of practice

The draft code of practice entitled "Voluntary Retention of Communications Data under Part 11: Anti-terrorism, Crime and Security Act 2001—Voluntary Code of Practice", laid before each House of Parliament on 11th September 2003, relating to the retention by communications providers of communications data obtained by or held by them, shall come into force on the day after the day on which this Order is made.

The Electronic Commerce (EC Directive) (Extension) Regulations 2004

(SI 2004/1178)

1 Citation and commencement

These Regulations may be cited as the Electronic Commerce (EC Directive) (Extension) Regulations 2004 and shall come into force on 14th May 2004.

2 Application of the E-Commerce Regulations

The Electronic Commerce (EC Directive) Regulations 2002 shall apply to the Sexual Offences Act 2003 notwithstanding regulation 3(2) of those Regulations.

The Financial Services (Distance Marketing) Regulations 2004

(SI 2004/2095)

1 Citation, commencement and extent

These Regulations may be cited as the Financial Services (Distance Marketing) Regulations 2004 and come into force on 31st October 2004.

2 Interpretation

(1) In these Regulations—

"the 1974 Act" means the Consumer Credit Act 1974;

"the 2000 Act" means the Financial Services and Markets Act 2000;

"the Authority" means the Financial Services Authority;

"appointed representative" has the same meaning as in section 39(2) of the 2000 Act (exemption of appointed representatives);

"authorised person" has the same meaning as in section 31(2) of the 2000 Act (authorised persons);

"breach" means a contravention by a supplier of a prohibition in, or a failure by a supplier to comply with a requirement of, these Regulations;

"business" includes a trade or profession;

"consumer" means any individual who, in contracts to which these Regulations apply, is acting for purposes which are outside any business he may carry on;

"court" in relation to England and Wales and Northern Ireland means a county court or the High Court, and in relation to Scotland means the Sheriff Court or the Court of Session;

"credit" includes a cash loan and any other form of financial accommodation, and for this purpose "cash" includes money in any form;

"designated professional body" has the same meaning as in section 326(2) of the 2000 Act (designation of professional bodies);

"the Directive" means Directive 2002/65/EC of the European Parliament and of the Council of 23 September 2002 concerning the distance marketing of consumer financial services and amending Council Directive 90/619/EEC and Directives 97/7/EC and 98/27/EC;

"distance contract" means any contract concerning one or more financial services concluded between a supplier and a consumer under an organised distance sales or service-provision scheme run by the supplier or by an intermediary, who, for the purpose of that contract, makes exclusive use of one or more means of distance communication up to and including the time at which the contract is concluded;

"durable medium" means any instrument which enables a consumer to store information addressed personally to him in a way accessible for future reference for a period of time adequate for the purposes of the information and which allows the unchanged reproduction of the information stored;

"EEA supplier" means a supplier who is a national of an EEA State, or a company or firm (within the meaning of Article 48 of the Treaty establishing the European Community) formed in accordance with the law of an EEA State;

"EEA State" means a State which is a contracting party to the Agreement on the European Economic Area signed at Oporto on 2nd May 1992, as adjusted by the Protocol signed at Brussels on 17th March 1993;

"exempt regulated activity" has the same meaning as in section 325(2) of the 2000 Act;

"financial service" means any service of a banking, credit, insurance, personal pension, investment or payment nature;

"means of distance communication" means any means which, without the simultaneous physical presence of the supplier and the consumer, may be used for the marketing of a service between those parties;

"the OFT" means the Office of Fair Trading;

"regulated activity" has the same meaning as in section 22 of the 2000 Act (the classes of activity and categories of investment);

"Regulated Activities Order" means the Financial Services and Markets Act 2000 (Regulated Activities) Order 2001;

"rule" means a rule—

(a) made by the Authority under the 2000 Act, or

(b) made by a designated professional body, and approved by the Authority, under section 332 of the 2000 Act,

as the context requires;

"supplier" means any person who, acting in his commercial or professional capacity, is the contractual provider of services.

(2) In these Regulations, subject to paragraph (1), any expression used in these Regulations which is also used in the Directive has the same meaning as in the Directive.

3   Scope of these Regulations

(1) Regulations 7 to 14 apply, subject to regulations 4 and 5, in relation to distance contracts made on or after 31st October 2004.

(2) Regulation 15 applies in relation to financial services supplied on or after 31st October 2004 under an organised distance sales or service-provision scheme run by the supplier or by an intermediary, who, for the purpose of that supply, makes exclusive use of one or more means of distance communication up to and including the time at which the financial services are supplied.

4. (1) Where an EEA State, other than the United Kingdom, has transposed the Directive or has obligations in its domestic law corresponding to those provided for in the Directive—

    (a) regulations 7 to 14 do not apply in relation to any contract made between an EEA supplier contracting from an establishment in that EEA State and a consumer in the United Kingdom, and

    (b) regulation 15 does not apply to any supply of financial services by an EEA supplier from an establishment in that EEA State to a consumer in the United Kingdom,

if the provisions by which that State has transposed the Directive, or the obligations in the domestic law of that State corresponding to those provided for in the Directive, as the case may be, apply to that contract or that supply.

    (2) Subject to paragraph (5) and regulation 6(3) and (4)—

    (a) regulations 7 to 11 do not apply in relation to any contract made by a supplier who is an authorised person, the making or performance of which constitutes or is part of a regulated activity carried on by him;

    (b) regulation 15 does not apply to any supply of financial services by a supplier who is an authorised person, where that supply constitutes or is part of a regulated activity carried on by him.

    (3) Subject to regulation 6(3) and (4)—

    (a) regulations 7 and 8 do not apply in relation to any contract made by a supplier who is an appointed representative, the making or performance of which constitutes or is part of a regulated activity (other than an exempt regulated activity) carried on by him;

    (b) regulation 15 does not apply to any supply of financial services by a supplier who is an appointed representative, where that supply constitutes or is part of a regulated activity (other than an exempt regulated activity) carried on by him.

    (4) Subject to regulation 6(3) and (4)—

    (a) regulations 7 and 8 do not apply in relation to any contract where—

      (i) the supplier is bound, or is controlled or managed by one or more persons who are bound, by rules of a designated professional body which are equivalent to those regulations, and

      (ii) the making or performance of that contract constitutes or is part of an exempt regulated activity carried on by the supplier;

    (b) regulation 15 does not apply to any supply of financial services where—

      (i) the supplier is bound, or is controlled or managed by one or more persons who are bound, by rules of a designated professional body which are equivalent to that regulation, and

      (ii) that supply constitutes or is part of an exempt regulated activity carried on by the supplier.

    (5) Paragraph (2) does not apply in relation to any contract or supply of financial services made by a supplier who is the operator, trustee or depositary of a scheme which is a recognised scheme by virtue of section 264 of the 2000 Act (schemes constituted in other EEA States), where the making or performance of the contract or the supply of the financial services constitutes or is part of a regulated activity for which he has permission in that capacity.

    (6) In paragraph (5)—

"the operator", "trustee" and "depositary" each has the same meaning as in section 237(2) of the 2000 Act (other definitions); and

"permission" has the same meaning as in section 266 of that Act (disapplication of rules).

5. (1) Where a consumer and a supplier enter an initial service agreement and—

    (a) successive operations of the same nature, or

    (b) a series of separate operations of the same nature,

are subsequently performed between them over time and within the framework of that agreement, then, if any of regulations 7 to 14 apply, they apply only to the initial service agreement.

(2) Where a consumer and a supplier do not enter an initial service agreement and—

(a) successive operations of the same nature, or

(b) a series of separate operations of the same nature,

are performed between them over time, then, if regulations 7 and 8 apply, they apply only—

    (i) when the first operation is performed, and

    (ii) to any operation which is performed more than one year after the previous operation.

(3) For the purposes of this regulation, "initial service agreement" includes, for example, an agreement for the provision of—

(a) a bank account;

(b) a credit card; or

(c) portfolio management services.

(4) For the purposes of this regulation, "operations" includes, for example—

(a) deposits to or withdrawals from a bank account;

(b) payments by a credit card;

(c) transactions carried out within the framework of an initial service agreement for portfolio management services; and

(d) subscriptions to new units of the same collective investment fund,

but does not include adding new elements to an existing initial service agreement, for example adding the possibility of using an electronic payment instrument together with an existing bank account.

6 Financial services marketed by an intermediary

(1) This regulation applies where a financial service is marketed by an intermediary.

(2) These Regulations have effect as if—

(a) each reference to a supplier in the definition of "breach" in regulation 2(1) were a reference to a supplier or an intermediary;

(b) the reference to the supplier in the definition of "means of distance communication" in regulation 2(1), each reference to the supplier in regulations 7, 8(1) and (2), 10 and 11(3)(b), and the first reference to the supplier in regulation 8(4), were a reference to the intermediary;

(c) the reference to the supplier in regulation 8(3) were a reference to the supplier or the intermediary;

(d) for regulation 11(2) there were substituted—

"(2) Paragraph (1) does not apply to a distance contract if the intermediary has not complied with regulation 8(1) (and the supplier has not done what the intermediary was required to do by regulation 8(1)), unless—

    (a) the circumstances fall within regulation 8(1)(b); and

    (b) either—

        (i) the intermediary has complied with regulation 7(1) and (2) or, if applicable, regulation 7(4)(b), and with regulation 7(5), or

        (ii) the supplier has done what the intermediary was required to do by regulation 7(1) and (2) or, if applicable, regulation 7(4)(b), and by regulation 7(5).";

(e) the reference to a supplier in regulation 22(1) were a reference to an intermediary; and

(f) each reference to the supplier in paragraphs 2, 4, 5 and 19 of Schedule 1 were a reference to the supplier and the intermediary.

(3) Notwithstanding paragraphs (2) to (4) of regulation 4, regulations 7 and 8 apply in relation to the intermediary unless—

(a) the intermediary is an authorised person and the marketing of the financial service constitutes or is part of a regulated activity carried on by him;

(b) the intermediary is an appointed representative and the marketing of the financial service constitutes or is part of a regulated activity (other than an exempt regulated activity) carried on by him; or

    (c) the intermediary is not an authorised person, but—
      (i)   he is bound, or is controlled or managed by one or more persons who are bound, by rules of a designated professional body which are equivalent to regulations 7 and 8, and
      (ii) the marketing of the financial service constitutes or is part of an exempt regulated activity carried on by him.

(4) Notwithstanding paragraphs (2) to (4) of regulation 4, regulation 15 applies to the intermediary unless—
    (a) the intermediary is an authorised person and is acting in the course of a regulated activity carried on by him;
    (b) the intermediary is an appointed representative and is acting in the course of a regulated activity (other than an exempt regulated activity) carried on by him; or
    (c) the intermediary is not an authorised person, but—
      (i)   he is bound, or is controlled or managed by one or more persons who are bound, by rules of a designated professional body which are equivalent to regulation 15, and
      (ii) he is acting in the course of an exempt regulated activity carried on by him.

7   Information required prior to the conclusion of the contract

(1) Subject to paragraph (4), in good time prior to the consumer being bound by any distance contract, the supplier shall provide to the consumer the information specified in Schedule 1.

(2) The supplier shall provide the information specified in Schedule 1 in a clear and comprehensible manner appropriate to the means of distance communication used, with due regard in particular to the principles of good faith in commercial transactions and the principles governing the protection of those who are unable to give their consent such as minors.

(3) Subject to paragraph (4), the supplier shall make clear his commercial purpose when providing the information specified in Schedule 1.

(4) In the case of a voice telephone communication—
    (a) the supplier shall make clear his identity and the commercial purpose of any call initiated by him at the beginning of any conversation with the consumer; and
    (b) if the consumer explicitly consents, only the information specified in Schedule 2 need be given.

(5) The supplier shall ensure that the information he provides to the consumer pursuant to this regulation, regarding the contractual obligations which would arise if the distance contract were concluded, accurately reflects the contractual obligations which would arise under the law presumed to be applicable to that contract.

8   Written and additional information

(1) The supplier under a distance contract shall communicate to the consumer on paper, or in another durable medium which is available and accessible to the consumer, all the contractual terms and conditions and the information specified in Schedule 1, either—
    (a) in good time prior to the consumer being bound by that distance contract; or
    (b) immediately after the conclusion of the contract, where the contract has been concluded at the consumer's request using a means of distance communication which does not enable provision in accordance with sub-paragraph (a) of the contractual terms and conditions and the information specified in Schedule 1.

(2) The supplier shall communicate the contractual terms and conditions to the consumer on paper, if the consumer so requests at any time during their contractual relationship.

(3) Paragraph (2) does not apply if the supplier has already communicated the contractual terms and conditions to the consumer on paper during that contractual relationship, and those terms and conditions have not changed since they were so communicated.

(4) The supplier shall change the means of distance communication with the consumer if the consumer so requests at any time during his contractual relationship with the supplier, unless that is incompatible with the distance contract or the nature of the financial service provided to the consumer.

9   Right to cancel

(1) Subject to regulation 11, if within the cancellation period set out in regulation 10 notice of cancellation is properly given by the consumer to the supplier, the notice of cancellation shall operate to cancel the distance contract.

(2) Cancelling the contract has the effect of terminating the contract at the time at which the notice of cancellation is given.

(3) For the purposes of these Regulations, a notice of cancellation is a notification given—

    (a) orally (where the supplier has informed the consumer that notice of cancellation may be given orally),

    (b) in writing, or

    (c) in another durable medium available and accessible to the supplier,

which, however expressed, indicates the intention of the consumer to cancel the contract by that notification.

(4) Notice of cancellation given under this regulation by a consumer to a supplier is to be treated as having been properly given if the consumer—

    (a) gives it orally to the supplier (where the supplier has informed the consumer that notice of cancellation may be given orally);

    (b) leaves it at the address of the supplier last known to the consumer and addressed to the supplier by name (in which case it is to be taken to have been given on the day on which it was left);

    (c) sends it by post to the address of the supplier last known to the consumer and addressed to the supplier by name (in which case it is to be taken to have been given on the day on which it was posted);

    (d) sends it by facsimile to the business facsimile number of the supplier last known to the consumer (in which case it is to be taken to have been given on the day on which it was sent);

    (e) sends it by electronic mail to the business electronic mail address of the supplier last known to the consumer (in which case it is to be taken to have been given on the day on which it is sent); or

    (f) by other electronic means—

        (i)   sends it to an internet address or web-site which the supplier has notified

        (ii)   the consumer may be used for the purpose, or

        (iii) indicates it on such a web-site in accordance with instructions which are on the web-site or which the supplier has provided to the consumer, (in which case it is to be taken to have been given on the day on which it is sent to that address or web-site or indicated on that web-site).

(5) The references in paragraph (4)(b) and (c) to the address of the supplier shall, in the case of a supplier which is a body corporate, be treated as including a reference to the address of the secretary or clerk of that body.

(6) The references in paragraph (4)(b) and (c) to the address of the supplier shall, in the case of a supplier which is a partnership, be treated as including a reference to the address of a partner or a person having control or management of the partnership business.

(7) In this regulation—

    (a) every reference to the supplier includes a reference to any other person previously notified by or on behalf of the supplier to the consumer as a person to whom notice of cancellation may be given;

    (b) the references to giving notice of cancellation orally include giving such notice by voice telephone communication, where the supplier has informed the consumer that notice of cancellation may be given in that way; and

    (c) "electronic mail" has the same meaning as in regulation 2(1) of the Privacy and Electronic Communications (EC Directive) Regulations 2003 (interpretation).

10   Cancellation period

(1) For the purposes of regulation 9, the cancellation period begins on the day on which the distance contract is concluded ("conclusion day") and ends as provided for in paragraphs (2) to (5).

(2) Where the supplier complies with regulation 8(1) on or before conclusion day, the cancellation period ends on the expiry of fourteen calendar days beginning with the day after conclusion day.

(3) Where the supplier does not comply with regulation 8(1) on or before conclusion day, but subsequently communicates to the consumer on paper, or in another durable medium which is available and accessible to the consumer, all the contractual terms and conditions and the information required under regulation 8(1), the cancellation period ends on the expiry of fourteen calendar days beginning with the day after the day on which the consumer receives the last of those terms and conditions and that information.

(4) In the case of a distance contract relating to life insurance, for the references to conclusion day in paragraphs (2) and (3) there are substituted references to the day on which the consumer is informed that the distance contract has been concluded.

(5) In the case of a distance contract relating to life insurance or a personal pension, for the references to fourteen calendar days in paragraphs (2) and (3) there are substituted references to thirty calendar days.

11   Exceptions to the right to cancel

(1) Subject to paragraphs (2) and (3), regulation 9 does not confer on a consumer a right to cancel a distance contract which is—

(a) a contract for a financial service where the price of that service depends on fluctuations in the financial market outside the supplier's control, which may occur during the cancellation period, such as services related to—

    (i)   foreign exchange,

    (ii)   money market instruments,

    (iii)   transferable securities,

    (iv)   units in collective investment undertakings,

    (v)   financial-futures contracts, including equivalent cash-settled instruments,

    (vi)   forward interest-rate agreements,

    (vii)   interest-rate, currency and equity swaps,

    (viii) options to acquire or dispose of any instruments referred to in sub-paragraphs (i) to (vii), including cash-settled instruments and options on currency and on interest rates;

(b) a contract whose performance has been fully completed by both parties at the consumer's express request before the consumer gives notice of cancellation;

(c) a contract which—

    (i)   is a connected contract of insurance within the meaning of article 72B(1) of the Regulated Activities Order (activities carried on by a provider of relevant goods or services),

    (ii)   covers travel risks within the meaning of article 72B(1)(d)(ii) of that Order, and

    (iii)   has a total duration of less than one month;

(d) a contract under which a supplier provides credit to a consumer and the consumer's obligation to repay is secured by a legal mortgage on land;

(e) a credit agreement cancelled under regulation 15(1) of the Consumer Protection (Distance Selling) Regulations 2000 (automatic cancellation of a related credit agreement);

(f) a credit agreement cancelled under section 6A of the Timeshare Act 1992 (automatic cancellation of timeshare credit agreement); or

(g) a restricted-use credit agreement (within the meaning of the 1974 Act) to finance the purchase of land or an existing building, or an agreement for a bridging loan in connection with the purchase of land or an existing building.

(2) Paragraph (1) does not apply to a distance contract if the supplier has not complied with regulation 8(1), unless—

    (a) the circumstances fall within regulation 8(1)(b); and

    (b) the supplier has complied with regulation 7(1) and (2) or, if applicable, regulation 7(4)(b), and with regulation 7(5).

(3) Where—

    (a) the conditions in sub-paragraphs (a) and (b) of paragraph (2) are satisfied in relation to a distance contract falling within paragraph (1),

    (b) the supplier has not complied with regulation 8(1), and

    (c) the consumer has not, by the end of the sixth day after the day on which the distance contract is concluded, received all the contractual terms and conditions and the information required under regulation 8(1),

the consumer may cancel the contract under regulation 9 during the period beginning on the seventh day after the day on which the distance contract is concluded and ending when he receives the last of the contractual terms and conditions and the information required under regulation 8(1).

12   Automatic cancellation of an attached distance contract

(1) For the purposes of this regulation, where there is a distance contract for the provision of a financial service by a supplier to a consumer ("the main contract") and there is a further distance contract ("the secondary contract") for the provision to that consumer of a further financial service by—

    (a) the same supplier, or

    (b) a third party, the further financial service being provided pursuant to an agreement between the third party and the supplier under the main contract,

then the secondary contract (referred to in these Regulations as an "attached contract") is attached to the main contract if any of the conditions in paragraph (2) are satisfied.

(2) The conditions referred to in paragraph (1) are—

    (a) the secondary contract is entered into in compliance with a term of the main contract;

    (b) the main contract is, or is to be, financed by the secondary contract;

    (c) the main contract is a debtor-creditor-supplier agreement within the meaning of the 1974 Act, and the secondary contract is, or is to be, financed by the main contract;

    (d) the secondary contract is entered into by the consumer to induce the supplier to enter into the main contract;

    (e) performance of the secondary contract requires performance of the main contract.

(3) Where a main contract is cancelled by a notice of cancellation given under regulation 9—

    (a) the cancellation of the main contract also operates to cancel, at the time at which the main contract is cancelled, any attached contract which is not a contract or agreement of a type listed in regulation 11(1); and

    (b) the supplier under the main contract shall, if he is not the supplier under the attached contract, forthwith on receipt of the notice of cancellation inform the supplier under the attached contract.

(4) Paragraph (3)(a) does not apply to an attached contract if, at or before the time at which the notice of cancellation in respect of the main contract is given, the consumer has given and not withdrawn a notice to the supplier under the main contract that cancellation of the main contract is not to operate to cancel that attached contract.

(5) Where a main contract made by an authorised person, the making or performance of which constitutes or is part of a regulated activity carried on by him, is cancelled under rules made by the Authority corresponding to regulation 9—

    (a) the cancellation of the main contract also operates to cancel, at the time at which the main contract is cancelled, any attached contract which is not a contract or agreement of a type listed in regulation 11(1); and

    (b) the supplier under the main contract shall, if he is not the supplier under the attached contract, inform the supplier under the attached contract forthwith on receiving notification of the consumer's intention to cancel the main contract by that notification.

(6) Paragraph (5)(a) does not apply to an attached contract if, at or before the time at which the consumer gives notification of his intention to cancel the main contract by that notification, the consumer has given and not withdrawn a notice to the supplier under the main contract that cancellation of the main contract is not to operate to cancel that attached contract.

13   Payment for services provided before cancellation

(1) This regulation applies where a cancellation event occurs in relation to a distance contract.

(2) In this regulation, "cancellation event" means the cancellation of a distance contract under regulation 9 or 12.

(3) The supplier shall refund any sum paid by or on behalf of the consumer under or in relation to the contract to the person by whom it was paid, less any charge made in accordance with paragraph (6), as soon as possible and in any event within a period not exceeding 30 calendar days beginning with—

  (a) the day on which the cancellation event occurred; or

  (b) if the supplier proves that this is later—

    (i)   in the case of a contract cancelled under regulation 9, the day on which the supplier in fact received the notice of cancellation, or

    (ii) in the case of an attached contract under which the supplier is not the supplier under the main contract, the day on which, pursuant to regulation 12(3)(b) or (5)(b), he was in fact informed by the supplier under the main contract of the cancellation of the main contract.

(4) The reference in paragraph (3) to any sum paid on behalf of the consumer includes any sum paid by any other person ("the creditor"), who is not the supplier, under an agreement between the consumer and the creditor by which the creditor provides the consumer with credit of any amount.

(5) Where any security has been provided in relation to the contract, the security (so far as it has been provided) shall, on cancellation under regulation 9 or 12, be treated as never having had effect; and any property lodged solely for the purposes of the security as so provided shall be returned forthwith by the person with whom it is lodged.

(6) Subject to paragraphs (7), (8) and (9), the supplier may make a charge for any service actually provided by the supplier in accordance with the contract.

(7) The charge shall not exceed an amount which is in proportion to the extent of the service provided to the consumer prior to the time at which the cancellation event occurred (including the service of arranging to provide the financial service) in comparison with the full coverage of the contract, and in any event shall not be such that it could be construed as a penalty.

(8) The supplier may not make any charge unless he can prove on the balance of probabilities that the consumer was informed about the amount payable in accordance with—

  (a) regulation 7(1) and paragraph 13 of Schedule 1,

  (b) regulation 7(4) and paragraph 5 of Schedule 2, or

  (c) rules corresponding to those provisions, as the case may be.

(9) The supplier may not make any charge if, without the consumer's prior request, he commenced performance of the contract prior to the expiry of the relevant cancellation period.

(10) In paragraph (9), the relevant cancellation period is the cancellation period which—

  (a) in the case of a main contract, is applicable to that contract, or

  (b) in the case of an attached contract, would be applicable to that contract if that contract were a main contract,

under regulation 10, or under rules corresponding to that regulation, as the case may be.

(11) The consumer shall, as soon as possible and in any event within a period not exceeding 30 calendar days beginning with the day on which the cancellation event occurred—

  (a) refund any sum paid by or on behalf of the supplier under or in relation to that contract to the person by whom it was paid; and

  (b) either restore to the supplier any property of which he has acquired possession under that contract, or deliver or send that property to any person to whom, under regulation 9, a notice of cancellation could have been given in respect of that contract.

(12) Breach of a duty imposed by paragraph (11) on a consumer is actionable as a breach of statutory duty.

14 Payment by card

(1) Subject to paragraph (2), where—

(a) a payment card has been issued to an individual who, when entering the contract for the provision of that card, was acting for purposes which were outside any business he may carry on ("the card-holder"), and

(b) fraudulent use is made of that card to make a payment under or in connection with a distance contract to which these Regulations apply, by another person who is neither acting, nor to be treated as acting, as the card-holder's agent,

the card-holder may request cancellation of that payment, and is entitled to be recredited with the sum paid, or to have it returned, by the card issuer.

(2) Where paragraph (1) applies and, in any proceedings, the card-holder alleges that any use made of the payment card was not authorised by him, it is for the card issuer to prove that the use was so authorised.

(3) Paragraph (1) does not apply if the contract for the provision of the payment card is an agreement to which section 83(1) of the 1974 Act (liability for misuse of credit facilities) applies.

(4) After subsection (3B) of section 84 of the 1974 Act (misuse of credit-tokens) insert—

"(3C) Subsections (1) and (2) shall not apply to any use, in connection with a distance contract within the meaning of the Financial Services (Distance Marketing) Regulations 2004, of a card which is a credit-token.".

(5) For the purposes of this regulation—

"card issuer" means the owner of the card;

"payment card" includes a credit card, a charge card, a debit card and a store card.

15 Unsolicited services

(1) A person ("the recipient") who receives unsolicited financial services for purposes other than those of his business from another person who supplies those services in the course of his business, shall not thereby become subject to any obligation (to make payment, or otherwise).

(2) Where, in the course of any business—

(a) unsolicited financial services are supplied for purposes other than those of the recipient's business, and

(b) a person includes with the supply of those services a demand for payment, or an assertion of a present or prospective right to payment in respect of those services,

that person is guilty of an offence and liable, on summary conviction, to a fine not exceeding level 4 on the standard scale.

(3) A person who, not having reasonable cause to believe that there is a right to payment, in the course of any business and with a view to obtaining payment for what he knows are unsolicited financial services supplied as mentioned in paragraph (2)—

(a) threatens to bring any legal proceedings,

(b) places or causes to be placed the name of any person on a list of defaulters or debtors or threatens to do so, or

(c) invokes or causes to be invoked any other collection procedure or threatens to do so,

is guilty of an offence and liable, on summary conviction, to a fine not exceeding level 5 on the standard scale.

(4) In this regulation, "unsolicited" means, in relation to financial services supplied to any person, that they are supplied without any prior request made by or on behalf of that person.

(5) For the purposes of this regulation, a person who sends to a recipient an invoice or similar document which—

(a) states the amount of a payment, and

(b) does not comply with the requirements, applicable to invoices and similar documents, of regulations made under section 3A of the Unsolicited Goods and Services Act 1971 (contents and form of notes of agreement, invoices and similar documents) or, as the case may be, article 6 of the Unsolicited Goods and Services (Northern Ireland) Order 1976 (contents and form of notes of agreement, invoices and similar documents),

is to be regarded as asserting a right to the payment.

(6) Section 3A of the Unsolicited Goods and Services Act 1971 applies for the purposes of this regulation in its application to England, Wales and Scotland as it applies for the purposes of that Act.

(7) Article 6 of the Unsolicited Goods and Services (Northern Ireland) Order 1976 applies for the purposes of this regulation in its application to Northern Ireland as it applies for the purposes of that Order.

(8) This regulation is without prejudice to any right a supplier may have at any time, by contract or otherwise, to renew a distance contract with a consumer without any request made by or on behalf of that consumer prior to the renewal of that contract.

16 Prevention of contracting-out

(1) A term contained in any contract is void if, and to the extent that, it is inconsistent with the application of a provision of these Regulations to a distance contract or the application of regulation 15 to a supply of unsolicited financial services.

(2) Where a provision of these Regulations specifies a duty or liability of the consumer in certain circumstances, a term contained in a contract is inconsistent with that provision if it purports to impose, directly or indirectly, an additional or greater duty or liability on him in those circumstances.

(3) These Regulations apply notwithstanding any contract term which applies or purports to apply the law of a State which is not an EEA State if the contract or supply has a close connection with the territory of an EEA State.

17 Enforcement authorities

(1) For the purposes of regulations 18 to 21—

  (a) in relation to any alleged breach concerning a specified contract, the Authority is the enforcement authority;

  (b) in relation to any alleged breach concerning a contract under which the supplier is a local authority, but which is not a specified contract, the OFT is the enforcement authority;

  (c) in relation to any other alleged breach—

    (i) the OFT, and

    (ii) in Great Britain every local weights and measures authority, and in Northern Ireland the Department of Enterprise, Trade and Investment, is an enforcement authority.

(2) For the purposes of paragraph (1) and regulation 22(6), each of the following is a specified contract—

  (a) a contract the making or performance of which constitutes or is part of a regulated activity carried on by the supplier;

  (b) a contract for the provision of a debit card;

  (c) a contract relating to the issuing of electronic money by a supplier to whom the Authority has given a certificate under article 9C of the Regulated Activities Order (persons certified as small issuers etc.);

  (d) a contract the effecting or carrying out of which is excluded from article 10(1) or (2) of the Regulated Activities Order (effecting and carrying out contracts of insurance) by article 12 of that order (breakdown insurance), where the supplier is a person who does not otherwise carry on an activity of the kind specified by article 10 of that order;

  (e) a contract under which a supplier provides credit to a consumer and the obligation of the consumer to repay is secured by a first legal mortgage on land;

  (f) a contract, made before 14th January 2005, for insurance mediation activity other than in respect of a contract of long-term care insurance.

(3) For the purposes of the application of this regulation and regulations 18 to 22 in relation to breaches of, and offences under, regulation 15, "contract"—

    (a) wherever it appears in this regulation other than in the expression "contract of long-term care insurance", and

    (b) in regulation 22(6),

is to be taken to mean "supply of financial services".

(4) For the purposes of this regulation—

"contract of long-term care insurance" has the same meaning as in the Financial Services and Markets Act 2000 (Regulated Activities) (Amendment) (No. 2) Order 2003;

"insurance mediation activity" means any activity which is not a regulated activity at the time the contract is made but will be a regulated activity of the kind specified by article 21, 25(1) or (2), 39A or 53 of the Regulated Activities Order when the amendments to that order made by the Financial Services and Markets Act 2000 (Regulated Activities) (Amendment) (No. 2) Order 2003 come into force;

"local authority" means—

    (a) in England and Wales, a local authority within the meaning of the Local Government Act 1972, the Greater London Authority, the Common Council of the City of London or the Council of the Isles of Scilly,

    (b) in Scotland, a council constituted under section 2 of the Local Government etc. (Scotland) Act 1994, and

    (c) in Northern Ireland, a district council within the meaning of the Local Government Act (Northern Ireland) 1972.

18   Consideration of complaints

(1) An enforcement authority shall consider any complaint made to it about a breach unless—

    (a) the complaint appears to that authority to be frivolous or vexatious; or

    (b) that authority is aware that another enforcement authority has notified the OFT that it agrees to consider the complaint.

(2) If an enforcement authority notifies the OFT that it agrees to consider a complaint made to another enforcement authority, the first mentioned authority shall be under a duty to consider the complaint.

19   Injunctions to secure compliance with these Regulations

(1) Subject to paragraph (2), an enforcement authority may apply for an injunction (including an interim injunction) against any person who appears to that authority to be responsible for a breach.

(2) An enforcement authority, other than the OFT or the Authority, may apply for an injunction only where—

    (a) that authority has notified the OFT, at least fourteen days before the date on which the application is to be made, of its intention to apply; or

    (b) the OFT consents to the application being made within a shorter period.

(3) On an application made under this regulation, the court may grant an injunction on such terms as it thinks fit to secure compliance with these Regulations.

(4) An enforcement authority which has a duty under regulation 18 to consider a complaint shall give reasons for its decision to apply or not to apply, as the case may be, for an injunction.

(5) In deciding whether or not to apply for an injunction in respect of a breach, an enforcement authority may, if it considers it appropriate to do so, have regard to any undertaking as to compliance with these Regulations given to it or to another enforcement authority by or on behalf of any person.

(6) In the application of this regulation to Scotland, for references to an "injunction" or an "interim injunction" there are substituted references to an "interdict" or an "interim interdict" respectively.

20   Notification of undertakings and orders to the OFT

An enforcement authority, other than the OFT and the Authority, shall notify the OFT of—

    (a) any undertaking given to it by or on behalf of any person who appears to it to be responsible for a breach;

(b) the outcome of any application made by it under regulation 19 and the terms of any undertaking given to, or order made by, the court; and

(c) the outcome of any application made by it to enforce a previous order of the court.

21 Publication, information and advice

(1) The OFT shall arrange for the publication, in such form and manner as it considers appropriate, of details of any undertaking or order notified to it under regulation 20.

(2) Each of the OFT and the Authority shall arrange for the publication in such form and manner
as it considers appropriate of—

(a) details of any undertaking as to compliance with these Regulations given to it by or on
behalf of any person;

(b) details of any application made by it under regulation 19(a), and of the terms of any
undertaking given to, or order made by, the court; and

(c) details of any application made by it to enforce a previous order of the court.

(3) Each of the OFT and the Authority may arrange for the dissemination, in such form and manner as it considers appropriate, of such information and advice concerning the operation of these
Regulations as may appear to it to be expedient to give to the public and to all persons likely to be
affected by these Regulations.

22 Offences

(1) A supplier under a distance contract who fails to comply with regulation 7(3) or (4)(a) or
regulation 8(2) or (4) is guilty of an offence and liable, on summary conviction, to a fine not exceeding level 3 on the standard scale.

(2) If an offence under paragraph (1), or under regulation 15(2) or (3), committed by a body
corporate is shown—

(a) to have been committed with the consent or connivance of any director, manager, secretary or other similar officer of the body corporate, or any person who was purporting to act
in any such capacity, or

(b) to be attributable to any neglect on his part,

he as well as the body corporate is guilty of the offence and liable to be proceeded against and punished accordingly.

(3) If the affairs of a body corporate are managed by its members, paragraph (2) applies in relation to the acts and defaults of a member in connection with his functions of management as if he were
a director of the body.

(4) If an offence under paragraph (1), or under regulation 15(2) or (3), committed by a partnership is shown—

(a) to have been committed with the consent or connivance of any partner, or any person who
was purporting to act as a partner, or

(b) to be attributable to any neglect on his part,

he as well as the partnership is guilty of an offence and liable to be proceeded against and punished
accordingly.

(5) If an offence under paragraph (1), or under regulation 15(2) or (3), committed by an unincorporated association (other than a partnership) is shown—

(a) to have been committed with the consent or connivance of an officer of the association or
a member of its governing body, or any person who was purporting to act in any such capacity, or

(b) to be attributable to any neglect on his part,

he as well as the association is guilty of an offence and liable to be proceeded against and punished
accordingly.

(6) Except in Scotland—

(a) the Authority may institute proceedings for an offence under these Regulations which
relates to a specified contract;

  (b) the OFT, and—
    (i) in Great Britain, every local weights and measures authority,
    (ii) in Northern Ireland, the Department of Enterprise, Trade and Investment, may insti-
    tute proceedings for any other offence under these Regulations.

23 Functions of the Authority

The functions conferred on the Authority by these Regulations shall be treated as if they were conferred by the 2000 Act.

24 Amendment of the Unfair Terms in Consumer Contracts Regulations 1999

(1) The Unfair Terms in Consumer Contracts Regulations 1999 are amended as follows.
(2) After regulation 3(1) (interpretation), insert—
"(1A) The references—
  (a) in regulation 4(1) to a seller or a supplier, and
  (b) in regulation 8(1) to a seller or supplier,
include references to a distance supplier and to an intermediary.
(1B) In paragraph (1A) and regulation 5(6)—
'distance supplier' means—
  (a) a supplier under a distance contract within the meaning of the Financial Ser vices (Distance
    Marketing) Regulations 2004, or
  (b) a supplier of unsolicited financial services within regulation 15 of those Regulations; and
'intermediary' has the same meaning as in those Regulations."
(3) After regulation 5(5) (unfair terms), insert—
"(6) Any contractual term providing that a consumer bears the burden of proof in respect of
showing whether a distance supplier or an intermediary complied with any or all of the obligations
placed upon him resulting from the Directive and any rule or enactment implementing it shall always
be regarded as unfair.
(7) In paragraph (6)—
'the Directive' means Directive 2002/65/EC of the European Parliament and of the Council of 23
September 2002 concerning the distance marketing of consumer financial services and amending
Council Directive 90/619/EEC and Directives 97/7/EC and 98/27/EC; and
'rule' means a rule made by the Financial Services Authority under the Financial Services and
Markets Act 2000 or by a designated professional body within the meaning of section 326(2) of that
Act.".

25 *(Amends the Consumer Protection (Distance Selling) Regulations 2000, earlier)*

26 Amendment of the Enterprise Act 2002

In Part 1 of Schedule 13 to the Enterprise Act 2002 (listed directives), after paragraph 9 insert—
 "(9A) Directive 2002/65/EC of the European Parliament and of the Council of 23 September
2002 concerning the distance marketing of consumer financial services and amending Council
Directive 90/619/EEC and Directives *97/7/EC* and 98/27/EC".

27 Amendment of the Enterprise Act 2002 (Part 8 Community Infringements Specified UK Laws) Order 2003

In the table in the Schedule to the Enterprise Act 2002 (Part 8 Community Infringements Specified
UK Laws) Order 2003 (listed directives), after the entry for Directive 2000/31/EC ("Directive on elec-
tronic commerce") insert—
 "Directive 2002/65/EC of the European Parliament and of the Council of 23 September 2002
concerning the distance marketing of consumer financial services and amending Council Directive
90/619/EEC and Directives 97/7/EC and 98/27/EC. Financial Services (Distance Marketing)
Regulations 2004; rules corresponding to any provisions of those Regulations made by the Financial
Services Authority or a designated professional body within the meaning of section 326(2) of the
Financial Services and Markets Act 2000."

28 Amendment of the Enterprise Act 2002 (Part 8 Notice to OFT of Intended Prosecution Specified Enactments, Revocation and Transitional Provision) Order 2003

In the table in the Schedule to the Enterprise Act 2002 (Part 8 Notice to OFT of Intended Prosecution Specified Enactments, Revocation and Transitional Provision) Order 2003, after the entry for the Fair Trading Act 1973 insert—

"Financial Services (Distance Marketing) Regulations 2004. All offences under those Regulations."

29 Transitional provisions

(1) In relation to any contract made before 31st May 2005 which is a consumer credit agreement within the meaning of the 1974 Act and a regulated agreement within the meaning of that Act—

    (a) regulations 7, 8, 10 and 11 apply subject to the modifications in paragraphs (2) to (5); and

    (b) references in these Regulations to regulations 7, 8, 10 and 11 or to provisions contained in them shall be construed accordingly.

(2) In regulation 7—

    (a) in paragraphs (1) to (3), before "Schedule 1" at each place where it occurs insert "paragraph 13 of"; and

    (b) in paragraph (4)(b), before "Schedule 2" insert "paragraph 5 of".

(3) In regulation 8(1), for "contractual terms and conditions and the information specified in" at each place where it occurs substitute "information specified in paragraph 13 of".

(4) In regulation 10(3), omit—

    (a) "the contractual terms and conditions and"; and

    (b) "those terms and conditions and".

(5) In regulation 11(3), omit "the contractual terms and conditions and" at each place where it occurs.

Regulations 7(1) and 8(1)   SCHEDULE 1

Information required prior to the conclusion of the contract

1. The identity and the main business of the supplier, the geographical address at which the supplier is established and any other geographical address relevant to the consumer's relations with the supplier.

2. Where the supplier has a representative established in the consumer's State of residence, the identity of that representative and the geographical address relevant to the consumer's relations with him.

3. Where the consumer's dealings are with any professional other than the supplier, the identity of that professional, the capacity in which he is acting with respect to the consumer, and the geographical address relevant to the consumer's relations with that professional.

4. Where the supplier is registered in a trade or similar public register, the particulars of the register in which the supplier is entered and his registration number or an equivalent means of identification in that register.

5. Where the supplier's activity is subject to an authorisation scheme, the particulars of the relevant supervisory authority.

6. A description of the main characteristics of the financial service.

7. The total price to be paid by the consumer to the supplier for the financial service, including all related fees, charges and expenses, and all taxes paid via the supplier or, where an exact price cannot be indicated, the basis for the calculation of the price enabling the consumer to verify it.

8. Where relevant, notice indicating that: (i) the financial service is related to instruments involving special risks related to their specific features or the operations to be executed or whose price depends on fluctuations in the financial markets outside the supplier's control; and (ii) historical performances are no indicators for future performances.

9. Notice of the possibility that other taxes or costs may exist that are not paid via the supplier or imposed by him.

10. Any limitations of the period for which the information provided is valid.

11. The arrangements for payment and for performance.

12. Any specific additional cost for the consumer of using the means of distance communication, if such additional cost is charged.

13. Whether or not there is a right of cancellation and, where there is a right of cancellation, its duration and the conditions for exercising it, including information on the amount which the consumer may be required to pay in accordance with regulation 13, as well as the consequences of not exercising that right.

14. The minimum duration of the distance contract in the case of financial services to be performed indefinitely or recurrently.

15. Information on any rights the parties may have to terminate the distance contract early or unilaterally by virtue of the terms of the contract, including any penalties imposed by the contract in such cases.

16. Practical instructions for exercising the right to cancel in accordance with regulation 9 indicating, among other things, the address at which the notice of cancellation should be left or to which it should be sent by post, and any facsimile number or electronic mail address to which it should be sent.

17. The EEA State or States whose laws are taken by the supplier as a basis for the establishment of relations with the consumer prior to the conclusion of the distance contract.

18. Any contractual clause on the law applicable to the distance contract or on the competent court.

19. In which language, or languages: (i) the contractual terms and conditions, and the prior information specified in this Schedule, are supplied; and (ii) the supplier, with the agreement of the consumer, undertakes to communicate during the duration of the distance contract.

20. Whether or not there is an out-of-court complaint and redress mechanism for the consumer and, if so, the methods for having access to it.

21. The existence of guarantee funds or other compensation arrangements, except to the extent that they are required by Directive 94/19/EC of the European Parliament and of the Council of 30 May 1994 on deposit guarantee schemes[26] or Directive 97/9/EC of the European Parliament and of the Council of 3 March 1997 on investor compensation schemes.

Regulation 7(4)(B) **SCHEDULE 2**

Information required in the case of voice telephone communications

1. The identity of the person in contact with the consumer and his link with the supplier.

2. A description of the main characteristics of the financial service.

3. The total price to be paid by the consumer to the supplier for the financial service including all taxes paid via the supplier or, if an exact price cannot be indicated, the basis for the calculation of the price enabling the consumer to verify it.

4. Notice of the possibility that other taxes or costs may exist that are not paid via the supplier or imposed by him.

5. Whether or not there is a right to cancel and, where there is such a right, its duration and the conditions for exercising it, including information on the amount which the consumer may be required to pay in accordance with regulation 13, as well as the consequences of not exercising that right.

6. That other information is available on request and the nature of that information.

The Freedom of Information and Data Protection (Appropriate Limit and Fees) Regulations 2004

(SI 2004/3244)

1 Citation and commencement
These Regulations may be cited as the Freedom of Information and Data Protection (Appropriate Limit and Fees) Regulations 2004 and come into force on 1st January 2005.

2 Interpretation
In these Regulations—
"the 2000 Act" means the Freedom of Information Act 2000;
"the 1998 Act" means the Data Protection Act 1998; and
"the appropriate limit" is to be construed in accordance with the provision made in regulation 3.

3 The appropriate limit
(1) This regulation has effect to prescribe the appropriate limit referred to in section 9A(3) and (4) of the 1998 Act and the appropriate limit referred to in section 12(1) and (2) of the 2000 Act.

(2) In the case of a public authority which is listed in Part I of Schedule 1 to the 2000 Act, the appropriate limit is £600.

(3) In the case of any other public authority, the appropriate limit is £450.

4 Estimating the cost of complying with a request-general
(1) This regulation has effect in any case in which a public authority proposes to estimate whether the cost of complying with a relevant request would exceed the appropriate limit.

(2) A relevant request is any request to the extent that it is a request—
(a) for unstructured personal data within the meaning of section 9A(1) of the 1998 Act, and to which section 7(1) of that Act would, apart from the appropriate limit, to any extent apply, or
(b) information to which section 1(1) of the 2000 Act would, apart from the appropriate limit, to any extent apply.

(3) In a case in which this regulation has effect, a public authority may, for the purpose of its estimate, take account only of the costs it reasonably expects to incur in relation to the request in—
(a) determining whether it holds the information,
(b) locating the information, or a document which may contain the information,
(c) retrieving the information, or a document which may contain the information, and
(d) extracting the information from a document containing it.

(4) To the extent to which any of the costs which a public authority takes into account are attributable to the time which persons undertaking any of the activities mentioned in paragraph (3) on behalf of the authority are expected to spend on those activities, those costs are to be estimated at a rate of £25 per person per hour.

The Electronic Commerce Directive (Terrorism Act 2006) Regulations 2007

(SI 2007/1550)

Citation and commencement
1. These Regulations may be cited as the Electronic Commerce Directive (Terrorism Act 2006) Regulations 2007 and shall come into force on 21st June 2007.

Interpretation

2.—(1) In these Regulations—

"the Act" means the Terrorism Act 2006;

"article" has the meaning given in section 20(2) of the Act;

"the Directive" means Directive 2000/31/EC of the European Parliament and of the Council of 8th June 2000 on certain legal aspects of information society services, in particular electronic commerce, in the Internal Market (Directive on electronic commerce);

"information society services"—

(a) has the meaning given in Article 2(a) of the Directive (which refers to Article 1(2) of Directive 98/34/EC of the European Parliament and of the Council of 22nd June 1998 laying down a procedure for the provision of information in the field of technical standards and regulations); and

(b) is summarised in recital 17 of the Directive as covering "any service normally provided for remuneration, at a distance, by means of electronic equipment for the processing (including digital compression) and storage of data, and at the individual request of a recipient of a service";

"recipient of the service" means any person who, for professional ends or otherwise, uses an information society service, in particular for the purposes of seeking information or making it accessible;

"record" has the meaning given in section 20(2) of the Act;

"relevant offence" is an offence under section 1 or 2 of the Act;

"service provider" means a person providing an information society service;

"statement" is to be construed in accordance with section 20(6) of the Act.

(2) For the purposes of these Regulations—

(a) a service provider is established in a particular EEA state if he effectively pursues an economic activity using a fixed establishment in that EEA state for an indefinite period and he is a national of an EEA state or a company or firm as mentioned in Article 48 of the EEC Treaty;

(b) the presence or use in a particular place of equipment or other technical means of providing an information society service does not, of itself, constitute the establishment of a service provider;

(c) where it cannot be determined from which of a number of establishments a given information society service is provided, that service is to be regarded as provided from the establishment where the service provider has the centre of his activities relating to the service,

and references to a person being established in any place must be construed accordingly.

Internal market: UK service providers

3.—(1) If—

(a) in the course of providing information society services, a service provider established in the United Kingdom does anything in an EEA state other than the United Kingdom, and

(b) his action, if done in a part of the United Kingdom, would constitute a relevant offence,

he shall be guilty in that part of the United Kingdom of the offence.

(2) If paragraph (1) applies—

(a) proceedings for the offence may be taken at any place in the United Kingdom; and

(b) the offence may for all incidental purposes be treated as having been committed at any such place.

(3) Paragraph (1) does not apply to a case to which section 17 of the Act applies.

(4) If a person commits a relevant offence only by virtue of paragraph (1) he is liable—

(a) on conviction on indictment, to imprisonment for a term not exceeding two years;

(b) on summary conviction, to imprisonment for a term not exceeding the appropriate period or to a fine not exceeding the appropriate amount.

(5) The appropriate period is—

(a) in the case of a conviction in England and Wales if the offence is committed after the commencement of section 154(1) of the Criminal Justice Act 2003, 12 months;

(b) in any other case, three months.

(6) The appropriate amount is—
    (a) if calculated on a daily basis, £100 per day;
    (b) if not calculated on a daily basis, level 5 on the standard scale.

Internal market: non-UK service providers

4.—(1) Proceedings for a relevant offence shall not be instituted against a non-UK service provider unless the derogation condition is satisfied.

(2) A notice under section 3(3) of the Act shall not be given to a non-UK service provider unless the derogation and cooperation conditions are satisfied.

(3) The derogation condition is that the step mentioned in paragraph (1) or (2) (as the case may be)—
    (a) is necessary to pursue any of the public interest objectives;
    (b) relates to an information society service that prejudices that objective or presents a serious and grave risk of prejudice to it; and
    (c) is proportionate to that objective.

(4) The public interest objectives are—
    (a) public policy, in particular the prevention, investigation, detection and prosecution of a relevant offence;
    (b) public security, including the safeguarding of national security and defence.

(5) The cooperation condition is that—
    (a) a constable has requested the EEA state in which the service provider is established to take appropriate measures and the EEA state has failed to do so; and
    (b) a constable has notified the Commission and the EEA state that it is proposed to take the step mentioned in paragraph (2).

(6) The requirement in paragraph (2) to satisfy the cooperation condition does not apply if—
    (a) it appears to a constable that the step mentioned in paragraph (2) should be taken as a matter of urgency; and
    (b) in the shortest possible time after that step is taken, a constable notifies the Commission and the EEA state in which the service provider is established that the step has been taken, indicating the reason for the urgency.

(7) Appropriate measures are measures which appear to the constable to have equivalent effect under the law of the EEA state to the giving of a notice under section 3(3) of the Act.

(8) In this regulation—
    (a) "the Commission" means the Commission of the European Communities;
    (b) "non-UK service provider" means a service provider who is established in an EEA state other than the United Kingdom.

Exception for mere conduits

5.—(1) A service provider is not capable of being guilty of a relevant offence in respect of anything done in the course of providing so much of an information society service as consists in—
    (a) the provision of access to a communication network; or
    (b) the transmission in a communication network of information provided by a recipient of the service,
if the transmission condition is satisfied.

(2) The transmission condition is that the service provider does not—
    (a) initiate the transmission;
    (b) select the recipient of the transmission; or
    (c) select or modify the information contained in the transmission.

(3) Paragraph (1)(b) does not apply if the information is information to which regulation 6 applies.

(4) For the purposes of this regulation, the provision of access to a communication network and the transmission of information in the network includes the automatic, intermediate and transient storage of information for the purpose of carrying out the transmission in the network.

(5) Paragraph (4) does not apply if the information is stored for longer than is reasonably necessary for the transmission.

Exception for caching

6.—(1) This regulation applies to information which—

(a) is provided by a recipient of the service; and

(b) is the subject of automatic, intermediate and temporary storage which is solely for the purpose of making the onward transmission of the information to other recipients of the service at their request more efficient.

(2) A service provider is not capable of being guilty of a relevant offence in respect of anything done in the course of providing so much of an information society service as consists in the transmission in a communication network of information to which this regulation applies if—

(a) the service provider does not modify the information;

(b) he complies with any conditions attached to having access to the information; and

(c) in a case to which paragraph (3) applies, the service provider expeditiously removes the information or disables access to it.

(3) This paragraph applies if the service provider obtains actual knowledge that—

(a) the information at the initial source of the transmission has been removed from the network;

(b) access to such information has been disabled; or

(c) a court or administrative authority has ordered the removal from the network of, or the disablement of access to, such information.

Exception for hosting

7.—(1) A service provider is not capable of being guilty of a relevant offence in respect of anything done in the course of providing so much of an information society service as consists in the storage of information provided by a recipient of the service if—

(a) the service provider did not know when the information was provided that it was unlawfully terrorism-related; or

(b) upon obtaining actual knowledge that the information was unlawfully terrorism-related, the service provider expeditiously removed the information or disabled access to it.

(2) For the purposes of paragraph (1), information is unlawfully terrorism-related if it is constituted by a statement, or contained in an article or record, which is unlawfully terrorism-related by virtue of section 3(7) of the Act.

(3) Paragraph (1) does not apply if the recipient of the service is acting under the authority or control of the service provider.

Part III

EU Law*

Directive 95/46/EC of the European Parliament and of the Council of 24 October 1995 on the protection of individuals with regard to the processing of personal data and on the free movement of such data

THE EUROPEAN PARLIAMENT AND THE COUNCIL OF THE EUROPEAN UNION,

Having regard to the Treaty establishing the European Community, and in particular Article 100a thereof,

Having regard to the proposal from the Commission[1],

Having regard to the opinion of the Economic and Social Committee[2],

Acting in accordance with the procedure referred to in Article 189b of the Treaty[3],

(1) Whereas the objectives of the Community, as laid down in the Treaty, as amended by the Treaty on European Union, include creating an ever closer union among the peoples of Europe, fostering closer relations between the States belonging to the Community, ensuring economic and social progress by common action to eliminate the barriers which divide Europe, encouraging the constant improvement of the living conditions of its peoples, preserving and strengthening peace and liberty and promoting democracy on the basis of the fundamental rights recognized in the constitution and laws of the Member States and in the European Convention for the Protection of Human Rights and Fundamental Freedoms;

(2) Whereas data-processing systems are designed to serve man; whereas they must, whatever the nationality or residence of natural persons, respect their fundamental rights and freedoms, notably the right to privacy, and contribute to economic and social progress, trade expansion and the well-being of individuals;

(3) Whereas the establishment and functioning of an internal market in which, in accordance with Article 7a of the Treaty, the free movement of goods, persons, services and capital is ensured require not only that personal data should be able to flow freely from one Member State to another, but also that the fundamental rights of individuals should be safeguarded;

(4) Whereas increasingly frequent recourse is being had in the Community to the processing of personal data in the various spheres of economic and social activity; whereas the progress made in information technology is making the processing and exchange of such data considerably easier;

(5) Whereas the economic and social integration resulting from the establishment and functioning of the internal market within the meaning of Article 7a of the Treaty will necessarily lead to a

---

* Only European Community official Documents printed in the Official Journal of the European Union are deemed authentic.

[1] OJ No C 277, 5.11.1990, p. 3 and OJ No C 311, 27.11.1992, p. 30.

[2] OJ No C 159, 17.6.1991, p. 38.

[3] Opinion of the European Parliament of 11 March 1992 (OJ No C 94, 13.4.1992, p. 198), confirmed on 2 December 1993 (OJ No C 342, 20.12.1993, p. 30); Council common position of 20 February 1995 (OJ No C 93, 13.4.1995, p. 1) and Decision of the European Parliament of 15 June 1995 (OJ No C 166, 3.7.1995).

substantial increase in cross-border flows of personal data between all those involved in a private or public capacity in economic and social activity in the Member States; whereas the exchange of personal data between undertakings in different Member States is set to increase; whereas the national authorities in the various Member States are being called upon by virtue of Community law to collaborate and exchange personal data so as to be able to perform their duties or carry out tasks on behalf of an authority in another Member State within the context of the area without internal frontiers as constituted by the internal market;

(6) Whereas, furthermore, the increase in scientific and technical cooperation and the coordinated introduction of new telecommunications networks in the Community necessitate and facilitate cross-border flows of personal data;

(7) Whereas the difference in levels of protection of the rights and freedoms of individuals, notably the right to privacy, with regard to the processing of personal data afforded in the Member States may prevent the transmission of such data from the territory of one Member State to that of another Member State; whereas this difference may therefore constitute an obstacle to the pursuit of a number of economic activities at Community level, distort competition and impede authorities in the discharge of their responsibilities under Community law; whereas this difference in levels of protection is due to the existence of a wide variety of national laws, regulations and administrative provisions;

(8) Whereas, in order to remove the obstacles to flows of personal data, the level of protection of the rights and freedoms of individuals with regard to the processing of such data must be equivalent in all Member States; whereas this objective is vital to the internal market but cannot be achieved by the Member States alone, especially in view of the scale of the divergences which currently exist between the relevant laws in the Member States and the need to coordinate the laws of the Member States so as to ensure that the cross-border flow of personal data is regulated in a consistent manner that is in keeping with the objective of the internal market as provided for in Article 7a of the Treaty; whereas Community action to approximate those laws is therefore needed;

(9) Whereas, given the equivalent protection resulting from the approximation of national laws, the Member States will no longer be able to inhibit the free movement between them of personal data on grounds relating to protection of the rights and freedoms of individuals, and in particular the right to privacy; whereas Member States will be left a margin for manoeuvre, which may, in the context of implementation of the Directive, also be exercised by the business and social partners; whereas Member States will therefore be able to specify in their national law the general conditions governing the lawfulness of data processing; whereas in doing so the Member States shall strive to improve the protection currently provided by their legislation; whereas, within the limits of this margin for manoeuvre and in accordance with Community law, disparities could arise in the implementation of the Directive, and this could have an effect on the movement of data within a Member State as well as within the Community;

(10) Whereas the object of the national laws on the processing of personal data is to protect fundamental rights and freedoms, notably the right to privacy, which is recognized both in Article 8 of the European Convention for the Protection of Human Rights and Fundamental Freedoms and in the general principles of Community law; whereas, for that reason, the approximation of those laws must not result in any lessening of the protection they afford but must, on the contrary, seek to ensure a high level of protection in the Community;

(11) Whereas the principles of the protection of the rights and freedoms of individuals, notably the right to privacy, which are contained in this Directive, give substance to and amplify those contained in the Council of Europe Convention of 28 January 1981 for the Protection of Individuals with regard to Automatic Processing of Personal Data;

(12) Whereas the protection principles must apply to all processing of personal data by any person whose activities are governed by Community law; whereas there should be excluded the processing of data carried out by a natural person in the exercise of activities which are exclusively personal or domestic, such as correspondence and the holding of records of addresses;

(13) Whereas the acitivities referred to in Titles V and VI of the Treaty on European Union regarding public safety, defence, State security or the acitivities of the State in the area of criminal

laws fall outside the scope of Community law, without prejudice to the obligations incumbent upon Member States under Article 56 (2), Article 57 or Article 100a of the Treaty establishing the European Community; whereas the processing of personal data that is necessary to safeguard the economic well-being of the State does not fall within the scope of this Directive where such processing relates to State security matters;

(14) Whereas, given the importance of the developments under way, in the framework of the information society, of the techniques used to capture, transmit, manipulate, record, store or communicate sound and image data relating to natural persons, this Directive should be applicable to processing involving such data;

(15) Whereas the processing of such data is covered by this Directive only if it is automated or if the data processed are contained or are intended to be contained in a filing system structured according to specific criteria relating to individuals, so as to permit easy access to the personal data in question;

(16) Whereas the processing of sound and image data, such as in cases of video surveillance, does not come within the scope of this Directive if it is carried out for the purposes of public security, defence, national security or in the course of State activities relating to the area of criminal law or of other activities which do not come within the scope of Community law;

(17) Whereas, as far as the processing of sound and image data carried out for purposes of journalism or the purposes of literary or artistic expression is concerned, in particular in the audiovisual field, the principles of the Directive are to apply in a restricted manner according to the provisions laid down in Article 9;

(18) Whereas, in order to ensure that individuals are not deprived of the protection to which they are entitled under this Directive, any processing of personal data in the Community must be carried out in accordance with the law of one of the Member States; whereas, in this connection, processing carried out under the responsibility of a controller who is established in a Member State should be governed by the law of that State;

(19) Whereas establishment on the territory of a Member State implies the effective and real exercise of activity through stable arrangements; whereas the legal form of such an establishment, whether simply branch or a subsidiary with a legal personality, is not the determining factor in this respect; whereas, when a single controller is established on the territory of several Member States, particularly by means of subsidiaries, he must ensure, in order to avoid any circumvention of national rules, that each of the establishments fulfils the obligations imposed by the national law applicable to its activities;

(20) Whereas the fact that the processing of data is carried out by a person established in a third country must not stand in the way of the protection of individuals provided for in this Directive; whereas in these cases, the processing should be governed by the law of the Member State in which the means used are located, and there should be guarantees to ensure that the rights and obligations provided for in this Directive are respected in practice;

(21) Whereas this Directive is without prejudice to the rules of territoriality applicable in criminal matters;

(22) Whereas Member States shall more precisely define in the laws they enact or when bringing into force the measures taken under this Directive the general circumstances in which processing is lawful; whereas in particular Article 5, in conjunction with Articles 7 and 8, allows Member States, independently of general rules, to provide for special processing conditions for specific sectors and for the various categories of data covered by Article 8;

(23) Whereas Member States are empowered to ensure the implementation of the protection of individuals both by means of a general law on the protection of individuals as regards the processing of personal data and by sectorial laws such as those relating, for example, to statistical institutes;

(24) Whereas the legislation concerning the protection of legal persons with regard to the processing data which concerns them is not affected by this Directive;

(25) Whereas the principles of protection must be reflected, on the one hand, in the obligations imposed on persons, public authorities, enterprises, agencies or other bodies responsible for

processing, in particular regarding data quality, technical security, notification to the supervisory authority, and the circumstances under which processing can be carried out, and, on the other hand, in the right conferred on individuals, the data on whom are the subject of processing, to be informed that processing is taking place, to consult the data, to request corrections and even to object to processing in certain circumstances;

(26) Whereas the principles of protection must apply to any information concerning an identified or identifiable person; whereas, to determine whether a person is identifiable, account should be taken of all the means likely reasonably to be used either by the controller or by any other person to identify the said person; whereas the principles of protection shall not apply to data rendered anonymous in such a way that the data subject is no longer identifiable; whereas codes of conduct within the meaning of Article 27 may be a useful instrument for providing guidance as to the ways in which data may be rendered anonymous and retained in a form in which identification of the data subject is no longer possible;

(27) Whereas the protection of individuals must apply as much to automatic processing of data as to manual processing; whereas the scope of this protection must not in effect depend on the techniques used, otherwise this would create a serious risk of circumvention; whereas, nonetheless, as regards manual processing, this Directive covers only filing systems, not unstructured files; whereas, in particular, the content of a filing system must be structured according to specific criteria relating to individuals allowing easy access to the personal data; whereas, in line with the definition in Article 2(c), the different criteria for determining the constituents of a structured set of personal data, and the different criteria governing access to such a set, may be laid down by each Member State; whereas files or sets of files as well as their cover pages, which are not structured according to specific criteria, shall under no circumstances fall within the scope of this Directive;

(28) Whereas any processing of personal data must be lawful and fair to the individuals concerned; whereas, in particular, the data must be adequate, relevant and not excessive in relation to the purposes for which they are processed; whereas such purposes must be explicit and legitimate and must be determined at the time of collection of the data; whereas the purposes of processing further to collection shall not be incompatible with the purposes as they were originally specified;

(29) Whereas the further processing of personal data for historical, statistical or scientific purposes is not generally to be considered incompatible with the purposes for which the data have previously been collected provided that Member States furnish suitable safeguards; whereas these safeguards must in particular rule out the use of the data in support of measures or decisions regarding any particular individual;

(30) Whereas, in order to be lawful, the processing of personal data must in addition be carried out with the consent of the data subject or be necessary for the conclusion or performance of a contract binding on the data subject, or as a legal requirement, or for the performance of a task carried out in the public interest or in the exercise of official authority, or in the legitimate interests of a natural or legal person, provided that the interests or the rights and freedoms of the data subject are not overriding; whereas, in particular, in order to maintain a balance between the interests involved while guaranteeing effective competition, Member States may determine the circumstances in which personal data may be used or disclosed to a third party in the context of the legitimate ordinary business activities of companies and other bodies; whereas Member States may similarly specify the conditions under which personal data may be disclosed to a third party for the purposes of marketing whether carried out commercially or by a charitable organization or by any other association or foundation, of a political nature for example, subject to the provisions allowing a data subject to object to the processing of data regarding him, at no cost and without having to state his reasons;

(31) Whereas the processing of personal data must equally be regarded as lawful where it is carried out in order to protect an interest which is essential for the data subject's life;

(32) Whereas it is for national legislation to determine whether the controller performing a task carried out in the public interest or in the exercise of official authority should be a public administration or another natural or legal person governed by public law, or by private law such as a professional association;

(33) Whereas data which are capable by their nature of infringing fundamental freedoms or privacy should not be processed unless the data subject gives his explicit consent; whereas, however, derogations from this prohibition must be explicitly provided for in respect of specific needs, in particular where the processing of these data is carried out for certain health-related purposes by persons subject to a legal obligation of professional secrecy or in the course of legitimate activities by certain associations or foundations the purpose of which is to permit the exercise of fundamental freedoms;

(34) Whereas Member States must also be authorized, when justified by grounds of important public interest, to derogate from the prohibition on processing sensitive categories of data where important reasons of public interest so justify in areas such as public health and social protection-especially in order to ensure the quality and cost-effectiveness of the procedures used for settling claims for benefits and services in the health insurance system-scientific research and government statistics; whereas it is incumbent on them, however, to provide specific and suitable safeguards so as to protect the fundamental rights and the privacy of individuals;

(35) Whereas, moreover, the processing of personal data by official authorities for achieving aims, laid down in constitutional law or international public law, of officially recognized religious associations is carried out on important grounds of public interest;

(36) Whereas where, in the course of electoral activities, the operation of the democratic system requires in certain Member States that political parties compile data on people's political opinion, the processing of such data may be permitted for reasons of important public interest, provided that appropriate safeguards are established;

(37) Whereas the processing of personal data for purposes of journalism or for purposes of literary or artistic expression, in particular in the audiovisual field, should qualify for exemption from the requirements of certain provisions of this Directive in so far as this is necessary to reconcile the fundamental rights of individuals with freedom of information and notably the right to receive and impart information, as guaranteed in particular in Article 10 of the European Convention for the Protection of Human Rights and Fundamental Freedoms; whereas Member States should therefore lay down exemptions and derogations necessary for the purpose of balance between fundamental rights as regards general measures on the legitimacy of data processing, measures on the transfer of data to third countries and the power of the supervisory authority; whereas this should not, however, lead Member States to lay down exemptions from the measures to ensure security of processing; whereas at least the supervisory authority responsible for this sector should also be provided with certain ex-post powers, e.g. to publish a regular report or to refer matters to the judicial authorities;

(38) Whereas, if the processing of data is to be fair, the data subject must be in a position to learn of the existence of a processing operation and, where data are collected from him, must be given accurate and full information, bearing in mind the circumstances of the collection;

(39) Whereas certain processing operations involve data which the controller has not collected directly from the data subject; whereas, furthermore, data can be legitimately disclosed to a third party, even if the disclosure was not anticipated at the time the data were collected from the data subject; whereas, in all these cases, the data subject should be informed when the data are recorded or at the latest when the data are first disclosed to a third party;

(40) Whereas, however, it is not necessary to impose this obligation if the data subject already has the information; whereas, moreover, there will be no such obligation if the recording or disclosure are expressly provided for by law or if the provision of information to the data subject proves impossible or would involve disproportionate efforts, which could be the case where processing is for historical, statistical or scientific purposes; whereas, in this regard, the number of data subjects, the age of the data, and any compensatory measures adopted may be taken into consideration;

(41) Whereas any person must be able to exercise the right of access to data relating to him which are being processed, in order to verify in particular the accuracy of the data and the lawfulness of the processing; whereas, for the same reasons, every data subject must also have the right to know the logic involved in the automatic processing of data concerning him, at least in the case of the automated decisions referred to in Article 15 (1); whereas this right must not adversely affect trade

secrets or intellectual property and in particular the copyright protecting the software; whereas these considerations must not, however, result in the data subject being refused all information;

(42) Whereas Member States may, in the interest of the data subject or so as to protect the rights and freedoms of others, restrict rights of access and information; whereas they may, for example, specify that access to medical data may be obtained only through a health professional;

(43) Whereas restrictions on the rights of access and information and on certain obligations of the controller may similarly be imposed by Member States in so far as they are necessary to safeguard, for example, national security, defence, public safety, or important economic or financial interests of a Member State or the Union, as well as criminal investigations and prosecutions and action in respect of breaches of ethics in the regulated professions; whereas the list of exceptions and limitations should include the tasks of monitoring, inspection or regulation necessary in the three last-mentioned areas concerning public security, economic or financial interests and crime prevention; whereas the listing of tasks in these three areas does not affect the legitimacy of exceptions or restrictions for reasons of State security or defence;

(44) Whereas Member States may also be led, by virtue of the provisions of Community law, to derogate from the provisions of this Directive concerning the right of access, the obligation to inform individuals, and the quality of data, in order to secure certain of the purposes referred to above;

(45) Whereas, in cases where data might lawfully be processed on grounds of public interest, official authority or the legitimate interests of a natural or legal person, any data subject should nevertheless be entitled, on legitimate and compelling grounds relating to his particular situation, to object to the processing of any data relating to himself; whereas Member States may nevertheless lay down national provisions to the contrary;

(46) Whereas the protection of the rights and freedoms of data subjects with regard to the processing of personal data requires that appropriate technical and organizational measures be taken, both at the time of the design of the processing system and at the time of the processing itself, particularly in order to maintain security and thereby to prevent any unauthorized processing; whereas it is incumbent on the Member States to ensure that controllers comply with these measures; whereas these measures must ensure an appropriate level of security, taking into account the state of the art and the costs of their implementation in relation to the risks inherent in the processing and the nature of the data to be protected;

(47) Whereas where a message containing personal data is transmitted by means of a telecommunications or electronic mail service, the sole purpose of which is the transmission of such messages, the controller in respect of the personal data contained in the message will normally be considered to be the person from whom the message originates, rather than the person offering the transmission services; whereas, nevertheless, those offering such services will normally be considered controllers in respect of the processing of the additional personal data necessary for the operation of the service;

(48) Whereas the procedures for notifying the supervisory authority are designed to ensure disclosure of the purposes and main features of any processing operation for the purpose of verification that the operation is in accordance with the national measures taken under this Directive;

(49) Whereas, in order to avoid unsuitable administrative formalities, exemptions from the obligation to notify and simplification of the notification required may be provided for by Member States in cases where processing is unlikely adversely to affect the rights and freedoms of data subjects, provided that it is in accordance with a measure taken by a Member State specifying its limits; whereas exemption or simplification may similarly be provided for by Member States where a person appointed by the controller ensures that the processing carried out is not likely adversely to affect the rights and freedoms of data subjects; whereas such a data protection official, whether or not an employee of the controller, must be in a position to exercise his functions in complete independence;

(50) Whereas exemption or simplification could be provided for in cases of processing operations whose sole purpose is the keeping of a register intended, according to national law, to provide information to the public and open to consultation by the public or by any person demonstrating a legitimate interest;

(51) Whereas, nevertheless, simplification or exemption from the obligation to notify shall not release the controller from any of the other obligations resulting from this Directive;

(52) Whereas, in this context, ex post facto verification by the competent authorities must in general be considered a sufficient measure;

(53) Whereas, however, certain processing operation are likely to pose specific risks to the rights and freedoms of data subjects by virtue of their nature, their scope or their purposes, such as that of excluding individuals from a right, benefit or a contract, or by virtue of the specific use of new technologies; whereas it is for Member States, if they so wish, to specify such risks in their legislation;

(54) Whereas with regard to all the processing undertaken in society, the amount posing such specific risks should be very limited; whereas Member States must provide that the supervisory authority, or the data protection official in cooperation with the authority, check such processing prior to it being carried out; whereas following this prior check, the supervisory authority may, according to its national law, give an opinion or an authorization regarding the processing; whereas such checking may equally take place in the course of the preparation either of a measure of the national parliament or of a measure based on such a legislative measure, which defines the nature of the processing and lays down appropriate safeguards;

(55) Whereas, if the controller fails to respect the rights of data subjects, national legislation must provide for a judicial remedy; whereas any damage which a person may suffer as a result of unlawful processing must be compensated for by the controller, who may be exempted from liability if he proves that he is not responsible for the damage, in particular in cases where he establishes fault on the part of the data subject or in case of force majeure; whereas sanctions must be imposed on any person, whether governed by private of public law, who fails to comply with the national measures taken under this Directive;

(56) Whereas cross-border flows of personal data are necessary to the expansion of international trade; whereas the protection of individuals guaranteed in the Community by this Directive does not stand in the way of transfers of personal data to third countries which ensure an adequate level of protection; whereas the adequacy of the level of protection afforded by a third country must be assessed in the light of all the circumstances surrounding the transfer operation or set of transfer operations;

(57) Whereas, on the other hand, the transfer of personal data to a third country which does not ensure an adequate level of protection must be prohibited;

(58) Whereas provisions should be made for exemptions from this prohibition in certain circumstances where the data subject has given his consent, where the transfer is necessary in relation to a contract or a legal claim, where protection of an important public interest so requires, for example in cases of international transfers of data between tax or customs administrations or between services competent for social security matters, or where the transfer is made from a register established by law and intended for consultation by the public or persons having a legitimate interest; whereas in this case such a transfer should not involve the entirety of the data or entire categories of the data contained in the register and, when the register is intended for consultation by persons having a legitimate interest, the transfer should be made only at the request of those persons or if they are to be the recipients;

(59) Whereas particular measures may be taken to compensate for the lack of protection in a third country in cases where the controller offers appropriate safeguards; whereas, moreover, provision must be made for procedures for negotiations between the Community and such third countries;

(60) Whereas, in any event, transfers to third countries may be effected only in full compliance with the provisions adopted by the Member States pursuant to this Directive, and in particular Article 8 thereof;

(61) Whereas Member States and the Commission, in their respective spheres of competence, must encourage the trade associations and other representative organizations concerned to draw up codes of conduct so as to facilitate the application of this Directive, taking account of the specific characteristics of the processing carried out in certain sectors, and respecting the national provisions adopted for its implementation;

(62) Whereas the establishment in Member States of supervisory authorities, exercising their functions with complete independence, is an essential component of the protection of individuals with regard to the processing of personal data;

(63) Whereas such authorities must have the necessary means to perform their duties, including powers of investigation and intervention, particularly in cases of complaints from individuals, and powers to engage in legal proceedings; whereas such authorities must help to ensure transparency of processing in the Member States within whose jurisdiction they fall;

(64) Whereas the authorities in the different Member States will need to assist one another in performing their duties so as to ensure that the rules of protection are properly respected throughout the European Union;

(65) Whereas, at Community level, a Working Party on the Protection of Individuals with regard to the Processing of Personal Data must be set up and be completely independent in the performance of its functions; whereas, having regard to its specific nature, it must advise the Commission and, in particular, contribute to the uniform application of the national rules adopted pursuant to this Directive;

(66) Whereas, with regard to the transfer of data to third countries, the application of this Directive calls for the conferment of powers of implementation on the Commission and the establishment of a procedure as laid down in Council Decision 87/373/EEC[4];

(67) Whereas an agreement on a modus vivendi between the European Parliament, the Council and the Commission concerning the implementing measures for acts adopted in accordance with the procedure laid down in Article 189b of the EC Treaty was reached on 20 December 1994;

(68) Whereas the principles set out in this Directive regarding the protection of the rights and freedoms of individuals, notably their right to privacy, with regard to the processing of personal data may be supplemented or clarified, in particular as far as certain sectors are concerned, by specific rules based on those principles;

(69) Whereas Member States should be allowed a period of not more than three years from the entry into force of the national measures transposing this Directive in which to apply such new national rules progressively to all processing operations already under way; whereas, in order to facilitate their cost-effective implementation, a further period expiring 12 years after the date on which this Directive is adopted will be allowed to Member States to ensure the conformity of existing manual filing systems with certain of the Directive's provisions; whereas, where data contained in such filing systems are manually processed during this extended transition period, those systems must be brought into conformity with these provisions at the time of such processing;

(70) Whereas it is not necessary for the data subject to give his consent again so as to allow the controller to continue to process, after the national provisions taken pursuant to this Directive enter into force, any sensitive data necessary for the performance of a contract concluded on the basis of free and informed consent before the entry into force of these provisions;

(71) Whereas this Directive does not stand in the way of a Member State's regulating marketing activities aimed at consumers residing in territory in so far as such regulation does not concern the protection of individuals with regard to the processing of personal data;

(72) Whereas this Directive allows the principle of public access to official documents to be taken into account when implementing the principles set out in this Directive,

HAVE ADOPTED THIS DIRECTIVE:

Chapter I General Provisions

Article 1 Object of the Directive

1. In accordance with this Directive, Member States shall protect the fundamental rights and freedoms of natural persons, and in particular their right to privacy with respect to the processing of personal data.

---

[4] OJ No L 197, 18.7.1987, p. 33.

2. Member States shall neither restrict nor prohibit the free flow of personal data between Member States for reasons connected with the protection afforded under paragraph 1.

Article 2   Definitions

For the purposes of this Directive:

(a) "personal data" shall mean any information relating to an identified or identifiable natural person ("data subject"); an identifiable person is one who can be identified, directly or indirectly, in particular by reference to an identification number or to one or more factors specific to his physical, physiological, mental, economic, cultural or social identity;

(b) "processing of personal data" ("processing") shall mean any operation or set of operations which is performed upon personal data, whether or not by automatic means, such as collection, recording, organization, storage, adaptation or alteration, retrieval, consultation, use, disclosure by transmission, dissemination or otherwise making available, alignment or combination, blocking, erasure or destruction;

(c) "personal data filing system" ("filing system") shall mean any structured set of personal data which are accessible according to specific criteria, whether centralized, decentralized or dispersed on a functional or geographical basis;

(d) "controller" shall mean the natural or legal person, public authority, agency or any other body which alone or jointly with others determines the purposes and means of the processing of personal data; where the purposes and means of processing are determined by national or Community laws or regulations, the controller or the specific criteria for his nomination may be designated by national or Community law;

(e) "processor" shall mean a natural or legal person, public authority, agency or any other body which processes personal data on behalf of the controller;

(f) "third party" shall mean any natural or legal person, public authority, agency or any other body other than the data subject, the controller, the processor and the persons who, under the direct authority of the controller or the processor, are authorized to process the data;

(g) "recipient" shall mean a natural or legal person, public authority, agency or any other body to whom data are disclosed, whether a third party or not; however, authorities which may receive data in the framework of a particular inquiry shall not be regarded as recipients;

(h) "the data subject's consent" shall mean any freely given specific and informed indication of his wishes by which the data subject signifies his agreement to personal data relating to him being processed.

Article 3   Scope

1. This Directive shall apply to the processing of personal data wholly or partly by automatic means, and to the processing otherwise than by automatic means of personal data which form part of a filing system or are intended to form part of a filing system.

2. This Directive shall not apply to the processing of personal data:

— in the course of an activity which falls outside the scope of Community law, such as those provided for by Titles V and VI of the Treaty on European Union and in any case to processing operations concerning public security, defence, State security (including the economic well-being of the State when the processing operation relates to State security matters) and the activities of the State in areas of criminal law,

— by a natural person in the course of a purely personal or household activity.

Article 4   National law applicable

1. Each Member State shall apply the national provisions it adopts pursuant to this Directive to the processing of personal data where:

(a) the processing is carried out in the context of the activities of an establishment of the controller on the territory of the Member State; when the same controller is established on the territory of several Member States, he must take the necessary measures to ensure that each of these establishments complies with the obligations laid down by the national law applicable;

(b) the controller is not established on the Member State's territory, but in a place where its national law applies by virtue of international public law;

(c) the controller is not established on Community territory and, for purposes of processing personal data makes use of equipment, automated or otherwise, situated on the territory of the said Member State, unless such equipment is used only for purposes of transit through the territory of the Community.

2. In the circumstances referred to in paragraph 1 (c), the controller must designate a representative established in the territory of that Member State, without prejudice to legal actions which could be initiated against the controller himself.

Chapter II General Rules on the Lawfulness of the Processing of Personal Data

Article 5

Member States shall, within the limits of the provisions of this Chapter, determine more precisely the conditions under which the processing of personal data is lawful.

Section I Principles Relating to Data Quality

Article 6

1. Member States shall provide that personal data must be:

   (a) processed fairly and lawfully;

   (b) collected for specified, explicit and legitimate purposes and not further processed in a way incompatible with those purposes. Further processing of data for historical, statistical or scientific purposes shall not be considered as incompatible provided that Member States provide appropriate safeguards;

   (c) adequate, relevant and not excessive in relation to the purposes for which they are collected and/or further processed;

   (d) accurate and, where necessary, kept up to date; every reasonable step must be taken to ensure that data which are inaccurate or incomplete, having regard to the purposes for which they were collected or for which they are further processed, are erased or rectified;

   (e) kept in a form which permits identification of data subjects for no longer than is necessary for the purposes for which the data were collected or for which they are further processed. Member States shall lay down appropriate safeguards for personal data stored for longer periods for historical, statistical or scientific use.

2. It shall be for the controller to ensure that paragraph 1 is complied with.

Section II Criteria for Making Data Processing Legitimate

Article 7

1. Member States shall provide that personal data may be processed only if:

   (a) the data subject has unambiguously given his consent; or

   (b) processing is necessary for the performance of a contract to which the data subject is party or in order to take steps at the request of the data subject prior to entering into a contract; or

   (c) processing is necessary for compliance with a legal obligation to which the controller is subject; or

   (d) processing is necessary in order to protect the vital interests of the data subject; or

   (e) processing is necessary for the performance of a task carried out in the public interest or in the exercise of official authority vested in the controller or in a third party to whom the data are disclosed; or

(f) processing is necessary for the purposes of the legitimate interests pursued by the controller or by the third party or parties to whom the data are disclosed, except where such interests are overridden by the interests for fundamental rights and freedoms of the data subject which require protection under Article 1 (1).

Section III Special Categories of Processing

Article 8 The processing of special categories of data

1. Member States shall prohibit the processing of personal data revealing racial or ethnic origin, political opinions, religious or philosophical beliefs, trade-union membership, and the processing of data concerning health or sex life.

2. Paragraph 1 shall not apply where:

(a) the data subject has given his explicit consent to the processing of those data, except where the laws of the Member State provide that the prohibition referred to in paragraph 1 may not be lifted by the data subject's giving his consent; or

(b) processing is necessary for the purposes of carrying out the obligations and specific rights of the controller in the field of employment law in so far as it is authorized by national law providing for adequate safeguards; or

(c) processing is necessary to protect the vital interests of the data subject or of another person where the data subject is physically or legally incapable of giving his consent; or

(d) processing is carried out in the course of its legitimate activities with appropriate guarantees by a foundation, association or any other non-profit-seeking body with a political, philosophical, religious or trade-union aim and on condition that the processing relates solely to the members of the body or to persons who have regular contact with it in connection with its purposes and that the data are not disclosed to a third party without the consent of the data subjects; or

(e) the processing relates to data which are manifestly made public by the data subject or is necessary for the establishment, exercise or defence of legal claims.

3. Paragraph 1 shall not apply where processing of the data is required for the purposes of preventive medicine, medical diagnosis, the provision of care or treatment or the management of health-care services, and where those data are processed by a health professional subject under national law or rules established by national competent bodies to the obligation of professional secrecy or by another person also subject to an equivalent obligation of secrecy.

4. Subject to the provision of suitable safeguards, Member States may, for reasons of substantial public interest, lay down exemptions in addition to those laid down in paragraph 2 either by national law or by decision of the supervisory authority.

5. Processing of data relating to offences, criminal convictions or security measures may be carried out only under the control of official authority, or if suitable specific safeguards are provided under national law, subject to derogations which may be granted by the Member State under national provisions providing suitable specific safeguards. However, a complete register of criminal convictions may be kept only under the control of official authority.

Member States may provide that data relating to administrative sanctions or judgements in civil cases shall also be processed under the control of official authority.

6. Derogations from paragraph 1 provided for in paragraphs 4 and 5 shall be notified to the Commission.

7. Member States shall determine the conditions under which a national identification number or any other identifier of general application may be processed.

Article 9 Processing of personal data and freedom of expression

Member States shall provide for exemptions or derogations from the provisions of this Chapter, Chapter IV and Chapter VI for the processing of personal data carried out solely for journalistic purposes or the purpose of artistic or literary expression only if they are necessary to reconcile the right to privacy with the rules governing freedom of expression.

Section IV Information to be Given to the Data Subject

Article 10   Information in cases of collection of data from the data subject

Member States shall provide that the controller or his representative must provide a data subject from whom data relating to himself are collected with at least the following information, except where he already has it:

(a) the identity of the controller and of his representative, if any;

(b) the purposes of the processing for which the data are intended;

(c) any further information such as

— the recipients or categories of recipients of the data,

— whether replies to the questions are obligatory or voluntary, as well as the possible consequences of failure to reply,

— the existence of the right of access to and the right to rectify the data concerning him

in so far as such further information is necessary, having regard to the specific circumstances in which the data are collected, to guarantee fair processing in respect of the data subject.

Article 11   Information where the data have not been obtained from the data subject

1. Where the data have not been obtained from the data subject, Member States shall provide that the controller or his representative must at the time of undertaking the recording of personal data or if a disclosure to a third party is envisaged, no later than the time when the data are first disclosed provide the data subject with at least the following information, except where he already has it:

(a) the identity of the controller and of his representative, if any;

(b) the purposes of the processing;

(c) any further information such as

— the categories of data concerned,

— the recipients or categories of recipients,

— the existence of the right of access to and the right to rectify the data concerning him

in so far as such further information is necessary, having regard to the specific circumstances in which the data are processed, to guarantee fair processing in respect of the data subject.

2. Paragraph 1 shall not apply where, in particular for processing for statistical purposes or for the purposes of historical or scientific research, the provision of such information proves impossible or would involve a disproportionate effort or if recording or disclosure is expressly laid down by law. In these cases Member States shall provide appropriate safeguards.

Section V The Data Subject's Right of Access to Data

Article 12   Right of access

Member States shall guarantee every data subject the right to obtain from the controller:

(a) without constraint at reasonable intervals and without excessive delay or expense:

— confirmation as to whether or not data relating to him are being processed and information at least as to the purposes of the processing, the categories of data concerned, and the recipients or categories of recipients to whom the data are disclosed,

— communication to him in an intelligible form of the data undergoing processing and of any available information as to their source,

— knowledge of the logic involved in any automatic processing of data concerning him at least in the case of the automated decisions referred to in Article 15 (1);

(b) as appropriate the rectification, erasure or blocking of data the processing of which does not comply with the provisions of this Directive, in particular because of the incomplete or inaccurate nature of the data;

(c) notification to third parties to whom the data have been disclosed of any rectification, erasure or blocking carried out in compliance with (b), unless this proves impossible or involves a disproportionate effort.

Section VI Exemptions and Restrictions

Article 13 Exemptions and restrictions

1. Member States may adopt legislative measures to restrict the scope of the obligations and rights provided for in Articles 6 (1), 10, 11 (1), 12 and 21 when such a restriction constitutes a necessary measures to safeguard:

(a) national security;

(b) defence;

(c) public security;

(d) the prevention, investigation, detection and prosecution of criminal offences, or of breaches of ethics for regulated professions;

(e) an important economic or financial interest of a Member State or of the European Union, including monetary, budgetary and taxation matters;

(f) a monitoring, inspection or regulatory function connected, even occasionally, with the exercise of official authority in cases referred to in (c), (d) and (e);

(g) the protection of the data subject or of the rights and freedoms of others.

2. Subject to adequate legal safeguards, in particular that the data are not used for taking measures or decisions regarding any particular individual, Member States may, where there is clearly no risk of breaching the privacy of the data subject, restrict by a legislative measure the rights provided for in Article 12 when data are processed solely for purposes of scientific research or are kept in personal form for a period which does not exceed the period necessary for the sole purpose of creating statistics.

Section VII The Data Subject's Right to Object

Article 14 The data subject's right to object

Member States shall grant the data subject the right:

(a) at least in the cases referred to in Article 7 (e) and (f), to object at any time on compelling legitimate grounds relating to his particular situation to the processing of data relating to him, save where otherwise provided by national legislation. Where there is a justified objection, the processing instigated by the controller may no longer involve those data;

(b) to object, on request and free of charge, to the processing of personal data relating to him which the controller anticipates being processed for the purposes of direct marketing, or to be informed before personal data are disclosed for the first time to third parties or used on their behalf for the purposes of direct marketing, and to be expressly offered the right to object free of charge to such disclosures or uses.

Member States shall take the necessary measures to ensure that data subjects are aware of the existence of the right referred to in the first subparagraph of (b).

Article 15 Automated individual decisions

1. Member States shall grant the right to every person not to be subject to a decision which produces legal effects concerning him or significantly affects him and which is based solely on automated processing of data intended to evaluate certain personal aspects relating to him, such as his performance at work, creditworthiness, reliability, conduct, etc.

2. Subject to the other Articles of this Directive, Member States shall provide that a person may be subjected to a decision of the kind referred to in paragraph 1 if that decision:

(a) is taken in the course of the entering into or performance of a contract, provided the request for the entering into or the performance of the contract, lodged by the data subject, has been satisfied or that there are suitable measures to safeguard his legitimate interests, such as arrangements allowing him to put his point of view; or

(b) is authorized by a law which also lays down measures to safeguard the data subject's legitimate interests.

Section VIII Confidentiality and Security of Processing

Article 16   Confidentiality of processing

Any person acting under the authority of the controller or of the processor, including the processor himself, who has access to personal data must not process them except on instructions from the controller, unless he is required to do so by law.

Article 17   Security of processing

1. Member States shall provide that the controller must implement appropriate technical and organizational measures to protect personal data against accidental or unlawful destruction or accidental loss, alteration, unauthorized disclosure or access, in particular where the processing involves the transmission of data over a network, and against all other unlawful forms of processing.

Having regard to the state of the art and the cost of their implementation, such measures shall ensure a level of security appropriate to the risks represented by the processing and the nature of the data to be protected.

2. The Member States shall provide that the controller must, where processing is carried out on his behalf, choose a processor providing sufficient guarantees in respect of the technical security measures and organizational measures governing the processing to be carried out, and must ensure compliance with those measures.

3. The carrying out of processing by way of a processor must be governed by a contract or legal act binding the processor to the controller and stipulating in particular that:
   — the processor shall act only on instructions from the controller,
   — the obligations set out in paragraph 1, as defined by the law of the Member State in which the processor is established, shall also be incumbent on the processor.

4. For the purposes of keeping proof, the parts of the contract or the legal act relating to data protection and the requirements relating to the measures referred to in paragraph 1 shall be in writing or in another equivalent form.

Section IX Notification

Article 18   Obligation to notify the supervisory authority

1. Member States shall provide that the controller or his representative, if any, must notify the supervisory authority referred to in Article 28 before carrying out any wholly or partly automatic processing operation or set of such operations intended to serve a single purpose or several related purposes.

2. Member States may provide for the simplification of or exemption from notification only in the following cases and under the following conditions:
   — where, for categories of processing operations which are unlikely, taking account of the data to be processed, to affect adversely the rights and freedoms of data subjects, they specify the purposes of the processing, the data or categories of data undergoing processing, the category or categories of data subject, the recipients or categories of recipient to whom the data are to be disclosed and the length of time the data are to be stored, and/or
   — where the controller, in compliance with the national law which governs him, appoints a personal data protection official, responsible in particular:
   — for ensuring in an independent manner the internal application of the national provisions taken pursuant to this Directive
   — for keeping the register of processing operations carried out by the controller, containing the items of information referred to in Article 21 (2), thereby ensuring that the rights and freedoms of the data subjects are unlikely to be adversely affected by the processing operations.

3. Member States may provide that paragraph 1 does not apply to processing whose sole purpose is the keeping of a register which according to laws or regulations is intended to provide information to the public and which is open to consultation either by the public in general or by any person demonstrating a legitimate interest.

4. Member States may provide for an exemption from the obligation to notify or a simplification of the notification in the case of processing operations referred to in Article 8 (2) (d).

5. Member States may stipulate that certain or all non-automatic processing operations involving personal data shall be notified, or provide for these processing operations to be subject to simplified notification.

Article 19   Contents of notification

1. Member States shall specify the information to be given in the notification. It shall include at least:
   (a) the name and address of the controller and of his representative, if any;
   (b) the purpose or purposes of the processing;
   (c) a description of the category or categories of data subject and of the data or categories of data relating to them;
   (d) the recipients or categories of recipient to whom the data might be disclosed;
   (e) proposed transfers of data to third countries;
   (f) a general description allowing a preliminary assessment to be made of the appropriateness of the measures taken pursuant to Article 17 to ensure security of processing.

2. Member States shall specify the procedures under which any change affecting the information referred to in paragraph 1 must be notified to the supervisory authority.

Article 20   Prior checking

1. Member States shall determine the processing operations likely to present specific risks to the rights and freedoms of data subjects and shall check that these processing operations are examined prior to the start thereof.

2. Such prior checks shall be carried out by the supervisory authority following receipt of a notification from the controller or by the data protection official, who, in cases of doubt, must consult the supervisory authority.

3. Member States may also carry out such checks in the context of preparation either of a measure of the national parliament or of a measure based on such a legislative measure, which define the nature of the processing and lay down appropriate safeguards.

Article 21   Publicizing of processing operations

1. Member States shall take measures to ensure that processing operations are publicized.

2. Member States shall provide that a register of processing operations notified in accordance with Article 18 shall be kept by the supervisory authority.

The register shall contain at least the information listed in Article 19 (1) (a) to (e).

The register may be inspected by any person.

3. Member States shall provide, in relation to processing operations not subject to notification, that controllers or another body appointed by the Member States make available at least the information referred to in Article 19 (1) (a) to (e) in an appropriate form to any person on request.

Member States may provide that this provision does not apply to processing whose sole purpose is the keeping of a register which according to laws or regulations is intended to provide information to the public and which is open to consultation either by the public in general or by any person who can provide proof of a legitimate interest.

Chapter III Judicial Remedies, Liability and Sanctions

Article 22   Remedies

Without prejudice to any administrative remedy for which provision may be made, inter alia before the supervisory authority referred to in Article 28, prior to referral to the judicial authority, Member

States shall provide for the right of every person to a judicial remedy for any breach of the rights guaranteed him by the national law applicable to the processing in question.

Article 23   Liability

1. Member States shall provide that any person who has suffered damage as a result of an unlawful processing operation or of any act incompatible with the national provisions adopted pursuant to this Directive is entitled to receive compensation from the controller for the damage suffered.

2. The controller may be exempted from this liability, in whole or in part, if he proves that he is not responsible for the event giving rise to the damage.

Article 24   Sanctions

The Member States shall adopt suitable measures to ensure the full implementation of the provisions of this Directive and shall in particular lay down the sanctions to be imposed in case of infringement of the provisions adopted pursuant to this Directive.

Chapter IV   Transfer of Personal Data to Third Countries

Article 25   Principles

1. The Member States shall provide that the transfer to a third country of personal data which are undergoing processing or are intended for processing after transfer may take place only if, without prejudice to compliance with the national provisions adopted pursuant to the other provisions of this Directive, the third country in question ensures an adequate level of protection.

2. The adequacy of the level of protection afforded by a third country shall be assessed in the light of all the circumstances surrounding a data transfer operation or set of data transfer operations; particular consideration shall be given to the nature of the data, the purpose and duration of the proposed processing operation or operations, the country of origin and country of final destination, the rules of law, both general and sectoral, in force in the third country in question and the professional rules and security measures which are complied with in that country.

3. The Member States and the Commission shall inform each other of cases where they consider that a third country does not ensure an adequate level of protection within the meaning of paragraph 2.

4. Where the Commission finds, under the procedure provided for in Article 31 (2), that a third country does not ensure an adequate level of protection within the meaning of paragraph 2 of this Article, Member States shall take the measures necessary to prevent any transfer of data of the same type to the third country in question.

5. At the appropriate time, the Commission shall enter into negotiations with a view to remedying the situation resulting from the finding made pursuant to paragraph 4.

6. The Commission may find, in accordance with the procedure referred to in Article 31 (2), that a third country ensures an adequate level of protection within the meaning of paragraph 2 of this Article, by reason of its domestic law or of the international commitments it has entered into, particularly upon conclusion of the negotiations referred to in paragraph 5, for the protection of the private lives and basic freedoms and rights of individuals.

Member States shall take the measures necessary to comply with the Commission's decision.

Article 26   Derogations

1. By way of derogation from Article 25 and save where otherwise provided by domestic law governing particular cases, Member States shall provide that a transfer or a set of transfers of personal data to a third country which does not ensure an adequate level of protection within the meaning of Article 25 (2) may take place on condition that:

    (a) the data subject has given his consent unambiguously to the proposed transfer; or

    (b) the transfer is necessary for the performance of a contract between the data subject and the controller or the implementation of pre-contractual measures taken in response to the data subject's request; or

(c) the transfer is necessary for the conclusion or performance of a contract concluded in the interest of the data subject between the controller and a third party; or

(d) the transfer is necessary or legally required on important public interest grounds, or for the establishment, exercise or defence of legal claims; or

(e) the transfer is necessary in order to protect the vital interests of the data subject; or

(f) the transfer is made from a register which according to laws or regulations is intended to provide information to the public and which is open to consultation either by the public in general or by any person who can demonstrate legitimate interest, to the extent that the conditions laid down in law for consultation are fulfilled in the particular case.

2. Without prejudice to paragraph 1, a Member State may authorize a transfer or a set of transfers of personal data to a third country which does not ensure an adequate level of protection within the meaning of Article 25 (2), where the controller adduces adequate safeguards with respect to the protection of the privacy and fundamental rights and freedoms of individuals and as regards the exercise of the corresponding rights; such safeguards may in particular result from appropriate contractual clauses.

3. The Member State shall inform the Commission and the other Member States of the authorizations it grants pursuant to paragraph 2.

If a Member State or the Commission objects on justified grounds involving the protection of the privacy and fundamental rights and freedoms of individuals, the Commission shall take appropriate measures in accordance with the procedure laid down in Article 31 (2).

Member States shall take the necessary measures to comply with the Commission's decision.

4. Where the Commission decides, in accordance with the procedure referred to in Article 31 (2), that certain standard contractual clauses offer sufficient safeguards as required by paragraph 2, Member States shall take the necessary measures to comply with the Commission's decision.

Chapter V Codes of Conduct

Article 27

1. The Member States and the Commission shall encourage the drawing up of codes of conduct intended to contribute to the proper implementation of the national provisions adopted by the Member States pursuant to this Directive, taking account of the specific features of the various sectors.

2. Member States shall make provision for trade associations and other bodies representing other categories of controllers which have drawn up draft national codes or which have the intention of amending or extending existing national codes to be able to submit them to the opinion of the national authority.

Member States shall make provision for this authority to ascertain, among other things, whether the drafts submitted to it are in accordance with the national provisions adopted pursuant to this Directive. If it sees fit, the authority shall seek the views of data subjects or their representatives.

3. Draft Community codes, and amendments or extensions to existing Community codes, may be submitted to the Working Party referred to in Article 29. This Working Party shall determine, among other things, whether the drafts submitted to it are in accordance with the national provisions adopted pursuant to this Directive. If it sees fit, the authority shall seek the views of data subjects or their representatives. The Commission may ensure appropriate publicity for the codes which have been approved by the Working Party.

Chapter VI Supervisory Authority and Working Party on the Protection of Individuals with Regard to the Processing of Personal Data

Article 28 Supervisory authority

1. Each Member State shall provide that one or more public authorities are responsible for monitoring the application within its territory of the provisions adopted by the Member States pursuant to this Directive.

These authorities shall act with complete independence in exercising the functions entrusted to them.

2. Each Member State shall provide that the supervisory authorities are consulted when drawing up administrative measures or regulations relating to the protection of individuals' rights and freedoms with regard to the processing of personal data.

3. Each authority shall in particular be endowed with:

— investigative powers, such as powers of access to data forming the subject-matter of processing operations and powers to collect all the information necessary for the performance of its supervisory duties,

— effective powers of intervention, such as, for example, that of delivering opinions before processing operations are carried out, in accordance with Article 20, and ensuring appropriate publication of such opinions, of ordering the blocking, erasure or destruction of data, of imposing a temporary or definitive ban on processing, of warning or admonishing the controller, or that of referring the matter to national parliaments or other political institutions,

— the power to engage in legal proceedings where the national provisions adopted pursuant to this Directive have been violated or to bring these violations to the attention of the judicial authorities.

Decisions by the supervisory authority which give rise to complaints may be appealed against through the courts.

4. Each supervisory authority shall hear claims lodged by any person, or by an association representing that person, concerning the protection of his rights and freedoms in regard to the processing of personal data. The person concerned shall be informed of the outcome of the claim. Each supervisory authority shall, in particular, hear claims for checks on the lawfulness of data processing lodged by any person when the national provisions adopted pursuant to Article 13 of this Directive apply. The person shall at any rate be informed that a check has taken place.

5. Each supervisory authority shall draw up a report on its activities at regular intervals. The report shall be made public.

6. Each supervisory authority is competent, whatever the national law applicable to the processing in question, to exercise, on the territory of its own Member State, the powers conferred on it in accordance with paragraph 3. Each authority may be requested to exercise its powers by an authority of another Member State.

The supervisory authorities shall cooperate with one another to the extent necessary for the performance of their duties, in particular by exchanging all useful information.

7. Member States shall provide that the members and staff of the supervisory authority, even after their employment has ended, are to be subject to a duty of professional secrecy with regard to confidential information to which they have access.

Article 29   Working party on the protection of individuals with regard to the processing of Personal Data

1. A Working Party on the Protection of Individuals with regard to the Processing of Personal Data, hereinafter referred to as "the Working Party", is hereby set up.

It shall have advisory status and act independently.

2. The Working Party shall be composed of a representative of the supervisory authority or authorities designated by each Member State and of a representative of the authority or authorities established for the Community institutions and bodies, and of a representative of the Commission.

Each member of the Working Party shall be designated by the institution, authority or authorities which he represents. Where a Member State has designated more than one supervisory authority, they shall nominate a joint representative. The same shall apply to the authorities established for Community institutions and bodies.

3. The Working Party shall take decisions by a simple majority of the representatives of the supervisory authorities.

4. The Working Party shall elect its chairman. The chairman's term of office shall be two years. His appointment shall be renewable.

5. The Working Party's secretariat shall be provided by the Commission.

6. The Working Party shall adopt its own rules of procedure.

7. The Working Party shall consider items placed on its agenda by its chairman, either on his own initiative or at the request of a representative of the supervisory authorities or at the Commission's request.

Article 30

1. The Working Party shall:
    (a) examine any question covering the application of the national measures adopted under this Directive in order to contribute to the uniform application of such measures;
    (b) give the Commission an opinion on the level of protection in the Community and in third countries;
    (c) advise the Commission on any proposed amendment of this Directive, on any additional or specific measures to safeguard the rights and freedoms of natural persons with regard to the processing of personal data and on any other proposed Community measures affecting such rights and freedoms;
    (d) give an opinion on codes of conduct drawn up at Community level.

2. If the Working Party finds that divergences likely to affect the equivalence of protection for persons with regard to the processing of personal data in the Community are arising between the laws or practices of Member States, it shall inform the Commission accordingly.

3. The Working Party may, on its own initiative, make recommendations on all matters relating to the protection of persons with regard to the processing of personal data in the Community.

4. The Working Party's opinions and recommendations shall be forwarded to the Commission and to the committee referred to in Article 31.

5. The Commission shall inform the Working Party of the action it has taken in response to its opinions and recommendations. It shall do so in a report which shall also be forwarded to the European Parliament and the Council. The report shall be made public.

6. The Working Party shall draw up an annual report on the situation regarding the protection of natural persons with regard to the processing of personal data in the Community and in third countries, which it shall transmit to the Commission, the European Parliament and the Council. The report shall be made public.

Chapter VII Community Implementing Measures

Article 31   The Committee

1. The Commission shall be assisted by a committee composed of the representatives of the Member States and chaired by the representative of the Commission.

2. The representative of the Commission shall submit to the committee a draft of the measures to be taken. The committee shall deliver its opinion on the draft within a time limit which the chairman may lay down according to the urgency of the matter.

The opinion shall be delivered by the majority laid down in Article 148 (2) of the Treaty. The votes of the representatives of the Member States within the committee shall be weighted in the manner set out in that Article. The chairman shall not vote.

The Commission shall adopt measures which shall apply immediately. However, if these measures are not in accordance with the opinion of the committee, they shall be communicated by the Commission to the Council forthwith. It that event:
    — the Commission shall defer application of the measures which it has decided for a period of three months from the date of communication,
    — the Council, acting by a qualified majority, may take a different decision within the time limit referred to in the first indent.

Final Provisions

Article 32

1. Member States shall bring into force the laws, regulations and administrative provisions necessary to comply with this Directive at the latest at the end of a period of three years from the date of its adoption.

When Member States adopt these measures, they shall contain a reference to this Directive or be accompanied by such reference on the occasion of their official publication. The methods of making such reference shall be laid down by the Member States.

2. Member States shall ensure that processing already under way on the date the national provisions adopted pursuant to this Directive enter into force, is brought into conformity with these provisions within three years of this date.

By way of derogation from the preceding subparagraph, Member States may provide that the processing of data already held in manual filing systems on the date of entry into force of the national provisions adopted in implementation of this Directive shall be brought into conformity with Articles 6, 7 and 8 of this Directive within 12 years of the date on which it is adopted. Member States shall, however, grant the data subject the right to obtain, at his request and in particular at the time of exercising his right of access, the rectification, erasure or blocking of data which are incomplete, inaccurate or stored in a way incompatible with the legitimate purposes pursued by the controller.

3. By way of derogation from paragraph 2, Member States may provide, subject to suitable safeguards, that data kept for the sole purpose of historical research need not be brought into conformity with Articles 6, 7 and 8 of this Directive.

4. Member States shall communicate to the Commission the text of the provisions of domestic law which they adopt in the field covered by this Directive.

Article 33

The Commission shall report to the Council and the European Parliament at regular intervals, starting not later than three years after the date referred to in Article 32 (1), on the implementation of this Directive, attaching to its report, if necessary, suitable proposals for amendments. The report shall be made public.

The Commission shall examine, in particular, the application of this Directive to the data processing of sound and image data relating to natural persons and shall submit any appropriate proposals which prove to be necessary, taking account of developments in information technology and in the light of the state of progress in the information society.

Article 34

This Directive is addressed to the Member States.

Done at Luxembourg, 24 October 1995.

For the European Parliament

The President

K. HAENSCH

For the Council

The President

L. ATIENZA SERNA

Directive 96/9/EC of the European Parliament and of the Council of 11 March 1996 on the legal protection of databases

THE EUROPEAN PARLIAMENT AND THE COUNCIL OF THE EUROPEAN UNION,

Having regard to the Treaty establishing the European Community, and in particular Article 57 (2), 66 and 100a thereof, Having regard to the proposal from the Commission[1],

[1] OJ No C 156, 23.6.1992, p. 4 and OJ No C 308, 15.11.1993, p. 1.

Having regard to the opinion of the Economic and Social Committee[2],

Acting in accordance with the procedure laid down in Article 189b of the Treaty[3],

(1) Whereas databases are at present not sufficiently protected in all Member States by existing legislation; whereas such protection, where it exists, has different attributes;

(2) Whereas such differences in the legal protection of databases offered by the legislation of the Member States have direct negative effects on the functioning of the internal market as regards databases and in particular on the freedom of natural and legal persons to provide online database goods and services on the basis of harmonized legal arrangements throughout the Community; whereas such differences could well become more pronounced as Member States introduce new legislation in this field, which is now taking on an increasingly international dimension;

(3) Whereas existing differences distorting the functioning of the internal market need to be removed and new ones prevented from arising, while differences not adversely affecting the functioning of the internal market or the development of an information market within the Community need not be removed or prevented from arising;

(4) Whereas copyright protection for databases exists in varying forms in the Member States according to legislation or case-law, and whereas, if differences in legislation in the scope and conditions of protection remain between the Member States, such unharmonized intellectual property rights can have the effect of preventing the free movement of goods or services within the Community;

(5) Whereas copyright remains an appropriate form of exclusive right for authors who have created databases;

(6) Whereas, nevertheless, in the absence of a harmonized system of unfair-competition legislation or of case-law, other measures are required in addition to prevent the unauthorized extraction and/or re-utilization of the contents of a database;

(7) Whereas the making of databases requires the investment of considerable human, technical and financial resources while such databases can be copied or accessed at a fraction of the cost needed to design them independently;

(8) Whereas the unauthorized extraction and/or re-utilization of the contents of a database constitute acts which can have serious economic and technical consequences;

(9) Whereas databases are a vital tool in the development of an information market within the Community; whereas this tool will also be of use in many other fields;

(10) Whereas the exponential growth, in the Community and worldwide, in the amount of information generated and processed annually in all sectors of commerce and industry calls for investment in all the Member States in advanced information processing systems;

(11) Whereas there is at present a very great imbalance in the level of investment in the database sector both as between the Member States and between the Community and the world's largest database-producing third countries;

(12) Whereas such an investment in modern information storage and processing systems will not take place within the Community unless a stable and uniform legal protection regime is introduced for the protection of the rights of makers of databases;

(13) Whereas this Directive protects collections, sometimes called "compilations", of works, data or other materials which are arranged, stored and accessed by means which include electronic, electromagnetic or electro-optical processes or analogous processes;

(14) Whereas protection under this Directive should be extended to cover non-electronic databases;

(15) Whereas the criteria used to determine whether a database should be protected by copyright should be defined to the fact that the selection or the arrangement of the contents of the database is the author's own intellectual creation; whereas such protection should cover the structure of the database;

---

[2] OJ No C 19, 25.1.1993, p. 3.

[3] Opinion of the European Parliament of 23 June 1993 (OJ No C 194, 19.7.1993, p. 144), Common Position of the Council of 10 July 1995 (OJ No C 288, 30.10.1995, p. 14), Decision of the European Parliament of 14 December 1995 (OJ No C 17, 22.1.1996) and Council Decision of 26 February 1996.

(16) Whereas no criterion other than originality in the sense of the author's intellectual creation should be applied to determine the eligibility of the database for copyright protection, and in particular no aesthetic or qualitative criteria should be applied;

(17) Whereas the term "database" should be understood to include literary, artistic, musical or other collections of works or collections of other material such as texts, sound, images, numbers, facts, and data; whereas it should cover collections of independent works, data or other materials which are systematically or methodically arranged and can be individually accessed; whereas this means that a recording or an audiovisual, cinematographic, literary or musical work as such does not fall within the scope of this Directive;

(18) Whereas this Directive is without prejudice to the freedom of authors to decide whether, or in what manner, they will allow their works to be included in a database, in particular whether or not the authorization given is exclusive; whereas the protection of databases by the sui generis right is without prejudice to existing rights over their contents, and whereas in particular where an author or the holder of a related right permits some of his works or subject matter to be included in a database pursuant to a non-exclusive agreement, a third party may make use of those works or subject matter subject to the required consent of the author or of the holder of the related right without the sui generis right of the maker of the database being invoked to prevent him doing so, on condition that those works or subject matter are neither extracted from the database nor re-utilized on the basis thereof;

(19) Whereas, as a rule, the compilation of several recordings of musical performances on a CD does not come within the scope of this Directive, both because, as a compilation, it does not meet the conditions for copyright protection and because it does not represent a substantial enough investment to be eligible under the sui generis right;

(20) Whereas protection under this Directive may also apply to the materials necessary for the operation or consultation of certain databases such as thesaurus and indexation systems;

(21) Whereas the protection provided for in this Directive relates to databases in which works, data or other materials have been arranged systematically or methodically; whereas it is not necessary for those materials to have been physically stored in an organized manner;

(22) Whereas electronic databases within the meaning of this Directive may also include devices such as CD-ROM and CD-i;

(23) Whereas the term "database" should not be taken to extend to computer programs used in the making or operation of a database, which are protected by Council Directive 91/250/EEC of 14 May 1991 on the legal protection of computer programs[4];

(24) Whereas the rental and lending of databases in the field of copyright and related rights are governed exclusively by Council Directive 92/100/EEC of 19 November 1992 on rental right and lending right and on certain rights related to copyright in the field of intellectual property[5];

(25) Whereas the term of copyright is already governed by Council Directive 93/98/EEC of 29 October 1993 harmonizing the term of protection of copyright and certain related rights[6];

(26) Whereas works protected by copyright and subject matter protected by related rights, which are incorporated into a database, remain nevertheless protected by the respective exclusive rights and may not be incorporated into, or extracted from, the database without the permission of the rightholder or his successors in title;

(27) Whereas copyright in such works and related rights in subject matter thus incorporated into a database are in no way affected by the existence of a separate right in the selection or arrangement of these works and subject matter in a database;

(28) Whereas the moral rights of the natural person who created the database belong to the author and should be exercised according to the legislation of the Member States and the provisions of the Berne Convention for the Protection of Literary and Artistic Works; whereas such moral rights remain outside the scope of this Directive;

---

[4] OJ No L 122, 17.5.1991, p. 42. Directive as last amended by Directive 93/98/EEC (OJ No L 290, 24.11.1993, p. 9.)
[5] OJ No L 346, 27.11.1992, p. 61.   [6] OJ No L 290, 24.11.1993, p. 9.

(29) Whereas the arrangements applicable to databases created by employees are left to the discretion of the Member States; whereas, therefore nothing in this Directive prevents Member States from stipulating in their legislation that where a database is created by an employee in the execution of his duties or following the instructions given by his employer, the employer exclusively shall be entitled to exercise all economic rights in the database so created, unless otherwise provided by contract;

(30) Whereas the author's exclusive rights should include the right to determine the way in which his work is exploited and by whom, and in particular to control the distribution of his work to unauthorized persons;

(31) Whereas the copyright protection of databases includes making databases available by means other than the distribution of copies;

(32) Whereas Member States are required to ensure that their national provisions are at least materially equivalent in the case of such acts subject to restrictions as are provided for by this Directive;

(33) Whereas the question of exhaustion of the right of distribution does not arise in the case of on-line databases, which come within the field of provision of services; whereas this also applies with regard to a material copy of such a database made by the user of such a service with the consent of the rightholder; whereas, unlike CD-ROM or CD-i, where the intellectual property is incorporated in a material medium, namely an item of goods, every on-line service is in fact an act which will have to be subject to authorization where the copyright so provides;

(34) Whereas, nevertheless, once the rightholder has chosen to make available a copy of the database to a user, whether by an on-line service or by other means of distribution, that lawful user must be able to access and use the database for the purposes and in the way set out in the agreement with the rightholder, even if such access and use necessitate performance of otherwise restricted acts;

(35) Whereas a list should be drawn up of exceptions to restricted acts, taking into account the fact that copyright as covered by this Directive applies only to the selection or arrangements of the contents of a database; whereas Member States should be given the option of providing for such exceptions in certain cases; whereas, however, this option should be exercised in accordance with the Berne Convention and to the extent that the exceptions relate to the structure of the database; whereas a distinction should be drawn between exceptions for private use and exceptions for reproduction for private purposes, which concerns provisions under national legislation of some Member States on levies on blank media or recording equipment;

(36) Whereas the term "scientific research" within the meaning of this Directive covers both the natural sciences and the human sciences;

(37) Whereas Article 10 (1) of the Berne Convention is not affected by this Directive;

(38) Whereas the increasing use of digital recording technology exposes the database maker to the risk that the contents of his database may be copied and rearranged electronically, without his authorization, to produce a database of identical content which, however, does not infringe any copyright in the arrangement of his database;

(39) Whereas, in addition to aiming to protect the copyright in the original selection or arrangement of the contents of a database, this Directive seeks to safeguard the position of makers of databases against misappropriation of the results of the financial and professional investment made in obtaining and collection the contents by protecting the whole or substantial parts of a database against certain acts by a user or competitor;

(40) Whereas the object of this sui generis right is to ensure protection of any investment in obtaining, verifying or presenting the contents of a database for the limited duration of the right; whereas such investment may consist in the deployment of financial resources and/or the expending of time, effort and energy;

(41) Whereas the objective of the sui generis right is to give the maker of a database the option of preventing the unauthorized extraction and/or re-utilization of all or a substantial part of the contents of that database; whereas the maker of a database is the person who takes the initiative and the risk of investing; whereas this excludes subcontractors in particular from the definition of maker;

(42) Whereas the special right to prevent unauthorized extraction and/or re-utilization relates to acts by the user which go beyond his legitimate rights and thereby harm the investment; whereas the right to prohibit extraction and/or re-utilization of all or a substantial part of the contents relates not only to the manufacture of a parasitical competing product but also to any user who, through his acts, causes significant detriment, evaluated qualitatively or quantitatively, to the investment;

(43) Whereas, in the case of on-line transmission, the right to prohibit re-utilization is not exhausted either as regards the database or as regards a material copy of the database or of part thereof made by the addressee of the transmission with the consent of the rightholder;

(44) Whereas, when on-screen display of the contents of a database necessitates the permanent or temporary transfer of all or a substantial part of such contents to another medium, that act should be subject to authorization by the rightholder;

(45) Whereas the right to prevent unauthorized extraction and/or re-utilization does not in any way constitute an extension of copyright protection to mere facts or data;

(46) Whereas the existence of a right to prevent the unauthorized extraction and/or re-utilization of the whole or a substantial part of works, data or materials from a database should not give rise to the creation of a new right in the works, data or materials themselves;

(47) Whereas, in the interests of competition between suppliers of information products and services, protection by the sui generis right must not be afforded in such a way as to facilitate abuses of a dominant position, in particular as regards the creation and distribution of new products and services which have an intellectual, documentary, technical, economic or commercial added value; whereas, therefore, the provisions of this Directive are without prejudice to the application of Community or national competition rules;

(48) Whereas the objective of this Directive, which is to afford an appropriate and uniform level of protection of databases as a means to secure the remuneration of the maker of the database, is different from the aim of Directive 95/46/EC of the European Parliament and of the Council of 24 October 1995 on the protection of individuals with regard to the processing of personal data and on the free movement of such data[7], which is to guarantee free circulation of personal data on the basis of harmonized rules designed to protect fundamental rights, notably the right to privacy which is recognized in Article 8 of the European Convention for the Protection of Human Rights and Fundamental Freedoms; whereas the provisions of this Directive are without prejudice to data protection legislation;

(49) Whereas, notwithstanding the right to prevent extraction and/or re-utilization of all or a substantial part of a database, it should be laid down that the maker of a database or rightholder may not prevent a lawful user of the database from extracting and re-utilizing insubstantial parts; whereas, however, that user may not unreasonably prejudice either the legitimate interests of the holder of the sui generis right or the holder of copyright or a related right in respect of the works or subject matter contained in the database;

(50) Whereas the Member States should be given the option of providing for exceptions to the right to prevent the unauthorized extraction and/or re-utilization of a substantial part of the contents of a database in the case of extraction for private purposes, for the purposes of illustration for teaching or scientific research, or where extraction and/or re-utilization are/is carried out in the interests of public security or for the purposes of an administrative or judicial procedure; whereas such operations must not prejudice the exclusive rights of the maker to exploit the database and their purpose must not be commercial;

(51) Whereas the Member States, where they avail themselves of the option to permit a lawful user of a database to extract a substantial part of the contents for the purposes of illustration for teaching or scientific research, may limit that permission to certain categories of teaching or scientific research institution;

---

[7] OJ No L 281, 23.11.1995, p. 31.

(52) Whereas those Member States which have specific rules providing for a right comparable to the sui generis right provided for in this Directive should be permitted to retain, as far as the new right is concerned, the exceptions traditionally specified by such rules;

(53) Whereas the burden of proof regarding the date of completion of the making of a database lies with the maker of the database;

(54) Whereas the burden of proof that the criteria exist for concluding that a substantial modification of the contents of a database is to be regarded as a substantial new investment lies with the maker of the database resulting from such investment;

(55) Whereas a substantial new investment involving a new term of protection may include a substantial verification of the contents of the database;

(56) Whereas the right to prevent unauthorized extraction and/or re-utilization in respect of a database should apply to databases whose makers are nationals or habitual residents of third countries or to those produced by legal persons not established in a Member State, within the meaning of the Treaty, only if such third countries offer comparable protection to databases produced by nationals of a Member State or persons who have their habitual residence in the territory of the Community;

(57) Whereas, in addition to remedies provided under the legislation of the Member States for infringements of copyright or other rights, Member States should provide for appropriate remedies against unauthorized extraction and/or re-utilization of the contents of a database;

(58) Whereas, in addition to the protection given under this Directive to the structure of the database by copyright, and to its contents against unauthorized extraction and/or re-utilization under the sui generis right, other legal provisions in the Member States relevant to the supply of database goods and services continue to apply;

(59) Whereas this Directive is without prejudice to the application to databases composed of audiovisual works of any rules recognized by a Member State's legislation concerning the broadcasting of audiovisual programmes;

(60) Whereas some Member States currently protect under copyright arrangements databases which do not meet the criteria for eligibility for copyright protection laid down in this Directive; whereas, even if the databases concerned are eligible for protection under the right laid down in this Directive to prevent unauthorized extraction and/or re-utilization of their contents, the term of protection under that right is considerably shorter than that which they enjoy under the national arrangements currently in force; whereas harmonization of the criteria for determining whether a database is to be protected by copyright may not have the effect of reducing the term of protection currently enjoyed by the rightholders concerned; whereas a derogation should be laid down to that effect; whereas the effects of such derogation must be confined to the territories of the Member States concerned,

HAVE ADOPTED THIS DIRECTIVE:

Chapter I Scope

Article 1   Scope

1. This Directive concerns the legal protection of databases in any form.

2. For the purposes of this Directive, "database" shall mean a collection of independent works, data or other materials arranged in a systematic or methodical way and individually accessible by electronic or other means.

3. Protection under this Directive shall not apply to computer programs used in the making or operation of databases accessible by electronic means.

Article 2   Limitations on the scope

This Directive shall apply without prejudice to Community provisions relating to:

(a) the legal protection of computer programs;

(b) rental right, lending right and certain rights related to copyright in the field of intellectual property;

(c) the term of protection of copyright and certain related rights.

Chapter II Copyright

Article 3   Object of protection

1. In accordance with this Directive, databases which, by reason of the selection or arrangement of their contents, constitute the author's own intellectual creation shall be protected as such by copyright. No other criteria shall be applied to determine their eligibility for that protection.

2. The copyright protection of databases provided for by this Directive shall not extend to their contents and shall be without prejudice to any rights subsisting in those contents themselves.

Article 4   Database authorship

1. The author of a database shall be the natural person or group of natural persons who created the base or, where the legislation of the Member States so permits, the legal person designated as the rightholder by that legislation.

2. Where collective works are recognized by the legislation of a Member State, the economic rights shall be owned by the person holding the copyright.

3. In respect of a database created by a group of natural persons jointly, the exclusive rights shall be owned jointly.

Article 5   Restricted acts

In respect of the expression of the database which is protectable by copyright, the author of a database shall have the exclusive right to carry out or to authorize:

(a) temporary or permanent reproduction by any means and in any form, in whole or in part;

(b) translation, adaptation, arrangement and any other alteration;

(c) any form of distribution to the public of the database or of copies thereof. The first sale in the Community of a copy of the database by the rightholder or with his consent shall exhaust the right to control resale of that copy within the Community;

(d) any communication, display or performance to the public;

(e) any reproduction, distribution, communication, display or performance to the public of the results of the acts referred to in (b).

Article 6   Exceptions to restricted acts

1. The performance by the lawful user of a database or of a copy thereof of any of the acts listed in Article 5 which is necessary for the purposes of access to the contents of the databases and normal use of the contents by the lawful user shall not require the authorization of the author of the database. Where the lawful user is authorized to use only part of the database, this provision shall apply only to that part.

2. Member States shall have the option of providing for limitations on the rights set out in Article 5 in the following cases:

(a) in the case of reproduction for private purposes of a non-electronic database;

(b) where there is use for the sole purpose of illustration for teaching or scientific research, as long as the source is indicated and to the extent justified by the non-commercial purpose to be achieved;

(c) where there is use for the purposes of public security or for the purposes of an administrative or judicial procedure;

(d) where other exceptions to copyright which are traditionally authorized under national law are involved, without prejudice to points (a), (b) and (c).

3. In accordance with the Berne Convention for the protection of Literary and Artistic Works, this Article may not be interpreted in such a way as to allow its application to be used in a manner which unreasonably prejudices the rightholder's legitimate interests or conflicts with normal exploitation of the database.

Chapter III Sui Generis Right

Article 7   Object of protection

1. Member States shall provide for a right for the maker of a database which shows that there has been qualitatively and/or quantitatively a substantial investment in either the obtaining, verification or presentation of the contents to prevent extraction and/or re-utilization of the whole or of a substantial part, evaluated qualitatively and/or quantitatively, of the contents of that database.

2. For the purposes of this Chapter:

(a) "extraction" shall mean the permanent or temporary transfer of all or a substantial part of the contents of a database to another medium by any means or in any form;

(b) "re-utilization" shall mean any form of making available to the public all or a substantial part of the contents of a database by the distribution of copies, by renting, by on-line or other forms of transmission. The first sale of a copy of a database within the Community by the rightholder or with his consent shall exhaust the right to control resale of that copy within the Community;

Public lending is not an act of extraction or re-utilization.

3. The right referred to in paragraph 1 may be transferred, assigned or granted under contractual licence.

4. The right provided for in paragraph 1 shall apply irrespective of the eligibility of that database for protection by copyright or by other rights. Moreover, it shall apply irrespective of eligibility of the contents of that database for protection by copyright or by other rights. Protection of databases under the right provided for in paragraph 1 shall be without prejudice to rights existing in respect of their contents.

5. The repeated and systematic extraction and/or re-utilization of insubstantial parts of the contents of the database implying acts which conflict with a normal exploitation of that database or which unreasonably prejudice the legitimate interests of the maker of the database shall not be permitted.

Article 8   Rights and obligations of lawful users

1. The maker of a database which is made available to the public in whatever manner may not prevent a lawful user of the database from extracting and/or re-utilizing insubstantial parts of its contents, evaluated qualitatively and/or quantitatively, for any purposes whatsoever. Where the lawful user is authorized to extract and/or re-utilize only part of the database, this paragraph shall apply only to that part.

2. A lawful user of a database which is made available to the public in whatever manner may not perform acts which conflict with normal exploitation of the database or unreasonably prejudice the legitimate interests of the maker of the database.

3. A lawful user of a database which is made available to the public in any manner may not cause prejudice to the holder of a copyright or related right in respect of the works or subject matter contained in the database.

Article 9   Exceptions to the sui generis right

Member States may stipulate that lawful users of a database which is made available to the public in whatever manner may, without the authorization of its maker, extract or re-utilize a substantial part of its contents:

(a) in the case of extraction for private purposes of the contents of a non-electronic database;

(b) in the case of extraction for the purposes of illustration for teaching or scientific research, as long as the source is indicated and to the extent justified by the non-commercial purpose to be achieved;

(c) in the case of extraction and/or re-utilization for the purposes of public security or an administrative or judicial procedure.

Article 10   Term of protection

1. The right provided for in Article 7 shall run from the date of completion of the making of the database. It shall expire fifteen years from the first of January of the year following the date of completion.

2. In the case of a database which is made available to the public in whatever manner before expiry of the period provided for in paragraph 1, the term of protection by that right shall expire fifteen years from the first of January of the year following the date when the database was first made available to the public.

3. Any substantial change, evaluated qualitatively or quantitatively, to the contents of a database, including any substantial change resulting from the accumulation of successive additions, deletions or alterations, which would result in the database being considered to be a substantial new investment, evaluated qualitatively or quantitatively, shall qualify the database resulting from that investment for its own term of protection.

Article 11   Beneficiaries of protection under the sui generis right

1. The right provided for in Article 7 shall apply to database whose makers or right-holders are nationals of a Member State or who have their habitual residence in the territory of the Community.

2. Paragraph 1 shall also apply to companies and firms formed in accordance with the law of a Member State and having their registered office, central administration or principal place of business within the Community; however, where such a company or firm has only its registered office in the territory of the Community, its operations must be genuinely linked on an ongoing basis with the economy of a Member State.

3. Agreements extending the right provided for in Article 7 to databases made in third countries and falling outside the provisions of paragraphs 1 and 2 shall be concluded by the Council acting on a proposal from the Commission. The term of any protection extended to databases by virtue of that procedure shall not exceed that available pursuant to Article 10.

Chapter IV Common Provisions

Article 12   Remedies

Member States shall provide appropriate remedies in respect of infringements of the rights provided for in this Directive.

Article 13   Continued application of other legal provisions

This Directive shall be without prejudice to provisions concerning in particular copyright, rights related to copyright or any other rights or obligations subsisting in the data, works or other materials incorporated into a database, patent rights, trade marks, design rights, the protection of national treasures, laws on restrictive practices and unfair competition, trade secrets, security, confidentiality, data protection and privacy, access to public documents, and the law of contract.

Article 14   Application over time

1. Protection pursuant to this Directive as regards copyright shall also be available in respect of databases created prior to the date referred to Article 16 (1) which on that date fulfil the requirements laid down in this Directive as regards copyright protection of databases.

2. Notwithstanding paragraph 1, where a database protected under copyright arrangements in a Member State on the date of publication of this Directive does not fulfil the eligibility criteria for copyright protection laid down in Article 3 (1), this Directive shall not result in any curtailing in that Member State of the remaining term of protection afforded under those arrangements.

3. Protection pursuant to the provisions of this Directive as regards the right provided for in Article 7 shall also be available in respect of databases the making of which was completed not more than fifteen years prior to the date referred to in Article 16 (1) and which on that date fulfil the requirements laid down in Article 7.

4. The protection provided for in paragraphs 1 and 3 shall be without prejudice to any acts concluded and rights acquired before the date referred to in those paragraphs.

5. In the case of a database the making of which was completed not more than fifteen years prior to the date referred to in Article 16 (1), the term of protection by the right provided for in Article 7 shall expire fifteen years from the first of January following that date.

Article 15 Binding nature of certain provisions

Any contractual provision contrary to Articles 6 (1) and 8 shall be null and void.

Article 16 Final provisions

1. Member States shall bring into force the laws, regulations and administrative provisions necessary to comply with this Directive before 1 January 1998.

When Member States adopt these provisions, they shall contain a reference to this Directive or shall be accompanied by such reference on the occasion of their official publication. The methods of making such reference shall be laid down by Member States.

2. Member States shall communicate to the Commission the text of the provisions of domestic law which they adopt in the field governed by this Directive.

3. Not later than at the end of the third year after the date referred to in paragraph 1, and every three years thereafter, the Commission shall submit to the European Parliament, the Council and the Economic and Social Committee a report on the application of this Directive, in which, inter alia, on the basis of specific information supplied by the Member States, it shall examine in particular the application of the sui generis right, including Articles 8 and 9, and shall verify especially whether the application of this right has led to abuse of a dominant position or other interference with free competition which would justify appropriate measures being taken, including the establishment of non-voluntary licensing arrangements. Where necessary, it shall submit proposals for adjustment of this Directive in line with developments in the area of databases.

Article 17

This Directive is addressed to the Member States.

Done at Strasbourg, 11 March 1996.

For the European Parliament

The President

K. HÄNSCH

For the Council

The President

L. DINI

Directive 97/7/EC of the European Parliament and of the Council of 20 May 1997 on the protection of consumers in respect of distance contracts

THE EUROPEAN PARLIAMENT AND THE COUNCIL OF THE EUROPEAN UNION,

Having regard to the Treaty establishing the European Community, and in particular Article 100a thereof,

Having regard to the proposal from the Commission[1],

Having regard to the opinion of the Economic and Social Committee[2],

Acting in accordance with the procedure laid down in Article 189b of the Treaty[3], in the light of the joint text approved by the Conciliation Committee on 27 November 1996,

---

[1] OJ No C 156, 23.6.1992, p. 14 and OJ No C 308, 15.11.1993, p. 18.

[2] OJ No C 19, 25.1.1993, p. 111.

[3] Opinion of the European Parliament of 26 May 1993 (OJ No C 176, 28.6.1993, p. 95), Council common position of 29 June 1995 (OJ No C 288, 30.10.1995, p. 1) and Decision of the European Parliament of 13 December 1995 (OJ No C 17, 22.1.1996, p. 51). Decision of the European Parliament of 16 January 1997 and Council Decision of 20 January 1997.

(1) Whereas, in connection with the attainment of the aims of the internal market, measures must be taken for the gradual consolidation of that market;

(2) Whereas the free movement of goods and services affects not only the business sector but also private individuals; whereas it means that consumers should be able to have access to the goods and services of another Member State on the same terms as the population of that State;

(3) Whereas, for consumers, cross-border distance selling could be one of the main tangible results of the completion of the internal market, as noted, inter alia, in the communication from the Commission to the Council entitled "Towards a single market in distribution"; whereas it is essential to the smooth operation of the internal market for consumers to be able to have dealings with a business outside their country, even if it has a subsidiary in the consumer's country of residence;

(4) Whereas the introduction of new technologies is increasing the number of ways for consumers to obtain information about offers anywhere in the Community and to place orders; whereas some Member States have already taken different or diverging measures to protect consumers in respect of distance selling, which has had a detrimental effect on competition between businesses in the internal market; whereas it is therefore necessary to introduce at Community level a minimum set of common rules in this area;

(5) Whereas paragraphs 18 and 19 of the Annex to the Council resolution of 14 April 1975 on a preliminary programme of the European Economic Community for a consumer protection and information policy[4] point to the need to protect the purchasers of goods or services from demands for payment for unsolicited goods and from high-pressure selling methods;

(6) Whereas paragraph 33 of the communication from the Commission to the Council entitled "A new impetus for consumer protection policy", which was approved by the Council resolution of 23 June 1986[5], states that the Commission will submit proposals regarding the use of new information technologies enabling consumers to place orders with suppliers from their homes;

(7) Whereas the Council resolution of 9 November 1989 on future priorities for relaunching consumer protection policy[6] calls upon the Commission to give priority to the areas referred to in the Annex to that resolution; whereas that Annex refers to new technologies involving teleshopping; whereas the Commission has responded to that resolution by adopting a three-year action plan for consumer protection policy in the European Economic Community (1990–1992); whereas that plan provides for the adoption of a Directive;

(8) Whereas the languages used for distance contracts are a matter for the Member States;

(9) Whereas contracts negotiated at a distance involve the use of one or more means of distance communication; whereas the various means of communication are used as part of an organized distance sales or service-provision scheme not involving the simultaneous presence of the supplier and the consumer; whereas the constant development of those means of communication does not allow an exhaustive list to be compiled but does require principles to be defined which are valid even for those which are not as yet in widespread use;

(10) Whereas the same transaction comprising successive operations or a series of separate operations over a period of time may give rise to different legal descriptions depending on the law of the Member States; whereas the provisions of this Directive cannot be applied differently according to the law of the Member States, subject to their recourse to Article 14; whereas, to that end, there is therefore reason to consider that there must at least be compliance with the provisions of this Directive at the time of the first of a series of successive operations or the first of a series of separate operations over a period of time which may be considered as forming a whole, whether that operation or series of operations are the subject of a single contract or successive, separate contracts;

(11) Whereas the use of means of distance communication must not lead to a reduction in the information provided to the consumer; whereas the information that is required to be sent to the consumer should therefore be determined, whatever the means of communication used; whereas the information supplied must also comply with the other relevant Community rules, in particular those in Council Directive 84/450/EEC of 10 September 1984 relating to the approximation of the laws,

[4] OJ No C 92, 25.4.1975, p. 1.   [5] OJ No C 167, 5.7.1986, p. 1.   [6] OJ No C 294, 22.11.1989, p. 1.

regulations and administrative provisions of the Member States concerning misleading advertising[7]; whereas, if exceptions are made to the obligation to provide information, it is up to the consumer, on a discretionary basis, to request certain basic information such as the identity of the supplier, the main characteristics of the goods or services and their price;

(12) Whereas in the case of communication by telephone it is appropriate that the consumer receive enough information at the beginning of the conversation to decide whether or not to continue;

(13) Whereas information disseminated by certain electronic technologies is often ephemeral in nature insofar as it is not received on a permanent medium; whereas the consumer must therefore receive written notice in good time of the information necessary for proper performance of the contract;

(14) Whereas the consumer is not able actually to see the product or ascertain the nature of the service provided before concluding the contract; whereas provision should be made, unless otherwise specified in this Directive, for a right of withdrawal from the contract; whereas, if this right is to be more than formal, the costs, if any, borne by the consumer when exercising the right of withdrawal must be limited to the direct costs for returning the goods; whereas this right of withdrawal shall be without prejudice to the consumer's rights under national laws, with particular regard to the receipt of damaged products and services or of products and services not corresponding to the description given in the offer of such products or services; whereas it is for the Member States to determine the other conditions and arrangements following exercise of the right of withdrawal;

(15) Whereas it is also necessary to prescribe a time limit for performance of the contract if this is not specified at the time of ordering;

(16) Whereas the promotional technique involving the dispatch of a product or the provision of a service to the consumer in return for payment without a prior request from, or the explicit agreement of, the consumer cannot be permitted, unless a substitute product or service is involved;

(17) Whereas the principles set out in Articles 8 and 10 of the European Convention for the Protection of Human Rights and Fundamental Freedoms of 4 November 1950 apply; whereas the consumer's right to privacy, particularly as regards freedom from certain particularly intrusive means of communication, should be recognized; whereas specific limits on the use of such means should therefore be stipulated; whereas Member States should take appropriate measures to protect effectively those consumers, who do not wish to be contacted through certain means of communication, against such contacts, without prejudice to the particular safeguards available to the consumer under Community legislation concerning the protection of personal data and privacy;

(18) Whereas it is important for the minimum binding rules contained in this Directive to be supplemented where appropriate by voluntary arrangements among the traders concerned, in line with Commission recommendation 92/295/EEC of 7 April 1992 on codes of practice for the protection of consumers in respect of contracts negotiated at a distance[8];

(19) Whereas in the interest of optimum consumer protection it is important for consumers to be satisfactorily informed of the provisions of this Directive and of codes of practice that may exist in this field;

(20) Whereas non-compliance with this Directive may harm not only consumers but also competitors; whereas provisions may therefore be laid down enabling public bodies or their representatives, or consumer organizations which, under national legislation, have a legitimate interest in consumer protection, or professional organizations which have a legitimate interest in taking action, to monitor the application thereof;

(21) Whereas it is important, with a view to consumer protection, to address the question of cross-border complaints as soon as this is feasible; whereas the Commission published on 14 February 1996 a plan of action on consumer access to justice and the settlement of consumer disputes in the internal market; whereas that plan of action includes specific initiatives to promote out-of-court procedures;

---

[7] OJ No L 250, 19.9.1984, p. 17.   [8] OJ No L 156, 10.6.1992, p. 21.

whereas objective criteria (Annex II) are suggested to ensure the reliability of those procedures and provision is made for the use of standardized claims forms (Annex III);

(22) Whereas in the use of new technologies the consumer is not in control of the means of communication used; whereas it is therefore necessary to provide that the burden of proof may be on the supplier;

(23) Whereas there is a risk that, in certain cases, the consumer may be deprived of protection under this Directive through the designation of the law of a non-member country as the law applicable to the contract; whereas provisions should therefore be included in this Directive to avert that risk;

(24) Whereas a Member State may ban, in the general interest, the marketing on its territory of certain goods and services through distance contracts; whereas that ban must comply with Community rules; whereas there is already provision for such bans, notably with regard to medicinal products, under Council Directive 89/552/EEC of 3 October 1989 on the coordination of certain provisions laid down by law, regulation or administrative action in Member States concerning the pursuit of television broadcasting activities[9] and Council Directive 92/28/EEC of 31 March 1992 on the advertising of medicinal products for human use,[10]

HAVE ADOPTED THIS DIRECTIVE:

Article 1   Object

The object of this Directive is to approximate the laws, regulations and administrative provisions of the Member States concerning distance contracts between consumers and suppliers.

Article 2   Definitions

For the purposes of this Directive:

(1) "distance contract" means any contract concerning goods or services concluded between a supplier and a consumer under an organized distance sales or service-provision scheme run by the supplier, who, for the purpose of the contract, makes exclusive use of one or more means of distance communication up to and including the moment at which the contract is concluded;

(2) "consumer" means any natural person who, in contracts covered by this Directive, is acting for purposes which are outside his trade, business or profession;

(3) "supplier" means any natural or legal person who, in contracts covered by this Directive, is acting in his commercial or professional capacity;

(4) "means of distance communication" means any means which, without the simultaneous physical presence of the supplier and the consumer, may be used for the conclusion of a contract between those parties. An indicative list of the means covered by this Directive is contained in Annex I;

(5) "operator of a means of communication" means any public or private natural or legal person whose trade, business or profession involves making one or more means of distance communication available to suppliers.

Article 3   Exemptions

1. This Directive shall not apply to contracts:
   — relating to financial services, a non-exhaustive list of which is given in Annex II,
   — concluded by means of automatic vending machines or automated commercial premises,
   — concluded with telecommunications operators through the use of public payphones,
   — concluded for the construction and sale of immovable property or relating to other immovable property rights, except for rental,
   — concluded at an auction.
2. Articles 4, 5, 6 and 7 (1) shall not apply:
   — to contracts for the supply of foodstuffs, beverages or other goods intended for everyday consumption supplied to the home of the consumer, to his residence or to his workplace by regular roundsmen,

---

[9] OJ No L 298, 17.10.1989, p. 23.   [10] 10 OJ No L 113, 30.4.1992, p. 13.

— to contracts for the provision of accommodation, transport, catering or leisure services, where the supplier undertakes, when the contract is concluded, to provide these services on a specific date or within a specific period; exceptionally, in the case of outdoor leisure events, the supplier can reserve the right not to apply Article 7 (2) in specific circumstances.

Article 4   Prior information

1. In good time prior to the conclusion of any distance contract, the consumer shall be provided with the following information:

  (a) the identity of the supplier and, in the case of contracts requiring payment in advance, his address;

  (b) the main characteristics of the goods or services;

  (c) the price of the goods or services including all taxes;

  (d) delivery costs, where appropriate;

  (e) the arrangements for payment, delivery or performance;

  (f) the existence of a right of withdrawal, except in the cases referred to in Article 6 (3);

  (g) the cost of using the means of distance communication, where it is calculated other than at the basic rate;

  (h) the period for which the offer or the price remains valid;

  (i) where appropriate, the minimum duration of the contract in the case of contracts for the supply of products or services to be performed permanently or recurrently.

2. The information referred to in paragraph 1, the commercial purpose of which must be made clear, shall be provided in a clear and comprehensible manner in any way appropriate to the means of distance communication used, with due regard, in particular, to the principles of good faith in commercial transactions, and the principles governing the protection of those who are unable, pursuant to the legislation of the Member States, to give their consent, such as minors.

3. Moreover, in the case of telephone communications, the identity of the supplier and the commercial purpose of the call shall be made explicitly clear at the beginning of any conversation with the consumer.

Article 5   Written confirmation of information

1. The consumer must receive written confirmation or confirmation in another durable medium available and accessible to him of the information referred to in Article 4(1) (a) to (f), in good time during the performance of the contract, and at the latest at the time of delivery where goods not for delivery to third parties are concerned, unless the information has already been given to the consumer prior to conclusion of the contract in writing or on another durable medium available and accessible to him. In any event the following must be provided:

— written information on the conditions and procedures for exercising the right of withdrawal, within the meaning of Article 6, including the cases referred to in the first indent of Article 6 (3),

— the geographical address of the place of business of the supplier to which the consumer may address any complaints,

— information on after-sales services and guarantees which exist,

— the conclusion for cancelling the contract, where it is of unspecified duration or a duration exceeding one year.

2. Paragraph 1 shall not apply to services which are performed through the use of a means of distance communication, where they are supplied on only one occasion and are invoiced by the operator of the means of distance communication. Nevertheless, the consumer must in all cases be able to obtain the geographical address of the place of business of the supplier to which he may address any complaints.

Article 6   Right of withdrawal

1. For any distance contract the consumer shall have a period of at least seven working days in which to withdraw from the contract without penalty and without giving any reason. The only charge

that may be made to the consumer because of the exercise of his right of withdrawal is the direct cost of returning the goods. The period for exercise of this right shall begin:

— in the case of goods, from the day of receipt by the consumer where the obligations laid down in Article 5 have been fulfilled,

— in the case of services, from the day of conclusion of the contract or from the day on which the obligations laid down in Article 5 were fulfilled if they are fulfilled after conclusion of the contract, provided that this period does not exceed the three-month period referred to in the following subparagraph.

If the supplier has failed to fulfil the obligations laid down in Article 5, the period shall be three months. The period shall begin:

— in the case of goods, from the day of receipt by the consumer,

— in the case of services, from the day of conclusion of the contract.

If the information referred to in Article 5 is supplied within this three-month period, the seven working day period referred to in the first subparagraph shall begin as from that moment.

2. Where the right of withdrawal has been exercised by the consumer pursuant to this Article, the supplier shall be obliged to reimburse the sums paid by the consumer free of charge. The only charge that may be made to the consumer because of the exercise of his right of withdrawal is the direct cost of returning the goods. Such reimbursement must be carried out as soon as possible and in any case within 30 days.

3. Unless the parties have agreed otherwise, the consumer may not exercise the right of withdrawal provided for in paragraph 1 in respect of contracts:

— for the provision of services if performance has begun, with the consumer's agreement, before the end of the seven working day period referred to in paragraph 1,

— for the supply of goods or services the price of which is dependent on fluctuations in the financial market which cannot be controlled by the supplier,

— for the supply of goods made to the consumer's specifications or clearly personalized or which, by reason of their nature, cannot be returned or are liable to deteriorate or expire rapidly,

— for the supply of audio or video recordings or computer software which were unsealed by the consumer,

— for the supply of newspapers, periodicals and magazines,

— for gaming and lottery services.

4. The Member States shall make provision in their legislation to ensure that:

— if the price of goods or services is fully or partly covered by credit granted by the supplier, or

— if that price is fully or partly covered by credit granted to the consumer by a third party on the basis of an agreement between the third party and the supplier,

the credit agreement shall be cancelled, without any penalty, if the consumer exercises his right to withdraw from the contract in accordance with paragraph 1.

Member States shall determine the detailed rules for cancellation of the credit agreement.

Article 7   Performance

1. Unless the parties have agreed otherwise, the supplier must execute the order within a maximum of 30 days from the day following that on which the consumer forwarded his order to the supplier.

2. Where a supplier fails to perform his side of the contract on the grounds that the goods or services ordered are unavailable, the consumer must be informed of this situation and must be able to obtain a refund of any sums he has paid as soon as possible and in any case within 30 days.

3. Nevertheless, Member States may lay down that the supplier may provide the consumer with goods or services of equivalent quality and price provided that this possibility was provided for prior to the conclusion of the contract or in the contract. The consumer shall be informed of this possibility in a clear and comprehensible manner. The cost of returning the goods following exercise of the right of withdrawal shall, in this case, be borne by the supplier, and the consumer must be informed of this. In such cases the supply of goods or services may not be deemed to constitute inertia selling within the meaning of Article 9.

Article 8   Payment by card

Member States shall ensure that appropriate measures exist to allow a consumer:

— to request cancellation of a payment where fraudulent use has been made of his payment card in connection with distance contracts covered by this Directive,

— in the event of fraudulent use, to be recredited with the sums paid or have them returned.

Article 9   Inertia selling

Member States shall take the measures necessary to:

— prohibit the supply of goods or services to a consumer without their being ordered by the consumer beforehand, where such supply involves a demand for payment,

— exempt the consumer from the provision of any consideration in cases of unsolicited supply, the absence of a response not constituting consent.

Article 10   Restrictions on the use of certain means of distance communication

1. Use by a supplier of the following means requires the prior consent of the consumer:

— automated calling system without human intervention (automatic calling machine),

— facsimile machine (fax).

2. Member States shall ensure that means of distance communication, other than those referred to in paragraph 1, which allow individual communications may be used only where there is no clear objection from the consumer.

Article 11   Judicial or administrative redress

1. Member States shall ensure that adequate and effective means exist to ensure compliance with this Directive in the interests of consumers.

2. The means referred to in paragraph 1 shall include provisions whereby one or more of the following bodies, as determined by national law, may take action under national law before the courts or before the competent administrative bodies to ensure that the national provisions for the implementation of this Directive are applied:

(a) public bodies or their representatives;

(b) consumer organizations having a legitimate interest in protecting consumers;

(c) professional organizations having a legitimate interest in acting.

3. (a) Member States may stipulate that the burden of proof concerning the existence of prior information, written confirmation, compliance with time-limits or consumer consent can be placed on the supplier.

(b) Member States shall take the measures needed to ensure that suppliers and operators of means of communication, where they are able to do so, cease practices which do not comply with measures adopted pursuant to this Directive.

4. Member States may provide for voluntary supervision by self-regulatory bodies of compliance with the provisions of this Directive and recourse to such bodies for the settlement of disputes to be added to the means which Member States must provide to ensure compliance with the provisions of this Directive.

Article 12   Binding nature

1. The consumer may not waive the rights conferred on him by the transposition of this Directive into national law.

2. Member States shall take the measures needed to ensure that the consumer does not lose the protection granted by this Directive by virtue of the choice of the law of a non-member country as the law applicable to the contract if the latter has close connection with the territory of one or more Member States.

Article 13   Community rules

1. The provisions of this Directive shall apply insofar as there are no particular provisions in rules of Community law governing certain types of distance contracts in their entirety.

2. Where specific Community rules contain provisions governing only certain aspects of the supply of goods or provision of services, those provisions, rather than the provisions of this Directive, shall apply to these specific aspects of the distance contracts.

Article 14   Minimal clause

Member States may introduce or maintain, in the area covered by this Directive, more stringent provisions compatible with the Treaty, to ensure a higher level of consumer protection. Such provisions shall, where appropriate, include a ban, in the general interest, on the marketing of certain goods or services, particularly medicinal products, within their territory by means of distance contracts, with due regard for the Treaty.

Article 15   Implementation

1. Member States shall bring into force the laws, regulations and administrative provisions necessary to comply with this Directive no later than three years after it enters into force. They shall forthwith inform the Commission thereof.

2. When Member States adopt the measures referred to in paragraph 1, these shall contain a reference to this Directive or shall be accompanied by such reference on the occasion of their official publication. The procedure for such reference shall be laid down by Member States.

3. Member States shall communicate to the Commission the text of the provisions of national law which they adopt in the field governed by this Directive.

4. No later than four years after the entry into force of this Directive the Commission shall submit a report to the European Parliament and the Council on the implementation of this Directive, accompanied if appropriate by a proposal for the revision thereof.

Article 16   Consumer information

Member States shall take appropriate measures to inform the consumer of the national law transposing this Directive and shall encourage, where appropriate, professional organizations to inform consumers of their codes of practice.

Article 17   Complaints systems

The Commission shall study the feasibility of establishing effective means to deal with consumers' complaints in respect of distance selling. Within two years after the entry into force of this Directive the Commission shall submit a report to the European Parliament and the Council on the results of the studies, accompanied if appropriate by proposals.

Article 18

This Directive shall enter into force on the day of its publication in the Official Journal of the European Communities.

Article 19

This Directive is addressed to the Member States.
Done at Brussels, 20 May 1997.
For the European Parliament
The President
J.M. GIL-ROBLES
For the Council
The President
J. VAN AARTSEN

Annex I

Means of communication covered by Article 2 (4)
— Unaddressed printed matter
— Addressed printed matter
— Standard letter

— Press advertising with order form
— Catalogue
— Telephone with human intervention
— Telephone without human intervention (automatic calling machine, audiotext)
— Radio
— Videophone (telephone with screen)
— Videotex (microcomputer and television screen) with keyboard or touch screen
— Electronic mail
— Facsimile machine (fax)
— Television (teleshopping).

Annex II

Financial services within the meaning of Article 3 (1)
— Investment services
— Insurance and reinsurance operations
— Banking services
— Operations relating to dealings in futures or options.

Such services include in particular:
— *investment services referred to in the Annex to Directive 93/22/EEC*[1]; services of collective investment undertakings,
— services covered by the activities subject to mutual recognition referred to in the Annex to Directive 89/646/EEC[2];
— operations covered by the insurance and reinsurance activities referred to in:
— Article 1 of Directive 73/239/EEC[3],
— the Annex to Directive 79/267/EEC[4],
— Directive 64/225/EEC[5],
— Directives 92/49/EEC[6] and 92/96/EEC[7].

Statement by the Council and the Parliament re Article 6(1)

The Council and the Parliament note that the Commission will examine the possibility and desirability of harmonizing the method of calculating the cooling-off period under existing consumer-protection legislation, notably Directive 85/577/EEC of 20 December 1985 on the protection of consumers in respect of contracts negotiated away from commercial establishments ("door-to-door sales")[8].

Statement by the Commission re Article 3 (1), first indent

The Commission recognizes the importance of protecting consumers in respect of distance contracts concerning financial services and has published a Green Paper entitled "Financial services: meeting consumers' expectations". In the light of reactions to the Green Paper the Commission will examine ways of incorporating consumer protection into the policy on financial services and the possible legislative implications and, if need be, will submit appropriate proposals.

---

[1] OJ No L 141, 11.6.1993, p. 27.
[2] OJ No L 386, 30.12.1989, p. 1. Directive as amended by Directive 92/30/EEC (OJ No L 110, 28.4.1992, p. 52.
[3] OJ No L 228, 16.8.1973, p. 3. Directive as last amended by Directive 92/49/EEC (OJ No L 228, 11.8.1992, p. 1.
[4] OJ No L 63, 13.3.1979, p. 1. Directive as last amended by Directive 90/619/EEC (OJ No L 330, 29.11.1990, p. 50.
[5] OJ No 56, 4.4.1964, p. 878/64. Directive as amended by the 1973 Act of Accession.
[6] OJ No L 228, 11.8.1992, p. 1.
[7] OJ No L 360, 9.12.1992, p. 1.
[8] OJ No L 372, 31.12.1985, p. 31.

Directive 1999/93/EC of the European Parliament and of the Council of 13 December 1999 on a Community framework for electronic signatures

THE EUROPEAN PARLIAMENT AND THE COUNCIL OF THE EUROPEAN UNION,

Having regard to the Treaty establishing the European Community, and in particular Articles 47(2), 55 and 95 thereof,

Having regard to the proposal from the Commission[1],

Having regard to the opinion of the Economic and Social Committee[2],

Having regard to the opinion of the Committee of the Regions[3],

Acting in accordance with the procedure laid down in Article 251 of the Treaty[4],

Whereas:

(1) On 16 April 1997 the Commission presented to the European Parliament, the Council, the Economic and Social Committee and the Committee of the Regions a Communication on a European Initiative in Electronic Commerce;

(2) On 8 October 1997 the Commission presented to the European Parliament, the Council, the Economic and Social Committee and the Committee of the Regions a Communication on ensuring security and trust in electronic communication-towards a European framework for digital signatures and encryption;

(3) On 1 December 1997 the Council invited the Commission to submit as soon as possible a proposal for a Directive of the European Parliament and of the Council on digital signatures;

(4) Electronic communication and commerce necessitate "electronic signatures" and related services allowing data authentication; divergent rules with respect to legal recognition of electronic signatures and the accreditation of certification-service providers in the Member States may create a significant barrier to the use of electronic communications and electronic commerce; on the other hand, a clear Community framework regarding the conditions applying to electronic signatures will strengthen confidence in, and general acceptance of, the new technologies; legislation in the Member States should not hinder the free movement of goods and services in the internal market;

(5) The interoperability of electronic-signature products should be promoted; in accordance with Article 14 of the Treaty, the internal market comprises an area without internal frontiers in which the free movement of goods is ensured; essential requirements specific to electronic-signature products must be met in order to ensure free movement within the internal market and to build trust in electronic signatures, without prejudice to Council Regulation (EC) No 3381/94 of 19 December 1994 setting up a Community regime for the control of exports of dual-use goods[5] and Council Decision 94/942/CFSP of 19 December 1994 on the joint action adopted by the Council concerning the control of exports of dual-use goods[6];

(6) This Directive does not harmonise the provision of services with respect to the confidentiality of information where they are covered by national provisions concerned with public policy or public security;

(7) The internal market ensures the free movement of persons, as a result of which citizens and residents of the European Union increasingly need to deal with authorities in Member States other than the one in which they reside; the availability of electronic communication could be of great service in this respect;

---

[1] OJ C 325, 23.10.1998, p. 5.   [2] OJ C 40, 15.2.1999, p. 29.   [3] OJ C 93, 6.4.1999, p. 33.

[4] Opinion of the European Parliament of 13 January 1999 (OJ C 104, 14.4.1999, p. 49), Council Common Position of 28 June 1999 (OJ C 243, 27.8.1999, p. 33) and Decision of the European Parliament of 27 October 1999 (not yet published in the Official Journal). Council Decision of 30 November 1999.

[5] OJ L 367, 31.12.1994, p. 1. Regulation as amended by Regulation (EC) No 837/95 (OJ L 90, 21.4.1995, p. 1).

[6] OJ L 367, 31.12.1994, p. 8. Decision as last amended by Decision 99/193/CFSP (OJ L 73, 19.3.1999, p. 1).

(8) Rapid technological development and the global character of the Internet necessitate an approach which is open to various technologies and services capable of authenticating data electronically;

(9) Electronic signatures will be used in a large variety of circumstances and applications, resulting in a wide range of new services and products related to or using electronic signatures; the definition of such products and services should not be limited to the issuance and management of certificates, but should also encompass any other service and product using, or ancillary to, electronic signatures, such as registration services, time-stamping services, directory services, computing services or consultancy services related to electronic signatures;

(10) The internal market enables certification-service-providers to develop their cross-border activities with a view to increasing their competitiveness, and thus to offer consumers and businesses new opportunities to exchange information and trade electronically in a secure way, regardless of frontiers; in order to stimulate the Community-wide provision of certification services over open networks, certification-service-providers should be free to provide their services without prior authorisation; prior authorisation means not only any permission whereby the certification-service-provider concerned has to obtain a decision by national authorities before being allowed to provide its certification services, but also any other measures having the same effect;

(11) Voluntary accreditation schemes aiming at an enhanced level of service-provision may offer certification-service-providers the appropriate framework for developing further their services towards the levels of trust, security and quality demanded by the evolving market; such schemes should encourage the development of best practice among certification-service-providers; certification-service-providers should be left free to adhere to and benefit from such accreditation schemes;

(12) Certification services can be offered either by a public entity or a legal or natural person, when it is established in accordance with the national law; whereas Member States should not prohibit certification-service-providers from operating outside voluntary accreditation schemes; it should be ensured that such accreditation schemes do not reduce competition for certification services;

(13) Member States may decide how they ensure the supervision of compliance with the provisions laid down in this Directive; this Directive does not preclude the establishment of private-sector-based supervision systems; this Directive does not oblige certification-service-providers to apply to be supervised under any applicable accreditation scheme;

(14) It is important to strike a balance between consumer and business needs;

(15) Annex III covers requirements for secure signature-creation devices to ensure the functionality of advanced electronic signatures; it does not cover the entire system environment in which such devices operate; the functioning of the internal market requires the Commission and the Member States to act swiftly to enable the bodies charged with the conformity assessment of secure signature devices with Annex III to be designated; in order to meet market needs conformity assessment must be timely and efficient;

(16) This Directive contributes to the use and legal recognition of electronic signatures within the Community; a regulatory framework is not needed for electronic signatures exclusively used within systems, which are based on voluntary agreements under private law between a specified number of participants; the freedom of parties to agree among themselves the terms and conditions under which they accept electronically signed data should be respected to the extent allowed by national law; the legal effectiveness of electronic signatures used in such systems and their admissibility as evidence in legal proceedings should be recognised;

(17) This Directive does not seek to harmonise national rules concerning contract law, particularly the formation and performance of contracts, or other formalities of a non-contractual nature concerning signatures; for this reason the provisions concerning the legal effect of electronic signatures should be without prejudice to requirements regarding form laid down in national law with regard to the conclusion of contracts or the rules determining where a contract is concluded;

(18) The storage and copying of signature-creation data could cause a threat to the legal validity of electronic signatures;

(19) Electronic signatures will be used in the public sector within national and Community administrations and in communications between such administrations and with citizens and economic operators, for example in the public procurement, taxation, social security, health and justice systems;

(20) Harmonised criteria relating to the legal effects of electronic signatures will preserve a coherent legal framework across the Community; national law lays down different requirements for the legal validity of hand-written signatures; whereas certificates can be used to confirm the identity of a person signing electronically; advanced electronic signatures based on qualified certificates aim at a higher level of security; advanced electronic signatures which are based on a qualified certificate and which are created by a secure-signature-creation device can be regarded as legally equivalent to hand-written signatures only if the requirements for hand-written signatures are fulfilled;

(21) In order to contribute to the general acceptance of electronic authentication methods it has to be ensured that electronic signatures can be used as evidence in legal proceedings in all Member States; the legal recognition of electronic signatures should be based upon objective criteria and not be linked to authorisation of the certification-service-provider involved; national law governs the legal spheres in which electronic documents and electronic signatures may be used; this Directive is without prejudice to the power of a national court to make a ruling regarding conformity with the requirements of this Directive and does not affect national rules regarding the unfettered judicial consideration of evidence;

(22) Certification-service-providers providing certification-services to the public are subject to national rules regarding liability;

(23) The development of international electronic commerce requires cross-border arrangements involving third countries; in order to ensure interoperability at a global level, agreements on multilateral rules with third countries on mutual recognition of certification services could be beneficial;

(24) In order to increase user confidence in electronic communication and electronic commerce, certification-service-providers must observe data protection legislation and individual privacy;

(25) Provisions on the use of pseudonyms in certificates should not prevent Member States from requiring identification of persons pursuant to Community or national law;

(26) The measures necessary for the implementation of this Directive are to be adopted in accordance with Council Decision 1999/468/EC of 28 June 1999 laying down the procedures for the exercise of implementing powers conferred on the Commission[7];

(27) Two years after its implementation the Commission will carry out a review of this Directive so as, inter alia, to ensure that the advance of technology or changes in the legal environment have not created barriers to achieving the aims stated in this Directive; it should examine the implications of associated technical areas and submit a report to the European Parliament and the Council on this subject;

(28) In accordance with the principles of subsidiarity and proportionality as set out in Article 5 of the Treaty, the objective of creating a harmonised legal framework for the provision of electronic signatures and related services cannot be sufficiently achieved by the Member States and can therefore be better achieved by the Community; this Directive does not go beyond what is necessary to achieve that objective,

HAVE ADOPTED THIS DIRECTIVE:

Article 1 Scope

The purpose of this Directive is to facilitate the use of electronic signatures and to contribute to their legal recognition. It establishes a legal framework for electronic signatures and certain certification-services in order to ensure the proper functioning of the internal market.

It does not cover aspects related to the conclusion and validity of contracts or other legal obligations where there are requirements as regards form prescribed by national or Community law nor does it affect rules and limits, contained in national or Community law, governing the use of documents.

---

[7] OJ L 184, 17.7.1999, p. 23.

Article 2   Definitions

For the purpose of this Directive:

1. "electronic signature" means data in electronic form which are attached to or logically associated with other electronic data and which serve as a method of authentication;

2. "advanced electronic signature" means an electronic signature which meets the following requirements:

    (a) it is uniquely linked to the signatory;

    (b) it is capable of identifying the signatory;

    (c) it is created using means that the signatory can maintain under his sole control; and

    (d) it is linked to the data to which it relates in such a manner that any subsequent change of the data is detectable;

3. "signatory" means a person who holds a signature-creation device and acts either on his own behalf or on behalf of the natural or legal person or entity he represents;

4. "signature-creation data" means unique data, such as codes or private cryptographic keys, which are used by the signatory to create an electronic signature;

5. "signature-creation device" means configured software or hardware used to implement the signature-creation data;

6. "secure-signature-creation device" means a signature-creation device which meets the requirements laid down in Annex III;

7. "signature-verification-data" means data, such as codes or public cryptographic keys, which are used for the purpose of verifying an electronic signature;

8. "signature-verification device" means configured software or hardware used to implement the signature-verification-data;

9. "certificate" means an electronic attestation which links signature-verification data to a person and confirms the identity of that person;

10. "qualified certificate" means a certificate which meets the requirements laid down in Annex I and is provided by a certification-service-provider who fulfils the requirements laid down in Annex II;

11. "certification-service-provider" means an entity or a legal or natural person who issues certificates or provides other services related to electronic signatures;

12. "electronic-signature product" means hardware or software, or relevant components thereof, which are intended to be used by a certification-service-provider for the provision of electronic-signature services or are intended to be used for the creation or verification of electronic signatures;

13. "voluntary accreditation" means any permission, setting out rights and obligations specific to the provision of certification services, to be granted upon request by the certification-service-provider concerned, by the public or private body charged with the elaboration of, and supervision of compliance with, such rights and obligations, where the certification-service-provider is not entitled to exercise the rights stemming from the permission until it has received the decision by the body.

Article 3   Market access

1. Member States shall not make the provision of certification services subject to prior authorisation.

2. Without prejudice to the provisions of paragraph 1, Member States may introduce or maintain voluntary accreditation schemes aiming at enhanced levels of certification-service provision. All conditions related to such schemes must be objective, transparent, proportionate and non-discriminatory. Member States may not limit the number of accredited certification-service-providers for reasons which fall within the scope of this Directive.

3. Each Member State shall ensure the establishment of an appropriate system that allows for supervision of certification-service-providers which are established on its territory and issue qualified certificates to the public.

4. The conformity of secure signature-creation-devices with the requirements laid down in Annex III shall be determined by appropriate public or private bodies designated by Member States.

The Commission shall, pursuant to the procedure laid down in Article 9, establish criteria for Member States to determine whether a body should be designated.

A determination of conformity with the requirements laid down in Annex III made by the bodies referred to in the first subparagraph shall be recognised by all Member States.

5. The Commission may, in accordance with the procedure laid down in Article 9, establish and publish reference numbers of generally recognised standards for electronic-signature products in the Official Journal of the European Communities. Member States shall presume that there is compliance with the requirements laid down in Annex II, point (f), and Annex III when an electronic signature product meets those standards.

6. Member States and the Commission shall work together to promote the development and use of signature-verification devices in the light of the recommendations for secure signature-verification laid down in Annex IV and in the interests of the consumer.

7. Member States may make the use of electronic signatures in the public sector subject to possible additional requirements. Such requirements shall be objective, transparent, proportionate and non-discriminatory and shall relate only to the specific characteristics of the application concerned. Such requirements may not constitute an obstacle to cross-border services for citizens.

Article 4   Internal market principles

1. Each Member State shall apply the national provisions which it adopts pursuant to this Directive to certification-service-providers established on its territory and to the services which they provide. Member States may not restrict the provision of certification-services originating in another Member State in the fields covered by this Directive.

2. Member States shall ensure that electronic-signature products which comply with this Directive are permitted to circulate freely in the internal market.

Article 5   Legal effects of electronic signatures

1. Member States shall ensure that advanced electronic signatures which are based on a qualified certificate and which are created by a secure-signature-creation device:

    (a) satisfy the legal requirements of a signature in relation to data in electronic form in the same manner as a handwritten signature satisfies those requirements in relation to paper-based data; and (b) are admissible as evidence in legal proceedings.

2. Member States shall ensure that an electronic signature is not denied legal effectiveness and admissibility as evidence in legal proceedings solely on the grounds that it is:

    — in electronic form, or
    — not based upon a qualified certificate, or
    — not based upon a qualified certificate issued by an accredited certification-service-provider, or
    — not created by a secure signature-creation device.

Article 6   Liability

1. As a minimum, Member States shall ensure that by issuing a certificate as a qualified certificate to the public or by guaranteeing such a certificate to the public a certification-service-provider is liable for damage caused to any entity or legal or natural person who reasonably relies on that certificate:

    (a) as regards the accuracy at the time of issuance of all information contained in the qualified certificate and as regards the fact that the certificate contains all the details prescribed for a qualified certificate;

    (b) for assurance that at the time of the issuance of the certificate, the signatory identified in the qualified certificate held the signature-creation data corresponding to the signature-verification data given or identified in the certificate;

    (c) for assurance that the signature-creation data and the signature-verification data can be used in a complementary manner in cases where the certification- service-provider generates them both;

unless the certification-service-provider proves that he has not acted negligently.

2. As a minimum Member States shall ensure that a certification-service-provider who has issued a certificate as a qualified certificate to the public is liable for damage caused to any entity or legal or natural person who reasonably relies on the certificate for failure to register revocation of the certificate unless the certification-service-provider proves that he has not acted negligently.

3. Member States shall ensure that a certification-service-provider may indicate in a qualified certificate limitations on the use of that certificate. provided that the limitations are recognisable to third parties. The certification-service-provider shall not be liable for damage arising from use of a qualified certificate which exceeds the limitations placed on it.

4. Member States shall ensure that a certification-service-provider may indicate in the qualified certificate a limit on the value of transactions for which the certificate can be used, provided that the limit is recognisable to third parties.

The certification-service-provider shall not be liable for damage resulting from this maximum limit being exceeded.

5. The provisions of paragraphs 1 to 4 shall be without prejudice to Council Directive 93/13/EEC of 5 April 1993 on unfair terms in consumer contracts[8].

Article 7   International aspects

1. Member States shall ensure that certificates which are issued as qualified certificates to the public by a certification-service-provider established in a third country are recognised as legally equivalent to certificates issued by a certification-service-provider established within the Community if:

(a) the certification-service-provider fulfils the requirements laid down in this Directive and has been accredited under a voluntary accreditation scheme established in a Member State; or

(b) a certification-service-provider established within the Community which fulfils the requirements laid down in this Directive guarantees the certificate; or

(c) the certificate or the certification-service-provider is recognised under a bilateral or multilateral agreement between the Community and third countries or international organisations.

2. In order to facilitate cross-border certification services with third countries and legal recognition of advanced electronic signatures originating in third countries, the Commission shall make proposals, where appropriate, to achieve the effective implementation of standards and international agreements applicable to certification services. In particular, and where necessary, it shall submit proposals to the Council for appropriate mandates for the negotiation of bilateral and multilateral agreements with third countries and international organisations. The Council shall decide by qualified majority.

3. Whenever the Commission is informed of any difficulties encountered by Community undertakings with respect to market access in third countries, it may, if necessary, submit proposals to the Council for an appropriate mandate for the negotiation of comparable rights for Community undertakings in these third countries. The Council shall decide by qualified majority.

Measures taken pursuant to this paragraph shall be without prejudice to the obligations of the Community and of the Member States under relevant international agreements.

Article 8   Data protection

1. Member States shall ensure that certification-service-providers and national bodies responsible for accreditation or supervision comply with the requirements laid down in Directive 95/46/EC of the European Parliament and of the Council of 24 October 1995 on the protection of individuals with regard to the processing of personal data and on the free movement of such data[9].

2. Member States shall ensure that a certification-service-provider which issues certificates to the public may collect personal data only directly from the data subject, or after the explicit consent of the data subject, and only insofar as it is necessary for the purposes of issuing and maintaining the

---

[8] OJ L 95, 21.4.1993, p. 29.   [9] OJ L 281, 23.11.1995, p. 31.

certificate. The data may not be collected or processed for any other purposes without the explicit consent of the data subject.

3. Without prejudice to the legal effect given to pseudonyms under national law, Member States shall not prevent certification-service-providers from indicating in the certificate a pseudonym instead of the signatory's name.

Article 9   Committee

1. The Commission shall be assisted by an "Electronic-Signature Committee", hereinafter referred to as "the committee".

2. Where reference is made to this paragraph, Articles 4 and 7 of Decision 1999/468/EC shall apply, having regard to the provisions of Article 8 thereof.

The period laid down in Article 4(3) of Decision 1999/468/EC shall be set at three months.

3. The Committee shall adopt its own rules of procedure.

Article 10   Tasks of the committee

The committee shall clarify the requirements laid down in the Annexes of this Directive, the criteria referred to in Article 3(4) and the generally recognised standards for electronic signature products established and published pursuant to Article 3(5), in accordance with the procedure laid down in Article 9(2).

Article 11   Notification

1. Member States shall notify to the Commission and the other Member States the following:
   (a) information on national voluntary accreditation schemes, including any additional requirements pursuant to Article 3(7);
   (b) the names and addresses of the national bodies responsible for accreditation and supervision as well as of the bodies referred to in Article 3(4);
   (c) the names and addresses of all accredited national certification-service-providers.

2. Any information supplied under paragraph 1 and changes in respect of that information shall be notified by the Member States as soon as possible.

Article 12   Review

1. The Commission shall review the operation of this Directive and report thereon to the European Parliament and to the Council by 19 July 2003 at the latest.

2. The review shall inter alia assess whether the scope of this Directive should be modified, taking account of technological, market and legal developments. The report shall in particular include an assessment, on the basis of experience gained, of aspects of harmonisation. The report shall be accompanied, where appropriate, by legislative proposals.

Article 13   Implementation

1. Member States shall bring into force the laws, regulations and administrative provisions necessary to comply with this Directive before 19 July 2001. They shall forthwith inform the Commission thereof.

When Member States adopt these measures, they shall contain a reference to this Directive or shall be accompanied by such a reference on the occasion of their official publication. The methods of making such reference shall be laid down by the Member States.

2. Member States shall communicate to the Commission the text of the main provisions of domestic law which they adopt in the field governed by this Directive.

Article 14   Entry into force

This Directive shall enter into force on the day of its publication in the Official Journal of the European Communities.

Article 15   Addressees

This Directive is addressed to the Member States.

Done at Brussels, 13 December 1999.

For the European Parliament

The President
N. FONTAINE
For the Council
The President
S. HASSI

Annex I

Requirements for qualified certificates

Qualified certificates must contain:
- (a) an indication that the certificate is issued as a qualified certificate;
- (b) the identification of the certification-service-provider and the State in which it is established;
- (c) the name of the signatory or a pseudonym, which shall be identified as such;
- (d) provision for a specific attribute of the signatory to be included if relevant, depending on the purpose for which the certificate is intended;
- (e) signature-verification-data which correspond to signature-creation data under the control of the signatory;
- (f) an indication of the beginning and end of the period of validity of the certificate;
- (g) the identity code of the certificate;
- (h) the advanced electronic signature of the certification-service-provider issuing it;
- (i) limitations on the scope of use of the certificate, if applicable; and
- (j) limits on the value of transactions for which the certificate can be used, if applicable.

Annex II

Requirements for certification-service-providers issuing qualified certificates

Certification-service-providers must:
- (a) demonstrate the reliability necessary for providing certification services;
- (b) ensure the operation of a prompt and secure directory and a secure and immediate revocation service;
- (c) ensure that the date and time when a certificate is issued or revoked can be determined precisely;
- (d) verify, by appropriate means in accordance with national law, the identity and, if applicable, any specific attributes of the person to which a qualified certificate is issued;
- (e) employ personnel who possess the expert knowledge, experience, and qualifications necessary for the services provided, in particular competence at managerial level, expertise in electronic signature techology and familiarity with proper security procedures; they must also apply administrative and management procedures which are adequate and correspond to recognised standards;
- (f) use trustworthy systems and products which are protected against modification and ensure the technical and cryptographic security of the process supported by them;
- (g) take measures against forgery of certificates, and, in cases where the certification-service-provider generates signature-creation-data, guarantee confidentiality during the process of generating such data;
- (h) maintain sufficient financial resources to operate in conformity with the requirements laid down in the Directive, in particular to bear the risk of liability for damages, for example, by obtaining appropriate insurance;
- (i) record all relevant information concerning a qualified certificate for an appropriate period of time, in particular for the purpose of providing evidence of certification for the purposes of legal proceedings. Such recording may be done electronically;

(j) not store or copy signature-creation data of the person to whom the certification-service-provider provided key management services;

(k) before entering into a contractual relationship with a person seeking a certificate to support his electronic signature inform that person by a durable means of communication of the precise terms and conditions regarding the use of the certificate, including any limitations on its use, the existence of a voluntary accreditation scheme and procedures for complaints and dispute settlement. Such information, which may be transmitted electronically, must be in writing and in redily understandable language. Relevant parts of this information must also be made available on request to third-parties relying on the certificate;

(l) use trustworthy systems to store certificates in a verifiable form so that:
— only authorised persons can make entries and changes,
— information can be checked for authenticity,
— certificates are publicly available for retrieval in only those cases for which the certificate-holder's consent has been obtained, and
— any technical changes compromising these security requirements are apparent to the operator.

Annex III

Requirements for secure signature-creation devices

1. Secure signature-creation devices must, by appropriate technical and procedural means, ensure at the least that:

(a) the signature-creation-data used for signature generation can practically occur only once, and that their secrecy is reasonably assured;

(b) the signature-creation-data used for signature generation cannot, with reasonable assurance, be derived and the signature is protected against forgery using currently available technology;

(c) the signature-creation-data used for signature generation can be reliably protected by the legitimate signatory against the use of others.

2. Secure signature-creation devices must not alter the data to be signed or prevent such data from being presented to the signatory prior to the signature process.

Annex IV

Recommendations for secure signature verification

During the signature-verification process it should be ensured with reasonable certainty that:

(a) the data used for verifying the signature correspond to the data displayed to the verifier;

(b) the signature is reliably verified and the result of that verification is correctly displayed;

(c) the verifier can, as necessary, reliably establish the contents of the signed data;

(d) the authenticity and validity of the certificate required at the time of signature verification are reliably verified;

(e) the result of verification and the signatory's identity are correctly displayed;

(f) the use of a pseudonym is clearly indicated; and

(g) any security-relevant changes can be detected.

Directive 2000/31/EC of the European Parliament and of the Council of 8 June 2000 on certain legal aspects of information society services, in particular electronic commerce, in the Internal Market ("Directive on electronic commerce")

THE EUROPEAN PARLIAMENT AND THE COUNCIL OF THE EUROPEAN UNION,

Having regard to the Treaty establishing the European Community, and in particular Articles 47(2), 55 and 95 thereof,

Having regard to the proposal from the Commission[1],

Having regard to the opinion of the Economic and Social Committee[2],

Acting in accordance with the procedure laid down in Article 251 of the Treaty[3],

Whereas:

(1) The European Union is seeking to forge ever closer links between the States and peoples of Europe, to ensure economic and social progress; in accordance with Article 14(2) of the Treaty, the internal market comprises an area without internal frontiers in which the free movements of goods, services and the freedom of establishment are ensured; the development of information society services within the area without internal frontiers is vital to eliminating the barriers which divide the European peoples.

(2) The development of electronic commerce within the information society offers significant employment opportunities in the Community, particularly in small and medium-sized enterprises, and will stimulate economic growth and investment in innovation by European companies, and can also enhance the competitiveness of European industry, provided that everyone has access to the Internet.

(3) Community law and the characteristics of the Community legal order are a vital asset to enable European citizens and operators to take full advantage, without consideration of borders, of the opportunities afforded by electronic commerce; this Directive therefore has the purpose of ensuring a high level of Community legal integration in order to establish a real area without internal borders for information society services.

(4) It is important to ensure that electronic commerce could fully benefit from the internal market and therefore that, as with Council Directive 89/552/EEC of 3 October 1989 on the coordination of certain provisions laid down by law, regulation or administrative action in Member States concerning the pursuit of television broadcasting activities[4], a high level of Community integration is achieved.

(5) The development of information society services within the Community is hampered by a number of legal obstacles to the proper functioning of the internal market which make less attractive the exercise of the freedom of establishment and the freedom to provide services; these obstacles arise from divergences in legislation and from the legal uncertainty as to which national rules apply to such services; in the absence of coordination and adjustment of legislation in the relevant areas, obstacles might be justified in the light of the case-law of the Court of Justice of the European Communities; legal uncertainty exists with regard to the extent to which Member States may control services originating from another Member State.

(6) In the light of Community objectives, of Articles 43 and 49 of the Treaty and of secondary Community law, these obstacles should be eliminated by coordinating certain national laws and by clarifying certain legal concepts at Community level to the extent necessary for the proper functioning

---

[1] OJ C 30, 5.2.1999, p. 4.

[2] OJ C 169, 16.6.1999, p. 36.

[3] Opinion of the European Parliament of 6 May 1999 (OJ C 279, 1.10.1999, p. 389), Council common position of 28 February 2000 (OJ C 128, 8.5.2000, p. 32) and Decision of the European Parliament of 4 May 2000 (not yet published in the Official Journal).

[4] OJ L 298, 17.10.1989, p. 23. Directive as amended by Directive 97/36/EC of the European Parliament and of the Council (OJ L 202, 30.7.1997, p. 60).

of the internal market; by dealing only with certain specific matters which give rise to problems for the internal market, this Directive is fully consistent with the need to respect the principle of subsidiarity as set out in Article 5 of the Treaty.

(7) In order to ensure legal certainty and consumer confidence, this Directive must lay down a clear and general framework to cover certain legal aspects of electronic commerce in the internal market.

(8) The objective of this Directive is to create a legal framework to ensure the free movement of information society services between Member States and not to harmonise the field of criminal law as such.

(9) The free movement of information society services can in many cases be a specific reflection in Community law of a more general principle, namely freedom of expression as enshrined in Article 10(1) of the Convention for the Protection of Human Rights and Fundamental Freedoms, which has been ratified by all the Member States; for this reason, directives covering the supply of information society services must ensure that this activity may be engaged in freely in the light of that Article, subject only to the restrictions laid down in paragraph 2 of that Article and in Article 46(1) of the Treaty; this Directive is not intended to affect national fundamental rules and principles relating to freedom of expression.

(10) In accordance with the principle of proportionality, the measures provided for in this Directive are strictly limited to the minimum needed to achieve the objective of the proper functioning of the internal market; where action at Community level is necessary, and in order to guarantee an area which is truly without internal frontiers as far as electronic commerce is concerned, the Directive must ensure a high level of protection of objectives of general interest, in particular the protection of minors and human dignity, consumer protection and the protection of public health; according to Article 152 of the Treaty, the protection of public health is an essential component of other Community policies.

(11) This Directive is without prejudice to the level of protection for, in particular, public health and consumer interests, as established by Community acts; amongst others, Council Directive 93/13/EEC of 5 April 1993 on unfair terms in consumer contracts[5] and Directive 97/7/EC of the European Parliament and of the Council of 20 May 1997 on the protection of consumers in respect of distance contracts[6] form a vital element for protecting consumers in contractual matters; those Directives also apply in their entirety to information society services; that same Community acquis, which is fully applicable to information society services, also embraces in particular Council Directive 84/450/EEC of 10 September 1984 concerning misleading and comparative advertising[7], Council Directive 87/102/EEC of 22 December 1986 for the approximation of the laws, regulations and administrative provisions of the Member States concerning consumer credit[8], Council Directive 93/22/EEC of 10 May 1993 on investment services in the securities field[9], Council Directive 90/314/EEC of 13 June 1990 on package travel, package holidays and package tours[10], Directive 98/6/EC of the European Parliament and of the Council of 16 February 1998 on consumer production in the indication of prices of products offered to consumers[11], Council Directive 92/59/EEC of 29 June 1992 on general product safety[12], Directive 94/47/EC of the European Parliament and of the Council of 26 October 1994 on the protection of purchasers in respect of certain aspects on contracts relating to the purchase of the right to use immovable properties on a timeshare basis[13], Directive 98/27/EC of the European Parliament and of the Council of 19 May 1998 on injunctions for the protection of consumers' interests[14], Council Directive 85/374/EEC of 25 July 1985 on the approximation of the laws, regulations

---

[5] OJ L 95, 21.4.1993, p. 29.   [6] OJ L 144, 4.6.1999, p. 19.

[7] OJ L 250, 19.9.1984, p. 17. Directive as amended by Directive 97/55/EC of the European Parliament and of the Council (OJ L 290, 23.10.1997, p. 18).

[8] OJ L 42, 12.2.1987, p. 48. Directive as last amended by Directive 98/7/EC of the European Parliament and of the Council (OJ L 101, 1.4.1998, p. 17).

[9] OJ L 141, 11.6.1993, p. 27. Directive as last amended by Directive 97/9/EC of the European Parliament and of the Council (OJ L 84, 26.3.1997, p. 22).

[10] OJ L 158, 23.6.1990, p. 59.   [11] OJ L 80, 18.3.1998, p. 27.   [12] OJ L 228, 11.8.1992, p. 24.

[13] OJ L 280, 29.10.1994, p. 83.

[14] OJ L 166, 11.6.1998, p. 51. Directive as amended by Directive 1999/44/EC (OJ L 171, 7.7.1999, p. 12).

and administrative provisions concerning liability for defective products[15], Directive 1999/44/EC of the European Parliament and of the Council of 25 May 1999 on certain aspects of the sale of consumer goods and associated guarantees[16], the future Directive of the European Parliament and of the Council concerning the distance marketing of consumer financial services and Council Directive 92/28/EEC of 31 March 1992 on the advertising of medicinal products[17]; this Directive should be without prejudice to Directive 98/43/EC of the European Parliament and of the Council of 6 July 1998 on the approximation of the laws, regulations and administrative provisions of the Member States relating to the advertising and sponsorship of tobacco products[18] adopted within the framework of the internal market, or to directives on the protection of public health; this Directive complements information requirements established by the abovementioned Directives and in particular Directive 97/7/EC.

(12) It is necessary to exclude certain activities from the scope of this Directive, on the grounds that the freedom to provide services in these fields cannot, at this stage, be guaranteed under the Treaty or existing secondary legislation; excluding these activities does not preclude any instruments which might prove necessary for the proper functioning of the internal market; taxation, particularly value added tax imposed on a large number of the services covered by this Directive, must be excluded form the scope of this Directive.

(13) This Directive does not aim to establish rules on fiscal obligations nor does it pre-empt the drawing up of Community instruments concerning fiscal aspects of electronic commerce.

(14) The protection of individuals with regard to the processing of personal data is solely governed by Directive 95/46/EC of the European Parliament and of the Council of 24 October 1995 on the protection of individuals with regard to the processing of personal data and on the free movement of such data[19] and Directive 97/66/EC of the European Parliament and of the Council of 15 December 1997 concerning the processing of personal data and the protection of privacy in the telecommunications sector[20] which are fully applicable to information society services; these Directives already establish a Community legal framework in the field of personal data and therefore it is not necessary to cover this issue in this Directive in order to ensure the smooth functioning of the internal market, in particular the free movement of personal data between Member States; the implementation and application of this Directive should be made in full compliance with the principles relating to the protection of personal data, in particular as regards unsolicited commercial communication and the liability of intermediaries; this Directive cannot prevent the anonymous use of open networks such as the Internet.

(15) The confidentiality of communications is guaranteed by Article 5 Directive 97/66/EC; in accordance with that Directive, Member States must prohibit any kind of interception or surveillance of such communications by others than the senders and receivers, except when legally authorised.

(16) The exclusion of gambling activities from the scope of application of this Directive covers only games of chance, lotteries and betting transactions, which involve wagering a stake with monetary value; this does not cover promotional competitions or games where the purpose is to encourage the sale of goods or services and where payments, if they arise, serve only to acquire the promoted goods or services.

(17) The definition of information society services already exists in Community law in Directive 98/34/EC of the European Parliament and of the Council of 22 June 1998 laying down a procedure for the provision of information in the field of technical standards and regulations and of rules on information society services[21] and in Directive 98/84/EC of the European Parliament and of the Council of 20 November 1998 on the legal protection of services based on, or consisting of, conditional access[22]; this definition covers any service normally provided for remuneration, at a distance, by means of electronic equipment for the processing (including digital compression) and storage of data, and at the individual request of a recipient of a service; those services referred to in the indicative list

[15] OJ L 210, 7.8.1985, p. 29. Directive as amended by Directive 1999/34/EC (OJ L 141, 4.6.1999, p. 20).
[16] OJ L 171, 7.7.1999, p. 12.   [17] OJ L 113, 30.4.1992, p. 13.   [18] OJ L 213, 30.7.1998, p. 9.
[19] OJ L 281, 23.11.1995, p. 31.   [20] OJ L 24, 30.1.1998, p. 1.
[21] OJ L 204, 21.7.1998, p. 37. Directive as amended by Directive 98/48/EC (OJ L 217, 5.8.1998, p. 18).
[22] OJ L 320, 28.11.1998, p. 54.

in Annex V to Directive 98/34/EC which do not imply data processing and storage are not covered by this definition.

(18) Information society services span a wide range of economic activities which take place on-line; these activities can, in particular, consist of selling goods on-line; activities such as the delivery of goods as such or the provision of services off-line are not covered; information society services are not solely restricted to services giving rise to on-line contracting but also, in so far as they represent an economic activity, extend to services which are not remunerated by those who receive them, such as those offering on-line information or commercial communications, or those providing tools allowing for search, access and retrieval of data; information society services also include services consisting of the transmission of information via a communication network, in providing access to a communication network or in hosting information provided by a recipient of the service; television broadcasting within the meaning of Directive EEC/89/552 and radio broadcasting are not information society services because they are not provided at individual request; by contrast, services which are transmitted point to point, such as video-on-demand or the provision of commercial communications by electronic mail are information society services; the use of electronic mail or equivalent individual communications for instance by natural persons acting outside their trade, business or profession including their use for the conclusion of contracts between such persons is not an information society service; the contractual relationship between an employee and his employer is not an information society service; activities which by their very nature cannot be carried out at a distance and by electronic means, such as the statutory auditing of company accounts or medical advice requiring the physical examination of a patient are not information society services.

(19) The place at which a service provider is established should be determined in conformity with the case-law of the Court of Justice according to which the concept of establishment involves the actual pursuit of an economic activity through a fixed establishment for an indefinite period; this requirement is also fulfilled where a company is constituted for a given period; the place of establishment of a company providing services via an Internet website is not the place at which the technology supporting its website is located or the place at which its website is accessible but the place where it pursues its economic activity; in cases where a provider has several places of establishment it is important to determine from which place of establishment the service concerned is provided; in cases where it is difficult to determine from which of several places of establishment a given service is provided, this is the place where the provider has the centre of his activities relating to this particular service.

(20) The definition of "recipient of a service" covers all types of usage of information society services, both by persons who provide information on open networks such as the Internet and by persons who seek information on the Internet for private or professional reasons.

(21) The scope of the coordinated field is without prejudice to future Community harmonisation relating to information society services and to future legislation adopted at national level in accordance with Community law; the coordinated field covers only requirements relating to on-line activities such as on-line information, on-line advertising, on-line shopping, on-line contracting and does not concern Member States' legal requirements relating to goods such as safety standards, labelling obligations, or liability for goods, or Member States' requirements relating to the delivery or the transport of goods, including the distribution of medicinal products; the coordinated field does not cover the exercise of rights of pre-emption by public authorities concerning certain goods such as works of art.

(22) Information society services should be supervised at the source of the activity, in order to ensure an effective protection of public interest objectives; to that end, it is necessary to ensure that the competent authority provides such protection not only for the citizens of its own country but for all Community citizens; in order to improve mutual trust between Member States, it is essential to state clearly this responsibility on the part of the Member State where the services originate; moreover, in order to effectively guarantee freedom to provide services and legal certainty for suppliers and recipients of services, such information society services should in principle be subject to the law of the Member State in which the service provider is established.

(23) This Directive neither aims to establish additional rules on private international law relating to conflicts of law nor does it deal with the jurisdiction of Courts; provisions of the applicable law designated by rules of private international law must not restrict the freedom to provide information society services as established in this Directive.

(24) In the context of this Directive, notwithstanding the rule on the control at source of information society services, it is legitimate under the conditions established in this Directive for Member States to take measures to restrict the free movement of information society services.

(25) National courts, including civil courts, dealing with private law disputes can take measures to derogate from the freedom to provide information society services in conformity with conditions established in this Directive.

(26) Member States, in conformity with conditions established in this Directive, may apply their national rules on criminal law and criminal proceedings with a view to taking all investigative and other measures necessary for the detection and prosecution of criminal offences, without there being a need to notify such measures to the Commission.

(27) This Directive, together with the future Directive of the European Parliament and of the Council concerning the distance marketing of consumer financial services, contributes to the creating of a legal framework for the on-line provision of financial services; this Directive does not pre-empt future initiatives in the area of financial services in particular with regard to the harmonisation of rules of conduct in this field; the possibility for Member States, established in this Directive, under certain circumstances of restricting the freedom to provide information society services in order to protect consumers also covers measures in the area of financial services in particular measures aiming at protecting investors.

(28) The Member States' obligation not to subject access to the activity of an information society service provider to prior authorisation does not concern postal services covered by Directive 97/67/EC of the European Parliament and of the Council of 15 December 1997 on common rules for the development of the internal market of Community postal services and the improvement of quality of service[23] consisting of the physical delivery of a printed electronic mail message and does not affect voluntary accreditation systems, in particular for providers of electronic signature certification service.

(29) Commercial communications are essential for the financing of information society services and for developing a wide variety of new, charge-free services; in the interests of consumer protection and fair trading, commercial communications, including discounts, promotional offers and promotional competitions or games, must meet a number of transparency requirements; these requirements are without prejudice to Directive 97/7/EC; this Directive should not affect existing Directives on commercial communications, in particular Directive 98/43/EC.

(30) The sending of unsolicited commercial communications by electronic mail may be undesirable for consumers and information society service providers and may disrupt the smooth functioning of interactive networks; the question of consent by recipient of certain forms of unsolicited commercial communications is not addressed by this Directive, but has already been addressed, in particular, by Directive 97/7/EC and by Directive 97/66/EC; in Member States which authorise unsolicited commercial communications by electronic mail, the setting up of appropriate industry filtering initiatives should be encouraged and facilitated; in addition it is necessary that in any event unsolicited commercial communities are clearly identifiable as such in order to improve transparency and to facilitate the functioning of such industry initiatives; unsolicited commercial communications by electronic mail should not result in additional communication costs for the recipient.

(31) Member States which allow the sending of unsolicited commercial communications by electronic mail without prior consent of the recipient by service providers established in their territory have to ensure that the service providers consult regularly and respect the opt-out registers in which natural persons not wishing to receive such commercial communications can register themselves.

---

[23] OJ L 15, 21.1.1998, p. 14.

(32) In order to remove barriers to the development of cross-border services within the Community which members of the regulated professions might offer on the Internet, it is necessary that compliance be guaranteed at Community level with professional rules aiming, in particular, to protect consumers or public health; codes of conduct at Community level would be the best means of determining the rules on professional ethics applicable to commercial communication; the drawing-up or, where appropriate, the adaptation of such rules should be encouraged without prejudice to the autonomy of professional bodies and associations.

(33) This Directive complements Community law and national law relating to regulated professions maintaining a coherent set of applicable rules in this field.

(34) Each Member State is to amend its legislation containing requirements, and in particular requirements as to form, which are likely to curb the use of contracts by electronic means; the examination of the legislation requiring such adjustment should be systematic and should cover all the necessary stages and acts of the contractual process, including the filing of the contract; the result of this amendment should be to make contracts concluded electronically workable; the legal effect of electronic signatures is dealt with by Directive 1999/93/EC of the European Parliament and of the Council of 13 December 1999 on a Community framework for electronic signatures[24]; the acknowledgement of receipt by a service provider may take the form of the on-line provision of the service paid for.

(35) This Directive does not affect Member States' possibility of maintaining or establishing general or specific legal requirements for contracts which can be fulfilled by electronic means, in particular requirements concerning secure electronic signatures.

(36) Member States may maintain restrictions for the use of electronic contracts with regard to contracts requiring by law the involvement of courts, public authorities, or professions exercising public authority; this possibility also covers contracts which require the involvement of courts, public authorities, or professions exercising public authority in order to have an effect with regard to third parties as well as contracts requiring by law certification or attestation by a notary.

(37) Member States' obligation to remove obstacles to the use of electronic contracts concerns only obstacles resulting from legal requirements and not practical obstacles resulting from the impossibility of using electronic means in certain cases.

(38) Member States' obligation to remove obstacles to the use of electronic contracts is to be implemented in conformity with legal requirements for contracts enshrined in Community law.

(39) The exceptions to the provisions concerning the contracts concluded exclusively by electronic mail or by equivalent individual communications provided for by this Directive, in relation to information to be provided and the placing of orders, should not enable, as a result, the by-passing of those provisions by providers of information society services.

(40) Both existing and emerging disparities in Member States' legislation and case-law concerning liability of service providers acting as intermediaries prevent the smooth functioning of the internal market, in particular by impairing the development of cross-border services and producing distortions of competition; service providers have a duty to act, under certain circumstances, with a view to preventing or stopping illegal activities; this Directive should constitute the appropriate basis for the development of rapid and reliable procedures for removing and disabling access to illegal information; such mechanisms could be developed on the basis of voluntary agreements between all parties concerned and should be encouraged by Member States; it is in the interest of all parties involved in the provision of information society services to adopt and implement such procedures; the provisions of this Directive relating to liability should not preclude the development and effective operation, by the different interested parties, of technical systems of protection and identification and of technical surveillance instruments made possible by digital technology within the limits laid down by Directives 95/46/EC and 97/66/EC.

(41) This Directive strikes a balance between the different interests at stake and establishes principles upon which industry agreements and standards can be based.

---

[24] OJ L 13, 19.1.2000, p. 12.

(42) The exemptions from liability established in this Directive cover only cases where the activity of the information society service provider is limited to the technical process of operating and giving access to a communication network over which information made available by third parties is transmitted or temporarily stored, for the sole purpose of making the transmission more efficient; this activity is of a mere technical, automatic and passive nature, which implies that the information society service provider has neither knowledge of nor control over the information which is transmitted or stored.

(43) A service provider can benefit from the exemptions for 'mere conduit' and for 'caching' when he is in no way involved with the information transmitted; this requires among other things that he does not modify the information that he transmits; this requirement does not cover manipulations of a technical nature which take place in the course of the transmission as they do not alter the integrity of the information contained in the transmission.

(44) A service provider who deliberately collaborates with one of the recipients of his service in order to undertake illegal acts goes beyond the activities of "mere conduit" or "caching" and as a result cannot benefit from the liability exemptions established for these activities.

(45) The limitations of the liability of intermediary service providers established in this Directive do not affect the possibility of injunctions of different kinds; such injunctions can in particular consist of orders by courts or administrative authorities requiring the termination or prevention of any infringement, including the removal of illegal information or the disabling of access to it.

(46) In order to benefit from a limitation of liability, the provider of an information society service, consisting of the storage of information, upon obtaining actual knowledge or awareness of illegal activities has to act expeditiously to remove or to disable access to the information concerned; the removal or disabling of access has to be undertaken in the observance of the principle of freedom of expression and of procedures established for this purpose at national level; this Directive does not affect Member States' possibility of establishing specific requirements which must be fulfilled expeditiously prior to the removal or disabling of information.

(47) Member States are prevented from imposing a monitoring obligation on service providers only with respect to obligations of a general nature; this does not concern monitoring obligations in a specific case and, in particular, does not affect orders by national authorities in accordance with national legislation.

(48) This Directive does not affect the possibility for Member States of requiring service providers, who host information provided by recipients of their service, to apply duties of care, which can reasonably be expected from them and which are specified by national law, in order to detect and prevent certain types of illegal activities.

(49) Member States and the Commission are to encourage the drawing-up of codes of conduct; this is not to impair the voluntary nature of such codes and the possibility for interested parties of deciding freely whether to adhere to such codes.

(50) It is important that the proposed directive on the harmonisation of certain aspects of copyright and related rights in the information society and this Directive come into force within a similar time scale with a view to establishing a clear framework of rules relevant to the issue of liability of intermediaries for copyright and relating rights infringements at Community level.

(51) Each Member State should be required, where necessary, to amend any legislation which is liable to hamper the use of schemes for the out-of-court settlement of disputes through electronic channels; the result of this amendment must be to make the functioning of such schemes genuinely and effectively possible in law and in practice, even across borders.

(52) The effective exercise of the freedoms of the internal market makes it necessary to guarantee victims effective access to means of settling disputes; damage which may arise in connection with information society services is characterised both by its rapidity and by its geographical extent; in view of this specific character and the need to ensure that national authorities do not endanger the mutual confidence which they should have in one another, this Directive requests Member States to ensure that appropriate court actions are available; Member States should examine the need to provide access to judicial procedures by appropriate electronic means.

(53) Directive 98/27/EC, which is applicable to information society services, provides a mechanism relating to actions for an injunction aimed at the protection of the collective interests of consumers; this mechanism will contribute to the free movement of information society services by ensuring a high level of consumer protection.

(54) The sanctions provided for under this Directive are without prejudice to any other sanction or remedy provided under national law; Member States are not obliged to provide criminal sanctions for infringement of national provisions adopted pursuant to this Directive.

(55) This Directive does not affect the law applicable to contractual obligations relating to consumer contracts; accordingly, this Directive cannot have the result of depriving the consumer of the protection afforded to him by the mandatory rules relating to contractual obligations of the law of the Member State in which he has his habitual residence.

(56) As regards the derogation contained in this Directive regarding contractual obligations concerning contracts concluded by consumers, those obligations should be interpreted as including information on the essential elements of the content of the contract, including consumer rights, which have a determining influence on the decision to contract.

(57) The Court of Justice has consistently held that a Member State retains the right to take measures against a service provider that is established in another Member State but directs all or most of his activity to the territory of the first Member State if the choice of establishment was made with a view to evading the legislation that would have applied to the provider had he been established on the territory of the first Member State.

(58) This Directive should not apply to services supplied by service providers established in a third country; in view of the global dimension of electronic commerce, it is, however, appropriate to ensure that the Community rules are consistent with international rules; this Directive is without prejudice to the results of discussions within international organisations (amongst others WTO, OECD, Uncitral) on legal issues.

(59) Despite the global nature of electronic communications, coordination of national regulatory measures at European Union level is necessary in order to avoid fragmentation of the internal market, and for the establishment of an appropriate European regulatory framework; such coordination should also contribute to the establishment of a common and strong negotiating position in international forums.

(60) In order to allow the unhampered development of electronic commerce, the legal framework must be clear and simple, predictable and consistent with the rules applicable at international level so that it does not adversely affect the competitiveness of European industry or impede innovation in that sector.

(61) If the market is actually to operate by electronic means in the context of globalisation, the European Union and the major non-European areas need to consult each other with a view to making laws and procedures compatible.

(62) Cooperation with third countries should be strengthened in the area of electronic commerce, in particular with applicant countries, the developing countries and the European Union's other trading partners.

(63) The adoption of this Directive will not prevent the Member States from taking into account the various social, societal and cultural implications which are inherent in the advent of the information society; in particular it should not hinder measures which Member States might adopt in conformity with Community law to achieve social, cultural and democratic goals taking into account their linguistic diversity, national and regional specificities as well as their cultural heritage, and to ensure and maintain public access to the widest possible range of information society services; in any case, the development of the information society is to ensure that Community citizens can have access to the cultural European heritage provided in the digital environment.

(64) Electronic communication offers the Member States an excellent means of providing public services in the cultural, educational and linguistic fields.

(65) The Council, in its resolution of 19 January 1999 on the consumer dimension of the information society[25], stressed that the protection of consumers deserved special attention in this field; the Commission will examine the degree to which existing consumer protection rules provide insufficient protection in the context of the information society and will identify, where necessary, the deficiencies of this legislation and those issues which could require additional measures; if need be, the Commission should make specific additional proposals to resolve such deficiencies that will thereby have been identified,

HAVE ADOPTED THIS DIRECTIVE:

Chapter I General Provisions

Article 1 Objective and scope

1. This Directive seeks to contribute to the proper functioning of the internal market by ensuring the free movement of information society services between the Member States.

2. This Directive approximates, to the extent necessary for the achievement of the objective set out in paragraph 1, certain national provisions on information society services relating to the internal market, the establishment of service providers, commercial communications, electronic contracts, the liability of intermediaries, codes of conduct, out-of-court dispute settlements, court actions and cooperation between Member States.

3. This Directive complements Community law applicable to information society services without prejudice to the level of protection for, in particular, public health and consumer interests, as established by Community acts and national legislation implementing them in so far as this does not restrict the freedom to provide information society services.

4. This Directive does not establish additional rules on private international law nor does it deal with the jurisdiction of Courts.

5. This Directive shall not apply to:
   (a) the field of taxation;
   (b) questions relating to information society services covered by Directives 95/46/ EC and 97/66/EC;
   (c) questions relating to agreements or practices governed by cartel law;
   (d) the following activities of information society services:
   — the activities of notaries or equivalent professions to the extent that they involve a direct and specific connection with the exercise of public authority,
   — the representation of a client and defence of his interests before the courts,
   — gambling activities which involve wagering a stake with monetary value in games of chance, including lotteries and betting transactions.

6. This Directive does not affect measures taken at Community or national level, in the respect of Community law, in order to promote cultural and linguistic diversity and to ensure the defence of pluralism.

Article 2 Definitions

For the purpose of this Directive, the following terms shall bear the following meanings:
   (a) "information society services": services within the meaning of Article 1(2) of Directive 98/34/EC as amended by Directive 98/48/EC;
   (b) "service provider": any natural or legal person providing an information society service;
   (c) "established service provider": a service provider who effectively pursues an economic activity using a fixed establishment for an indefinite period. The presence and use of the technical means and technologies required to provide the service do not, in themselves, constitute an establishment of the provider;

---

[25] OJ C 23, 28.1.1999, p. 1.

(d) "recipient of the service": any natural or legal person who, for professional ends or otherwise, uses an information society service, in particular for the purposes of seeking information or making it accessible;

(e) "consumer": any natural person who is acting for purposes which are outside his or her trade, business or profession;

(f) "commercial communication": any form of communication designed to promote, directly or indirectly, the goods, services or image of a company, organisation or person pursuing a commercial, industrial or craft activity or exercising a regulated profession. The following do not in themselves constitute commercial communications:

— information allowing direct access to the activity of the company, organisation or person, in particular a domain name or an electronic-mail address,

— communications relating to the goods, services or image of the company, organisation or person compiled in an independent manner, particularly when this is without financial consideration;

(g) "regulated profession": any profession within the meaning of either Article 1(d) of Council Directive 89/48/EEC of 21 December 1988 on a general system for the recognition of higher-education diplomas awarded on completion of professional education and training of at least three-years' duration[26] or of Article 1(f) of Council Directive 92/51/EEC of 18 June 1992 on a second general system for the recognition of professional education and training to supplement Directive 89/ 48/EEC[27];

(h) "coordinated field": requirements laid down in Member States' legal systems applicable to information society service providers or information society services, regardless of whether they are of a general nature or specifically designed for them.

(i) The coordinated field concerns requirements with which the service provider has to comply in respect of:

— the taking up of the activity of an information society service, such as requirements concerning qualifications, authorisation or notification,

— the pursuit of the activity of an information society service, such as requirements concerning the behaviour of the service provider, requirements regarding the quality or content of the service including those applicable to advertising and contracts, or requirements concerning the liability of the service provider;

(ii) The coordinated field does not cover requirements such as:

— requirements applicable to goods as such,

— requirements applicable to the delivery of goods,

— requirements applicable to services not provided by electronic means.

Article 3   Internal market

1. Each Member State shall ensure that the information society services provided by a service provider established on its territory comply with the national provisions applicable in the Member State in question which fall within the coordinated field.

2. Member States may not, for reasons falling within the coordinated field, restrict the freedom to provide information society services from another Member State.

3. Paragraphs 1 and 2 shall not apply to the fields referred to in the Annex.

4. Member States may take measures to derogate from paragraph 2 in respect of a given information society service if the following conditions are fulfilled:

(a) the measures shall be:

(i) necessary for one of the following reasons:

— public policy, in particular the prevention, investigation, detection and prosecution of criminal offences, including the protection of minors and the fight against

---

[26] OJ L 19, 24.1.1989, p. 16.

[27] OJ L 209, 24.7.1992, p. 25. Directive as last amended by Commission Directive 97/38/EC (OJ L 184, 12.7.1997, p. 31).

any incitement to hatred on grounds of race, sex, religion or nationality, and violations of human dignity concerning individual persons,

— the protection of public health, public security, including the safeguarding of national security and defence,

— the protection of consumers, including investors;

(ii) taken against a given information society service which prejudices the objectives referred to in point (i) or which presents a serious and grave risk of prejudice to those objectives;

(iii) proportionate to those objectives;

(b) before taking the measures in question and without prejudice to court proceedings, including preliminary proceedings and acts carried out in the framework of a criminal investigation, the Member State has:

— asked the Member State referred to in paragraph 1 to take measures and the latter did not take such measures, or they were inadequate,

— notified the Commission and the Member State referred to in paragraph 1 of its intention to take such measures.

5. Member States may, in the case of urgency, derogate from the conditions stipulated in paragraph 4(b). Where this is the case, the measures shall be notified in the shortest possible time to the Commission and to the Member State referred to in paragraph 1, indicating the reasons for which the Member State considers that there is urgency.

6. Without prejudice to the Member State's possibility of proceeding with the measures in question, the Commission shall examine the compatibility of the notified measures with Community law in the shortest possible time; where it comes to the conclusion that the measure is incompatible with Community law, the Commission shall ask the Member State in question to refrain from taking any proposed measures or urgently to put an end to the measures in question.

Chapter II Principles

Section 1

Establishment and information requirements

Article 4 Principle excluding prior authorisation

1. Member States shall ensure that the taking up and pursuit of the activity of an information society service provider may not be made subject to prior authorisation or any other requirement having equivalent effect.

2. Paragraph 1 shall be without prejudice to authorisation schemes which are not specifically and exclusively targeted at information society services, or which are covered by Directive 97/13/EC of the European Parliament and of the Council of 10 April 1997 on a common framework for general authorisations and individual licences in the field of telecommunications services[28].

Article 5 General information to be provided

1. In addition to other information requirements established by Community law, Member States shall ensure that the service provider shall render easily, directly and permanently accessible to the recipients of the service and competent authorities, at least the following information:

(a) the name of the service provider;

(b) the geographic address at which the service provider is established;

(c) the details of the service provider, including his electronic mail address, which allow him to be contacted rapidly and communicated with in a direct and effective manner;

---

[28] OJ L 117, 7.5.1997, p. 15.

(d) where the service provider is registered in a trade or similar public register, the trade register in which the service provider is entered and his registration number, or equivalent means of identification in that register;

(e) where the activity is subject to an authorisation scheme, the particulars of the relevant supervisory authority;

(f) as concerns the regulated professions:
— any professional body or similar institution with which the service provider is registered,
— the professional title and the Member State where it has been granted,
— a reference to the applicable professional rules in the Member State of establishment and the means to access them;

(g) where the service provider undertakes an activity that is subject to VAT, the identification number referred to in Article 22(1) of the sixth Council Directive 77/388/EEC of 17 May 1977 on the harmonisation of the laws of the Member States relating to turnover taxes— Common system of value added tax: uniform basis of assessment[29].

2. In addition to other information requirements established by Community law, Member States shall at least ensure that, where information society services refer to prices, these are to be indicated clearly and unambiguously and, in particular, must indicate whether they are inclusive of tax and delivery costs.

Section 2

Commercial communications

Article 6   Information to be provided

In addition to other information requirements established by Community law, Member States shall ensure that commercial communications which are part of, or constitute, an information society service comply at least with the following conditions:

(a) the commercial communication shall be clearly identifiable as such;

(b) the natural or legal person on whose behalf the commercial communication is made shall be clearly identifiable;

(c) promotional offers, such as discounts, premiums and gifts, where permitted in the Member State where the service provider is established, shall be clearly identifiable as such, and the conditions which are to be met to qualify for them shall be easily accessible and be presented clearly and unambiguously;

(d) promotional competitions or games, where permitted in the Member State where the service provider is established, shall be clearly identifiable as such, and the conditions for participation shall be easily accessible and be presented clearly and unambiguously.

Article 7   Unsolicited commercial communication

1. In addition to other requirements established by Community law, Member States which permit unsolicited commercial communication by electronic mail shall ensure that such commercial communication by a service provider established in their territory shall be identifiable clearly and unambiguously as such as soon as it is received by the recipient.

2. Without prejudice to Directive 97/7/EC and Directive 97/66/EC, Member States shall take measures to ensure that service providers undertaking unsolicited commercial communications by electronic mail consult regularly and respect the opt-out registers in which natural persons not wishing to receive such commercial communications can register themselves.

Article 8   Regulated professions

1. Member States shall ensure that the use of commercial communications which are part of, or constitute, an information society service provided by a member of a regulated profession is permitted

---

[29] OJ L 145, 13.6.1977, p. 1. Directive as last amended by Directive 1999/85/EC (OJ L 277, 28.10.1999, p. 34).

subject to compliance with the professional rules regarding, in particular, the independence, dignity and honour of the profession, professional secrecy and fairness towards clients and other members of the profession.

2. Without prejudice to the autonomy of professional bodies and associations, Member States and the Commission shall encourage professional associations and bodies to establish codes of conduct at Community level in order to determine the types of information that can be given for the purposes of commercial communication in conformity with the rules referred to in paragraph 1.

3. When drawing up proposals for Community initiatives which may become necessary to ensure the proper functioning of thc Internal Market with regard to the information referred to in paragraph 2, the Commission shall take due account of codes of conduct applicable at Community level and shall act in close cooperation with the relevant professional associations and bodies.

4. This Directive shall apply in addition to Community Directives concerning access to, and the exercise of, activities of the regulated professions.

Section 3

Contracts concluded by electronic means

Article 9   Treatment of contracts

1. Member States shall ensure that their legal system allows contracts to be concluded by electronic means. Member States shall in particular ensure that the legal requirements applicable to the contractual process neither create obstacles for the use of electronic contracts nor result in such contracts being deprived of legal effectiveness and validity on account of their having been made by electronic means.

2. Member States may lay down that paragraph 1 shall not apply to all or certain contracts falling into one of the following categories:

    (a) contracts that create or transfer rights in real estate, except for rental rights;

    (b) contracts requiring by law the involvement of courts, public authorities or professions exercising public authority;

    (c) contracts of suretyship granted and on collateral securities furnished by persons acting for purposes outside their trade, business or profession;

    (d) contracts governed by family law or by the law of succession.

3. Member States shall indicate to the Commission the categories referred to in paragraph 2 to which they do not apply paragraph 1. Member States shall submit to the Commission every five years a report on the application of paragraph 2 explaining the reasons why they consider it necessary to maintain the category referred to in paragraph 2(b) to which they do not apply paragraph 1.

Article 10   Information to be provided

1. In addition to other information requirements established by Community law, Member States shall ensure, except when otherwise agreed by parties who are not consumers, that at least the following information is given by the service provider clearly, comprehensibly and unambiguously and prior to the order being placed by the recipient of the service:

    (a) the different technical steps to follow to conclude the contract;

    (b) whether or not the concluded contract will be filed by the service provider and whether it will be accessible;

    (c) the technical means for identifying and correcting input errors prior to the placing of the order;

    (d) the languages offered for the conclusion of the contract.

2. Member States shall ensure that, except when otherwise agreed by parties who are not consumers, the service provider indicates any relevant codes of conduct to which he subscribes and information on how those codes can be consulted electronically.

3. Contract terms and general conditions provided to the recipient must be made available in a way that allows him to store and reproduce them.

4. Paragraphs 1 and 2 shall not apply to contracts concluded exclusively by exchange of electronic mail or by equivalent individual communications.

Article 11   Placing of the order

1. Member States shall ensure, except when otherwise agreed by parties who are not consumers, that in cases where the recipient of the service places his order through technological means, the following principles apply:

— the service provider has to acknowledge the receipt of the recipient's order without undue delay and by electronic means,

— the order and the acknowledgement of receipt are deemed to be received when the parties to whom they are addressed are able to access them.

2. Member States shall ensure that, except when otherwise agreed by parties who are not consumers, the service provider makes available to the recipient of the service appropriate, effective and accessible technical means allowing him to identify and correct input errors, prior to the placing of the order.

3. Paragraph 1, first indent, and paragraph 2 shall not apply to contracts concluded exclusively by exchange of electronic mail or by equivalent individual communications.

Section 4

Liability of intermediary service providers

Article 12   "Mere conduit"

1. Where an information society service is provided that consists of the transmission in a communication network of information provided by a recipient of the service, or the provision of access to a communication network, Member States shall ensure that the service provider is not liable for the information transmitted, on condition that the provider:

(a) does not initiate the transmission;

(b) does not select the receiver of the transmission; and does not select or modify the information contained in the transmission.

2. The acts of transmission and of provision of access referred to in paragraph 1 include the automatic, intermediate and transient storage of the information transmitted in so far as this takes place for the sole purpose of carrying out the transmission in the communication network, and provided that the information is not stored for any period longer than is reasonably necessary for the transmission.

3. This Article shall not affect the possibility for a court or administrative authority, in accordance with Member States' legal systems, of requiring the service provider to terminate or prevent an infringement.

Article 13   "Caching"

1. Where an information society service is provided that consists of the transmission in a communication network of information provided by a recipient of the service, Member States shall ensure that the service provider is not liable for the automatic, intermediate and temporary storage of that information, performed for the sole purpose of making more efficient the information's onward transmission to other recipients of the service upon their request, on condition that:

(a) the provider does not modify the information;

(b) the provider complies with conditions on access to the information;

(c) the provider complies with rules regarding the updating of the information, specified in a manner widely recognised and used by industry;

(d) the provider does not interfere with the lawful use of technology, widely recognised and used by industry, to obtain data on the use of the information; and

(e) the provider acts expeditiously to remove or to disable access to the information it has stored upon obtaining actual knowledge of the fact that the information at the initial source of the transmission has been removed from the network, or access to it has been disabled, or that a court or an administrative authority has ordered such removal or disablement.

2. This Article shall not affect the possibility for a court or administrative authority, in accordance with Member States' legal systems, of requiring the service provider to terminate or prevent an infringement.

Article 14   Hosting

1. Where an information society service is provided that consists of the storage of information provided by a recipient of the service, Member States shall ensure that the service provider is not liable for the information stored at the request of a recipient of the service, on condition that:

> (a) the provider does not have actual knowledge of illegal activity or information and, as regards claims for damages, is not aware of facts or circumstances from which the illegal activity or information is apparent; or
>
> (b) the provider, upon obtaining such knowledge or awareness, acts expeditiously to remove or to disable access to the information.

2. Paragraph 1 shall not apply when the recipient of the service is acting under the authority or the control of the provider.

3. This Article shall not affect the possibility for a court or administrative authority, in accordance with Member States' legal systems, of requiring the service provider to terminate or prevent an infringement, nor does it affect the possibility for Member States of establishing procedures governing the removal or disabling of access to information.

Article 15   No general obligation to monitor

1. Member States shall not impose a general obligation on providers, when providing the services covered by Articles 12, 13 and 14, to monitor the information which they transmit or store, nor a general obligation actively to seek facts or circumstances indicating illegal activity.

2. Member States may establish obligations for information society service providers promptly to inform the competent public authorities of alleged illegal activities undertaken or information provided by recipients of their service or obligations to communicate to the competent authorities, at their request, information enabling the identification of recipients of their service with whom they have storage agreements.

Chapter III Implementation

Article 16   Codes of conduct

1. Member States and the Commission shall encourage:

> (a) the drawing up of codes of conduct at Community level, by trade, professional and consumer associations or organisations, designed to contribute to the proper implementation of Articles 5 to 15;
>
> (b) the voluntary transmission of draft codes of conduct at national or Community level to the Commission;
>
> (c) the accessibility of these codes of conduct in the Community languages by electronic means;
>
> (d) the communication to the Member States and the Commission, by trade, professional and consumer associations or organisations, of their assessment of the application of their codes of conduct and their impact upon practices, habits or customs relating to electronic commerce;
>
> (e) the drawing up of codes of conduct regarding the protection of minors and human dignity.

2. Member States and the Commission shall encourage the involvement of associations or organisations representing consumers in the drafting and implementation of codes of conduct affecting their interests and drawn up in accordance with paragraph 1(a). Where appropriate, to take account of their specific needs, associations representing the visually impaired and disabled should be consulted.

Article 17   Out-of-court dispute settlement

1. Member States shall ensure that, in the event of disagreement between an information society service provider and the recipient of the service, their legislation does not hamper the use of out-of-court schemes, available under national law, for dispute settlement, including appropriate electronic means.

2. Member States shall encourage bodies responsible for the out-of-court settlement of, in particular, consumer disputes to operate in a way which provides adequate procedural guarantees for the parties concerned.

3. Member States shall encourage bodies responsible for out-of-court dispute settlement to inform the Commission of the significant decisions they take regarding information society services and to transmit any other information on the practices, usages or customs relating to electronic commerce.

Article 18   Court actions

1. Member States shall ensure that court actions available under national law concerning information society services' activities allow for the rapid adoption of measures, including interim measures, designed to terminate any alleged infringement and to prevent any further impairment of the interests involved.

2. The Annex to Directive 98/27/EC shall be supplemented as follows:

"11. Directive 2000/31/EC of the European Parliament and of the Council of 8 June 2000 on certain legal aspects on information society services, in particular electronic commerce, in the internal market (Directive on electronic commerce) (OJ L 178, 17.7.2000, p. 1)".

Article 19   Cooperation

1. Member States shall have adequate means of supervision and investigation necessary to implement this Directive effectively and shall ensure that service providers supply them with the requisite information.

2. Member States shall cooperate with other Member States; they shall, to that end, appoint one or several contact points, whose details they shall communicate to the other Member States and to the Commission.

3. Member States shall, as quickly as possible, and in conformity with national law, provide the assistance and information requested by other Member States or by the Commission, including by appropriate electronic means.

4. Member States shall establish contact points which shall be accessible at least by electronic means and from which recipients and service providers may:

      (a) obtain general information on contractual rights and obligations as well as on the complaint and redress mechanisms available in the event of disputes, including practical aspects involved in the use of such mechanisms;

      (b) obtain the details of authorities, associations or organisations from which they may obtain further information or practical assistance.

5. Member States shall encourage the communication to the Commission of any significant administrative or judicial decisions taken in their territory regarding disputes relating to information society services and practices, usages and customs relating to electronic commerce. The Commission shall communicate these decisions to the other Member States.

Article 20   Sanctions

Member States shall determine the sanctions applicable to infringements of national provisions adopted pursuant to this Directive and shall take all measures necessary to ensure that they are enforced. The sanctions they provide for shall be effective, proportionate and dissuasive.

Chapter IV   Final Provisions

Article 21   Re-examination

1. Before 17 July 2003, and thereafter every two years, the Commission shall submit to the European Parliament, the Council and the Economic and Social Committee a report on the application

of this Directive, accompanied, where necessary, by proposals for adapting it to legal, technical and economic developments in the field of information society services, in particular with respect to crime prevention, the protection of minors, consumer protection and to the proper functioning of the internal market.

2. In examining the need for an adaptation of this Directive, the report shall in particular analyse the need for proposals concerning the liability of providers of hyperlinks and location tool services, "notice and take down" procedures and the attribution of liability following the taking down of content. The report shall also analyse the need for additional conditions for the exemption from liability, provided for in Articles 12 and 13, in the light of technical developments, and the possibility of applying the internal market principles to unsolicited commercial communications by electronic mail.

Article 22   Transposition

1. Member States shall bring into force the laws, regulations and administrative provisions necessary to comply with this Directive before 17 January 2002. They shall forthwith inform the Commission thereof.

2. When Member States adopt the measures referred to in paragraph 1, these shall contain a reference to this Directive or shall be accompanied by such reference at the time of their official publication. The methods of making such reference shall be laid down by Member States.

Article 23   Entry into force

This Directive shall enter into force on the day of its publication in the Official Journal of the European Communities.

Article 24   Addressees

This Directive is addressed to the Member States.

Done at Luxemburg, 8 June 2000.
For the European Parliament
The President
N. Fontaine
For the Council
The President
G. d'Oliveira Martins

Annex

Derogations from Article 3

As provided for in Article 3(3), Article 3(1) and (2) do not apply to:
— copyright, neighbouring rights, rights referred to in Directive 87/54/EEC[1] and Directive 96/9/EC[2] as well as industrial property rights,
— the emission of electronic money by institutions in respect of which Member States have applied one of the derogations provided for in Article 8(1) of Directive 2000/46/EC[3],
— Article 44(2) of Directive 85/611/EEC[4],
— Article 30 and Title IV of Directive 92/49/EEC[5], Title IV of Directive 92/96/EEC[6],
— Articles 7 and 8 of Directive 88/35 7/EEC[7] and Article 4 of Directive 90/619/EEC[8],
— the freedom of the parties to choose the law applicable to their contract,
— contractual obligations concerning consumer contacts,

---

[1] OJ L 24, 27.1.1987, p. 36.   [2] OJ L 77, 27.3.1996, p. 20.   [3] Not yet published in the Official Journal.
[4] OJ L 375, 31.12.1985, p. 3. Directive as last amended by Directive 95/26/EC (OJ L 168, 18.7.1995, p. 7.
[5] OJ L 228, 11.8.1992, p. 1. Directive as last amended by Directive 95/26/EC.
[6] OJ L 360, 9.12.1992, p. 2. Directive as last amended by Directive 95/26/EC.
[7] OJ L 172, 4.7.1988, p. 1. Directive as last amended by Directive 92/49/EC.
[8] OJ L 330, 29.11.1990, p. 50. Directive as last amended by Directive 92/96/EC.

— formal validity of contracts creating or transferring rights in real estate where such contracts are subject to mandatory formal requirements of the law of the Member State where the real estate is situated,

— the permissibility of unsolicited commercial communications by electronic mail.

Directive 2001/29/EC of the European Parliament and of the Council of 22 May 2001 on the harmonisation of certain aspects of copyright and related rights in the information society

THE EUROPEAN PARLIAMENT AND THE COUNCIL OF THE EUROPEAN UNION,

Having regard to the Treaty establishing the European Community, and in particular Articles 47(2), 55 and 95 thereof,

Having regard to the proposal from the Commission[1],

Having regard to the opinion of the Economic and Social Committee[2],

Acting in accordance with the procedure laid down in Article 251 of the Treaty[3],

Whereas:

(1) The Treaty provides for the establishment of an internal market and the institution of a system ensuring that competition in the internal market is not distorted. Harmonisation of the laws of the Member States on copyright and related rights contributes to the achievement of these objectives.

(2) The European Council, meeting at Corfu on 24 and 25 June 1994, stressed the need to create a general and flexible legal framework at Community level in order to foster the development of the information society in Europe. This requires, inter alia, the existence of an internal market for new products and services. Important Community legislation to ensure such a regulatory framework is already in place or its adoption is well under way. Copyright and related rights play an important role in this context as they protect and stimulate the development and marketing of new products and services and the creation and exploitation of their creative content.

(3) The proposed harmonisation will help to implement the four freedoms of the internal market and relates to compliance with the fundamental principles of law and especially of property, including intellectual property, and freedom of expression and the public interest.

(4) A harmonised legal framework on copyright and related rights, through increased legal certainty and while providing for a high level of protection of intellectual property, will foster substantial investment in creativity and innovation, including network infrastructure, and lead in turn to growth and increased competitiveness of European industry, both in the area of content provision and information technology and more generally across a wide range of industrial and cultural sectors. This will safeguard employment and encourage new job creation.

(5) Technological development has multiplied and diversified the vectors for creation, production and exploitation. While no new concepts for the protection of intellectual property are needed, the current law on copyright and related rights should be adapted and supplemented to respond adequately to economic realities such as new forms of exploitation.

(6) Without harmonisation at Community level, legislative activities at national level which have already been initiated in a number of Member States in order to respond to the technological challenges might result in significant differences in protection and thereby in restrictions on the free movement of services and products incorporating, or based on, intellectual property, leading to a refragmentation of the internal market and legislative inconsistency. The impact of such legislative

---

[1] OJ C 108, 7.4.1998, p. 6 and OJ C 180, 25.6.1999, p. 6.   [2] OJ C 407, 28.12.1998, p. 30.

[3] Opinion of the European Parliament of 10 February 1999 (OJ C 150, 28.5.1999, p. 171), Council Common Position of 28 September 2000 (OJ C 344, 1.12.2000, p. 1) and Decision of the European Parliament of 14 February 2001 (not yet published in the Official Journal). Council Decision of 9 April 2001.

differences and uncertainties will become more significant with the further development of the information society, which has already greatly increased transborder exploitation of intellectual property. This development will and should further increase. Significant legal differences and uncertainties in protection may hinder economies of scale for new products and services containing copyright and related rights.

(7) The Community legal framework for the protection of copyright and related rights must, therefore, also be adapted and supplemented as far as is necessary for the smooth functioning of the internal market. To that end, those national provisions on copyright and related rights which vary considerably from one Member State to another or which cause legal uncertainties hindering the smooth functioning of the internal market and the proper development of the information society in Europe should be adjusted, and inconsistent national responses to the technological developments should be avoided, whilst differences not adversely affecting the functioning of the internal market need not be removed or prevented.

(8) The various social, societal and cultural implications of the information society require that account be taken of the specific features of the content of products and services.

(9) Any harmonisation of copyright and related rights must take as a basis a high level of protection, since such rights are crucial to intellectual creation. Their protection helps to ensure the maintenance and development of creativity in the interests of authors, performers, producers, consumers, culture, industry and the public at large. Intellectual property has therefore been recognised as an integral part of property.

(10) If authors or performers are to continue their creative and artistic work, they have to receive an appropriate reward for the use of their work, as must producers in order to be able to finance this work. The investment required to produce products such as phonograms, films or multimedia products, and services such as "on-demand" services, is considerable. Adequate legal protection of intellectual property rights is necessary in order to guarantee the availability of such a reward and provide the opportunity for satisfactory returns on this investment.

(11) A rigorous, effective system for the protection of copyright and related rights is one of the main ways of ensuring that European cultural creativity and production receive the necessary resources and of safeguarding the independence and dignity of artistic creators and performers.

(12) Adequate protection of copyright works and subject-matter of related rights is also of great importance from a cultural standpoint. Article 151 of the Treaty requires the Community to take cultural aspects into account in its action.

(13) A common search for, and consistent application at European level of, technical measures to protect works and other subject-matter and to provide the necessary information on rights are essential insofar as the ultimate aim of these measures is to give effect to the principles and guarantees laid down in law.

(14) This Directive should seek to promote learning and culture by protecting works and other subject-matter while permitting exceptions or limitations in the public interest for the purpose of education and teaching.

(15) The Diplomatic Conference held under the auspices of the World Intellectual Property Organisation (WIPO) in December 1996 led to the adoption of two new Treaties, the "WIPO Copyright Treaty" and the "WIPO Performances and Phonograms Treaty", dealing respectively with the protection of authors and the protection of performers and phonogram producers. Those Treaties update the international protection for copyright and related rights significantly, not least with regard to the so-called "digital agenda", and improve the means to fight piracy world-wide. The Community and a majority of Member States have already signed the Treaties and the process of making arrangements for the ratification of the Treaties by the Community and the Member States is under way. This Directive also serves to implement a number of the new international obligations.

(16) Liability for activities in the network environment concerns not only copyright and related rights but also other areas, such as defamation, misleading advertising, or infringement of trademarks, and is addressed horizontally in Directive 2000/31/EC of the European Parliament and of the Council of 8 June 2000 on certain legal aspects of information society services, in particular electronic

commerce, in the internal market ("Directive on electronic commerce")[4], which clarifies and harmonises various legal issues relating to information society services including electronic commerce. This Directive should be implemented within a timescale similar to that for the implementation of the Directive on electronic commerce, since that Directive provides a harmonised framework of principles and provisions relevant inter alia to important parts of this Directive. This Directive is without prejudice to provisions relating to liability in that Directive.

(17) It is necessary, especially in the light of the requirements arising out of the digital environment, to ensure that collecting societies achieve a higher level of rationalisation and transparency with regard to compliance with competition rules.

(18) This Directive is without prejudice to the arrangements in the Member States concerning the management of rights such as extended collective licences.

(19) The moral rights of rightholders should be exercised according to the legislation of the Member States and the provisions of the Berne Convention for the Protection of Literary and Artistic Works, of the WIPO Copyright Treaty and of the WIPO Performances and Phonograms Treaty. Such moral rights remain outside the scope of this Directive.

(20) This Directive is based on principles and rules already laid down in the Directives currently in force in this area, in particular Directives 91/250/EEC[5], 92/100/EEC[6], 93/83/EEC[7], 93/98/EEC[8] and 96/9/EC[9] and it develops those principles and rules and places them in the context of the information society. The provisions of this Directive should be without prejudice to the provisions of those Directives, unless otherwise provided in this Directive.

(21) This Directive should define the scope of the acts covered by the reproduction right with regard to the different beneficiaries. This should be done in conformity with the acquis communautaire. A broad definition of these acts is needed to ensure legal certainty within the internal market.

(22) The objective of proper support for the dissemination of culture must not be achieved by sacrificing strict protection of rights or by tolerating illegal forms of distribution of counterfeited or pirated works.

(23) This Directive should harmonise further the author's right of communication to the public. This right should be understood in a broad sense covering all communication to the public not present at the place where the communication originates. This right should cover any such transmission or retransmission of a work to the public by wire or wireless means, including broadcasting. This right should not cover any other acts.

(24) The right to make available to the public subject-matter referred to in Article 3(2) should be understood as covering all acts of making available such subject-matter to members of the public not present at the place where the act of making available originates, and as not covering any other acts.

(25) The legal uncertainty regarding the nature and the level of protection of acts of on-demand transmission of copyright works and subject-matter protected by related rights over networks should be overcome by providing for harmonised protection at Community level. It should be made clear that all rightholders recognised by this Directive should have an exclusive right to make available to the public copyright works or any other subject-matter by way of interactive on-demand transmissions. Such interactive on-demand transmissions are characterised by the fact that members of the public may access them from a place and at a time individually chosen by them.

---

[4] OJ L 178, 17.7.2000, p. 1.

[5] Council Directive 91/250/EEC of 14 May 1991 on the legal protection of computer programs (OJ L 122, 17.5.1991, p. 42). Directive as amended by Directive 93/98/EEC.

[6] Council Directive 92/100/EEC of 19 November 1992 on rental right and lending right and on certain rights related to copyright in the field of intellectual property (OJ L 346, 27.11.1992, p. 61). Directive as amended by Directive 93/98/EEC.

[7] Council Directive 93/83/EEC of 27 September 1993 on the coordination of certain rules concerning copyright and rights related to copyright applicable to satellite broadcasting and cable retransmission (OJ L 248, 6.10.1993, p. 15).

[8] Council Directive 93/98/EEC of 29 October 1993 harmonising the term of protection of copyright and certain related rights (OJ L 290, 24.11.1993, p. 9).

[9] Directive 96/9/EC of the European Parliament and of the Council of 11 March 1996 on the legal protection of databases (OJ L 77, 27.3.1996, p. 20).

(26) With regard to the making available in on-demand services by broadcasters of their radio or television productions incorporating music from commercial phonograms as an integral part thereof, collective licensing arrangements are to be encouraged in order to facilitate the clearance of the rights concerned.

(27) The mere provision of physical facilities for enabling or making a communication does not in itself amount to communication within the meaning of this Directive.

(28) Copyright protection under this Directive includes the exclusive right to control distribution of the work incorporated in a tangible article. The first sale in the Community of the original of a work or copies thereof by the rightholder or with his consent exhausts the right to control resale of that object in the Community. This right should not be exhausted in respect of the original or of copies thereof sold by the rightholder or with his consent outside the Community. Rental and lending rights for authors have been established in Directive 92/100/EEC. The distribution right provided for in this Directive is without prejudice to the provisions relating to the rental and lending rights contained in Chapter I of that Directive.

(29) The question of exhaustion does not arise in the case of services and on-line services in particular. This also applies with regard to a material copy of a work or other subject-matter made by a user of such a service with the consent of the rightholder. Therefore, the same applies to rental and lending of the original and copies of works or other subject-matter which are services by nature. Unlike CD-ROM or CD-I, where the intellectual property is incorporated in a material medium, namely an item of goods, every on-line service is in fact an act which should be subject to authorisation where the copyright or related right so provides.

(30) The rights referred to in this Directive may be transferred, assigned or subject to the granting of contractual licences, without prejudice to the relevant national legislation on copyright and related rights.

(31) A fair balance of rights and interests between the different categories of right-holders, as well as between the different categories of rightholders and users of protected subject-matter must be safeguarded. The existing exceptions and limitations to the rights as set out by the Member States have to be reassessed in the light of the new electronic environment. Existing differences in the exceptions and limitations to certain restricted acts have direct negative effects on the functioning of the internal market of copyright and related rights. Such differences could well become more pronounced in view of the further development of transborder exploitation of works and cross-border activities. In order to ensure the proper functioning of the internal market, such exceptions and limitations should be defined more harmoniously. The degree of their harmonisation should be based on their impact on the smooth functioning of the internal market.

(32) This Directive provides for an exhaustive enumeration of exceptions and limitations to the reproduction right and the right of communication to the public. Some exceptions or limitations only apply to the reproduction right, where appropriate. This list takes due account of the different legal traditions in Member States, while, at the same time, aiming to ensure a functioning internal market. Member States should arrive at a coherent application of these exceptions and limitations, which will be assessed when reviewing implementing legislation in the future.

(33) The exclusive right of reproduction should be subject to an exception to allow certain acts of temporary reproduction, which are transient or incidental reproductions, forming an integral and essential part of a technological process and carried out for the sole purpose of enabling either efficient transmission in a network between third parties by an intermediary, or a lawful use of a work or other subject-matter to be made. The acts of reproduction concerned should have no separate economic value on their own. To the extent that they meet these conditions, this exception should include acts which enable browsing as well as acts of caching to take place, including those which enable transmission systems to function efficiently, provided that the intermediary does not modify the information and does not interfere with the lawful use of technology, widely recognised and used by industry, to obtain data on the use of the information. A use should be considered lawful where it is authorised by the rightholder or not restricted by law.

(34) Member States should be given the option of providing for certain exceptions or limitations for cases such as educational and scientific purposes, for the benefit of public institutions such as

libraries and archives, for purposes of news reporting, for quotations, for use by people with disabilities, for public security uses and for uses in administrative and judicial proceedings.

(35) In certain cases of exceptions or limitations, rightholders should receive fair compensation to compensate them adequately for the use made of their protected works or other subject-matter. When determining the form, detailed arrangements and possible level of such fair compensation, account should be taken of the particular circumstances of each case. When evaluating these circumstances, a valuable criterion would be the possible harm to the rightholders resulting from the act in question. In cases where rightholders have already received payment in some other form, for instance as part of a licence fee, no specific or separate payment may be due. The level of fair compensation should take full account of the degree of use of technological protection measures referred to in this Directive. In certain situations where the prejudice to the rightholder would be minimal, no obligation for payment may arise.

(36) The Member States may provide for fair compensation for rightholders also when applying the optional provisions on exceptions or limitations which do not require such compensation.

(37) Existing national schemes on reprography, where they exist, do not create major barriers to the internal market. Member States should be allowed to provide for an exception or limitation in respect of reprography.

(38) Member States should be allowed to provide for an exception or limitation to the reproduction right for certain types of reproduction of audio, visual and audio-visual material for private use, accompanied by fair compensation. This may include the introduction or continuation of remuneration schemes to compensate for the prejudice to rightholders. Although differences between those remuneration schemes affect the functioning of the internal market, those differences, with respect to analogue private reproduction, should not have a significant impact on the development of the information society. Digital private copying is likely to be more widespread and have a greater economic impact. Due account should therefore be taken of the differences between digital and analogue private copying and a distinction should be made in certain respects between them.

(39) When applying the exception or limitation on private copying, Member States should take due account of technological and economic developments, in particular with respect to digital private copying and remuneration schemes, when effective technological protection measures are available. Such exceptions or limitations should not inhibit the use of technological measures or their enforcement against circumvention.

(40) Member States may provide for an exception or limitation for the benefit of certain non-profit making establishments, such as publicly accessible libraries and equivalent institutions, as well as archives. However, this should be limited to certain special cases covered by the reproduction right. Such an exception or limitation should not cover uses made in the context of on-line delivery of protected works or other subject-matter. This Directive should be without prejudice to the Member States' option to derogate from the exclusive public lending right in accordance with Article 5 of Directive 92/100/EEC. Therefore, specific contracts or licences should be promoted which, without creating imbalances, favour such establishments and the disseminative purposes they serve.

(41) When applying the exception or limitation in respect of ephemeral recordings made by broadcasting organisations it is understood that a broadcaster's own facilities include those of a person acting on behalf of and under the responsibility of the broadcasting organisation.

(42) When applying the exception or limitation for non-commercial educational and scientific research purposes, including distance learning, the non-commercial nature of the activity in question should be determined by that activity as such. The organisational structure and the means of funding of the establishment concerned are not the decisive factors in this respect.

(43) It is in any case important for the Member States to adopt all necessary measures to facilitate access to works by persons suffering from a disability which constitutes an obstacle to the use of the works themselves, and to pay particular attention to accessible formats.

(44) When applying the exceptions and limitations provided for in this Directive, they should be exercised in accordance with international obligations. Such exceptions and limitations may not be applied in a way which prejudices the legitimate interests of the rightholder or which conflicts with

the normal exploitation of his work or other subject-matter. The provision of such exceptions or limitations by Member States should, in particular, duly reflect the increased economic impact that such exceptions or limitations may have in the context of the new electronic environment. Therefore, the scope of certain exceptions or limitations may have to be even more limited when it comes to certain new uses of copyright works and other subject-matter.

(45) The exceptions and limitations referred to in Article 5(2), (3) and (4) should not, however, prevent the definition of contractual relations designed to ensure fair compensation for the rightholders insofar as permitted by national law.

(46) Recourse to mediation could help users and rightholders to settle disputes. The Commission, in cooperation with the Member States within the Contact Committee, should undertake a study to consider new legal ways of settling disputes concerning copyright and related rights.

(47) Technological development will allow rightholders to make use of technological measures designed to prevent or restrict acts not authorised by the rightholders of any copyright, rights related to copyright or the sui generis right in databases. The danger, however, exists that illegal activities might be carried out in order to enable or facilitate the circumvention of the technical protection provided by these measures. In order to avoid fragmented legal approaches that could potentially hinder the functioning of the internal market, there is a need to provide for harmonised legal protection against circumvention of effective technological measures and against provision of devices and products or services to this effect.

(48) Such legal protection should be provided in respect of technological measures that effectively restrict acts not authorised by the rightholders of any copyright, rights related to copyright or the sui generis right in databases without, however, preventing the normal operation of electronic equipment and its technological development. Such legal protection implies no obligation to design devices, products, components or services to correspond to technological measures, so long as such device, product, component or service does not otherwise fall under the prohibition of Article 6. Such legal protection should respect proportionality and should not prohibit those devices or activities which have a commercially significant purpose or use other than to circumvent the technical protection. In particular, this protection should not hinder research into cryptography.

(49) The legal protection of technological measures is without prejudice to the application of any national provisions which may prohibit the private possession of devices, products or components for the circumvention of technological measures.

(50) Such a harmonised legal protection does not affect the specific provisions on protection provided for by Directive 91/250/EEC. In particular, it should not apply to the protection of technological measures used in connection with computer programs, which is exclusively addressed in that Directive. It should neither inhibit nor prevent the development or use of any means of circumventing a technological measure that is necessary to enable acts to be undertaken in accordance with the terms of Article 5(3) or Article 6 of Directive 91/250/EEC. Articles 5 and 6 of that Directive exclusively determine exceptions to the exclusive rights applicable to computer programs.

(51) The legal protection of technological measures applies without prejudice to public policy, as reflected in Article 5, or public security. Member States should promote voluntary measures taken by rightholders, including the conclusion and implementation of agreements between rightholders and other parties concerned, to accommodate achieving the objectives of certain exceptions or limitations provided for in national law in accordance with this Directive. In the absence of such voluntary measures or agreements within a reasonable period of time, Member States should take appropriate measures to ensure that rightholders provide beneficiaries of such exceptions or limitations with appropriate means of benefiting from them, by modifying an implemented technological measure or by other means. However, in order to prevent abuse of such measures taken by rightholders, including within the framework of agreements, or taken by a Member State, any technological measures applied in implementation of such measures should enjoy legal protection.

(52) When implementing an exception or limitation for private copying in accordance with Article 5(2)(b), Member States should likewise promote the use of voluntary measures to accommodate achieving the objectives of such exception or limitation. If, within a reasonable period of time,

no such voluntary measures to make reproduction for private use possible have been taken, Member States may take measures to enable beneficiaries of the exception or limitation concerned to benefit from it. Voluntary measures taken by right-holders, including agreements between rightholders and other parties concerned, as well as measures taken by Member States, do not prevent rightholders from using technological measures which are consistent with the exceptions or limitations on private copying in national law in accordance with Article 5(2)(b), taking account of the condition of fair compensation under that provision and the possible differentiation between various conditions of use in accordance with Article 5(5), such as controlling the number of reproductions. In order to prevent abuse of such measures, any technological measures applied in their implementation should enjoy legal protection.

(53) The protection of technological measures should ensure a secure environment for the provision of interactive on-demand services, in such a way that members of the public may access works or other subject-matter from a place and at a time individually chosen by them. Where such services are governed by contractual arrangements, the first and second subparagraphs of Article 6(4) should not apply. Non-interactive forms of online use should remain subject to those provisions.

(54) Important progress has been made in the international standardisation of technical systems of identification of works and protected subject-matter in digital format. In an increasingly networked environment, differences between technological measures could lead to an incompatibility of systems within the Community. Compatibility and interoperability of the different systems should be encouraged. It would be highly desirable to encourage the development of global systems.

(55) Technological development will facilitate the distribution of works, notably on networks, and this will entail the need for rightholders to identify better the work or other subject-matter, the author or any other rightholder, and to provide information about the terms and conditions of use of the work or other subject-matter in order to render easier the management of rights attached to them. Rightholders should be encouraged to use markings indicating, in addition to the information referred to above, inter alia their authorisation when putting works or other subject-matter on networks.

(56) There is, however, the danger that illegal activities might be carried out in order to remove or alter the electronic copyright-management information attached to it, or otherwise to distribute, import for distribution, broadcast, communicate to the public or make available to the public works or other protected subject-matter from which such information has been removed without authority. In order to avoid fragmented legal approaches that could potentially hinder the functioning of the internal market, there is a need to provide for harmonised legal protection against any of these activities.

(57) Any such rights-management information systems referred to above may, depending on their design, at the same time process personal data about the consumption patterns of protected subject-matter by individuals and allow for tracing of on-line behaviour. These technical means, in their technical functions, should incorporate privacy safeguards in accordance with Directive 95/46/EC of the European Parliament and of the Council of 24 October 1995 on the protection of individuals with regard to the processing of personal data and the free movement of such data[10].

(58) Member States should provide for effective sanctions and remedies for infringements of rights and obligations as set out in this Directive. They should take all the measures necessary to ensure that those sanctions and remedies are applied. The sanctions thus provided for should be effective, proportionate and dissuasive and should include the possibility of seeking damages and/or injunctive relief and, where appropriate, of applying for seizure of infringing material.

(59) In the digital environment, in particular, the services of intermediaries may increasingly be used by third parties for infringing activities. In many cases such intermediaries are best placed to bring such infringing activities to an end. Therefore, without prejudice to any other sanctions and remedies available, rightholders should have the possibility of applying for an injunction against an intermediary who carries a third party's infringement of a protected work or other subject-matter in a

---

[10] OJ L 281, 23.11.1995, p. 31.

network. This possibility should be available even where the acts carried out by the intermediary are exempted under Article 5. The conditions and modalities relating to such injunctions should be left to the national law of the Member States.

(60) The protection provided under this Directive should be without prejudice to national or Community legal provisions in other areas, such as industrial property, data protection, conditional access, access to public documents, and the rule of media exploitation chronology, which may affect the protection of copyright or related rights.

(61) In order to comply with the WIPO Performances and Phonograms Treaty, Directives 92/100/EEC and 93/98/EEC should be amended,

HAVE ADOPTED THIS DIRECTIVE:

Chapter I Objective and Scope

Article 1 Scope

1. This Directive concerns the legal protection of copyright and related rights in the framework of the internal market, with particular emphasis on the information society.

2. Except in the cases referred to in Article 11, this Directive shall leave intact and shall in no way affect existing Community provisions relating to:

    (a) the legal protection of computer programs;

    (b) rental right, lending right and certain rights related to copyright in the field of intellectual property;

    (c) copyright and related rights applicable to broadcasting of programmes by satellite and cable retransmission;

    (d) the term of protection of copyright and certain related rights;

    (e) the legal protection of databases.

Chapter II Rights and Exceptions

Article 2 Reproduction right

Member States shall provide for the exclusive right to authorise or prohibit direct or indirect, temporary or permanent reproduction by any means and in any form, in whole or in part:

    (a) for authors, of their works;

    (b) for performers, of fixations of their performances;

    (c) for phonogram producers, of their phonograms;

    (d) for the producers of the first fixations of films, in respect of the original and copies of their films;

    (e) for broadcasting organisations, of fixations of their broadcasts, whether those broadcasts are transmitted by wire or over the air, including by cable or satellite.

Article 3 Right of communication to the public of works and right of making available to the public other subject-matter

1. Member States shall provide authors with the exclusive right to authorise or prohibit any communication to the public of their works, by wire or wireless means, including the making available to the public of their works in such a way that members of the public may access them from a place and at a time individually chosen by them.

2. Member States shall provide for the exclusive right to authorise or prohibit the making available to the public, by wire or wireless means, in such a way that members of the public may access them from a place and at a time individually chosen by them:

    (a) for performers, of fixations of their performances;

    (b) for phonogram producers, of their phonograms;

    (c) for the producers of the first fixations of films, of the original and copies of their films;

    (d) for broadcasting organisations, of fixations of their broadcasts, whether these broadcasts are transmitted by wire or over the air, including by cable or satellite.

3. The rights referred to in paragraphs 1 and 2 shall not be exhausted by any act of communication to the public or making available to the public as set out in this Article.

Article 4   Distribution right

1. Member States shall provide for authors, in respect of the original of their works or of copies thereof, the exclusive right to authorise or prohibit any form of distribution to the public by sale or otherwise.

2. The distribution right shall not be exhausted within the Community in respect of the original or copies of the work, except where the first sale or other transfer of ownership in the Community of that object is made by the rightholder or with his consent.

Article 5   Exceptions and limitations

1. Temporary acts of reproduction referred to in Article 2, which are transient or incidental [and] an integral and essential part of a technological process and whose sole purpose is to enable:

> (a) a transmission in a network between third parties by an intermediary, or
> (b) a lawful use

of a work or other subject-matter to be made, and which have no independent economic significance, shall be exempted from the reproduction right provided for in Article 2.

2. Member States may provide for exceptions or limitations to the reproduction right provided for in Article 2 in the following cases:

> (a) in respect of reproductions on paper or any similar medium, effected by the use of any kind of photographic technique or by some other process having similar effects, with the exception of sheet music, provided that the rightholders receive fair compensation;
> (b) in respect of reproductions on any medium made by a natural person for private use and for ends that are neither directly nor indirectly commercial, on condition that the rightholders receive fair compensation which takes account of the application or non-application of technological measures referred to in Article 6 to the work or subject-matter concerned;
> (c) in respect of specific acts of reproduction made by publicly accessible libraries, educational establishments or museums, or by archives, which are not for direct or indirect economic or commercial advantage;
> (d) in respect of ephemeral recordings of works made by broadcasting organisations by means of their own facilities and for their own broadcasts; the preservation of these recordings in official archives may, on the grounds of their exceptional documentary character, be permitted;
> (e) in respect of reproductions of broadcasts made by social institutions pursuing non-commercial purposes, such as hospitals or prisons, on condition that the rightholders receive fair compensation.

3. Member States may provide for exceptions or limitations to the rights provided for in Articles 2 and 3 in the following cases:

> (a) use for the sole purpose of illustration for teaching or scientific research, as long as the source, including the author's name, is indicated, unless this turns out to be impossible and to the extent justified by the non-commercial purpose to be achieved;
> (b) uses, for the benefit of people with a disability, which are directly related to the disability and of a non-commercial nature, to the extent required by the specific disability;
> (c) reproduction by the press, communication to the public or making available of published articles on current economic, political or religious topics or of broadcast works or other subject-matter of the same character, in cases where such use is not expressly reserved, and as long as the source, including the author's name, is indicated, or use of works or other subject-matter in connection with the reporting of current events, to the extent justified by the informatory purpose and as long as the source, including the author's name, is indicated, unless this turns out to be impossible;
> (d) quotations for purposes such as criticism or review, provided that they relate to a work or other subject-matter which has already been lawfully made available to the public,

that, unless this turns out to be impossible, the source, including the author's name, is indicated, and that their use is in accordance with fair practice, and to the extent required by the specific purpose;

(e) use for the purposes of public security or to ensure the proper performance or reporting of administrative, parliamentary or judicial proceedings;

(f) use of political speeches as well as extracts of public lectures or similar works or subject-matter to the extent justified by the informatory purpose and provided that the source, including the author's name, is indicated, except where this turns out to be impossible;

(g) use during religious celebrations or official celebrations organised by a public authority;

(h) use of works, such as works of architecture or sculpture, made to be located permanently in public places;

(i) incidental inclusion of a work or other subject-matter in other material;

(j) use for the purpose of advertising the public exhibition or sale of artistic works, to the extent necessary to promote the event, excluding any other commercial use;

(k) use for the purpose of caricature, parody or pastiche;

(l) use in connection with the demonstration or repair of equipment;

(m) use of an artistic work in the form of a building or a drawing or plan of a building for the purposes of reconstructing the building;

(n) use by communication or making available, for the purpose of research or private study, to individual members of the public by dedicated terminals on the premises of establishments referred to in paragraph 2(c) of works and other subject-matter not subject to purchase or licensing terms which are contained in their collections;

(o) use in certain other cases of minor importance where exceptions or limitations already exist under national law, provided that they only concern analogue uses and do not affect the free circulation of goods and services within the Community, without prejudice to the other exceptions and limitations contained in this Article.

4. Where the Member States may provide for an exception or limitation to the right of reproduction pursuant to paragraphs 2 and 3, they may provide similarly for an exception or limitation to the right of distribution as referred to in Article 4 to the extent justified by the purpose of the authorised act of reproduction.

5. The exceptions and limitations provided for in paragraphs 1, 2, 3 and 4 shall only be applied in certain special cases which do not conflict with a normal exploitation of the work or other subject-matter and do not unreasonably prejudice the legitimate interests of the rightholder.

Chapter III Protection of Technological Measures and Rights-Management Information

Article 6 Obligations as to technological measures

1. Member States shall provide adequate legal protection against the circumvention of any effective technological measures, which the person concerned carries out in the knowledge, or with reasonable grounds to know, that he or she is pursuing that objective.

2. Member States shall provide adequate legal protection against the manufacture, import, distribution, sale, rental, advertisement for sale or rental, or possession for commercial purposes of devices, products or components or the provision of services which:

(a) are promoted, advertised or marketed for the purpose of circumvention of, or

(b) have only a limited commercially significant purpose or use other than to circumvent, or

(c) are primarily designed, produced, adapted or performed for the purpose of enabling or facilitating the circumvention of,

any effective technological measures.

3. For the purposes of this Directive, the expression "technological measures" means any technology, device or component that, in the normal course of its operation, is designed to prevent or restrict acts, in respect of works or other subject-matter, which are not authorised by the rightholder of any

copyright or any right related to copyright as provided for by law or the sui generis right provided for in Chapter III of Directive 96/9/EC. Technological measures shall be deemed "effective" where the use of a protected work or other subject-matter is controlled by the rightholders through application of an access control or protection process, such as encryption, scrambling or other transformation of the work or other subject-matter or a copy control mechanism, which achieves the protection objective.

4. Notwithstanding the legal protection provided for in paragraph 1, in the absence of voluntary measures taken by rightholders, including agreements between rightholders and other parties concerned, Member States shall take appropriate measures to ensure that rightholders make available to the beneficiary of an exception or limitation provided for in national law in accordance with Article 5(2)(a), (2)(c), (2)(d), (2)(e), (3)(a), (3)(b) or (3)(e) the means of benefiting from that exception or limitation, to the extent necessary to benefit from that exception or limitation and where that beneficiary has legal access to the protected work or subject-matter concerned.

A Member State may also take such measures in respect of a beneficiary of an exception or limitation provided for in accordance with Article 5(2)(b), unless reproduction for private use has already been made possible by rightholders to the extent necessary to benefit from the exception or limitation concerned and in accordance with the provisions of Article 5(2)(b) and (5), without preventing rightholders from adopting adequate measures regarding the number of reproductions in accordance with these provisions.

The technological measures applied voluntarily by rightholders, including those applied in implementation of voluntary agreements, and technological measures applied in implementation of the measures taken by Member States, shall enjoy the legal protection provided for in paragraph 1.

The provisions of the first and second subparagraphs shall not apply to works or other subject-matter made available to the public on agreed contractual terms in such a way that members of the public may access them from a place and at a time individually chosen by them.

When this Article is applied in the context of Directives 92/100/EEC and 96/9/EC, this paragraph shall apply mutatis mutandis.

Article 7   Obligations concerning rights-management information

1. Member States shall provide for adequate legal protection against any person knowingly performing without authority any of the following acts:

    (a) the removal or alteration of any electronic rights-management information;

    (b) the distribution, importation for distribution, broadcasting, communication or making available to the public of works or other subject-matter protected under this Directive or under Chapter III of Directive 96/9/EC from which electronic rights-management information has been removed or altered without authority,

if such person knows, or has reasonable grounds to know, that by so doing he is inducing, enabling, facilitating or concealing an infringement of any copyright or any rights related to copyright as provided by law, or of the sui generis right provided for in Chapter III of Directive 96/9/EC.

2. For the purposes of this Directive, the expression "rights-management information" means any information provided by rightholders which identifies the work or other subject-matter referred to in this Directive or covered by the sui generis right provided for in Chapter III of Directive 96/9/EC, the author or any other rightholder, or information about the terms and conditions of use of the work or other subject-matter, and any numbers or codes that represent such information.

The first subparagraph shall apply when any of these items of information is associated with a copy of, or appears in connection with the communication to the public of, a work or other subject-matter referred to in this Directive or covered by the sui generis right provided for in Chapter III of Directive 96/9/EC.

Chapter IV Common Provisions

Article 8   Sanctions and remedies

1. Member States shall provide appropriate sanctions and remedies in respect of infringements of the rights and obligations set out in this Directive and shall take all the measures necessary to

ensure that those sanctions and remedies are applied. The sanctions thus provided for shall be effective, proportionate and dissuasive.

2. Each Member State shall take the measures necessary to ensure that rightholders whose interests are affected by an infringing activity carried out on its territory can bring an action for damages and/or apply for an injunction and, where appropriate, for the seizure of infringing material as well as of devices, products or components referred to in Article 6(2).

3. Member States shall ensure that rightholders are in a position to apply for an injunction against intermediaries whose services are used by a third party to infringe a copyright or related right.

Article 9　Continued application of other legal provisions

This Directive shall be without prejudice to provisions concerning in particular patent rights, trade marks, design rights, utility models, topographies of semi-conductor products, type faces, conditional access, access to cable of broadcasting services, protection of national treasures, legal deposit requirements, laws on restrictive practices and unfair competition, trade secrets, security, confidentiality, data protection and privacy, access to public documents, the law of contract.

Article 10　Application over time

1. The provisions of this Directive shall apply in respect of all works and other subject-matter referred to in this Directive which are, on 22 December 2002, protected by the Member States' legislation in the field of copyright and related rights, or which meet the criteria for protection under the provisions of this Directive or the provisions referred to in Article 1(2).

2. This Directive shall apply without prejudice to any acts concluded and rights acquired before 22 December 2002.

Article 11　Technical adaptations

1. Directive 92/100/EEC is hereby amended as follows:
   (a) Article 7 shall be deleted;
   (b) Article 10(3) shall be replaced by the following: "3. The limitations shall only be applied in certain special cases which do not conflict with a normal exploitation of the subject-matter and do not unreasonably prejudice the legitimate interests of the rightholder."

2. Article 3(2) of Directive 93/98/EEC shall be replaced by the following: "2. The rights of producers of phonograms shall expire 50 years after the fixation is made. However, if the phonogram has been lawfully published within this period, the said rights shall expire 50 years from the date of the first lawful publication. If no lawful publication has taken place within the period mentioned in the first sentence, and if the phonogram has been lawfully communicated to the public within this period, the said rights shall expire 50 years from the date of the first lawful communication to the public.

However, where through the expiry of the term of protection granted pursuant to this paragraph in its version before amendment by Directive 2001/29/EC of the European Parliament and of the Council of 22 May 2001 on the harmonisation of certain aspects of copyright and related rights in the information society[11] the rights of producers of phonograms are no longer protected on 22 December 2002, this paragraph shall not have the effect of protecting those rights anew."

Article 12　Final provisions

1. Not later than 22 December 2004 and every three years thereafter, the Commission shall submit to the European Parliament, the Council and the Economic and Social Committee a report on the application of this Directive, in which, inter alia, on the basis of specific information supplied by the Member States, it shall examine in particular the application of Articles 5, 6 and 8 in the light of the development of the digital market. In the case of Article 6, it shall examine in particular whether that Article confers a sufficient level of protection and whether acts which are permitted by law are being adversely affected by the use of effective technological measures. Where necessary, in particular to ensure the functioning of the internal market pursuant to Article 14 of the Treaty, it shall submit proposals for amendments to this Directive.

---

[11]　OJ L 167, 22.6.2001, p. 10.

2. Protection of rights related to copyright under this Directive shall leave intact and shall in no way affect the protection of copyright.

3. A contact committee is hereby established. It shall be composed of representatives of the competent authorities of the Member States. It shall be chaired by a representative of the Commission and shall meet either on the initiative of the chairman or at the request of the delegation of a Member State.

4. The tasks of the committee shall be as follows:
    (a) to examine the impact of this Directive on the functioning of the internal market, and to highlight any difficulties;
    (b) to organise consultations on all questions deriving from the application of this Directive;
    (c) to facilitate the exchange of information on relevant developments in legislation and case-law, as well as relevant economic, social, cultural and technological developments;
    (d) to act as a forum for the assessment of the digital market in works and other items, including private copying and the use of technological measures.

Article 13   Implementation

1. Member States shall bring into force the laws, regulations and administrative provisions necessary to comply with this Directive before 22 December 2002. They shall forthwith inform the Commission thereof. When Member States adopt these measures, they shall contain a reference to this Directive or shall be accompanied by such reference on the occasion of their official publication. The methods of making such reference shall be laid down by Member States.

2. Member States shall communicate to the Commission the text of the provisions of domestic law which they adopt in the field governed by this Directive.

Article 14   Entry into force

This Directive shall enter into force on the day of its publication in the Official Journal of the European Communities.

Article 15   Addressees

This Directive is addressed to the Member States.

Done at Brussels, 22 May 2001.
For the European Parliament
The President
N. Fontaine
For the Council
The President
M. Winberg

Directive 2002/58/EC of the European Parliament and of the Council of 12 July 2002 concerning the processing of personal data and the protection of privacy in the electronic communications sector (Directive on privacy and electronic communications)

THE EUROPEAN PARLIAMENT AND THE COUNCIL OF THE EUROPEAN UNION,

Having regard to the Treaty establishing the European Community, and in particular Article 95 thereof,

Having regard to the proposal from the Commission[1],

---

[1] OJ C 365 E, 19.12.2000, p. 223.

Having regard to the opinion of the Economic and Social Committee[2],

Having consulted the Committee of the Regions,

Acting in accordance with the procedure laid down in Article 251 of the Treaty[3],

Whereas:

(1) Directive 95/46/EC of the European Parliament and of the Council of 24 October 1995 on the protection of individuals with regard to the processing of personal data and on the free movement of such data[4] requires Member States to ensure the rights and freedoms of natural persons with regard to the processing of personal data, and in particular their right to privacy, in order to ensure the free flow of personal data in the Community.

(2) This Directive seeks to respect the fundamental rights and observes the principles recognised in particular by the Charter of fundamental rights of the European Union. In particular, this Directive seeks to ensure full respect for the rights set out in Articles 7 and 8 of that Charter.

(3) Confidentiality of communications is guaranteed in accordance with the international instruments relating to human rights, in particular the European Convention for the Protection of Human Rights and Fundamental Freedoms, and the constitutions of the Member States.

(4) Directive 97/66/EC of the European Parliament and of the Council of 15 December 1997 concerning the processing of personal data and the protection of privacy in the telecommunications sector[5] translated the principles set out in Directive 95/46/EC into specific rules for the telecommunications sector. Directive 97/66/EC has to be adapted to developments in the markets and technologies for electronic communications services in order to provide an equal level of protection of personal data and privacy for users of publicly available electronic communications services, regardless of the technologies used. That Directive should therefore be repealed and replaced by this Directive.

(5) New advanced digital technologies are currently being introduced in public communications networks in the Community, which give rise to specific requirements concerning the protection of personal data and privacy of the user. The development of the information society is characterised by the introduction of new electronic communications services. Access to digital mobile networks has become available and affordable for a large public. These digital networks have large capacities and possibilities for processing personal data. The successful cross-border development of these services is partly dependent on the confidence of users that their privacy will not be at risk.

(6) The Internet is overturning traditional market structures by providing a common, global infrastructure for the delivery of a wide range of electronic communications services. Publicly available electronic communications services over the Internet open new possibilities for users but also new risks for their personal data and privacy.

(7) In the case of public communications networks, specific legal, regulatory and technical provisions should be made in order to protect fundamental rights and freedoms of natural persons and legitimate interests of legal persons, in particular with regard to the increasing capacity for automated storage and processing of data relating to subscribers and users.

(8) Legal, regulatory and technical provisions adopted by the Member States concerning the protection of personal data, privacy and the legitimate interest of legal persons, in the electronic communication sector, should be harmonised in order to avoid obstacles to the internal market for electronic communication in accordance with Article 14 of the Treaty. Harmonisation should be limited to requirements necessary to guarantee that the promotion and development of new electronic communications services and networks between Member States are not hindered.

(9) The Member States, providers and users concerned, together with the competent Community bodies, should cooperate in introducing and developing the relevant technologies where this is necessary to apply the guarantees provided for by this Directive and taking particular account of the

[2] OJ C 123, 25.4.2001, p. 53.
[3] Opinion of the European Parliament of 13 November 2001 (not yet published in the Official Journal), Council Common Position of 28 January 2002 (OJ C 113 E, 14.5.2002, p. 39) and Decision of the European Parliament of 30 May 2002 (not yet published in the Official Journal). Council Decision of 25 June 2002.
[4] OJ L 281, 23.11.1995, p. 31.   [5] OJ L 24, 30.1.1998, p. 1.

objectives of minimising the processing of personal data and of using anonymous or pseudonymous data where possible.

(10) In the electronic communications sector, Directive 95/46/EC applies in particular to all matters concerning protection of fundamental rights and freedoms, which are not specifically covered by the provisions of this Directive, including the obligations on the controller and the rights of individuals. Directive 95/46/EC applies to non-public communications services.

(11) Like Directive 95/46/EC, this Directive does not address issues of protection of fundamental rights and freedoms related to activities which are not governed by Community law. Therefore it does not alter the existing balance between the individual's right to privacy and the possibility for Member States to take the measures referred to in Article 15(1) of this Directive, necessary for the protection of public security, defence, State security (including the economic well-being of the State when the activities relate to State security matters) and the enforcement of criminal law. Consequently, this Directive does not affect the ability of Member States to carry out lawful interception of electronic communications, or take other measures, if necessary for any of these purposes and in accordance with the European Convention for the Protection of Human Rights and Fundamental Freedoms, as interpreted by the rulings of the European Court of Human Rights. Such measures must be appropriate, strictly proportionate to the intended purpose and necessary within a democratic society and should be subject to adequate safeguards in accordance with the European Convention for the Protection of Human Rights and Fundamental Freedoms.

(12) Subscribers to a publicly available electronic communications service may be natural or legal persons. By supplementing Directive 95/46/EC, this Directive is aimed at protecting the fundamental rights of natural persons and particularly their right to privacy, as well as the legitimate interests of legal persons. This Directive does not entail an obligation for Member States to extend the application of Directive 95/46/EC to the protection of the legitimate interests of legal persons, which is ensured within the framework of the applicable Community and national legislation.

(13) The contractual relation between a subscriber and a service provider may entail a periodic or a one-off payment for the service provided or to be provided. Prepaid cards are also considered as a contract.

(14) Location data may refer to the latitude, longitude and altitude of the user's terminal equipment, to the direction of travel, to the level of accuracy of the location information, to the identification of the network cell in which the terminal equipment is located at a certain point in time and to the time the location information was recorded.

(15) A communication may include any naming, numbering or addressing information provided by the sender of a communication or the user of a connection to carry out the communication. Traffic data may include any translation of this information by the network over which the communication is transmitted for the purpose of carrying out the transmission. Traffic data may, inter alia, consist of data referring to the routing, duration, time or volume of a communication, to the protocol used, to the location of the terminal equipment of the sender or recipient, to the network on which the communication originates or terminates, to the beginning, end or duration of a connection. They may also consist of the format in which the communication is conveyed by the network.

(16) Information that is part of a broadcasting service provided over a public communications network is intended for a potentially unlimited audience and does not constitute a communication in the sense of this Directive. However, in cases where the individual subscriber or user receiving such information can be identified, for example with video-on-demand services, the information conveyed is covered within the meaning of a communication for the purposes of this Directive.

(17) For the purposes of this Directive, consent of a user or subscriber, regardless of whether the latter is a natural or a legal person, should have the same meaning as the data subject's consent as defined and further specified in Directive 95/46/EC. Consent may be given by any appropriate method enabling a freely given specific and informed indication of the user's wishes, including by ticking a box when visiting an Internet website.

(18) Value added services may, for example, consist of advice on least expensive tariff packages, route guidance, traffic information, weather forecasts and tourist information.

(19) The application of certain requirements relating to presentation and restriction of calling and connected line identification and to automatic call forwarding to subscriber lines connected to analogue exchanges should not be made mandatory in specific cases where such application would prove to be technically impossible or would require a disproportionate economic effort. It is important for interested parties to be informed of such cases and the Member States should therefore notify them to the Commission.

(20) Service providers should take appropriate measures to safeguard the security of their services, if necessary in conjunction with the provider of the network, and inform subscribers of any special risks of a breach of the security of the network. Such risks may especially occur for electronic communications services over an open network such as the Internet or analogue mobile telephony. It is particularly important for subscribers and users of such services to be fully informed by their service provider of the existing security risks which lie outside the scope of possible remedies by the service provider. Service providers who offer publicly available electronic communications services over the Internet should inform users and subscribers of measures they can take to protect the security of their communications for instance by using specific types of software or encryption technologies. The requirement to inform subscribers of particular security risks does not discharge a service provider from the obligation to take, at its own costs, appropriate and immediate measures to remedy any new, unforeseen security risks and restore the normal security level of the service. The provision of information about security risks to the subscriber should be free of charge except for any nominal costs which the subscriber may incur while receiving or collecting the information, for instance by downloading an electronic mail message. Security is appraised in the light of Article 17 of Directive 95/46/EC.

(21) Measures should be taken to prevent unauthorised access to communications in order to protect the confidentiality of communications, including both the contents and any data related to such communications, by means of public communications networks and publicly available electronic communications services. National legislation in some Member States only prohibits intentional unauthorised access to communications.

(22) The prohibition of storage of communications and the related traffic data by persons other than the users or without their consent is not intended to prohibit any automatic, intermediate and transient storage of this information in so far as this takes place for the sole purpose of carrying out the transmission in the electronic communications network and provided that the information is not stored for any period longer than is necessary for the transmission and for traffic management purposes, and that during the period of storage the confidentiality remains guaranteed. Where this is necessary for making more efficient the onward transmission of any publicly accessible information to other recipients of the service upon their request, this Directive should not prevent such information from being further stored, provided that this information would in any case be accessible to the public without restriction and that any data referring to the individual subscribers or users requesting such information are erased.

(23) Confidentiality of communications should also be ensured in the course of lawful business practice. Where necessary and legally authorised, communications can be recorded for the purpose of providing evidence of a commercial transaction. Directive 95/46/EC applies to such processing. Parties to the communications should be informed prior to the recording about the recording, its purpose and the duration of its storage. The recorded communication should be erased as soon as possible and in any case at the latest by the end of the period during which the transaction can be lawfully challenged.

(24) Terminal equipment of users of electronic communications networks and any information stored on such equipment are part of the private sphere of the users requiring protection under the European Convention for the Protection of Human Rights and Fundamental Freedoms. So-called spyware, web bugs, hidden identifiers and other similar devices can enter the user's terminal without their knowledge in order to gain access to information, to store hidden information or to trace the activities of the user and may seriously intrude upon the privacy of these users. The use of such devices should be allowed only for legitimate purposes, with the knowledge of the users concerned.

(25) However, such devices, for instance so-called "cookies", can be a legitimate and useful tool, for example, in analysing the effectiveness of website design and advertising, and in verifying the identity of users engaged in on-line transactions. Where such devices, for instance cookies, are intended for a legitimate purpose, such as to facilitate the provision of information society services, their use should be allowed on condition that users are provided with clear and precise information in accordance with Directive 95/46/EC about the purposes of cookies or similar devices so as to ensure that users are made aware of information being placed on the terminal equipment they are using. Users should have the opportunity to refuse to have a cookie or similar device stored on their terminal equipment. This is particularly important where users other than the original user have access to the terminal equipment and thereby to any data containing privacy-sensitive information stored on such equipment. Information and the right to refuse may be offered once for the use of various devices to be installed on the user's terminal equipment during the same connection and also covering any further use that may be made of those devices during subsequent connections. The methods for giving information, offering a right to refuse or requesting consent should be made as user-friendly as possible. Access to specific website content may still be made conditional on the well-informed acceptance of a cookie or similar device, if it is used for a legitimate purpose.

(26) The data relating to subscribers processed within electronic communications networks to establish connections and to transmit information contain information on the private life of natural persons and concern the right to respect for their correspondence or concern the legitimate interests of legal persons. Such data may only be stored to the extent that is necessary for the provision of the service for the purpose of billing and for interconnection payments, and for a limited time. Any further processing of such data which the provider of the publicly available electronic communications services may want to perform, for the marketing of electronic communications services or for the provision of value added services, may only be allowed if the subscriber has agreed to this on the basis of accurate and full information given by the provider of the publicly available electronic communications services about the types of further processing it intends to perform and about the subscriber's right not to give or to withdraw his/her consent to such processing. Traffic data used for marketing communications services or for the provision of value added services should also be erased or made anonymous after the provision of the service. Service providers should always keep subscribers informed of the types of data they are processing and the purposes and duration for which this is done.

(27) The exact moment of the completion of the transmission of a communication, after which traffic data should be erased except for billing purposes, may depend on the type of electronic communications service that is provided. For instance for a voice telephony call the transmission will be completed as soon as either of the users terminates the connection. For electronic mail the transmission is completed as soon as the addressee collects the message, typically from the server of his service provider.

(28) The obligation to erase traffic data or to make such data anonymous when it is no longer needed for the purpose of the transmission of a communication does not conflict with such procedures on the Internet as the caching in the domain name system of IP addresses or the caching of IP addresses to physical address bindings or the use of log-in information to control the right of access to networks or services.

(29) The service provider may process traffic data relating to subscribers and users where necessary in individual cases in order to detect technical failure or errors in the transmission of communications. Traffic data necessary for billing purposes may also be processed by the provider in order to detect and stop fraud consisting of unpaid use of the electronic communications service.

(30) Systems for the provision of electronic communications networks and services should be designed to limit the amount of personal data necessary to a strict minimum. Any activities related to the provision of the electronic communications service that go beyond the transmission of a communication and the billing thereof should be based on aggregated, traffic data that cannot be related to subscribers or users. Where such activities cannot be based on aggregated data, they should be considered as value added services for which the consent of the subscriber is required.

(31) Whether the consent to be obtained for the processing of personal data with a view to providing a particular value added service should be that of the user or of the subscriber, will depend on the data to be processed and on the type of service to be provided and on whether it is technically, procedurally and contractually possible to distinguish the individual using an electronic communications service from the legal or natural person having subscribed to it.

(32) Where the provider of an electronic communications service or of a value added service subcontracts the processing of personal data necessary for the provision of these services to another entity, such subcontracting and subsequent data processing should be in full compliance with the requirements regarding controllers and processors of personal data as set out in Directive 95/46/EC. Where the provision of a value added service requires that traffic or location data are forwarded from an electronic communications service provider to a provider of value added services, the subscribers or users to whom the data are related should also be fully informed of this forwarding before giving their consent for the processing of the data.

(33) The introduction of itemised bills has improved the possibilities for the subscriber to check the accuracy of the fees charged by the service provider but, at the same time, it may jeopardise the privacy of the users of publicly available electronic communications services. Therefore, in order to preserve the privacy of the user, Member States should encourage the development of electronic communication service options such as alternative payment facilities which allow anonymous or strictly private access to publicly available electronic communications services, for example calling cards and facilities for payment by credit card. To the same end, Member States may ask the operators to offer their subscribers a different type of detailed bill in which a certain number of digits of the called number have been deleted.

(34) It is necessary, as regards calling line identification, to protect the right of the calling party to withhold the presentation of the identification of the line from which the call is being made and the right of the called party to reject calls from unidentified lines. There is justification for overriding the elimination of calling line identification presentation in specific cases. Certain subscribers, in particular help lines and similar organisations, have an interest in guaranteeing the anonymity of their callers. It is necessary, as regards connected line identification, to protect the right and the legitimate interest of the called party to withhold the presentation of the identification of the line to which the calling party is actually connected, in particular in the case of forwarded calls. The providers of publicly available electronic communications services should inform their subscribers of the existence of calling and connected line identification in the network and of all services which are offered on the basis of calling and connected line identification as well as the privacy options which are available. This will allow the subscribers to make an informed choice about the privacy facilities they may want to use. The privacy options which are offered on a per-line basis do not necessarily have to be available as an automatic network service but may be obtainable through a simple request to the provider of the publicly available electronic communications service.

(35) In digital mobile networks, location data giving the geographic position of the terminal equipment of the mobile user are processed to enable the transmission of communications. Such data are traffic data covered by Article 6 of this Directive. However, in addition, digital mobile networks may have the capacity to process location data which are more precise than is necessary for the transmission of communications and which are used for the provision of value added services such as services providing individualised traffic information and guidance to drivers. The processing of such data for value added services should only be allowed where subscribers have given their consent. Even in cases where subscribers have given their consent, they should have a simple means to temporarily deny the processing of location data, free of charge.

(36) Member States may restrict the users' and subscribers' rights to privacy with regard to calling line identification where this is necessary to trace nuisance calls and with regard to calling line identification and location data where this is necessary to allow emergency services to carry out their tasks as effectively as possible. For these purposes, Member States may adopt specific provisions to entitle providers of electronic communications services to provide access to calling line identification and location data without the prior consent of the users or subscribers concerned.

(37) Safeguards should be provided for subscribers against the nuisance which may be caused by automatic call forwarding by others. Moreover, in such cases, it must be possible for subscribers to stop the forwarded calls being passed on to their terminals by simple request to the provider of the publicly available electronic communications service.

(38) Directories of subscribers to electronic communications services are widely distributed and public. The right to privacy of natural persons and the legitimate interest of legal persons require that subscribers are able to determine whether their personal data are published in a directory and if so, which. Providers of public directories should inform the subscribers to be included in such directories of the purposes of the directory and of any particular usage which may be made of electronic versions of public directories especially through search functions embedded in the software, such as reverse search functions enabling users of the directory to discover the name and address of the subscriber on the basis of a telephone number only.

(39) The obligation to inform subscribers of the purpose(s) of public directories in which their personal data are to be included should be imposed on the party collecting the data for such inclusion. Where the data may be transmitted to one or more third parties, the subscriber should be informed of this possibility and of the recipient or the categories of possible recipients. Any transmission should be subject to the condition that the data may not be used for other purposes than those for which they were collected. If the party collecting the data from the subscriber or any third party to whom the data have been transmitted wishes to use the data for an additional purpose, the renewed consent of the subscriber is to be obtained either by the initial party collecting the data or by the third party to whom the data have been transmitted.

(40) Safeguards should be provided for subscribers against intrusion of their privacy by unsolicited communications for direct marketing purposes in particular by means of automated calling machines, telefaxes, and e-mails, including SMS messages. These forms of unsolicited commercial communications may on the one hand be relatively easy and cheap to send and on the other may impose a burden and/or cost on the recipient. Moreover, in some cases their volume may also cause difficulties for electronic communications networks and terminal equipment. For such forms of unsolicited communications for direct marketing, it is justified to require that prior explicit consent of the recipients is obtained before such communications are addressed to them. The single market requires a harmonised approach to ensure simple, Community-wide rules for businesses and users.

(41) Within the context of an existing customer relationship, it is reasonable to allow the use of electronic contact details for the offering of similar products or services, but only by the same company that has obtained the electronic contact details in accordance with Directive 95/46/EC. When electronic contact details are obtained, the customer should be informed about their further use for direct marketing in a clear and distinct manner, and be given the opportunity to refuse such usage. This opportunity should continue to be offered with each subsequent direct marketing message, free of charge, except for any costs for the transmission of this refusal.

(42) Other forms of direct marketing that are more costly for the sender and impose no financial costs on subscribers and users, such as person-to-person voice telephony calls, may justify the maintenance of a system giving subscribers or users the possibility to indicate that they do not want to receive such calls. Nevertheless, in order not to decrease existing levels of privacy protection, Member States should be entitled to uphold national systems, only allowing such calls to subscribers and users who have given their prior consent.

(43) To facilitate effective enforcement of Community rules on unsolicited messages for direct marketing, it is necessary to prohibit the use of false identities or false return addresses or numbers while sending unsolicited messages for direct marketing purposes.

(44) Certain electronic mail systems allow subscribers to view the sender and subject line of an electronic mail, and also to delete the message, without having to download the rest of the electronic mail's content or any attachments, thereby reducing costs which could arise from downloading unsolicited electronic mails or attachments. These arrangements may continue to be useful in certain cases as an additional tool to the general obligations established in this Directive.

(45) This Directive is without prejudice to the arrangements which Member States make to protect the legitimate interests of legal persons with regard to unsolicited communications for direct marketing purposes. Where Member States establish an opt-out register for such communications to legal persons, mostly business users, the provisions of Article 7 of Directive 2000/31/EC of the European Parliament and of the Council of 8 June 2000 on certain legal aspects of information society services, in particular electronic commerce, in the internal market (Directive on electronic commerce)[6] are fully applicable.

(46) The functionalities for the provision of electronic communications services may be integrated in the network or in any part of the terminal equipment of the user, including the software. The protection of the personal data and the privacy of the user of publicly available electronic communications services should be independent of the configuration of the various components necessary to provide the service and of the distribution of the necessary functionalities between these components. Directive 95/46/EC covers any form of processing of personal data regardless of the technology used. The existence of specific rules for electronic communications services alongside general rules for other components necessary for the provision of such services may not facilitate the protection of personal data and privacy in a technologically neutral way. It may therefore be necessary to adopt measures requiring manufacturers of certain types of equipment used for electronic communications services to construct their product in such a way as to incorporate safeguards to ensure that the personal data and privacy of the user and subscriber are protected. The adoption of such measures in accordance with Directive 1999/5/EC of the European Parliament and of the Council of 9 March 1999 on radio equipment and telecommunications terminal equipment and the mutual recognition of their conformity[7] will ensure that the introduction of technical features of electronic communication equipment including software for data protection purposes is harmonised in order to be compatible with the implementation of the internal market.

(47) Where the rights of the users and subscribers are not respected, national legislation should provide for judicial remedies. Penalties should be imposed on any person, whether governed by private or public law, who fails to comply with the national measures taken under this Directive.

(48) It is useful, in the field of application of this Directive, to draw on the experience of the Working Party on the Protection of Individuals with regard to the Processing of Personal Data composed of representatives of the supervisory authorities of the Member States, set up by Article 29 of Directive 95/46/EC.

(49) To facilitate compliance with the provisions of this Directive, certain specific arrangements are needed for processing of data already under way on the date that national implementing legislation pursuant to this Directive enters into force,

HAVE ADOPTED THIS DIRECTIVE:

Article 1 Scope and aim

1. This Directive harmonises the provisions of the Member States required to ensure an equivalent level of protection of fundamental rights and freedoms, and in particular the right to privacy, with respect to the processing of personal data in the electronic communication sector and to ensure the free movement of such data and of electronic communication equipment and services in the Community.

2. The provisions of this Directive particularise and complement Directive 95/46/EC for the purposes mentioned in paragraph 1. Moreover, they provide for protection of the legitimate interests of subscribers who are legal persons.

3. This Directive shall not apply to activities which fall outside the scope of the Treaty establishing the European Community, such as those covered by Titles V and VI of the Treaty on European Union, and in any case to activities concerning public security, defence, State security (including the economic well-being of the State when the activities relate to State security matters) and the activities of the State in areas of criminal law.

[6] OJ L 178, 17.7.2000, p. 1.   [7] OJ L 91, 7.4.1999, p. 10.

Article 2 Definitions

Save as otherwise provided, the definitions in Directive 95/46/EC and in Directive 2002/21/ EC of the European Parliament and of the Council of 7 March 2002 on a common regulatory framework for electronic communications networks and services (Framework Directive)[8] shall apply. The following definitions shall also apply:

    (a) "user" means any natural person using a publicly available electronic communications service, for private or business purposes, without necessarily having subscribed to this service;

    (b) "traffic data" means any data processed for the purpose of the conveyance of a communication on an electronic communications network or for the billing thereof;

    (c) "location data" means any data processed in an electronic communications network, indicating the geographic position of the terminal equipment of a user of a publicly available electronic communications service;

    (d) "communication" means any information exchanged or conveyed between a finite number of parties by means of a publicly available electronic communications service. This does not include any information conveyed as part of a broadcasting service to the public over an electronic communications network except to the extent that the information can be related to the identifiable subscriber or user receiving the information;

    (e) "call" means a connection established by means of a publicly available telephone service allowing two-way communication in real time;

    (f) "consent" by a user or subscriber corresponds to the data subject's consent in Directive 95/46/EC;

    (g) "value added service" means any service which requires the processing of traffic data or location data other than traffic data beyond what is necessary for the transmission of a communication or the billing thereof;

    (h) "electronic mail" means any text, voice, sound or image message sent over a public communications network which can be stored in the network or in the recipient's terminal equipment until it is collected by the recipient.

Article 3   Services concerned

1. This Directive shall apply to the processing of personal data in connection with the provision of publicly available electronic communications services in public communications networks in the Community.

2. Articles 8, 10 and 11 shall apply to subscriber lines connected to digital exchanges and, where technically possible and if it does not require a disproportionate economic effort, to subscriber lines connected to analogue exchanges.

3. Cases where it would be technically impossible or require a disproportionate economic effort to fulfil the requirements of Articles 8, 10 and 11 shall be notified to the Commission by the Member States.

Article 4   Security

1. The provider of a publicly available electronic communications service must take appropriate technical and organisational measures to safeguard security of its services, if necessary in conjunction with the provider of the public communications network with respect to network security. Having regard to the state of the art and the cost of their implementation, these measures shall ensure a level of security appropriate to the risk presented.

2. In case of a particular risk of a breach of the security of the network, the provider of a publicly available electronic communications service must inform the subscribers concerning such risk and, where the risk lies outside the scope of the measures to be taken by the service provider, of any possible remedies, including an indication of the likely costs involved.

---

[8] OJ L 108, 24.4.2002, p. 33.

Article 5   Confidentiality of the communications

1. Member States shall ensure the confidentiality of communications and the related traffic data by means of a public communications network and publicly available electronic communications services, through national legislation. In particular, they shall prohibit listening, tapping, storage or other kinds of interception or surveillance of communications and the related traffic data by persons other than users, without the consent of the users concerned, except when legally authorised to do so in accordance with Article 15(1). This paragraph shall not prevent technical storage which is necessary for the conveyance of a communication without prejudice to the principle of confidentiality.

2. Paragraph 1 shall not affect any legally authorised recording of communications and the related traffic data when carried out in the course of lawful business practice for the purpose of providing evidence of a commercial transaction or of any other business communication.

3. Member States shall ensure that the use of electronic communications networks to store information or to gain access to information stored in the terminal equipment of a subscriber or user is only allowed on condition that the subscriber or user concerned is provided with clear and comprehensive information in accordance with Directive 95/46/EC, inter alia about the purposes of the processing, and is offered the right to refuse such processing by the data controller. This shall not prevent any technical storage or access for the sole purpose of carrying out or facilitating the transmission of a communication over an electronic communications network, or as strictly necessary in order to provide an information society service explicitly requested by the subscriber or user.

Article 6   Traffic data

1. Traffic data relating to subscribers and users processed and stored by the provider of a public communications network or publicly available electronic communications service must be erased or made anonymous when it is no longer needed for the purpose of the transmission of a communication without prejudice to paragraphs 2, 3 and 5 of this Article and Article 15(1).

2. Traffic data necessary for the purposes of subscriber billing and interconnection payments may be processed. Such processing is permissible only up to the end of the period during which the bill may lawfully be challenged or payment pursued.

3. For the purpose of marketing electronic communications services or for the provision of value added services, the provider of a publicly available electronic communications service may process the data referred to in paragraph 1 to the extent and for the duration necessary for such services or marketing, if the subscriber or user to whom the data relate has given his/her consent. Users or subscribers shall be given the possibility to withdraw their consent for the processing of traffic data at any time.

4. The service provider must inform the subscriber or user of the types of traffic data which are processed and of the duration of such processing for the purposes mentioned in paragraph 2 and, prior to obtaining consent, for the purposes mentioned in paragraph 3.

5. Processing of traffic data, in accordance with paragraphs 1, 2, 3 and 4, must be restricted to persons acting under the authority of providers of the public communications networks and publicly available electronic communications services handling billing or traffic management, customer enquiries, fraud detection, marketing electronic communications services or providing a value added service, and must be restricted to what is necessary for the purposes of such activities.

6. Paragraphs 1, 2, 3 and 5 shall apply without prejudice to the possibility for competent bodies to be informed of traffic data in conformity with applicable legislation with a view to settling disputes, in particular interconnection or billing disputes.

Article 7   Itemised billing

1. Subscribers shall have the right to receive non-itemised bills.

2. Member States shall apply national provisions in order to reconcile the rights of subscribers receiving itemised bills with the right to privacy of calling users and called subscribers, for example by ensuring that sufficient alternative privacy enhancing methods of communications or payments are available to such users and subscribers.

Article 8   Presentation and restriction of calling and connected line identification

1. Where presentation of calling line identification is offered, the service provider must offer the calling user the possibility, using a simple means and free of charge, of preventing the presentation of the calling line identification on a per-call basis. The calling subscriber must have this possibility on a per-line basis.

2. Where presentation of calling line identification is offered, the service provider must offer the called subscriber the possibility, using a simple means and free of charge for reasonable use of this function, of preventing the presentation of the calling line identification of incoming calls.

3. Where presentation of calling line identification is offered and where the calling line identification is presented prior to the call being established, the service provider must offer the called subscriber the possibility, using a simple means, of rejecting incoming calls where the presentation of the calling line identification has been prevented by the calling user or subscriber.

4. Where presentation of connected line identification is offered, the service provider must offer the called subscriber the possibility, using a simple means and free of charge, of preventing the presentation of the connected line identification to the calling user.

5. Paragraph 1 shall also apply with regard to calls to third countries originating in the Community. Paragraphs 2, 3 and 4 shall also apply to incoming calls originating in third countries.

6. Member States shall ensure that where presentation of calling and/or connected line identification is offered, the providers of publicly available electronic communications services inform the public thereof and of the possibilities set out in paragraphs 1, 2, 3 and 4.

Article 9   Location data other than traffic data

1. Where location data other than traffic data, relating to users or subscribers of public communications networks or publicly available electronic communications services, can be processed, such data may only be processed when they are made anonymous, or with the consent of the users or subscribers to the extent and for the duration necessary for the provision of a value added service. The service provider must inform the users or subscribers, prior to obtaining their consent, of the type of location data other than traffic data which will be processed, of the purposes and duration of the processing and whether the data will be transmitted to a third party for the purpose of providing the value added service. Users or subscribers shall be given the possibility to withdraw their consent for the processing of location data other than traffic data at any time.

2. Where consent of the users or subscribers has been obtained for the processing of location data other than traffic data, the user or subscriber must continue to have the possibility, using a simple means and free of charge, of temporarily refusing the processing of such data for each connection to the network or for each transmission of a communication.

3. Processing of location data other than traffic data in accordance with paragraphs 1 and 2 must be restricted to persons acting under the authority of the provider of the public communications network or publicly available communications service or of the third party providing the value added service, and must be restricted to what is necessary for the purposes of providing the value added service.

Article 10   Exceptions

Member States shall ensure that there are transparent procedures governing the way in which a provider of a public communications network and/or a publicly available electronic communications service may override:

(a) the elimination of the presentation of calling line identification, on a temporary basis, upon application of a subscriber requesting the tracing of malicious or nuisance calls. In this case, in accordance with national law, the data containing the identification of the calling subscriber will be stored and be made available by the provider of a public communications network and/or publicly available electronic communications service;

(b) the elimination of the presentation of calling line identification and the temporary denial or absence of consent of a subscriber or user for the processing of location data, on a per-line basis for organisations dealing with emergency calls and recognised as such by a Member State, including law enforcement agencies, ambulance services and fire brigades, for the purpose of responding to such calls.

Article 11   Automatic call forwarding

Member States shall ensure that any subscriber has the possibility, using a simple means and free of charge, of stopping automatic call forwarding by a third party to the subscriber's terminal.

Article 12   Directories of subscribers

1. Member States shall ensure that subscribers are informed, free of charge and before they are included in the directory, about the purpose(s) of a printed or electronic directory of subscribers available to the public or obtainable through directory enquiry services, in which their personal data can be included and of any further usage possibilities based on search functions embedded in electronic versions of the directory.

2. Member States shall ensure that subscribers are given the opportunity to determine whether their personal data are included in a public directory, and if so, which, to the extent that such data are relevant for the purpose of the directory as determined by the provider of the directory, and to verify, correct or withdraw such data. Not being included in a public subscriber directory, verifying, correcting or withdrawing personal data from it shall be free of charge.

3. Member States may require that for any purpose of a public directory other than the search of contact details of persons on the basis of their name and, where necessary, a minimum of other identifiers, additional consent be asked of the subscribers.

4. Paragraphs 1 and 2 shall apply to subscribers who are natural persons. Member States shall also ensure, in the framework of Community law and applicable national legislation, that the legitimate interests of subscribers other than natural persons with regard to their entry in public directories are sufficiently protected.

Article 13   Unsolicited communications

1. The use of automated calling systems without human intervention (automatic calling machines), facsimile machines (fax) or electronic mail for the purposes of direct marketing may only be allowed in respect of subscribers who have given their prior consent.

2. Notwithstanding paragraph 1, where a natural or legal person obtains from its customers their electronic contact details for electronic mail, in the context of the sale of a product or a service, in accordance with Directive 95/46/EC, the same natural or legal person may use these electronic contact details for direct marketing of its own similar products or services provided that customers clearly and distinctly are given the opportunity to object, free of charge and in an easy manner, to such use of electronic contact details when they are collected and on the occasion of each message in case the customer has not initially refused such use.

3. Member States shall take appropriate measures to ensure that, free of charge, unsolicited communications for purposes of direct marketing, in cases other than those referred to in paragraphs 1 and 2, are not allowed either without the consent of the subscribers concerned or in respect of subscribers who do not wish to receive these communications, the choice between these options to be determined by national legislation.

4. In any event, the practice of sending electronic mail for purposes of direct marketing disguising or concealing the identity of the sender on whose behalf the communication is made, or without a valid address to which the recipient may send a request that such communications cease, shall be prohibited.

5. Paragraphs 1 and 3 shall apply to subscribers who are natural persons. Member States shall also ensure, in the framework of Community law and applicable national legislation, that the legitimate interests of subscribers other than natural persons with regard to unsolicited communications are sufficiently protected.

Article 14   Technical features and standardisation

1. In implementing the provisions of this Directive, Member States shall ensure, subject to paragraphs 2 and 3, that no mandatory requirements for specific technical features are imposed on

terminal or other electronic communication equipment which could impede the placing of equipment on the market and the free circulation of such equipment in and between Member States.

2. Where provisions of this Directive can be implemented only by requiring specific technical features in electronic communications networks, Member States shall inform the Commission in accordance with the procedure provided for by Directive 98/34/EC of the European Parliament and of the Council of 22 June 1998 laying down a procedure for the provision of information in the field of technical standards and regulations and of rules on information society services[9].

3. Where required, measures may be adopted to ensure that terminal equipment is constructed in a way that is compatible with the right of users to protect and control the use of their personal data, in accordance with Directive 1999/5/EC and Council Decision 87/95/EEC of 22 December 1986 on standardisation in the field of information technology and communications[10].

Article 15   Application of certain provisions of Directive 95/46/EC

1. Member States may adopt legislative measures to restrict the scope of the rights and obligations provided for in Article 5, Article 6, Article 8(1), (2), (3) and (4), and Article 9 of this Directive when such restriction constitutes a necessary, appropriate and proportionate measure within a democratic society to safeguard national security (i.e. State security), defence, public security, and the prevention, investigation, detection and prosecution of criminal offences or of unauthorised use of the electronic communication system, as referred to in Article 13(1) of Directive 95/46/EC. To this end, Member States may, inter alia, adopt legislative measures providing for the retention of data for a limited period justified on the grounds laid down in this paragraph. All the measures referred to in this paragraph shall be in accordance with the general principles of Community law, including those referred to in Article 6(1) and (2) of the Treaty on European Union.

2. The provisions of Chapter III on judicial remedies, liability and sanctions of Directive 95/46/EC shall apply with regard to national provisions adopted pursuant to this Directive and with regard to the individual rights derived from this Directive.

3. The Working Party on the Protection of Individuals with regard to the Processing of Personal Data instituted by Article 29 of Directive 95/46/EC shall also carry out the tasks laid down in Article 30 of that Directive with regard to matters covered by this Directive, namely the protection of fundamental rights and freedoms and of legitimate interests in the electronic communications sector.

Article 16   Transitional arrangements

1. Article 12 shall not apply to editions of directories already produced or placed on the market in printed or off-line electronic form before the national provisions adopted pursuant to this Directive enter into force.

2. Where the personal data of subscribers to fixed or mobile public voice telephony services have been included in a public subscriber directory in conformity with the provisions of Directive 95/46/EC and of Article 11 of Directive 97/66/EC before the national provisions adopted in pursuance of this Directive enter into force, the personal data of such subscribers may remain included in this public directory in its printed or electronic versions, including versions with reverse search functions, unless subscribers indicate otherwise, after having received complete information about purposes and options in accordance with Article 12 of this Directive.

Article 17   Transposition

1. Before 31 October 2003 Member States shall bring into force the provisions necessary to comply with this Directive. They shall forthwith inform the Commission thereof.

When Member States adopt those provisions, they shall contain a reference to this Directive or be accompanied by such a reference on the occasion of their official publication. The methods of making such reference shall be laid down by the Member States.

---

[9] OJ L 204, 21.7.1998, p. 37. Directive as amended by Directive 98/48/EC (OJ L 217, 5.8.1998, p. 18).
[10] OJ L 36, 7.2.1987, p. 31. Decision as last amended by the 1994 Act of Accession.

2. Member States shall communicate to the Commission the text of the provisions of national law which they adopt in the field governed by this Directive and of any subsequent amendments to those provisions.

Article 18   Review

The Commission shall submit to the European Parliament and the Council, not later than three years after the date referred to in Article 17(1), a report on the application of this Directive and its impact on economic operators and consumers, in particular as regards the provisions on unsolicited communications, taking into account the international environment. For this purpose, the Commission may request information from the Member States, which shall be supplied without undue delay. Where appropriate, the Commission shall submit proposals to amend this Directive, taking account of the results of that report, any changes in the sector and any other proposal it may deem necessary in order to improve the effectiveness of this Directive.

Article 19   Repeal

Directive 97/66/EC is hereby repealed with effect from the date referred to in Article 17(1). References made to the repealed Directive shall be construed as being made to this Directive.

Article 20   Entry into force

This Directive shall enter into force on the day of its publication in the Official Journal of the European Communities.

Article 21   Addressees

This Directive is addressed to the Member States.

Done at Brussels, 12 July 2002.
For the European Parliament
The President
P. Cox
For the Council
The President
T. Pedersen

Part IV

Other documents

Convention on Cybercrime[1]

BUDAPEST, 23.XI.2001

Preamble

The member States of the Council of Europe and the other States signatory hereto,

Considering that the aim of the Council of Europe is to achieve a greater unity between its members;

Recognising the value of fostering co-operation with the other States parties to this Convention;

Convinced of the need to pursue, as a matter of priority, a common criminal policy aimed at the protection of society against cybercrime, *inter alia,* by adopting appropriate legislation and fostering international co-operation;

Conscious of the profound changes brought about by the digitalisation, convergence and continuing globalisation of computer networks;

Concerned by the risk that computer networks and electronic information may also be used for committing criminal offences and that evidence relating to such offences may be stored and transferred by these networks;

Recognising the need for co-operation between States and private industry in combating cybercrime and the need to protect legitimate interests in the use and development of information technologies;

Believing that an effective fight against cybercrime requires increased, rapid and well-functioning international co-operation in criminal matters;

Convinced that the present Convention is necessary to deter action directed against the confidentiality, integrity and availability of computer systems, networks and computer data as well as the misuse of such systems, networks and data by providing for the criminalisation of such conduct, as described in this Convention, and the adoption of powers sufficient for effectively combating such criminal offences, by facilitating their detection, investigation and prosecution at both the domestic and international levels and by providing arrangements for fast and reliable international co-operation;

Mindful of the need to ensure a proper balance between the interests of law enforcement and respect for fundamental human rights as enshrined in the 1950 Council of Europe Convention for the Protection of Human Rights and Fundamental Freedoms, the 1966 United Nations International Covenant on Civil and Political Rights and other applicable international human rights treaties, which reaffirm the right of everyone to hold opinions without interference, as well as the right to freedom of expression, including the freedom to seek, receive, and impart information and ideas of all kinds, regardless of frontiers, and the rights concerning the respect for privacy;

---

[1] Entered into force on 1 July 2004.

Mindful also of the right to the protection of personal data, as conferred, for example, by the 1981 Council of Europe Convention for the Protection of Individuals with regard to Automatic Processing of Personal Data;

Considering the 1989 United Nations Convention on the Rights of the Child and the 1999 International Labour Organization Worst Forms of Child Labour Convention;

Taking into account the existing Council of Europe conventions on co-operation in the penal field, as well as similar treaties which exist between Council of Europe member States and other States, and stressing that the present Convention is intended to supplement those conventions in order to make criminal investigations and proceedings concerning criminal offences related to computer systems and data more effective and to enable the collection of evidence in electronic form of a criminal offence;

Welcoming recent developments which further advance international understanding and cooperation in combating cybercrime, including action taken by the United Nations, the OECD, the European Union and the G8;

Recalling Committee of Ministers Recommendations No. R (85) 10 concerning the practical application of the European Convention on Mutual Assistance in Criminal Matters in respect of letters rogatory for the interception of telecommunications, No. R (88) 2 on piracy in the field of copyright and neighbouring rights, No. R (87) 15 regulating the use of personal data in the police sector, No. R (95) 4 on the protection of personal data in the area of telecommunication services, with particular reference to telephone services, as well as No. R (89) 9 on computer-related crime providing guidelines for national legislatures concerning the definition of certain computer crimes and No. R (95) 13 concerning problems of criminal procedural law connected with information technology;

Having regard to Resolution No. 1 adopted by the European Ministers of Justice at their 21st Conference (Prague, 10 and 11 June 1997), which recommended that the Committee of Ministers support the work on cybercrime carried out by the European Committee on Crime Problems (CDPC) in order to bring domestic criminal law provisions closer to each other and enable the use of effective means of investigation into such offences, as well as to Resolution No. 3 adopted at the 23rd Conference of the European Ministers of Justice (London, 8 and 9 June 2000), which encouraged the negotiating parties to pursue their efforts with a view to finding appropriate solutions to enable the largest possible number of States to become parties to the Convention and acknowledged the need for a swift and efficient system of international co-operation, which duly takes into account the specific requirements of the fight against cybercrime;

Having also regard to the Action Plan adopted by the Heads of State and Government of the Council of Europe on the occasion of their Second Summit (Strasbourg, 10 and 11 October 1997), to seek common responses to the development of the new information technologies based on the standards and values of the Council of Europe;

Have agreed as follows:

Chapter I Use of Terms

Article 1 Definitions

For the purposes of this Convention:

(a) "computer system" means any device or a group of interconnected or related devices, one or more of which, pursuant to a program, performs automatic processing of data;

(b) "computer data" means any representation of facts, information or concepts in a form suitable for processing in a computer system, including a program suitable to cause a computer system to perform a function;

(c) "service provider" means:

    (i) any public or private entity that provides to users of its service the ability to communicate by means of a computer system, and

    (ii) any other entity that processes or stores computer data on behalf of such communication service or users of such service;

(d) "traffic data" means any computer data relating to a communication by means of a computer system, generated by a computer system that formed a part in the chain of communication, indicating the communication's origin, destination, route, time, date, size, duration, or type of underlying service.

Chapter II Measures to be Taken at the National Level

Section 1 Substantive Criminal Law

Title 1 *Offences against the confidentiality, integrity and availability of computer data and systems*

Article 2 Illegal access

Each Party shall adopt such legislative and other measures as may be necessary to establish as criminal offences under its domestic law, when committed intentionally, the access to the whole or any part of a computer system without right. A Party may require that the offence be committed by infringing security measures, with the intent of obtaining computer data or other dishonest intent, or in relation to a computer system that is connected to another computer system.

Article 3 Illegal interception

Each Party shall adopt such legislative and other measures as may be necessary to establish as criminal offences under its domestic law, when committed intentionally, the interception without right, made by technical means, of non-public transmissions of computer data to, from or within a computer system, including electromagnetic emissions from a computer system carrying such computer data. A Party may require that the offence be committed with dishonest intent, or in relation to a computer system that is connected to another computer system.

Article 4 Data interference

1. Each Party shall adopt such legislative and other measures as may be necessary to establish as criminal offences under its domestic law, when committed intentionally, the damaging, deletion, deterioration, alteration or suppression of computer data without right.

2. A Party may reserve the right to require that the conduct described in paragraph 1 result in serious harm.

Article 5 System interference

Each Party shall adopt such legislative and other measures as may be necessary to establish as criminal offences under its domestic law, when committed intentionally, the serious hindering without right of the functioning of a computer system by inputting, transmitting, damaging, deleting, deteriorating, altering or suppressing computer data.

Article 6 Misuse of devices

1. Each Party shall adopt such legislative and other measures as may be necessary to establish as criminal offences under its domestic law, when committed intentionally and without right:

    (a) the production, sale, procurement for use, import, distribution or otherwise making available of:

        (i) a device, including a computer program, designed or adapted primarily for the purpose of committing any of the offences established in accordance with the above Articles 2 through 5;

        (ii) a computer password, access code, or similar data by which the whole or any part of a computer system is capable of being accessed, with intent that it be used for the purpose of committing any of the offences established in Articles 2 through 5; and

    (b) the possession of an item referred to in paragraphs a.i or ii above, with intent that it be used for the purpose of committing any of the offences established in Articles 2 through 5. A Party may require by law that a number of such items be possessed before criminal liability attaches.

2. This article shall not be interpreted as imposing criminal liability where the production, sale, procurement for use, import, distribution or otherwise making available or possession referred to in paragraph 1 of this article is not for the purpose of committing an offence established in accordance with Articles 2 through 5 of this Convention, such as for the authorised testing or protection of a computer system.

3. Each Party may reserve the right not to apply paragraph 1 of this article, provided that the reservation does not concern the sale, distribution or otherwise making available of the items referred to in paragraph 1.a.ii of this article.

Title 2 Computer-related offences

Article 7 Computer-related forgery

Each Party shall adopt such legislative and other measures as may be necessary to establish as criminal offences under its domestic law, when committed intentionally and without right, the input, alteration, deletion, or suppression of computer data, resulting in inauthentic data with the intent that it be considered or acted upon for legal purposes as if it were authentic, regardless whether or not the data is directly readable and intelligible. A Party may require an intent to defraud, or similar dishonest intent, before criminal liability attaches.

Article 8 Computer-related fraud

Each Party shall adopt such legislative and other measures as may be necessary to establish as criminal offences under its domestic law, when committed intentionally and without right, the causing of a loss of property to another person by:

(a) any input, alteration, deletion or suppression of computer data;

(b) any interference with the functioning of a computer system,

with fraudulent or dishonest intent of procuring, without right, an economic benefit for oneself or for another person.

Title 3 Content-related offences

Article 9 Offences related to child pornography

1. Each Party shall adopt such legislative and other measures as may be necessary to establish as criminal offences under its domestic law, when committed intentionally and without right, the following conduct:

(a) producing child pornography for the purpose of its distribution through a computer system;

(b) offering or making available child pornography through a computer system;

(c) distributing or transmitting child pornography through a computer system;

(d) procuring child pornography through a computer system for oneself or for another person;

(e) possessing child pornography in a computer system or on a computer-data storage medium.

2. For the purpose of paragraph 1 above, the term "child pornography" shall include pornographic material that visually depicts:

(a) a minor engaged in sexually explicit conduct;

(b) a person appearing to be a minor engaged in sexually explicit conduct;

(c) realistic images representing a minor engaged in sexually explicit conduct.

3. For the purpose of paragraph 2 above, the term "minor" shall include all persons under 18 years of age. A Party may, however, require a lower age-limit, which shall be not less than 16 years.

4. Each Party may reserve the right not to apply, in whole or in part, paragraphs 1, sub-paragraphs d. and e, and 2, sub-paragraphs b. and c.

Title 4 Offences related to infringements of copyright and related rights

Article 10   Offences related to infringements of copyright and related rights

1. Each Party shall adopt such legislative and other measures as may be necessary to establish as criminal offences under its domestic law the infringement of copyright, as defined under the law of that Party, pursuant to the obligations it has undertaken under the Paris Act of 24 July 1971 revising the Berne Convention for the Protection of Literary and Artistic Works, the Agreement on Trade-Related Aspects of Intellectual Property Rights and the WIPO Copyright Treaty, with the exception of any moral rights conferred by such conventions, where such acts are committed wilfully, on a commercial scale and by means of a computer system.

2. Each Party shall adopt such legislative and other measures as may be necessary to establish as criminal offences under its domestic law the infringement of related rights, as defined under the law of that Party, pursuant to the obligations it has undertaken under the International Convention for the Protection of Performers, Producers of Phonograms and Broadcasting Organisations (Rome Convention), the Agreement on Trade-Related Aspects of Intellectual Property Rights and the WIPO Performances and Phonograms Treaty, with the exception of any moral rights conferred by such conventions, where such acts are committed wilfully, on a commercial scale and by means of a computer system.

3. A Party may reserve the right not to impose criminal liability under paragraphs 1 and 2 of this article in limited circumstances, provided that other effective remedies are available and that such reservation does not derogate from the Party's international obligations set forth in the international instruments referred to in paragraphs 1 and 2 of this article.

Title 5 Ancillary liability and sanctions

Article 11   Attempt and aiding or abetting

1. Each Party shall adopt such legislative and other measures as may be necessary to establish as criminal offences under its domestic law, when committed intentionally, aiding or abetting the commission of any of the offences established in accordance with Articles 2 through 10 of the present Convention with intent that such offence be committed.

2. Each Party shall adopt such legislative and other measures as may be necessary to establish as criminal offences under its domestic law, when committed intentionally, an attempt to commit any of the offences established in accordance with Articles 3 through 5, 7, 8, and 9.1.a and c. of this Convention.

3. Each Party may reserve the right not to apply, in whole or in part, paragraph 2 of this article.

Article 12   Corporate liability

1. Each Party shall adopt such legislative and other measures as may be necessary to ensure that legal persons can be held liable for a criminal offence established in accordance with this Convention, committed for their benefit by any natural person, acting either individually or as part of an organ of the legal person, who has a leading position within it, based on:

> (a) a power of representation of the legal person;
> (b) an authority to take decisions on behalf of the legal person;
> (c) an authority to exercise control within the legal person.

2. In addition to the cases already provided for in paragraph 1 of this article, each Party shall take the measures necessary to ensure that a legal person can be held liable where the lack of supervision or control by a natural person referred to in paragraph 1 has made possible the commission of a criminal offence established in accordance with this Convention for the benefit of that legal person by a natural person acting under its authority.

3. Subject to the legal principles of the Party, the liability of a legal person may be criminal, civil or administrative.

4. Such liability shall be without prejudice to the criminal liability of the natural persons who have committed the offence.

Article 13   Sanctions and measures

1. Each Party shall adopt such legislative and other measures as may be necessary to ensure that the criminal offences established in accordance with Articles 2 through 11 are punishable by effective, proportionate and dissuasive sanctions, which include deprivation of liberty.

2. Each Party shall ensure that legal persons held liable in accordance with Article 12 shall be subject to effective, proportionate and dissuasive criminal or non-criminal sanctions or measures, including monetary sanctions.

Section 2 Procedural Law

Title 1 Common provisions

Article 14   Scope of procedural provisions

1. Each Party shall adopt such legislative and other measures as may be necessary to establish the powers and procedures provided for in this section for the purpose of specific criminal investigations or proceedings.

2. Except as specifically provided otherwise in Article 21, each Party shall apply the powers and procedures referred to in paragraph 1 of this article to:

  (a) the criminal offences established in accordance with Articles 2 through 11 of this Convention;
  (b) other criminal offences committed by means of a computer system; and
  (c) the collection of evidence in electronic form of a criminal offence.

3. (a) Each Party may reserve the right to apply the measures referred to in Article 20 only to offences or categories of offences specified in the reservation, provided that the range of such offences or categories of offences is not more restricted than the range of offences to which it applies the measures referred to in Article 21. Each Party shall consider restricting such a reservation to enable the broadest application of the measure referred to in Article 20.

  (b) Where a Party, due to limitations in its legislation in force at the time of the adoption of the present Convention, is not able to apply the measures referred to in Articles 20 and 21 to communications being transmitted within a computer system of a service provider, which system:
  (i) is being operated for the benefit of a closed group of users, and
  (ii) does not employ public communications networks and is not connected with another computer system, whether public or private,
  that Party may reserve the right not to apply these measures to such communications. Each Party shall consider restricting such a reservation to enable the broadest application of the measures referred to in Articles 20 and 21.

Article 15   Conditions and safeguards

1. Each Party shall ensure that the establishment, implementation and application of the powers and procedures provided for in this Section are subject to conditions and safeguards provided for under its domestic law, which shall provide for the adequate protection of human rights and liberties, including rights arising pursuant to obligations it has undertaken under the 1950 Council of Europe Convention for the Protection of Human Rights and Fundamental Freedoms, the 1966 United Nations International Covenant on Civil and Political Rights, and other applicable international human rights instruments, and which shall incorporate the principle of proportionality.

2. Such conditions and safeguards shall, as appropriate in view of the nature of the procedure or power concerned, *inter alia,* include judicial or other independent supervision, grounds justifying application, and limitation of the scope and the duration of such power or procedure.

3. To the extent that it is consistent with the public interest, in particular the sound administration of justice, each Party shall consider the impact of the powers and procedures in this section upon the rights, responsibilities and legitimate interests of third parties.

Title 2 Expedited preservation of stored computer data

Article 16   Expedited preservation of stored computer data

1. Each Party shall adopt such legislative and other measures as may be necessary to enable its competent authorities to order or similarly obtain the expeditious preservation of specified computer data, including traffic data, that has been stored by means of a computer system, in particular where there are grounds to believe that the computer data is particularly vulnerable to loss or modification.

2. Where a Party gives effect to paragraph 1 above by means of an order to a person to preserve specified stored computer data in the person's possession or control, the Party shall adopt such legislative and other measures as may be necessary to oblige that person to preserve and maintain the integrity of that computer data for a period of time as long as necessary, up to a maximum of ninety days, to enable the competent authorities to seek its disclosure. A Party may provide for such an order to be subsequently renewed.

3. Each Party shall adopt such legislative and other measures as may be necessary to oblige the custodian or other person who is to preserve the computer data to keep confidential the undertaking of such procedures for the period of time provided for by its domestic law.

4. The powers and procedures referred to in this article shall be subject to Articles 14 and 15.

Article 17   Expedited preservation and partial disclosure of traffic data

1. Each Party shall adopt, in respect of traffic data that is to be preserved under Article 16, such legislative and other measures as may be necessary to:

    (a) ensure that such expeditious preservation of traffic data is available regardless of whether one or more service providers were involved in the transmission of that communication; and

    (b) ensure the expeditious disclosure to the Party's competent authority, or a person designated by that authority, of a sufficient amount of traffic data to enable the Party to identify the service providers and the path through which the communication was transmitted.

2. The powers and procedures referred to in this article shall be subject to Articles 14 and 15.

Title 3 Production order

Article 18   Production order

1. Each Party shall adopt such legislative and other measures as may be necessary to empower its competent authorities to order:

    (a) a person in its territory to submit specified computer data in that person's possession or control, which is stored in a computer system or a computer-data storage medium; and

    (b) a service provider offering its services in the territory of the Party to submit subscriber information relating to such services in that service provider's possession or control.

2. The powers and procedures referred to in this article shall be subject to Articles 14 and 15.

3. For the purpose of this article, the term "subscriber information" means any information contained in the form of computer data or any other form that is held by a service provider, relating to subscribers of its services other than traffic or content data and by which can be established:

    (a) the type of communication service used, the technical provisions taken thereto and the period of service;

    (b) the subscriber's identity, postal or geographic address, telephone and other access number, billing and payment information, available on the basis of the service agreement or arrangement;

    (c) any other information on the site of the installation of communication equipment, available on the basis of the service agreement or arrangement.

Title 4 Search and seizure of stored computer data

Article 19   **Search and seizure of stored computer data**

1. Each Party shall adopt such legislative and other measures as may be necessary to empower its competent authorities to search or similarly access:

    (a) a computer system or part of it and computer data stored therein; and

    (b) a computer-data storage medium in which computer data may be stored in its territory.

2. Each Party shall adopt such legislative and other measures as may be necessary to ensure that where its authorities search or similarly access a specific computer system or part of it, pursuant to paragraph 1.a, and have grounds to believe that the data sought is stored in another computer system or part of it in its territory, and such data is lawfully accessible from or available to the initial system, the authorities shall be able to expeditiously extend the search or similar accessing to the other system.

3. Each Party shall adopt such legislative and other measures as may be necessary to empower its competent authorities to seize or similarly secure computer data accessed according to paragraphs 1 or 2. These measures shall include the power to:

    (a) seize or similarly secure a computer system or part of it or a computer-data storage medium;

    (b) make and retain a copy of those computer data;

    (c) maintain the integrity of the relevant stored computer data;

    (d) render inaccessible or remove those computer data in the accessed computer system.

4. Each Party shall adopt such legislative and other measures as may be necessary to empower its competent authorities to order any person who has knowledge about the functioning of the computer system or measures applied to protect the computer data therein to provide, as is reasonable, the necessary information, to enable the undertaking of the measures referred to in paragraphs 1 and 2.

5. The powers and procedures referred to in this article shall be subject to Articles 14 and 15.

Title 5 Real-time collection of computer data

Article 20   **Real-time collection of traffic data**

1. Each Party shall adopt such legislative and other measures as may be necessary to empower its competent authorities to:

    (a) collect or record through the application of technical means on the territory of that Party, and

    (b) compel a service provider, within its existing technical capability:

        (i) to collect or record through the application of technical means on the territory of that Party; or

        (ii) to co-operate and assist the competent authorities in the collection or recording of,

traffic data, in real-time, associated with specified communications in its territory transmitted by means of a computer system.

2. Where a Party, due to the established principles of its domestic legal system, cannot adopt the measures referred to in paragraph 1.a, it may instead adopt legislative and other measures as may be necessary to ensure the real-time collection or recording of traffic data associated with specified communications transmitted in its territory, through the application of technical means on that territory.

3. Each Party shall adopt such legislative and other measures as may be necessary to oblige a service provider to keep confidential the fact of the execution of any power provided for in this article and any information relating to it.

4. The powers and procedures referred to in this article shall be subject to Articles 14 and 15.

Article 21   **Interception of content data**

1. Each Party shall adopt such legislative and other measures as may be necessary, in relation to a range of serious offences to be determined by domestic law, to empower its competent authorities to:

    (a) collect or record through the application of technical means on the territory of that Party, and

(b) compel a service provider, within its existing technical capability:

    (i)   to collect or record through the application of technical means on the territory of that Party, or

    (ii) to co-operate and assist the competent authorities in the collection or recording of, content data, in real-time, of specified communications in its territory transmitted by means of a computer system.

2. Where a Party, due to the established principles of its domestic legal system, cannot adopt the measures referred to in paragraph 1.a, it may instead adopt legislative and other measures as may be necessary to ensure the real-time collection or recording of content data on specified communications in its territory through the application of technical means on that territory.

3. Each Party shall adopt such legislative and other measures as may be necessary to oblige a service provider to keep confidential the fact of the execution of any power provided for in this article and any information relating to it.

4. The powers and procedures referred to in this article shall be subject to Articles 14 and 15.

Section 3 Jurisdiction

Article 22   Jurisdiction

1. Each Party shall adopt such legislative and other measures as may be necessary to establish jurisdiction over any offence established in accordance with Articles 2 through 11 of this Convention, when the offence is committed:

    (a) in its territory; or

    (b) on board a ship flying the flag of that Party; or

    (c) on board an aircraft registered under the laws of that Party; or

    (d) by one of its nationals, if the offence is punishable under criminal law where it was committed or if the offence is committed outside the territorial jurisdiction of any State.

2. Each Party may reserve the right not to apply or to apply only in specific cases or conditions the jurisdiction rules laid down in paragraphs 1.b through 1.d of this article or any part thereof.

3. Each Party shall adopt such measures as may be necessary to establish jurisdiction over the offences referred to in Article 24, paragraph 1, of this Convention, in cases where an alleged offender is present in its territory and it does not extradite him or her to another Party, solely on the basis of his or her nationality, after a request for extradition.

4. This Convention does not exclude any criminal jurisdiction exercised by a Party in accordance with its domestic law.

5. When more than one Party claims jurisdiction over an alleged offence established in accordance with this Convention, the Parties involved shall, where appropriate, consult with a view to determining the most appropriate jurisdiction for prosecution.

Chapter III International Co-Operation

Section 1 General Principles

Title 1 General principles relating to international co-operation

Article 23   General principles relating to international co-operation

The Parties shall co-operate with each other, in accordance with the provisions of this chapter, and through the application of relevant international instruments on international co-operation in criminal matters, arrangements agreed on the basis of uniform or reciprocal legislation, and domestic laws, to the widest extent possible for the purposes of investigations or proceedings concerning criminal offences related to computer systems and data, or for the collection of evidence in electronic form of a criminal offence.

Title 2 Principles relating to extradition

Article 24   Extradition

1. (a) This article applies to extradition between Parties for the criminal offences established in accordance with Articles 2 through 11 of this Convention, provided that they are punishable under the laws of both Parties concerned by deprivation of liberty for a maximum period of at least one year, or by a more severe penalty,

    (b) Where a different minimum penalty is to be applied under an arrangement agreed on the basis of uniform or reciprocal legislation or an extradition treaty, including the European Convention on Extradition (ETS No. 24), applicable between two or more parties, the minimum penalty provided for under such arrangement or treaty shall apply.

2. The criminal offences described in paragraph 1 of this article shall be deemed to be included as extraditable offences in any extradition treaty existing between or among the Parties. The Parties undertake to include such offences as extraditable offences in any extradition treaty to be concluded between or among them.

3. If a Party that makes extradition conditional on the existence of a treaty receives a request for extradition from another Party with which it does not have an extradition treaty, it may consider this Convention as the legal basis for extradition with respect to any criminal offence referred to in paragraph 1 of this article.

4. Parties that do not make extradition conditional on the existence of a treaty shall recognise the criminal offences referred to in paragraph 1 of this article as extraditable offences between themselves.

5. Extradition shall be subject to the conditions provided for by the law of the requested Party or by applicable extradition treaties, including the grounds on which the requested Party may refuse extradition.

6. If extradition for a criminal offence referred to in paragraph 1 of this article is refused solely on the basis of the nationality of the person sought, or because the requested Party deems that it has jurisdiction over the offence, the requested Party shall submit the case at the request of the requesting Party to its competent authorities for the purpose of prosecution and shall report the final outcome to the requesting Party in due course. Those authorities shall take their decision and conduct their investigations and proceedings in the same manner as for any other offence of a comparable nature under the law of that Party.

7. (a) Each Party shall, at the time of signature or when depositing its instrument of ratification, acceptance, approval or accession, communicate to the Secretary General of the Council of Europe the name and address of each authority responsible for making or receiving requests for extradition or provisional arrest in the absence of a treaty.

    (b) The Secretary General of the Council of Europe shall set up and keep updated a register of authorities so designated by the Parties. Each Party shall ensure that the details held on the register are correct at all times.

Title 3 General principles relating to mutual assistance

Article 25   General principles relating to mutual assistance

1. The Parties shall afford one another mutual assistance to the widest extent possible for the purpose of investigations or proceedings concerning criminal offences related to computer systems and data, or for the collection of evidence in electronic form of a criminal offence.

2. Each Party shall also adopt such legislative and other measures as may be necessary to carry out the obligations set forth in Articles 27 through 35.

3. Each Party may, in urgent circumstances, make requests for mutual assistance or communications related thereto by expedited means of communication, including fax or e-mail, to the extent that such means provide appropriate levels of security and authentication (including the use of encryption, where necessary), with formal confirmation to follow, where required by the requested

Party. The requested Party shall accept and respond to the request by any such expedited means of communication.

4. Except as otherwise specifically provided in articles in this chapter, mutual assistance shall be subject to the conditions provided for by the law of the requested Party or by applicable mutual assistance treaties, including the grounds on which the requested Party may refuse co-operation. The requested Party shall not exercise the right to refuse mutual assistance in relation to the offences referred to in Articles 2 through 11 solely on the ground that the request concerns an offence which it considers a fiscal offence.

5. Where, in accordance with the provisions of this chapter, the requested Party is permitted to make mutual assistance conditional upon the existence of dual criminality, that condition shall be deemed fulfilled, irrespective of whether its laws place the offence within the same category of offence or denominate the offence by the same terminology as the requesting Party, if the conduct underlying the offence for which assistance is sought is a criminal offence under its laws.

Article 26   Spontaneous information

1. A Party may, within the limits of its domestic law and without prior request, forward to another Party information obtained within the framework of its own investigations when it considers that the disclosure of such information might assist the receiving Party in initiating or carrying out investigations or proceedings concerning criminal offences established in accordance with this Convention or might lead to a request for co-operation by that Party under this chapter.

2. Prior to providing such information, the providing Party may request that it be kept confidential or only used subject to conditions. If the receiving Party cannot comply with such request, it shall notify the providing Party, which shall then determine whether the information should nevertheless be provided. If the receiving Party accepts the information subject to the conditions, it shall be bound by them.

Title 4   Procedures pertaining to mutual assistance requests in the absence of applicable international agreements

Article 27   Procedures pertaining to mutual assistance requests in the absence of applicable international agreements

1. Where there is no mutual assistance treaty or arrangement on the basis of uniform or reciprocal legislation in force between the requesting and requested Parties, the provisions of paragraphs 2 through 9 of this article shall apply. The provisions of this article shall not apply where such treaty, arrangement or legislation exists, unless the Parties concerned agree to apply any or all of the remainder of this article in lieu thereof.

2. (a) Each Party shall designate a central authority or authorities responsible for sending and answering requests for mutual assistance, the execution of such requests or their transmission to the authorities competent for their execution.

(b) The central authorities shall communicate directly with each other;

(c) Each Party shall, at the time of signature or when depositing its instrument of ratification, acceptance, approval or accession, communicate to the Secretary General of the Council of Europe the names and addresses of the authorities designated in pursuance of this paragraph;

(d) The Secretary General of the Council of Europe shall set up and keep updated a register of central authorities designated by the Parties. Each Party shall ensure that the details held on the register are correct at all times.

3. Mutual assistance requests under this article shall be executed in accordance with the procedures specified by the requesting Party, except where incompatible with the law of the requested Party.

4. The requested Party may, in addition to the grounds for refusal established in Article 25, paragraph 4, refuse assistance if:

(a) the request concerns an offence which the requested Party considers a political offence or an offence connected with a political offence, or

(b) it considers that execution of the request is likely to prejudice its sovereignty, security, *ordre public* or other essential interests.

5. The requested Party may postpone action on a request if such action would prejudice criminal investigations or proceedings conducted by its authorities.

6. Before refusing or postponing assistance, the requested Party shall, where appropriate after having consulted with the requesting Party, consider whether the request may be granted partially or subject to such conditions as it deems necessary.

7. The requested Party shall promptly inform the requesting Party of the outcome of the execution of a request for assistance. Reasons shall be given for any refusal or postponement of the request. The requested Party shall also inform the requesting Party of any reasons that render impossible the execution of the request or are likely to delay it significantly.

8. The requesting Party may request that the requested Party keep confidential the fact of any request made under this chapter as well as its subject, except to the extent necessary for its execution. If the requested Party cannot comply with the request for confidentiality, it shall promptly inform the requesting Party, which shall then determine whether the request should nevertheless be executed.

9. (a) In the event of urgency, requests for mutual assistance or communications related thereto may be sent directly by judicial authorities of the requesting Party to such authorities of the requested Party. In any such cases, a copy shall be sent at the same time to the central authority of the requested Party through the central authority of the requesting Party.

   (b) Any request or communication under this paragraph may be made through the International Criminal Police Organisation (Interpol).

   (c) Where a request is made pursuant to sub-paragraph a. of this article and the authority is not competent to deal with the request, it shall refer the request to the competent national authority and inform directly the requesting Party that it has done so.

   (d) Requests or communications made under this paragraph that do not involve coercive action may be directly transmitted by the competent authorities of the requesting Party to the competent authorities of the requested Party.

   (e) Each party may, at the time of signature or when depositing its instrument of ratification, acceptance, approval or accession, inform the Secretary General of the Council of Europe that, for reasons of efficiency, requests made under this paragraph are to be addressed to its central authority.

Article 28   Confidentiality and limitation on use

1. When there is no mutual assistance treaty or arrangement on the basis of uniform or reciprocal legislation in force between the requesting and the requested Parties, the provisions of this article shall apply. The provisions of this article shall not apply where such treaty, arrangement or legislation exists, unless the Parties concerned agree to apply any or all of the remainder of this article in lieu thereof.

2. The requested Party may make the supply of information or material in response to a request dependent on the condition that it is:

   (a) kept confidential where the request for mutual legal assistance could not be complied with in the absence of such condition, or

   (b) not used for investigations or proceedings other than those stated in the request.

3. If the requesting Party cannot comply with a condition referred to in paragraph 2, it shall promptly inform the other Party, which shall then determine whether the information should nevertheless be provided. When the requesting Party accepts the condition, it shall be bound by it.

4. Any Party that supplies information or material subject to a condition referred to in paragraph 2 may require the other Party to explain, in relation to that condition, the use made of such information or material.

Section 2 Specific Provisions

Title 1 *Mutual assistance regarding provisional measures*

Article 29   Expedited preservation of stored computer data

1. A Party may request another Party to order or otherwise obtain the expeditious preservation of data stored by means of a computer system, located within the territory of that other Party and in respect of which the requesting Party intends to submit a request for mutual assistance for the search or similar access, seizure or similar securing, or disclosure of the data.

2. A request for preservation made under paragraph 1 shall specify:
   (a) the authority seeking the preservation;
   (b) the offence that is the subject of a criminal investigation or proceedings and a brief summary of the related facts;
   (c) the stored computer data to be preserved and its relationship to the offence;
   (d) any available information identifying the custodian of the stored computer data or the location of the computer system;
   (e) the necessity of the preservation; and
   (f) that the Party intends to submit a request for mutual assistance for the search or similar access, seizure or similar securing, or disclosure of the stored computer data.

3. Upon receiving the request from another Party, the requested Party shall take all appropriate measures to preserve expeditiously the specified data in accordance with its domestic law. For the purposes of responding to a request, dual criminality shall not be required as a condition to providing such preservation.

4. A Party that requires dual criminality as a condition for responding to a request for mutual assistance for the search or similar access, seizure or similar securing, or disclosure of stored data may, in respect of offences other than those established in accordance with Articles 2 through 11 of this Convention, reserve the right to refuse the request for preservation under this article in cases where it has reasons to believe that at the time of disclosure the condition of dual criminality cannot be fulfilled.

5. In addition, a request for preservation may only be refused if:
   (a) the request concerns an offence which the requested Party considers a political offence or an offence connected with a political offence, or
   (b) the requested Party considers that execution of the request is likely to prejudice its sovereignty, security, *ordre public* or other essential interests.

6. Where the requested Party believes that preservation will not ensure the future availability of the data or will threaten the confidentiality of or otherwise prejudice the requesting Party's investigation, it shall promptly so inform the requesting Party, which shall then determine whether the request should nevertheless be executed.

7. Any preservation effected in response to the request referred to in paragraph 1 shall be for a period not less than sixty days, in order to enable the requesting Party to submit a request for the search or similar access, seizure or similar securing, or disclosure of the data. Following the receipt of such a request, the data shall continue to be preserved pending a decision on that request.

Article 30   Expedited disclosure of preserved traffic data

1. Where, in the course of the execution of a request made pursuant to Article 29 to preserve traffic data concerning a specific communication, the requested Party discovers that a service provider in another State was involved in the transmission of the communication, the requested Party shall expeditiously disclose to the requesting Party a sufficient amount of traffic data to identify that service provider and the path through which the communication was transmitted.

2. Disclosure of traffic data under paragraph 1 may only be withheld if:
   (a) the request concerns an offence which the requested Party considers a political offence or an offence connected with a political offence; or

(b) the requested Party considers that execution of the request is likely to prejudice its sovereignty, security, *ordre public* or other essential interests.

Title 2 Mutual assistance regarding investigative powers

Article 31   Mutual assistance regarding accessing of stored computer data

1. A Party may request another Party to search or similarly access, seize or similarly secure, and disclose data stored by means of a computer system located within the territory of the requested Party, including data that has been preserved pursuant to Article 29.

2. The requested Party shall respond to the request through the application of international instruments, arrangements and laws referred to in Article 23, and in accordance with other relevant provisions of this chapter.

3. The request shall be responded to on an expedited basis where:
   (a) there are grounds to believe that relevant data is particularly vulnerable to loss or modification; or
   (b) the instruments, arrangements and laws referred to in paragraph 2 otherwise provide for expedited co-operation.

Article 32   Trans-border access to stored computer data with consent or where publicly available

A Party may, without the authorisation of another Party:
   (a) access publicly available (open source) stored computer data, regardless of where the data is located geographically; or
   (b) access or receive, through a computer system in its territory, stored computer data located in another Party, if the Party obtains the lawful and voluntary consent of the person who has the lawful authority to disclose the data to the Party through that computer system.

Article 33   Mutual assistance in the real-time collection of traffic data

1. The Parties shall provide mutual assistance to each other in the real-time collection of traffic data associated with specified communications in their territory transmitted by means of a computer system. Subject to the provisions of paragraph 2, this assistance shall be governed by the conditions and procedures provided for under domestic law.

2. Each Party shall provide such assistance at least with respect to criminal offences for which real-time collection of traffic data would be available in a similar domestic case.

Article 34   Mutual assistance regarding the interception of content data

The Parties shall provide mutual assistance to each other in the real-time collection or recording of content data of specified communications transmitted by means of a computer system to the extent permitted under their applicable treaties and domestic laws.

Title 3 24/7 Network

Article 35   24/7 Network

1. Each Party shall designate a point of contact available on a twenty-four hour, seven-day-a-week basis, in order to ensure the provision of immediate assistance for the purpose of investigations or proceedings concerning criminal offences related to computer systems and data, or for the collection of evidence in electronic form of a criminal offence. Such assistance shall include facilitating, or, if permitted by its domestic law and practice, directly carrying out the following measures:
   (a) the provision of technical advice;
   (b) the preservation of data pursuant to Articles 29 and 30;
   (c) the collection of evidence, the provision of legal information, and locating of suspects.

2. (a) A Party's point of contact shall have the capacity to carry out communications with the point of contact of another Party on an expedited basis,
   (b) If the point of contact designated by a Party is not part of that Party's authority or authorities responsible for international mutual assistance or extradition, the point of contact

shall ensure that it is able to co-ordinate with such authority or authorities on an expedited basis.

3. Each Party shall ensure that trained and equipped personnel are available, in order to facilitate the operation of the network.

Chapter IV Final Provisions

Article 36　Signature and entry into force

1. This Convention shall be open for signature by the member States of the Council of Europe and by non-member States which have participated in its elaboration.

2. This Convention is subject to ratification, acceptance or approval. Instruments of ratification, acceptance or approval shall be deposited with the Secretary General of the Council of Europe.

3. This Convention shall enter into force on the first day of the month following the expiration of a period of three months after the date on which five States, including at least three member States of the Council of Europe, have expressed their consent to be bound by the Convention in accordance with the provisions of paragraphs 1 and 2.

4. In respect of any signatory State which subsequently expresses its consent to be bound by it, the Convention shall enter into force on the first day of the month following the expiration of a period of three months after the date of the expression of its consent to be bound by the Convention in accordance with the provisions of paragraphs 1 and 2.

Article 37　Accession to the Convention

1. After the entry into force of this Convention, the Committee of Ministers of the Council of Europe, after consulting with and obtaining the unanimous consent of the Contracting States to the Convention, may invite any State which is not a member of the Council and which has not participated in its elaboration to accede to this Convention. The decision shall be taken by the majority provided for in Article 20.d. of the Statute of the Council of Europe and by the unanimous vote of the representatives of the Contracting States entitled to sit on the Committee of Ministers.

2. In respect of any State acceding to the Convention under paragraph 1 above, the Convention shall enter into force on the first day of the month following the expiration of a period of three months after the date of deposit of the instrument of accession with the Secretary General of the Council of Europe.

Article 38　Territorial application

1. Any State may, at the time of signature or when depositing its instrument of ratification, acceptance, approval or accession, specify the territory or territories to which this Convention shall apply.

2. Any State may, at any later date, by a declaration addressed to the Secretary General of the Council of Europe, extend the application of this Convention to any other territory specified in the declaration. In respect of such territory the Convention shall enter into force on the first day of the month following the expiration of a period of three months after the date of receipt of the declaration by the Secretary General.

3. Any declaration made under the two preceding paragraphs may, in respect of any territory specified in such declaration, be withdrawn by a notification addressed to the Secretary General of the Council of Europe. The withdrawal shall become effective on the first day of the month following the expiration of a period of three months after the date of receipt of such notification by the Secretary General.

Article 39　Effects of the Convention

1. The purpose of the present Convention is to supplement applicable multilateral or bilateral treaties or arrangements as between the Parties, including the provisions of:
　　— the European Convention on Extradition, opened for signature in Paris, on 13 December 1957 (ETS No. 24);
　　— the European Convention on Mutual Assistance in Criminal Matters, opened for signature in Strasbourg, on 20 April 1959 (ETS No. 30);

— the Additional Protocol to the European Convention on Mutual Assistance in Criminal Matters, opened for signature in Strasbourg, on 17 March 1978 (ETS No. 99).

2. If two or more Parties have already concluded an agreement or treaty on the matters dealt with in this Convention or have otherwise established their relations on such matters, or should they in future do so, they shall also be entitled to apply that agreement or treaty or to regulate those relations accordingly. However, where Parties establish their relations in respect of the matters dealt with in the present Convention other than as regulated therein, they shall do so in a manner that is not inconsistent with the Convention's objectives and principles.

3. Nothing in this Convention shall affect other rights, restrictions, obligations and responsibilities of a Party.

Article 40   Declarations

By a written notification addressed to the Secretary General of the Council of Europe, any State may, at the time of signature or when depositing its instrument of ratification, acceptance, approval or accession, declare that it avails itself of the possibility of requiring additional elements as provided for under Articles 2, 3, 6 paragraph 1.b, 7, 9 paragraph 3, and 27, paragraph 9.e.

Article 41   Federal clause

1. A federal State may reserve the right to assume obligations under Chapter II of this Convention consistent with its fundamental principles governing the relationship between its central government and constituent States or other similar territorial entities provided that it is still able to co-operate under Chapter III.

2. When making a reservation under paragraph 1, a federal State may not apply the terms of such reservation to exclude or substantially diminish its obligations to provide for measures set forth in Chapter II. Overall, it shall provide for a broad and effective law enforcement capability with respect to those measures.

3. With regard to the provisions of this Convention, the application of which comes under the jurisdiction of constituent States or other similar territorial entities, that are not obliged by the constitutional system of the federation to take legislative measures, the federal government shall inform the competent authorities of such States of the said provisions with its favourable opinion, encouraging them to take appropriate action to give them effect.

Article 42   Reservations

By a written notification addressed to the Secretary General of the Council of Europe, any State may, at the time of signature or when depositing its instrument of ratification, acceptance, approval or accession, declare that it avails itself of the reservation(s) provided for in Article 4, paragraph 2, Article 6, paragraph 3, Article 9, paragraph 4, Article 10, paragraph 3, Article 11, paragraph 3, Article 14, paragraph 3, Article 22, paragraph 2, Article 29, paragraph 4, and Article 41, paragraph 1. No other reservation may be made.

Article 43   Status and withdrawal of reservations

1. A Party that has made a reservation in accordance with Article 42 may wholly or partially withdraw it by means of a notification addressed to the Secretary General of the Council of Europe. Such withdrawal shall take effect on the date of receipt of such notification by the Secretary General. If the notification states that the withdrawal of a reservation is to take effect on a date specified therein, and such date is later than the date on which the notification is received by the Secretary General, the withdrawal shall take effect on such a later date.

2. A Party that has made a reservation as referred to in Article 42 shall withdraw such reservation, in whole or in part, as soon as circumstances so permit.

3. The Secretary General of the Council of Europe may periodically enquire with Parties that have made one or more reservations as referred to in Article 42 as to the prospects for withdrawing such reservation(s).

Article 44   Amendments

1. Amendments to this Convention may be proposed by any Party, and shall be communicated by the Secretary General of the Council of Europe to the member States of the Council of Europe, to the non-member States which have participated in the elaboration of this Convention as well as to any State which has acceded to, or has been invited to accede to, this Convention in accordance with the provisions of Article 37.

2. Any amendment proposed by a Party shall be communicated to the European Committee on Crime Problems (CDPC), which shall submit to the Committee of Ministers its opinion on that proposed amendment.

3. The Committee of Ministers shall consider the proposed amendment and the opinion submitted by the CDPC and, following consultation with the non-member States Parties to this Convention, may adopt the amendment.

4. The text of any amendment adopted by the Committee of Ministers in accordance with paragraph 3 of this article shall be forwarded to the Parties for acceptance.

5. Any amendment adopted in accordance with paragraph 3 of this article shall come into force on the thirtieth day after all Parties have informed the Secretary General of their acceptance thereof.

Article 45   Settlement of disputes

1. The European Committee on Crime Problems (CDPC) shall be kept informed regarding the interpretation and application of this Convention.

2. In case of a dispute between Parties as to the interpretation or application of this Convention, they shall seek a settlement of the dispute through negotiation or any other peaceful means of their choice, including submission of the dispute to the CDPC, to an arbitral tribunal whose decisions shall be binding upon the Parties, or to the International Court of Justice, as agreed upon by the Parties concerned.

Article 46   Consultations of the Parties

1. The Parties shall, as appropriate, consult periodically with a view to facilitating:
   (a) the effective use and implementation of this Convention, including the identification of any problems thereof, as well as the effects of any declaration or reservation made under this Convention;
   (b) the exchange of information on significant legal, policy or technological developments pertaining to cybercrime and the collection of evidence in electronic form;
   (c) consideration of possible supplementation or amendment of the Convention.

2. The European Committee on Crime Problems (CDPC) shall be kept periodically informed regarding the result of consultations referred to in paragraph 1.

3. The CDPC shall, as appropriate, facilitate the consultations referred to in paragraph 1 and take the measures necessary to assist the Parties in their efforts to supplement or amend the Convention. At the latest three years after the present Convention enters into force, the European Committee on Crime Problems (CDPC) shall, in co-operation with the Parties, conduct a review of all of the Convention's provisions and, if necessary, recommend any appropriate amendments.

4. Except where assumed by the Council of Europe, expenses incurred in carrying out the provisions of paragraph 1 shall be borne by the Parties in the manner to be determined by them.

5. The Parties shall be assisted by the Secretariat of the Council of Europe in carrying out their functions pursuant to this article.

Article 47   Denunciation

1. Any Party may, at any time, denounce this Convention by means of a notification addressed to the Secretary General of the Council of Europe.

2. Such denunciation shall become effective on the first day of the month following the expiration of a period of three months after the date of receipt of the notification by the Secretary General.

Article 48   Notification
The Secretary General of the Council of Europe shall notify the member States of the Council of Europe, the non-member States which have participated in the elaboration of this Convention as well as any State which has acceded to, or has been invited to accede to, this Convention of:
   (a) any signature;
   (b) the deposit of any instrument of ratification, acceptance, approval or accession;
   (c) any date of entry into force of this Convention in accordance with Articles 36 and 37;
   (d) any declaration made under Article 40 or reservation made in accordance with Article 42;
   (e) any other act, notification or communication relating to this Convention.
In witness whereof the undersigned, being duly authorised thereto, have signed this Convention.

   Done at Budapest, this 23rd day of November 2001, in English and in French, both texts being equally authentic, in a single copy which shall be deposited in the archives of the Council of Europe. The Secretary General of the Council of Europe shall transmit certified copies to each member State of the Council of Europe, to the non-member States which have participated in the elaboration of this Convention, and to any State invited to accede to it.

First Additional Protocol to the Convention on Cybercrime concerning the criminalisation of acts of a racist and xenophobic nature committed through computer systems[1]

The member States of the Council of Europe and the other Parties to the Convention on Cybercrime, opened for signature in Budapest on 23 November 2001, signatory hereto;
   Considering that the aim of the Council of Europe is to achieve a greater unity between its members;
   Recalling that all human beings are born free and equal in dignity and rights;
   Stressing the need to secure a full and effective implementation of all human rights without any discrimination or distinction, as enshrined in European and other international instruments;
   Convinced that acts of a racist and xenophobic nature constitute a violation of Human Rights and a threat to the Rule of Law and democratic stability;
   Considering that national and international law need to provide adequate legal responses to propaganda of a racist and xenophobic nature through computer systems;
   Aware of the fact that propaganda to such acts is often subject to criminalisation in national legislation;
   Having regard to the Convention on Cybercrime, which provides for modern and flexible means of international co-operation and convinced of the need to harmonise substantive law provisions concerning the fight against racist and xenophobic propaganda;
   Aware that computer systems offer an unprecedented means of facilitating freedom of expression and communication around the globe;
   Recognising that the freedom of expression constitutes one of the essential foundations of a democratic society, one of the basic conditions for its progress and for the development of every human being;
   Concerned however by the risk that such computer systems are misused or abused to disseminate racist and xenophobic propaganda;
   Mindful of the need to ensure a proper balance between freedom of expression and an effective fight against acts of a racist and xenophobic nature;
   Recognising that this Protocol is not intended to affect established principles relating to freedom of expression in national legal systems;

[1] Entered into force on 1 March 2006.

Taking into account the relevant international legal instruments in this field, in particular the European Convention on Human Rights and Protocol No. 12 thereto, the existing Council of Europe conventions on co-operation in the penal field, in particular the Convention on Cybercrime, the International Convention on the Elimination of All Forms of Racial Discrimination of 21 December 1965, the Joint Action of 15 July 1996 of the European Union adopted by the Council on the basis of Article k.3 of the Treaty of the European Union, concerning action to combat racism and xenophobia;

Welcoming the recent developments which further advance international understanding and co-operation in combating cybercrime, as well as racism and xenophobia;

Having regard to the Action Plan adopted by the Heads of State and Government of the Council of Europe on the occasion of their second Summit (Strasbourg, 10–11 October 1997) to seek common responses to the developments of the new technologies based on the standards and values of the Council of Europe;

Have agreed as follows:

Chapter I   Common Provisions

Article 1   Purpose

The purpose of this Protocol is to supplement, as between the Parties to the Protocol, the provisions of the Convention on Cybercrime, opened for signature in Budapest on 23 November 2001 (hereinafter referred to as "the Convention"), as regards the criminalisation of acts of a racist and xenophobic nature committed through computer systems.

Article 2   Definition

1. For the purposes of this Protocol:
   — "Racist and xenophobic material" means any written material, any image or any other representation of thoughts or theories, which advocates, promotes or incites hatred, discrimination or violence, against any individual or group of individuals, based on race, colour, descent or national or ethnic origin, as well as religion if used as a pretext for any of these factors.

2. The terms and expressions used in this Protocol shall be interpreted in the same manner as such terms and expressions are interpreted under the Convention.

Chapter II   Measures to be Taken at National Level

Article 3   Dissemination of racist and xenophobic material in a computer system

1. Each Party shall adopt such legislative and other measures as may be necessary to establish as criminal offences under its domestic law, when committed intentionally and without right, the following conduct:
   — distributing or otherwise making available racist and xenophobic material to the public through a computer system.

2. A Party may reserve the right not to attach criminal liability to conduct as defined by paragraph 1 of this Article, where the material, as defined in Article 2, paragraph 1, advocates promotes or incites discrimination that is not associated with hatred or violence, provided that other effective remedies are available.

3. Notwithstanding paragraph 2, a Party may reserve the right not to apply paragraph 1 in relation to those cases of discrimination for which, due to established principles of its national legal system concerning freedom of expression, it cannot provide for effective remedies as referred to in paragraph 2.

Article 4   Racist and xenophobic motivated threat

Each Party shall adopt such legislative and other measures as may be necessary to establish as criminal offences under its domestic law, when committed intentionally and without right, the following conduct:

— threatening, through a computer system, with the commission of a serious criminal offence as defined under its domestic law, (i) persons for the reason that they belong to a group, distinguished by race, colour, descent or national or ethnic origin, as well as religion, if used as a pretext for any of these factors, or (ii) a group of persons which is distinguished by any of these characteristics.

Article 5   Racist and xenophobic motivated insult

1. Each Party shall adopt such legislative and other measures as may be necessary to establish as criminal offences under its domestic law, when committed intentionally and without right, the following conduct:

— insulting publicly, through a computer system, (i) persons for the reason that they belong to a group, distinguished by race, colour, descent or national or ethnic origin, as well as religion, if used as a pretext for any of these factors, or (ii) a group of persons which is distinguished by any of these characteristics.

2. A Party may either
   (i)   require that the offence referred to in paragraph 1 has the effect that the person or group of persons referred to in paragraph 1 is exposed to hatred, contempt or ridicule, or otherwise
   (ii) reserve the right not to apply, in whole or in part, paragraph 1.

Article 6   Denial, gross minimisation, approval or justification of genocide or crimes against humanity

1. Each Party shall adopt such legislative measures as may be necessary to establish the following conduct as criminal offences under its domestic law, when committed intentionally and without right:

— distributing or otherwise making available through a computer system to the public material which denies, grossly minimises, approves or justifies acts constituting genocide or crimes against humanity, as defined by international law and recognised as such by final and binding decisions of the International Military Tribunal, established by the London Agreement of 8 April 1945, or of any other international court, established by relevant international instruments and whose jurisdiction is recognised by that Party.

2. A Party may either
   (i)   require that the denial or the gross minimisation referred to in paragraph 1 is committed with the intent to incite hatred, discrimination or violence against any individual or group of individuals, based on race, colour, descent or national or ethnic origin, as well as religion if used as a pretext for any of these factors, or otherwise
   (ii) reserve the right not to apply, in whole or in part, paragraph 1.

Article 7   Aiding and abetting

1. Each Party shall adopt such legislative and other measures as may be necessary to establish as criminal offences under its domestic law, when committed intentionally and without right, aiding or abetting the commission of any of the offences established in accordance with this Protocol, with intent that such offence be committed.

Chapter III Relations between the Convention and this Protocol

Article 8   Relations between the Convention and this Protocol

1. Article 1, Articles 12 and 13, Articles 22, 41, 44, 45 and 46 of the Convention shall apply, *mutatis mutandis,* to this Protocol.

2. The Parties shall extend the scope of application of the measures defined in Articles 14 to 21 and Articles 23 to 35 of the Convention to Articles 2 to 7 of this Protocol.

Chapter IV Final Provisions

Article 9   Expression of consent to be bound

1. This Protocol shall be open for signature by the States which have signed the Convention, which may express their consent to be bound by either:

    (a) signature without reservation as to ratification, acceptance or approval; or

    (b) signature subject to ratification, acceptance or approval, followed by ratification, acceptance or approval.

2. A State may not sign this Protocol without reservation as to ratification, acceptance or approval, or deposit an instrument of ratification, acceptance or approval, unless it has already deposited or simultaneously deposits an instrument of ratification, acceptance or approval of the Convention.

3. The instruments of ratification, acceptance or approval shall be deposited with the Secretary General of the Council of Europe.

Article 10   Entry into force

1. This Protocol shall come into force on the first day of the month following the expiration of a period of three months after the date on which five States have expressed their consent to be bound by the Protocol, in accordance with the provisions of Article 9.

2. In respect of any State which subsequently expresses its consent to be bound by it, the Protocol shall come into force on the first day of the month following the expiration of a period of three months after the date of its signature without reservation as to ratification, acceptance or approval or deposit of its instrument of ratification, acceptance or approval.

Article 11   Accession

1. After the entry into force of this Protocol, any State which has acceded to the Convention may also accede to the Protocol.

2. Accession shall be effected by the deposit with the Secretary General of the Council of Europe of an instrument of accession which shall take effect on the first day of the month following the expiration of a period of three months after the date of its deposit.

Article 12   Reservations and declarations

1. Reservations and declarations made by a Party to a provision of the Convention shall be applicable also to this Protocol, unless that Party otherwise declares at the time of signature or when depositing its instrument of ratification, acceptance, approval or accession.

2. By a written notification addressed to the Secretary General of the Council of Europe, any Party may, at the time of signature or when depositing its instrument of ratification, acceptance, approval or accession, declare that it avails itself of the reservation(s) provided for in Articles 3, 5 and 6 of this Protocol. At the same time, a Party may avail itself, with respect to the provisions of this Protocol, of the reservation(s) provided for in Article 22, paragraph 2 and Article 41, paragraph 1, of the Convention irrespective of the implementation made by that Party under the Convention. No other reservations may be made.

Article 13   Status and withdrawal of reservations

1. A Party that has made a reservation in accordance with Article 12 shall withdraw such reservation, in whole or in part, as soon as circumstances so permit. Such withdrawal shall take effect on the date of receipt of such notification by the Secretary General. If the notification states that the withdrawal of a reservation is to take effect on a date specified therein, and such date is later than the date on which the notification is received by the Secretary General, the withdrawal shall take effect on such a later date.

2. The Secretary General of the Council of Europe may periodically enquire with Parties that have made one or more reservations in accordance with Article 12 as to the prospects for withdrawing such reservation(s).

Article 14   Territorial application

1. Any Party may at the time of signature or when depositing its instrument of ratification, acceptance, approval or accession specify the territory or territories to which this Protocol shall apply.

2. Any Party may, at any later date, by a declaration addressed to the Secretary General of the Council of Europe, extend the application of this Protocol to any other territory specified in the declaration. In respect of such territory, the Protocol shall enter into force on the first day of the month following the expiration of a period of three months after the date of receipt of such declaration by the Secretary General.

3. Any declaration made under the two preceding paragraphs may, in respect of any territory specified in such declaration, be withdrawn by a notification addressed to the Secretary General. The withdrawal shall become effective on the first day of the month following the expiration of a period of three months after the date of receipt of such notification by the Secretary General.

Article 15   Denunciation

1. Any Party may, at any time, denounce this Protocol by means of a notification addressed to the Secretary General of the Council of Europe.

2. Such denunciation shall become effective on the first day of the month following the expiration of a period of three months after the date of receipt of the notification by the Secretary General.

Article 16   Notification

The Secretary General of the Council of Europe shall notify the member States of the Council of Europe, the non-member States which have participated in the elaboration of this Protocol as well as any State which has acceded to, or has been invited to accede to, this Protocol of:

    a. any signature;

    b. the deposit of any instrument of ratification, acceptance, approval or accession;

    c. any date of entry into force of this Protocol in accordance with Articles 9, 10 and 11;

    d. any other act, notification or communication relating to this Protocol.

In witness whereof the undersigned, being duly authorised thereto, have signed this Protocol.

Done at ... , this ... , in English and in French, both texts being equally authentic, in a single copy which shall be deposited in the archives of the Council of Europe. The Secretary General of the Council of Europe shall transmit certified copies to each member State of the Council of Europe, to the non-member States which have participated in the elaboration of this Protocol, and to any State invited to accede to it.

Agreement on Trade-related Aspects of Intellectual Property Rights

(1994)

Members,

Desiring to reduce distortions and impediments to international trade, and taking into account the need to promote effective and adequate protection of intellectual property rights, and to ensure that measures and procedures to enforce intellectual property rights do not themselves become barriers to legitimate trade;

Recognizing, to this end, the need for new rules and disciplines concerning:

    (a) the applicability of the basic principles of GATT 1994 and of relevant international intellectual property agreements or conventions;

    (b) the provision of adequate standards and principles concerning the availability, scope and use of trade-related intellectual property rights;

    (c) the provision of effective and appropriate means for the enforcement of trade-related intellectual property rights, taking into account differences in national legal systems;

(d) the provision of effective and expeditious procedures for the multilateral prevention and settlement of disputes between governments; and

(e) transitional arrangements aiming at the fullest participation in the results of the negotiations;

Recognizing the need for a multilateral framework of principles, rules and disciplines dealing with international trade in counterfeit goods;

Recognizing that intellectual property rights are private rights;

Recognizing the underlying public policy objectives of national systems for the protection of intellectual property, including developmental and technological objectives;

Recognizing also the special needs of the least-developed country Members in respect of maximum flexibility in the domestic implementation of laws and regulations in order to enable them to create a sound and viable technological base;

Emphasizing the importance of reducing tensions by reaching strengthened commitments to resolve disputes on trade-related intellectual property issues through multilateral procedures;

Desiring to establish a mutually supportive relationship between the WTO and the World Intellectual Property Organization (referred to in this Agreement as "WIPO") as well as other relevant international organizations;

Hereby agree as follows:

PART I GENERAL PROVISIONS AND BASIC PRINCIPLES

Article 1 Nature and Scope of Obligations

1. Members shall give effect to the provisions of this Agreement. Members may, but shall not be obliged to, implement in their law more extensive protection than is required by this Agreement, provided that such protection does not contravene the provisions of this Agreement. Members shall be free to determine the appropriate method of implementing the provisions of this Agreement within their own legal system and practice.

2. For the purposes of this Agreement, the term "intellectual property" refers to all categories of intellectual property that are the subject of Sections 1 through 7 of Part II.

3. Members shall accord the treatment provided for in this Agreement to the nationals of other Members.[1] In respect of the relevant intellectual property right, the nationals of other Members shall be understood as those natural or legal persons that would meet the criteria for eligibility for protection provided for in the Paris Convention (1967), the Berne Convention (1971), the Rome Convention and the Treaty on Intellectual Property in Respect of Integrated Circuits, were all Members of the WTO members of those conventions.[2] Any Member availing itself of the possibilities provided in paragraph 3 of Article 5 or paragraph 2 of Article 6 of the Rome Convention shall make a notification as foreseen in those provisions to the Council for Trade-Related Aspects of Intellectual Property Rights (the "Council for TRIPS").

Article 2 Intellectual property Conventions

1. In respect of Parts II, III and IV of this Agreement, Members shall comply with Articles 1 through 12, and Article 19, of the Paris Convention (1967).

---

[1] When "nationals" are referred to in this Agreement, they shall be deemed, in the case of a separate customs territory Member of the WTO, to mean persons, natural or legal, who are domiciled or who have a real and effective industrial or commercial establishment in that customs territory.

[2] In this Agreement, "Paris Convention" refers to the Paris Convention for the Protection of Industrial Property; "Paris Convention (1967)" refers to the Stockholm Act of this Convention of 14 July 1967. "Berne Convention" refers to the Berne Convention for the Protection of Literary and Artistic Works; "Berne Convention (1971)" refers to the Paris Act of this Convention of 24 July 1971. "Rome Convention" refers to the International Convention for the Protection of Performers, Producers of Phonograms and Broadcasting Organizations, adopted at Rome on 26 October 1961. "Treaty on Intellectual Property in Respect of Integrated Circuits" (IPIC Treaty) refers to the Treaty on Intellectual Property in Respect of Integrated Circuits, adopted at Washington on 26 May 1989. "WTO Agreement" refers to the Agreement Establishing the WTO.

2. Nothing in Parts I to IV of this Agreement shall derogate from existing obligations that Members may have to each other under the Paris Convention, the Berne Convention, the Rome Convention and the Treaty on Intellectual Property in Respect of Integrated Circuits.

Article 3   National treatment

1. Each Member shall accord to the nationals of other Members treatment no less favourable than that it accords to its own nationals with regard to the protection[3] of intellectual property, subject to the exceptions already provided in, respectively, the Paris Convention (1967), the Berne Convention (1971), the Rome Convention or the Treaty on Intellectual Property in Respect of Integrated Circuits. In respect of performers, producers of phonograms and broadcasting organizations, this obligation only applies in respect of the rights provided under this Agreement. Any Member availing itself of the possibilities provided in Article 6 of the Berne Convention (1971) or paragraph 1(b) of Article 16 of the Rome Convention shall make a notification as foreseen in those provisions to the Council for TRIPS.

2. Members may avail themselves of the exceptions permitted under paragraph 1 in relation to judicial and administrative procedures, including the designation of an address for service or the appointment of an agent within the jurisdiction of a Member, only where such exceptions are necessary to secure compliance with laws and regulations which are not inconsistent with the provisions of this Agreement and where such practices are not applied in a manner which would constitute a disguised restriction on trade.

Article 4   Most-favoured-nation treatment

With regard to the protection of intellectual property, any advantage, favour, privilege or immunity granted by a Member to the nationals of any other country shall be accorded immediately and unconditionally to the nationals of all other Members. Exempted from this obligation are any advantage, favour, privilege or immunity accorded by a Member:

(a) deriving from international agreements on judicial assistance or law enforcement of a general nature and not particularly confined to the protection of intellectual property;

(b) granted in accordance with the provisions of the Berne Convention (1971) or the Rome Convention authorizing that the treatment accorded be a function not of national treatment but of the treatment accorded in another country;

(c) in respect of the rights of performers, producers of phonograms and broadcasting organizations not provided under this Agreement;

(d) deriving from international agreements related to the protection of intellectual property which entered into force prior to the entry into force of the WTO Agreement, provided that such agreements are notified to the Council for TRIPS and do not constitute an arbitrary or unjustifiable discrimination against nationals of other Members.

Article 5   Multilateral agreements on acquisition or maintenance of Protection

The obligations under Articles 3 and 4 do not apply to procedures provided in multilateral agreements concluded under the auspices of WIPO relating to the acquisition or maintenance of intellectual property rights.

Article 6   Exhaustion

For the purposes of dispute settlement under this Agreement, subject to the provisions of Articles 3 and 4 nothing in this Agreement shall be used to address the issue of the exhaustion of intellectual property rights.

Article 7   Objectives

The protection and enforcement of intellectual property rights should contribute to the promotion of technological innovation and to the transfer and dissemination of technology, to the mutual

---

[3] For the purposes of Articles 3 and 4, "protection" shall include matters affecting the availability, acquisition, scope, maintenance and enforcement of intellectual property rights as well as those matters affecting the use of intellectual property rights specifically addressed in this Agreement.

advantage of producers and users of technological knowledge and in a manner conducive to social and economic welfare, and to a balance of rights and obligations.

Article 8   Principles

1. Members may, in formulating or amending their laws and regulations, adopt measures necessary to protect public health and nutrition, and to promote the public interest in sectors of vital importance to their socio-economic and technological development, provided that such measures are consistent with the provisions of this Agreement.

2. Appropriate measures, provided that they are consistent with the provisions of this Agreement, may be needed to prevent the abuse of intellectual property rights by right holders or the resort to practices which unreasonably restrain trade or adversely affect the international transfer of technology.

PART II STANDARDS CONCERNING THE AVAILABILITY, SCOPE AND USE OF INTELLECTUAL PROPERTY RIGHTS

Section 1 Copyright And Related Rights

Article 9   Relation to the Berne Convention

1. Members shall comply with Articles 1 through 21 of the Berne Convention (1971) and the Appendix thereto. However, Members shall not have rights or obligations under this Agreement in respect of the rights conferred under Article *6bis* of that Convention or of the rights derived therefrom.

2. Copyright protection shall extend to expressions and not to ideas, procedures, methods of operation or mathematical concepts as such.

Article 10   Computer programs and compilations of data

1. Computer programs, whether in source or object code, shall be protected as literary works under the Berne Convention (1971).

2. Compilations of data or other material, whether in machine readable or other form, which by reason of the selection or arrangement of their contents constitute intellectual creations shall be protected as such. Such protection, which shall not extend to the data or material itself, shall be without prejudice to any copyright subsisting in the data or material itself.

Article 12   Term of protection

Whenever the term of protection of a work, other than a photographic work or a work of applied art, is calculated on a basis other than the life of a natural person, such term shall be no less than 50 years from the end of the calendar year of authorized publication, or, failing such authorized publication within 50 years from the making of the work, 50 years from the end of the calendar year of making.

...

Section 5 Patents

Article 27   Patentable subject matter

1. Subject to the provisions of paragraphs 2 and 3, patents shall be available for any inventions, whether products or processes, in all fields of technology, provided that they are new, involve an inventive step and are capable of industrial application.[4] Subject to paragraph 4 of Article 65, paragraph 8 of Article 70 and paragraph 3 of this Article, patents shall be available and patent rights enjoyable without discrimination as to the place of invention, the field of technology and whether products are imported or locally produced.

---

[4] For the purposes of this Article, the terms "inventive step" and "capable of industrial application" may be deemed by a Member to be synonymous with the terms "non-obvious" and "useful" respectively.

2. Members may exclude from patentability inventions, the prevention within their territory of the commercial exploitation of which is necessary to protect *ordre public* or morality, including to protect human, animal or plant life or health or to avoid serious prejudice to the environment, provided that such exclusion is not made merely because the exploitation is prohibited by their law.

3. Members may also exclude from patentability:

(a) diagnostic, therapeutic and surgical methods for the treatment of humans or animals;

(b) plants and animals other than micro-organisms, and essentially biological processes for the production of plants or animals other than non-biological and microbiological processes. However, Members shall provide for the protection of plant varieties either by patents or by an effective *sui generis* system or by any combination thereof. The provisions of this subparagraph shall be reviewed four years after the date of entry into force of the WTO Agreement.

...

PART III ENFORCEMENT OF INTELLECTUAL PROPERTY RIGHTS

Section 1 General Obligations

Article 41

1. Members shall ensure that enforcement procedures as specified in this Part are available under their law so as to permit effective action against any act of infringement of intellectual property rights covered by this Agreement, including expeditious remedies to prevent infringements and remedies which constitute a deterrent to further infringements. These procedures shall be applied in such a manner as to avoid the creation of barriers to legitimate trade and to provide for safeguards against their abuse.

2. Procedures concerning the enforcement of intellectual property rights shall be fair and equitable. They shall not be unnecessarily complicated or costly, or entail unreasonable time-limits or unwarranted delays.

3. Decisions on the merits of a case shall preferably be in writing and reasoned. They shall be made available at least to the parties to the proceeding without undue delay. Decisions on the merits of a case shall be based only on evidence in respect of which parties were offered the opportunity to be heard.

4. Parties to a proceeding shall have an opportunity for review by a judicial authority of final administrative decisions and, subject to jurisdictional provisions in a Member's law concerning the importance of a case, of at least the legal aspects of initial judicial decisions on the merits of a case. However, there shall be no obligation to provide an opportunity for review of acquittals in criminal cases.

5. It is understood that this Part does not create any obligation to put in place a judicial system for the enforcement of intellectual property rights distinct from that for the enforcement of law in general, nor does it affect the capacity of Members to enforce their law in general. Nothing in this Part creates any obligation with respect to the distribution of resources as between enforcement of intellectual property rights and the enforcement of law in general.

Uniform Domain Name Dispute Resolution Policy

(as approved by ICANN on 24 October 1999)

1   Purpose

This Uniform Domain Name Dispute Resolution Policy (the "Policy") has been adopted by the Internet Corporation for Assigned Names and Numbers ("ICANN"), is incorporated by reference into your

Registration Agreement, and sets forth the terms and conditions in connection with a dispute between you and any party other than us (the registrar) over the registration and use of an Internet domain name registered by you. Proceedings under Paragraph 4 of this Policy will be conducted according to the Rules for Uniform Domain Name Dispute Resolution Policy (the "Rules of Procedure"), which are available at www.icann.org/udrp/udrp-rules-24oct99.htm, and the selected administrative-dispute-resolution service provider's supplemental rules.

2   Your representations

By applying to register a domain name, or by asking us to maintain or renew a domain name registration, you hereby represent and warrant to us that (a) the statements that you made in your Registration Agreement are complete and accurate; (b) to your knowledge, the registration of the domain name will not infringe upon or otherwise violate the rights of any third party; (c) you are not registering the domain name for an unlawful purposes; and (d) you will not knowingly use the domain name in violation of any applicable laws or regulations. It is your responsibility to determine whether your domain name registration infringes or violates someone else's rights.

3   Cancellations, Transfers, and Changes

We will cancel, transfer or otherwise make changes to domain name registrations under the following circumstances:

(a) subject to the provisions of Paragraph 8, our receipt of written or appropriate electronic instructions from you or your authorized agent to take such action;

(b) our receipt of an order from a court or arbitral tribunal, in each case of competent jurisdiction, requiring such action; and/or

(c) our receipt of a decision of an Administrative Panel requiring such action in any administrative proceeding to which you were a party and which was conducted under this Policy or a later version of this Policy adopted by ICANN. (See Paragraph 4(i) and (k) below.)

We may also cancel, transfer or otherwise make changes to a domain name registration in accordance with the terms of your Registration Agreement or other legal requirements.

4   Mandatory administrative proceeding

This Paragraph sets forth the type of disputes for which you are required to submit to a mandatory administrative proceeding. These proceedings will be conducted before one of the administrative-dispute-resolution service providers listed at www.icann.org/udrp/approvedproviders.htm (each, a "Provider").

Applicable Disputes. You are required to submit to a mandatory administrative proceeding in the event that a third party (a "complainant") asserts to the applicable Provider, in compliance with the Rules of Procedure, that

(i)   your domain name is identical or confusingly similar to a trademark or

(ii) service mark in which the complainant has rights; and you have no rights or legitimate interests in respect of the domain name; and

(iii) your domain name has been registered and is being used in bad faith.

In the administrative proceeding, the complainant must prove that each of these three elements are present.

Evidence of Registration and Use in Bad Faith. For the purposes of Paragraph 4(a)(iii), the following circumstances, in particular but without limitation, if found by the Panel to be present, shall be evidence of the registration and use of a domain name in bad faith:

(i)   circumstances indicating that you have registered or you have acquired the domain name primarily for the purpose of selling, renting, or otherwise transferring the domain name registration to the complainant who is the owner of the trademark or service mark or to a competitor of that complainant, for valuable consideration in excess of your documented out-of-pocket costs directly related to the domain name; or

(ii)   you have registered the domain name in order to prevent the owner of the trademark or service mark from reflecting the mark in a corresponding domain name, provided that you have engaged in a pattern of such conduct; or

(iii)   you have registered the domain name primarily for the purpose of disrupting the business of a competitor; or

(iv)   by using the domain name, you have intentionally attempted to attract, for commercial gain, Internet users to your web site or other on-line location, by creating a likelihood of confusion with the complainant's mark as to the source, sponsorship, affiliation, or endorsement of your web site or location or of a product or service on your web site or location.

How to Demonstrate Your Rights to and Legitimate Interests in the Domain Name in Responding to a Complaint. When you receive a complaint, you should refer to Paragraph 5 of the Rules of Procedure in determining how your response should be prepared. Any of the following circumstances, in particular but without limitation, if found by the Panel to be proved based on its evaluation of all evidence presented, shall demonstrate your rights or legitimate interests to the domain name for purposes of Paragraph 4(a)(ii):

(i)   before any notice to you of the dispute, your use of, or demonstrable preparations to use, the domain name or a name corresponding to the domain name in connection with a bona fide offering of goods or services; or

(ii)   you (as an individual, business, or other organization) have been commonly known by the domain name, even if you have acquired no trademark or service mark rights; or

(iii)   you are making a legitimate non-commercial or fair use of the domain name, without intent for commercial gain to misleadingly divert consumers or to tarnish the trademark or service mark at issue.

Selection of Provider. The complainant shall select the Provider from among those approved by ICANN by submitting the complaint to that Provider. The selected Provider will administer the proceeding, except in cases of consolidation as described in Paragraph 4(f).

Initiation of Proceeding and Process and Appointment of Administrative Panel. The Rules of Procedure state the process for initiating and conducting a proceeding and for appointing the panel that will decide the dispute (the "Administrative Panel").

Consolidation. In the event of multiple disputes between you and a complainant, either you or the complainant may petition to consolidate the disputes before a single Administrative Panel. This petition shall be made to the first Administrative Panel appointed to hear a pending dispute between the parties. This Administrative Panel may consolidate before it any or all such disputes in its sole discretion, provided that the disputes being consolidated are governed by this Policy or a later version of this Policy adopted by ICANN.

Fees. All fees charged by a Provider in connection with any dispute before an Administrative Panel pursuant to this Policy shall be paid by the complainant, except in cases where you elect to expand the Administrative Panel from one to three panelists as provided in Paragraph 5(b)(iv) of the Rules of Procedure, in which case all fees will be split evenly by you and the complainant.

Our Involvement in Administrative Proceedings. We do not, and will not, participate in the administration or conduct of any proceeding before an Administrative Panel. In addition, we will not be liable as a result of any decisions rendered by the Administrative Panel.

Remedies. The remedies available to a complainant pursuant to any proceeding before an Administrative Panel shall be limited to requiring the cancellation of your domain name or the transfer of your domain name registration to the complainant.

Notification and Publication. The Provider shall notify us of any decision made by an Administrative Panel with respect to a domain name you have registered with us. All decisions under this Policy will be published in full over the Internet, except when an Administrative Panel determines in an exceptional case to redact portions of its decision.

Availability of Court Proceedings. The mandatory administrative proceeding requirements set forth in Paragraph 4 shall not prevent either you or the complainant from submitting the dispute to a court of competent jurisdiction for independent resolution before such mandatory administrative proceeding is commenced or after such proceeding is concluded. If an Administrative Panel decides that your domain name registration should be canceled or transferred, we will wait ten (10) business days (as observed in the location of our principal office) after we are informed by the applicable Provider of the Administrative Panel's decision before implementing that decision. We will then implement the decision unless we have received from you during that ten (10) business day period official documentation (such as a copy of a complaint, file-stamped by the clerk of the court) that you have commenced a lawsuit against the complainant in a jurisdiction to which the complainant has submitted under Paragraph 3(b)(xiii) of the Rules of Procedure. (In general, that jurisdiction is either the location of our principal office or of your address as shown in our Whois database. See Paragraphs 1 and 3(b) (xiii) of the Rules of Procedure for details.) If we receive such documentation within the ten (10) business day period, we will not implement the Administrative Panel's decision, and we will take no further action, until we receive (i) evidence satisfactory to us of a resolution between the parties; (ii) evidence satisfactory to us that your lawsuit has been dismissed or withdrawn; or (iii) a copy of an order from such court dismissing your lawsuit or ordering that you do not have the right to continue to use your domain name.

5   All other disputes and litigation

All other disputes between you and any party other than us regarding your domain name registration that are not brought pursuant to the mandatory administrative proceeding provisions of Paragraph 4 shall be resolved between you and such other party through any court, arbitration or other proceeding that may be available.

6   Our involvement in disputes

We will not participate in any way in any dispute between you and any party other than us regarding the registration and use of your domain name. You shall not name us as a party or otherwise include us in any such proceeding. In the event that we are named as a party in any such proceeding, we reserve the right to raise any and all defenses deemed appropriate, and to take any other action necessary to defend ourselves.

7   Maintaining the status quo

We will not cancel, transfer, activate, deactivate, or otherwise change the status of any domain name registration under this Policy except as provided in Paragraph 3 above.

8   Transfers during a dispute

Transfers of a Domain Name to a New Holder. You may not transfer your domain name registration to another holder (i) during a pending administrative proceeding brought pursuant to Paragraph 4 or for a period of fifteen (15) business days (as observed in the location of our principal place of business) after such proceeding is concluded; or (ii) during a pending court proceeding or arbitration commenced regarding your domain name unless the party to whom the domain name registration is being transferred agrees, in writing, to be bound by the decision of the court or arbitrator. We reserve the right to cancel any transfer of a domain name registration to another holder that is made in violation of this subparagraph.

Changing Registrars. You may not transfer your domain name registration to another registrar during a pending administrative proceeding brought pursuant to Paragraph 4 or for a period of fifteen (15) business days (as observed in the location of our principal place of business) after such proceeding is concluded. You may transfer administration of your domain name registration to another registrar during a pending court action or arbitration, provided that the domain name you have registered with us shall continue to be subject to the proceedings commenced against you in accordance with the terms of this Policy. In the event that you transfer a domain name registration to us during the pendency of a court action or arbitration, such dispute shall remain subject to the domain name dispute policy of the registrar from which the domain name registration was transferred.

9   Policy modifications

We reserve the right to modify this Policy at any time with the permission of ICANN. We will post our revised Policy at <URL> at least thirty (30) calendar days before it becomes effective. Unless this Policy has already been invoked by the submission of a complaint to a Provider, in which event the version of the Policy in effect at the time it was invoked will apply to you until the dispute is over, all such changes will be binding upon you with respect to any domain name registration dispute, whether the dispute arose before, on or after the effective date of our change. In the event that you object to a change in this Policy, your sole remedy is to cancel your domain name registration with us, provided that you will not be entitled to a refund of any fees you paid to us. The revised Policy will apply to you until you cancel your domain name registration.

Rules for Uniform Domain Name Dispute Resolution Policy (the "Rules")

(as approved by ICANN on 24 October 1999)

Administrative proceedings for the resolution of disputes under the Uniform Dispute Resolution Policy adopted by ICANN shall be governed by these Rules and also the Supplemental Rules of the Provider administering the proceedings, as posted on its web site.

1   Definitions

In these Rules:

Complainant means the party initiating a complaint concerning a domain-name registration.

ICANN refers to the Internet Corporation for Assigned Names and Numbers.

Mutual Jurisdiction means a court jurisdiction at the location of either (a) the principal office of the Registrar (provided the domain-name holder has submitted in its Registration Agreement to that jurisdiction for court adjudication of disputes concerning or arising from the use of the domain name) or (b) the domain-name holder's address as shown for the registration of the domain name in Registrar's Whois database at the time the complaint is submitted to the Provider.

Panel means an administrative panel appointed by a Provider to decide a complaint concerning a domain-name registration.

Panelist means an individual appointed by a Provider to be a member of a Panel.

Party means a Complainant or a Respondent.

Policy means the Uniform Domain Name Dispute Resolution Policy that is incorporated by reference and made a part of the Registration Agreement.

Provider means a dispute-resolution service provider approved by ICANN. A list of such Providers appears at www.icann.org/udrp/approved-providers.htm.

Registrar means the entity with which the Respondent has registered a domain name that is the subject of a complaint.

Registration Agreement means the agreement between a Registrar and a domain-name holder.

Respondent means the holder of a domain-name registration against which a complaint is initiated.

Reverse Domain Name Hijacking means using the Policy in bad faith to attempt to deprive a registered domain-name holder of a domain name.

Supplemental Rules means the rules adopted by the Provider administering a proceeding to supplement these Rules. Supplemental Rules shall not be inconsistent with the Policy or these Rules and shall cover such topics as fees, word and page limits and guidelines, the means for communicating with the Provider and the Panel, and the form of cover sheets.

2 Communications

(a) When forwarding a complaint to the Respondent, it shall be the Provider's responsibility to employ reasonably available means calculated to achieve actual notice to Respondent. Achieving actual notice, or employing the following measures to do so, shall discharge this responsibility:

  (i) sending the complaint to all postal-mail and facsimile addresses (A) shown in the domain name's registration data in Registrar's Whois database for the registered domain-name holder, the technical contact, and the administrative contact and (B) supplied by Registrar to the Provider for the registration's billing contact; and

  (ii) sending the complaint in electronic form (including annexes to the extent available in that form) by e-mail to:

  (A) the e-mail addresses for those technical, administrative, and billing contacts;

  (B) postmaster@ <the contested domain name>; and

  (C) if the domain name (or "www." followed by the domain name) resolves to an active web page (other than a generic page the Provider concludes is maintained by a registrar or ISP for parking domain-names registered by multiple domain-name holders), any e-mail address shown or e-mail links on that web page; and

  (iii) sending the complaint to any address the Respondent has notified the Provider it prefers and, to the extent practicable, to all other addresses provided to the Provider by Complainant under Paragraph 3(b)(v).

(b) Except as provided in Paragraph 2(a), any written communication to Complainant or Respondent provided for under these Rules shall be made by the preferred means stated by the Complainant or Respondent, respectively (see Paragraphs 3(b)(iii) and 5(b)(iii)), or in the absence of such specification:

  (i) by telecopy or facsimile transmission, with a confirmation of transmission; or

  (ii) by postal or courier service, postage pre-paid and return receipt requested; or

  (iii) electronically via the Internet, provided a record of its transmission is available.

(c) Any communication to the Provider or the Panel shall be made by the means and in the manner (including number of copies) stated in the Provider's Supplemental Rules.

(d) Communications shall be made in the language prescribed in Paragraph 11. E-mail communications should, if practicable, be sent in plaintext.

(e) Either Party may update its contact details by notifying the Provider and the Registrar.

(f) Except as otherwise provided in these Rules, or decided by a Panel, all communications provided for under these Rules shall be deemed to have been made:

  (i) if delivered by telecopy or facsimile transmission, on the date shown on the confirmation of transmission; or

  (ii) if by postal or courier service, on the date marked on the receipt; or

  (iii) if via the Internet, on the date that the communication was transmitted, provided that the date of transmission is verifiable.

(g) Except as otherwise provided in these Rules, all time periods calculated under these Rules to begin when a communication is made shall begin to run on the earliest date that the communication is deemed to have been made in accordance with Paragraph 2(f).

(h) Any communication by

  (i) a Panel to any Party shall be copied to the Provider and to the other Party;

  (ii) the Provider to any Party shall be copied to the other Party; and

  (iii) a Party shall be copied to the other Party, the Panel and the Provider, as the case may be.

(i) It shall be the responsibility of the sender to retain records of the fact and circumstances of sending, which shall be available for inspection by affected parties and for reporting purposes.

(j) In the event a Party sending a communication receives notification of nondelivery of the communication, the Party shall promptly notify the Panel (or, if no Panel is yet appointed, the Provider) of the circumstances of the notification.

Further proceedings concerning the communication and any response shall be as directed by the Panel (or the Provider).

3   The Complaint

(a) Any person or entity may initiate an administrative proceeding by submitting a complaint in accordance with the Policy and these Rules to any Provider approved by ICANN. (Due to capacity constraints or for other reasons, a Provider's ability to accept complaints may be suspended at times. In that event, the Provider shall refuse the submission. The person or entity may submit the complaint to another Provider.)

(b) The complaint shall be submitted in hard copy and (except to the extent not available for annexes) in electronic form and shall:

   (i)   Request that the complaint be submitted for decision in accordance with the Policy and these Rules;

   (ii) Provide the name, postal and e-mail addresses, and the telephone and telefax numbers of the Complainant and of any representative authorized to act for the Complainant in the administrative proceeding;

   (iii) Specify a preferred method for communications directed to the Complainant in the administrative proceeding (including person to be contacted, medium, and address information) for each of (A) electronic-only material and (B) material including hard copy;

   (iv) Designate whether Complainant elects to have the dispute decided by a single-member or a three-member Panel and, in the event Complainant elects a three-member Panel, provide the names and contact details of three candidates to serve as one of the Panelists (these candidates may be drawn from any ICANN-approved Provider's list of panelists);

   (v)   Provide the name of the Respondent (domain-name holder) and all information (including any postal and e-mail addresses and telephone and telefax numbers) known to Complainant regarding how to contact Respondent or any representative of Respondent, including contact information based on pre-complaint dealings, in sufficient detail to allow the Provider to send the complaint as described in Paragraph 2(a);

   (vi) Specify the domain name(s) that is/are the subject of the complaint;

   (vii) Identify the Registrar(s) with whom the domain name(s) is/are registered at the time the complaint is filed;

   (viii) Specify the trademark(s) or service mark(s) on which the complaint is based and, for each mark, describe the goods or services, if any, with which the mark is used (Complainant may also separately describe other goods and services with which it intends, at the time the complaint is submitted, to use the mark in the future.);

   (ix) Describe, in accordance with the Policy, the grounds on which the complaint is made including, in particular,

      (1) the manner in which the domain name(s) is/are identical or confusingly similar to a trademark or service mark in which the Complainant has rights; and

      (2) why the Respondent (domain-name holder) should be considered as having no rights or legitimate interests in respect of the domain name(s) that is/are the subject of the complaint; and

      (3) why the domain name(s) should be considered as having been registered and being used in bad faith

      (The description should, for elements (2) and (3), discuss any aspects of Paragraphs 4(b) and 4(c) of the Policy that are applicable. The description shall comply with any word or page limit set forth in the Provider's Supplemental Rules.);

    (x)   Specify, in accordance with the Policy, the remedies sought;

    (xi) Identify any other legal proceedings that have been commenced or terminated in connection with or relating to any of the domain name(s) that are the subject of the complaint;

    (xii) State that a copy of the complaint, together with the cover sheet as prescribed by the Provider's Supplemental Rules, has been sent or transmitted to the Respondent (domain-name holder), in accordance with Paragraph 2(b);

    (xiii) State that Complainant will submit, with respect to any challenges to a decision in the administrative proceeding canceling or transferring the domain name, to the jurisdiction of the courts in at least one specified Mutual Jurisdiction;

    (xiv) Conclude with the following statement followed by the signature of the Complainant or its authorized representative:

"Complainant agrees that its claims and remedies concerning the registration of the domain name, the dispute, or the dispute's resolution shall be solely against the domain-name holder and waives all such claims and remedies against (a) the dispute-resolution provider and panelists, except in the case of deliberate wrongdoing, (b) the registrar, (c) the registry administrator, and (d) the Internet Corporation for Assigned Names and Numbers, as well as their directors, officers, employees, and agents."

"Complainant certifies that the information contained in this Complainant is to the best of Complainant's knowledge complete and accurate, that this Complaint is not being presented for any improper purpose, such as to harass, and that the assertions in this Complaint are warranted under these Rules and under applicable law, as it now exists or as it may be extended by a good-faith and reasonable argument"; and

    (xv) Annex any documentary or other evidence, including a copy of the Policy applicable to the domain name(s) in dispute and any trademark or service mark registration upon which the complaint relies, together with a schedule indexing such evidence.

(c) The complaint may relate to more than one domain name, provided that the domain names are registered by the same domain-name holder.

4 Notification of complaint

(a) The Provider shall review the complaint for administrative compliance with the Policy and these Rules and, if in compliance, shall forward the complaint (together with the explanatory cover sheet prescribed by the Provider's Supplemental Rules) to the Respondent, in the manner prescribed by Paragraph 2(a), within three (3) calendar days following receipt of the fees to be paid by the Complaint in accordance with Paragraph 19.

(b) If the Provider finds the complaint to be administratively deficient, it shall promptly notify the Complainant and the Respondent of the nature of the deficiencies identified. The Complainant shall have five (5) calendar days within which to correct any such deficiencies, after which the administrative proceeding will be deemed withdrawn without prejudice to submission of a different complaint by Complainant.

(c) The date of commencement of the administrative proceeding shall be the date on which the Provider completes its responsibilities under Paragraph 2(a) in connection with forwarding the Complaint to the Respondent.

(d) The Provider shall immediately notify the Complainant, the Respondent, the concerned Registrar(s), and ICANN of the date of commencement of the administrative proceeding.

5 The response

(a) Within twenty (20) days of the date of commencement of the administrative proceeding the Respondent shall submit a response to the Provider.

(b) The response shall be submitted in hard copy and (except to the extent not available for annexes) in electronic form and shall:

    (i)   Respond specifically to the statements and allegations contained in the complaint and include any and all bases for the Respondent (domain-name holder) to retain registration and use of the disputed domain name (This portion of the response shall comply with any word or page limit set forth in the Provider's Supplemental Rules.);

(ii) Provide the name, postal and e-mail addresses, and the telephone and telefax numbers of the Respondent (domain-name holder) and of any representative authorized to act for the Respondent in the administrative proceeding;

(iii) Specify a preferred method for communications directed to the Respondent in the administrative proceeding (including person to be contacted, medium, and address information) for each of (A) electronic-only material and (B) material including hard copy;

(iv) If Complainant has elected a single-member panel in the Complaint (see Paragraph 3(b)(iv)), state whether Respondent elects instead to have the dispute decided by a three-member panel;

(v) If either Complainant or Respondent elects a three-member Panel, provide the names and contact details of three candidates to serve as one of the Panelists (these candidates may be drawn from any ICANN-approved Provider's list of panelists);

(vi) Identify any other legal proceedings that have been commenced or terminated in connection with or relating to any of the domain name(s) that are the subject of the complaint;

(vii) State that a copy of the response has been sent or transmitted to the Complainant, in accordance with Paragraph 2(b); and

(viii) Conclude with the following statement followed by the signature of the Respondent or its authorized representative:
"Respondent certifies that the information contained in this Response is to the best of Respondent's knowledge complete and accurate, that this Response is not being presented for any improper purpose, such as to harass, and that the assertions in this Response are warranted under these Rules and under applicable law, as it now exists or as it may be extended by a good-faith and reasonable argument"; and

(ix) Annex any documentary or other evidence upon which the Respondent relies, together with a schedule indexing such documents.

(c) If Complainant has elected to have the dispute decided by a single-member Panel and Respondent elects a three-member Panel, Respondent shall be required to pay one-half of the applicable fee for a three-member Panel as set forth in the Provider's Supplemental Rules. This payment shall be made together with the submission of the response to the Provider. In the event that the required payment is not made, the dispute shall be decided by a single-member Panel.

(d) At the request of the Respondent, the Provider may, in exceptional cases, extend the period of time for the filing of the response. The period may also be extended by written stipulation between the Parties, provided the stipulation is approved by the Provider.

(e) If a Respondent does not submit a response, in the absence of exceptional circumstances, the Panel shall decide the dispute based upon the complaint.

6 Appointment of the panel and timing of decision

(a) Each Provider shall maintain and publish a publicly available list of panelists and their qualifications.

(b) If neither the Complainant nor the Respondent has elected a three-member Panel (Paragraphs 3(b)(iv) and 5(b)(iv)), the Provider shall appoint, within five (5) calendar days following receipt of the response by the Provider, or the lapse of the time period for the submission thereof, a single Panelist from its list of panelists. The fees for a single-member Panel shall be paid entirely by the Complainant.

(c) If either the Complainant or the Respondent elects to have the dispute decided by a three-member Panel, the Provider shall appoint three Panelists in accordance with the procedures identified in Paragraph 6(e). The fees for a three-member Panel shall be paid in their entirety by the Complainant, except where the election for a three-member Panel was made by the Respondent, in which case the applicable fees shall be shared equally between the Parties.

(d) Unless it has already elected a three-member Panel, the Complainant shall submit to the Provider, within five (5) calendar days of communication of a response in which the Respondent elects a three-member Panel, the names and contact details of three candidates to serve as one of the Panelists. These candidates may be drawn from any ICANN-approved Provider's list of panelists.

(e) In the event that either the Complainant or the Respondent elects a three-member Panel, the Provider shall endeavor to appoint one Panelist from the list of candidates provided by each of the Complainant and the Respondent. In the event the Provider is unable within five (5) calendar days to secure the appointment of a Panelist on its customary terms from either Party's list of candidates, the Provider shall make that appointment from its list of panelists. The third Panelist shall be appointed by the Provider from a list of five candidates submitted by the Provider to the Parties, the Provider's selection from among the five being made in a manner that reasonably balances the preferences of both Parties, as they may specify to the Provider within five (5) calendar days of the Provider's submission of the five-candidate list to the Parties.

(f) Once the entire Panel is appointed, the Provider shall notify the Parties of the Panelists appointed and the date by which, absent exceptional circumstances, the Panel shall forward its decision on the complaint to the Provider.

7   Impartiality and independence

A Panelist shall be impartial and independent and shall have, before accepting appointment, disclosed to the Provider any circumstances giving rise to justifiable doubt as to the Panelist's impartiality or independence. If, at any stage during the administrative proceeding, new circumstances arise that could give rise to justifiable doubt as to the impartiality or independence of the Panelist, that Panelist shall promptly disclose such circumstances to the Provider. In such event, the Provider shall have the discretion to appoint a substitute Panelist.

8   Communication between parties and the panel

No Party or anyone acting on its behalf may have any unilateral communication with the Panel. All communications between a Party and the Panel or the Provider shall be made to a case administrator appointed by the Provider in the manner prescribed in the Provider's Supplemental Rules.

9   Transmission of the file to the panel

The Provider shall forward the file to the Panel as soon as the Panelist is appointed in the case of a Panel consisting of a single member, or as soon as the last Panelist is appointed in the case of a three-member Panel.

10   General powers of the panel

(a) The Panel shall conduct the administrative proceeding in such manner as it considers appropriate in accordance with the Policy and these Rules.

(b) In all cases, the Panel shall ensure that the Parties are treated with equality and that each Party is given a fair opportunity to present its case.

(c) The Panel shall ensure that the administrative proceeding takes place with due expedition. It may, at the request of a Party or on its own motion, extend, in exceptional cases, a period of time fixed by these Rules or by the Panel.

(d) The Panel shall determine the admissibility, relevance, materiality and weight of the evidence.

(e) A Panel shall decide a request by a Party to consolidate multiple domain name disputes in accordance with the Policy and these Rules.

11   Language of proceedings

(a) Unless otherwise agreed by the Parties, or specified otherwise in the Registration Agreement, the language of the administrative proceeding shall be the language of the

Registration Agreement, subject to the authority of the Panel to determine otherwise, having regard to the circumstances of the administrative proceeding.

(b) The Panel may order that any documents submitted in languages other than the language of the administrative proceeding be accompanied by a translation in whole or in part into the language of the administrative proceeding.

12   Further statements

In addition to the complaint and the response, the Panel may request, in its sole discretion, further statements or documents from either of the Parties.

13   In-person hearings

There shall be no in-person hearings (including hearings by teleconference, videoconference, and web conference), unless the Panel determines, in its sole discretion and as an exceptional matter, that such a hearing is necessary for deciding the complaint.

14   Default

(a) In the event that a Party, in the absence of exceptional circumstances, does not comply with any of the time periods established by these Rules or the Panel, the Panel shall proceed to a decision on the complaint.

(b) If a Party, in the absence of exceptional circumstances, does not comply with any provision of, or requirement under, these Rules or any request from the Panel, the Panel shall draw such inferences therefrom as it considers appropriate.

15   Panel decisions

(a) A Panel shall decide a complaint on the basis of the statements and documents submitted and in accordance with the Policy, these Rules and any rules and principles of law that it deems applicable.

(b) In the absence of exceptional circumstances, the Panel shall forward its decision on the complaint to the Provider within fourteen (14) days of its appointment pursuant to Paragraph 6.

(c) In the case of a three-member Panel, the Panel's decision shall be made by a majority.

(d) The Panel's decision shall be in writing, provide the reasons on which it is based, indicate the date on which it was rendered and identify the name(s) of the Panelist(s).

(e) Panel decisions and dissenting opinions shall normally comply with the guidelines as to length set forth in the Provider's Supplemental Rules. Any dissenting opinion shall accompany the majority decision. If the Panel concludes that the dispute is not within the scope of Paragraph 4(a) of the Policy, it shall so state. If after considering the submissions the Panel finds that the complaint was brought in bad faith, for example in an attempt at Reverse Domain Name Hijacking or was brought primarily to harass the domain-name holder, the Panel shall declare in its decision that the complaint was brought in bad faith and constitutes an abuse of the administrative proceeding.

16   Communication of decision to parties

(a) Within three (3) calendar days after receiving the decision from the Panel, the Provider shall communicate the full text of the decision to each Party, the concerned Registrar(s), and ICANN. The concerned Registrar(s) shall immediately communicate to each Party, the Provider, and ICANN the date for the implementation of the decision in accordance with the Policy.

(b) Except if the Panel determines otherwise (see Paragraph 4(j) of the Policy), the Provider shall publish the full decision and the date of its implementation on a publicly accessible web site. In any event, the portion of any decision determining a complaint to have been brought in bad faith (see Paragraph 15(e) of these Rules) shall be published.

17   Settlement or other grounds for termination

(a) If, before the Panel's decision, the Parties agree on a settlement, the Panel shall terminate the administrative proceeding.

    (b) If, before the Panel's decision is made, it becomes unnecessary or impossible to continue the administrative proceeding for any reason, the Panel shall terminate the administrative proceeding, unless a Party raises justifiable grounds for objection within a period of time to be determined by the Panel.

18   Effect of court proceedings

    (a) In the event of any legal proceedings initiated prior to or during an administrative proceeding in respect of a domain-name dispute that is the subject of the complaint, the Panel shall have the discretion to decide whether to suspend or terminate the administrative proceeding, or to proceed to a decision.

    (b) In the event that a Party initiates any legal proceedings during the pendency of an administrative proceeding in respect of a domain-name dispute that is the subject of the complaint, it shall promptly notify the Panel and the Provider. See Paragraph 8 above.

19   Fees

    (a) The Complainant shall pay to the Provider an initial fixed fee, in accordance with the Provider's Supplemental Rules, within the time and in the amount required. A Respondent electing under Paragraph 5(b)(iv) to have the dispute decided by a three-member Panel, rather than the single-member Panel elected by the Complainant, shall pay the Provider one-half the fixed fee for a three-member Panel. See Paragraph 5(c). In all other cases, the Complainant shall bear all of the Provider's fees, except as prescribed under Paragraph 19(d). Upon appointment of the Panel, the Provider shall refund the appropriate portion, if any, of the initial fee to the Complainant, as specified in the Provider's Supplemental Rules.

    (b) No action shall be taken by the Provider on a complaint until it has received from Complainant the initial fee in accordance with Paragraph 19(a).

    (c) If the Provider has not received the fee within ten (10) calendar days of receiving the complaint, the complaint shall be deemed withdrawn and the administrative proceeding terminated.

    (d) In exceptional circumstances, for example in the event an in-person hearing is held, the Provider shall request the Parties for the payment of additional fees, which shall be established in agreement with the Parties and the Panel.

20   Exclusion of liability

Except in the case of deliberate wrongdoing, neither the Provider nor a Panelist shall be liable to a Party for any act or omission in connection with any administrative proceeding under these Rules.

21   Amendments

The version of these Rules in effect at the time of the submission of the complaint to the Provider shall apply to the administrative proceeding commenced thereby. These Rules may not be amended without the express written approval of ICANN.

Nominet Dispute Resolution Service Policy

(Version 2, September 2004)

1.   Definitions

Abusive Registration means a Domain Name which either:

    i.   was registered or otherwise acquired in a manner which, at the time when the registration or acquisition took place, took unfair advantage of or was unfairly detrimental to the Complainant's Rights; OR

    ii. has been used in a manner which took unfair advantage of or was unfairly detrimental to the Complainant's Rights;

Complainant means a third party who asserts to us the elements set out in paragraph 2 of this Policy and according to the Procedure, or, if there are multiple complainants, the "lead complainant" (see Procedure paragraph 3(b));

Contract means the contract between us and the Respondent, made up of our Terms and Conditions, the Rules for .uk domain and sub-domains, this Policy and the Procedure;

Days means unless otherwise stated any day other than Saturday, Sunday or any Bank or public holiday in England and Wales;

Decision means the decision reached by an Expert and where applicable includes decisions of an appeal panel;

Dispute Resolution Service means the service provided by us according to this Policy and the Procedure;

Domain Name means a domain name registered in any sub-domain of the .uk domain;

Expert means the expert(s) we appoint under paragraphs 8 or 18 of the Procedure;

Informal Mediation means impartial mediation which we conduct to facilitate an acceptable resolution to the dispute;

ISP means the internet service provider through which the Domain Name in dispute has been registered or is hosted;

Party means a Complainant or Respondent and "Parties" has a corresponding meaning;

Procedure means the Procedure for the conduct of proceedings under the Dispute Resolution Service;

Respondent means the person (including a legal person) in whose name or on whose behalf a Domain Name is registered and against whom the Complainant makes a complaint;

Rights includes, but is not limited to, rights enforceable under English law. However, a Complainant will be unable to rely on rights in a name or term which is wholly descriptive of the Complainant's business;

we means Nominet UK (company no. 3203859) whose registered office is at Sandford Gate, Sandy Lane West, Littlemore, Oxford, OX4 6LB and "us" and "our" have corresponding meanings.

2. Dispute Resolution Service

    a. A Respondent must submit to proceedings under the Dispute Resolution Service if a Complainant asserts to us, according to the Procedure, that:

        i. The Complainant has Rights in respect of a name or mark which is identical or similar to the Domain Name; and

        ii. The Domain Name, in the hands of the Respondent, is an Abusive Registration.

    b. The Complainant is required to prove to the Expert that both elements are present on the balance of probabilities.

    c. We recommend that both Parties use our guidance and help information, which can be found on our website.

3. Evidence of Abusive Registration

    a. A non-exhaustive list of factors which may be evidence that the Domain Name is an Abusive Registration is as follows:

        i. Circumstances indicating that the Respondent has registered or otherwise acquired the Domain Name primarily:

            A. for the purposes of selling, renting or otherwise transferring the Domain Name to the Complainant or to a competitor of the Complainant, for valuable consideration in excess of the Respondent's documented out-of-pocket costs directly associated with acquiring or using the Domain Name;

            B. as a blocking registration against a name or mark in which the Complainant has Rights; or

            C. for the purpose of unfairly disrupting the business of the Complainant;

        ii. Circumstances indicating that the Respondent is using the Domain Name in a way which has confused people or businesses into believing that the Domain Name is registered to, operated or authorised by, or otherwise connected with the Complainant;

iii. The Complainant can demonstrate that the Respondent is engaged in a pattern of registrations where the Respondent is the registrant of domain names (under .uk or otherwise) which correspond to well known names or trade marks in which the Respondent has no apparent rights, and the Domain Name is part of that pattern;

iv. It is independently verified that the Respondent has given false contact details to us; or

v. The domain name was registered as a result of a relationship between the Complainant and the Respondent, and the Complainant:

   A. has been using the domain name registration exclusively; and

   B. paid for the registration and/or renewal of the domain name registration.

b. Failure on the Respondent's part to use the Domain Name for the purposes of e-mail or a web-site is not in itself evidence that the Domain Name is an Abusive Registration.

c. There shall be a presumption of Abusive Registration if the Complainant proves that Respondent has been found to have made an Abusive Registration in three (3) or more Dispute Resolution Service cases in the two (2) years before the Complaint was filed. This presumption can be rebutted (see paragraph 4 (c)).

4. How the Respondent may demonstrate in its response that the Domain Name is not an Abusive Registration

a. A non-exhaustive list of factors which may be evidence that the Domain Name is not an Abusive Registration is as follows:

i. Before being aware of the Complainant's cause for complaint (not necessarily the "complaint" under the DRS), the Respondent has

   A. used or made demonstrable preparations to use the Domain Name or a Domain Name which is similar to the Domain Name in connection with a genuine offering of goods or services;

   B. been commonly known by the name or legitimately connected with a mark which is identical or similar to the Domain Name;

   C. made legitimate non-commercial or fair use of the Domain Name; or

ii. The Domain Name is generic or descriptive and the Respondent is making fair use of it;

iii. In relation to paragraph 3(a)(v); that the Registrant's holding of the Domain Name is consistent with an express term of a written agreement entered into by the Parties; or

iv. In relation to paragraphs 3(a)(iii) and/or 3(c); that the Domain Name is not part of a wider pattern or series of registrations because the Domain Name is of a significantly different type or character to the other domain names registered by the Respondent.

b. Fair use may include sites operated solely in tribute to or in criticism of a person or business.

c. If paragraph 3(c) applies, to succeed the Respondent must rebut the presumption by proving in the Response that the registration of the Domain Name is not an Abusive Registration.

5. Informal Mediation

a. After we have received the Parties' submissions under the Procedure, we will initiate and conduct a period of Informal Mediation under paragraph 7 of the Procedure.

6. Without prejudice

a. Documents and information which are "without prejudice" (or are marked as being "without prejudice") may be used in submissions and may be considered by the Expert except that the Expert will not consider such materials if:

i. they are generated within Informal Mediation; or

ii. the Expert believes that it is in the interests of justice that the document or information be excluded from consideration.

7. Appointment of Expert

a. If an acceptable resolution cannot be found by Informal Mediation we will notify the Parties that we will appoint an Expert when the Complainant has paid the applicable fees set out in paragraph 21(a) of the Procedure and within the time specified in paragraph 21(c) of the Procedure. The Expert will come to a written Decision.

8. **Notification and publication**
   a. We will communicate a Decision to the Parties according to paragraph 17 of the Procedure and will publish all Decisions in full on our web site.
   b. Fees are payable by the Complainant or otherwise according to paragraph 22 of the Procedure only if an acceptable resolution has not been reached by Informal Mediation and once we have notified the Parties that an Expert is to be appointed.
   c. Decisions may contain the contact details of the Parties and the Parties' consent to contact details being displayed in this way.

9. **Exclusion of liability**
   a. Neither we nor our directors, officers, employees or servants nor any Expert shall be liable to a party for anything done or omitted in connection with any proceedings under the Dispute Resolution Service unless the act or omission is shown to have been in bad faith.

10. **Appeal, repeat complaints and availability of court proceedings**
   a. Either Party will have the right to appeal a Decision under paragraph 18 of the Procedure. The appeal panel will consider appeals on the basis of a full review of the matter and may review procedural matters.
   b. We may refer questions of interpretation of the Policy and Procedure to the appeal panel. Any decision rendered as a result of our referral will not affect any Decision previously made under the Dispute Resolution Service.
   c. We will publish decisions of the appeal panel. Appeal decisions will not have precedent value, but will be of persuasive value to Experts in future decisions.
   d. The operation of the Dispute Resolution Service will not prevent either the Complainant or the Respondent from submitting the dispute to a court of competent jurisdiction.
   e. If a complaint has reached the Decision stage on a previous occasion it will not be reconsidered (but it may be appealed, see paragraph 10(a) and Procedure paragraph 18) by an Expert. If the Expert finds that the complaint is a resubmission of an earlier complaint he or she shall reject the complaint without a consideration of its merits.
   f. In determining whether a complaint is a resubmission of an earlier complaint, or contains a material difference that justifies a re-hearing the Expert shall consider the following questions:
      i. Are the Complainant, the Respondent and the domain name in issue the same as in the earlier case?
      ii. Does the substance of the complaint relate to acts that occurred prior to or subsequent to the close of submissions in the earlier case?
      iii. If the substance of the complaint relates to acts that occurred prior to the close of submissions in the earlier case, are there any exceptional grounds for the rehearing or reconsideration, bearing in mind the need to protect the integrity and smooth operation of the Policy and Procedure?
      iv. If the substance of the complaint relates to acts that occurred subsequent to the close of submissions in the earlier decision, acts on which the re-filed complaint is based should not be, in substance, the same as the acts on which the previous complaint was based.
   g. A non-exhaustive list of examples which may be exceptional enough to justify a re-hearing under paragraph 10(f)(iii) include:
      i. serious misconduct on the part of the Expert, a party, witness or lawyer;
      ii. false evidence having been offered to the Expert;
      iii. the discovery of credible and material evidence which could not have been reasonably foreseen or known for the Complainant to have included it in the evidence in support of the earlier complaint;
      iv. a breach of natural justice; and
      v. the avoidance of an unconscionable result.

11. Implementation of Expert Decisions

a. If the Expert makes a Decision that a Domain Name registration should be cancelled, suspended, transferred or otherwise amended, we will implement that Decision by making any necessary changes to the Register according to the process set out in paragraph 17 of the Procedure. We will use the details set out in the Complaint form unless you specify other details to us in good time.

12. Other action by us

a. We will not cancel, transfer, activate, deactivate or otherwise change any Domain Name registration except as set out in paragraph 11 above and as provided under paragraphs 6.3 or 16 to 19 of the Terms and Conditions.

13. Transfers during a dispute

a. A Respondent may not transfer a Domain Name registration:

   i. if the electronic form of a complaint has been received by our Dispute Resolution Service staff and the matter is pending the receipt of a valid paper copy to confirm the complaint (to a maximum of five (5) Days); or

   ii. whilst proceedings under the Dispute Resolution Service are ongoing in relation to the Domain Name or for a period of ten (10) Days after their conclusion, unless to the Complainant as a result of a settlement reached between the Parties and approved by us whether or not pursuant to Informal Mediation; or

   iii. whilst a court proceeding or arbitration in respect of the Domain Name registration is ongoing in a court of competent jurisdiction.

We reserve the right to reverse any transfer of a Domain Name registration which does not comply with this paragraph.

b. A Respondent may not without the Complainant's consent (which the Complainant will not unreasonably withhold) transfer the hosting of a Domain Name to another ISP whilst proceedings under the Dispute Resolution Service are ongoing in relation to the Domain Name or for a period of ten (10) Days after the conclusion of the Dispute Resolution Service.

14. Modifications to the Policy and Procedure of the Dispute Resolution Service

a. The internet is an emerging and evolving medium and the regulatory and administrative framework under which we operate is constantly developing. For these reasons we reserve the right to make reasonable modifications to the Policy and Procedure at any time. We will only do so when we have good reason. Except where we are acting in pursuance of a statutory requirement or a court order, changes will be implemented following a process of open public consultation. Each such change will be published in advance (where practicable, 30 calendar days in advance) on our web site: http://www.nominet.org.uk/ and will become binding and effective upon the date specified therein.

b. The Respondent will be bound by the Policy and Procedure which are current at the time the Dispute Resolution Service is commenced until the dispute is concluded.

Procedure for the conduct of proceedings under the Dispute Resolution Service

(NOMINET Rules of Procedure, Version 2, September 2004)

1. Definitions

Abusive Registration means a Domain Name which either:

   i. was registered or otherwise acquired in a manner which, at the time when the registration or acquisition took place, took unfair advantage of or was unfairly detrimental to the Complainant's Rights; OR

   ii. has been used in a manner which took unfair advantage of or was unfairly detrimental to the Complainant's Rights;

Complainant means a third party who asserts to us the elements set out in paragraph 2 of the Policy and according to this Procedure, or, if there are multiple Complainants, the "lead complainant" (see paragraph 3(b));

Contract means the contract between us and the Respondent, made up of our Terms and Conditions, the Rules for .uk domain and sub-domains, the Policy and this Procedure;

Days means unless otherwise stated any day other than Saturday, Sunday or any Bank or public holiday in England and Wales;

Decision means the decision reached by an Expert and where applicable includes decisions of an appeal panel;

Dispute Resolution Service means the service provided by us according to the Policy and this Procedure;

Domain Name means a domain name registered in any sub-domain of the .uk domain;

Expert means the expert(s) we appoint under paragraphs 8 or 18 of this Procedure;

Informal Mediation means impartial mediation which we conduct to facilitate an acceptable resolution to the dispute;

ISP means the internet service provider through which the Domain Name in dispute has been registered or is hosted;

Party means a Complainant or Respondent and "Parties" has a corresponding meaning;

Policy means Nominet's Dispute Resolution Service Policy;

Respondent means the person (including a legal person) in whose name or on whose behalf a Domain Name is registered and against whom the Complainant makes a complaint;

Reverse Domain Name Hijacking means using the Policy in bad faith in an attempt to deprive a registered domain-name holder of a domain name;

Rights includes, but is not limited to, rights enforceable under English law. However, a Complainant will be unable to rely on rights in a name or term which is wholly descriptive of the Complainant's business;

We means Nominet UK (company no. 3203859) whose registered office is at Minerva House, Edmund Halley Road, Oxford Science Park, Oxford, OX4 4DQ and "us" and "our" have corresponding meanings.

2. Communication

   a. We will send a complaint (see paragraph 3) to the Respondent by using, in our discretion, any of the following means:

      i. sending the complaint by first class post, fax or e-mail to the Respondent at the contact details shown as the registrant or other contacts in our Domain Name register database entry for the Domain Name in dispute;

      ii. sending the complaint in electronic form (including attachments to the extent available in that form) by e-mail to;

         A. postmaster@<the Domain Name in dispute>; or

         B. if the Domain Name resolves to an active web page (other than a generic page which we conclude is maintained by an ISP for parking Domain Names), to any e-mail address shown or e-mail links on that web page so far as this is practicable; or

      iii. sending the complaint to any addresses provided to us by the Complainant under paragraph 3(b)(iii) so far as this is practicable.

   b. Except as set out in paragraph 2(a) above, all written communication to a Party or a Party's representative under the Policy or this Procedure shall be made by fax, first class post or e-mail.

   c. Communication shall be made in English. E-mail communications should be sent in plain text so far as this is practicable.

   d. During the course of proceedings under the Dispute Resolution Service, if either Party wishes to change its contact details it must notify us of all changes.

e. Except as otherwise provided in this Procedure or as otherwise decided by us or if appointed, the Expert, all communications provided for under this Procedure shall be deemed to have been received:

    i.   if sent by facsimile, on the date transmitted; or

    ii. if sent by first class post, on the second Day after posting; or

    iii. if sent via the Internet, on the date that the communication was transmitted;

    iv. and, unless otherwise provided in this Procedure, the time periods provided for under the Policy and this Procedure shall be calculated accordingly.

f. Any communication (except for communications relating to Informal Mediation) between:

    i.   us and any Party shall be copied by us to the other Party and if appointed, the Expert, subject to paragraph (13), below; and

    ii. a Party to another Party shall be copied by the sender to us and we will copy such correspondence to the Expert, if appointed.

3. The Complaint

a. Any person or entity may submit a complaint to us in accordance with the Policy and this Procedure. In exceptional circumstances, we may have to suspend our ability to accept complaints. If so, we will post a message to that effect on our web site which will indicate when the suspension is likely to be lifted.

b. More than one person or entity may jointly make a complaint. Where this occurs the joint Complainants must:

    i.   all sign the hard copy of the complaint (or have it signed on their behalf);

    ii. specify one of the Complainants, or a single representative, who will be the "lead Complainant" who will receive correspondence on behalf of all the Complainants and is entitled to act on behalf of them all (e.g. in Informal Mediation); and

    iii. specify which Complainant the Complainants wish to become the sole registrant of each Domain Name(s) which are the subject of the complaint if the Complainants are successful (this does not bind the Expert).

c. The Complainant must send the complaint to us in hard copy and (except to the extent not available for attachments) in electronic form. The complaint shall:—

    i.   not exceed 2000 words (not including the text set out in paragraph 3(c)(ix) below and annexes);

    ii. specify whether the Complainant wishes to be contacted direct or through an authorised representative, and set out the e-mail address, telephone number, fax number and postal address which should be used;

    iii. set out any of the Respondent's contact details which are known to the Complainant;

    iv. specify the Domain Name which is the subject of the dispute and the name or mark which is identical or similar to the Domain Name and in which the Complainant asserts it has Rights;

    v. describe in accordance with the Policy the grounds on which the complaint is made including in particular: what Rights the Complainant asserts in the name or mark; why the Domain Name should be considered to be an Abusive Registration in the hands of the Respondent; and discuss any applicable aspects of paragraph 3 of the Policy, as well as any other grounds which support the Complainant's assertion;

    vi. specify whether the Complainant is seeking to have the Domain Name transferred, suspended, cancelled or otherwise amended;

    vii. tell us whether any legal proceedings have been commenced or terminated in connection with the Domain Name which is the subject of the complaint;

    viii. state that the Complainant will submit to the exclusive jurisdiction of the English courts with respect to any legal proceedings seeking to reverse the effect of a Decision requiring the suspension, cancellation, transfer or other amendment to a Domain

Name registration, and that the Complainant agrees that any such legal proceedings will be governed by English law;

ix. conclude with the following statement followed by the signature of the Complainant or its authorised representative:—

"The Complainant agrees that its claims and remedies concerning the registration of the Domain Name, the dispute, or the dispute's resolution shall be solely against the Respondent and that neither Nominet UK nor its directors, officers, employees or servants nor any Expert shall be liable for anything done or omitted in connection with any proceedings under the Dispute Resolution Service unless the act or omission is shown to have been in bad faith.";

"The information contained in this complaint is to the best of the Complainant's knowledge true and complete. This complaint is not being presented in bad faith and the matters stated in this complaint comply with the Procedure and applicable law."; and

"If the Expert orders a transfer of the domain name(s) then I agree to be bound by Nominet's Terms and Conditions for the Registration of Domain Names, and in particular the provisions relating to Nominet's processing of personal data."

x. attach three copies of any documentary or other evidence on which the Complainant relies including correspondence and any trade mark registration and/or evidence of use of or reputation in a name or mark, together with an index of the material attached.

d. The complaint may relate to more than one Domain Name, provided that those Domain Names are registered in the name of the Respondent.

4. Notification of Complaint

a. We will check that the complaint complies with the Policy and this Procedure and, if so, we will forward it to the Respondent together with our explanatory coversheet within three (3) Days of our receipt of the complaint.

b. If we find that the complaint does not comply with the Policy and this Procedure, we will promptly notify the Complainant of the deficiencies we have identified. The Complainant shall have three (3) Days from receipt of notification within which to correct the deficiencies and return the complaint to us, failing which we will deem the complaint to be withdrawn. This will not prevent the Complainant submitting a different complaint to us.

c. Proceedings under the Dispute Resolution Service will commence on the earliest date upon which the complaint is deemed to have been received by the Respondent in accordance with paragraph 2(e) of this Procedure. We will promptly notify the Parties of the date of commencement of such proceedings.

5. The Response

a. Within fifteen (15) Days of the date of commencement of proceedings under the Dispute Resolution Service, the Respondent shall submit a response to us.

b. Within three (3) Days following our receipt of the response, we will forward the response to the Complainant.

c. The Respondent must send the response to us in hard copy and (except to the extent not available for attachments) in electronic form to us at the addresses set out in our explanatory coversheet. The response shall:

i. not exceed 2000 words (not including the text set out in paragraph 5(c)(v) and annexes);

ii. include any grounds the Respondent wishes to rely upon to rebut the Complainant's assertions under 3(c)(v) above including any relevant factors set out in paragraph 4 of the Policy;

iii. specify whether the Respondent wishes to be contacted direct or through an authorised representative, and set out the e-mail address, telephone number, fax number and postal address which should be used;

    iv. tell us whether any legal proceedings have been commenced or terminated in connection with the Domain Name which is the subject of the complaint;

    v. conclude with the following statement followed by the signature of the Respondent or its authorised representative:—

> *"The information contained in this response is to the best of the Respondent's knowledge true and complete and the matters stated in this response comply with the Procedure and applicable law."*; and

    vi. attach three copies of any documentary or other evidence on which the Respondent relies including correspondence and any trade mark registration and/or evidence of use of or reputation in a name or mark together with an index of the material attached.

d. If the Respondent does not submit a response, we will notify the Parties that we will appoint the Expert on our receipt from the Complainant of the applicable fees according to paragraph 21 and in the absence of exceptional circumstances.

6. Reply by the Complainant

a. Within five (5) Days of receiving the response from us, the Complainant may submit to us a reply to the Respondent's response, which shall not exceed 2000 words (not including annexes). If a reply is submitted it must be submitted in hard copy (including three copies of all annexes) and as far as possible in electronic form to us. If the Complainant does not submit a reply to us within five (5) Days we will proceed to Informal Mediation.

7. Informal Mediation

a. Within three (3) Days of our receipt of the Complainant's reply (or the expiry of the deadline to do so), we will begin to conduct Informal Mediation. Informal Mediation will be conducted in a manner which we, in our sole discretion, consider appropriate. No Informal Mediation will occur if the Respondent does not file a Response.

b. Negotiations conducted between the Parties during Informal Mediation (including any information obtained from or in connection to negotiations) shall be confidential, that is they will not be shown to the Expert. Neither we nor any Party may reveal details of such negotiations to any third parties unless a court of competent jurisdiction orders disclosure, or we or either Party are required to do so by applicable laws or regulations. Neither Party shall use any information gained during mediation for any ulterior or collateral purpose or include it in any submission likely to be seen by any Expert, judge or arbitrator in this dispute or any later dispute or litigation.

c. If the Parties reach a settlement during Informal Mediation then the existence, nature and terms of the settlement shall be confidential, unless the Parties specifically agree otherwise or a court of competent jurisdiction orders otherwise.

d. No binding verbal agreements can be reached as part of the Informal Mediation: any settlement reached by the Parties must be in writing or similar electronic form to be enforceable.

e. If the Parties do not achieve an acceptable resolution through Informal Mediation within ten (10) Days, we will send notice to the Parties that we will appoint an Expert when the Complainant has paid the applicable fees set out under paragraph 21(a) within the time limit specified in paragraph 21(c). We will tell the Expert whether or not Informal Mediation occurred, but we will not tell the Expert what happened during Informal Mediation or why it failed to resolve the dispute.

f. No Party may ask us (including our directors, officers, employees, contractors, agents and any Expert) to reveal information or materials gained as a result of any Informal Mediation under the Dispute Resolution Service unless such disclosure has been ordered by a court of competent jurisdiction. Neither Party shall call the Expert or us (including our directors, officers, employees, contractors, or agents) as a witness (either in person or to produce documents or other materials) in any proceedings which arise from, or are in connection with, the matters discussed in the mediation.

8. **Appointment of the Expert and timing of decision**
   a. If we do not receive the Complainant's request to refer the matter to an Expert together with the applicable fees within ten (10) Days of the Complainant's receipt of the notice referred to in paragraph 7(e) above, we will deem the complaint to be withdrawn. This will not prevent the Complainant submitting a different complaint to us.
   b. Within five (5) Days of our receipt of the applicable fees from the Complainant, we will appoint an Expert on a rotational basis from our list of Experts.
   c. We will maintain and publish a list of Experts and their qualifications.
   d. Once we have appointed the Expert, we will notify the Parties of the name of the Expert appointed and the date by which, except in exceptional circumstances, the Expert will forward his or her Decision to us.

9. **Impartiality and independence**
   a. The Expert shall be impartial and independent and both before accepting the appointment and during the proceedings will disclose to us any circumstances giving rise to justifiable doubt as to his or her impartiality or independence. We will have the discretion to appoint a substitute Expert if necessary in which case we will adjust the timetable accordingly.

10. **Communication between Parties and the Expert**
    a. A Party and the Expert must not communicate directly. All communication between a Party and the Expert must be made through us.

11. **Transmission of the file to the Expert**
    a. We will forward the file except for documents relating to Informal Mediation to the Expert as soon as the Expert is appointed.

12. **General powers of Nominet and the Expert**
    a. We, or the Expert if appointed, may in exceptional cases extend any period of time in proceedings under the Dispute Resolution Service.
    b. The Expert shall determine the admissibility, relevance, materiality and weight of the evidence.
    c. We shall decide a request by a Party to consolidate multiple Domain Name disputes in accordance with the Policy and this Procedure.

13. **Further statement**
    a. In addition to the complaint, the response and if applicable the reply and any appeal, the Expert may request further statements or documents from the Parties. The Expert will not be obliged to consider any statements or documents from the Parties which he or she has not received according to the Policy or this Procedure or which he or she has not requested.
    b. Any communication with us intended to be passed to the Expert which is not part of the standard process (e.g. other than a complaint, response, reply, submissions requested by the Expert, appeal notice or appeal notice response) is a "non-standard submission". Any non-standard submission must contain as a separate, first paragraph, a brief explanation of why there is an exceptional need for the non-standard submission. We will pass this explanation to the Expert, and the remainder will only be passed to the Expert at his or her sole discretion. If there is no explanation, we may not pass on the document or information.

14. **In person hearings**
    a. No in person hearings (including hearings by conference call, video conference and web conference) will be held unless the Expert determines in his or her sole discretion and in exceptional cases, that such a hearing is necessary to enable him or her to come to a Decision.

15. **Default**
    a. If we find that a submission by a Party exceeds the word limit, we will return the submission to that Party who will within three (3) Days return a submission to us which complies with the word limits. If we do not receive the submission back from:

     i. the Complainant, we will deem the complaint to be withdrawn, which will not stop the Complainant from submitting a different complaint; or

    ii. the Respondent, we will notify the Parties that we will appoint the Expert when the Complainant has paid the applicable fees set out in paragraph 21 and in the absence of exceptional circumstances. Once appointed the Expert will decide the dispute based upon the complaint and evidence attached to it.

b. If, in the absence of exceptional circumstances, a Party does not comply with any time period laid down in the Policy or this Procedure, the Expert will proceed to a Decision on the complaint. If the Expert has not been appointed Nominet shall take any action which it deems appropriate in its sole discretion, unless prescribed by this Procedure.

c. If, in the absence of exceptional circumstances, a Party does not comply with any provision in the Policy or this Procedure or any request by us or the Expert, the Expert will draw such inferences from the Party's non compliance as he or she considers appropriate.

16. Expert Decision

a. The Expert will decide a complaint on the basis of the Parties' submissions, the Policy and the Procedure.

b. Unless exceptional circumstances apply, an Expert shall forward his or her Decision to us within ten (10) Days of his or her appointment pursuant to paragraph 8.

c. The Decision shall be in writing and signed, provide the reasons on which it is based, indicate the date on which it was made and identify the name of the Expert.

d. If the Expert concludes that the dispute is not within the scope of paragraph 2 of the Policy, he or she shall state that this is the case. If, after considering the submissions, the Expert finds that the complaint was brought in bad faith, for example in an attempt at Reverse Domain Name Hijacking, the Expert shall state this finding in the Decision. If the Complainant is found on three separate occasions within a 2-year period to have brought a complaint in bad faith, Nominet will not accept any further complaints from that Complainant for a period of 2 years.

17. Communication of Decision to Parties and implementation of Decision

a. Within three (3) Days of our receipt of a Decision from the Expert, we will communicate the full text of the Decision to each Party and the date for the implementation of the Decision in accordance with the Policy.

b. We will publish the full Decision and the date that any action which the Decision requires will be taken, on our website.

c. If the Expert makes a Decision that a Domain Name registration should be cancelled, suspended, transferred or otherwise amended, we will implement that Decision by making any necessary changes to the Domain Name register database after ten (10) Days of the date that the parties were notified, unless, during the ten (10) Days following the date that the parties were notified we receive from either Party:

     i. an appeal or statement of intention to appeal complying with paragraph 18 of the Procedure, in which case we will take no further action in respect of the Domain Name until the appeal is concluded; or

    ii. official documentation showing that the Party has issued and served (or in the case of service outside England and Wales, commenced the process of serving) legal proceedings against the other Party in respect of the domain name. In this case, we will take no further action in respect of the Domain Name unless we receive:

       A. evidence which satisfies us that the Parties have reached a settlement; or

       B. evidence which satisfies us that such proceedings have been dismissed, withdrawn or are otherwise unsuccessful.

18. Appeal

a. Either Party shall have the right to appeal a Decision by submitting either:

   i. a statement of the intention to appeal (see paragraph 18(b)), plus the non-refundable deposit (see paragraph 21(e)), which must be followed within fifteen (15) Days by an appeal notice (see paragraph 18(c)) and the balance of the fee (see paragraph 21(e)); or

   ii. an appeal notice (see paragraph 18(c)) and the whole fee (see paragraph 21(e)).

b. A statement of intention to appeal should only contain sufficient information to make it clear that an appeal is requested. The statement of intention to appeal should not contain the actual grounds or reasons for appeal.

c. An appeal notice should not exceed 1000 words, should set out detailed grounds and reasons for the appeal, but shall contain no new evidence or annexes.

d. Within three (3) Days of our receipt of the:

   i. statement of the intention to appeal and deposit; or

   ii. appeal notice and the full fee

   we will forward the statement of intention to appeal or appeal notice (as the case may be) to the other Party.

e. Within ten (10) Days of receiving the appeal notice from us, the other Party may submit to us an appeal notice response (paragraph 18(f)).

f. An appeal notice response must not exceed 1000 words, should set out detailed grounds and reasons why the appeal should be rejected but should contain no new evidence or annexes.

g. Following the filing of an appeal notice response (or the expiry of the deadline to do so) we will appoint an appeal panel of three Experts. The test of impartiality shall apply to each appeal Expert; subject to this the appeal panel shall consist of:

   i. the chairman of the group of Experts, or at his or her discretion, an Expert of his or her choice; and

   ii. the next available two Independent Experts appointed by rotation from our list.

h. The appeal panel should not normally take into consideration any new evidence presented in an appeal notice or appeal notice response, unless they believe that it is in the interests of justice to do so.

i. So far as is appropriate in the circumstances paragraphs 16 and 17 apply equally to appeal Decisions, except that:

   i. appeal Decisions should be returned by the appeal panel to us within thirty (30) days of the appointment of the last panellist, but this deadline may be extended by up to ten (10) Days by agreement with us; and

   ii. appeal Decisions cannot be subject to any appeal within the Dispute Resolution Service.

19. Settlement or other grounds for termination

a. If, before a Decision is made the Parties agree and notify us of a settlement which we approve, whether or not pursuant to Informal Mediation, we will terminate proceedings under the Dispute Resolution Service.

b. If, before a Decision is made, it becomes unnecessary or impossible to continue proceedings under the Dispute Resolution Service for any reason, we will terminate proceedings under the Dispute Resolution Service unless a Party raises justifiable grounds for objection within a period of time which we will determine.

20. Effect of court proceedings

a. If legal proceedings relating to a Domain Name which is the subject of a complaint are issued in a court of competent jurisdiction before or during the course of proceedings under the Dispute Resolution Service and are brought to our attention, we will suspend the proceedings, pending the outcome of the legal proceedings.

b. A Party must promptly notify us if it initiates legal proceedings in a court of competent jurisdiction in relating to a Domain Name which is the subject of a complaint during the course of proceedings under the Dispute Resolution Service.

21. Fees

a. The applicable fees in respect of the referral of proceedings under the Dispute Resolution Service to an Expert are £750 + VAT for disputes involving 1–5 Domain Names and only one Complainant. For disputes involving 6 or more Domain Names, and/or more than one Complainant, we will set a fee in consultation with the Complainant. Fees are calculated on a cost-recovery basis, and are passed on in their entirety to the Expert(s). Nominet does not charge for its mediation or administration services in respect of the Dispute Resolution Service.

b. Fees are payable by the Complainant only if an acceptable resolution has not been reached and we notify the Parties that an Expert is to be appointed.

c. If we have not received the fees from the Complainant as set out in paragraph 21(a) above within ten (10) Days of receipt by the Complainant of notice from us that an Expert is to be appointed under paragraphs 5(d), 7(e) or 15(a)(ii) we will deem the complaint to be withdrawn.

d. In exceptional circumstances, for example if an in person hearing is held, we will request that the Parties pay additional fees to be agreed between us, the Parties and the Expert.

e. The applicable fees for the submission of an appeal are £3,000 + VAT. If the option is used to pay a deposit and the balance, the deposit is £300 + VAT and non-refundable, and the balance is £2,700 + VAT. If the deposit is paid, and the balance of the fee and/or appeal notice are not filed in time, that appeal is deemed withdrawn and the case will be closed.

22. Exclusion of liability

a. Neither we nor our directors, officers, employees or servants nor any Expert shall be liable to a party for anything done or omitted in connection with any proceedings under the Dispute Resolution Service unless the act or omission is shown to have been in bad faith.

23. Modifications to the Policy and Procedure of the Dispute Resolution Service

a. The internet is an emerging and evolving medium and the regulatory and administrative framework under which we operate is constantly developing. For these reasons we reserve the right to make reasonable modifications to the Policy and Procedure at any time. We will only do so when we have good reason. Except where we are acting in pursuance of a statutory requirement or a court order, changes will be implemented following a process of open public consultation. Each such change will be published in advance (where practicable, thirty (30) calendar days in advance) on our web site: http://www.nominet.org.uk/ and will become binding and effective upon the date specified therein.

b. The Respondent will be bound by the Policy and Procedure which are current at the time the Dispute Resolution Service is commenced until the dispute is concluded.

WIPO Copyright Treaty adopted by the Diplomatic Conference on 20 December 1996

Preamble

The Contracting Parties,

Desiring to develop and maintain the protection of the rights of authors in their literary and artistic works in a manner as effective and uniform as possible,

Recognizing the need to introduce new international rules and clarify the interpretation of certain existing rules in order to provide adequate solutions to the questions raised by new economic, social, cultural and technological developments,

Recognizing the profound impact of the development and convergence of information and communication technologies on the creation and use of literary and artistic works,

Emphasizing the outstanding significance of copyright protection as an incentive for literary and artistic creation,

Recognizing the need to maintain a balance between the rights of authors and the larger public interest, particularly education, research and access to information, as reflected in the Berne Convention,

Have agreed as follows:

Article 1   Relation to the Berne convention

(1) This Treaty is a special agreement within the meaning of Article 20 of the Berne Convention for the Protection of Literary and Artistic Works, as regards Contracting Parties that are countries of the Union established by that Convention. This Treaty shall not have any connection with treaties other than the Berne Convention, nor shall it prejudice any rights and obligations under any other treaties.

(2) Nothing in this Treaty shall derogate from existing obligations that Contracting Parties have to each other under the Berne Convention for the Protection of Literary and Artistic Works.

(3) Hereinafter, "Berne Convention" shall refer to the Paris Act of July 24, 1971, of the Berne Convention for the Protection of Literary and Artistic Works.

(4) Contracting Parties shall comply with Articles 1 to 21 and the Appendix of the Berne Convention.

Article 2   Scope of copyright protection

Copyright protection extends to expressions and not to ideas, procedures, methods of operation or mathematical concepts as such.

Article 3   Application of Articles 2 to 6 of the Berne Convention

Contracting Parties shall apply *mutatis mutandis* the provisions of Articles 2 to 6 of the Berne Convention in respect of the protection provided for in this Treaty.

Article 4   Computer programs

Computer programs are protected as literary works within the meaning of Article 2 of the Berne Convention. Such protection applies to computer programs, whatever may be the mode or form of their expression.

Article 5   Compilations of data (Databases)

Compilations of data or other material, in any form, which by reason of the selection or arrangement of their contents constitute intellectual creations, are protected as such. This protection does not extend to the data or the material itself and is without prejudice to any copyright subsisting in the data or material contained in the compilation.

Article 6   Right of distribution

(1) Authors of literary and artistic works shall enjoy the exclusive right of authorizing the making available to the public of the original and copies of their works through sale or other transfer of ownership.

(2) Nothing in this Treaty shall affect the freedom of Contracting Parties to determine the conditions, if any, under which the exhaustion of the right in paragraph (1) applies after the first sale or other transfer of ownership of the original or a copy of the work with the authorization of the author.

Article 7   Right of rental

(1) Authors of
    (i)   computer programs;

    (ii) cinematographic works; and

    (iii) works embodied in phonograms, as determined in the national law of Contracting Parties,

shall enjoy the exclusive right of authorizing commercial rental to the public of the originals or copies of their works.

    (2) Paragraph (1) shall not apply

    (i) in the case of computer programs, where the program itself is not the essential object of the rental; and

    (ii) in the case of cinematographic works, unless such commercial rental has led to widespread copying of such works materially impairing the exclusive right of reproduction.

    (3) Notwithstanding the provisions of paragraph (1), a Contracting Party that, on April 15, 1994, had and continues to have in force a system of equitable remuneration of authors for the rental of copies of their works embodied in phonograms may maintain that system provided that the commercial rental of works embodied in phonograms is not giving rise to the material impairment of the exclusive right of reproduction of authors.

Article 8   Right of communication to the public

Without prejudice to the provisions of Articles 11(1)(ii), 11bis(1)(i) and (ii), 11ter(1)(ii), 14(1)(ii) and 14bis(1) of the Berne Convention, authors of literary and artistic works shall enjoy the exclusive right of authorizing any communication to the public of their works, by wire or wireless means, including the making available to the public of their works in such a way that members of the public may access these works from a place and at a time individually chosen by them.

Article 9   Duration of the protection of photographic works

In respect of photographic works, the Contracting Parties shall not apply the provisions of Article 7(4) of the Berne Convention.

Article 10   Limitations and exceptions

    (1) Contracting Parties may, in their national legislation, provide for limitations of or exceptions to the rights granted to authors of literary and artistic works under this Treaty in certain special cases that do not conflict with a normal exploitation of the work and do not unreasonably prejudice the legitimate interests of the author.

    (2) Contracting Parties shall, when applying the Berne Convention, confine any limitations of or exceptions to rights provided for therein to certain special cases that do not conflict with a normal exploitation of the work and do not unreasonably prejudice the legitimate interests of the author.

Article 11   Obligations concerning technological measures

Contracting Parties shall provide adequate legal protection and effective legal remedies against the circumvention of effective technological measures that are used by authors in connection with the exercise of their rights under this Treaty or the Berne Convention and that restrict acts, in respect of their works, which are not authorized by the authors concerned or permitted by law.

Article 12   Obligations concerning rights management information

    (1) Contracting Parties shall provide adequate and effective legal remedies against any person knowingly performing any of the following acts knowing, or with respect to civil remedies having reasonable grounds to know, that it will induce, enable, facilitate or conceal an infringement of any right covered by this Treaty or the Berne Convention:

    (i) to remove or alter any electronic rights management information without authority;

    (ii) to distribute, import for distribution, broadcast or communicate to the public, without authority, works or copies of works knowing that electronic rights management information has been removed or altered without authority.

    (2) As used in this Article, "rights management information" means information which identifies the work, the author of the work, the owner of any right in the work, or information about the terms and conditions of use of the work, and any numbers or codes that represent such information, when

any of these items of information is attached to a copy of a work or appears in connection with the communication of a work to the public.

Article 13 Application in time

Contracting Parties shall apply the provisions of Article 18 of the Berne Convention to all protection provided for in this Treaty.

Article 14 Provisions on enforcement of rights

(1) Contracting Parties undertake to adopt, in accordance with their legal systems, the measures necessary to ensure the application of this Treaty.

(2) Contracting Parties shall ensure that enforcement procedures are available under their law so as to permit effective action against any act of infringement of rights covered by this Treaty, including expeditious remedies to prevent infringements and remedies which constitute a deterrent to further infringements.

...

Article 22 No reservations to the Treaty

No reservation to this Treaty shall be admitted.

Article 23 Denunciation of the Treaty

This Treaty may be denounced by any Contracting Party by notification addressed to the Director General of WIPO. Any denunciation shall take effect one year from the date on which the Director General of WIPO received the notification.

Article 24 Languages of the treaty

(1) This Treaty is signed in a single original in English, Arabic, Chinese, French, Russian and Spanish languages, the versions in all these languages being equally authentic.

(2) An official text in any language other than those referred to in paragraph (1) shall be established by the Director General of WIPO on the request of an interested party, after consultation with all the interested parties. For the purposes of this paragraph, "interested party" means any Member State of WIPO whose official language, or one of whose official languages, is involved and the European Community, and any other intergovernmental organization that may become party to this Treaty, if one of its official languages is involved.

Article 25 Depositary

The Director General of WIPO is the depositary of this Treaty.

Agreed Statements Concerning the WIPO Copyright Treaty adopted by the Diplomatic Conference on 20 December 1996

Concerning Article 1(4):

The reproduction right, as set out in Article 9 of the Berne Convention, and the exceptions permitted thereunder, fully apply in the digital environment, in particular to the use of works in digital form. It is understood that the storage of a protected work in digital form in an electronic medium constitutes a reproduction within the meaning of Article 9 of the Berne Convention.

Concerning Article 3:

It is understood that, in applying Article 3 of this Treaty, the expression "country of the Union" in Articles 2 to 6 of the Berne Convention will be read as if it were a reference to a Contracting Party to this Treaty, in the application of those Berne Articles in respect of protection provided for in this Treaty. It is also understood that the expression "country outside the Union" in those Articles in the Berne Convention will, in the same circumstances, be read as if it were a reference to a country that is not a Contracting Party to this Treaty, and that "this Convention" in Articles 2(8), 2bis(2), 3, 4 and 5 of the Berne Convention will be read as if it were a reference to the Berne Convention and this Treaty. Finally, it is understood that a reference in Articles 3 to 6 of the Berne Convention to a "national of one of the countries of the Union" will, when these Articles are applied to this Treaty, mean, in regard to an intergovernmental organization that is a Contracting Party to this Treaty, a national of one of the countries that is member of that organization.

Concerning Article 4:

The scope of protection for computer programs under Article 4 of this Treaty, read with Article 2, is consistent with Article 2 of the Berne Convention and on a par with the relevant provisions of the TRIPS Agreement.

Concerning Article 5:

The scope of protection for compilations of data (databases) under Article 5 of this Treaty, read with Article 2, is consistent with Article 2 of the Berne Convention and on a par with the relevant provisions of the TRIPS Agreement.

Concerning Articles 6 and 7:

As used in these Articles, the expressions "copies" and "original and copies," being subject to the right of distribution and the right of rental under the said Articles, refer exclusively to fixed copies that can be put into circulation as tangible objects.

Concerning Article 7:

It is understood that the obligation under Article 7(1) does not require a Contracting Party to provide an exclusive right of commercial rental to authors who, under that Contracting Party's law, are not granted rights in respect of phonograms. It is understood that this obligation is consistent with Article 14(4) of the TRIPS Agreement.

Concerning Article 8:

It is understood that the mere provision of physical facilities for enabling or making a communication does not in itself amount to communication within the meaning of this Treaty or the Berne Convention. It is further understood that nothing in Article 8 precludes a Contracting Party from applying Article 11bis(2).

Concerning Article 10:

It is understood that the provisions of Article 10 permit Contracting Parties to carry forward and appropriately extend into the digital environment limitations and exceptions in their national laws which have been considered acceptable under the Berne Convention. Similarly, these provisions should be understood to permit Contracting Parties to devise new exceptions and limitations that are appropriate in the digital network environment.

It is also understood that Article 10(2) neither reduces nor extends the scope of applicability of the limitations and exceptions permitted by the Berne Convention.

Concerning Article 12:

It is understood that the reference to "infringement of any right covered by this Treaty or the Berne Convention" includes both exclusive rights and rights of remuneration.

It is further understood that Contracting Parties will not rely on this Article to devise or implement rights management systems that would have the effect of imposing formalities which are not permitted under the Berne Convention or this Treaty, prohibiting the free movement of goods or impeding the enjoyment of rights under this Treaty.

UNCITRAL Model Law on Electronic Commerce[*]

(Resolution of the General Assembly of the United Nations, 16.XII.1996)

PART ONE ELECTRONIC COMMERCE IN GENERAL

Chapter I General Provisions

Article 1   Sphere of application[1]

This Law[2] applies to any kind of information in the form of a data message used in the context[3] of commercial[4] activities.

Article 2   Definitions

For the purposes of this Law:

(a) "Data message" means information generated, sent, received or stored by electronic, optical or similar means including, but not limited to, electronic data interchange (EDI), electronic mail, telegram, telex or telecopy;

(b) "Electronic data interchange (EDI)" means the electronic transfer from computer to computer of information using an agreed standard to structure the information;

(c) "Originator" of a data message means a person by whom, or on whose behalf, the data message purports to have been sent or generated prior to storage, if any, but it does not include a person acting as an intermediary with respect to that data message;

(d) "Addressee" of a data message means a person who is intended by the originator to receive the data message, but does not include a person acting as an intermediary with respect to that data message;

(e) "Intermediary", with respect to a particular data message, means a person who, on behalf of another person, sends, receives or stores that data message or provides other services with respect to that data message;

(f) "Information system" means a system for generating, sending, receiving, storing or otherwise processing data messages.

Article 3   Interpretation

(1) In the interpretation of this Law, regard is to be had to its international origin and to the need to promote uniformity in its application and the observance of good faith.

(2) Questions concerning matters governed by this Law which are not expressly settled in it are to be settled in conformity with the general principles on which this Law is based.

Article 4   Variation by agreement

(1) As between parties involved in generating, sending, receiving, storing or otherwise processing data messages, and except as otherwise provided, the provisions of chapter III may be varied by agreement.

(2) Paragraph (1) does not affect any right that may exist to modify by agreement any rule of law referred to in chapter II.

---

[*] In the text of this model law, "[...]" denotes where individual nations have scope to modify the terms of the model law.

[1] UNCITRAL suggests the following text for States that might wish to limit the applicability of this Law to international data messages: "This Law applies to a data message as defined in paragraph (1) of article 2 where the data message relates to international commerce."

[2] "This Law does not override any rule of law intended for the protection of consumers".

[3] UNICITRAL suggests the following text for States that might wish to extend the applicability of this Law: "This Law applies to any kind of information in the form of a data message, except in the following situations: [...].

[4] "The term 'commercial' should be given a wide interpretation so as to cover matters arising from all relationships of a commercial nature, whether contractual or not. Relationships of a commercial nature include, but are not limited to, the following transactions: any trade transaction for the supply or exchange of goods or services; distribution agreement; commercial representation or agency; factoring; leasing; construction of works; consulting; engineering; licensing; investment; financing; banking; insurance; exploitation agreement or concession; joint venture and other forms of industrial or business cooperation; carriage of goods or passengers by air, sea, rail or road".

Chapter II Application of Legal Requirements to Data Messages

Article 5 Legal recognition of data messages

Information shall not be denied legal effect, validity or enforceability solely on the grounds that it is in the form of a data message.

[Article 5 *bis* Incorporation by reference

Information shall not be denied legal effect, validity or enforceability solely on the grounds that it is not contained in the data message purporting to give rise to such legal effect, but is merely referred to in that data message.]

Article 6 Writing

(1) Where the law requires information to be in writing, that requirement is met by a data message if the information contained therein is accessible so as to be usable for subsequent reference.

(2) Paragraph (1) applies whether the requirement therein is in the form of an obligation or whether the law simply provides consequences for the information not being in writing.

(3) The provisions of this article do not apply to the following: [...].

Article 7 Signature

(1) Where the law requires a signature of a person, that requirement is met in relation to a data message if:

(a) a method is used to identify that person and to indicate that person's approval of the information contained in the data message; and

(b) that method is as reliable as was appropriate for the purpose for which the data message was generated or communicated, in the light of all the circumstances, including any relevant agreement.

(2) Paragraph (1) applies whether the requirement therein is in the form of an obligation or whether the law simply provides consequences for the absence of a signature.

(3) The provisions of this article do not apply to the following: [...].

Article 8 Original

(1) Where the law requires information to be presented or retained in its original form, that requirement is met by a data message if:

(a) there exists a reliable assurance as to the integrity of the information from the time when it was first generated in its final form, as a data message or otherwise; and

(b) where it is required that information be presented, that information is capable of being displayed to the person to whom it is to be presented.

(2) Paragraph (1) applies whether the requirement therein is in the form of an obligation or whether the law simply provides consequences for the information not being presented or retained in its original form.

(3) For the purposes of subparagraph (a) of paragraph (1):

(a) the criteria for assessing integrity shall be whether the information has remained complete and unaltered, apart from the addition of any endorsement and any change which arises in the normal course of communication, storage and display; and

(b) the standard of reliability required shall be assessed in the light of the purpose for which the information was generated and in the light of all the relevant circumstances.

(4) The provisions of this article do not apply to the following: [...].

Article 9 Admissibility and evidential weight of data messages

(1) In any legal proceedings, nothing in the application of the rules of evidence shall apply so as to deny the admissibility of a data message in evidence:

(a) on the sole ground that it is a data message; or,

(b) if it is the best evidence that the person adducing it could reasonably be expected to obtain, on the grounds that it is not in its original form.

(2) Information in the form of a data message shall be given due evidential weight. In assessing the evidential weight of a data message, regard shall be had to the reliability of the manner in which the data message was generated, stored or communicated, to the reliability of the manner in which the integrity of the information was maintained, to the manner in which its originator was identified, and to any other relevant factor.

Article 10   Retention of data messages

(1) Where the law requires that certain documents, records or information be retained, that requirement is met by retaining data messages, provided that the following conditions are satisfied:

  (a) the information contained therein is accessible so as to be usable for subsequent reference; and

  (b) the data message is retained in the format in which it was generated, sent or received, or in a format which can be demonstrated to represent accurately the information generated, sent or received; and

  (c) such information, if any, is retained as enables the identification of the origin and destination of a data message and the date and time when it was sent or received.

(2) An obligation to retain documents, records or information in accordance with paragraph (1) does not extend to any information the sole purpose of which is to enable the message to be sent or received.

(3) A person may satisfy the requirement referred to in paragraph (1) by using the services of any other person, provided that the conditions set forth in subparagraphs (a), (b) and (c) of paragraph (1) are met.

Chapter III Communication of Data Messages

Article 11   Formation and validity of contracts

(1) In the context of contract formation, unless otherwise agreed by the parties, an offer and the acceptance of an offer may be expressed by means of data messages. Where a data message is used in the formation of a contract, that contract shall not be denied validity or enforceability on the sole ground that a data message was used for that purpose.

(2) The provisions of this article do not apply to the following: [...].

Article 12   Recognition by parties of data messages

(1) As between the originator and the addressee of a data message, a declaration of will or other statement shall not be denied legal effect, validity or enforceability solely on the grounds that it is in the form of a data message.

(2) The provisions of this article do not apply to the following: [...].

Article 13   Attribution of data messages

(1) A data message is that of the originator if it was sent by the originator itself.

(2) As between the originator and the addressee, a data message is deemed to be that of the originator if it was sent:

  (a) by a person who had the authority to act on behalf of the originator in respect of that data message; or

  (b) by an information system programmed by, or on behalf of, the originator to operate automatically.

(3) As between the originator and the addressee, an addressee is entitled to regard a data message as being that of the originator, and to act on that assumption, if:

  (a) in order to ascertain whether the data message was that of the originator, the addressee properly applied a procedure previously agreed to by the originator for that purpose; or

  (b) the data message as received by the addressee resulted from the actions of a person whose relationship with the originator or with any agent of the originator enabled that person to gain access to a method used by the originator to identify data messages as its own.

(4) Paragraph (3) does not apply:

    (a) as of the time when the addressee has both received notice from the originator that the data message is not that of the originator, and had reasonable time to act accordingly; or

    (b) in a case within paragraph (3)(b), at any time when the addressee knew or should have known, had it exercised reasonable care or used any agreed procedure, that the data message was not that of the originator.

(5) Where a data message is that of the originator or is deemed to be that of the originator, or the addressee is entitled to act on that assumption, then, as between the originator and the addressee, the addressee is entitled to regard the data message as received as being what the originator intended to send, and to act on that assumption. The addressee is not so entitled when it knew or should have known, had it exercised reasonable care or used any agreed procedure, that the transmission resulted in any error in the data message as received.

(6) The addressee is entitled to regard each data message received as a separate data message and to act on that assumption, except to the extent that it duplicates another data message and the addressee knew or should have known, had it exercised reasonable care or used any agreed procedure, that the data message was a duplicate.

Article 14   Acknowledgement of receipt

(1) Paragraphs (2) to (4) of this article apply where, on or before sending a data message, or by means of that data message, the originator has requested or has agreed with the addressee that receipt of the data message be acknowledged.

(2) Where the originator has not agreed with the addressee that the acknowledgement be given in a particular form or by a particular method, an acknowledgement may be given by

    (a) any communication by the addressee, automated or otherwise, or

    (b) any conduct of the addressee,

sufficient to indicate to the originator that the data message has been received.

(3) Where the originator has stated that the data message is conditional on receipt of the acknowledgement, the data message is treated as though it has never been sent, until the acknowledgement is received.

(4) Where the originator has not stated that the data message is conditional on receipt of the acknowledgement, and the acknowledgement has not been received by the originator within the time specified or agreed or, if no time has been specified or agreed, within a reasonable time, the originator:

    (a) may give notice to the addressee stating that no acknowledgement has been received and specifying a reasonable time by which the acknowledgement must be received; and

    (b) if the acknowledgement is not received within the time specified in subparagraph (a), may, upon notice to the addressee, treat the data message as though it had never been sent, or exercise any other rights it may have.

(5) Where the originator receives the addressee's acknowledgement of receipt, it is presumed that the related data message was received by the addressee. That presumption does not imply that the data message corresponds to the message received.

(6) Where the received acknowledgement states that the related data message met technical requirements, either agreed upon or set forth in applicable standards, it is presumed that those requirements have been met.

(7) Except in so far as it relates to the sending or receipt of the data message, this article is not intended to deal with the legal consequences that may flow either from that data message or from the acknowledgement of its receipt.

Article 15   Time and place of dispatch and receipt of data messages

(1) Unless otherwise agreed between the originator and the addressee, the dispatch of a data message occurs when it enters an information system outside the control of the originator or of the person who sent the data message on behalf of the originator.

(2) Unless otherwise agreed between the originator and the addressee, the time of receipt of a data message is determined as follows:

    (a) if the addressee has designated an information system for the purpose of receiving data messages, receipt occurs:

        (i) at the time when the data message enters the designated information system; or

        (ii) if the data message is sent to an information system of the addressee that is not the designated information system, at the time when the data message is retrieved by the addressee;

    (b) if the addressee has not designated an information system, receipt occurs when the data message enters an information system of the addressee.

(3) Paragraph (2) applies notwithstanding that the place where the information system is located may be different from the place where the data message is deemed to be received under paragraph (4).

(4) Unless otherwise agreed between the originator and the addressee, a data message is deemed to be dispatched at the place where the originator has its place of business, and is deemed to be received at the place where the addressee has its place of business. For the purposes of this paragraph:

    (a) if the originator or the addressee has more than one place of business, the place of business is that which has the closest relationship to the underlying transaction or, where there is no underlying transaction, the principal place of business;

    (b) if the originator or the addressee does not have a place of business, reference is to be made to its habitual residence.

(5) The provisions of this article do not apply to the following: [...].

PART TWO ELECTRONIC COMMERCE IN SPECIFIC AREAS

Chapter I Carriage of Goods

Article 16 Actions related to contracts of carriage of goods

Without derogating from the provisions of part one of this Law, this chapter applies to any action in connection with, or in pursuance of, a contract of carriage of goods, including but not limited to:

    (a) (i) furnishing the marks, number, quantity or weight of goods;

        (ii) stating or declaring the nature or value of goods;

        (iii) issuing a receipt for goods;

        (iv) confirming that goods have been loaded;

    (b) (i) notifying a person of terms and conditions of the contract;

        (ii) giving instructions to a carrier;

    (c) (i) claiming delivery of goods;

        (ii) authorizing release of goods;

        (iii) giving notice of loss of, or damage to, goods;

    (d) giving any other notice or statement in connection with the performance of the contract;

    (e) undertaking to deliver goods to a named person or a person authorized to claim delivery;

    (f) granting, acquiring, renouncing, surrendering, transferring or negotiating rights in goods;

    (g) acquiring or transferring rights and obligations under the contract.

Article 17 Transport documents

(1) Subject to paragraph (3), where the law requires that any action referred to in article 16 be carried out in writing or by using a paper document, that requirement is met if the action is carried out by using one or more data messages.

(2) Paragraph (1) applies whether the requirement therein is in the form of an obligation or whether the law simply provides consequences for failing either to carry out the action in writing or to use a paper document.

(3) If a right is to be granted to, or an obligation is to be acquired by, one person and no other person, and if the law requires that, in order to effect this, the right or obligation must be conveyed to that person by the transfer, or use of, a paper document, that requirement is met if the right or obligation is conveyed by using one or more data messages, provided that a reliable method is used to render such data message or messages unique.

(4) For the purposes of paragraph (3), the standard of reliability required shall be assessed in the light of the purpose for which the right or obligation was conveyed and in the light of all the circumstances, including any relevant agreement.

(5) Where one or more data messages are used to effect any action in subparagraphs (f) and (g) of article 16, no paper document used to effect any such action is valid unless the use of data messages has been terminated and replaced by the use of paper documents. A paper document issued in these circumstances shall contain a statement of such termination. The replacement of data messages by paper documents shall not affect the rights or obligations of the parties involved.

(6) If a rule of law is compulsorily applicable to a contract of carriage of goods which is in, or is evidenced by, a paper document, that rule shall not be inapplicable to such a contract of carriage of goods which is evidenced by one or more data messages by reason of the fact that the contract is evidenced by such data message or messages instead of by a paper document.

(7) The provisions of this article do not apply to the following: [...].

Index